THE ADVANCED INTEL MICROPROCESSORS

80286, 80386, and 80486

BARRY B. BREY
DeVry Institute of Technology

Merrill, an imprint of
Macmillan Publishing Company
New York

Maxwell Macmillan Canada
Toronto

Maxwell Macmillan International
New York   Oxford   Singapore   Sydney

Editor: Dave Garza
Production Editor: Louise N. Sette
Art Coordinator: Pete Robison
Text Designer: Debra A. Fargo
Cover Designer: Cathleen Norz
Production Buyer: Patricia A. Tonneman

This book was set in Times Roman by Publication Services and was printed and bound by Book Press Inc., a Quebecor America Book Group Company. The cover was printed by Book Press, Inc., a Quebecor America Book Group Company.

Macmillan Publishing Company
866 Third Avenue
New York, NY 10022

Macmillan Publishing Company is part of the Maxwell Communication Group of Companies.

Maxwell Macmillan Canada, Inc.
1200 Eglinton Avenue East, Suite 200
Don Mills, Ontario M3C 3N1

Library of Congress Cataloging-in-Publication Data
Brey, Barry B.
    The advanced Intel microprocessors : 80286, 80386, and 80486 /
    Barry B. Brey.
        p   cm.
    Includes index.
    ISBN 0–02–314245–6
    1. Intel 80286 (Microprocessor) 2. Intel 80386 (Microprocessor)
    3. Intel 80486 (Microprocessor) I. Title.
    QA76.8.I2927B74   1992
004.165—dc20
                                         92–11880
                                          CIP

Printing: 2 3 4 5 6 7 8 9 Year: 3 4 5 6 7

MERRILL'S INTERNATIONAL SERIES IN ENGINEERING TECHNOLOGY

INTRODUCTION TO ENGINEERING TECHNOLOGY

Pond, *Introduction to Engineering Technology, 2nd Edition*, 0-02-396031-0

ELECTRONICS TECHNOLOGY

Electronics Reference

Adamson, *The Electronics Dictionary for Technicians*, 0-02-300820-2
Berlin, *The Illustrated Electronics Dictionary*, 0-675-20451-8
Reis, *Becoming an Electronics Technician: Securing Your High-Tech Future*, 0-02-399231-X

DC/AC Circuits

Boylestad, *DC/AC: The Basics*, 0-675-20918-8
Boylestad, *Introductory Circuit Analysis, 6th Edition*, 0-675-21181-6
Ciccarelli, *Circuit Modeling: Exercises and Software, 2nd Edition*, 0-02-322455-X
Floyd, *Electric Circuits Fundamentals, 2nd Edition*, 0-675-21408-4
Floyd, *Electronics Fundamentals: Circuits, Devices, and Applications, 2nd Edition*, 0-675-21310-X
Floyd, *Principles of Electric Circuits, 4th Edition*, 0-02-338501-4
Floyd, *Principles of Electric Circuits: Electron Flow Version, 3rd Edition*, 0-02-338531-6
Keown, *PSpice and Circuit Analysis*, 0-675-22135-8
Monssen, *PSpice with Circuit Analysis* 0-675-21376-2
Tocci, *Introduction to Electric Circuit Analysis, 2nd Edition*, 0-675-20002-4

Devices and Linear Circuits

Berlin & Getz, *Fundamentals of Operational Amplifiers and Linear Integrated Circuits*, 0-675-21002-X
Berube, *Electronic Devices and Circuits Using MICRO-CAP II*, 0-02-309160-6
Berube, *Electronic Devices and Circuits Using MICRO-CAP III*, 0-02-309151-7
Bogart, *Electronic Devices and Circuits, 3rd Edition*, 0-02-311701-X
Tocci, *Electronic Devices: Conventional Flow Version, 3rd Edition*, 0-675-21150-6
Floyd, *Electronic Devices, 3rd Edition*, 0-675-22170-6
Floyd, *Electronic Devices: Electron Flow Version*, 0-02-338540-5
Floyd, *Fundamentals of Linear Circuits*, 0-02-338481-6
Schwartz, *Survey of Electronics, 3rd Edition*, 0-675-20162-4
Stanley, *Operational Amplifiers with Linear Integrated Circuits, 2nd Edition*, 0-675-20660-X
Tocci & Oliver, *Fundamentals of Electronic Devices, 4th Edition*, 0-675-21259-6

Digital Electronics

Floyd, *Digital Fundamentals, 4th Edition*, 0-675-21217-0
McCalla, *Digital Logic and Computer Design*, 0-675-21170-0
Reis, *Digital Electronics through Project Analysis* 0-675-21141-7
Tocci, *Fundamentals of Pulse and Digital Circuits, 3rd Edition*, 0-675-20033-4

Microprocessor Technology

Antonakos, *The 68000 Microprocessor: Hardware and Software Principles and Applications, 2nd Edition*, 0-02-303603-6
Antonakos, *The 8088 Microprocessor*, 0-675-22173-0
Brey, *The Advanced Intel Microprocessors*, 0-02-314245-6
Brey, *The Intel Microprocessors: 8086/8088, 80186, 80286, 80386, and 80486: Architecture, Programming, and Interfacing, 2nd Edition*, 0-675-21309-6
Brey, *Microprocessors and Peripherals: Hardware, Software, Interfacing, and Applications, 2nd Edition*, 0-675-20884-X
Gaonkar, *Microprocessor Architecture, Programming, and Applications with the 8085/8080A, 2nd Edition*, 0-675-20675-6
Gaonkar, *The Z80 Microprocessor: Architecture, Interfacing, Programming, and Design, 2nd Edition*, 0-02-340484-1
Goody, *Programming and Interfacing the 8086/8088 Microprocessor: A Product- Development Laboratory Process*, 0-675-21312-6
MacKenzie, *The 8051 Microcontroller*, 0-02-373650-X
Miller, *The 68000 Family of Microprocessors: Architecture, Programming, and Applications, 2nd Edition*, 0-02-381560-4
Quinn, *The 6800 Microprocessor*, 0-675-20515-8
Subbarao, *16/32 Bit Microprocessors: 68000/68010/68020 Software, Hardware, and Design Applications*, 0-675-21119-0

Electronic Communications

Monaco, *Introduction to Microwave Technology*, 0-675-21030-5
Monaco, *Preparing for the FCC Radio-Telephone Operator's License Examination*, 0-675-21313-4
Schoenbeck, *Electronic Communications: Modulation and Transmission, 2nd Edition*, 0-675-21311-8
Young, *Electronic Communication Techniques, 2nd Edition*, 0-675-21045-3
Zanger & Zanger, *Fiber Optics: Communication and Other Applications*, 0-675-20944-7

Microcomputer Servicing

Adamson, *Microcomputer Repair*, 0-02-300825-3
Asser, Stigliano, & Bahrenburg, *Microcomputer Servicing: Practical Systems and Troubleshooting, 2nd Edition*, 0-02-304241-9
Asser, Stigliano, & Bahrenburg, *Microcomputer Theory and Servicing, 2nd Edition*, 0-02-304231-1

Programming

Adamson, *Applied Pascal for Technology*,
0-675-20771-1
Adamson, *Structured BASIC Applied to Technology, 2nd Edition*, 0-02-300827-X
Adamson, *Structured C for Technology*, 0-675-20993-5
Adamson, *Structured C for Technology (with disk)*,
0-675-21289-8
Nashelsky & Boylestad, *BASIC Applied to Circuit Analysis*, 0-675-20161-6

Instrumentation and Measurement

Berlin & Getz, *Principles of Electronic Instrumentation and Measurement*, 0-675-20449-6
Buchla & McLachlan, *Applied Electronic Instrumentation and Measurement*, 0-675-21162-X
Gillies, *Instrumentation and Measurements for Electronic Technicians, 2nd Edition*, 0-02-343051-6

Transform Analysis

Kulathinal, *Transform Analysis and Electronic Networks with Applications*, 0-675-20765-7

Biomedical Equipment Technology

Aston, *Principles of Biomedical Instrumentation and Measurement*, 0-675-20943-9

Mathematics

Monaco, *Essential Mathematics for Electronics Technicians*, 0-675-21172-7
Davis, *Technical Mathematics*, 0-675-20338-4
Davis, *Technical Mathematics with Calculus*,
0-675-20965-X

INDUSTRIAL ELECTRONICS/ INDUSTRIAL TECHNOLOGY

Bateson, *Introduction to Control System Technology, 4th Edition*, 0-02-306463-3
Fuller, *Robotics: Introduction, Programming, and Projects*,
0-675-21078-X
Goetsch, *Industrial Safety: In the Age of High Technology*,
0-02-344207-7
Goetsch, *Industrial Supervision: In the Age of High Technology*, 0-675-22137-4
Horath, *Computer Numerical Control Programming of Machines*, 0-02-357201-9
Hubert, *Electric Machines: Theory, Operation, Applications, Adjustment, and Control*, 0-675-20765-7
Humphries, *Motors and Controls*, 0-675-20235-3
Hutchins, *Introduction to Quality: Management, Assurance, and Control*, 0-675-20896-3
Laviana, *Basic Computer Numerical Control Programming*
0-675-21298-7

Reis, *Electronic Project Design and Fabrication, 2nd Edition*,
0-02-399230-1
Rosenblatt & Friedman, *Direct and Alternating Current Machinery, 2nd Edition*, 0-675-20160-8
Smith, *Statistical Process Control and Quality Improvement*,
0-675-21160-3
Webb, *Programmable Logic Controllers: Principles and Applications, 2nd Edition*, 0-02-424970-X
Webb & Greshock, *Industrial Control Electronics, 2nd Edition*,
0-02-424864-9

MECHANICAL/CIVIL TECHNOLOGY

Keyser, *Materials Science in Engineering, 4th Edition*,
0-675-20401-1
Kraut, *Fluid Mechanics for Technicians*, 0-675-21330-4
Mott, *Applied Fluid Mechanics, 3rd Edition*, 0-675-21026-7
Mott, *Machine Elements in Mechanical Design, 2nd Edition*,
0-675-22289-3
Rolle, *Thermodynamics and Heat Power, 3rd Edition*,
0-675-21016-X
Spiegel & Limbrunner, *Applied Statics and Strength of Materials*, 0-675-21123-9
Wolansky & Akers, *Modern Hydraulics: The Basics at Work*,
0-675-20987-0
Wolf, *Statics and Strength of Materials: A Parallel Approach to Understanding Structures*, 0-675-20622-7

DRAFTING TECHNOLOGY

Cooper, *Introduction to VersaCAD*, 0-675-21164-6
Goetsch & Rickman, *Computer-Aided Drafting with AutoCAD*,
0-675-20915-3
Kirkpatrick & Kirkpatrick, *AutoCAD for Interior Design and Space Planning*, 0-02-364455-9
Kirkpatrick, *The AutoCAD Book: Drawing, Modeling, and Applications, 2nd Edition*, 0-675-22288-5
Lamit and Lloyd, *Drafting for Electronics, 2nd Edition*,
0-02-367342-7
Lamit and Paige, *Computer-Aided Design and Drafting*,
0-675-20475-5
Maruggi, *Technical Graphics: Electronics Worktext, 2nd Edition*, 0-675-21378-9
Maruggi, *The Technology of Drafting*, 0-675-20762-2
Sell, *Basic Technical Drawing*, 0-675-21001-1

TECHNICAL WRITING

Croft, *Getting a Job: Resume Writing, Job Application Letters, and Interview Strategies*, 0-675-20917-X
Panares, *A Handbook of English for Technical Students*,
0-675-20650-2
Pfeiffer, *Proposal Writing: The Art of Friendly Persuasion*,
0-675-20988-9
Pfeiffer, *Technical Writing: A Practical Approach*,
0-675-21221-9
Roze, *Technical Communications: The Practical Craft*,
0-675-20641-3
Weisman, *Basic Technical Writing, 6th Edition*, 0-675-21256-1

In awe of it all!

PREFACE

This text is written for the student in a course of study that requires a thorough knowledge of the Intel family of microprocessors beginning with the Intel 80286. It is a very practical reference text for anyone interested in all aspects of this important microprocessor family, as well as anyone functioning or striving to function today in a field of study that uses computers. Intel microprocessors have gained wide applications in many areas of electronics, communications, control systems, and particularly in desktop computer systems.

Organization and Coverage

In order to cultivate a comprehensive approach to learning, each chapter of the text begins with a set of objectives that briefly define the contents of the chapter. This is followed by the body of the chapter, which includes many programming and hardware applications that illustrate the main topics of the chapter. At the end of each chapter, a numerical summary, which doubles as a study guide, reviews the information presented in the chapter. Finally, questions and problems are provided to promote practice and mental exercise with the concepts presented in the chapter.

This text is divided into two main parts. The first presents the microprocessor as a programmable device. Chapters 1–6 explain the function of each instruction and also illustrate many example programs. Example programs, using the Microsoft Macro Assembler program, provide an opportunity to learn how to program the Intel family of microprocessors. Chapter 6 concentrates on using the assembler, linker, library, macros, DOS function, and BIOS functions. The basic foundation presented in the first six chapters is required to understand the second part of the text (Chapters 7–13), which explains how the microprocessor functions in its environment. The microprocessor's environment includes its memory and I/O system. Interfacing is explained so that the microprocessor can be connected to virtually any device that exists. Through this comprehensive approach, the student will become proficient in microprocessor programming, interfacing, and application.

Approach

Because the Intel family of microprocessors is quite diverse, this text initially concentrates on the 80286 microprocessor. Other family members, which include the 80386 and 80486, are compared and contrasted with the 80286 in Chapter 13. This entire series of microprocessors is very similar, which allows more advanced versions to be learned once the basic 80286 is understood.

In addition to fully explaining the programming, operation, and interfacing of the microprocessor, this text also explains the programming and operation of the numeric coprocessor (80287/80387). The numeric coprocessor functions in a system to provide access to floating-point calculations that are important in applications such as control systems, video graphics, and computer-aided design (CAD). The numeric coprocessor allows a program to access complex arithmetic operations that are otherwise difficult to achieve with normal microprocessor programming.

Through this approach, the operation of the microprocessor, programming, interfacing, and the advanced family members, a working and practical background is attainable. On completion of a course of study based on this text, you should be able to:

1. Develop control software to control an application interface to the 80286, 80386, or 80486 microprocessor. Generally, the software developed will also function on the earlier 8086/8088 microprocessor. This software also includes DOS-based applications.
2. Program the numeric coprocessor (80287/80387) to solve complex equations.
3. Interface memory subsystems to the microprocessor.
4. Interface peripheral devices to the microprocessor to control I/O devices using direct, interrupt, or DMA techniques as they apply.
5. Explain the differences between the family members and highlight the features of each member.

Content Overview

Chapter 1 introduces the Intel family of microprocessors with an emphasis on the 80286 microprocessor. This first chapter serves to introduce the microprocessor, its history, its operation, and the methods used to store data in a microprocessor-based system. Once an understanding of these basic machines is grasped, Chapters 2–5 explain how each instruction functions with the 80286 microprocessor. As instructions are explained, simple applications are presented to illustrate the operation of the instructions and develop basic programming concepts.

Once the basis for programming is developed, Chapter 6 provides applications using the assembler program. These applications include programming using DOS and BIOS function calls. Disk files are explained, as are the keyboard and video operation on a personal computer system. This chapter provides the tools required to develop virtually any program on a personal computer system.

Chapter 7 introduces the 80286 as a component in a digital system. This chapter provides details on the connection of the microprocessor to its system through bus buffers and latches. It also provides details on ancillary components required for a functioning 80286-based system. The electrical characteristics are provided at this point so the microprocessor can be interfaced to memory and I/O components in later chapters.

Once the operation, pinout, and electrical characteristics of the microprocessor are understood, Chapter 8 interfaces the microprocessor to a memory system. Memory interface is accomplished through the use of TTL decoders, PROM decoders, and PAL* decoders. This chapter also describes the operation of common memory components such as EPROM, SRAM, and DRAM, and how to interface them.

Chapters 9–11 provide a complete coverage of I/O interfacing to the microprocessor. The first of these chapters explains the operation of the I/O instructions and basic serial, parallel, ADC, and DAC interfacing. Common I/O subsystems include keyboards, displays, and printer interfaces.

Once these basic I/O devices are understood, Chapters 10 and 11 provide additional details on interrupt and DMA-processed I/O. They also explain the operation and programming of programmable interrupt and DMA controllers. Chapter 11 also explains how disk and video systems function in a computer system.

Advanced material on the 80287/80387 numeric coprocessor and the 80386/80486 microprocessors appears in Chapters 12 and 13. These advanced topics include memory management, coprocessor programming, cache memory, and memory paging.

Appendixes are included to enhance the application of the text. These include:

Appendix A. A complete listing of the DOS INT 21H function calls. This appendix also details the use of the assembler program and many of the BIOS function calls.

Appendix B. Complete listing of all 80286/80386/80486 instructions including many examples, execution times, and machine coding in hexadecimal.

Appendix C. Many instructions change the flag bits. This appendix lists only the instructions that change the flags and also shows which flags change.

Appendix D. The personal computer contains either an 8-bit or a 16-bit bus structure. This appendix provides the pinouts of the ISA (IBM standard architecture) pin connections of the bus connectors.

Appendix E. Answers for the even-numbered questions and problems are provided in this appendix.

I am grateful to the following reviewers for their helpful suggestions for making this work as useful as possible for students and teachers alike: Richard Cihkey (New England Tech Institute), Jane Craig (ITT Technical Institute), Michael J. Batchelder (South Dakota School of Mines and Technology), and Edward R. Enfield (Texas State Technical College at Waco).

---

*PAL is a programmable array logic device that is a registered trademark of Monolithic Memories, Inc.

CONTENTS

CHAPTER 1

Introduction to the Intel Family of Microprocessors

INTRODUCTION

This chapter introduces the Intel family of microprocessors: the 80286, 80386, and 80486. The 80286 is a 16-bit microprocessor found in many personal and business computer systems. The 80386 and 80486 are both 32-bit microprocessors found in more costly and higher speed personal and business computer systems. The 80386 and 80486 perform tasks reserved for mainframe computer systems just a few years ago. Often the 80486 operates at a comparable throughput to many recent mainframe computer systems. Currently the 80486 microprocessor is finding application in *massively parallel* processing systems where up to one thousand 80486 microprocessors are paralleled to perform at supercomputer speeds.

In the introduction to microprocessors, we explain the evolution of the microprocessor, its architecture, and memory structures. We also present the programming model and data formats used with the microprocessor and its programs. In the next three chapters, we introduce the instruction set for the Intel family and expound each instruction.

OBJECTIVES

Upon completion of this chapter, you will be able to:

1. Describe the evolution of the microprocessor.
2. Detail the operation of a microprocessor in a computer system.
3. Explain the structure of the memory and internal registers of the 80286 microprocessor.
4. Compare the memory systems of the 80286, 80386, and 80486 microprocessors.
5. Define the terms memory segment and offset address.

6. Calculate the effective address for the next step in a program using the contents of the instruction pointer (IP) and code segment (CS) register.
7. Explain the difference between real and protected mode operation.
8. Describe the memory organization of the personal computer and indicate the location and purpose of extended and expanded memory, the transient program area, and the system area.
9. Convert between decimal, binary signed and unsigned integer, BCD, ASCII, and floating-point formats.
10. Identify the data types byte, word, double word, quad word, and ten bytes.
11. Provide an overview of the 80286 instruction set.

1-1   THE EVOLUTION OF THE MICROPROCESSOR

Before discussing the 80286, 80386, and 80486 microprocessors, we must first understand what events led to the development of these microprocessors and their predecessors. This section details the entire spectrum of microprocessors and their historical evolution. It also lists popular early microprocessors produced by various manufacturers.

The 4-Bit Microprocessor

In 1971, Intel Corporation released the world's first microprocessor—the Intel 4004, a 4-bit microprocessor. This integrated, programmable controller on a chip was meager by today's standards. It addressed a mere 4,096 four-bit memory locations. Its instruction set contained only 45 different instructions. It was fabricated with *P*-channel MOSFET technology that caused it to execute instructions at the slow rate of 50 KIPS (*kilo-instructions per second*).

At first, applications abounded for this device. The 4-bit microprocessor debuted in early video game systems and small microprocessor-based control systems. The main problems with this early microprocessor were its speed, word size, and memory size. Its evolution ended when Intel released the 4040, an updated version of the earlier 4004. The 4040 operated at a higher speed because it was fabricated using NMOS logic, although it lacked improvements in word and memory size. Other companies, in particular Texas Instruments (TMS-1000), also produced 4-bit microprocessors. The 4-bit microprocessor still survives in low-end applications such as microwave ovens and small control systems, and is produced by most major microprocessor manufacturers.

The 8-Bit Microprocessor

Later in 1971, realizing that the microprocessor was a commercially viable product, Intel Corporation released the 8008—an 8-bit microprocessor. The expanded memory size (16K bytes) and additional instructions (a total of 48) provided an opportunity for its application in more advanced systems. (A *byte* is an 8-bit-wide binary number and a computer *K* is 1,024. Often, memory size is rated in *K bytes*.)

As engineers began developing more demanding uses for the 8008 micro-processor, its somewhat small memory size and instruction set limited its useful-ness. Intel recognized the limitations of the 8008 and, in 1973, introduced the 8080 microprocessor—the first modern 8-bit microprocessor. The flood gates opened and the 8080 ushered in the age of the microprocessor. Soon, many other companies began to introduce their versions of the 8-bit microprocessor. Table 1–1 lists several of these early microprocessors and their manufacturers. Of these early microproces-sor producers, only Intel and Motorola continue to enjoy success with newer and improved microprocessors.

What was special about the 8080? Not only could it address more memory and execute more instructions, but it executed them 10 times faster than the 8008. An addition, which took 20 μs (50,000 instructions per second) on an 8008-based system, took only 2.0 μs (500,000 instructions per second) on an 8080-based system. Also, the 8080 was compatible with TTL (*transistor–transistor logic*), while the 8008 was not directly compatible. The 8080 could address four times more memory (64K bytes) than the 8008. These improvements are responsible for introducing the era of the 8080, and the continuing era of the microprocessor.

In 1977, Intel Corporation introduced an updated version of the 8080—the 8085. Although only slightly more advanced than an 8080, the 8085 executes soft-ware at an even higher speed. An addition, which took 2.0 μs (500,000 instructions per second) on the 8080, requires only 1.3 μs (769,230 instructions per second) on the 8085. The main advantages of the 8085 are its internal clock generator, in-ternal system controller, and higher clock frequency. Intel has managed to sell well over 100,000,000 copies of the 8085 microprocessor. Applications that contain the 8085 are still being designed and may well continue to be popular well into the future.

The 16-Bit Microprocessor

In 1978, Intel released the 8086 microprocessor and a year or so later the 8088. Both devices are 16-bit microprocessors, which execute instructions in as little as 400 ns (2.5 *MIPS,* or 2.5 millions of instructions per second). This represents a major improvement over the execution speed of the 8085. In addition, the 8086 and 8088 address 1M byte of memory, 16 times more memory than the 8085. (A *1M memory* contains 1,024K locations.) These higher execution speeds and larger memory sizes allow the 8086 and 8088 to replace smaller minicomputers in many applications.

TABLE 1–1   Early 8-bit microprocessors

Manufacturer	Part Number
Fairchild	F-8
Intel	8080
MOS Technology	6502
Motorola	MC6800
National Semiconductor	IMP-8
Rockwell International	PPS-8

The increase in memory size and additional instructions of the 8086 and 8088 have led to many sophisticated applications for microprocessors. Improvements to the instruction set included a multiply and divide instruction, which was missing from all prior versions of the microprocessor. Also the number of instructions increased from 45 on the 4004, to 246 on the 8085, to well over 20,000 variations on the 8086 and 8088 microprocessors. These additional instructions ease the task of developing efficient and sophisticated applications even though their sheer number is at first overwhelming.

The 16-bit microprocessor evolved because of the need for larger memory systems. Applications such as spreadsheets, word processors, spelling checkers, and computer-based thesauruses were memory intensive and required more than the 64K bytes of memory found in 8-bit microprocessors. The 16-bit 8086 and 8088 provided 1M byte of memory for these applications. Soon even 1M byte of memory proved limiting for large spreadsheets and other applications. This led to the introduction of the 80286 microprocessor, by Intel in 1983.

The 80286 Microprocessor.   The 80286 microprocessor is almost identical to the 8086 and 8088 except it can address a 16M byte memory instead of 1M byte. The instruction set of the 80286 is almost identical to the 8086 and 8088 except for a few additional instructions that manage the extra 15M bytes of memory. The clock speed of the 80286 was increased so it could execute some instructions in as little as 250 ns (4.0 MIPS) with the 8.0-MHz version.

The 16-bit microprocessor also provides more internal register storage than the 8-bit microprocessor. These additional registers allow software to be written more efficiently.

The 32-Bit Microprocessor

Applications began to demand faster microprocessor speeds, more memory, and wider data widths. This led Intel Corporation to introduce the 80386 in 1986. The 80386, which is a full 32-bit microprocessor that contains a 32-bit data bus and a 32-bit memory address, represented a major overhaul of the microprocessor. The 80386 addresses up to 4G bytes of memory. (*One G* of memory contains 1,024 M locations.)

Applications that require higher microprocessor speeds include systems using a GUI, or a *graphical user interface*. Modern graphical displays often contain 256,000 or more picture elements *(pixels)*. (The VGA display has a resolution of 640 pixels per line with 480 lines.) In order to display one screen of information, each picture element must be changed. This requires a high-speed microprocessor. Many new software packages use this type of video interface. These packages require high microprocessor speeds for quick and efficient manipulation of video text or graphical data. The most striking system, which requires high-speed computing for its graphical display, is Microsoft Corporation's Windows* version 3.0.

The 32-bit microprocessor is needed because of the size of its data bus, which transfers real numbers that require 32-bit-wide memory. In order to efficiently process

---

*Windows® is a registered trademark of Microsoft Corporation.

32-bit real numbers, the microprocessor must be able to pass them between itself and memory. If they pass through an 8-bit data bus, it takes four read or write cycles, but when passed through a 32-bit data bus, only one read or write cycle is required. This significantly increases the speed of any program that manipulates real numbers. Most high-level languages, spreadsheets, and database management systems use real numbers.

Besides providing higher clocking speeds, the 80386 includes a memory management unit, which allows memory resources to be allocated and managed by the operating system. Earlier microprocessors left memory management to the software. The 80386 includes hardware circuitry for memory management and assignment.

The 80486 Microprocessor. In 1989, Intel released the 80486 microprocessor, which incorporated the 80386 microprocessor, and 80387 numeric coprocessor, and an 8K byte cache memory into one integrated package. Although the 80486 is not radically different from the 80386, it does include one major change. The internal structure of the 80486 is modified from the 80386, so about half its instructions execute in one clock. Because the 80486 is available in a 33-MHz version, about half the instructions execute in 33.3 ns (33 MIPS). The average speed improvement is about 50 percent over the 80386 operated at the same clock frequency.

Table 1–2 lists many microprocessors produced by Intel and Motorola, with information about their word and memory sizes. Other companies produce microprocessors, but none have had the success of Intel and to a lesser degree Motorola.

TABLE 1–2 Many modern microprocessors

Manufacturer	Part Number	Data Bus Width	Memory Size
Intel	8048	8	2K internal
	8051	8	8K internal
	8085A	8	64K
	8086	16	1M
	8088	8	1M
	8096	16	8K internal
	80186	16	1M
	80188	8	1M
	80286	16	16M
	80386DX	32	4G
	80386SL	16	32M
	80386SX	16	16M
	80486DX	32	4G
	80486SX	32	4G
Motorola	6800	8	64K
	6805	8	2K
	6809	8	64K
	68000	16	16M
	68008	8	1M or 4M
	68010	16	16M
	68020	32	4G
	68030	32	4G
	68040	32	4G

1–2   BASIC 80286 ARCHITECTURE

Efficient programming and interfacing depend upon a clear understanding of the basic microprocessor architecture. This section provides a detailed description of the basic architecture of the 80286 microprocessor, while later chapters detail the architecture of the 80386 and 80486.

Internal 80286 Architecture

Like early microprocessors, the 80286 fetches its instructions from the memory, but it does so in an entirely new way. Early microprocessors fetched an instruction from memory and executed it, then fetched the next instruction. This process continued in round-robin fashion as long as the microprocessor executed software. The 80286 still fetches instructions from memory, but as one instruction executes, the microprocessor has already fetched the next and has begun to process it.

Figure 1–1(a) illustrates the operation of an earlier microprocessor, such as the Intel 8085 or Motorola 6800. The instruction is first fetched or read from memory. Next, the microprocessor decodes the instruction and executes it. This sequence continues with many areas in the timing where the system bus is idle, such as during the decoding of each instruction and during the execution of certain instructions. The 80286 microprocessor makes use of most of the bus idle time.

Figure 1–1(b) illustrates the sequence of events as a program is executed by the 80286 microprocessor. The microprocessor still fetches, decodes, and executes instructions. The difference is, while it is fetching one instruction, it is decoding a second and executing a third. This form of operation is called a *pipeline*. Information feeds into the microprocessor through the system buses where the microprocessor decodes it and passes it to the execution unit for execution. All of these operations occur sequentially so different sections of the microprocessor can process different stages, of different instructions, simultaneously.

The Internal Structure.   The 80286 contains four internal processing sections that correspond to the four phases of operation pictured in Figure 1–1(b). These four internal units are the *bus unit* (BU), *instruction unit* (IU), *execution unit* (EU), and *address unit* (AU). All four units simultaneously process different phases of different instructions. The pipeline interconnects these units. The pipe connects from the memory to the bus unit, from the bus unit to the instruction unit, from the instruction unit to the execution unit, and from the execution unit to the address unit. Figure 1–2 illustrates the internal organization of the 80286 microprocessor.

The Bus Unit (BU).   The *bus unit* controls the system buses and distributes information between the microprocessor and memory or input/output (I/O). It also passes information between itself and the address unit, execution unit, and instruction unit.

One important feature of the bus unit is the prefetch queue. (The term *queue* is British and it is used by the British to describe the way that people line up for a bus. In Great Britain people queue up for the bus.) The prefetch queue separates the bus unit from the instruction unit. The prefetch queue stores and then passes

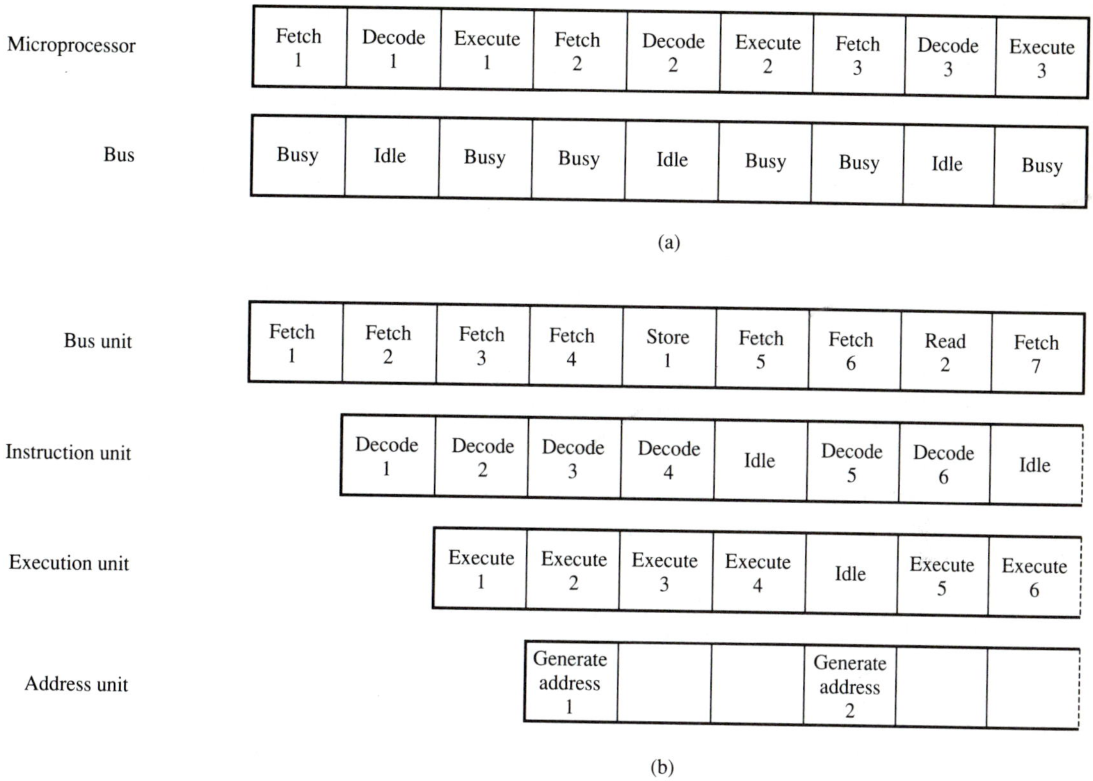

Microprocessor	Fetch 1	Decode 1	Execute 1	Fetch 2	Decode 2	Execute 2	Fetch 3	Decode 3	Execute 3
Bus	Busy	Idle	Busy	Busy	Idle	Busy	Busy	Idle	Busy

(a)

Bus unit	Fetch 1	Fetch 2	Fetch 3	Fetch 4	Store 1	Fetch 5	Fetch 6	Read 2	Fetch 7
Instruction unit		Decode 1	Decode 2	Decode 3	Decode 4	Idle	Decode 5	Decode 6	Idle
Execution unit			Execute 1	Execute 2	Execute 3	Execute 4	Idle	Execute 5	Execute 6
Address unit			Generate address 1			Generate address 2			

(b)

FIGURE 1–1 (a) The operation of an early microprocessor such as the 8085A. (b) The operation of the 80286 pipelined microprocessor.

opcodes from the BU to the IU. The prefetch queue in the 80286 stores 6 bytes of opcodes. If the BU becomes idle, it fetches instructions from the memory and fills the prefetch queue with several instructions. This one feature alone accounts for a large percentage of the increased speed of the 80286 microprocessor. The prefetch queue is often called a *look-ahead buffer* or *instruction cache.*

The Instruction Unit (IU). The instruction unit receives opcodes from the BU through the prefetch queue and decodes them. These decoded instructions pass into another queue called an *instruction queue* located between the IU and the execution unit. This queue is three instructions deep and again increases the performance of the 80286.

The Execution Unit (EU). The execution unit receives the decoded instruction from the instruction queue. The execution unit executes instructions that it receives from the queue and uses the BU to transfer data between the 80286 and the memory and I/O.

The Address Unit (AU). The address unit generates all addresses for memory and I/O accesses. The AU passes the address to the BU so memory and I/O are accessed; it also performs memory management using a variety of address translation techniques

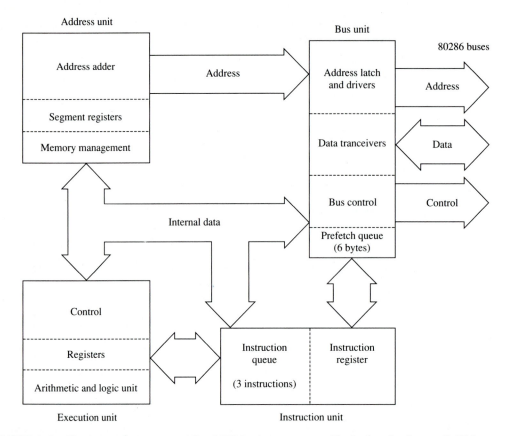

FIGURE 1–2   The internal structure of the 80286 microprocessor illustrating the bus unit (BU), instruction unit (IU), execution unit (EU), and the address unit (AU).

that convert the *linear address,* which is generated by software, into a *physical address* that accesses a physical memory or I/O location.

80286 System Architecture

Figure 1–3 illustrates the system architecture of the 80286 microprocessor-based system. The system contains the 80286 microprocessor, a clock generator (82284), a system bus controller (82288), memory, and I/O devices. Communications between the microprocessor and the system occur via the address, data, and control buses. The address bus provides memory and I/O with an address that selects a unique memory location or I/O device. The data bus transfers data between the microprocessor and the memory or I/O. The control bus provides control signals that cause a read or a write and select memory or an I/O device.

Address Bus.   The *address bus* in the 80286 contains 24 bits or connections labeled A23–A0. The A0 position is the least significant address bus connection. A 24-bit address allows the 80286 to address up to 16M bytes of memory space. Each memory

FIGURE 1–3 The 80286 system architecture using the 82284 clock generator and the 82288 bus controller.

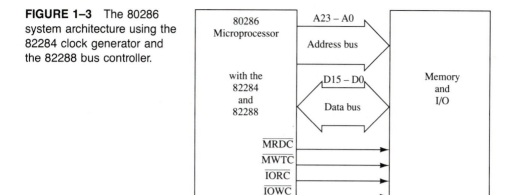

location (address) is numbered in hexadecimal and holds one byte of data. The first byte of memory is numbered 000000_{16} and the last byte is numbered $FFFFFF_{16}$. The address bus also addresses the I/O devices in the system, but only 16 of its 24 bits select an I/O device. Address bus connections A15–A0 provide the address for up to 64K different I/O devices. The I/O devices are addressed using locations 0000_{16} through $FFFF_{16}$.

Data Bus. The 80286 contains a set of 16 lines that function as a *data bus*. These connections (D15–D0) transfer a byte or word of data between the microprocessor and the memory or I/O. The data bus also functions during an interrupt acknowledge to fetch the interrupt-type number through bus connections D7–D0.

Data transfers, through the 16-bit data bus, occur 8 or 16 bits at a time. If an 8-bit number is transferred, only half the data bus performs the transfer. All even-addressed data bytes pass through D7–D0, and all odd-addressed data bytes pass through D15–D8.

Control Bus. The *control bus* controls the memory and I/O attached to the address and data buses of the 80286. The 82288 system bus controller generates the control bus signals. Most microprocessor-based systems contain four main control bus signals: $\overline{MRDC}$, $\overline{MWTC}$, $\overline{IORC}$, and $\overline{IOWC}$.

The $\overline{MRDC}$ (*memory read*) and $\overline{MWTC}$ (*memory write*) signals control the reading and writing of memory data. The $\overline{IORC}$ (*I/O read*) and $\overline{IOWC}$ (*I/O write*) control signals control the reading and writing of I/O data.

The microprocessor accesses a memory location by placing a physical address on the address bus. It next issues either a memory read or memory write signal to activate the memory device. Finally the memory responds by either sending data to the microprocessor for a read, or accepting data from the microprocessor for a write. Note that the data moved between the memory and the microprocessor travel through the data bus.

The microprocessor accesses an I/O device by sending the device address to the I/O device through the address bus (A15–A0). It next issues either an I/O read or I/O write signal to activate the I/O device. Finally the I/O device responds by moving data between itself and the microprocessor through the data bus connections.

1–3   MEMORY FOR THE 80286, 80386, AND 80486 MICROPROCESSORS

Memory for the microprocessor appears to a programmer as logical memory, and to the hardware system as physical memory. The memory maps for the 80286 and the 80386/80486 differ in size. The memory maps for these microprocessors are presented in this section of the text so software can be developed for any of these machines.

The Linear Memory System

Memory appears to the programmer differently than to the circuitry. This programmer's view of the memory system is often called the *linear memory*. Linear memory allows the programmer to develop software that is upward compatible from the 80286 to the 80386 and 80486. In fact, software written for the 8086 and 8088 are also upward compatible with these microprocessors. Figure 1–4 illustrates the logical memory map of the 80286, 80386, and 80486 microprocessors. Notice that memory addresses are in hexadecimal and extend from location 000000H–FFFFFFH on the 80286 (16M bytes) and from location 00000000H–FFFFFFFFH on the 80386 and 80486 (4G bytes). These memory addresses are often referred to as *linear* or *logical addresses*. Each logical memory location is always 8 bits wide. (*Note:* The letter H shows that a number is hexadecimal or base 16. The hexadecimal number system uses the numerals 0–9 and letter A, B, C, D, E, and F to represent the numbers 10 through 15.)

FIGURE 1–4   The logical memory maps of the (a) 80286 and (b) 80386 and 80486 microprocessors.

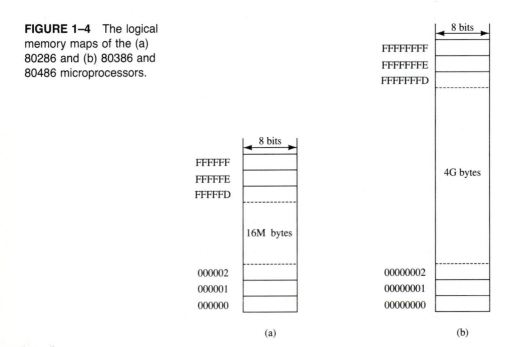

We represent data as bytes (8 bits) or words (16 bits) in the 80286 system. A word is two consecutive memory locations (2 bytes). Data appears as bytes, words, or double-words (32 bits) in the 80386 and 80486 systems. A double-word is four consecutive bytes of logical memory. Whenever multiple-byte data (words or double-words) appear in the memory, the least significant portion is always stored in the lowest numbered memory locations. For example, if memory locations 001000H and 001001H contain the word FA23H, location 001000 stores the 23H and location 001001H holds the FAH. If a double-word of 12345678H is stored at memory location 00100000H–00100003H, then locations 00100000H = 78H, 00100001H = 56H, 00100002H = 34H, and 00100003H = 12H.

The Physical Memory System

The physical memory systems of the 80286 and the 80386 and 80486 differ in width. *Physical memory* is the memory system as viewed by the hardware of the microprocessor. Physical memory is addressed by a physical memory address. The 80286 uses a 16-bit-wide memory system, and the 80386 and 80486 use a 32-bit-wide memory system. For programming, there is no difference—memory is always considered 8 bits wide. This makes all versions of the microprocessor, from the 8086 upward to the 80486, compatible. This upward compatibility has led to the success of this line of microprocessor because software written in 1978 for the 8086 functions on the latest version of the 80486.

80286 Physical Memory. The 80286 physical memory map appears in Figure 1–5. This memory is 16 bits wide and contains two 8-bit-wide banks of memory. Each memory bank contains 8M bytes of memory for a total space of 16M bytes. The

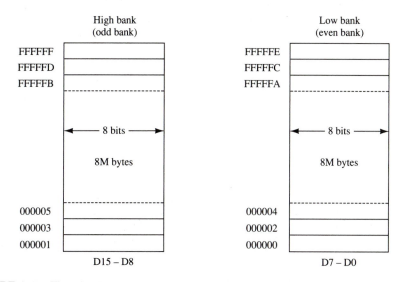

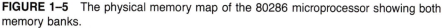

FIGURE 1–5 The physical memory map of the 80286 microprocessor showing both memory banks.

high bank connects to the most-significant data bus half and the low bank to the least-significant half. The high bank always contains odd-numbered memory bytes, and the low bank contains even-numbered bytes.

This organization allows the 80286 to access any byte of memory or any word in one read or write operation. An 8-bit write to memory location 000001H activates the high bank so data are written into a single 8-bit memory location. A 16-bit write causes both memory banks to activate, writing two bytes of data. All 16-bit data are customarily stored at even-numbered memory locations so the microprocessor can write data to two banks simultaneously. If 16-bit data are stored at an odd location, the microprocessor writes the odd byte first, and then the even byte. This requires twice as much time and should be avoided.

80386 and 80486 Physical Memory.   Memory for the 80386 and 80486 microprocessors is identical, and the physical memory map for both machines appears in Figure 1–6. These microprocessors address a physical memory space that is 32 bits wide and contains four 8-bit memory banks. Four banks appear in these microprocessors so data can be written as a byte, word, or double-word.

Each memory bank connects to 8 bits of the 32-bit data bus. A word is stored at location 00000000H or 00000002H, but not usually at location 00000001H or 00000003H. A double-word is normally stored at locations 00000000H, 00000004H, 00000008H, etc. Each bank contains up to 1G bytes of data, allowing up to 4G bytes to be accessed in the four memory banks. Please note that even though these microprocessors address 4G bytes of memory, many computer systems containing them only allow 16M or 32M bytes of total memory. Eventually software applications and lower memory prices will push this limit toward 4G bytes.

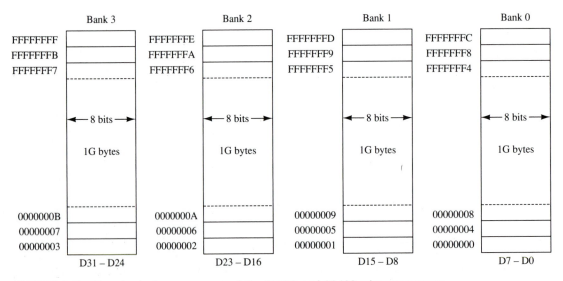

FIGURE 1–6   The physical memory map of the 80386 and 80486 microprocessors.

1–4   THE 80286 PROGRAMMING MODEL

All programming methods depend upon a clear understanding of the internal structure of the 80286 microprocessor. This section of the text illustrates the programming model and explains how memory addresses are formed through a segment and an offset address. It also introduces the idea of memory management. Memory management is fully explained in Chapter 5, which discusses program control instructions.

The 80386 and 80486 programming models are upward compatible with the 80286. The 80386 and 80486 programming models appear in later chapters, which deal with these improved versions of the 80286.

Figure 1–7 illustrates the programming model of the 80286 microprocessor. Incidentally, the programming model of the 80286 is almost identical with the older 8088 and 8086 microprocessors. The main difference is the memory-

FIGURE 1–7 The programming model of the 80286 microprocessor. (Note that the registers used for memory management are not shown with this general programming model.)

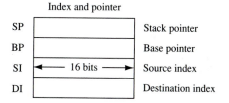

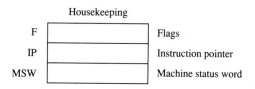

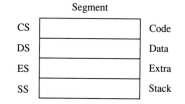

management register, called the machine status word (MSW). The MSW allows the microprocessors to control the memory system above location 0FFFFFH. This area of memory and this register are not available in the 8086 and 8088. Otherwise the 80286 is identical to the 8086 and 8088.

The internal structure of the 80286 has four groups of registers: *general-purpose registers, index and pointer registers, housekeeping registers,* and *segment registers.* These registers are accessed by software. Additional registers also exist that allow memory management. One is the MSW and others, which do not appear in the programming model, are considered invisible to the program. The *program-invisible* memory-management registers are depicted and described with memory management in Chapter 5.

General-Purpose Registers

The general-purpose registers function in any way the programmer wishes. Each general-purpose register is addressable as a 16-bit register (AX, BX, CX, and DX) or as an 8-bit register (AH, AL, BH, BL, CH, CL, DH, and DL). Some instructions explained in later chapters also use the general-purpose registers for specific tasks. For this reason each register has a name (*accumulator, base index, count,* and *data*). In assembly language programming, the general-purpose registers are always referenced with their two-letter designation. For example, the accumulator is referred to as AX or as AH or as AL.

The primary functions of the general-purpose registers are:

AX   (*Accumulator*)—often holds the temporary result after an arithmetic or logic operation. The accumulator also holds the product after a multiplication and the dividend before a division.

BX   (*Base*)—holds the offset address of a memory location when used as an indirect address. Also used with the XLAT instruction to address a lookup table by holding the base address of the table.

CX   (*Count*)—contains a count for instructions such as the shift and rotate count (CL) for the shift and rotate instructions. It also holds the count (CX) for the repeat prefixes of string instructions and the LOOP instructions.

DX   (*Data*)—a general-purpose register that holds the most-significant part of the 32-bit product after a 16-bit multiplication. It also holds the most-significant part of the 32-bit dividend before a 16-bit division and the I/O port number for variable I/O instructions. The AX register holds the least-significant parts of the 32-bit product or dividend.

Index and Pointer Registers

Although the index and pointer registers are also general purpose in nature, they are most often used to index or point to a memory location. The base index register (see general-purpose registers) is also often used to address memory data.

The function of each index and pointer register follows:

SP   (*Stack Pointer*)—addresses data within the stack segment for the LIFO (last-in, first-out) stack. Some instructions that use the SP are: PUSH, PUSHA, PUSHF, POP, POPA, POPF, CALL, and RETurn. The stack pointer contains the offset address of the data located in the stack segment.

BP   (*Base Pointer*)—a general-purpose pointer used to address data within the stack segment.

SI   (*Source Index*)—used with the string instructions to address source data in the data segment. Also used for general-purpose memory addressing in the data segment.

DI   (*Destination Index*)—normally used to address data with the string instructions in the extra segment. Also used for general-purpose memory addressing in the data segment.

Segment Registers

Segment registers are unique to the Intel family of microprocessors and first appeared in the 8086/8088 microprocessor. They were designed to allow relocatable software. Relocation is explained after describing the purpose and the use of the segment register.

The address bus of the 80286 is 24 bits wide. The 80286 operates in two distinct modes: real and protected. Real mode operation causes the 80286 to behave like an 8086/8088 microprocessor. In real mode, the 80286 uses a 20-bit address that appears on pins A19–A0. Address connections A23–A20 are 0000_2 during real mode operation. Segment registers hold a segment address in the real mode. In protected mode operation, the 80286 has access to all 16M bytes of memory through its 24-bit address bus. In protected mode operation the segment register contains a selector, not a segment address. Selectors are described with the memory manager. This portion of the text assumes that real mode operation is in effect.

In the 80286 microprocessor a *segment* is a block of memory (up to 64K bytes in length) addressed by a special register called a *segment register*. Figure 1–8 shows segments in the memory of the 80286 microprocessor. Four separate segments coexist in the memory space: *code segment, data segment, stack segment,* and *extra segment*. The *index registers* and *pointer registers* index or point to data located within a memory segment.

Each segment register holds a 16-bit segment address, which helps to form a 20-bit address that accesses a 64K byte memory segment located in the 1M byte memory system. The 20-bit memory address is formed by appending the contents of the segment register with a 0000_2 (0H) on its least-significant end. So a segment register that contains a 2000H actually addresses memory location 20000H. Table 1–3 provides examples of the contents of segment registers and the segment addresses generated by them.

Memory segments may overlap completely or may be spaced as closely as 16 bytes. (The 16-byte spacing is often called a *paragraph*.) If an 80286 system

FIGURE 1–8 An example memory map illustrating the contents of each segment register and the location of the segments in the memory.

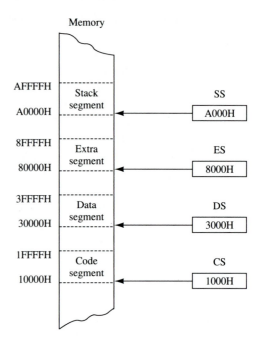

contains only 64K bytes of memory, we load all four segment registers with 0000H, and all segments overlap. Segment size usually determines segment placement in a system. Figure 1–9 illustrates a memory map using three segments: code, data, and stack. In this example, the code segment is 2K bytes in length, the data segment is 1K byte in length, and the stack segment is 256 bytes in length. Note the segment register contents and the compactness of this map.

Each segment register functions with one or more index or pointer registers to generate an effective address. The index register, pointer register, or a value following the instruction contains the offset address. The *offset address* adds to the beginning location of the segment to generate the *effective address*. At times we write the effective address as DS:BX if we are using the data segment as the segment address and the BX register as the offset. An SS:BP indicates the stack segment using the base pointer as an offset address.

TABLE 1–3 The contents of segment registers and the 64K byte block of memory addressed by them

Segment Register	Memory Address Range
0100H	01000H–10FFFH
0101H	01010H–1100FH
1234H	12340H–2233FH
2000H	20000H–2FFFFH

FIGURE 1–9 An example showing segments that are overlapped. Here the code segment begins at location 10000H and extends to 1FFFFH, but it is overlapped at location 10800H by the data segment and location 10C00H by the stack segment.

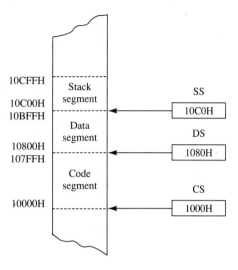

Figure 1–10 shows how a memory address is generated within a segment by adding the offset address to the starting address of a segment. In this example, the data segment register (DS) contains a 1000H, so the data segment begins at memory location 10000H. Because the offset address is a 0010H, held in BX, the effective address is at memory location 10010H (1000H × 10H + 0010H).

FIGURE 1–10 An example memory map depicting how address 10010H is referenced when DS = 1000H and BX contains an offset address of 0010H.

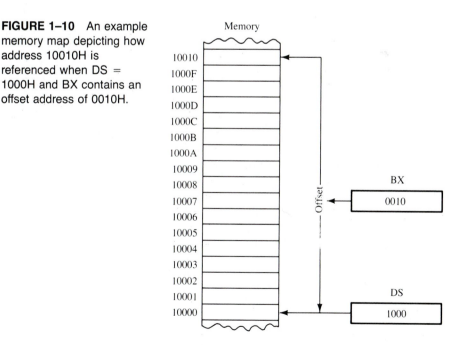

Segment registers normally function with a specific index or pointer register, but the default segment register can be overridden, as discussed in Chapter 3. The normal or *default* segment assignments are briefly described in the following list.

CS   (*Code Segment*)—a 64k byte section of the memory that contains the program or code. The code segment register changes for some jump, call, or return instrucitons. The address of the next instruction executed by the 80286 is generated by adding the contents of the instruction pointer (IP) to the contents of CS × 10H.

DS   (*Data Segment*)—a 64k byte section of the memory that contains data referenced by most instructions and many addressing modes. Data are usually moved into or out of the memory via the data segment. The effective address of the data is generated by adding the contents of an index or pointer register (BX, SI, or DI) to the contents of DS × 10H.

SS   (*Stack Segment*)—a 64K byte section of the memory used for the LIFO stack. The effective stack address is a combination of the contents of the stack pointer (SP) plus SS × 10H. For example, if SS contains a 1000H and SP contains a 0000H, the stack address is at memory location 10000H. Data referenced with the base pointer (BP) are normally found in the stack segment.

ES   (*Extra Segment*)—a special segment that is normally used only with the string instructions. When a string instruction executes, the destination index register (DI) plus ES × 10H forms the destination address. The source address is located by the source index (SI) plus DS × 10H.

Table 1–4 shows the normal or default segment register assignments and the alternate assignments. More information on address generation and the addressing modes appears in Chapter 2.

Segment registers allow software to be relocated without changing anything but the number contained in the segment register. Suppose a segment contains two bytes of data. Offset address 0000H contains a 06H and offset address 0001H contains a 1AH. At present the contents of the data segment register contains a 1000H. This

TABLE 1–4 Default and alternate address generation

Reference	Default Segment	Alternate Segment	Offset
Instruction fetch	CS	None	IP
Stack operation	SS	None	SP
Data (except for the following)	DS	CS, ES, or SS	BX, SI, DI, or 16-bit offset
String source	DS	CS, ES, or SS	SI
String destination	ES	None	DI
Base pointer	SS	CS, ES, or SS	BP

segment begins at location 10000H, where the 06H is stored, and ends at location 10001H, where the 1AH is stored.

This segment can be relocated if the data are moved to a new area of memory and the contents of the segment register are changed. Suppose the data segment is changed to a 1100H. This means this memory segment now begins at location 11000H. If the 06H and 1AH are moved to this new area of memory, the offset addresses do not change. Offset address 0000H now addresses location 11000H and offset address 0001H addresses location 11001H. Software is written to address memory via the offset address. If the offset address does not change when a memory segment is moved, the segment is considered relocatable because no change is required to the program using the data.

Housekeeping Registers

The 80286 housekeeping registers consist of the flags, instruction pointer (IP), and the machine status word (MSW). The term housekeeping refers to a register that is present and essential to the operation of the microprocessor, yet seldom directly addressed by an instruction.

The Flag Register. The *flag register,* also called a status register, is a 16-bit register that contains 11 active bits of information. The rightmost eight bits contain general user flags (SF, PF, AF, ZF, and SF). The leftmost eight bits contain additional flag bits (TF, IF, DF, OF, IOPL bits, and NT), which are mainly system flag bits except OF and DF.

Figure 1–11 illustrates the relative bit positions of each flag bit. The unused flag bits are reserved and should not be used for an application. The flag bits function as follows:

CF   (*Carry Flag*)—indicates a carry or a borrow following an arithmetic operation. *Carry* changes with some shift and rotate instructions and when the multiply instruction executes.

PF   (*Parity Flag*)—refers to the parity of the result of an arithmetic or logic operation. If the result contains an even number of ones, the parity bit sets (1) to indicate even parity. If the result contains an odd number of ones, the parity bit clears (0) to indicate odd parity.

AF   (*Auxiliary Carry Flag*)—holds a carry or borrow between half-bytes of an 8-bit arithmetic or logic operation using the AL register. This flag is used to adjust the result of BCD (binary-coded decimal) arithmetic.

ZF   (*Zero Flag*)—indicates whether the result of an arithmetic or logic operation is zero. If ZF = 1, the result is zero.

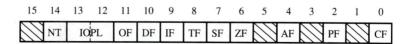

FIGURE 1–11   The 80286 flag register.

SF   (*Sign Flag*)—indicates the sign of the result of an arithmetic or logic operation. A logic 1 in the sign flag indicates a negative result.

TF   (*Trap Flag*)—causes the 80286 to enter a single-step debugging mode of operation. More detail on the TF bit and software that uses it is explained in Chapter 10.

IF   (*Interrupt Flag*)—enables or disables the INTR (interrupt request) input pin. If IF = 1, then INTR is enabled.

DF   (*Direction Flag*)—selects autoincrement or autodecrement operation for the destination index (DI) and source index (SI) in string instructions. If DF = 0, SI and/or DI are incremented during the execution of a string instruction.

OF   (*Overflow Flag*)—indicates an arithmetic overflow after an addition or subtraction. For example, if 7FH (+ 127) and 01H (+ 1) are added, and they are signed numbers, the result is 80H (−128). Because −128 is not the correct signed result, the OF flag sets (1) to indicate an overflow.

IOPL   (*I/O Privilege Level*)—used in protected mode operation to indicate the maximum current privilege level allowed before I/O instructions begin generating privilege violation exceptions (vector type 13). This flag bit is not present on an 8086 or 8088 microprocessor.

NT   (*Nested Task*)—used in protected mode operation to show that a task is nested within another task. This bit is tested by the interrupt return instruction. This flag bit is not present on an 8086 or 8088 microprocessor.

The Instruction Pointer (IP).   The instructor pointer register and the code segment register locate the next instruction in the program. Each time the 80286 fetches an instruction from the memory, CS × 10H and IP add to form the address of the instruction executed by the 80286. This register is modified by some of the instructions.

The Machine Status Word (MSW).   The 80286 microprocessor uses the machine status word (MSW) in the protected mode operation. The binary bit pattern of the MSW appears in Figure 1–12. Only the rightmost four bits of this register are currently in use for the 80286 microprocessor. The unused bits are reserved for use in future products such as the 80386 and 80486, where this register is called *control register 0*.

The MSW places the 80286 into the protected mode of operation if the PE bit is set. *Protected mode operation* allows access to memory above 0FFFFFH. This protected mode memory, at locations 100000H–FFFFFFH, is often called *extended memory.*

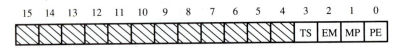

FIGURE 1–12   The 80286 machine status word (MSW) register.

The purpose of each MSW bit position follows:

PE   (*Protected Mode Enable*)—enables protected mode operation of the 80286 microprocessor. We enter protected mode by setting the PE bit, but cannot be exited by clearing it. To leave protected mode and return to real mode, the microprocessor must be reset.

MP   (*Monitor Processor Extension*)—allows WAIT instructions to cause a processor extension not present interrupt (vector 7). This bit shows that the coprocessor is not present.

EM   (*Emulate Coprocessor*)—shows the coprocessor is not present and that the coprocessor must be emulated with software.

TS   (*Task Switched*)—indicates the next instruction using the coprocessor will cause a type 7 exception. Both the TS and MP bits are set to indicate a coprocessor is present in a system. Otherwise software must be provided to emulate the function of the coprocessor.

Introduction to Protected Mode Operation

The 80286 operates in either the real or protected mode. In the real mode, it functions like an 8086/8088 microprocessor, allowing it to access only the first 1M bytes of the memory system. In the protected mode, the 80286 accesses all 16M bytes of memory through a memory-management scheme. We briefly introduce this scheme at this point and fully explain it in Chapter 5.

Protected mode addressing is identical with real mode addressing if only the first 1M bytes of memory are considered. The effective address is still generated using the segment register and an offset address. A program that functions in the real mode also functions in the protected mode without making any changes to any of the instructions. The difference with protected mode is the way a segment register addresses a memory segment.

In protected mode, the segment register holds a selector instead of a segment address. The *selector* chooses a descriptor and the descriptor describes the location of, access rights to, and function of the memory segment. Figure 1–13 illustrates the format of the segment register in protected mode. Notice it still contains a 16-bit number as it did in the real mode. The difference is that in the real mode, the segment number addresses an area of the memory. In protected mode, the segment number (called a selector) addresses a descriptor, which addresses an area of the memory.

The selector contains a 13-bit number, which indexes an entry in either a local descriptor table or a global descriptor table. The TI bit indicates whether the table is global (TI = 0) or local (TI = 1). Besides selecting a descriptor, the segment register also contains a 2-bit field that indicates the requested privilege level (RPL).

15	14	13	12	11	10	9	8	7	6	5	4	3	2	1	0
Selector													TI	RPL	

FIGURE 1–13 The format of a segment register used as a selector in the 80286 protected mode operation.

FIGURE 1–14 The 8-byte-long 80286 descriptor that contains the 24-bit address of the segment, the length of the segment, and the access rights.

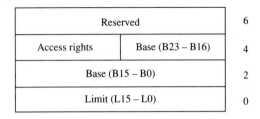

Reserved		6
Access rights	Base (B23 – B16)	4
Base (B15 – B0)		2
Limit (L15 – L0)		0

Segments in the 80286 protected mode have four privilege levels from 00 to 11. A privilege level of 00 is the highest and most protected, and 11 is the lowest and available to other privilege levels.

Figure 1–14 illustrates the format of a descriptor used to address a memory segment. The 80286 *descriptor* always contains a 24-bit base address that allows it to address any location in the 16M bytes available in the 80286 protected mode memory system. It also contains a 16-bit limit, which indicates the length of the segment of memory from 1 byte to 64K bytes. The *limit* contains the offset address of the last byte of the segment. The remainder of the descriptor contains the access rights byte and a reserved word that is only used in the 80386 and 80486 microprocessors. This reserved word contains part of a 32-bit base address and also part of a 20-bit segment limit in the 80386 or 80486 microprocessor.

In protected mode, the selector chooses a descriptor from a table located in the memory. The descriptor indicates the memory locations of the segment, 000000H–FFFFFFH, and the length of the segment from 1 byte to 64K bytes. Figure 1–15 shows how a segment of memory is addressed using a selector and descriptor from a descriptor table in the protected mode. This example addresses memory locations 2A1200H–2A1300H as a segment of memory located well above the real mode memory space.

The *access rights* byte indicates the type of segment (data, code, or stack) and the privilege level. The access rights byte also indicates whether the descriptor and its memory segment have been accessed. More detail of descriptors and protected mode operation appears in Chapter 5. Remember that all instructions are treated the same in either real or protected mode operation. For general-purpose programming, the type of segment addressing scheme is usually a domain of the operating system instead of user software.

Personal Computers.   Because the IBM personal computer (IBM PC) and clones are so popular today, we present a discussion of the memory organization of these systems. Figure 1–16 illustrates the organization of the memory system of the PC. Note that the memory contains three main parts: the *transient program area* (TPA), the *system area,* and *extended memory.* The TPA and system area appear in all IBM PCs and clones. Extended memory only appears in 80286-, 80386-, and 80486-based systems and requires protected mode operation for access. A system based on an 8086/8088 is called a PC (personal computer) or XT (extended architecture), and a system based on the 80286, 80386, or 80486 is often called an AT (advanced architecture).

The transient program area, at locations 00000H–9FFFFH (the first 640K bytes), is where all software are loaded into the machine for execution. This includes

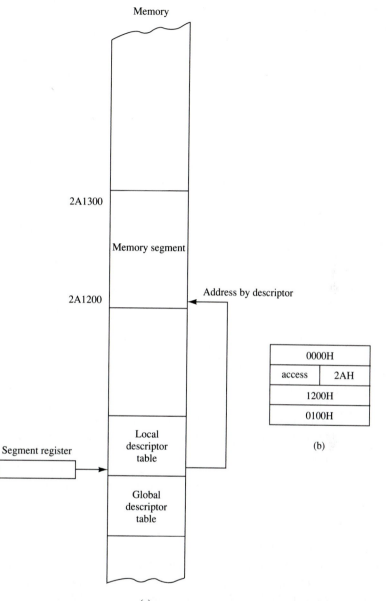

FIGURE 1–15 The protected mode addressing scheme of the 80286 microprocessor. (a) The selector addresses a descriptor in the local descriptor table. (b) The descriptor contains a base address of 2A1200H and a limit of 0100H that addresses a memory segment from location 2A1200H to location 2A1300H.

FIGURE 1–16 The memory
map of the IBM PC and all
clones of this machine.

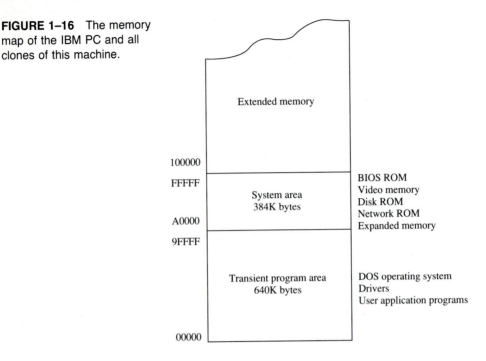

the operating system (MS-DOS* or PC-DOS†) and all the drivers that operate the computer's peripheral devices. The TPA contains read/write memory.

The system area contains the video display RAM and ROM memory used for the video display system. One important area of ROM contained in the system area is the BIOS (*basic I/O system*). The BIOS contains software that allows the computer to control the video, disk, and I/O devices. The BIOS makes the computer compatible with other computers because the functions it performs are universal to all computers. Other ROM memory exists for the video system, disk system, network cards, and fax cards.

One additional section of the system area is called *expanded memory.* The expanded memory usually occupies a 64K byte unused opening or *page frame* in the system area. This memory system expands the basic TPA beyond 640K bytes. Expanded memory can be used in the PC, XT, or AT types of computer systems. Expansion is accomplished by filling the 64K-byte page frame in the system area with many pages of memory. Figure 1–17 shows how a 1M byte expanded memory occupies the 64K page frame at locations D0000H–DFFFFH in the system area. Note that expanded memory is available as a 64K page at a time in this system-area window. The location of the page frame may vary from one system to another due to the location of other ROM memory. A driver pages through the expanded memory when supported by software program.

---

*MS-DOS® is a trademark of Microsoft Corporation.
†PC-DOS® is a trademark of IBM Corporation.

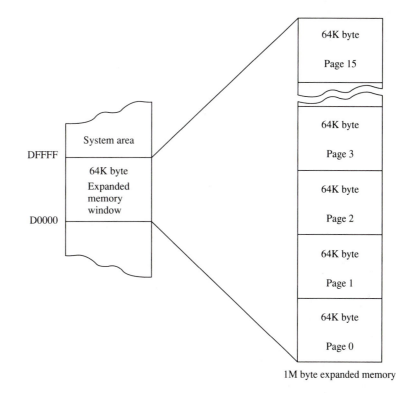

FIGURE 1–17 The expanded memory system using locations D0000H–DFFFFH as a page frame.

The extended memory system begins at location 100000H and continues to the top of the memory. In a system based upon the 80286 or 80386SX, extended memory begins at location 0100000H and extends to location FFFFFFH for a total of 15M bytes of extended memory. In a system based upon the 80386DX, 80486DX, or 80486SX, extended memory begins at location 00010000H and extends to location FFFFFFFFH for a total of 4,095M bytes of extended memory. At present few computers or programs support more than 16M or 32M bytes of total system memory.

1–5   DATA FORMATS

Successful programming depends on a clear understanding of data formats. In this section, we describe the common data formats used with the 80286, 80386, and 80486 microprocessors. Data appear as ASCII, BCD, signed and unsigned integers, and floating-point numbers (real numbers).

ASCII Data

ASCII (American Standard Code for Information Interchange) data (see Table 1–5) represents alphanumeric characters in the memory of a computer system. The *ASCII*

TABLE 1–5 The ASCII code

Second	0X	1X	2X	3X	4X	5X	6X	7X
				First				
X0	NUL	DLE	SP	0	@	P	`	p
X1	SOH	DC1	!	1	A	Q	a	q
X2	STX	DC2	"	2	B	R	b	r
X3	ETX	DC3	#	3	C	S	c	s
X4	EOT	DC4	$	4	D	T	d	t
X5	ENQ	NAK	%	5	E	U	e	u
X6	ACK	SYN	&	6	F	V	f	v
X7	BEL	ETB	'	7	G	W	g	w
X8	BS	CAN	(	8	H	X	h	x
X9	HT	EM	)	9	I	Y	i	y
XA	LF	SUB	*	:	J	Z	j	z
XB	VT	ESC	+	;	K	[	k	{
XC	FF	FS	,	<	L	\	l	¦
XD	CR	GS	-	=	M	]	m	}
XE	SO	RS	.	>	N	^	n	~
XF	SI	US	/	?	O	_	o	▦

code is a 7-bit code with the eighth and most-significant bit used to hold parity in some systems. If ASCII data are used with a printer, the most-significant bit is a 0 for alphanumeric printing, and 1 for graphics printing. In the PC, extended characters are selected by a logic 1 in the leftmost bit. Table 1–6 shows the extended characters using code 80H–FFH. The extended characters store foreign letters and punctuation,

TABLE 1–6 Extended ASCII characters

Second	8X	9X	AX	BX	CX	DX	EX	FX
				First				
X0			á	▦	└	⊥	α	≡
X1			í	▨	┴	╤	β	±
X2			ó	▦	┬	╥	Γ	≥
X3			ú	│	├	╙	π	≤
X4			ñ	┤	─	╘	Σ	
X5			Ñ	╡	┼	╒	σ	
X6			a	╢	╞	╓	μ	÷
X7			o	╖	╟	╫	τ	≈
X8			¿	╕	╚	╪	Φ	°
X9			⌐	╣	╔	┘	Θ	•
XA			¬	║	╩	┌	Ω	·
XB			½	╗	╦	■	δ	√
XC			¼	╝	╠	▄	∞	η
XD			¡	╜	=	▐	φ	2
XE			«	╛	╬	▌	ε	■
XF			»	┐	╧	▀	∩	

Greek characters, mathematical characters, box drawing characters, and other special characters.

The ASCII control characters, also listed in Table 1–5, perform control functions in a computer system. These include clear screen, backspace, and line fed. To enter the control codes through the computer keyboard, the control key is held down while typing a letter. To obtain the control code 01H, type a control A, a 02H is obtained by a control B, etc.

To use Table 1–5 for converting alphanumeric or control characters into ASCII characters, first locate the alphanumeric code for conversion. Next follow up the column to the hexadecimal numbers listed across the top for the first digit of the hexadecimal ASCII code. Follow the column to the left for the second digit. For example, the letter A is ASCII code 41H.

BCD (Binary-Coded Decimal) Data

Binary-coded decimal (BCD) information is stored in either packed or unpacked forms. Packed BCD data are stored as two digits per byte and unpacked BCD data are stored as one digit per byte. The range of BCD data extends from 0000 to 1001, or 0–9.

Table 1–7 shows some decimal numbers converted to both the packed and unpacked BCD forms. Applications that require BCD data are point-of-sales terminals and almost any device that performs a minimum amount of simple arithmetic. If a system requires complex arithmetic, BCD data are seldom used because there is no simple and efficient method of performing complex BCD arithmetic.

Byte-Sized Data

Byte-sized data are stored as unsigned and signed integers. Figure 1–18 illustrates both the unsigned and signed forms of the byte-sized integer. The only difference between both forms is the weight of the leftmost bit position. Its value is 128 for the unsigned integer and −128 for the signed integer. In the signed integer format, the leftmost bit represents the sign bit of the number as well as a weight of −128. For example, an 80H represents a value of 128 as an unsigned number, while as a signed number it represents a value of −128. Unsigned integers range in value from 00H to FFH (0–255). Signed integers range in value from −128 to 0 to +127.

Although negative signed numbers are represented in this way, they are stored in the *two's complement form*. The method of evaluating a signed number, using the weights of each bit position, is much easier than the act of two's complementing a number to find its value. This is especially true in the world of calculators designed for programmers.

TABLE 1–7 Packed and unpacked BCD data

Decimal	Packed		Unpacked		
12	0001 0010		0000 0001	0000 0010	
623	0000 0110	0010 0011	0000 0110	0000 0010	0000 0011
910	0000 1001	0001 0000	0000 1001	0000 0001	0000 0000

FIGURE 1–18   8-bit integers. (a) An unsigned 8-bit integer. (b) A signed 8-bit integer.

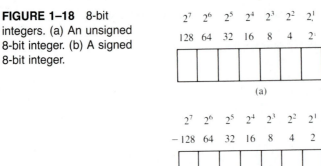

Whenever a number is two's complemented, its sign changes from negative to positive or positive to negative. For example, the number 00001000 is a +8. Its negative value (−8) is found by two's complementing the +8. To form a two's complement, we first one's complement the number. We one's complement a number by inverting each bit of a number. Once the one's complement is formed, the two's complement is found by adding a one to the one's complement. Example 1–1 shows how numbers are two's complemented using this technique.

EXAMPLE 1–1

+ 8 = 00001000

$$\begin{array}{r} 11110111 \ \text{(one's complement)} \\ + \qquad\qquad 1 \\ \hline \text{- 8} = \ 11111000 \ \text{(two's complement)} \end{array}$$

Word-Sized Data

A *word* (16-bits) is formed with two bytes of data. The least-significant byte is always stored in the lowest numbered memory location, and the most-significant byte in the highest. Figure 1–19(a) shows the weights of each bit position in a word of data, and Figure 1–19(b) shows how the number 1234H appears when stored in the memory. The only difference between a signed and an unsigned word is the leftmost bit position. In the unsigned form, the leftmost bit is unsigned, and in the signed form its weight is a −32,768. As with byte-sized signed data, the signed word is in two's complement form when representing a negative number.

Double-Word-Sized Data

Double-word-sized data require four bytes to store because they are a 32-bit number. Double-word data appear as a product after a multiplication and also as a

FIGURE 1–19 16-bit integers. (a) The binary weights of each bit position in a 16-bit word of data. Recall that if the number is signed, the weight of the leftmost bit position is negative. (b) A 1234H stored in the memory beginning at location 10000H.

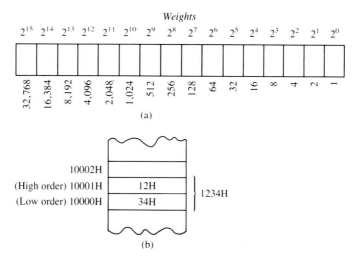

dividend before a division. Figure 1–20 shows the form used to store double words in the memory and the binary weights of each bit position.

Figure 1–21 shows how an address (segment and offset) is stored in a 32-bit section of the memory. Notice that the offset address appears in the two lowest numbered memory locations with the least-significant byte stored first. Following the offset address is the segment address stored in the next two bytes of memory. The segment number is also stored with its least-significant byte first.

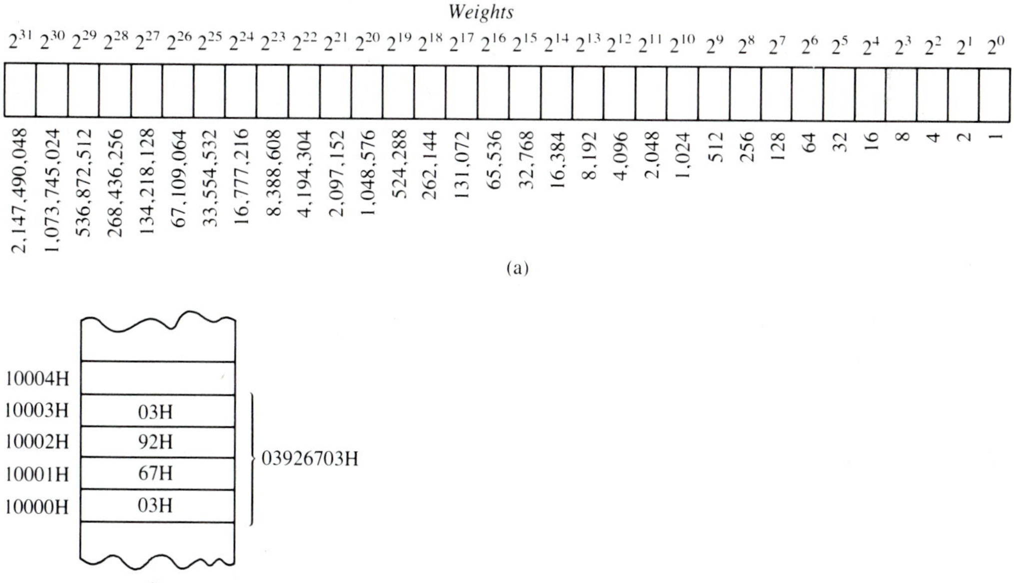

FIGURE 1–20 32-bit integers. (a) The binary weights of each bit position in a 32-bit double word of data. (b) A 03926703H stored in the memory beginning at location 10000H.

FIGURE 1–21   An example memory map illustrating how memory address 11300H is stored in the memory. The segment number is 1100H and the offset address is 0300H. Notice that the offset address is stored first, followed by the segment address.

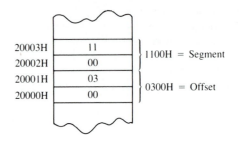

Real Numbers

Because many high-level languages use the 80286, 80386, and 80486 microprocessors, real numbers are often encountered. A real number, or as it is often called, a *floating-point number,* contains two parts: a *mantissa* and an *exponent.* Figure 1–22 depicts both the 4- and 8-byte forms of real numbers as they are stored in any Intel system. Note that the 4-byte real number is called *single-precision* and the 8-byte form is called *double-precision.* The form presented here is the same form specified by the IEEE standard, IEEE-754, version 10.0. This standard has been adopted as the standard form of real number with virtually all high-level programming languages and many applications packages. Figure 1–22(a) shows the single-precision form that contains a sign-bit, an 8-bit exponent, and a 24-bit fraction (mantissa).

Simple arithmetic indicates that it should take 33 bits to store all three pieces of data. Not true—the 24-bit mantissa contains an implied (hidden) one-bit that allows the mantissa to represent 24 bits while being stored in only 23 bits. The *hidden bit* is the first bit of the normalized real number. When normalizing a number, it is adjusted so its value is at least 1, but less than 2. For example, if we convert a 12 to binary (1100) and normalize it, the result is a 1.1×2^3. The 1 is not stored in the

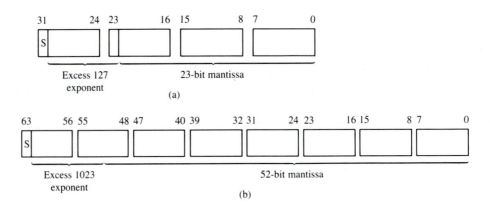

FIGURE 1–22   Real or floating-point data storage. (a) The 4-byte short form of a real number. (b) The 8-byte long form of a real number.

TABLE 1–8   Single-precision real numbers

Decimal	Binary	Normalized	Sign	Biased Exponent	Mantissa
+12	1100	1.1×2^3	0	10000010	1000000 00000000 00000000
−12	1100	-1.1×2^3	1	10000010	1000000 00000000 00000000
+100	1100100	1.1001×2^6	0	10000101	1001000 00000000 00000000
−1.75	1.11	-1.11×2^0	1	01111111	1100000 00000000 00000000
+0.25	.01	1.0×2^{-2}	0	01111101	0000000 00000000 00000000
+0.0	0	0	0	00000000	0000000 00000000 00000000

23-bit mantissa portion of the number. The 1 is the hidden one-bit. Table 1–8 shows the single-precision form of this number and others.

The exponent is stored as a biased exponent. With the single-precision form of the real number, the bias is 127 (7FH), and with the double-precision form, it is 1023 (3FFH). The *bias* adds to the exponent before it is stored into the exponent portion of the floating-point number. In the previous example there is an exponent of 2^3, represented as a biased exponent of $127 + 3$ or 130 (82H) in the short form or as 1026 (402H) in the long form.

There are two exceptions to the rules for floating-point numbers. The number 0.0 is stored as all zeros; the number infinity is stored as all ones. The sign-bit indicates a ± 0.0 or a $\pm \infty$.

1–6   THE INSTRUCTION SET

The 80286 instruction set is identical, except for the memory management instructions presented here and in Chapter 5, to the older 8086 and 8088 microprocessors that only function in the real mode. The main difference between the older 8086/8088 and the 80286 is the memory-management unit that allows the 80286 to operate in protected mode. All instructions beginning with the 8086/8088 are upward compatible to the 80486 microprocessor.

This section provides an overview of each general category of the instruction set and each instruction. Usage of each instruction is further explained in Chapters 2–5. The categories of the instruction set described are: data transfer, arithmetic, bit manipulation, string, program transfer, and processor control.

Data Transfer

The 80286 instruction set includes 16 data transfer instructions. These instructions transfer data between registers, between a register and a memory location, and between the microprocessor and the stack memory system. Two instructions (IN and OUT) transfer bytes or words between the microprocessor and the I/O devices in the

TABLE 1–9 80286 data transfer instructions

Opcode	Function
IN	Inputs data to accumulator from I/O device
LAHF	Moves flags into AH
LEA	Loads effective address
LDS	Loads DS and word register with a 32-bit address
LES	Loads ES and word register with a 32-bit address
MOV	Moves byte or word
OUT	Outputs data from accumulator to I/O device
POP	Pops word from stack
POPA*	Pops all general and pointer registers from stack
POPF	Pops flags from stack
PUSH	Pushes word onto stack
PUSHA*	Pushes all general and pointer registers onto stack
PUSHF	Pushes flags onto stack
SAHF	Loads flags from AH
XCHG	Exchanges bytes or words
XLAT	Translates data from a lookup table

Note: PUSHA and POPA are not available on the earlier 8086 or 8088 microprocessors.

computer system. Table 1–9 lists the data transfer instructions and briefly describes the operating characteristics of each. Of all the data transfer instructions, the MOV, PUSH, and POP instructions are the most commonly used in programs.

Arithmetic

The 80286 can add, subtract, multiply, and divide data as either bytes or words. The system adds and subtracts by using signed or unsigned bytes or words and BCD or ASCII data. It multiplies and divides 8- and 16-bit data on signed, unsigned, or ASCII numbers. Table 1–10 lists the arithmetic instructions found in the 80286 microprocessor. Incidentally, these are the same instructions found in the 8086 and 8088 microprocessors.

Bit Manipulation

Twelve instructions provide binary bit manipulation capabilities to the 80286 as well as the older 8086 and 8088 microprocessors. These instructions include: logic operations, shifts, and rotates. A brief description of each instruction and its symbolic coding appears in Table 1–11.

String Instructions

The string instructions manipulate strings (long lists) of data in the memory. Each *string* contains either bytes or words and can be up to 64K bytes in length. The string instructions use the DI and SI registers to address data and the CX register as a counter. String instructions occur once unless they are prefixed with a REP, REPE/REPZ, or REPNE/REPNZ. If prefixed, the string instruction repeats up to the

TABLE 1–10 80286 arithmetic instructions

Opcode	Function
AAA	Adjusts ASCII after addition
AAD	Adjusts ASCII before division
AAM	Adjusts ASCII after multiplication
AAS	Adjusts ASCII after subtraction
ADC	Adds bytes or words with carry
ADD	Adds bytes or words
CBW	Converts byte to a word
CMP	Compares bytes or word
CWD	Converts word to a double word
DAA	Adjust BCD after addition
DAS	Adjusts BCD after subtraction
DEC	Subtracts 1 from byte or word
DIV	Divides unsigned byte or word
IDIV	Divides signed byte or word
IMUL	Multiplies signed byte or word
INC	Adds 1 to byte or word
MUL	Multiplies unsigned byte or word
NEG	Changes sign of byte or word
SBB	Subtracts bytes or words with borrow
SUB	Subtracts bytes or words

number of times contained in the CX register. Table 1–12 lists the string instructions available in the 80286 microprocessor.

Program Transfer

Program transfer instructions include jump, call, and return. These instructions provide the microprocessor with the ability to make decisions. The decision-making instructions, conditional jumps, function similarly to the IF statement found in high-level languages. Table 1–13 lists all the program transfer instructions found on the

TABLE 1–11 80286 bit manipulation instructions

Opcode	Function
AND	ANDs bytes or words
NOT	Inverts bytes or words
OR	ORs bytes or words
RCL	Rotate left through carry
RCR	Rotate right through carry
ROL	Rotate left
ROR	Rotate right
SAR	Shift right, arithmetic
SHL/SAL	Shift left, logical/arithmetic
SHR	Shift right, logical
TEST	Tests bytes or words (AND)
XOR	Exclusive-ORs bytes or words

TABLE 1–12 80286 string instructions

Opcode	Function
CMPS	Compares bytes or words in memory
INS*	Inputs bytes or words
LODS	Loads AL or AX with byte or word
MOVS	Moves bytes or words
OUTS*	Outputs bytes or words
SCAS	Compares bytes or words with memory
STOS	Stores AL or AX in byte or word

*Note: INS and OUTS are not available on the earlier 8086 or 8088 microprocessors.

TABLE 1–13 80286 program transfer instructions

Opcode	Function
BOUND*	Tests boundary
CALL	Calls subroutine
ENTER*	Enter procedure
INT	Interrupt
INT 3	Type 3 interrupt
INTO	Interrupts on overflow
IRET	Interrupt return
JA/JNBE	Jumps if above/jumps if not below or equal
JAE/JNB	Jumps if above or equal/jumps if not below
JB/JNAE	Jumps if below/jumps if not above or equal
JBE/JNA	Jumps if below or equal/jumps if not above
JC	Jumps if carry set
JCXZ	Jumps if CX = 0
JE/JZ	Jumps if equal/jumps if zero
JG/JNLE	Jumps if greater than/jumps if not less than or equal
JGE/JNL	Jumps if greater than or equal/jumps if not less than
JL/JNGE	Jumps if less than/jumps if not greater than or equal
JLE/JNG	Jumps if less than or equal/jumps if not greater than
JMP	Jumps to another part of program
JNC	Jumps if carry cleared
JNE/JNZ	Jumps if not equal/jumps if not zero
JNO	Jumps if no overflow
JNP/JPO	Jumps if no parity/jumps if parity odd
JNS	Jumps if no sign
JO	Jumps if overflow
JP/JPE	Jumps if parity/jumps if parity even
JS	Jumps if sign set
LEAVE*	Leave procedure
LOOP	Loops CX times
LOOPE/LOOPZ	Loops while equal/loops while zero
LOOPNE/LOOPNZ	Loops while not equal/loops while not zero
RET	Returns from subroutine

*Note: The BOUND, ENTER, and LEAVE instructions do not appear in the 8086 or 8088 instruction set.

TABLE 1–14 80286 processor control instruction

Opcode	Function
CLC	Clears carry flag
CLD	Clears direction flag
CLI	Clears interrupt flag
CMC	Complements carry flag
ESC	Provides coprocessor escape
HLT	Halts until a reset or interrupt
LOCK	Locks the bus during the next instruction
NOP	Performs no operation
STC	Sets carry flag
STD	Sets direction flag
STI	Sets interrupt flag
WAIT	Waits for $\overline{\text{BUSY}}$* pin $= 0$

Note: On the 8086/8088 this pin is labeled $\overline{\text{TEST}}$.

80286, 8086, and 8088 microprocessors. Note that BOUND, ENTER, and LEAVE appear in the 80286 instruction set.

Processor Control

The processor control instructions are the most changed group of instructions from the 8086/8088 microprocessor to the 80286 microprocessor. The 8086/8088 contained 12 processor control instructions that still function on the 80286 microprocessor. These 12 instructions are listed in Table 1–14.

Besides these basic processor control instructions, the 80286 contains other instructions that primarily control the memory-management unit for protected mode operations. These additional 80286 instructions appear in Table 1–15.

TABLE 1–15 Addition 80286 processor control instructions

Opcode	Function
ARPL	Adjusts requested privilege level
CTS	Clears task-switched flag
LAR	Loads access rights
LGDT	Loads global descriptor table register
LIDT	Loads interrupt descriptor table register
LLDT	Loads local descriptor table register
LMSW	Loads machine status register
LTR	Loads task register
SGDT	Stores global descriptor table register
SIDT	Stores interrupt descriptor table register
SLDT	Stores local descriptor table register
STR	Stores task register
SMSW	Stores machine status register
LSL	Loads segment limit
VERR	Verifies read access
VERW	Verifies write access

1–7   SUMMARY

1. The life of the 4-bit microprocessor was limited because of its inferior speed, instruction set, and memory size.

2. The 8-bit microprocessor solved many problems encountered with the 4-bit microprocessor until recently. Microprocessors have begun replacing minicomputers in many applications that require 16- and 32-bit data widths, additional instructions, and much more memory. This requirement has seen the end of the 8-bit microprocessor used as a computer system. The 8-bit microprocessor still finds wide application in dedicated task control systems and most likely will for many years to come.

3. The 16-bit microprocessor is very popular today in personal computers, control systems, and microprocessor-based workstations. This popularity stems from the additional memory, instructions, and speed found in the 16-bit microprocessor.

4. The 32-bit microprocessor is finding its place because of the applications that require high-level languages that use floating-point arithmetic. Floating-point numbers are stored as 32-bit numbers in single-precision form. A 32-bit microprocessor accesses these numbers in a very short time.

5. The 16-bit microprocessor has a new internal organization that allows it to execute instructions at a higher speed because of a pipeline. The pipe passes information between internal sections, allowing the microprocessor to be partially executing more than one instruction at a time.

6. When comparing older 16-bit architectures, such as the 8086/8088, to the 80286, there is little external difference. Both machines have the same basic instruction set, except the 80286 has a few additional instructions for memory management.

7. Logical memory is the memory system as seen by the programmer. Logical memory is 8 bits wide, with each byte numbered in hexadecimal. The 80286 logical memory map begins at location 000000H and extends to location FFFFFFH (16M bytes of memory). The 80386 and 80486 logical memories extend from location 00000000H to FFFFFFFFH (4G bytes of memory).

8. The physical memory system of the 80286 differs from the 80386 and 80486. The 80286 has a 16-bit-wide memory that contains two 8-bit banks. Each 80286 memory bank holds up to 8M bytes of memory. The 80386 and 80486 memory is 32 bits wide and is organized in four 8-bit-wide banks that each hold 1G byte of memory.

9. The programming model of the 80286 contains four general-purpose registers (AX, BX, CX, and DX) that are 16 bits wide. These general-purpose registers are also addressable as 8-bit registers (AH, AL, BH, BL, CH, CL, DH, and DL).

10. The 80286 contains four index and pointer registers that hold the offset address of memory data. These index and pointer registers are 16-bit registers SP, BP, SI, and DI.

11. Four segment registers exist in the 80286 microprocessor (CS, DS, ES, and SS). The program or code is located in the code segment, and various other data are located in the data, extra, and stack memory segments. Each memory segment is a 64K byte section of the memory system.

12. A segment register and an offset address generate the effective memory address. The contents of the segment register (with a 0H appended to the rightmost end) and the offset address add to form the effective address when the 80286 operates in the real mode. In the protected mode, the segment register addresses a descriptor that contains the 20-bit start of a segment. This 20-bit address adds to the offset address to generate the effective address in protected mode.

13. The housekeeping registers consist of the flags, instruction pointer (IP), and the machine status word. The flag register contains bits that indicate certain conditions and select certain options for the microprocessor. The instruction pointer contains the offset address within the code segment used to address the next instruction in the program. The machine status word PE bit switches the microprocessor from the real mode to the protected mode.

14. Real mode operation of the 80286 causes it to function as an 8086 or 8088 microprocessor. Real mode operation limits the amount of available memory to 1M byte. Protected mode operation allows the 80286 to address 16M bytes of memory.

15. Data formats for the 80286 consist of bytes (8-bits), words (16-bits), and double words (32-bits). These different sizes of data can hold unsigned or signed binary numbers, BCD numbers, ASCII data, or floating-point numbers.

16. Real numbers (floating-point) are expressed as either single-precision numbers that are 4 bytes (short) in width or as double-precision numbers that are 8 bytes (long) in width. A real number contains two major components: an exponent and a mantissa.

17. The 80286 instruction set is almost completely compatible with earlier 16-bit microprocessors such as the 8086 and 8088. The instruction types include data transfer, arithmetic, bit manipulation, string operations, program transfer, and processor control.

1–8   QUESTIONS AND PROBLEMS

1. What were some problems associated with the early 4-bit microprocessors?
2. List a few applications of the early 4-bit microprocessor.
3. What improvements in microprocessor technology led to the arrival of the 8-bit microprocessor?
4. Compare execution speeds of the 4-, 8-, 16-, and 32-bit microprocessors.
5. How much memory can the 80286 microprocessor address?
6. How much memory can the 80486 microprocessor address?
7. What is the purpose of the AU (address unit) within the 80286 microprocessor?
8. What is the purpose of the IU (instruction unit) within the 80286 microprocessor?
9. Why is a queue placed between the BU (bus unit) and the IU inside the 80286 microprocessor?
10. How does the pipeline aid in execution of software in the 80286 microprocessor?
11. What three buses connect the memory and I/O to the 80286 microprocessor?
12. Memory is numbered from _____ to _____ in the 80286 microprocessor.

13. Memory is numbered from _____ to _____ in the 80486 microprocessor.
14. A word requires _____ bytes of memory.
15. A double word requires _____ bytes of memory.
16. What are the differences between the 80286 logical and physical memory systems?
17. What are the differences between the 80386 logical and physical memory systems?
18. An 80486 memory bank can store _____ bytes of memory.
19. How many 8-bit general-purpose registers are available in the 80286 microprocessor? What are their two-letter names?
20. How many 16-bit general-purpose registers are available in the 80286 microprocessor? What are their two-letter names?
21. Why is the CX register called the count register?
22. Why is the DX register called the data register?
23. List the four index and pointer registers and explain their normal function.
24. The effective address is formed by a segment address and an _____ address.
25. Segment registers address a segment in the memory system. How is this possible when a segment register is only 16 bits wide and the real mode memory address is 20 bits wide?
26. Describe the difference, about the memory size, between protected and real mode operation of the 80286 microprocessor.
27. Can segments overlap?
28. If a segment is not placed directly on top of another segment, what is the closest spacing between segments?
29. If IP = 1000H and CS = 2000H, the actual address of the next instruction in a program is _____.
30. If SS = 1234H and SP = 2000H, the current address of the stack memory is _____.
31. What two pointers address, by default, data in the stack memory segment?
32. The string source (SI) is located in the _____ segment and the string destination (DI) is located in the _____ segment.
33. How many flag bits contain information?
34. List and describe the purpose of each flag bit.
35. A byte = _____ bits, a word = _____ bits, and a double word = _____ bits.
36. Extended memory begins at what memory location?
37. The expanded memory page frame appears in which major section of the microprocessor memory?
38. What is the purpose of the transient program area in a personal computer?
39. What is the purpose of the system area in a personal computer?
40. In protected mode, the segment register contains what information?
41. A descriptor describes what information about a memory segment?
42. What is the limit in a descriptor?
43. Convert the following unsigned binary numbers into their decimal equivalents:
    a. 1000 0000
    b. 0101 0001

    c. 1010 0111

    d. 0010 0010

    e. 1111 1111

44. Assume that the binary numbers in Question 43 represent signed numbers and convert them to signed decimal equivalents.

45. Convert the following decimal numbers in both packed and unpacked BCD equivalents:

    a. 92

    b. 432

    c. 1009

    d. 23

    e. 3421

46. Using the ASCII coding chart of Table 1–5, convert the following alphanumeric words and phrases into ASCII code:

    a. Well?

    b. Water is cold!

    c. So what?

    d. Shall we?

    e. Who said so?

47. Show how the following hexadecimal numbers are stored in a word or a double word beginning at memory location 10000H:

    a. 82H (word)

    b. 5678H (word)

    c. ABCD1234H (double word)

    d. 23H (double word)

    e. AF82H (double word)

48. Show how the memory address 1000:1234H is stored in a double word beginning at location 04000H.

49. Convert the following decimal numbers into single-precision floating-point form:

    a. +10

    b. −11

    c. +101.125

    d. −65.0625

    e. +300.09375

50. Convert the following 32-bit binary single-precision floating-point numbers into decimal equivalents:

    a. 0 10000010 10000000000000000000000

    b. 1 01111110 00000000000000000000000

    c. 0 10000101 11010000000000000000000

    d. 1 01111100 10100000000000000000000

    e. 1 10000010 11111000000000000000000

51. What instruction grouping moves data from one internal register to another?

52. What instruction grouping clears the carry flag bit?

CHAPTER 2

Addressing Modes

INTRODUCTION

Efficient software development for the 80286, and other family members, requires a complete familiarity with the addressing modes applied to each instruction. In this chapter, we use the MOV (move data) instruction to describe the data-addressing modes. The MOV instruction transfers bytes or words of data between registers or between registers and memory. In describing the program memory-addressing modes, we use the call and jump instructions that modify the flow of the program.

The data-addressing modes include register, immediate, direct, register indirect, base-plus-index, register relative, and base relative–plus–index. The program memory-addressing modes include program relative, direct, and indirect. The operation of the stack memory is explained so the PUSH and POP instructions are understood.

OBJECTIVES

Upon completion of this chapter, you will be able to:

1. Explain the operation of each data-addressing mode.
2. Use the data-addressing modes to form assembly language statements.
3. Explain the operation of each program memory-addressing mode.
4. Use the program memory-addressing modes to form assembly and machine language statements.
5. Select the appropriate addressing mode to accomplish a given task.
6. Describe the sequence of events that place data onto the stack or remove data from the stack.

2–1   DATA-ADDRESSING MODES

Because the MOV instruction is a simple and flexible 80286 instruction, it provides a basis for the explanation of the data-addressing modes. Figure 2–1 illustrates the MOV instruction and defines the direction of data flow. The source is to the right and the destination is to the left, next to the opcode MOV. This is at first awkward because we naturally assume things move from left to right, where here they move from right to left. (An *opcode* tells the microprocessor which operation to perform.) A comma always separates the destination from source in an instruction.

In Figure 2–1, the MOV AX,BX instruction transfers the word contents of the source register (BX) into the destination register (AX). The source *never* changes, but the destination *usually* changes.*

Figure 2–2 shows all variations of the data-addressing modes using the MOV instruction. This illustration helps show how each data-addressing is formulated with the MOV instruction. These are the same data-addressing modes found with the 8086/8088 microprocessor. The 80286 data-addressing modes are:

1. *Register Addressing* —used to transfer a byte or word from the source register or memory location to the destination register or memory location. (*Example:* The MOV CX,DX instruction copies the word-sized contents of register DX into register CX.)
2. *Immediate Addressing* —transfers an immediate byte or word of data into the destination register or memory location. (*Example:* The MOV AL,22H instruction copies the byte-sized 22H into register AL.)
3. *Direct Addressing* —moves a byte or word between a memory location and a register. (*Example:* The MOV CX,LIST instruction copies the word-sized contents of memory location LIST into register CX.)
4. *Register Indirect Addressing* —used to transfer a byte or word between a register and a memory location addressed by an index or base register. The index and base registers are: BP, BX, DI, and SI. (*Example:* The MOV AX,[BX] instruction copies the word-sized data from the data segment offset address pointed to by BX into register AX.)

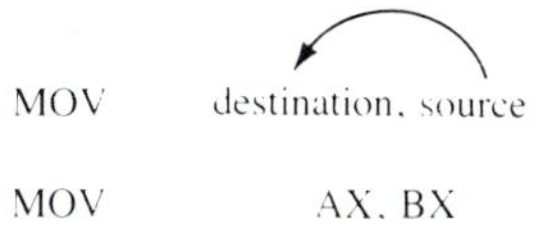

FIGURE 2–1   The MOV
AX,BX instruction illustrating
the direction of flow.

MOV   destination, source

MOV   AX, BX

---

*The exceptions are the CMP and TEST instructions that never change the destination. These instructions are described in later chapters.

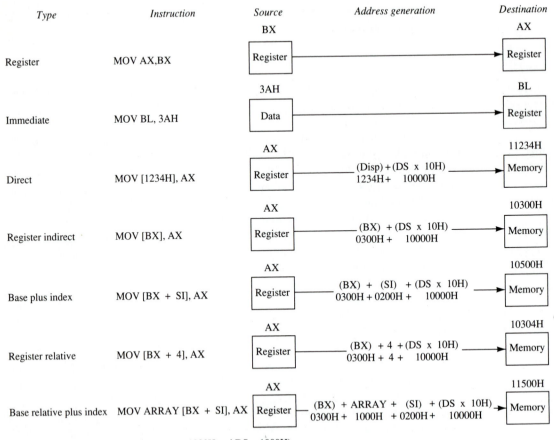

(Notes: BX = 0300H, SI = 0200H, Array = 1000H and DS = 1000H)

FIGURE 2–2   80286 data-addressing modes.

5. *Base-Plus-Index Addressing* —transfers a byte or word between a register and the memory location addressed by a base register (BP or BX) plus an index register (DI or SI). (*Example:* The MOV [BX+DI],CL instruction copies the byte-sized contents of register CL into the memory location addressed by BX plus DI located in the data segment.)

6. *Register Relative Addressing* —moves a byte or word between a register and the memory location addressed by an index or base register plus a displacement. (*Example:* MOV AX,[BX+4] or MOV AX,ARRAY[BX]. The first instruction copies a word of data from an address in the data segment, formed by BX plus 4, into the AX register. The second instruction transfers the contents of the memory location in an ARRAY plus the contents of BX into register AX.)

7. *Base Relative-Plus-Index Addressing* —used to transfer a byte or word between a register and the memory location addressed by a base and an index register plus a displacement. (*Example:* MOV AX,ARRAY[BX+DI] or MOV AX,[BX+DI+4]. These instructions both copy a word of data from a memory location into register

AX. The first instruction uses an address formed by adding ARRAY, BX, and DI and the second by adding BX, DI, and 4.)

2-2   REGISTER ADDRESSING

Register addressing is an easy addressing mode to master once the many registers inside the 80286 are learned. The 80286 contains the following 8-bit registers used with register addressing: AH, AL, BH, BL, CH, CL, DH, and DL. It also contains the following 16-bit registers: AX, BX, CX, DX, SP, BP, SI, and DI. Some MOV instructions and the PUSH and POP instructions use the 16-bit segment registers (CS, ES, DS, and SS) for register addressing. It is important that instructions use registers that are of uniform size. Never mix an 8-bit register with a 16-bit register because this is not allowed by the 80286 instruction set.

Table 2–1 shows some different versions of register move instructions. It is impossible to show all variations of register addressing because there are so many possible combinations. For example, just the 8-bit subset of the MOV instruction has 64 different permutations. About the only type of register MOV instruction not allowed, is a segment-to-segment register MOV instruction. Note that the code segment register may not be changed by a MOV instruction. The reason is that the address of the next instruction is found in both IP and CS. If just CS is changed, the next instruction's address is unpredictable.

Figure 2–3 shows the function of the MOV BX,CX instruction. Note that the source does not change, but the destination does. Here, a 1234H moves from register CX into register BX. This data transfer erases the old contents (76AFH) of register BX. In fact, the contents of the destination register or destination memory location change for all instructions, except the CMP and TEST instructions.

TABLE 2–1 Examples of the register-addressed instructions

Assembly Language	Operation
MOV AL,BL	Copies BL into AL
MOV CH,CL	Copies CL into CH
MOV AX,CX	Copies CX into AX
MOV SP,BP	Copies BP into SP
MOV DS,AX	Copies AX into DS
MOV SI,DI	Copies DI into SI
MOV BX,ES	Copies ES into BX
MOV ES,DS	Not allowed (segment-to-segment)
MOV BL,BX	Not allowed (mixed sizes)
MOV CS,AX	Not allowed (the code segment register may not be used as a destination register)

FIGURE 2–3 The effect of executing the MOV BX,CX instruction at the point just before the BX register changes. Note that the 1234H is copied from the CX register and is about to enter the BX register. Once 1234H enters the BX register, the 764FH currently in BX is lost.

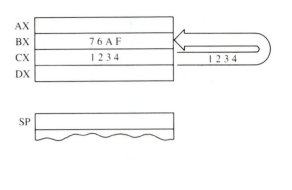

2–3   IMMEDIATE ADDRESSING

Another data-addressing mode is immediate addressing. The term *immediate* implies that the data immediately follows the hexadecimal opcode in the memory. Immediate addressing operates upon a byte or word of data. The MOV immediate instruction transfers a copy of the immediate data into a register or a memory location. Figure 2–4 shows the operation of a MOV AX,3456H instruction. This instruction copies the 3456H from the instruction, located in the memory, into register AX. As with the MOV instruction illustrated in Figure 2–3, the source data overwrites the destination data.

In symbolic assembly language, the symbol # precedes immediate data with some 80286 assemblers. The MOV AX,#3456H instruction is an example. Most 80286 assemblers do not use the # symbol but represent immediate data as in the MOV AX,3456H instruction. In this text we will not use the # symbol for immediate data.

The symbolic assembler portrays immediate data in many ways. The letter H appends hexadecimal data. If hexadecimal data begin with a letter, we start them with a 0. For example, to represent an F2H, we use 0F2H in assembly language. Decimal data are represented as is, and require no special codes or adjustments. An example is the 100 decimal in the MOV AL,100 instruction. An ASCII coded character or characters may be depicted in the immediate form if the ASCII data are enclosed in apostrophes. An example is the MOV BH,'A' instruction, which moves an ASCII-coded A into register BH. Be careful to use the apostrophe (') for ASCII

FIGURE 2–4 The effect of executing a MOV AX,3456H instruction. Here the data, which follow the opcode B8, are moved from the memory into the AX register. The operation is shown at the point just before register AX changes.

TABLE 2–2 Examples of immediate addressing using the MOV instruction

Assembly Language	Operation
MOV BL,44	Moves a 44 decimal (2CH) into BL
MOV AX,44H	Moves a 44 hexadecimal into AX
MOV SI,0	Moves a 0000H into SI
MOV CH,100	Moves a 100 (64H) into CH
MOV AL,'A'	Moves an ASCII A (41H) into AL
MOV AX,'AB'	Moves an ASCII BA* (4241H) into AX
MOV CL,11001110B	Moves a binary 11001110 into CL

Note: This is not an error. The ASCII characters are stored as a BA, so care should be exercised when using a word-sized pair of ASCII characters.

data and not a single quotation mark ('). Table 2–2 shows many different MOV instructions that apply immediate data.

2–4 DIRECT DATA ADDRESSING

Most commands use direct data addressing. Direct data addressing is applied to many instructions in a typical program. There are two basic forms of direct data addressing: (1) direct addressing that only applies to a MOV between a memory location and AL or AX, and (2) displacement addressing for almost any instruction in the 80286 instruction set.

Direct Addressing

Direct addressing is only allowed with a MOV instruction that transfers data between a memory location, located within the data segment, and either the AL (8-bit) or AX (16-bit) register. This instruction is always a 3-byte-long instruction.

The MOV AL,DATA instruction, as represented by most 80286 assemblers, transfers a copy of the byte stored at memory location DATA (1234H), within the data segment, into the AL register. Memory location DATA is a *symbolic memory location*. A few assemblers represent this instruction as a MOV AL,[1234H]. The [1234H] is an *absolute memory location* that is not always allowed by the assembler. Figure 2–5 shows how this instruction transfers a copy of the byte-sized contents of

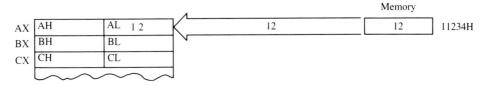

FIGURE 2–5 The effect of executing the MOV AL,[1234H] instruction if DS = 1000H. Here the AL register is shown after the data (12) have destroyed the previous contents of register AL.

TABLE 2–3 The four possible direct addressed instructions

Assembly Language	Operation
MOV AL,NUMBER	Copies the byte contents of memory address NUMBER located in the data segment into AL
MOV AX,COW	Copies the word contents of memory address COW in the data segment into AX
MOV NEWS,AL	Copies AL into memory location NEWS in the data segment
MOV THERE,AX	Copies AX into memory location THERE in the data segment

memory location 11234H into AL. We form the effective address by adding 1234H (the offset address) to 10000H (the data segment address).

Table 2–3 lists all four possible direct addressed instructions. These instructions often appear in programs, so Intel decided to make them special 3-byte-long instructions. All other instructions that move data from a memory location to a register, called *displacement addressed instructions,* require 4 bytes of memory for storage in a program.

Displacement Addressing

Displacement addressing is almost identical with direct addressing, except that the instruction is 4 bytes wide instead of 3. This type of direct data addressing is much more flexible because most 80286 instructions can use it.

Figure 2–6 shows the operation of the MOV CL,[1234H] instruction. This instruction operates in the same manner as the MOV AL,[1234H] instruction of Figure 2–5. The difference only becomes apparent upon examination of the assembled versions of these two instructions. The MOV AL,[1234H] instruction is 3 bytes and the MOV CL,[1234H] instruction is 4 bytes, as illustrated in Example 2–1.

EXAMPLE 2–1

```
0000 A0 1234 R          MOV    AL,[1234H]
0003 8A 0E 1234 R       MOV    CL,[1234H]
```

Table 2–4 lists some MOV displacement forms of direct addressing. Not all forms are listed because there are many MOV instructions of this type.

FIGURE 2–6   The effect of executing the MOV CL,[1234H] instruction if DS = 1000H. Here the CL register is shown after the data (8A) have destroyed the previous contents of CL.

TABLE 2–4 Examples of direct data addressing using a displacement

Assembly Language	Operation
MOV CH,DOG	Copies the contents of memory location DOG from the data segment to register CH. The actual offset address of DOG is calculated by the assembler
MOV CH,[1000H]	Copies the contents of memory location 1000H from the data segment into register CH
MOV DATA,BP	BP is copied into memory location DATA within the data segment
MOV NUMBER,SP	SP is copied into memory location NUMBER within the data segment

2–5 REGISTER INDIRECT ADDRESSING

Register indirect addressing allows data to be addressed at any memory location by any of the following registers: BP, BX, DI, and SI. For example, if register BX contains a 1000H and the MOV AX,[BX] instruction executes, the data at memory location 1000H in the data segment is copied into register AX. If DS = 0100H, this instruction addresses the word stored at memory location 2000H and 2001H and transfers it into register AX (see Figure 2–7). The [ ] symbols denote indirect

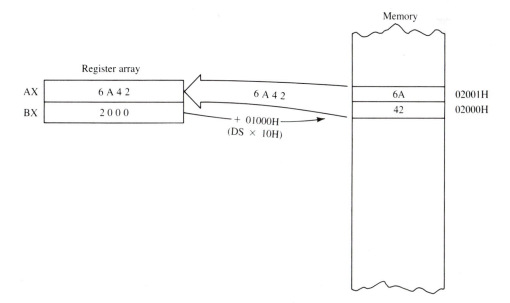

FIGURE 2–7 The effect of executing the MOV AX,[BX] instruction if DS = 0100H and BX = 1000H. Here the AX register is shown after the data (6A42H) have destroyed the previous contents of AX.

TABLE 2–5 Example instructions using register indirect addressing

Assembly Language	Operation
MOV CX,[BX]	A word from the memory location address by BX within the data segment moves into register CX
MOV [BP],DL	A byte is copied from register DL into the memory location addressed by BP within the stack segment
MOV [DI],BH	A byte is copied from register BH into the memory location addressed by DI within the data segment
MOV [DI],[BX]	Memory-to-memory moves are not allowed except with string instructions

addressing in 80286 assembly language. Some typical instructions using indirect addressing appear in Table 2–5.

BP, BX, DI, and SI

When using register indirect addressing or any other addressing mode that uses BX, DI, or SI to address memory, these registers address data in the data segment. If register BP addresses memory, it uses the stack segment. These are considered the default settings for these four index and base registers.

Indirect addressing often allows a program to refer to tabular data located in the memory system. For example, suppose that you must create a table of information that contains 50 samples taken from a digital voltmeter. Figure 2–8 shows the table and the BX register used to address each location in the table sequentially. To do this, you need to load the starting location of the table into the BX register with a MOV immediate instruction. After initializing the starting address of the table, you then use register indirect addressing to store the 50 samples sequentially.

EXAMPLE 2–2

```
                    ;instructions that read 50 bytes of data from the DATA_PORT
                    ;and store them in the TABLE
                    ;
0000 BB 0000 R           MOV    BX,OFFSET TABLE    ;address TABLE
0003 B9 0032             MOV    CX,50              ;load counter

0006                AGAIN:

0006 E4 2A               IN     AL,DATA_PORT       ;read voltmeter
0008 88 07               MOV    [BX],AL            ;save data
000A 43                  INC    BX                 ;address next
000B E2 F9               LOOP   AGAIN              ;repeat 50 times
```

The sequence shown in Example 2–2 loads register BX with the starting address of the table and initializes the count, located in register CX, to 50. The OFFSET

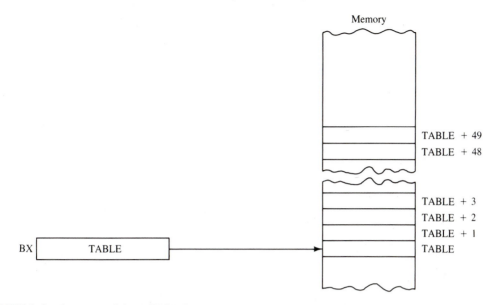

FIGURE 2–8 An array of data (TABLE) containing 50 bytes that are indirectly addressed through the BX register.

directive tells the assembler to load BX with the offset address of memory location TABLE and not the contents of TABLE. For example, the MOV BX,DATA instruction copies the contents of memory location DATA into BX, while the MOV BX,OFFSET DATA instruction copies the address of DATA into BX. When the OFFSET directive is used with the MOV instruction, the assembler calculates the address and then uses a move immediate instruction to load the address into the specified 16-bit register.

Once the counter and pointer are initialized, a repeat-until CX = 0 loop executes. Here data are input (IN) from the voltmeter and then stored in the memory location indirectly addressed by register BX. Next, BX increments (*adds one*) to the next table locations, and finally the LOOP instruction repeats the LOOP 50 times. The LOOP instruction decrements (*subtracts one*) the counter (CX) and if CX is not zero, LOOP jumps to memory location AGAIN. If CX becomes zero, no jump occurs and the sequence of instructions ends.

2–6   BASE-PLUS-INDEX ADDRESSING

Base-plus-index addressing is similar to indirect addressing because it indirectly addresses memory data. This type of addressing uses one base register (BP or BX) and one index register (DI or SI) to indirectly address memory. Often the base register holds the beginning location of a memory array, while the index register holds the relative position of an element in the array. Remember that whenever BP addresses memory data, both the stack segment register and BP form the effective address.

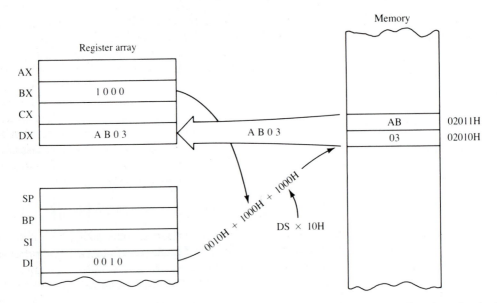

FIGURE 2–9 An example showing how the base-plus-index mode of addressing functions for the MOV DX,[BX+DI] instruction. Notice that memory address 02010H is referenced by this instruction because DS (0100H), BX (1000H), and DI (0010H) are summed to generate this address.

Addressing Data with Base-Plus-Index Addressing

Figure 2–9 shows how data are addressed by the MOV DX,[BX+DI] instruction. In this example, BX = 1000H, DI = 0010H, and DS = 0100H, which translate into memory address 02010H. This instruction transfers a copy of the word from location 02010h into the DX register. Table 2–6 lists some instructions used for base-plus-index addressing.

TABLE 2–6 Examples of base-plus-index addressing

Assembly Language	Operation
MOV CX,[BX+DI]	The word contents of the memory location addressed by BX plus DI within the data segment are copied into register CX
MOV CH,[BP+SI]	The byte contents of the memory location addressed by BP plus SI within the stack segment are copied into register CH
MOV [BX+SI],SP	The word contents of SP are stored in the data segment at the location addressed by BX plus SI
MOV [BP+DI],CX	The word contents of CX are stored in the stack segment at the memory location addressed by BP plus DI

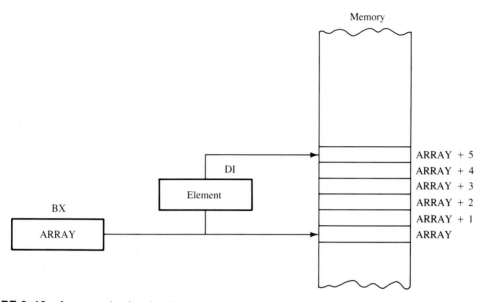

FIGURE 2–10 An example showing base-plus-index addressing. Here an element (DI) of an array of data (BX) is accessed.

Addressing Arrays of Data Using Base-Plus-Index Addressing

A major use of the base-plus-index mode of addressing is to address elements in a memory array. Suppose that we need to address the elements in an array located in the data segment at memory location ARRAY. To accomplish this, we need to load the BX register (base) with the beginning address of the array and DI (index) with the element number to be accessed. Figure 2–10 shows the use of BX and DI to access an element in an array of data.

EXAMPLE 2–3

```
                        ;using the base-plus-index addressing mode
                        ;
0000  BB 0000 R         MOV    BX,OFFSET ARRAY    ;address ARRAY
0003  BF 0010           MOV    DI,10H             ;element 10H
0006  8A 01             MOV    AL,[BX+DI]         ;get data
0008  BF 0020           MOV    DI,20H             ;element 20H
000B  88 01             MOV    [BX+DI],AL         ;save data
```

A short program listed in Example 2–3 moves array element 10H into array element 20H. Notice that the array element number, loaded into the DI register, addresses the array element.

2–7   **REGISTER RELATIVE ADDRESSING**

Register relative addressing is similar to base-plus-index addressing and displacement addressing discussed earlier. In register relative addressing, the data in a segment of memory are addressed by adding the displacement to the contents of a base or an index register (BP, BX, DI, or SI). Figure 2–11 shows the operation of the MOV AX,[BX+1000H] instruction. In this example, BX = 0100H and DS = 0200H, so the address generated is the sum of DS × 10H, BX, and the displacement of 1000H or 03100H. Remember that BX, DI, or SI address the data segment and BP addresses the stack segment. Table 2–7 lists a few instructions that use register relative addressing.

The displacement can be a number added to the register within the [], as in the MOV AL,[DI+2] instruction, or it can be a displacement subtracted from the register, as in MOV AL,[SI−1]. A displacement also can be an offset address appended to the front of the [ ] as in MOV AL,DATA[DI]. Both forms of displacement also can appear simultaneously as in the MOV AL,DATA[DI+3] instruction. In all cases both forms of the displacement add to the base or base-and-index register within the []. The value of the displacement is limited to a 16-bit signed number or ±32K.

Array Data with Register Relative Addressing

It is possible to address array data with register relative addressing much as one does with base-plus-index addressing. In Figure 2–12, we illustrate register relative

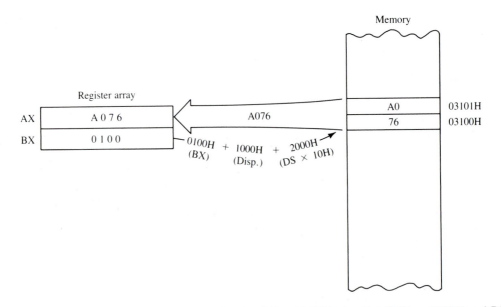

FIGURE 2–11   The effect of executing the MOV AX,[BX+1000H] instruction if BX = 0100H and DS = 0200H.

TABLE 2–7 Examples of register relative addressing

Assembly Language	Operation
MOV AX,[DI+100H]	The word contents of the data segment memory location addressed by DI plus 100H are copied into register AX
MOV ARRAY[SI],BL	The byte contents of BL are copied into the data segment at the location addressed by ARRAY plus SI
MOV LIST[SI+2],CL	The byte contents of CL are copied into the data segment at the location addressed by the sum of LIST, SI, and 2
MOV DI,SETS[BX]	DI is loaded from the data segment location addressed by SETS plus BX

addressing with the same example we used for base-plus-index addressing. This shows how the displacement ARRAY adds to index register DI to generate a reference to an array element.

Example 2–4 shows how this new addressing mode can transfer the contents of array element 10H into array element 20H. Notice the similarity between this example and Example 2–3. The main difference is that in Example 2–4 we do not use register BX to address memory area ARRAY; instead, we use ARRAY as a displacement to accomplish the same task.

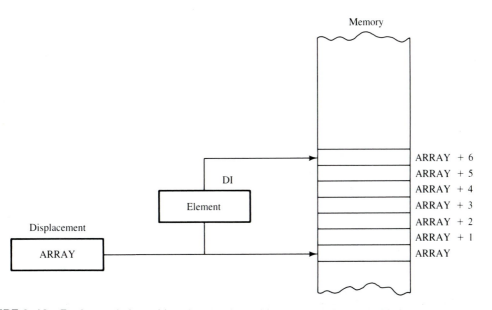

FIGURE 2–12 Register relative addressing used to address an element of ARRAY. The displacement addresses the start of the array, and the contents of DI (the element) select an element of the array.

EXAMPLE 2–4

```
                        ;using the register relative addressing mode
                        ;
0000  BF 0010           MOV   DI,10H             ;element 10H
0003  8A 85 0000 R      MOV   AL,ARRAY[DI]       ;get data
0007  BF 0020           MOV   DI,20H             ;element 20H
000   88 85 0000 R      MOV   ARRAY[DI],AL       ;save data
```

2–8   BASE RELATIVE-PLUS-INDEX ADDRESSING

The final data addressing mode available to the 80286 is the base relative-plus-index addressing mode. This mode is similar to the base-plus-index addressing mode, but adds a displacement besides using a base register and an index register to form the memory address. This type of addressing mode often addresses a two-dimensional array of memory data.

Data with Base Relative-Plus-Index Addressing

Base relative-plus-index addressing is the least used addressing mode. Figure 2–13 shows how data are references if the instruction executed by the 80286 is a MOV

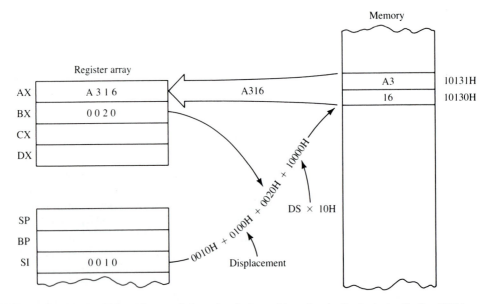

FIGURE 2–13   An example of base relative-plus-index addressing is illustrated with the MOV AX,[BX+SI+100H] instruction. This instruction moves data from memory to the AX register. The memory address is the sum of DS × 10H, 100H, BX, and SI.

AX,[BX+SI+100H]. The displacement of 100H adds to BX and SI to form the offset address within the data segment. Registers BX = 0020H, SI = 0010H, and DS = 1000H, so the effective address for this instruction is 10130H—the sum of these registers plus a displacement of 100H. This addressing mode is too complex for frequent use in a program. Some typical instructions using base relative-plus-index addressing appear in Table 2–8.

Arrays with Base Relative-Plus-Index Addressing

Suppose that a file of many records exists in memory and each record contains many elements. This displacement addresses the file, the base register addresses a record, and the index register addresses an element of a record. Figure 2–14 illustrates this very complex form of addressing.

Example 2–5 provides a program that copies element 0 of record A into element 2 of record C using the base relative-plus-index mode of addressing.

EXAMPLE 2–5

```
                          ;using the base relative-plus-index addressing mode
                          ;
0000  BB 0000 R                   MOV    BX,OFFSET RECA      ;address record A
0003  BF 0000                     MOV    DI,0                ;element 0
0006  8A 81 0000 R                MOV    AL,FILE[BX+DI]      ;get data
000A  BB 0064 R                   MOV    BX,OFFSET RECC      ;address record C
000D  BF 0002                     MOV    DI,2                ;element 2
0010  88 81 0000 R                MOV    FILE[BX+DI],AL      ;save data
```

Assembly Language	Operation
MOV DH,[BX+DI+20H]	DH is loaded from the data segment location addressed by the sum of BX, DI, and 20H
MOV AX,FILE[BX+DI]	AX is loaded from the data segment location addressed by the sum of FILE, BX, and DI
MOV LIST[BP+DI],CL	CL is stored at the stack segment location addressed by the sum of LIST, BP, and DI
MOV LIST[BP+SI+4],DH	DH is stored at the stack segment location addressed by the sum of LIST, BP, SI, and 4

TABLE 2–8 Examples of base relative-plus-index instructions

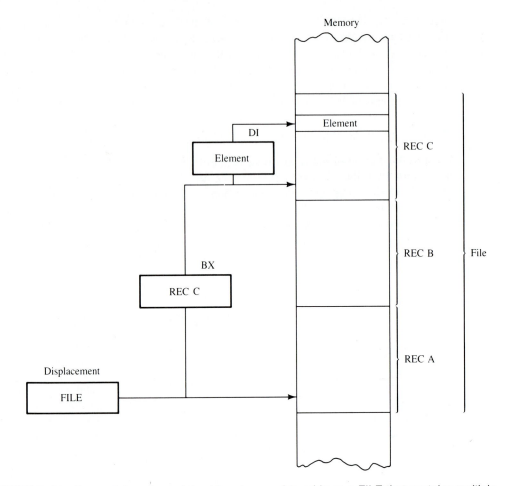

FIGURE 2–14 Base relative-plus-index addressing used to address a FILE that contains multiple records (REC); each record contains many elements.

2–9   PROGRAM MEMORY-ADDRESSING MODES

Program memory-addressing modes, used with the JMP and CALL instructions, consist of three distinct forms: direct, relative, and indirect. This section introduces these three addressing forms, using the JMP instruction to illustrate their operation.

Direct Program Memory Addressing

Direct program memory addressing is what most early microprocessors used for all jumps and calls. Direct program memory addressing is also used in high-level languages as GOTO and GOSUB instructions. The 80286 can use this form of addressing, but doesn't use it nearly as often as relative and indirect program addressing.

Opcode	Offset—low	Offset—high	Segment—low	Segment—high
EA	00	00	00	10

FIGURE 2–15 The 5-byte machine language instruction for a JMP [10000H] instruction. The opcode is followed by the offset address (0000H) and then the code segment address (1000H).

The instructions for direct program memory addressing store the address with the opcode. For example, if a program jumps to memory location 10000H for the next instruction, the address (10000H) is stored following the opcode in the memory. Figure 2–15 shows the direct *intersegment* JMP instruction and the four bytes required to store the address 10000H. A JMP 10000H instruction loads CS with 1000H and IP with 0000H to jump to memory location 10000H for the next instruction. (An *intersegment* jump is a jump to any memory location within the memory system.) We often call the direct jump a *far* jump because it can jump to any memory location for the next instruction.

The only other instruction that uses direct program addressing is the intersegment CALL instruction. Usually, the name of a memory address, called a *label,* refers to the location that is called or jumped to instead of the actual numeric address. When using a label with the CALL or JMP instruction, most assemblers select the best form of program addressing.

Relative Program Memory Addressing

Relative program memory addressing is not available in many early microprocessors, but it is available to the 80286 microprocessor. The term *relative* means "relative to the instruction pointer (IP)." For example, if a JMP instruction skips the next two bytes of memory, the address in relation to the instruction pointer is a 2 that adds to the instruction pointer. This develops the address of the next program instruction. An example of the relative JMP instruction is shown in Figure 2–16. Notice that the JMP instruction is a 1-byte instruction with a 1-byte or a 2-byte displacement that adds to the instruction pointer. A 1-byte displacement is used in *short* jumps, and a 2-byte displacement is used with *near* jumps and calls. Both types are considered intrasegment jumps. (An *intrasegment* jump is a jump anywhere within the current code segment.)

Relative JMP and CALL instructions contain either an 8-bit or a 16-bit signed displacement that allows a forward memory reference or a reverse memory reference. All assemblers automatically find the distance of the displacement and select the proper 1- or 2-byte form. If the distance is too far for a 2-byte displacement, some

FIGURE 2–16 A JMP [2] instruction, which will skip over the next two bytes in the program. In this example, the program continues at location 10004H.

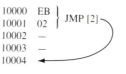

```
10000   EB  ⎫
10001   02  ⎬ JMP [2]
10002   —  ⎭
10003   —
10004   ◄
```

TABLE 2–9 Examples of indirect program addressing

Assembly Language	Operation
JMP AX	Jump to the location addressed by AX in the current code segment
JMP CX	Jump to the location addressed by CX in the current code segment
JMP [BX]	Jump to the current code segment location to the address stored at the data segment location plus BX
JMP [DI+2]	Jump to the current code segment location to the address stored at the data segment location plus DI + 2
JMP TABLE[BX]	Jump to the current code segment location addressed by the contents of TABLE plus BX

assemblers use the direct jump. An 8-bit displacement (*short*) has a value between +127 and −128, while a 16-bit displacement (*near*) has a value between ±32K.

Indirect Program Memory Addressing

The 80286 allows several forms of indirect program memory addressing for the JMP and CALL instruction. Table 2–9 lists some acceptable indirect program jump instructions, which can use any 16-bit register (AX, BX, CX, DX, SP, BP, DI, or SI), any relative register ([BP], [BX], [DI], or [SI]), and any relative register with a displacement.

If a 16-bit register forms the address of a JMP instruction, the jump is near. For example, if the BX register contains a 1000H and a JMP BX instruction executes, the microprocessor jumps to offset address 1000H in the current code segment.

If a relative register holds the address, the JMP is also considered an indirect jump. For example, a JMP [BX] refers to memory location within the data segment at the offset address contained in BX. At this offset address is a 16-bit number that is used as the offset address in the intrasegment jump.

Figure 2–17 shows a jump table that is stored beginning at memory location TABLE. This jump table is referenced by the short program of Example 2–6. In this example, the BX register is loaded with a 4, so when it combines in the JMP TABLE[BX] instruction with TABLE, the effective address is the contents of the second entry in the jump table.

FIGURE 2–17 A jump table that is used to allow the program to select different jump addresses for different values in the BX register.

```
TABLE   DW   L0C0      Addresses of four
        DW   L0C1      different programs.
        DW   L0C2   (Each address is a 2-byte
        DW   L0C3         offset.)
```

EXAMPLE 2–6

```
                            ;using indirect addressing for a jump
                            ;
0000 BB 0004                MOV   BX,4                ;address LOC2
0003 FF A7 23A1 R           JMP   TABLE[BX]           ;jump to LOC2
```

2–10   STACK MEMORY ADDRESSING

The stack is an important part of the memory system in all microprocessors. It holds data temporarily and stores return addresses for subroutines. The stack memory

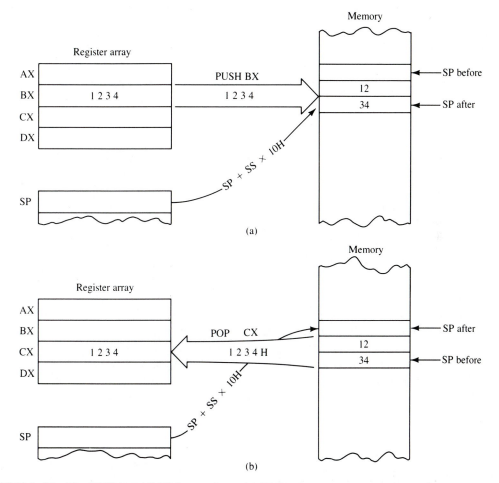

FIGURE 2–18 The PUSH and POP instructions. (a) PUSH BX places the contents of the BX register onto the stack addressed by the SP + SS × 10H. (b) POP CX removes data from the stack at the location addressed by SP + SS × 10H and places the data into the CX register.

TABLE 2–10 Examples of PUSH and POP instructions

Assembly Language	Operation
POPF	Removes a word from the stack and places into the flags
PUSHF	Stores a copy of the flag word on the stack
PUSH AX	Stores a copy of AX on the stack
POP BX	Removes a word from the stack and places it into BX
PUSH DS	Stores a copy of DS on the stack
POP CS	Illegal instruction
PUSH [BX]	Stores a copy of the word contents of the memory location addressed by BX in the data segment on the stack
PUSHA	Stores a copy of registers AX, BX, CX, DX, SP, BP, SI, and DI on the stack
POPA	Removes data from the stack and places it into DI, SI, BP, SP, DX, CX, BX, and AX

is a LIFO (last-in, first-out) memory in the 80286 microprocessor. Data are placed onto the stack with a PUSH instruction and removed with a POP instruction. The CALL instruction uses the stack to hold the return address for subroutines and a RET (return) instruction to remove the return address from the stack.

The 80286 stack memory is maintained by two registers: the *stack pointer* (SP) and the *stack segment register* (SS). Whenever a word of data is pushed onto the stack [see Figure 2–18(a)], the high-order 8 bits are placed in the location addressed by SP − 1. The low-order 8 bits are placed in the location addressed by SP − 2. The SP is then decremented by 2, so the next word of data is stored in the next available stack memory location. The SP register always points to an area of memory located within the stack segment. SP adds to SS × 10H to form the stack memory address.

Whenever data are popped from the stack [see Figure 2–18(b)], the low-order 8 bits are removed from the location addressed by SP. The high-order 8 bits are removed from the location addressed by SP + 1. The SP register is then incremented by 2. Table 2–10 lists some of the PUSH and POP instructions available in the 80286 microprocessor. Note that PUSH and POP always store or retrieve *words* of data— never bytes. Data may be pushed onto the stack from any 16-bit register or segment register. Data may be popped off the stack into any 16-bit register or any segment register except CS. The reason that we may not pop data from the stack into CS is that this only changes part of the address of the next instruction.

2–11   SUMMARY

1. The data-addressing modes include register, immediate, direct, register indirect, base-plus index, register relative, and base relative-plus-index addressing.

2. The program memory-addressing modes include direct, relative, and indirect addressing.
3. Table 2–11 lists all data-addressing modes available to the 80286 microprocessor.
4. The MOV instruction copies the contents of the source address into the destination address. The source operand never changes for any instruction.
5. Register addressing specifies any 8-bit register (AH, AL, BH, BL, CH, CL, DH, or DL) or any 16-bit register (AX, BX, CX, DX, SP, BP, SI, or DI). The segment registers (CS, DS, ES, or SS) are also addressable for moving data between a segment register and a 16-bit register/memory location or for PUSH and POP.

TABLE 2–11 80286 data-addressing modes

Assembly Language	Address Generation
MOV AL,BL	Register addressing
MOV AL,LIST	(DS × 10H) + LIST
MOV AL,12	Immediate data of 12 decimal
MOV AL,[BP]	(SS × 10H) + BP
MOV AL,[BX]	(DS × 10H) + BX
MOV AL,[DI]	(DS × 10H) + DI
MOV AL,[SI]	(DS × 10H) + SI
MOV AL,[BP+2]	(SS × 10H) + BP + 2
MOV AL,[BX−4]	(DS × 10H) + BX − 4
MOV AL,[DI+1000H]	(DS × 10H) + DI + 1000H
MOV AL,[SI+300H]	(DS × 10H) + SI + 0300H
MOV AL,LIST[BP]	(SS × 10H) + BP + LIST
MOV AL,LIST[BX]	(DS × 10H) + BX + LIST
MOV AL,LIST[DI]	(DS × 10H) + DI + LIST
MOV AL,LIST[SI]	(DS × 10H) + SI + LIST
MOV AL,LIST[BP+2]	(SS × 10H) + BP + LIST + 2
MOV AL,LIST[BX−6]	(DS × 10H) + BX + LIST − 6
MOV AL,LIST[DI+100H]	(DS × 10H) + DI + LIST + 100H
MOV AL,LIST[SI+20H]	(DS × 10H) + SI + LIST + 20H
MOV AL,[BP+DI]	(SS × 10H) + BP + DI
MOV AL,[BP+SI]	(SS × 10H) + BP + SI
MOV AL,[BX+DI]	(DS × 10H) + BX + DI
MOV AL,[BX+SI]	(DS × 10H) + BX + SI
MOV AL,[BP+DI+2]	(SS × 10H) + BP + DI + 2
MOV AL,[BP+SI−4]	(SS × 10H) + BP + SI − 4
MOV AL,[BX+DI+30H]	(DS × 10H) + BX + DI + 30H
MOV AL,[BX+SI+10H]	(DS × 10H) + BX + SI + 10H
MOV AL,LIST[BP+DI]	(SS × 10H) + BP + DI + LIST
MOV AL,LIST[BP+SI]	(SS × 10H) + BP + SI + LIST
MOV AL,LIST[BX+DI]	(DS × 10H) + BX + DI + LIST
MOV AL,LIST[BX+SI]	(DS × 10H) + BX + SI + LIST
MOV AL,LIST[BP+DI+2]	(SS × 10H) + BP + DI + LIST + 2
MOV AL,LIST[BP+SI−7]	(SS × 10H) + BP + SI + LIST − 7
MOV AL,LIST[BX+DI−10H]	(DS × 10H) + BX + DI + LIST − 10H
MOV AL,LIST[BX+SI+1AFH]	(DS × 10H) + BX + SI + LIST + 1AFH

6. The MOV instruction that uses immediate addressing transfers the byte or word immediately following the opcode into a register or a memory location. Immediate addressing manipulates constant data in a program.

7. Direct addressing occurs in two forms in the 80286 microprocessor: (1) direct addressing and (2) displacement addressing. Both forms of addressing are identical, except direct addressing is used to transfer data between either AX or AL and memory, while displacement addressing is used with any register-memory transfer. Direct addressing requires 3 bytes of memory, while displacement addressing requires 4 bytes.

8. Register indirect addressing allows data to be addressed at the memory location pointed to by either a base (BP and BX) or index register (DI and SI).

9. Base-plus-index addressing often addresses data in an array. The memory address for this mode is formed by adding a base register, index register, and the contents of a segment register times 10H.

10. Register relative addressing uses either a base or index register plus a displacement to access memory data.

11. Base relative-plus-index addressing is useful for addressing a two-dimensional memory array. The address is formed by adding a base register, an index register, displacement, and the contents of a segment register times 10H.

12. Direct program memory addressing is allowed with the JMP and CALL instructions to any location in the memory system. With this addressing mode, the offset address and segment address are stored with the instruction.

13. Relative program addressing allows a JMP or CALL instruction to branch forward or backward in the current code segment by ±32K bytes.

14. Indirect program addressing allows the JMP or CALL instructions to address another portion of the program or subroutine indirectly through a register or memory location.

15. The PUSH and POP instructions transfer a word between the stack and a register or memory location.

2–12   QUESTIONS AND PROBLEMS

1. What do the following MOV instructions accomplish?
   a. MOV AX,BX
   b. MOV BX,AX
   c. MOV BL,CH
   d. MOV SP,BP
   e. MOV AX,CS

2. List the 8-bit registers that are used for register addressing.

3. List the 16-bit registers that are used for register addressing.

4. List the 16-bit segment registers used by MOV, PUSH, and POP.

5. What is wrong with the MOV BL,CX instruction?

6. What is wrong with the MOV DS,SS instruction?

7. Select an instruction for each of the following tasks:
   a. copy BX into DX
   b. copy BL into CL
   c. copy SI into BX
   d. copy DS into AX
   e. copy AL into AH

8. Select an instruction for each of the following tasks:
   a. move a 12H into AL
   b. move a 123AH into AX
   c. move a 0CDH into CL
   d. move a 1000H into SI
   e. move a 1200H into BX

9. What special symbol is sometimes used to denote immediate data?

10. What is a displacement? How does it determine the memory address in a MOV [2000H],AL instruction?

11. What do the symbols [ ] indicate?

12. Given that DS = 0200H, BX = 0300H, and DI = 400H, determine the memory address accessed by each of the following instructions:
    a. MOV AL,[1234H]
    b. MOV AL,[BX]
    c. MOV [DI],AL

13. What is wrong with a MOV [BX],[DI] instruction?

14. Choose an instruction that requires BYTE PTR.

15. Choose an instruction that requires WORD PTR.

16. Explain the difference between MOV BX,DATA instruction and the MOV BX,OFFSET DATA instruction.

17. Given that DS = 1000H, SS = 2000H, BP = 1000H, and DI = 0100H, determine the memory address accessed by each of the following:
    a. MOV AL,[BP+DI]
    b. MOV CX,[DI]
    c. MOV DX,[BP]

18. Given that DS = 1200H, BX = 0100H, and SI = 0250H, determine the address accessed by each of the following instructions:
    a. MOV [100H],DL
    b. MOV [SI+100H],AL
    c. MOV DL,[BX+100H]

19. Given that DS = 1100H, BX = 0200H, LIST = 0250H, and SI = 0500H, determine the address accessed by each of the following instructions:
    a. MOV LIST[SI],DX
    b. MOV CL,LIST[BX+SI]
    c. MOV CH,[BX+SI]

20. Given that DS = 1300H, SS = 1400H, BP = 1500H, and SI = 0100H, determine the address accessed by each of the following instructions:
    a. MOV AL,[BP+200H]
    b. MOV AL,[BP+SI−200H]
    c. MOV AL,[SI−0100H]

21. Which 80286 base register addresses data in the stack segment?

22. List all three program memory-addressing modes.

23. How many bytes of memory store a direct jump instruction? What is stored in each of the bytes?

24. What is the difference between an intersegment and intrasegment jump?

25. If a near jump uses a signed 16-bit displacement, how can it jump to any memory location within the current code segment?

26. What is a far jump?

27. If a JMP instruction is stored at memory location 100H within the current code segment, it cannot be a _____ jump if it is jumping to memory location 200H within the current code segment.

28. Show which JMP instruction assembles (direct, short displacement, or long displacement) if the JMP THERE instruction is stored at memory address 10000H and the address of THERE is:
    a. 10020H
    b. 11000H
    c. 0FFFEH
    d. 30000H

29. Form a JMP instruction that jumps to the address pointed to by the BX register.

30. Select a JMP instruction that jumps to the location stored in memory at location TABLE. Assume that it is a near JMP.

31. How many bytes are stored on the stack by PUSH instructions?

32. Explain how the PUSH [DI] instruction functions.

CHAPTER 3

Data Movement Instructions

INTRODUCTION

In this chapter, we explain the 80286 data movement instructions. These instructions, except for a few, also function on the earlier 8086/8088 microprocessor in exactly the same manner as described in this chapter. The data movement instructions include MOV, PUSH, POP, XCHG, XLAT, IN, OUT, LEA, LDS, LES, LAHF, SAHF; and the string instructions include MOVS, LODS, STOS, INS, and OUTS. We present data movement instructions first because they are probably the most often used and the easiest to understand and master.

The 80286 microprocessor usually requires some type of assembler program that generates machine language because machine language instructions are too complex to generate by hand. This chapter describes some of the assembly language syntax and directives. (This text assumes that the user is developing software on an IBM personal computer or clone using the Microsoft MACRO assembler (MASM), Intel Assembler, Borland Turbo assembler (TASM), or similar software. Appendix A explains the assembler and provides detail on the linker program.)

OBJECTIVES

Upon completion of this chapter, you will be able to:

1. Explain the operation of each data movement instruction with applicable addressing modes.
2. Explain the purposes of the assembly language pseudo-operations and key words such as ALIGN, ASSUME, DB, DD, DW, END, ENDS, ENDP, EQU, OFFSET, ORG, PROC, PTR, and SEGMENT.
3. Given a specific data movement task, select the appropriate 80286 assembly language instructions to accomplish it.
4. Given a hexadecimal machine language instruction, determine the symbolic opcode, source, destination, and addressing mode.

5. Use the assembler to set up a data segment, stack segment, and a code segment.
6. Show how to set up a procedure using PROC and ENP.
7. Explain the difference between memory models and full-segment definitions for the MASM assembler.

3–1   MOV REVISITED

We used the MOV instruction in Chapter 2 to explain the 80286 addressing modes. In this chapter, we use it to explain the machine language forms available to the programmer for various addressing modes and instructions. We introduce machine code here because at times it may be necessary to interpret a machine language program generated by an assembler. This ability allows debugging or modification at the machine language level. It also shows how to convert between machine and assembly language instructions using Appendix B.

Machine Language

Machine language is the native binary code that the microprocessor understands as the instructions that control its operation. Machine language instructions, for the 80286, vary in length from 1 to 6 bytes. Although machine language appears complex, there is some order to this microprocessor's machine language. There are over 20,000 variations of machine language instructions for the 80286 microprocessor. This means there is no complete list of these variations. Because of this, some binary bits in machine language instructions are given, and the remainder must be determined for each variation of the instruction.

Byte one of any machine language instruction contains the *opcode,* which selects the operation (addition, subtraction, move, etc.) the microprocessor will perform. Figure 3–1 illustrates the general form of the first byte of many, but not all, 80286 machine language instructions. Here the first 6 bits of the first byte are the opcode. The remaining 2 bits indicate the *direction* (D) of the data flow and whether the data are a *byte* or a *word* (W).

If D = 1, data flow to the register (REG) field from the R/M field in byte two of the instruction. If D = 0, data flow to the R/M field from the REG field. If W = 1, the data size is a word, and if W = 0, the data size is a byte. The W bit appears in most instructions, while the D bit mainly appears in the MOV instruction and a few other instructions. Refer to Figure 3–2 for the binary bit pattern of byte two

FIGURE 3–1   Byte 1 of many machine language instructions, illustrating the position of the opcode, D, and W.

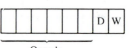

Opcode

FIGURE 3–2 Byte 2 of many machine language instructions, illustrating the position of the MOD, REG, and R/M fields.

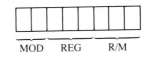

MOD   REG   R/M

of many instructions. This illustration shows the location of the REG (*register*), R/M (*register/memory*), and MOD (*mode*) fields.

MOD Field. The *MOD field* specifies the addressing mode (MOD) for the selected instruction. It determines the type of addressing and whether a displacement is present with the selected type. Table 3–1 lists the operand forms available to the MOD field. If the MOD field contains a 11, it selects the register addressing mode. This is where the R/M field, of the second byte, addresses a register. If the MOD field contains a 00, 01, or 10, the R/M field selects one of the data memory-addressing modes of operation. When MOD selects a memory-addressing mode, it indicates that the addressing mode contains no displacement (00), an 8-bit sign-extended displacement (01), or a 16-bit displacement (10). The MOV AL,[DI] instruction uses no displacement, a MOV AL,[DI+2] instruction uses an 8-bit displacement (+2), and a MOV AL,[DI+1000] instruction uses a 16-bit displacement (+1000).

All 8-bit displacements are sign extended into 16-bit displacements when the 80286 executes the instruction. If the 8-bit displacement is 00H–7FH (positive), it is sign extended to 0000H–007FH before adding to a segment address. If the 8-bit displacement is 80H–FFH (negative), it is sign extended to FF80H–FFFFH. To sign extend a number, its sign-bit is copied to the next higher order byte, which generates a 00H or FFH.

Register Assignments. Table 3–2 lists the register assignments for the REG field and the R/M field only when MOD = 11. This table contains two lists of register assignments: one is used when W = 1 for words, and the other is W = 0 for bytes.

Suppose that a 2-byte instruction, 8BECH, appears in a machine language program. This instruction is converted to binary and placed in the instruction format of bytes 1 and 2 as illustrated in Figure 3–3. The opcode is 100010. If you refer to Appendix B, which lists the machine language instructions, you will find that this is the opcode for a MOV instruction. Also notice that both the D and W bits are a logic 1, which means that a word moves into the register specified in the REG field. The REG field contains a 101, indicating register BP, so the MOV instruction moves data into register BP. Because the MOD field contains a 11, the R/M

TABLE 3–1 MOD field specifications

MOD	Function
00	No displacement
01	8-bit sign-extended displacement
10	16-bit displacement
11	R/M is a register

TABLE 3–2 REG and R/M (when MOD = 11) assignments

Code	W = 0 (Byte)	W = 1 (Word)
000	AL	AX
001	CL	CX
010	DL	DX
011	BL	BX
100	AH	SP
101	CH	BP
110	DH	SI
111	BH	DI

field also indicates a register. Here, R/M = 100 (SP), therefore this instruction moves data from SP into BP and is written in symbolic form as a MOV BP,SP instruction.

R/M Memory Addressing.   If the MOD field contains a 00, 01, or 10, the R/M field takes on a new meaning. Table 3–3 lists the memory-addressing modes for the R/M field when MOD is a 00, 01, or 10.

All the addressing modes represented in Chapter 2 appear in Table 3–3. The displacement, discussed in Chapter 2, is defined by the MOD field. If MOD = 00 and R/M = 101, the addressing mode is [DI]. If MOD = 01 or 10, the addressing mode is LIST [DI], [DI+33H], or LIST [DI+22H]. This example uses LIST, 33H, and 22H as arbitrary values for the displacement.

Figure 3–4 illustrates the machine language version of a MOV DL,[DI] instruction (8A15H). This instruction is two bytes long and has an opcode 100010, D = 1 (*to REG from R/M*), W = 0 (*byte*), MOD = 00 (*no displacement*), REG = 010 (*DL*), and R/M = 101 (*[DI]*). If the instruction changes to MOV DL,[DI+1], the MOD field changes to 01 for an 8-bit displacement, but the first two bytes of the instruction otherwise remain the same. The instruction now becomes 8A5501H instead of 8A15H. Notice that the 8-bit displacement appends to the first two bytes of the instruction to form a 3-byte instruction instead of two bytes. If the instruction is again changed to a MOV DL,[DI+1000H], the machine language form becomes a 8A750010H. Here the 16-bit displacement of 1000H (coded as 0010H) appends the opcode.

Special Addressing Mode.   There is a special addressing mode that does not appear in Tables 3–1, 3–2, or 3–3 that occurs whenever memory data are referenced by only the

FIGURE 3–3 The 8BEC instruction placed in the byte 1 and 2 formats of Figures 3–1 and 3–2. This machine language instruction is decoded as the symbolic instruction MOV BP,SP.

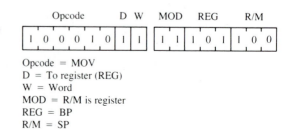

Opcode	D W	MOD	REG	R/M

| 1 | 0 | 0 | 0 | 1 | 0 | 1 | 1 | | 1 | 1 | 1 | 0 | 1 | 1 | 0 | 0 |

Opcode = MOV
D = To register (REG)
W = Word
MOD = R/M is register
REG = BP
R/M = SP

TABLE 3–3 R/M memory-addressing modes

Code	Function
000	DS:[BX+SI]
001	DS:[BX+DI]
010	SS:[BP+SI]
011	SS:[BP+DI]
100	DS:[SI]
101	DS:[DI]
110	SS:[BP]*
111	DS:[BX]

Note: See text under Special Addressing Mode.

displacement mode of addressing. Examples are the MOV [1000H],DL and MOV NUMB,DL instructions. The first instruction moves the contents of register DL into data segment memory location 1000H. The second instruction moves register DL into symbolic data segment memory location NUMB.

Whenever an instruction has only a displacement, the MOD field is always a 00 and the R/M field is always a 110. This combination normally shows that the instruction contains no displacement and uses addressing mode [BP]. You cannot actually use addressing mode [BP] without a displacement in machine language. The assembler takes care of this by using an 8-bit displacement (MOD = 01) of 00H whenever the [BP] addressing mode appears in an instruction. This means that the [BP] addressing mode assembles as a [BP+0] even though we use [BP].

Figure 3–5 shows the binary bit pattern required to encode the MOV [1000H],DL instruction in machine language. If the individual translating this symbolic instruction into machine language does not know about the special addressing mode, it would incorrectly translate to a MOV [BP],DL instruction. Figure 3–6 shows the actual form of the MOV [BP],DL instruction. Notice that this is a 3-byte instruction with a displacement of 00H.

An Immediate Instruction. Suppose we choose the MOV WORD PTR [BX+1000H],1234H instruction as an example of immediate addressing. This instruction moves a 1234H into the word-sized memory location addressed by the sum of 1000H, BX, and DS × 10H. This 6-byte instruction uses two bytes for the opcode, D, W, MOD, REG, and R/M fields. Two of the six bytes are the data of

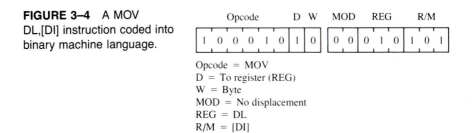

FIGURE 3–4 A MOV DL,[DI] instruction coded into binary machine language.

Opcode D W   MOD REG R/M

| 1 | 0 | 0 | 0 | 1 | 0 | 1 | 0 | 0 | 0 | 0 | 1 | 0 | 1 | 0 | 1 |

Opcode = MOV
D = To register (REG)
W = Byte
MOD = No displacement
REG = DL
R/M = [DI]

FIGURE 3–5 A MOV [1000H],DL instruction coded into binary machine language. Note that 2 additional bytes are required for the displacement of 1000H.

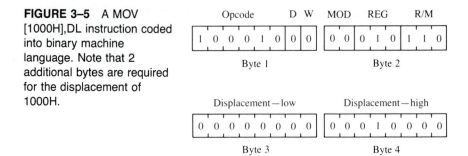

1234H. Two of the six bytes are the displacement of 1000H. Figure 3–7 shows the binary bit pattern for each byte of this instruction.

This instruction, in symbolic form, includes WORD PTR. The WORD PTR directive indicates to the assembler that the instruction uses a word-sized memory pointer. If the instruction moves a byte of immediate data, then BYTE PTR replaces WORD PTR in the instruction. Most instructions that refer to memory through a pointer do not need the BYTE PTR or WORD PTR directive. These are only necessary when it is not clear if the operation is a byte or a word. The MOV [BX],AL instruction is clearly a byte move, while the MOV [BX],1 instruction is not precise and could therefore be a byte- or a word-sized move. Here the instruction must be coded as either MOV BYTE PTR [BX],1 or MOV WORD PTR [BX],1. If not, the assembler flags it as an error because it cannot determine the intent of this instruction.

Segment MOV Instructions. If the contents of a segment register are moved by the MOV, PUSH, or POP instruction, a special set of register bits (REG field) selects the segment register (see Table 3–4).

Figure 3–8 shows a MOV BX,CS instruction converted to binary. The opcode for this type of MOV instruction is different for the prior MOV instructions. Segment registers can be moved between any 16-bit register or 16-bit memory location. For example, the MOV [DI],DS instruction stores the contents of DS into the memory location addressed by DI in the data segment.

FIGURE 3–6 The MOV [BP],DL instruction coded into binary machine language requires a 1-byte displacement of 00H in order for the 80286 to execute this instruction.

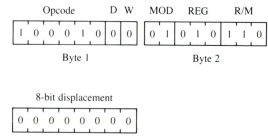

FIGURE 3–7 A MOV WORD PTR [BX+1000H],1234H instruction converted into binary machine language requires 6 bytes of memory: 2 for the instruction, 2 for the displacement of 1000H, and 2 for the immediate data of 1234H.

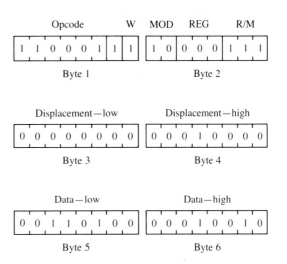

| Opcode | W | MOD | REG | R/M |

| 1 1 0 0 0 1 | 1 | 1 | | 1 0 | 0 0 0 | 1 1 1 |
| Byte 1 | | Byte 2 |

Displacement—low   Displacement—high

| 0 0 0 0 0 0 0 0 | 0 0 0 1 0 0 0 0 |
| Byte 3 | Byte 4 |

Data—low   Data—high

| 0 0 1 1 0 1 0 0 | 0 0 0 1 0 0 1 0 |
| Byte 5 | Byte 6 |

Note: D and REG are not used in immediate memory addressing.

Although this has not been a complete coverage of machine language coding, it should give you a good start in machine language programming. Remember, a program written in symbolic assembly language (assembly language) is rarely assembled by hand into binary machine language. An *assembler* converts symbolic assembly language into machine language. With the 80286 microprocessor and its 20,000 instruction variations, let us hope that an assembler is available for the conversion, because the process is very time-consuming, although not impossible.

TABLE 3–4 Segment register selection bits

Code	Segment Register
000	ES
001	CS*
010	SS
011	DS

Note: MOV CS,?? and POP CS are not allowed by the 80286.

FIGURE 3–8 A MOV BX,CS instruction converted into binary machine language. Here the REG is encoded as the CS register and R/M is encoded as the BX register. *Note:* W and D are not present in this instruction.

| Opcode | MOD | REG | R/M |

| 1 0 0 0 1 1 0 0 | 1 1 | 0 0 1 | 0 1 1 |

Note: W and D are not present in this instruction.

3–2   **PUSH/POP**

The PUSH and POP instructions are important instructions that store and retrieve data from the LIFO stack memory. The 80286 microprocessor has six forms of the PUSH and POP instructions: register, memory, immediate, segment register, flags, and all registers. The PUSH and POP immediate and the PUSH and POP all registers forms are not available in the earlier 8086/8088 microprocessor, but are available to the 80286, 80386, and 80486.

Register addressing allows the contents of any 16-bit register to be transferred to or from the stack. Memory addressing stores the contents of a 16-bit memory location on the stack or stack data into a memory location. Immediate addressing allows immediate data to be pushed onto the stack, but not popped off the stack. Segment register addressing allows the contents of any segment register to be pushed onto the stack or removed from the stack except the CS register. The CS register may be pushed, but data from the stack may never be popped into CS. The flags may be pushed or popped from that stack and the contents of all the registers may be pushed or popped.

PUSH

The PUSH instruction always transfers *two bytes* of data to the stack. The source of the data may be any internal 16-bit register, immediate data, any segment register, or any two bytes of memory data. There is also a PUSHA instruction that copies the contents of the internal register set, except the segment registers, to the stack. The PUSHA (*push all*) instruction copies the registers to the stack in the following order: AX, BX, CX, DX, SP, BP, DI, and SI. The PUSHF (*push flags*) instruction copies the contents of the flag register to the stack.

Whenever data are pushed onto the stack, the first (most significant) data byte moves into the stack segment memory location addressed by SP − 1. The second (least significant) data byte moves into the stack segment memory location addressed by SP − 2. After the data are stored by a PUSH, the contents of the SP register decrement by 2. Figure 3–9 shows the operation of the PUSH AX instruction. This instruction copies the contents of AX onto the stack where address SS:[SP − 1] = AH, SS:[SP − 2] = AL, and afterwards SP = SP − 2.

The PUSHA instruction pushes all the internal 16-bit registers onto the stack as illustrated in Figure 3–10. This instruction requires 16 bytes of stack memory space to store all eight 16-bit registers. After all registers are pushed, the contents of the SP register are decremented by 16. The PUSHA instruction is very useful when the entire register set (*microprocessor environment*) of the 80286 must be saved during a task.

The PUSH immediate data instruction has two different opcodes, but in both cases a 16-bit immediate number moves onto the stack. If the value of the immediate data are 00H–FFH, the opcode is a 6AH, and if the data are 0100H–FFFFH, the opcode is 68H. The PUSH 8 instruction assembles as a 6A08H, and the PUSH 1000H instructions assembles as 680010H.

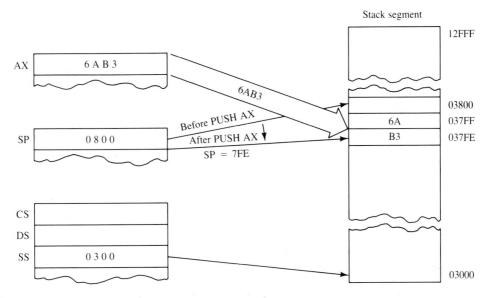

FIGURE 3–9 The effect of a PUSH AX instruction on the SP register and stack memory locations 037FFH and 037FEH.

Table 3–5 lists the forms of the PUSH instruction that include PUSHA and PUSHF. The table also lists the binary bit pattern of each byte in each instruction for use in machine language programming and conversions.

POP

The POP instruction performs the inverse operation of a PUSH instruction. The POP instruction removes data from the stack and places them into the target 16-bit register,

FIGURE 3–10 The stack format for the PUSHA instruction.

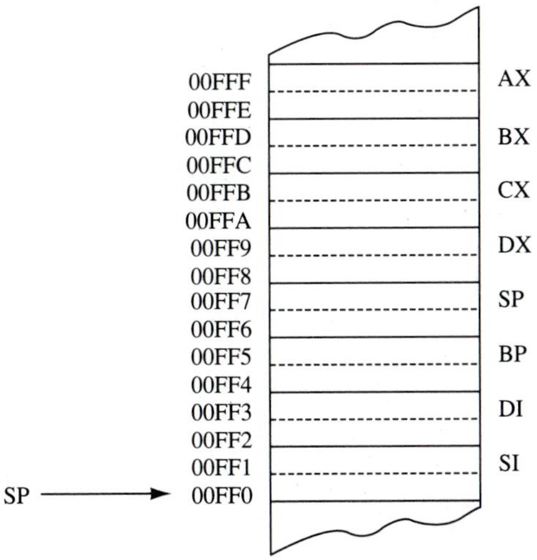

TABLE 3–5 The PUSH instructions

Symbolic	Byte 1	Byte 2	Example
PUSH reg	0101 0rrr		PUSH BX
PUSH mem	1111 1111	mm11 0aaa	PUSH [BX]
PUSH seg	000s s110		PUSH DS
PUSH imm	0110 10z0		PUSH 1200H
PUSHA	0110 0000		PUSHA
PUSHF	1001 1100		PUSHF

Note: aaa = any memory-addressing mode, mm = MOD code, rrr = any 16-bit register, ss = any segment register, and z = size of immediate data. The PUSHA and PUSH imm forms are not found in the 8086/8088 microprocessor's instruction set.

segment register, or a 16-bit memory location. The POP instruction is not available as an immediate POP. The POPF (*pop flags*) instruction removes a 16-bit number from the stack and places it into the flag register. The POPA (*pop all*) instruction removes 16 bytes of data from the stack and places them into the following registers in the order shown: SI, DI, BP, SP, DX, CX, BX, and AX. This is the reverse order from the way they are placed on the stack by the PUSHA instruction.

Suppose that a POP BX instruction executes. The first byte of data removed from the stack (the memory location addressed by SP in the stack segment) moves into register BL. The second byte is removed from stack segment memory location SP + 1, and placed into register BH. After both bytes are removed from the stack, the SP register increments by 2. Figure 3–11 shows how the POP BX instruction removes data from the stack and places them into register BX.

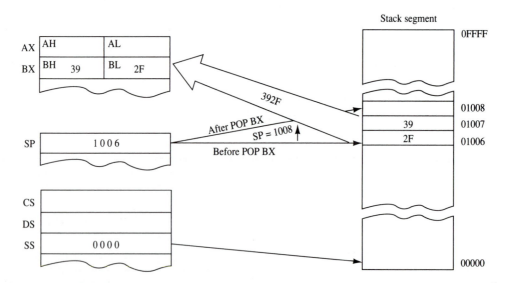

FIGURE 3–11 POP BX removes 2 bytes of data from the stack segment and places them into the BX register.

The opcodes used for the POP instruction, and all its variations, appear in Table 3–6. As in Table 3–5, this table also lists the binary machine language opcodes. Note that a POP CS instruction is not a valid instruction in the 80286 instruction set. If we allow a POP CS instruction to execute, only a portion of the address (CS) of the next instruction changes. This makes the POP CS instruction unpredictable and therefore not allowed.

Initializing the Stack

When the stack area is initialized, we load both the stack segment register (SS) and the stack pointer (SP) register. It is normal to designate an area of memory as the stack segment by loading SS with the bottom location of the stack segment.

For example, if the stack segment is to reside in memory locations 10000H–1FFFFH, SS is loaded with a 1000H. (Recall that we append the rightmost end of the stack segment register with a 0H.) To start the stack at the top of the 64K byte stack segment, the stack pointer (SP) is loaded with a 0000H. Figure 3–12 shows how this value causes data to be pushed onto the top of the stack segment with a PUSH CX instruction. Remember that all segments are *cyclic* in nature—that is, the top location of a segment is *contiguous* with the bottom location of the segment.

EXAMPLE 3–1

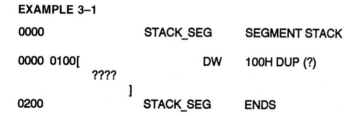

```
0000                    STACK_SEG      SEGMENT STACK

0000  0100[             DW      100H DUP (?)
        ????

      ]
0200                    STACK_SEG      ENDS
```

In assembly language, a stack segment is set up as illustrated in Example 3–1. The first statement identifies the start of the stack segment and the last statement identifies the end of the stack segment. The assembler and linker program places the correct stack segment address in SS and the length of the segment (top of the stack) into SP. There is no need to load these registers in your program unless you wish to change the initial values for some reason.

TABLE 3–6 The POP instructions

Symbolic	Byte 1	Byte 2	Example
POP reg	0101 1rrr		POP DI
POP mem	1000 1111	mm00 0aaa	POP [DI+2]
POP seg	000s s111		POP ES
POPA	0110 0001		POPA
POPF	1001 1101		POPF

Note: aaa = any memory-addressing mode, mm = MOD field, rrr = any 16-bit register, ss = any segment register. The POPA instruction is not found in the 8086/8088 instruction set.

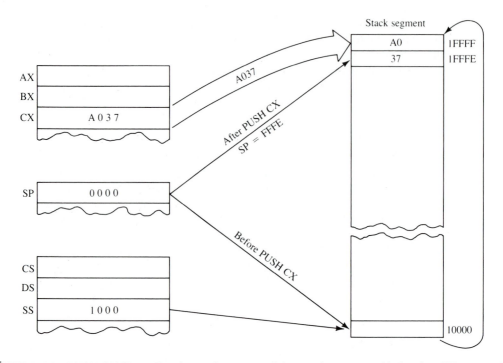

FIGURE 3–12 PUSH CX illustrating the cyclic nature of the stack segment. Notice that SP starts at 0000H and, after being decremented, ends up at FFFEH.

An alternative method for defining the stack segment is used with one of the memory models for the assembler (refer to Appendix A). Here (see Example 3–2) the .STACK statement, followed by the number of bytes allocated to the stack, defines the stack area. This is identical to Example 3–1. The .STACK statement also initializes both SS and SP.

If the stack is not specified using either method, a warning will appear when the program is linked. This warning may be ignored if the stack size is 256 bytes or less. The system automatically assigns (through DOS) a 256-byte section of memory to the stack.

EXAMPLE 3–2

```
.MODEL SMALL
.STACK 200H                    ;set stack size
```

3–3   LOAD-EFFECTIVE ADDRESS

There are three load-effective address instructions in the 80286 instruction set. The LEA instruction loads any 16-bit register with the address as determined by the addressing mode selected for the instruction. The LDS and LES variations load any 16-bit register with the offset address retrieved from a memory location and then load either DS or ES with a segment address retrieved from memory. Table 3–7 lists these three load-effective address instructions.

LEA

The LEA instruction loads a 16-bit register with the offset address of the data specified by the operand. As the first example in Table 3–7 shows, the operand address NUMB is loaded into register AX, not the contents of address NUMB.

By comparing LEA with MOV, we observe the following effect: LEA BX,[DI] loads the offset address specified by [DI] (contents of DI) into the BX register; MOV BX,[DI] loads the data stored at the memory location addressed by [DI] into register BX.

Earlier in the text, we presented several examples using the OFFSET pseudo-operation. The OFFSET directive performs the same function as an LEA instruction if the operand is a displacement. For example, the MOV BX,OFFSET LIST performs the same function as LEA BX,LIST. Both instructions load the offset address of memory location LIST into the BX register.

But why is the LEA instruction available if the OFFSET directive accomplishes the same task? First, OFFSET can only function with simple operands such as LIST. It may not be used for an operand such as [DI], LIST[SI]. The OFFSET directive is more efficient than the LEA instruction for simple operands. It takes the 80286 longer to execute the LEA BX,LIST than MOV BX,OFFSET LIST; it requires three clocks to execute the LEA BX,LIST instruction and only two clocks to execute MOV BX,OFFSET LIST. The reason that the MOV BX,OFFSET LIST instruction executes faster is because the assembler calculates the offset address of LIST, while with the LEA instruction, the microprocessor does the calculation as it executes the instruction. The MOV BX,OFFSET LIST instruction is actually assembled as a move immediate instruction and is more efficient.

Suppose that the 80286 executes an LEA BX,[DI] instruction and DI contains a 1000H. Because DI contains the offset address, the microprocessor transfers a copy of DI into BX. A MOV BX,DI instruction performs this task in less time and is often preferred to the LEA BX,[DI] instruction.

TABLE 3–7 The load-effective address instructions	*Symbolic*	*Function*
	LEA AX,NUMB	AX is loaded with the address of NUMB
	LDS DI,LIST	DI and DS are loaded with the address stored at LIST
	LES BX,CAT	BX and ES are loaded with the address stored at CAT

Another example is LEA SI,[BX+DI]. This instruction adds BX to DI and stores the sum in the SI register. The sum generated is a modulo-64K sum. If BX = 1000H and DI = 2000H, the offset address moved into SI is 3000H. If BX = 1000H and DI = FF00H, the offset address is 0F00H. Notice that the second result is a modulo-64K sum. (A modulo-64K sum drops any carry out of the 16-bit result.)

LDS and LES

The LDS and LES instructions load any 16-bit register with an offset address and either the DS or ES segment register with a segment address. These instructions use any of the memory-addressing modes to access a 32-bit section of memory that contains both the segment and offset address. These instructions may not use the register addressing mode (MOD = 11).

Figure 3–13 illustrates an example LDS BX,[DI] instruction. This instruction transfers the 32-bit number, addressed by DI in the data segment, into the BX and DS registers. The LDS and LES instructions obtain a new far address from memory. The offset address appears first, followed by the segment address. This format is used for storing all 32-bit memory addresses.

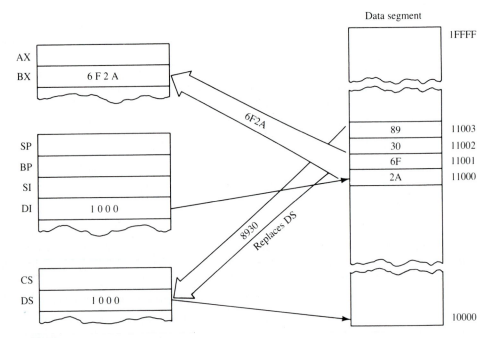

FIGURE 3–13   LDS BX,[DI] loads the BX register from locations 11000H and 11001H and the DS register from locations 11002H and 11003H. This instruction will change the data segment from 10000H–1FFFFH to 89300H–992FFH.

A far address can be stored in memory by the assembler. For example, the ADDR DD FAR PTR FROG instruction stores the offset and segment address (*far address*) of FROG in 32 bits of memory at location ADDR. The DD directive tells the assembler to store a *double word* (32-bit number) in memory address ADDR.

3–4 STRING DATA TRANSFERS

There are five string data transfer instructions—LODS, STOS, MOVS, INS, and OUTS. Each string instruction allows data transfers that are either a single byte or word, or a block of bytes or words. Before the string instructions are presented, the operation of the DF flag-bit (*direction*), DI, and SI must be understood as they apply to the string instructions.

Direction Flag (DF)

The direction flag (DF) selects auto-increment (DF = 0) or auto-decrement (DF = 1) operation for the DI and SI registers during string operations. The direction flag is only used with the string instructions. The CLD instruction *clears* the DF flag (DF = 0) and the STD instruction *sets* it (DF = 1). Therefore, the CLD instruction selects the auto-increment mode (DF = 0) and STD selects the auto-decrement mode (DF = 1).

Whenever a string instruction transfers a byte, the contents of DI and/or SI increment or decrement by 1. If a word is transferred, the contents of DI and/or SI increment or decrement by 2. Only the actual registers used by the string instruction increment or decrement. For example, the STOSB instruction uses the DI register to address a memory location. When STOSB executes, only DI increments or decrements without affecting SI. The same is true for the LODSB instruction, which uses the SI register to address memory data. LODSB only increments/decrements SI without affecting DI.

DI and SI

During the execution of a string instruction, memory accesses occur through either or both the DI and SI registers. The DI offset addresses data in the extra segment for all string instructions that use it. The SI offset address is located, by default, in the data segment. The segment assignment of SI may be changed with a segment override prefix as described later in this chapter. The DI segment assignment is *always* in the extra segment when a string instruction executes. This assignment cannot be changed. The reason that one pointer addresses data in the extra segment and the other in the data segment is so the MOVS instruction can move 64K bytes of data from one section of memory to another.

LODS

The LODS instruction loads either AL or AX with data stored at the data segment offset address indexed by the SI register. After loading AL with a byte or AX with a word, the contents of SI increment, if DF = 0, or decrement, if DF = 1. A 1 is added to or subtracted from SI for a byte LODS and a 2 is added or subtracted for a word LODS.

Table 3–8 lists the permissible forms of the LODS instruction. The LODSB (*loads a byte*) instruction causes a byte to be loaded into AL and the LODSW (*loads a word*) instruction causes a word to be loaded into AX. Although rare, as an alternative to LODSB and LODSW, LODS may be followed by either a byte-sized or word-sized operand to select a byte or word transfer. Operands are often defined as bytes, with DB, or as words, with DW. The DB pseudo-operation *defines byte(s)* and the DW pseudo-operation *defines word(s)*.

Figure 3–14 shows the effect of executing the LODSW instruction if the DF flag = 0, SI = 1000H, and DS = 1000H. Here a 16-bit number, stored at memory locations 11000H and 11001H moves into AX. Because DF = 0, and this is a word transfer, the contents of SI increment by 2 *after* AX loads with memory data.

STOS

The STOS instruction stores AL or AX at the extra segment memory location addressed by the DI register. Table 3–9 lists all forms of the STOS instruction. As with LODS, a STOS instruction may be appended with a B or W for a byte or word transfer. The STOSB (*stores a byte*) instruction stores the byte in AL at the extra segment memory location addressed by DI. The STOSW (*stores a word*) instruction stores AX in the extra segment memory location addressed by DI. After the byte (AL) or word (AX) is stored, the contents of DI increments or decrements.

STOS with a REP.   The *repeat prefix* (REP) may be added to any string instruction. The REP prefix causes CX to decrement by 1 each time the string instruction executes. After CX decrements, the string instruction repeats. If CX reaches a value of 0, the instruction terminates and the program continues with the next instruction. Thus, if

TABLE 3–8 Forms of the LODS instruction

Symbolic	Function
LODSB	AL = [SI]; SI = SI ± 1
LODSW	AX = [SI]; SI = SI ± 2
LODS LIST	AL = [SI]; SI = SI ± 1 (if LIST is a byte)
LODS DATA1	AX = [SI]; SI = SI ± 2 (if DATA1 is a word)

Note: SI addresses data in the data segment by default for LODS.

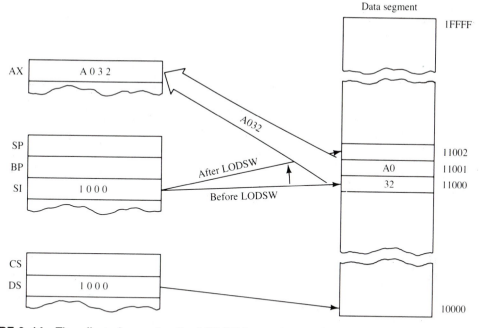

FIGURE 3–14 The effect of executing the LODSW instruction if DS = 1000H, SI = 1000H, D = 0, 11000H = 32, and 11001H = A0.

CX is loaded with a 100, and a REP STOSB instruction executes, the microprocessor automatically repeats the STOSB instruction 100 times. Since the DI register is incremented or decremented after each datum is stored, this instruction stores the contents of AL in a block of memory instead of a single byte of memory.

Suppose that 10 bytes of data, in an area of memory (BUFFER), must be cleared to 00H. This task is accomplished with a series of STOSB instructions (10

TABLE 3–9 Forms of the STOS instruction

Symbolic	Function
STOSB	[DI] = AL; DI = DI ± 1
STOSW	[DI] = AX; DI = DI ± 2
STOS LIST	[DI] = AL; DI = DI ± 1 (if LIST is a byte)
STOS DATA1	[DI] = AX; DI = DI ± 2 (if DATA1 is a word)

Note: DI addresses data in the extra segment.

of them) or with one STOSB prefixed by an REP, if CX is a 10. The program listed in Example 3–3 clears memory area BUFFER.

EXAMPLE 3–3

```
                         ;using REP STOSB to clear a BUFFER
                         ;
0000  BF 0000 R                  MOV    DI,OFFSET BUFFER    ;address BUFFER
0003  B9 000A                    MOV    CX,10               ;load count
0006  FC                         CLD                        ;auto-increment
0007  B0 00                      MOV    AL,0                ;clear AL
0009  F3/AA                      REP STOSB                  ;clear buffer
```

This short sequence of instructions addresses location BUFFER using the MOV DI,OFFSET BUFFER instruction. Though BUFFER is in the extra segment, the assembler still uses an offset address to address the memory. Notice how the REP prefix precedes the STOSB instruction in both assembly language and hexadecimal machine language. In machine language, the F3H is the REP prefix and AAH is the STOSB opcode.

A faster method of clearing this 10-byte buffer is to use the STOSW instruction with a count of five. Example 3–4 illustrates the same task as Example 3–3 except the count changes to a five and the STOSW instruction repeats instead of the STOSB instruction. Also register AX is cleared instead of register AL.

EXAMPLE 3–4

```
                         ;using REP STOSW to clear a BUFFER
                         ;
0000  BF 0000 R                  MOV    DI,OFFSET BUFFER    ;address BUFFER
0003  B9 0005                    MOV    CX,5                ;load count
0006  FC                         CLD                        ;auto-increment
0007  B8 0000                    MOV    AX,0                ;clear AX
000A  F3/AB                      REP STOSW                  ;clear buffer
```

MOVS

The most useful string data transfer instruction is the MOVS instruction because it transfers data from one memory location to another. This is a *memory-to-memory* transfer. The MOVS instruction transfers a byte or a word from the data segment location addressed by SI, to the extra segment location addressed by DI. As with the other string instructions, the pointers then increment or decrement as dictated by the direction flag. Table 3–10 lists all the permissible forms of the MOVS instruction. Note that only the source operand (SI), located in the data segment, may be overridden so another segment may be used. The destination operand (DI) must always be located in the extra segment.

Suppose that the contents of a 100-byte array must be transferred to another 100-byte array. The repeated MOVSB (*moves a byte*) instruction is ideal for this task as illustrated in Example 3–5.

EXAMPLE 3–5

```
                    ;using REP MOVSB to transfer data from LIST1
                    ;into LIST2
                    ;
0000  BE 0000 R             MOV    SI,OFFSET LIST1      ;address LIST1
0003  BF 0064 R             MOV    DI,OFFSET LIST2      ;address LIST2
0006  B9 0064               MOV    CX,100               ;load count
0009 FC                     CLD                         ;auto-increment
000A  F3/A4                 REP MOVSB                   ;transfer data
```

INS

The INS (*input string*) instruction (not available on the 8086/8088 microprocessor) transfers a byte or a word of data from an I/O device into the extra segment memory location addressed by the DI register. The *I/O address* is contained in the DX register. This instruction is useful for inputting a block of data from an external I/O device directly into the memory. One application transfers data from a disk drive to memory. Disk drives are often considered and interfaced as I/O devices in a computer system.

As with the prior string instructions, there are two basic forms of the INS. One, INSB, inputs data from an 8-bit I/O device and stores them in the byte-sized memory location indexed by SI. The other is INSW, which inputs 16-bit I/O data and stores them in a word-sized memory location. Both instructions can be repeated. This ability allows an entire block of input data to be stored in the memory from an I/O device. Table 3–11 lists the various forms of the INS instruction.

TABLE 3–10 Forms of the MOVS instruction

Symbolic	Function
MOVSB	[DI] = [SI]; DI = DI ± 1; SI = SI ± 1 (byte transferred)
MOVSW	[DI] = [SI]; DI = DI ± 2; SI = SI ± 2 (word transferred)
MOVS BYTE1,BYTE2	[DI] = [SI]; DI = DI ± 1; SI = SI ± 1 (if BYTE1 and BYTE2 are bytes)
MOVS WORD1,WORD2	[DI] = [SI]; DI = DI ± 2; SI = SI ± 2 (if WORD1 and WORD2 are words)

TABLE 3–11 Forms of the INS instruction

Symbolic	Function
INSB	[DI] = [DX]; DI = DI ± 1 (byte transferred)
INSW	[DI] = [DX]; DI = DI ± 2 (word transferred)
INS LIST	[DI] = [DX]; DI = DI ± 1 (if LIST is a byte)
INS DATA1	[DI] = [DX]; DI = DI ± 2 (if DATA1 is a word)

Note: [DX] indicates that DX contains the I/O device address. These instructions are not available on the 8086/8088 microprocessor.

Example 3–6 shows a short program that inputs 50 bytes from an I/O device whose address is 03ACH and stores the data in memory array LISTS. This software assumes that data are available from the I/O device at all times. Otherwise, the software must check to see if the I/O device is ready to transfer data, precluding the use of a REP prefix.

EXAMPLE 3–6

```
                     ;using REP INSB to input data to a memory array
                     ;
0000  BF 0000 R         MOV   DI,OFFSET LISTS   ;address array
0003  BA 03AC           MOV   DX,3ACH           ;address I/O
0006  FC                CLD                     ;auto-increment
0007  B9 0032           MOV   CX,50             ;load count
000A  F3/6C             REP INSB                ;input data
```

OUTS

The OUTS (*output string*) instruction (not available on the 8086/8088 microprocessor) transfers a byte or word of data from the data segment memory location address by SI to an I/O device. The I/O device is addressed by the DX register as it was with the INS instruction. Table 3–12 shows the variations available for the OUTS instruction.

Example 3–7 shows a short program that transfers data from a memory array to an I/O device. This software assumes that the I/O device is always ready for data.

TABLE 3–12 Forms of the OUTS instruction

Symbolic	Function
OUTSB	[DX] = [SI]; SI = SI ± 1 (byte transferred)
OUTSW	[DX] = [SI]; SI = SI ± 2 (word transferred)
OUTS LIST	[DX] = [SI]; SI = SI ± 1 (if LIST is a byte)
OUTS DATA1	[DX] = [SI]; SI = SI ± 2 (if DATA1 is a word)

Note: [DX] indicates that DX contains the I/O device address. These instructions are not available on the 8086/8088 microprocessor.

EXAMPLE 3–7

```
                        ;using REP OUTS to ouput data from a memory array
                        ;
0000  BE 0064 R         MOV    SI,OFFSET ARRAY    ;address array
0003  BA 03AC           MOV    DX,3ACH            ;address I/O
0006  FC                CLD                       ;auto-increment
0007  B9 0064           MOV    CX,100             ;load count
000A  F3/6E             REP OUTSB
```

3–5 MISCELLANEOUS DATA TRANSFER INSTRUCTIONS

Don't be fooled by the word "miscellaneous." The data transfer instructions detailed in this section—XCHG, LAHF, SAHF, XLAT, IN, and OUT—are, for the most part, extremely important instructions. Because they may not be used as often as a MOV instruction, they have been grouped together and represented in this section.

XCHG

The exchange instruction (XCHG) exchanges the contents of a register with the contents of any other register or memory location. The XCHG instruction cannot exchange segment registers or memory-to-memory data. Exchanges are byte-sized or word-sized and use any addressing mode discussed in Chapter 2 except immediate addressing. Table 3–13 shows the forms available for the XCHG instruction.

The XCHG instruction, using the 16-bit AX register with another 16-bit register, is the most efficient exchange. This instruction occupies one byte of memory. Other XCHG instructions require two or more bytes of memory, depending on the addressing mode selected.

When using a memory-addressing mode and the assembler, it doesn't matter which operand addresses memory. The XCHG AL,[DI] instruction is identical to the XCHG [DI],AL instruction as far as the assembler is concerned.

LAHF and SAHF

The LAHF and SAHF instructions are seldom used because they were designed as *bridge* instructions. These instructions allowed 8085 software to be translated

TABLE 3–13 Forms of the XCHG instruction

Symbolic	Byte 1	Byte 2
XCHG AX,reg	1001 0rrr	
XCHG reg,reg	1000 011w	11rr raaa
XCHG reg,mem	1000 011w	mmrr raaa

Notes: aaa = any memory-addressing mode, mm = mode (MOD), rrr = any register except a segment register, and w = word/byte.

into 8086 software. Because any software that required translation was probably completed years ago, these instructions have little application today. The LAHF instruction transfers the rightmost 8 bits of the flag register into the AH register. The SAHF instruction transfers the AH register into the rightmost 8 bits of the flag register.

XLAT

The XLAT (*translate*) instruction converts the contents of the AL register into a number stored in a memory table. This instruction performs the direct table lookup technique often used to convert one code to another. An XLAT instruction first adds the contents of AL to BX to form a memory address within the data segment. It then copies the contents of this address into AL. This is the only instruction that adds an 8-bit number to a 16-bit number.

Suppose that a 7-segment LED display lookup table is stored in memory at address TABLE. The XLAT instruction then translates the BCD number in AL to a 7-segment code in AL. Example 3–8 provides a short program that converts from a BCD code to 7-segment code. Figure 3–15 shows the operation of this example program if TABLE = 1000H, DS = 1000H, and the initial value of AL = 05H (a 5 BCD). After the translation, AL = 6DH.

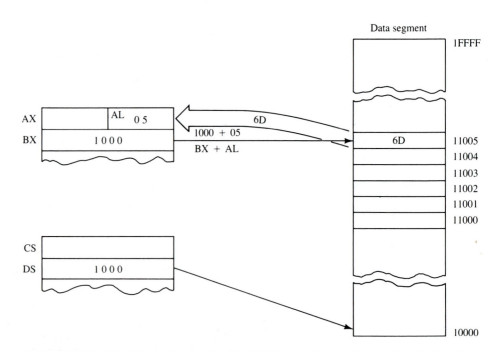

FIGURE 3–15 The effect of executing the XLAT instruction at the point just before the 6DH from memory location 11005H is gated into the AL register.

EXAMPLE 3–8

```
                         ;using XLAT to convert from BCD to 7-segment code
                         ;
0000  BB 1000 R                  MOV    BX,OFFSET TABLE    ;address TABLE
0003  D7                         XLAT                      ;convert
```

IN and OUT

Table 3–14 lists the forms of the IN and OUT instructions, which perform I/O operations. Notice that the contents of AL or AX *only* are transferred between the I/O device and the microprocessor. An IN instruction transfers data from an external I/O device to either AL or AX, and an OUT transfers data from AL or AX to an external I/O device.

Two forms of the I/O device (*port*) address exist for IN and OUT: fixed-port and variable-port. *Fixed-port addressing* allows data transfer between either AL or AX using an 8-bit I/O port address. It is called *fixed-port addressing* because the port number follows the instruction's opcode. Often instructions are stored in a ROM. A fixed-port instruction stored in a ROM has its port number permanently fixed because of the nature of read-only memory.

The port address appears on the address bus during an I/O operation. For the 8-bit fixed-port I/O instructions, the 8-bit port address is zero extended into a 16-bit address. For example, if the IN AL,6AH instruction executes, data from I/O address 6AH is input to AL. The address appears as a 16-bit 006AH on pins A0–A15 of the address bus. Address bus bits A16–A23 are undefined for an IN or OUT instruction.

Variable-port addressing allows data transfers between either AL or AX and a 16-bit port address. It is called *variable-port addressing* because the I/O port number is stored in register DX, which can be changed (*varied*) during the execution of a program. The 16-bit I/O port address appears on the address bus pin connections

TABLE 3–14 IN and OUT instructions

Symbolic	Function
IN AL,p8	8-bit data are input to AL from port p8
IN AX,p8	16-bit data are input to AX from port p8
IN AL,DX	8-bit data are input to AL from port DX
IN AX,DX	16-bit data are input to AX from port DX
OUT p8,AL	8-bit data are sent to port p8 from AL
OUT p8,AX	16-bit data are sent to port p8 from AX
OUT DX,AL	8-bit data are sent to port DX from AL
OUT DX,AX	16-bit data are sent to port DX from AX

Notes: p8 = an 8-bit I/O port number and DX = the 16-bit port address held in DX.

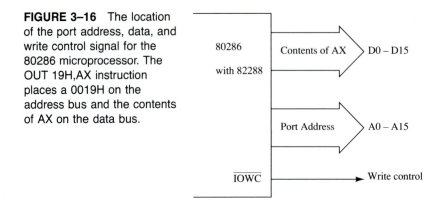

FIGURE 3–16 The location of the port address, data, and write control signal for the 80286 microprocessor. The OUT 19H,AX instruction places a 0019H on the address bus and the contents of AX on the data bus.

A0–A15. The IBM PC uses a 16-bit port address to access its I/O space. The I/O space for a PC is located at I/O port 0000H–03FFH. Some plug-in adapter cards may use I/O addresses above 03FFH.

Figure 3–16 illustrated the execution of the OUT 19H,AX instruction, which transfers the contents of AX to I/O port 19H. Notice that the I/O port number appears as a 0019H on the 16-bit address bus and that the data from AX appears on the 16-bit data bus of the 80286 microprocessor. The system control signal, $\overline{\text{IOWC}}$ (I/O write control) is a logic zero to enable the I/O device.

3–6   SEGMENT OVERRIDE PREFIX

The segment override prefix, which may be added to almost any 80286 instruction in any memory-addressing mode, allows the programmer to deviate from the default segment. The segment override prefix is an additional byte that appends to the front of an instruction to select an alternate segment register for the instruction. About the only instructions that cannot be prefixed are the jump and call instructions that must use the code segment register for address generation.

An example, the MOV AX,[DI] instruction, accesses data within the data segment by default. If required by a program, this can be changed by prefixing the instruction. Suppose that the data are in the extra segment instead of the data segment. This instruction addresses the extra segment if changed to MOV AX,ES:[DI].

Table 3–15 shows some altered instructions that address different memory segments than normal. Each time we prefix an instruction with a segment override prefix, the instruction becomes one byte longer. Although this is not a serious change to the length of the instruction, it does add to its execution time. Usually, we limit the use of the segment override prefix and remain in the default segments to write shorter and more efficient software.

TABLE 3–15 Instructions that include segment override prefixes

Symbolic	Segment Accessed	Normal Segment
MOV AX,DS:[BP]	Data segment	Stack segment
MOV AX,ES:[BP]	Extra segment	Stack segment
MOV AX,SS:[DI]	Stack segment	Data segment
MOV AX,CS:[SI]	Code segment	Data segment
MOV AX,ES:LIST	Extra segment	Data segment
LODS ES:DATA	Data segment	Extra segment

3–7   ASSEMBLER DETAILS

The assembler* for the 80286 microprocessor can be used in two ways. This section of the text presents both methods and explains how to organize a program's memory space using the assembler. It also explains the purpose and use of some of the more important directives used with this assembler. Appendix A provides additional detail about the assembler.

Directives

Before the format of an assembly language program is discussed, some details about the directives (pseudo-operations) that control the assembler must be learned. Some more common 80286 assembly language directives appear in Table 3–16. Directives indicate how an operand or section of a program is to be processed by the assembler. Some directives generate and store information in the memory, while others do not. The DB (define byte) directive stores bytes of data in the memory, while the BYTE PTR directive never stores data. The BYTE PTR directive indicates the size of the data references by a pointer or index register.

    Note that the assembler by default accepts only 8086/8088 instructions unless the software is preceded by the .286 or .286P directive. The .286 directive tells the assembler to use the 80286 instruction set in the real mode, while the .286P directive tells the assembler to use the 80286 protected-mode instruction set. Other similar directives are available for the 80386 and 80486 microprocessors, although not listed in Table 3–16.

Storing Data in a Memory Segment. The DB (define byte), DW (define word), and DD (define double word) directives are most often used with the 80286 to define and store memory data. If a numeric coprocessor is present in the system, the DQ (define quad word) and DT (define ten bytes) directives are also common. These directives use the label to identify a memory location and then the directive to indicate the size of the location.

---

*The assembler used in this text is the Microsoft Corporation macro assembler, which they call MASM.

TABLE 3–16 80286 assembler directives

Directive	Function
.286	Selects the 80286 instruction set
.286P	Selects the protected-mode 80286 instruction set
ALIGN 2	Starts the data in a segment at word or double-word boundaries
ASSUME	Indicates the names of each segment to the assembler; it does not load the segment registers
AT	Indicates what physical segment address is used with the SEGMENT statement
BYTE	Indicates a byte-sized operand as in BYTE PTR or THIS BYTE
DB	Defines byte(s) (8-bits)
DD	Defines double word(s) (32-bits)
DQ	Defines quad word(s) (64-bits)
DT	Defines ten bytes (80-bits)
DUP	Generates duplicates of characters or numbers
DW	Defines word(s) (16-bits)
DWORD	Indicates a double-word-sized operand as in THIS DWORD
END	Indicates the end of the program
ENDP	Indicates the end of a procedure
ENDS	Indicates the end of a segment
EQU	Equates data to a label
FAR	Specifies a far address as in JMP FAR PTR LISTS
NEAR	Specifies a near address as in JMP NEAR PTR HELP
OFFSET	Specifies an offset address
ORG	Sets the origin within a segment
PROC	Defines the beginning of a procedure
PTR	Indicates a memory pointer
SEGMENT	Defines the start of a memory segment
STACK	Indicates that a segment is a stack segment
THIS	Used with EQU to set a label to a byte, word, or double word
WORD	Acts as a word operand as in WORD PTR or THIS WORD

Note: Most of these directives function with most versions of the 80286 assembler.

EXAMPLE 3-9

```
                        ;using DB, DW, and DD
                        ;
0000                    LIST_SEG        SEGMENT

0000 01 02 03           DATA_ONE        DB      1,2,3        ;define bytes
0003 45                                 DB      45H          ;hexadecimal
0004 41                                 DB      'A'          ;ASCII
0005 F0                                 DB      11110000B    ;binary
0006 000C 000D          DATA_TWO        DW      12,13        ;define words
000A 0200                               DW      LIST1        ;symbolic
000C 2345                               DW      2345H        ;hexadecimal
000E 00000300          DATA_THREE       DD      300H         ;hexadecimal
0012 4007DF3B                           DD      2.123        ;real
0016 544269E1                           DD      3.34E+12     ;real
001A 00                 LISTA           DB      ?            ;reserve 1 byte
001B 000A[              LISTB           DB      10 DUP (?)   ;reserve 10 bytes
            ??

         ]
0025 00                                 ALIGN   2            ;set word boundary

0026 0100[              LISTC           DW      100H DUP (0)
            0000

         ]

0226 0016[             LIST_NINE        DD      22 DUP (?)
         ????????
                    ]

027E 0064[              SIXES           DB      100 DUP (6)
            06

         ]

02E2                    LIST_SEG        ENDS
                                        END
```

Example 3-9 shows a memory segment that contains various forms of data definition directives. The first statement indicates the start of the segment and its symbolic name. The last statement of the segment contains the ENDS directive that indicates the end of the segment. The name of the segment (LIST_SEG), can be anything that the programmer desires to call it.

This example shows various forms of data storage for bytes at DATA_ONE. More than one byte can be defined on a line in binary, hexadecimal, decimal, or ASCII code. The DATA_TWO label shows how to store various forms of word data. Double-words are stored at DATA_THREE and they include floating-point, single-precision real numbers.

Memory can be reserved for use in the future by using a ? as an operand for a DB, DW, or DD directive. When a ? is used in place of a numeric or ASCII value, the assembler sets aside a location and does not initialize it to any value. The DUP (duplicate) directive creates an array as shown in several ways in Example 3–9. A 10 DUP (?) reserves 10 locations of memory, but stores no specific value in any of the 10 locations. If a number appears within the () part of the DUP statement, the assembler initializes the reserved section of memory with data.

The ALIGN directive, used in this example, makes sure that the memory arrays are stored on word boundaries. An ALIGN 2 places data on word boundaries for an 80286 microprocessor and word data and an ALIGN 4 places them on double-word boundaries for an 80386 or 80486 and double-word data. It is important that word-sized data are placed at word boundaries and double-word-sized data at double-word boundaries. If not, the 80286, 80386, or 80486 spends more time than necessary accessing these data types. A word stored at an odd-numbered memory location takes twice as long to access as a word stored on an even-numbered memory location.

EQU and THIS. The equate directive (EQU) equates a numeric, ASCII, or label to another label. Equates make a program clearer and simplifies debugging. Example 3–10 shows several equate statements and a few instructions that show how they function in a program.

EXAMPLE 3–10

```
                        ;using equate
                        ;
= 000A                  TEN     EQU    10
= 0009                  NINE    EQU    9

0000  B0 0A                     MOV    AL,TEN
0002  04 09                     ADD    AL,NINE
```

The THIS directive always appears as THIS BYTE, THIS WORD, or THIS DWORD. In certain cases, data must be referred to as both a byte and a word. The assembler can only assign either a byte or a word address to a label. To assign a byte label to a word, we use the software listed in Example 3–11.

EXAMPLE 3–11

```
                        ;using THIS and ORG
                        ;
0000                    DATA_SEG        SEGMENT

0100                                    ORG    100H

= 0100                  DATA1   EQU    THIS BYTE
0100  0000              DATA2   DW     ?

0102                    DATA_SEG        ENDS

0000                    CODE_SEG        SEGMENT
```

```
                              ASSUME  CS:CODE_SEG,DS:DATA_SEG

0000 8A 1E 0100 R                 MOV    BL,DATA1
0004 A1 0100 R                    MOV    AX,DATA2
0007 8A 3E 0101 R                 MOV    BH,DATA1+1

000B               CODE_SEG       ENDS
```

This example also illustrates how the ORG (origin) statement changes the starting address of the data in the data segment to location 100H. The ASSUME statement tells the assembler what names have been chosen for the code, data, extra, and stack segments. Without the assume statement, the assembler assumes nothing and uses a prefix on all instructions that address memory data.

PROC and ENDP. The PROC and ENDP directives indicate the start and end of a procedure (*subroutine*). These directives force structure because the procedure is clearly defined. Both directives require a label to indicate the name of the subroutine. The PROC directive, which indicates the start of a procedure, must also be followed with either NEAR or FAR. A NEAR procedure is one that resides in the same code segment as the program. A FAR procedure may reside at any location in the memory system. We often call NEAR procedures *local,* and FAR procedures *global*. The term global denotes a procedure that can be used by any program, while local defines a procedure that is only used by the current program.

EXAMPLE 3–12

```
                   ;procedure that adds BX, CX, and DX with the sum
                   ;stored in AX
                   ;
0000               ADDEM   PROC  FAR

0000 03 D9                 ADD   BX,CX
0002 03 DA                 ADD   BX,DX
0004 8B C3                 MOV   AX,BX
0006 CB                    RET

0007               ADDEM   ENDP
```

Example 3–12 shows a procedure that adds BX, CX, and DX and stores the sum in register AX. Although this procedure is short, and may not be that useful, it does illustrate how to use the PROC and ENDP directives to delineate the procedure.

Memory Organization

The assembler uses two basic formats for developing software. One method uses models and the other uses full-segment definitions. Memory models are unique to the MASM assembler program. The full-segment definitions are common to most assemblers, including the *Intel assembler,* and are most often used for software development. The models are easier to use, but the full-segment definitions offer better control over the assembly language task and are recommended and used in other places in this text. We use full segments because they apply to all assemblers, where models do not.

Models.   There are many models that can be used with the MASM assembler from tiny to huge. Appendix A contains a table that lists all the models available for use with the assembler. To designate a model, we use the .MODEL statement followed by the size of the memory system. The tiny model requires that all software and data fit into one 64K byte memory segment and is useful for small programs. The small model requires that only one data segment be used with one code segment for a total of 128K bytes of memory. Other models are available up to the huge model.

EXAMPLE 3–13

```
                              .MODEL SMALL

                              .STACK 100H              ;define stack

                              .DATA                    ;define data

0000 0064[          LISTA     DB      100 DUP (?)
            ??
        ]

0064 0064[          LISTB     DB      100 DUP (?)
            ??
        ]

                              .CODE                    ;define code

0000 B8 ---- R      HERE:     MOV     AX,@DATA         ;load ES, DS
0003 8E C0                    MOV     ES,AX
0005 8E D8                    MOV     DS,AX

0007 FC                       CLD                      ;move data
0008 BE 0000 R                MOV     SI,OFFSET LISTA
000B BF 0064 R                MOV     DI,OFFSET LISTB
000E B9 0064                  MOV     CX,100
0011 F3/A4                    REP MOVSB

0013 B4 4C                    MOV     AH,4CH           ;exit to DOS
0015 CD 21                    INT     21H

                              END     HERE
```

Example 3–13 illustrates how the .MODEL statement defines the parameters of a short program that copies the contents of a 100-byte block of memory (LISTA) into a second 100-byte block of memory (LISTB).

Full-Segment Definitions. Example 3–14 illustrates the same program using full-segment definitions. This program appears longer but more structured than the model method of setting up a program. The first segment defined is the STACK_SEG that is clearly delineated with the SEGMENT and ENDS directives. Within these directives a DW 100 DUP (?) sets aside 100H words for the stack segment. Because the word STACK appears next to SEGMENT, the assembler and linker automatically load both the stack segment register (SS) and stack pointer (SP).

EXAMPLE 3–14

```
0000                    STACK_SEG       SEGMENT STACK

0000  0100[                             DW      100H DUP (?)
          ????
             ]

0200                    STACK_SEG       ENDS

0000                    DATA_SEG        SEGMENT 'DATA'

0000  0064[                     LISTA   DB      100 DUP (?)
        ??
           ]

0064  0064[                     LISTB   DB      100 DUP (?)
        ??
           ]

00C8                    DATA_SEG        ENDS

0000                    CODE_SEG        SEGMENT 'CODE'

                                ASSUME CS:CODE_SEG,DS:DATA_SEG,SS:STACK_SEG

0000                    MAIN    PROC    FAR

0000  B8 ---- R                 MOV     AX,DATA_SEG    ;load DS and ES
0003  8E C0                     MOV     ES,AX
0005  8E D8                     MOV     DS,AX

0007  FC                        CLD                    ;move data
0008  BE 0000 R                 MOV     SI,OFFSET LISTA
000B  BF 0064 R                 MOV     DI,OFFSET LISTB
000E  B9 0064                   MOV     CX,100
0011  F3/A4                     REP MOVSB

0013  B4 4C                     MOV     AH,4CH         ;exit to DOS
0015  CD 21                     INT     21H

0017                    MAIN    ENDP
```

```
0017              CODE_SEG       ENDS

                  END       MAIN
```

Next the data are defined in the DATA_SEG. Here two arrays of data appear as LISTA and LISTB. Each array contains 100 bytes of space for the program. The names of the segments in this program can be changed to any name. We include the group name 'DATA' so the Microsoft program codeview can be effectively used to debug this software. If the group name is not placed in a program, codeview can still be used to debug a program, but the program will not be debugged in symbolic form. Other group names, such as 'STACK' and 'CODE', are listed in Appendix A.

The CODE_SEG is organized as a far procedure because most software is procedure oriented. Before the program begins, the code segment contains the ASSUME statement. The ASSUME statement tells the assembler and linker that the name used for the code segment (CS) is CODE_SEG; it also tells the assembler and linker that the data segment is DATA_SEG and the stack segment is STACK_SEG. Also notice we include the group name 'CODE' for the code segment. Other group names appear in Appendix A with the models.

After the program loads both the extra segment register and data segment register with the location of the data segment, it transfers 100 bytes from LISTA to LISTB. Following this is a sequence of two instructions that return control back to DOS (the disk operating system).

The last statement in the program is END MAIN. The END statement indicates the end of the program and the location of the first instruction executed. Here we want the machine to execute the main procedure, so a label follows the END directive. In a file that is linked to another file, there is no label on the END directive.

A Sample Program

Example 3–15 provides a sample program that reads a character from the keyboard and displays it on the CRT screen. Although this program is trivial, it does illustrate a complete, workable program that functions on any personal computer using DOS from the earliest 8088-based system to the latest 80486-based system. This program also illustrates the use of a few DOS function calls. Appendix A lists the DOS function calls with their parameters. The BIOS function calls allow the use of the keyboard, printer, disk drives, and everything else that is available in your computer system.

EXAMPLE 3–15

```
                  ;program that reads a key and displays key
                  ;an @ key ends the program
                  ;
0000              CODE_SEG       SEGMENT 'CODE'

                        ASSUME   CS:CODE_SEG
```

```
0000                                    MAIN    PROC    FAR

0000 B4 06                                      MOV     AH,6        ;read key
0002 B2 FF                                       MOV     DL,0FFH
0004 CD 21                                       INT     21H
0006 74 F8                                        JE      MAIN        ;if no key

0008 3C 40                                       CMP     AL,'@'      ;test for @
000A 74 08                                        JE      MAIN1       ;if @

000C B4 06                                       MOV     AH,6        ;display key
000E 8A D0                                       MOV     DL,AL
0010 CD 21                                       INT     21H
0012 EB EC                                       JMP     MAIN        ;repeat

0014                                    MAIN1:

0014 B4 4C                                       MOV     AH,4CH      ;exit to DOS
0016 CD 21                                       INT     21H

0018                                    MAIN    ENDP

0018                    CODE_SEG        ENDS

                                        END     MAIN
```

This example program uses only a code segment because there are no data. A stack segment should appear, but has been left out because DOS automatically allocates a 256-byte stack for all programs. The only time that the stack is used in this example is for the INT 21H instructions that call a procedure in DOS. Note that when this program is linked, the linker signals that no stack segment is present. This warning may be ignored in this example because the stack is less than 256 bytes.

The program uses DOS functions 06H and 4CH. The function number is placed in AH before the INT 21H instruction executes. The 06H function reads the keyboard if DL = 0FFH or displays the ASCII contents of DL if it is not 0FFH. Upon close examination, the first section of the program moves a 06H into AH and a 0FFH into DL so a key is read from the keyboard. The INT 21H tests the keyboard and if no key is typed, it returns equal. The JE instruction tests the equal condition and jumps to MAIN if no key is typed.

When a key is typed, the program continues to the next step. This step compares the contents of AL with an @ symbol. Upon return from the INT 21H, the ASCII character of the typed key is found in AL. In this program if we type an @ symbol, the program ends. If we do not type an @ symbol the program continues by displaying the character typed on the keyboard with the next INT 21H instruction.

The second INT 21H instruction moves the ASCII character into DL so it can be displayed on the CRT screen. After displaying the character a JMP executes. This causes the program to continue at MAIN where it repeats reading a key.

If the @ symbol is typed, the program continues at MAIN1 where it executes the DOS function code number 4CH. This causes the program to return to the DOS prompt (A>) so the computer can be used for other tasks.

More information about the assembler and its application appears in Appendix A and in the next several chapters. The Appendix provides a complete overview of the assembler, linker, and DOS functions. It also provides a list of the BIOS (*basic I/O system*) functions. The information provided in the following chapters clarifies how to use the assembler for certain tasks at different levels of the text.

3–8   SUMMARY

1. Data movement instructions transfer data between registers, a register and memory, a register and the stack, memory and the stack, the accumulator and I/O, and the flags and the stack.
2. Data movement instructions include: MOV, PUSH, POP, XCHG, XLAT, IN, OUT, LEA, LSD, LES, LAHF, SAHF, and the string instructions: LODS, STOS, MOVS, INS, and OUTS.
3. The first byte of an 80286 instruction contains the opcode, which specifies the operation performed by the microprocessor.
4. The D bit, located in many instructions, selects the direction of data flow. If D = 1, the data flow from the REG field to the R/M field of the instruction. If D = 0, the data flow from the R/M field to the REG field.
5. The W bit, found in most instructions, selects the size of the data transfer. If W = 0, the data are byte-sized and if W = 1, the data are word-sized.
6. MOD selects the addressing mode of operation for a machine language instruction's R/M field. If MOD = 00, there is no displacement; if a 01, an 8-bit sign-extended displacement appears; if 10, a 16-bit displacement occurs; and if a 11, a register is used instead of a memory location.
7. A 3-bit binary register code specifies the REG and R/M fields when the MOD = 11. The 8-bit registers are: AH, AL, BH, BL, CH, CL, DH, and DL, and the 16-bit registers are: AX, BX, CX, DX, SP, BP, DI, and SI.
8. When the R/M field depicts a memory mode, a 3-bit code selects one of the following modes: [BX+DI], [BX+SI], [BP+DI], [BP+SI], [BX], [BP], [DI], or [SI].
9. All memory-addressing modes, by default, address data in the data segment unless BP addresses memory. The BP register addresses data in the stack segment.
10. The segment registers may be addressed only by the MOV, PUSH, or POP instruction. The MOV instruction may transfer a segment register to 16-bit register or vice versa. We do not allow the MOV CS,reg or POP CS instruction.
11. Data are transferred between a register or a memory location and the stack by the PUSH and POP instructions. Variations of these instructions allow immediate data to be pushed onto the stack, the flags to be transferred between the stack, and all the 16-bit registers transferred between the stack and the registers. When data are transferred to the stack, two bytes always move with the least-significant

byte placed at the SP location − 1 byte and the most-significant byte placed at the SP location − 2 bytes. After placing the data on the stack, SP decrements by 2.

12. Opcodes that transfer data between the stack and the flags are PUSHF and POPF. Opcodes that transfer all the 16-bit registers between the stack and the registers are PUSHA and POPA.

13. LEA, LDS, and LES instructions load a register or registers with an effective address. The LEA instruction loads any 16-bit register with an effective address, while LDS and LES load any 16-bit register and either DS or ES with the effective address.

14. String data transfer instructions use either or both DI and SI to address memory. The DI offset address is located in the extra segment and the SI offset address is located in the data segment.

15. The direction flag (DF) chooses the auto-increment or auto-decrement mode of operation for DI and SI for string instructions. If we clear DF with the CLD instruction, we select the auto-increment mode, and if we set DF with STD, we select the auto-decrement mode. Either or both DI and SI increment/decrement by 1 for a byte operation and by 2 for a word operation.

16. LODS loads AL or AX with data from the memory location addressed by SI, STOS stores AL or AX in the memory location addressed by DI, and MOVS transfers a byte or a word from the memory location addressed by SI into the location addressed by DI.

17. INS inputs data from an I/O device addressed by DX and stores it in the memory location addressed by DI, and OUTS outputs the contents of the memory location addressed by SI and sends it to the I/O device addressed by DX.

18. The REP prefix may be attached to any string instruction to repeat it. The REP prefix repeats the string instruction the number of times found in register CX.

19. Translate (XLAT) converts the data in AL into a number stored at the memory location address by BX plus AL.

20. IN and OUT transfer data between either AL or AX and an external I/O device. The address of the I/O device is either stored with the instruction (fixed port) or in register DX (variable port).

21. The segment override prefix selects a different segment register for a memory location than the default segment. For example, the MOV AX,[BX] instruction uses the data segment, but the MOV AX,ES:[BX] instruction uses the extra segment because of the ES: prefix.

22. Assembler directives DB (define byte), DW (define word), DD (define double-word), and DUP (duplicate) store data in the 80286 memory system.

23. The EQU (equate) directive allows data or labels to be equated to labels.

24. SEGMENT identifies the start of a memory segment and ENDS identifies the end of a segment.

25. ASSUME tells the assembler what segment names you have assigned to CS, DS, ES, and SS.

26. The PROC and ENDP directives indicate the start and end of a procedure.

27. Memory models can be used to shorten the program slightly, but they are more difficult to use for larger programs and programming in general. Memory models are not compatible with all assembler programs.

3-9   **QUESTIONS AND PROBLEMS**

1. The first byte of any 80286 instruction is the _____.
2. Describe the purpose of the D and W bits found in some machine language instructions.
3. The MOD field, in a machine language instruction, specifies what information?
4. If the register field (REG) of an instruction contains a 010 and W = 0, what register is selected?
5. What memory-addressing mode is specified by R/M = 001 with MOD = 00?
6. Identify the default segment register assigned to:
   a. SP
   b. BX
   c. DI
   d. BP
   e. SI
7. Convert an 8B07H from machine language to assembly language.
8. Convert an 8B1E004CH from machine language to assembly language.
9. If a MOV SI,[BX+2] instruction appears in a program, what is its machine language equivalent?
10. What is wrong with a MOV CS,AX instruction?
11. What type of MOV instruction might be 6 bytes in length?
12. PUSH and POP always transfer a _____-bit number between the stack and a register or memory location.
13. What segment register may not be popped from the stack?
14. What registers move onto the stack with the PUSHA instruction?
15. Describe the operation of each of the following instructions:
    a. PUSH AX
    b. POP SI
    c. PUSH [BX]
    d. PUSHF
    e. POP DS
    f. PUSH 4
16. Explain what happens when the PUSH BX instruction executes. Make sure to show where BH and BL are stored. (Assume that SP = 0100H and SS = 0200H.)
17. The POP instruction (except for POPA) increments SP by _____.
18. What values appear in SP and SS if the stack pointer addresses memory location 02200H?
19. Compare the operation of a MOV DI,NUMB instruction with a LEA DI, NUMB instruction.
20. What is the difference between a LEA SI,NUMB instruction and a MOV SI,OFFSET NUMB instruction?
21. Which is more efficient, a MOV with an OFFSET or a LEA instruction?
22. Describe how the LDS BX,NUMB instruction operates.
23. What is the difference between the LDS and LES instructions?

24. Develop a sequence of instructions that move the contents of data segment memory locations NUMB and NUMB + 1 into BX, DX, and SI.
25. What is the purpose of the direction flag?
26. Which instructions set and clear the direction flag?
27. The string instructions use DI and SI to address memory data in which memory segments?
28. Explain the operation of the LODSB instruction.
29. Explain the operation of the STOSW instruction.
30. Explain the operation of the OUTSB instruction.
31. What does the REP prefix accomplish and what type of instruction is it used with?
32. Develop a sequence of instructions that copy 12 bytes of data from an area of memory addressed by SOURCE into an area of memory addressed by DEST.
33. Where is the I/O address (port number) stored for an INSB instruction?
34. Select an assembly language instruction that exchanges the contents of the BX register with the SI register.
35. Would the LAHF and SAHF instructions normally appear in 80286 software?
36. Explain how the XLAT instruction transforms the contents of the AL register.
37. Write a short program that uses the XLAT instruction to convert the BCD numbers 0–9 into ASCII-coded numbers 30H–39H. Store the ASCII-coded data into a TABLE.
38. Explain what the IN AL,12H instruction accomplishes.
39. Explain how the OUT DX,AX instruction operates.
40. What is a segment override prefix?
41. Select an instruction that moves a byte of data from the memory location addressed by the BX register in the extra segment into the AH register.
42. Develop a sequence of instructions that exchanges the contents of AX with BX, CX with DX, and SI with DI.
43. What is an assembly language directive?
44. Describe the purpose of the following assembly language directives: DB, DW, and DD.
45. Select an assembly language directive that reserves 30 bytes of memory for array LIST1.
46. Describe the purpose of the EQU directive.
47. What is the purpose of the .286 directive?
48. What is the purpose of the .MODEL directive?
49. If the start of a segment is identified with .DATA, what type of memory organization is in effect?
50. If the SEGMENT directive identifies the start of a segment, what type of memory organization is in effect?
51. What does the INT 21H accomplish if AH contains a 4CH?
52. What directives indicate the start and end of a procedure?
53. Develop a near procedure that stores AL into four consecutive memory locations, within the data segment, as addressed by the DI register.
54. Develop a far procedure that copies word-sized memory location CS:DATA1 into AX, BX, CX, DX, and SI.

CHAPTER 4

Arithmetic and Logic Instructions

INTRODUCTION

In this chapter, we examine the arithmetic and logic instructions found in the 80286 instruction set. Arithmetic instructions include: addition, subtraction, multiplication, division, comparison, negation, incrementation, and decrementation. Logic instructions include: AND, OR, Exclusive-OR, NOT, shifts, rotates, and the logical compare (TEST).

We will also introduce string comparison instructions, which are used for scanning tabular data and for comparing sections of memory. Both tasks perform efficiently with the string scan and string comparison instructions.

If you are already familiar with an 8-bit microprocessor, you will recognize that the 80286 instruction set is superior. Even if this is your first microprocessor, you will quickly learn that the 80286 possesses a powerful and easy to use set of arithmetic and logic instructions.

OBJECTIVES

Upon completion of this chapter, you will be able to:

1. Use the 80286 arithmetic and logic instructions to accomplish simple binary, BCD, and ASCII arithmetic.
2. Use AND, OR, and Exclusive-OR to accomplish binary bit manipulation.
3. Use the shift and rotate instructions.
4. Check the contents of a table for a match with the string instructions.

4–1   ADDITION, SUBTRACTION, AND COMPARISON

The core grouping of arithmetic instructions found in any microprocessor includes addition, subtraction, and comparison. The 80286 microprocessor is no different. In this section we illustrate and define these instructions. We also show their use in manipulating register and memory data.

Addition

Addition takes many forms in the 80286 microprocessor. This section details the use of the ADD instruction for 8- and 16-bit binary addition. Another form of addition, called *add-with-carry* is introduced with the ADC instruction. Finally, the increment instruction (INC), a special type of add instruction, is presented. In Section 4–3 we examine other forms of addition, such as BCD and ASCII.

Table 4–1 illustrates the addressing modes available to the ADD instruction. (The addressing modes include almost all those mentioned in Chapter 2.) Since there are over 1,000 variations of the ADD instruction in the 80286 instruction set, it is impossible to list them in this table. The only types of addition not allowed are memory-to-memory and segment register. The segment registers can only be moved, pushed, or popped.

Register Addition. Example 4–1 shows a simple program that uses register addition to add the contents of several registers. In this example, we add contents of AX, BX, CX, and DX. This example forms a 16-bit result that is stored in the AX register.

TABLE 4–1 Addition instructions

Instruction	Comment
ADD AL,BL	AL = AL + BL
ADD CX,DI	CX = CX + DI
ADD CL,44H	CL = CL + 44H
ADD BX,35AFH	BX = BX + 35AFH
ADD [BX],AL	AL adds to contents of the data segment offset location addressed by BX and the result is stored in the same memory location
ADD CL,[BP]	The contents of the stack segment offset location addressed by BP add to CL and the result is stored in CL
ADD BX,[SI+2]	The word-sized contents of the data segment location addressed by SI + 2 add to BX and the result is stored in BX
ADD CL,TEMP	The contents of data segment location TEMP add to CL with the result stored in CL
ADD BX,TEMP[DI]	The word-sized contents of the data segment location addressed by TEMP + DI add to BX and the result is stored in the same memory location
ADD [BX+DI],DL	The data segment memory byte addressed by BX + DI is the sum of that byte plus DL
ADD BYTE PTR [DI],3	Add a 3 to the contents of the byte-sized memory location addressed by DI within the data segment

EXAMPLE 4–1

```
0000  03 C3                    ADD    AX,BX
0002  03 C1                    ADD    AX,CX
0004  03 C2                    ADD    AX,DX
```

Whenever arithmetic and logic instructions execute, the contents of the flag register change. The flags denote the result of the arithmetic operation. Any ADD instruction modifies the contents of the sign, zero, carry, auxiliary carry, parity, and overflow flags. The flag bits never change for most of the data transfer instructions presented in Chapter 3.

Immediate Addition.   Immediate addition is used whenever constant or known data are added. An 8-bit immediate addition appears in Example 4–2. In this example, we first load a 12H into DL. Next we add a 33H to the 12H. Both instructions are immediate instructions. After the addition, the sum (45H) moves into register DL and the flags change as follows:

$$ZF = 0 \text{ (result not zero)}$$
$$CF = 0 \text{ (no carry)}$$
$$AF = 0 \text{ (no half-carry)}$$
$$SF = 0 \text{ (result positive)}$$
$$PF = 0 \text{ (odd parity)}$$
$$OF = 0 \text{ (no overflow)}$$

EXAMPLE 4–2

```
0006  B2 12                    MOV    DL,12H
0008  80 C2 33                 ADD    DL,33H
```

Memory-to-Register Addition.   Suppose an application requires the addition of memory data to the AL register. Example 4–3 shows an example that adds two consecutive bytes of data, stored at data segment memory locations NUMB and NUMB+1, to the AL register.

EXAMPLE 4–3

```
0000  BF 0000 R                MOV    DI,OFFSET NUMB      ;address NUMB
0003  B0 00                    MOV    AL,0                ;clear sum
0005  02 05                    ADD    AL,[DI]             ;add NUMB
0007  02 45 01                 ADD    AL,[DI+1]           ;add NUMB+1
```

The sequence of instructions first loads the contents of the destination index register (DI) with offset address NUMB. The DI register used in this example addresses data in the data segment beginning at memory location NUMB. Next the ADD AL,[DI] instruction adds the contents of memory location NUMB to AL. This occurs because DI addresses memory location NUMB, and the instruction adds its contents to AL. Next, the ADD AL,[DI+1] instruction adds the contents of memory location NUMB+1 to the AL register. After both ADD instructions execute, the result appears in the AL register forming the sum of NUMB plus NUMB+1.

Array Addition.   Memory arrays contain lists of data. Suppose that an array of data (ARRAY) contains 10 bytes of data numbered from element number 0 through element number 9. Example 4–4 shows a program that adds the contents of array elements 3, 5, and 7. (The program and the array elements it adds are chosen to demonstrate the use of some of the addressing modes for the 80286 microprocessor.)

EXAMPLE 4–4

```
0000 B0 00              MOV   AL,0             ;clear sum
0002 BE 0003            MOV   SI,3             ;address element 3
0005 02 84 0002 R       ADD   AL,ARRAY[SI]     ;add element 3
0009 02 84 0004 R       ADD   AL,ARRAY[SI+2]   ;add element 5
000D 02 84 0006 R       ADD   AL,ARRAY[SI+4]   ;add element 7
```

This example clears AL to zero so it can be used to accumulate the sum. Next we load register SI with a 3 to initially address array element number three. The ADD AL,ARRAY[SI] instruction adds the contents of array element three to the sum in AL. Instructions that follow add array elements 5 and 7 to the sum in AL using the 3 in SI plus a displacement of 2 to address element 5 and a displacement of 4 to address element 7.

Increment Addition.   Increment addition (INC) adds 1 to a register or a memory location. Any register or memory location can be incremented except a segment register. Table 4–2 illustrates the possible forms of the increment instruction available to the 80286 microprocessor. As with other instructions presented thus far, it is impossible to show all variations of the INC instruction because of the large number available.

TABLE 4–2   Increment instructions

Instruction	Comment
INC BL	BL = BL + 1
INC SP	SP = SP + 1
INC BYTE PTR [BX]	The byte contents of the memory location addressed by BX in the data segment increment
INC WORD PTR [SI]	The word contents of the memory location addressed by SI in the data segment increment
INC DATA1	The contents of DATA1 increment

With indirect memory increments, the size of the data must be described using either the BYTE PTR or WORD PTR directives. The reason is that the assembler program cannot determine if, for example, the INC [DI] instruction is a byte-sized or word-sized increment. The INC BYTE PTR [DI] instruction clearly indicates byte-sized memory data and the INC WORD PTR [DI] instruction unquestionably indicates a word-sized memory data.

EXAMPLE 4–5

```
0000 BF 0000 R          MOV     DI,OFFSET NUMB          ;address NUMB
0003 B0 00              MOV     AL,0                    ;clear sum
0005 02 05              ADD     AL,[DI]                 ;add NUMB
0007 47                 INC     DI                      ;address NUMB+1
0008 02 05              ADD     AL,[DI]                 ;add NUMB+1
```

Example 4–5 shows how the program of Example 4–3 can be modified to use an increment for addressing NUMB and NUMB+1. Here, the INC DI instruction changes the contents of register DI from offset address NUMB to offset address NUMB+1. Both programs of Examples 4–3 and 4–5 add the contents of NUMB and NUMB+1. The difference between the programs is the way that these data are addressed through the contents of the DI register.

Increment instructions affect the flag bits as do most other arithmetic and logic operations. The only difference is that increment instructions do not affect the carry flag bit. The reason is that we often use the increment instructions in programs that depend on the contents of the carry flag.

Addition with Carry.   An addition-with-carry instruction (ADC) adds the bit in the carry flag (CF) to the operand data. This instruction mainly appears in software that adds numbers that are wider than 16 bits.

Table 4–3 lists several add-with-carry instructions with comments that explain their operation. Like the ADD instruction, ADC affects the flags after the addition.

Suppose that the 32-bit number in BX and AX is added to the 32-bit number in DX and CX. Figure 4–1 illustrates this addition so the placement and function of

TABLE 4–3   Add-with-carry instructions

Instruction	Comment
ADC AL,AH	AL = AL + AH + CF
ADC CX,BX	CX = CX + BX + CF
ADC [BX],DH	The byte contents of the memory location in the data segment addressed by BX are summed with DH and carry; the result is stored in memory
ADC BX,[BP+2]	BX and the word contents of the memory location in the stack segment addressed by BP are summed with carry; the result is stored in BX

FIGURE 4–1
Addition-with-carry showing
how the carry flag (CF) links
the two 16-bit additions into
one 32-bit addition.

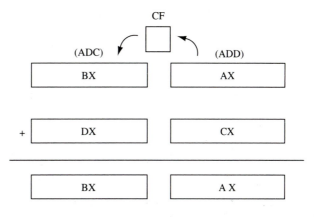

carry can be understood. This addition cannot be performed without adding the carry flag bit because the 80286 only adds 8- or 16-bit numbers. Example 4–6 shows how the addition occurs with a program. Here the contents of registers AX and CX add to form the least-significant 16 bits of the sum. This addition may or may not generate a carry. A carry appears if the sum is greater than FFFFH. Because it is impossible to predict a carry, the most-significant 16 bits of this addition are added with the carry flag using the ADC instruction. This program adds BX–AX to DX–CX with the sum appearing in BX–AX.

EXAMPLE 4–6

```
0000  03 C1            ADD    AX,CX
0002  13 DA            ADC    BX,DX
```

Subtraction

Many forms of the subtraction instruction (SUB) appear in the 80286 instruction set. These forms use any of the addressing modes and either 8- or 16-bit data. A special form of subtraction (decrement) subtracts a 1 from any register or memory location. Section 4–4 shows how BCD and ASCII data subtract. As with addition, numbers that are wider than 16-bits must often be subtracted. The subtract-with-borrow instruction (SBB) performs this type of subtraction.

Table 4–4 lists many addressing modes allowed with the subtract instruction (SUB). There are well over 1,000 possible subtraction instructions, far too many to list. About the only types of subtraction not allowed are memory-to-memory and segment register subtractions. Like other arithmetic instructions, the subtract instruction affects the flag bits.

Register Subtraction. Example 4–7 shows a program that performs register subtraction. This example subtracts the 16-bit contents of registers CX and DX from the contents of register BX. After each subtraction, the microprocessor modifies the contents of the flag register. As mentioned earlier, the flags change for most arithmetic and logic operations.

TABLE 4–4   Subtraction instructions

Instruction	Comment
SUB CL,BL	CL = CL − BL
SUB AX,SP	AX = AX − SP
SUB DH,6FH	DH = DH − 6FH
SUB AX,0CCCCH	AX = AX − 0CCCCH
SUB [DI],CH	CH subtracts from the byte contents of the data segment memory location addressed by DI
SUB CH,[BP]	The byte contents of the stack segment memory location addressed by BP subtract from CH
SUB AH,TEMP	The byte contents of the data segment memory location TEMP subtract from AH
SUB DI,TEMP [BX]	The word contents of the data segment memory location addressed by TEMP + BX subtract from DI

EXAMPLE 4–7

```
0000 2B D9              SUB    BX,CX
0002 2B DA              SUB    BX,DX
```

Immediate Subtraction.   As with addition, the 80286 also allows immediate operands for subtraction. Example 4–8 presents a short program that subtracts a 44H from a 22H. Here, we first load the 22H into CH using an immediate move instruction. Next, the SUB instruction, using immediate data 44H, subtracts a 44H from the 22H. After the subtraction, the difference (DEH) moves into the CH register. The flags change as follows for this subtraction:

$$ZF = 0 \text{ (result not zero)}$$

$$CF = 1 \text{ (borrow)}$$

$$AF = 1 \text{ (half-borrow)}$$

$$SF = 1 \text{ (result negative)}$$

$$PF = 1 \text{ (even parity)}$$

$$OF = 0 \text{ (no overflow)}$$

EXAMPLE 4–8

```
0000 B5 22              MOV    CH,22H
0002 80 ED 44           SUB    CH,44H
```

Both carry flags (CF and AF) hold borrows after a subtraction instead of carries, as after an addition. Notice in this example that there is no overflow. This example subtracted a 44H (+68) from a 22H (+34) resulting in a DEH (−34). Because the

TABLE 4–5 Decrement instructions

Instruction	Comment
DEC BH	BH = BH − 1
DEC SP	SP = SP − 1
DEC BYTE PTR [DI]	The byte contents of the data segment memory location addressed by DI decrements
DEC WORD PTR [BP]	The word contents of the stack segment memory location addressed by BP decrements
DEC NUMB	Decrements the contents of data segment memory location NUMB. The way that NUMB is defined determines whether this is a byte or word decrement

correct 8-bit signed result is a −34, there is no overflow in this example. An 8-bit overflow only occurs if the signed result is greater than +127 or less than −128.

Decrement Subtraction. Decrement subtraction (DEC) subtracts a 1 from a register or the contents of a memory location. Table 4–5 lists some decrement instructions that illustrate register and memory decrements.

The decrement memory data instructions require either BYTE PTR or WORD PTR because the assembler cannot distinguish a byte from a word when an index register addresses memory. For example, DEC [SI] is vague, because the assembler cannot determine if the location addressed by SI is a byte or a word. Using either DEC BYTE PTR [SI] or DEC WORD PTR [SI] reveals the size of the data.

Subtract with Borrow. A subtraction-with-borrow (SBB) instruction functions as a regular subtraction, except the carry flag (CF), which holds the borrow, also subtracts from the difference. The most common use for this instruction is for subtractions that are wider than 16 bits. Wide subtractions require that borrows propagate through the subtraction, just as wide additions propagated the carry.

Table 4–6 lists many SBB instructions with comments that define their operation. Like the SUB instruction, SBB affects the flags. Notice that the subtract from

TABLE 4–6 Subtract-with-borrow instructions

Instruction	Comment
SBB AH,AL	AH = AH − AL − CF
SBB AX,BX	AX = AX − BX − CF
SBB CL,3	CL = CL − 3 − CF
SBB BYTE PTR [DI],3	3 and CF subtract from the byte contents of the data segment memory location addressed by DI
SBB [DI],AL	AL and CF subtract from the byte contents of the data segment memory location addressed by DI
SBB DI,[BP+2]	The word contents of the stack segment memory location addressed by BP plus 2 and CF subtract from DI

memory immediate instruction in this table requires a BYTE PTR or WORD PTR directive.

When the 32-bit number held in BX and AX is subtracted from the 32-bit number held in SI and DI, the carry flag propagates the borrow between the two 16-bit subtractions required to perform this operation. Figure 4–2 shows how the borrow propagates through the carry flag (CF) for this task. Example 4–9 shows how this subtraction is performed by a program. With wide subtraction, the least significant 16-bit data are subtracted with the SUB instruction. All subsequent and more significant data are subtracted using the SBB instruction. The example uses the SUB instruction to subtract DI from AX, then SBB to subtract-with-borrow SI from BX.

EXAMPLE 4–9

```
0004 2B C7              SUB     AX,DI
0006 1B DE              SBB     BX,SI
```

Comparison

The comparison instruction (CMP) is a subtraction that does not change anything except the flag bits. A comparison is useful for checking the entire contents of a register or a memory location against another value. A CMP is normally followed by a conditional jump instruction, which tests the condition of the flag bits.

Table 4–7 lists a variety of comparison instructions that use the same addressing modes as the addition and subtraction instructions already presented. Similarly, the only disallowed forms of compare are memory-to-memory and segment register compares.

EXAMPLE 4–10

```
0000 3C 10              CMP     AL,10H    ;compare with 10H
0002 73 1C              JAE     SUBER     ;if 10H or above
```

Example 4–10 shows a comparison followed by a conditional jump instruction. In this example the contents of AL are compared with a 10H. The conditional jump

FIGURE 4–2
Subtraction-with-borrow showing how the carry flag (CF) propagates the borrow.

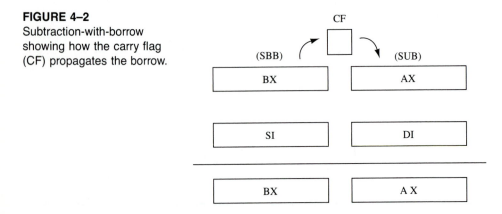

TABLE 4–7 Comparison instructions

Instruction	Comment
CMP CL,BL	Subtracts BL from CL; neither BL nor CL changes
CMP AX,SP	Subtracts SP from AX; neither AX nor SP changes
CMP AX,0CCCCH	Subtracts 0CCCCH from AX; AX does not change
CMP [DI],CH	Subtracts CH from the byte contents of the data segment memory location addressed by DI; neither CH nor memory changes
CMP CL,[BP]	Subtracts the byte contents of the stack segment memory location addressed by BP from CL; neither CL nor memory changes
CMP AH,TEMP	Subtracts the byte contents of the data segment memory location TEMP from AH; neither AH nor memory changes
CMP DI,TEMP [BX]	Subtracts the word contents of the data segment memory location addressed by TEMP plus BX from DI; neither DI nor memory changes

instructions that often follow the compare are JA (jump above) or JB (jump below). If the JA follows the compare, the jump occurs if the value in AL is above 10H; if the JB follows the compare, the jump occurs if the value in AL is below 10H. In this example, the JAE instruction follows the compare. This causes the program to continue at memory location SUBER if the value in AL is 10H or above. There is also a JBE (jump below or equal) instruction that could follow the compare to jump if the outcome is below or equal to 10H. Chapter 5 provides more detail on the compare instruction and the conditional jump instructions.

4–2 MULTIPLICATION AND DIVISION

Only the more modern microprocessors, such as the 80286 or earlier 8086/8088, contain multiplication and division instructions. Earlier 8-bit microprocessors were not able to multiply or divide directly. These tasks required a program that specifically multiplied or divided. Because microprocessor manufacturers were aware of this inadequacy, they incorporated multiplication and division instructions into the instruction sets of the newer microprocessors.

Multiplication

Multiplication, in the 80286 microprocessor, is performed on bytes or words and can be signed integer (IMUL) or unsigned (MUL). The product after a multiplication is always a double-width product. If we multiply two 8-bit numbers, they generate a 16-bit product, and, if we multiply two 16-bit numbers, they generate a 32-bit product.

Some flag bits (OF and CF) change when the multiply instruction executes, and produce predictable outcomes. The other flags also change, but their results are unpredictable and therefore are unused. In an 8-bit multiplication, if the most significant 8 bits of the result are 0, both CF and OF flag bits equal 0. These flag bits can be used to find whether the result is 8-bits wide or 16-bits wide. In a 16-bit multiplication, if the most significant 16 bits of the product are 0, both CF and OF clear to 0.

8-Bit Multiplication.   With 8-bit multiplication, whether signed or unsigned, the multiplicand is always in the AL register. The multiplier can be any 8-bit register or any memory location. Immediate multiplication is not allowed unless the special signed immediate multiplication instruction, discussed later in this section, appears in a program. The multiplication instruction contains one operand because it always multiplies the operand times the contents of register AL. An example is the MUL BL instruction. This instruction multiplies the unsigned contents of AL by the unsigned contents of BL and leaves the unsigned product in AX—a double-width product. Table 4–8 lists some 8-bit multiplication instructions.

Suppose that BL and CL each contain two 8-bit unsigned numbers. The numbers must be multiplied to form a 16-bit product stored in DX. This cannot be accomplished by a single instruction because we can only multiply a number times the AL register for an 8-bit multiplication. Example 4–11 shows a short program that generates DX = BL × CL. This example loads registers BL and CL with test data 5 and 10. The product, a 50, moves into DX from AX after the multiplication by the MOV DX,AX instruction.

EXAMPLE 4–11

```
0000 B3 05          MOV    BL,5      ;load data
0002 B1 0A          MOV    CL,10
0004 8A C1          MOV    AL,CL     ;position data
0006 F6 E3          MUL    BL        ;multiply
0008 8B D0          MOV    DX,AX     ;position product
```

TABLE 4–8 8-bit multiplication instructions

Instruction	Comment
MUL CL	AL is multiplied by CL; this unsigned multiplication leaves the product in AX
IMUL DH	AL is multiplied by DH; this signed multiplication leaves the product in AX
IMUL BYTE PTR [BX]	AL is multiplied by the byte contents of the data segment memory location addressed by BX; this unsigned multiplication leaves the product in AX
MUL TEMP	AL is multiplied by the contents of the data segment memory location TEMP; if TEMP is defined as an 8-bit number, the unsigned product is found in AX

For signed multiplication, the product is in true binary form, if positive, and in two's complement form, if negative. The same is true of all positive and negative signed numbers with the 80286 microprocessor. If the program of Example 4–11 multiplies two signed numbers, only the MUL instruction must be changed to IMUL.

16-Bit Multiplication. Word multiplication is very similar to byte multiplication. The differences are that AX contains the multiplicand instead of AL and the product appears in DX–AX instead of AX. The DX register always contains the most significant 16 bits of the product and AX the least significant 16 bits. As with 8-bit multiplication, the choice of the multiplier is up to the programmer. Table 4–9 shows several different 16-bit multiplication instructions.

Immediate Multiplication. The 8086/8088 microprocessor could not perform immediate multiplication, but the 80286 can by using a special version of the multiply instruction. Immediate multiplication must be signed multiplication, and the instruction format is different because it contains three operands. The first operand is the 16-bit destination register, the second operand is a register or memory location that contains the 16-bit multiplicand, and the third operand is either an 8-bit or 16-bit immediate data used as the multiplier.

The IMUL CX,DX,12H instruction multiplies 12H times DX and leaves a *16-bit* signed product in CX. If the immediate data are 8-bits, they sign extend into a 16-bit number before the multiplication occurs. Another example is IMUL BX,NUMBER,1000H, which multiplies NUMBER times 1000H and leaves the product in BX. Both the destination and multiplicand must be 16-bit numbers. Although this is immediate multiplication, the restrictions placed upon it limit its utility, especially the fact that it is a signed multiplication and the product is 16 bits wide.

Division

Like multiplication, division in the 80286 occurs on 8- or 16-bit numbers that are signed integers (IDIV) or unsigned (DIV) numbers. The dividend is always a double-width dividend that is divided by the operand. This means that an 8-bit division divides a 16-bit number by an 8-bit number, and a 16-bit division divides a 32-bit number by a 16-bit number. There is no immediate division instruction available to the 80286 microprocessor.

None of the flag bits change predictably for a division. A division can result in two different types of errors. One of these is an attempt to divide by zero and the

TABLE 4–9 16-bit multiplication instructions

Instruction	Comment
MUL CX	AX is multiplied by CX; the unsigned product is found in DX–AX
IMUL DI	AX is multiplied by DI; the signed product is found in DX–AX
MUL WORD PTR [SI]	AX is multiplied by the word contents of the data segment memory location addressed by SI; the unsigned product is found in DX–AX

other is a divide overflow. A *divide overflow* occurs when a small number divides into a large number. For example, suppose that AX = 3,000 and that we divide it by 2. Because the quotient for an 8-bit division appears in AL and 1,500 does not fit into AL, the result of 1,500 causes a divide overflow. In both cases the microprocessor generates an interrupt if a divide error occurs. Chapter 10 explains the divide-error-interrupt and all other interrupts for the 80286 microprocessor.

8-Bit Division.   An 8-bit division uses the AX register to store the dividend that is divided by the contents of any 8-bit register or memory location. The quotient moves into AL after the division, with AH containing a whole number remainder. For a signed division, the quotient is positive or negative, but the remainder is always a positive integer. For example, if AX = 0010H (+16) and BL = FDH (−3) and the IDIV BL instruction executes, AX = 01FBH. This represents a quotient of −5 with a remainder of 1. Table 4–10 lists some of the 8-bit division instructions.

With 8-bit division, the numbers are usually 8 bits wide. This means that one of them, the dividend, must be converted to a 16-bit-wide number in AX. This is accomplished differently for signed and unsigned numbers. For the unsigned number, the most significant 8 bits must be cleared to zero (*zero-extended*). For the signed number, the least significant 8 bits are sign extended into the most significant 8 bits. In the 80286 microprocessor a special instruction exists that sign extends AL into AH, or converts an 8-bit signed number in AL into a 16-bit signed number in AX. The CBW (*convert byte to word*) instruction performs this conversion.

EXAMPLE 4–12

```
0000 A0 0000 R          MOV    AL,NUMB        ;get NUMB
0003 B4 00              MOV    AH,0           ;zero-extend
0005 F6 36 0002 R       DIV    NUMB1          ;divide by NUMB1
0009 A2 0003 R          MOV    ANSQ,AL        ;save quotient
000C 88 26 0004 R       MOV    ANSR,AH        ;save remainder
```

Example 4–12 illustrates a short program that divides the unsigned byte contents of memory location NUMB by the unsigned contents of memory location NUMB1. Here we store the quotient in location ANSQ and the remainder in location ANSR.

TABLE 4–10   8-bit division instructions

Instruction	Comment
DIV CL	AX is divided by CL; the unsigned quotient is in AL and the remainder is in AH
IDIV BL	AX is divided by BL; the signed quotient is in AL and the remainder is in AH
DIV BYTE PTR [BP]	AX is divided by the byte contents of the stack segment memory location addressed by BP; the unsigned quotient is in AL and the remainder is in AH

Notice how the contents of location NUMB are retrieved from memory and then zero extended to form a 16-bit unsigned number for the dividend.

EXAMPLE 4–13

```
0000 A0 0000 R        MOV    AL,NUMB        ;get NUMB
0003 98               CBW                   ;sign-extend
0004 F6 3E 0002 R     IDIV   NUMB1          ;divide by NUMB1
0008 A2 0003 R        MOV    ANSQ,AL        ;save quotient
000B 88 26 0004 R     MOV    ANSR,AH        ;save remainder
```

Example 4–13 shows the same basic program except that the numbers are signed numbers. This means that instead of zero extending AL into AH, we sign extend it using the CBW instruction.

16-Bit Division. Sixteen-bit division is similar to 8-bit division except that instead of dividing into AX we divide into DX–AX, a 32-bit dividend. The quotient appears in AX and the remainder in DX after a 16-bit division. Table 4–11 lists some of the 16-bit division instructions.

As with 8-bit division, numbers must often be converted to the proper form for the dividend. If we start with a 16-bit unsigned number in AX, then DX must be cleared to 0. If AX is a 16-bit signed number, the CWD (*converted word to double word*) instruction sign extends it into a signed 32-bit number.

EXAMPLE 4–14

```
0000 B8 FF9C          MOV    AX,-100        ;load -100
0003 B9 0009          MOV    CX,9           ;load +9
0006 99               CWD                   ;sign-extend
0007 F7 F9            IDIV   CX
```

Example 4–14 shows the division of two 16-bit signed numbers. Here a −100 in AX is divided by a +9 in CX. The CWD instruction converts the −100 in AX

TABLE 4–11 16-bit division instructions

Instruction	Comment
DIV CX	DX–AX is divided by CX; the unsigned quotient is in AX and the remainder is in DX
IDIV SI	DX–AX is divided by SI; the signed quotient is in AX and the remainder is in DX
DIV NUMB	DX–AX is divided by the word contents of the data segment memory location NUMB; the unsigned quotient is in AX and the remainder is in DX

to a −100 in DX–AX before the division. After the division, the results appear in DX–AX as a quotient of −11 in AX and a remainder of 1 in DX.

The Remainder.   What do we do with the remainder after a division? There are a few possible choices. We could use the remainder to round the result or we could drop the remainder to truncate the result. If the division is unsigned, rounding requires that we compare the remainder with half the divisor to decide whether to round up the quotient. We could also convert the remainder to a fractional remainder.

EXAMPLE 4–15

```
0000  F6 F3              DIV    BL          ;divide
0002  02 E4              ADD    AH,AH       ;double remainder
0004  3A E3              CMP    AH,BL       ;test for rounding
0006  72 02              JB     NEXT
0008  FE C0              INC    AL          ;round

000A             NEXT:
```

Example 4–15 shows a sequence of instructions that divide AX by BL and round the result. This program doubles the remainder before comparing it with BL to decide whether or not to round the quotient. Here, an INC instruction rounds the contents of AL after the compare.

Suppose that we need a fractional remainder instead of an integer remainder. A fractional remainder is obtained by saving the quotient. Next the AL register is cleared to zero. The number remaining in AX is now divided by the original operand to generate a fractional remainder.

EXAMPLE 4–16

```
0000  B8 000D            MOV    AX,13       ;load 13
0003  B3 02              MOV    BL,2        ;load 2
0005  F6 F3              DIV    BL          ;13/2
0007  A2 0003 R          MOV    ANSQ,AL     ;save quotient
000A  B0 00              MOV    AL,0        ;clear AL
000C  F6 F3              DIV    BL          ;generate remainder
000E  A2 0004 R          MOV    ANSR,AL     ;save remainer
```

Example 4–16 shows how a 13 is divided by a 2. The 8-bit quotient is saved in memory location ANSQ and then AL is cleared. Next the contents of AX are again divided by 2 to generate a fractional remainder. After the division, the AL register equals an 80H. This is a 10000000_2. If the binary point (radix) is placed before the leftmost bit of AL, we have a fractional remainder of 0.10000000_2 or 0.5 decimal. The remainder is saved in memory location ANSR in this example.

4–3   BCD AND ASCII ARITHMETIC

The 80286 microprocessor allows arithmetic manipulation of both binary-coded decimal (BCD) and American Standard Code for Information Interchange (ASCII) data. This is accomplished by instructions that adjust the numbers for BCD and ASCII arithmetic.

The BCD operations occur in systems such as point-of-sale terminals (cash registers) and other systems that seldom require arithmetic. The ASCII operations are performed on ASCII data used by some programs. In most cases today, we rarely use BCD or ASCII arithmetic.

BCD Arithmetic

Two arithmetic techniques operate with BCD data: addition and subtraction. The 80286 instruction set provides two instructions that correct the result of a BCD addition and a BCD subtraction. The DAA (*decimal adjust after addition*) instruction follows BCD addition, and DAS (*decimal adjust after subtraction*) follows BCD subtraction. Both instructions correct the result of the addition or subtraction so it is a BCD number.

For BCD data, the numbers always appear in the packaged BCD form and are stored as two BCD digits per byte. The adjust instructions only function with the AL register after BCD addition and subtraction.

DAA Instruction.   The DAA instruction follows the ADD or ADC instruction to adjust the result into a BCD result. Suppose that DX and BX each contain 4-digit packed BCD numbers. Example 4–17 provides a short sample program that adds the BCD numbers in DX and BX and stores the result in CX.

EXAMPLE 4–17

```
0000  BA 1234          MOV   DX,1234H         ;load 1,234
0003  BB 3099          MOV   BX,3099H         ;load 3,099
0006  8A C3            MOV   AL,BL            ;sum BL with DL
0008  02 C2            ADD   AL,DL
000A  27               DAA                    ;adjust
000B  8A C8            MOV   CL,AL            ;answer to CL
000D  8A C7            MOV   AL,BH            ;sum BH with DH and CF
000F  12 C6            ADC   AL,DH
0011  27               DAA                    ;adjust
0012  8A E8            MOV   CH,AL            ;answer to CH
```

Because the DAA instruction only functions with the AL register, this addition must occur 8 bits at a time. After adding the BL and DL registers, the result is adjusted with a DAA instruction before being stored in CL. Next, we add BH and DH registers with carry, and the result again is adjusted with DAA before being stored in CH. In this example, a 1,234 adds to a 3,099 to generate a sum of 4,333 that moves into CX after the addition. Note that 1234 BCD is the same as 1234H.

DAS Instruction.   The DAS instruction functions the same way as the DAA instruction, except it follows a subtraction instead of an addition. Example 4–18 is basically the same as Example 4–15, except that it subtracts instead of adds DX and BX. The main difference in these programs is that the DAA instructions change to DAS and the ADD and ADC instructions change to SUB and SBB instructions.

EXAMPLE 4–18

```
0000  BA 1234          MOV    DX,1234H       ;load 1,234
0003  BB 3099          MOV    BX,3099H       ;load 3,099
0006  8A C3            MOV    AL,BL          ;subtract DL from BL
0008  2A C2            SUB    AL,DL
000A  2F               DAS                   ;adjust
000B  8A C8            MOV    CL,AL          ;answer to CL
000D  8A C7            MOV    AL,BH          ;subtract DH and CF from BH
000F  1A C6            SBB    AL,DH
0011  2F               DAS                   ;adjust
0012  8A E8            MOV    CH,AL          ;answer to CH
```

ASCII Arithmetic

The ASCII arithmetic instructions function with ASCII-coded numbers. These numbers range in value from 30H to 39H for the numbers 0–9. There are four instructions used with ASCII arithmetic operations: AAA (*ASCII adjust after addition*), AAD (*ASCII adjust before division*), AAM (*ASCII adjust after multiplication*), and AAS (*ASCII adjust after subtraction*). These instructions use register AX as the source and as the destination.

AAA Instruction.   The addition of two 1-digit ASCII-coded numbers will not result in any useful data. For example, if we add a 31H and 39H, the result is a 6AH. This ASCII addition (1+9) should produce a 2-digit ASCII result equivalent to a 10 decimal, which is a 31H and a 30H in ASCII code. If we execute the AAA instruction after this addition, the AX register will contain a 0100H. Although this is not ASCII code, it can be converted to ASCII code by adding 3030H, which generates 3130H. The AAA instruction clears AH if the result is less than 10 and adds a 1 to AH if the result is greater than 10.

EXAMPLE 4–19

```
0000  B8 0031          MOV    AX,31H         ;load ASCII 1
0003  04 39            ADD    AL,39H         ;add ASCII 9
0005  37               AAA                   ;adjust
0006  05 3030          ADD    AX,3030H       ;answer to ASCII
```

Example 4–19 shows how this ASCII addition functions in the 80286 micropro-cessor. Please note that we clear AH before the addition by using the MOV AX,31H instruction. The operand of 0031H places a 00H in AH and a 31H into AL.

AAD Instruction. While all the other adjust instructions follow their instructions the AAD instruction appears before a division. The AAD instruction requires that the AX register contain a 2-digit unpacked BCD number (not ASCII) before executing. After adjusting the AX register with AAD, it is divided by an unpacked BCD number to generate a single-digit result in AL with any remainder in AH.

EXAMPLE 4–20

```
0000 B3 09          MOV    BL,9         ;load divisor
0002 B8 0702        MOV    AX,0702H     ;load dividend
0005 D5 0A          AAD                 ;adjust
0007 F6 F3          DIV    BL
```

Example 4–20 illustrates how a 72 in unpacked BCD is divided by 9 to produce a quotient of 8. The 0702H loaded into the AX register is adjusted by the AAD instruction to 0048H. Notice that this converts a 2-digit unpacked BCD number into a binary number so it can be divided with the binary division instruction (DIV). The AAD instruction converts the unpacked BCD numbers between 00 and 99 into binary.

AAM Instruction. The AAM instruction follows the multiplication instruction after multiplying two 1-digit unpacked BCD numbers. Example 4–21 shows a short pro-gram that multiplies a 5 times a 5. The result after the multiplication is 0018H in the AX register. After adjusting the result with the AAM instruction, AX contains a 0205H. This is an unpacked BCD result of 25. If 3030H adds to 0205H, this becomes an ASCII result of 3235H.

EXAMPLE 4–21

```
0000 B0 05          MOV    AL,5         ;load multiplicand
0002 B1 05          MOV    CL,5         ;load multiplier
0004 F6 E1          MUL    CL
0006 D4 0A          AAM                 ;adjust
```

One side benefit of the AAM instruction is that AAM will convert from binary to unpacked BCD. If a binary number between 0000H and 0063H appears in the AX register, the AAM instruction converts it to BCD. For example, if AX contains a 0060H before AAM, it will contain a 0906H after AAM executes. This is the unpacked BCD equivalent to a 96. If 3030H is added to 0906H, we have just changed the result to ASCII.

AAS Instruction.   Like other ASCII adjust instructions, AAS adjusts the AX register after an ASCII subtraction. For example, suppose that a 35H subtracts from a 39H. The result will be a 04H, which requires no correction. Here AAS will modify neither AH nor AL. On the other hand, if 38H subtracts from 37H, then AL will equal 09H and the number in AH will decrement by 1. This decrement allows multiple-digit ASCII numbers to be subtracted from each other.

4–4   BASIC LOGIC INSTRUCTIONS

The basic logic instructions include: AND, OR, Exclusive-OR, and NOT. Another logic instruction is TEST, which is explained in this section of the text because the operation of the TEST instruction is a special form of the AND instruction. Also explained is the NEG instruction, which is similar to the NOT instruction.

Logic operations provide binary bit control in *low-level software*. The logic instructions allow bits to be set, cleared, or complemented. Low-level software appears in machine language or assembly language form and often controls the I/O devices in a system. All logic instructions affect the flag bits. Logic operations always clear the carry and overflow flags, while the other flags change to reflect the condition of the result.

When binary data are manipulated in a register or a memory location, the rightmost bit position is always numbered bit 0. Bit position numbers increase from bit 0 toward the left to bit 7 for a byte and to bit 15 for a word. A double word (32-bits) uses bit position 31 as its leftmost bit.

AND

The AND operation performs logical multiplication as illustrated by the truth table in Figure 4–3. Here two bits, A and B, are ANDed to produce the result X. As indicated by the truth table, X is a logic 1 only when both A and B are logic 1s. For all other input combinations of A and B, X is a logic 0. It is important to remember that 0 AND anything is always 0 and 1 AND 1 is always a 1.

FIGURE 4–3   The truth table demonstrating the AND operation (logical multiplication).

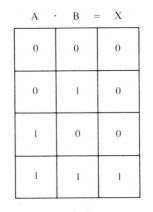

A	·	B	=	X
0		0		0
0		1		0
1		0		0
1		1		1

FIGURE 4–4 Here a mask (0000 1111) is ANDed with an unknown number. Notice how the leftmost 4 bits are masked off (cleared) to 0.

XXXX	XXXX	(Unknown pattern)
0000	1111	(Mask pattern)
0000	XXXX	(Result)

The AND instruction often replaces discrete AND gates if the speed of the logic circuit is not too great. With the 80286 microprocessor, the AND instruction often executes in about a microsecond. So if the circuit that the AND instruction replaces operates at a slower speed than a microsecond, the AND instruction is a logical replacement. This replacement saves a considerable amount of money. A single AND gate integrated circuit (7408) costs approximately 40 cents, while it costs less than 1/100 of a cent to store the AND instruction in a read-only memory.

The AND operation also clears bits of a binary number. The task of clearing a bit in a binary number is called *masking*. Figure 4–4 illustrates the process of masking. Notice that the leftmost four bits clear to 0, because 0 AND anything is 0. The bit positions that are ANDed with 1s do not change. This occurs because if a 1 ANDs with a 1, a 1 results, and if a 1 ANDs with a 0, a 0 results.

The AND instruction uses any addressing mode except memory-to-memory and segment register addressing. Refer to Table 4–12 for a list of some AND instructions and comments about their operation.

EXAMPLE 4–22

```
0000  BB 3135          MOV   BX,3135H          ;load ASCII
0003  81 E3 0F0F       AND   BX,0F0FH          ;mask BX
```

An ASCII coded number can be converted to BCD by using the AND instruction to mask off the leftmost four binary bit positions. This converts the ASCII

TABLE 4–12   AND instructions

Instruction	Comment
AND AL,BL	AL = AL AND BL
AND CX,DX	CX = CX AND DX
AND CL,33H	CL = CL AND 33H
AND DI,4FFFH	DI = DI AND 4FFFH
AND AX,[DI]	AX is ANDed with the word contents of the data segment memory location addressed by DI; the result moves into AX
AND ARRAY [SI],AL	The byte contents of the data segment memory location addressed by ARRAY plus SI is ANDed to AL; the result moves to memory

FIGURE 4–5 The truth table illustrating the OR operation (logical addition). Note that a + sign is used to indicate the OR operation.

A	+	B	=	X
0		0		0
0		1		1
1		0		1
1		1		1

30H to 39H to 0–9. Example 4–22 shows a short program that converts the ASCII contents of BX into BCD. The AND instruction in this example converts two digits from ASCII to BCD simultaneously.

OR

The OR operation performs logical addition and is often called the *Inclusive-OR function*. The OR function generates a 1 if any inputs are 1. A 0 appears at the output only when all inputs are 0. The truth table for the OR function appears in Figure 4–5. Here the inputs A and B OR together to produce the X output. It is important we remember that 1 ORed with anything yields a 1.

The OR instruction often replaces discrete OR gates. This results in a considerable savings, because a quad, 2-input OR gate (7432) costs about 40 cents, while the OR instruction costs less than 1/100 of a cent to store in a read-only memory.

Figure 4–6 shows how the OR gate sets (1) any bit of a binary number. Here an unknown number (XXXX XXXX) ORs with a 0000 1111 to produce a result of XXXX 1111. The rightmost four bits set, while the leftmost four bits remain unchanged. The OR operation sets any bit and the AND operation clears any bit.

The OR instruction uses any of the addressing modes allowed to any other instruction except segment register addressing. Table 4–13 illustrates several example OR instructions with comments about their operation.

Suppose that we multiply two BCD numbers and adjust them with the AAM instruction. The result appears in AX as a 2-digit unpacked BCD number. Example 4-23 illustrates this multiplication and shows how to change the result into a 2-digit ASCII-coded number using the OR instruction. Here, OR AX,3030H converts the 0305H found in AX to 3335H. The OR operation can be replaced with an ADD AX,3030H to obtain the same results.

FIGURE 4–6 A test pattern (0000 1111) is ORed with an unknown number to illustrate how the OR operation is used to selectively set bits.

```
   XXXX   XXXX    (Unknown pattern)
 + 0000   1111    (Test pattern)
   ────────────
   XXXX   1111    (Result)
```

TABLE 4–13 OR instructions

Instruction	Comment
OR AH,BL	AH = AH OR BL
OR SI,DX	SI = SI OR DX
OR DH,OA3H	DH = DH OR OA3H
OR SP,990DH	SP = SP OR 990DH
OR DX,[BX]	DX is ORed with the word contents of the data segment memory location addressed by BX
OR DATES [DI + 2],AL	The data segment memory location addressed by DATES plus DI plus 2 is ORed with AL

EXAMPLE 4–23

```
0000 B0 05          MOV    AL,5           ;load data
0002 B3 07          MOV    BL,7
0004 F6 E3          MUL    BL
0006 D4 0A          AAM                   ;adjust
0008 0D 3030        OR     AX,3030H       ;to ASCII
```

Exclusive-OR

The Exclusive-OR instruction (XOR) differs from Inclusive-OR (OR) in that a 1,1 condition of the OR function produces a 1, while the 1,1 condition of the Exclusive-OR operation produces a 0. The Exclusive-OR operation excludes this condition, while the Inclusive-OR includes it.

Figure 4–7 shows the truth table of the Exclusive-OR function. (Compare this figure with Figure 4–5 to appreciate the difference between these two OR functions.) If the inputs of the Exclusive-OR function are both 0 or both 1, the output is 0. If the inputs are different, the output is a 1. Because of this, the Exclusive-OR is sometimes called a *comparator*.

FIGURE 4–7 The truth table for the Exclusive-OR function. Notice that the ⊕ sign is used to indicate an Exclusive-OR operation.

A ⊕	B =	X
0	0	0
0	1	1
1	0	1
1	1	0

TABLE 4–14   Exclusive-OR instructions

Instruction	Comment
XOR CH,DL	CH = CH XOR DL
XOR SI,BX	SI = SI XOR BX
XOR CH,0EEH	CH = CH XOR 0EEH
XOR DI,00DDH	DI = DI XOR OODDH
XOR DX,[SI]	DX is XORed with the word contents of the data segment memory location addressed by SI; the result is left in DX
XOR DATES[DI + 2],AL	The byte contents of the data segment memory location addressed by DATES plus DI plus 2 are XORed with AL; the result is left in memory

The XOR instruction uses any addressing mode except segment register addressing. Table 4–14 lists various forms of the Exclusive-OR instruction with comments about their operation.

As with the AND and OR functions, Exclusive-OR also replaces discrete logic circuitry. The 7486 quad, 2-input Exclusive-OR gate is replaced by one XOR instruction. The 7486 costs about 40 cents, while the instruction costs less than 1/20 of a cent to store in the memory. Replacing just one 7486 saves a considerable amount of money, especially if we build many systems.

The Exclusive-OR instruction is useful if some bits of a register or memory location must be inverted. This instruction allows part of a number to be inverted or complemented. Figure 4–8 shows how just part of an unknown quantity can be inverted by XOR. Notice that when a 1 Exclusive-ORs with X, the result is $\overline{X}$. If a 0 Exclusive-ORs with X, the result is X.

Suppose that the leftmost 10 bits of the BX register must be inverted without changing the rightmost 6 bits. The XOR BX,0FFC0H instruction accomplishes this task. The AND instruction clears (0) bits, the OR instruction sets (1) bits, and now the Exclusive-OR instruction inverts bits. These three instructions allow a program to gain complete control over any bit, stored in any register or memory location. This is ideal for control system applications where equipment must be turned on (1), turned off (0), and toggled from on to off or off to on.

TEST

The TEST instruction performs the AND operation. The difference is that the AND instruction changes the destination operand, while the TEST instruction does not. A

FIGURE 4–8   A test pattern (0000 1111) Exclusive-ORed with an unknown quantity produces inversion in the bit positions where the test pattern contains logic 1.

	XXXX	XXXX	(Unknown pattern)
$\oplus$	0000	1111	(Test pattern)
	XXXX	$\overline{XXXX}$	(Result)

TEST only affects the condition of the flag register, which indicates the result of the test. The TEST instruction uses the same addressing modes as the AND instruction. Table 4–15 illustrates some forms of the TEST instruction with comments about the operation of each form.

The TEST instruction functions in the same manner as a CMP instruction. The difference is that the TEST instruction normally tests a single bit, while the CMP instruction tests the entire byte or word. The zero flag (ZF) is a logic 1 (indicating a zero result) if the bit under test is a zero, and ZF = 0 (indicating a nonzero result) if the bit under test is not zero.

Usually the TEST instruction is followed by either the JZ (*jump zero*) or JNZ (*jump not zero*) instruction. The destination operand is normally tested against immediate data. The value of immediate data is 1, to test the rightmost bit position, 2 to test the next bit, 4 for the next, and so forth.

Example 4–24 lists a short program that tests the rightmost and leftmost bit positions of the AL register. Here, 1 selects the rightmost bit and 128 selects the leftmost bit. The JNZ instruction follows each test to jump to different memory locations depending on the outcome of the tests. The JNZ instruction jumps to the operand address (RIGHT or LEFT in the example) if the bit under test is not zero.

EXAMPLE 4–24

```
0000 A8 01          TEST   AL,1              ;test right bit
0002 75 1C          JNZ    RIGHT             ;if set
0004 A8 80          TEST   AL,128            ;test left bit
0006 75 38          JNZ    LEFT              ;if set
```

NOT and NEG

Logical inversion or *one's complement* (NOT) and arithmetic sign inversion or *two's complement* (NEG) are the last two logic functions presented except for shift and rotate in the next section of the text. These are two of the few instructions that contain only one operand. Table 4–16 lists some variations of the NOT and NEG instructions. As with most other instructions, NOT and NEG can use any addressing mode except segment register addressing.

The NOT instruction inverts all bits of a byte or word. The NEG instruction two's complements a number, which means that the arithmetic sign of a signed

TABLE 4–15   TEST instructions

Instruction	Comment
TEST DL,DH	DL is ANDed with DH; neither DL nor DH changes; only the flags change
TEST CX,BX	CX is ANDed with BX; neither CX nor BX changes; only the flags change
TEST AH,4	AH is ANDed with 4; AH does not change; only the flags change

TABLE 4–16   NOT and NEG instructions

Instruction	Comment
NOT CH	CH is one's complemented
NEG CH	CH is two's complemented
NEG AX	AX is two's complemented
NOT TEMP	The contents of the data segment memory location addressed by TEMP are one's complemented. The size of TEMP is determined by how TEMP is defined
NOT BYTE PTR [BX]	The byte contents of the data segment memory location addresses by BX are one's complemented

number changes from positive to negative or negative to positive. The NOT function is considered logical and the NEG function is considered an arithmetic operation.

4–5   SHIFTS AND ROTATES

Shift and rotate instructions manipulate binary numbers at the binary bit level, as did the AND, OR, Exclusive-OR, and NOT instructions. Shifts and rotates find their most common application in low-level software used to control I/O devices. The 80286 microprocessor contains a complete set of shift and rotate instructions used to shift or rotate any memory data or register.

Shifts

Shift instructions position or move numbers to the left or right within a register or memory location. They also perform simple arithmetic such as multiplication by powers of 2^n (*left shift*) and division by powers of 2^{-n} (*right shift*). The 80286 instruction set contains four different shift instructions: two are *logical shifts* and two are *arithmetic shifts*. All four shift operations appear in Figure 4–9.

Notice in Figure 4–9 that there are two different right shifts and two different left shifts. The logical shifts move a 0 into the rightmost bit position for a logical left shift and a 0 into the leftmost bit position for a logical right shift. There are also two arithmetic shifts. The arithmetic and logical left shifts are identical. The arithmetic and logical right shifts are different because the arithmetic right shift copies the sign-bit through the number while the logical right shift copies a 0 through the number.

Logical shift operations function with unsigned numbers and arithmetic shifts function with signed numbers. Logical shifts multiply or divide unsigned data, and arithmetic shifts multiply or divide signed data. A shift left always multiplies by 2 for each bit position shifted, and a shift right always divides by 2 for each bit position shifted.

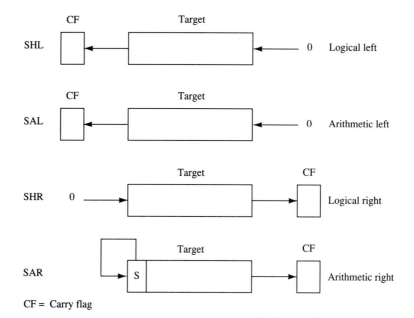

FIGURE 4–9 The four shift operations available in the 80286 instruction set. Note that the target is any 8- or 16-bit register or memory location except the segment registers. *Note:* CF = carry flag.

Table 4–17 illustrates some addressing modes allowed for the various shift instructions. There are two different forms of shifts that allow any register (except the segment register) or memory location to be shifted. One mode uses an immediate shift count, and the other uses register CL to hold the shift count. Note that CL must hold the shift count. When CL is the shift count, it does not change when the shift instruction executes. Note that the shift count is a modulo-32 count. This means that a shift count of 33 will shift the data one place (33/32 = remainder of 1).

Example 4–25 shows how the DX register shifts left 14 places in two different ways. The first method uses an immediate shift count of 14. The second method loads a 14 into CL and then uses CL as the shift count. Both instructions

TABLE 4–17 Shift instructions

Instruction	Comment
SHL AX,1	Logically shift AX left one place
SHR BX,12	Logically shift BX right 12 places
SAL DATA1,CL	Arithmetically shift DATA1, in the data segment, left the number of places contained in CL
SAR SI,2	Arithmetically shift SI right 2 places

Note: The 8086/8088 microprocessor allowed an immediate shift count of 1 only.

shift the contents of the DX register logically to the left 14 binary bit positions or places.

EXAMPLE 4–25

```
0000 C1 E2 0E               SHL    DX,14

                            or

0003 B1 0E                  MOV    CL,14
0005 D3 E2                  SHL    DX,CL
```

Suppose that the contents of AX must be multiplied by 10, as in Example 4–26. This can be done in two ways: by the MUL instruction or by shifts and additions. A number is doubled when it shifts left one binary place. When a number is doubled, then added to the number times 8, the result is 10 times the number. The number 10 decimal is 1010 in binary. A logic 1 appears in both the 2's and the 8's positions. If 2 times the number adds to 8 times the number, the result is 10 times the number. Using this technique, a program can be written to multiply by any constant. This technique often executes faster than the multiply instruction.

EXAMPLE 4–26

```
                    ;multiply AX by 10 (1010)
                    ;
0000 D1 E0              SHL    AX,1           ;AX times 2
0002 8B D8              MOV    BX,AX
0004 C1 E0 02           SHL    AX,2           ;AX times 8
0007 03 C3              ADD    AX,BX          ;10 x AX
                    ;
                    ;multiply AX by 18 (10010)
                    ;
0009 D1 E0              SHL    AX,1           ;AX times 2
000B 8B D8              MOV    BX,AX
000D C1 E0 03           SHL    AX,3           ;AX times 16
0010 03 D8              ADD    BX,AX
```

Rotates

Rotate instructions position binary data by rotating the information in a register or memory location either from one end to another or through the carry flag. They are often used to shift or position numbers that are wider than 16 bits in the 80286 microprocessor. The four rotate instructions available appear in Figure 4–10.

Numbers rotate through a register and a memory location and CF (carry) or through a register and memory location only. With either type of rotate instruction, the programmer can use either a left or a right rotate. Addressing modes used with rotate are the same as used with the shifts. A rotate count can be immediate or

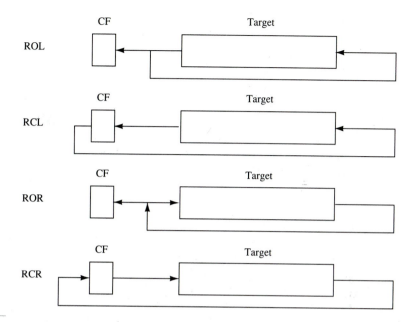

FIGURE 4–10 The four rotate operations available in the 80286 instruction set. Note that both the RCL and RCR instructions have data rotated through CF (carry) and that ROL and ROR rotate data only through the target.

located in register CL. Table 4–18 lists some of the possible rotate instructions. If CL is used for a rotate count, it does not change. As with shifts, the count in CL is a modulo-32 count.

EXAMPLE 4–27

```
0000 D1 E0          SHL   AX,1
0002 D1 D3          RCL   BX,1
0004 D1 D2          RCL   DX,1
```

TABLE 4–18   Rotate instructions

Instruction	Comment
ROL SI,4	SI rotates left 4 places
RCL BL,6	BL rotates left through CF 6 places
RCR AH,CL	AH rotates right through CF the number of places contained in CL
ROR WORD PTR [BP],2	The word contents of the stack segment memory location addressed by BP rotate right 2 places

Note: The 8086/8088 microprocessor can only use an immediate rotate count or 1.

Rotates are often used to shift wide numbers to the left or right. The program listed in Example 4–27 shifts the 48-bit number, in registers DX, BX, and AX, left one binary place. Notice that the least significant 16-bits (AX) shift left first. This shift moves its leftmost bit of AX into the CF flag bit. Next the rotate BX instruction rotates CF into BX and its leftmost bit moves into CF. The last instruction rotates CF into DX and the shift is complete.

4–6   STRING COMPARISONS

As we have seen in Chapter 3, the string instructions of the 80286 microprocessor are very powerful because they allow the programmer to manipulate large blocks of data with relative ease. Block data manipulation occurs with the string instructions MOVS, LODS, STOS, INS, and OUTS.

In this section, we discuss additional string instructions that allow a section of memory to be tested against a constant or against another section of memory. To accomplish these tasks we use the SCAS (*string scan*) or CMPS (*string compare*) instructions.

SCAS

The string scan instruction (SCAS) compares either the AL register with a byte block of memory or the AX register with a word block of memory. The SCAS instruction subtracts memory from AL or AX without affecting either the register or the memory location. The opcode used for byte comparison is *SCASB* and the opcode used for word comparison is *SCASW*. In both cases the contents of the memory location addressed by DI, in the extra segment, is compared with either AL or AX. Recall that this default segment cannot be changed with a segment override prefix.

Like the other string instructions, SCAS instructions use the direction flag (DF) to select either auto-increment or auto-decrement operation for DI. They also repeat if prefixed by a *conditional* repeat prefix. As with the other string instructions, DI addresses data in the extra segment.

EXAMPLE 4–28

```
0000 BF 0011 R        MOV    DI,OFFSET BLOCK    ;address data
0003 FC               CLD                       ;auto-increment
0004 B9 0064          MOV    CX,100             ;load counter
0007 32 C0            XOR    AL,AL              ;clear AL
0009 F2/AE            REPNE SCASB               ;search
```

Suppose a section of memory is 100 bytes in length and begins at location BLOCK. This section of memory must be tested to see if any location contains a 00H. The program in Example 4–28 shows how to search this part of memory for a 00H using the SCASB instruction. In this example, the SCASB instruction is prefixed with an REPNE (*repeat while not equal*). The REPNE prefix causes the SCASB instruction to repeat until *either* the CX register reaches 0, or until an equal condition exists as the outcome of the SCASB instruction's comparison. Another conditional repeat prefix is REPE (*repeat while equal*). With either repeat prefix, the contents of CX decrement without affecting the flag bits. The SCASB instruction changes the flags.

Suppose you must develop a program that skips ASCII-coded spaces in a memory array. This task appears in the procedure listed in Example 4–29. This procedure assumes that the DI register already addresses the ASCII-coded character string, and that the length of the string is 256 bytes or less. Because this program is to skip spaces (20H), the REPE (repeat while equal) prefix is used with a SCASB instruction. The SCASB instruction repeats the comparison, searching for a 20H, as long as an equal condition exists.

EXAMPLE 4–29

```
0000                    SKIP    PROC  FAR

0000 FC                         CLD                     ;auto-increment
0001 B9 0100                    MOV   CX,256            ;counter
0004 B0 20                      MOV   AL,20H            ;get space
0006 F3/AE                      REPE  SCASB             ;search
0008 CB                         RET

0009                    SKIP    ENDP
```

CMPS

The *compare strings* instruction (CMPS) always compares two sections of memory data as bytes (CMPSB) or words (CMPSW). The contents of the data segment location addressed by SI are compared with the contents of the extra segment location addressed by DI. The CMPS instruction increments or decrements both SI and DI. The CMPS instruction is normally used with either the REPE or REPNE prefix. Alternates to these prefixes are REPZ (repeat while zero) and REPNZ (repeat while not zero), but usually we use REPE or REPNE.

EXAMPLE 4–30

```
0000                    MATCH   PROC  FAR

0000 BE 0075 R                  MOV   SI,OFFSET LINE    ;address LINE
0003 BF 007F R                  MOV   DI,OFFSET TABLE   ;address TABLE
0006 FC                         CLD                     ;auto-increment
0007 B9 000A                    MOV   CX,10             ;counter
000A F3/A6                      REPE  CMPSB             ;search
000C CB                         RET

000D                    MATCH   ENDP
```

Example 4–30 illustrates a short procedure that compares two sections of memory searching for a match. The CMPSB instruction is prefixed with a REPE. This causes the search to continue as long as an equal condition exists. When the CX register becomes 0, or an unequal condition exists, the CMPSB instruction stops execution. If CX is zero or the flags indicate an equal condition, the two strings match. If CX is not zero or the flags indicate a not-equal condition, the strings do not match.

4–7   SUMMARY

1. Addition (ADD) can be either 8 or 16 bits. The ADD instruction allows any addressing mode except segment register addressing. All flags change when the ADD instruction executes. A different type of addition, add-with-carry (ADC), adds two operands and the contents of CF.

2. The increment instruction (INC) adds 1 to either a byte or a word of register or memory data. The INC instruction affects all the flag bits except the carry flag. The BYTE PTR and WORD PTR directives appear with the INC instruction when the contents of a memory location are addressed by a pointer.

3. Subtraction (SUB) is either a byte or a word and is performed on a register or a memory location. The only form of addressing not allowed by the SUB instruction is segment register addressing. The subtract instruction affects all the flags and subtracts CF if the SBB form is used.

4. The decrement (DEC) instruction subtracts 1 from the contents of a register or a memory location. The only addressing modes not allowed with DEC are immediate or segment register addressing. The DEC instruction does not affect the carry flag and is often used with BYTE PTR or WORD PTR.

5. The compare (CMP) instruction is a special form of subtraction that does not store the difference; instead the flags change to reflect the difference. Compare is used to compare an entire byte or word located in any register (except segment) or memory location.

6. Multiplication is a byte or word and can be signed (IMUL) or unsigned (MUL). The 8-bit multiplication always multiplies register AL by an operand with the product found in AX. The 16-bit multiplication always multiplies register AX by an operand with the product found in DX–AX. A special IMUL immediate instruction exists on the 80286 that contains three operands. For example, the IMUL BX,CX,3 instruction multiplies CX by 3 and leaves the product in BX.

7. Division is either a byte or word and can be signed (IDIV) or unsigned (DIV). For an 8-bit division, the AX register divides by the operand, after which the quotient appears in AL and the remainder in AH. In the 16-bit division, the DX–AX register divides by the operand, after which, the AX register contains the quotient and the DX the remainder.

8. BCD data add or subtract in packed form by adjusting the result of the addition with DAA or the subtraction with DAS. ASCII data are added, subtracted,

multiplied, or divided when the operations are adjusted with AAA, AAS, AAM, or AAD.

9. The AAM instruction has an interesting added feature that allows it to convert a binary number into unpacked BCD. This instruction converts a binary number between 00H and 63H into unpacked BCD in AX.

10. The AND, OR, and Exclusive-OR instructions perform logic functions on either a byte or word stored in a register or memory location. All flags change with these instructions, with carry (CF) and overflow (OF) cleared.

11. The TEST instruction performs the AND operation, but the logical product is lost. This instruction changes the flag bits to indicate the outcome of the test.

12. The NOT and NEG instructions perform logical inversion and arithmetic inversion. The NOT instruction one's complements an operand, and the NEG instruction two's complements an operand.

13. There are eight different shift and rotate instructions. Each of these instructions can shift or rotate a byte or a word or a register or memory data. These instructions have two operands. The first operand is the location of the data shifted or rotated, and the second is an immediate shift or rotate count or CL. If the second operand is CL, the CL register holds the shift or rotate count.

14. The scan string (SCAS) instruction compares either AL or AX with the contents of the extra segment memory location addressed by DI.

15. The string compare (CMPS) instruction compares the byte or word contents of two sections of memory. One section is addressed by DI, in the extra segment, and the other by SI, in the data segment.

16. The SCAS and CMPS instruction repeat with the REPE or REPNE prefixes. The REPE prefix repeats the string instruction while an equal condition exists, and the REPNE repeats the string instruction while an unequal condition exists.

4–8 QUESTIONS AND PROBLEMS

1. Select an ADD instruction that will:
   a. add BX to AX
   b. add 12H to AL
   c. add DI and BP
   d. add 22H to CX
   e. add the data addressed by SI to AL
   f. add CX to the data stored at memory location FROG

2. What is wrong with the ADD CL,AX instruction?

3. Is it possible to add CX to DS with the ADD instruction?

4. If AX = 1001H and DX = 20FFH, list the sum and the contents of each flag register bit after the ADD AX,DX instruction executes.

5. Develop a short sequence of instructions that adds AL, BL, CL, DL, and AH. Save the sum in the DH register.

6. Develop a short sequence of instructions that adds AX, BX, CX, DX, and SP. Save the sum in the DI register.

7. Select an instruction that adds BX to DX and that also adds the contents of the carry flag (CF) to the result.
8. Choose an instruction that adds a 1 to the contents of the SP register.
9. What is wrong with the INC [BX] instruction?
10. Select a SUB instruction that will:
    a. subtract BX from CX
    b. subtract 0EEH from DH
    c. subtract DI from SI
    d. subtract 3322H from SP
    e. subtract the data addressed by SI from CH
    f. subtract the data stored 10 words after the location addressed by SI from DX
    g. subtract AL from memory location FROG
11. If DL = 0F3H and BH = 72H, list the difference after BH subtracts from DL and show the contents of the flag register bits.
12. Write a short sequence of instructions that subtract the numbers in DI, SI, and BP from the AX register. Store the difference in register BX.
13. Choose an instruction that subtracts 1 from register BL.
14. Explain what the SBB [DI + 4],DX instruction accomplishes.
15. Explain the difference between a SUB and a CMP instruction.
16. When two 8-bit numbers multiply, in which register is the product found?
17. When two 16-bit numbers multiply, in which two registers is the product found? Show which register contains the most and least significant portions of the product.
18. When two numbers multiply, what happens to the OF and CF flag bits?
19. What is the difference between the IMUL and MUL instruction?
20. Write a sequence of instructions that will cube the 8-bit number found in DL, assuming DL contains a 5 initially. Make sure your result is a 16-bit number.
21. Describe the operation of the IMUL BX,DX,100H instruction.
22. When 8-bit numbers divide, in which register is the dividend found?
23. When two 16-bit numbers divide, in which register is the quotient found?
24. What type of errors are detected during division by the 80286 microprocessor?
25. Explain the difference between the IDIV and DIV instructions.
26. Where is the remainder found after an 8-bit division?
27. Write a short sequence of instructions that will divide the number in BL by the number in CL and then multiply the result by 2. The first answer must be a 16-bit number stored in the DX register.
28. What instructions are used with BCD arithmetic operations?
29. What instructions are used with ASCII arithmetic operations?
30. Explain how the AAM instruction converts from binary to BCD.
31. Develop a sequence of instructions that adds the 8-digit BCD number in AX and BX to the 8-digit BCD number in CX and DX. (AX and CX are the most-significant registers. The result must be found in CX and DX after the addition.)
32. Select an AND instruction that will:
    a. AND BX with DX and save the result in BX
    b. AND 0EAH with DH

    c. AND DI with BP and save the result in DI

    d. AND 1122H with AX

    e. AND the data addressed by BP with CX and save the result in memory

    f. AND the data stored in four words before the location addressed by SI with DX and save the result in DX

    g. AND AL with memory location WHAT and save the result at location WHAT

33. Develop a short sequence of instructions that will clear the three leftmost bits of DH without changing DH and store the result in BH.

34. Select an OR instruction that will:

    a. OR BL with AH and save the result in AH

    b. OR 88H with CX

    c. OR DX with SI and save the result in SI

    d. OR 1122H with BP

    e. OR the data addressed by BX with CX and save the result in memory

    f. OR the data stored 40 bytes after the location addressed by BP with AL and save the result in AL

    g. OR AH with memory location WHEN and save the result in WHEN

35. Develop a short sequence of instructions that will set the rightmost five bits of DI without changing DI. Save the result in SI.

36. Select the XOR instruction that will:

    a. XOR BH with AH and save the result in AH

    b. XOR 99H with CL

    c. XOR DX with DI and save the result in DX

    d. XOR 1A23H with SP

    e. XOR the data addressed by BX with DX and save the result in memory

    f. XOR the data stored 30 words after the location addressed by BP with DI and save the result in DI

    g. XOR DI with memory location WELL and save the result in DI

37. Develop a sequence of instructions that will set the rightmost four bits of AX, clear the leftmost three bits of AX, and invert bits 7, 8, and 9 of AX.

38. Describe the difference between AND and TEST.

39. Select an instruction that tests bit position 2 of register CH.

40. What is the difference between a NOT and a NEG?

41. Select the correct instruction to perform each of the following tasks:

    a. shift DI right three places with zeros moved into the leftmost bit

    b. move all bits in AL left one place, making sure that a 0 moves into the rightmost bit position

    c. rotate all the bits of AL left 3 places

    d. rotate carry right one place through DX

    e. move the DH register right one place, making sure that the sign of the result is the same as the sign of the original number

42. What does the SCASB instruction accomplish?

43. For string instructions, DI always addresses data in the _____ segment.

44. What is the purpose of the DF flag bit?

45. Explain what the REPE prefix does.
46. What condition or conditions will terminate the repeated string instruction REPNE SCASB?
47. Describe what the CMPSB instruction accomplishes.
48. Develop a sequence of instructions that will scan through a 300H byte section of memory called LIST searching for a 66H.

CHAPTER 5

Program Control Instructions

INTRODUCTION

The program control instructions direct the flow of a program. Program control instructions allow the flow of the program to change. These changes in flow occur after decisions made with the CMP or TEST instruction followed by a conditional jump instruction. This chapter explains all the program control instructions, including jumps, calls, returns, interrupts, and machine control instructions.

The operation of the 80286 microprocessor in protected mode is also completely explained in this chapter. Described are the internal registers and various other structures that apply to protected mode operation. We show how to define descriptors and descriptor tables and how to switch from real mode operation to protected mode operation.

OBJECTIVES

Upon completion of this chapter, you will be able to:

1. Use both conditional and unconditional jump instructions to control the flow of a program.
2. Use the call and return instructions to include procedures in the program structure.
3. Explain the operation of the interrupts and interrupt control instructions.
4. Explain the operation of the 80286 in protected mode.
5. Use machine control instructions to modify the flag bits.
6. Detail the function of the descriptor, task state segment, and gate for protected mode operation of the 80286 microprocessor.
7. Show how the 80286 defines the descriptor tables and performs the switch to protected mode operation.

5–1   ## THE JUMP GROUP

The main type of program control instruction, the jump (JMP), allows the programmer to skip sections of a program and branch to any part of the memory for the next instruction. The conditional jump instructions allow the programmer to make decisions based upon numerical tests. The results of these numerical tests are held in the flag bits, which are tested by the conditional jump instructions.

In this section of the text, we cover all jump instructions and illustrate their use with sample programs. We also revisit the LOOP and conditional LOOP instructions, first presented in Chapter 3, because they are also forms of the jump instruction.

Unconditional Jump (JMP)

Three types of unconditional jump instructions (refer to Figure 5–1) are available in the 80286 microprocessor's instruction set: short jump, near jump, and far jump. The *short jump* is a 2-byte instruction that allows jumps or branches to memory locations within +127 and −128 bytes from the memory location following the jump. The 3-byte *near jump* allows a branch or jump within ±32K bytes (anywhere) from the instruction in the current code segment. Finally, the 5-byte *far jump* allows a jump to any memory location within the entire memory system. The short and near jumps are often called *intrasegment jumps,* and the far jumps are often called *intersegment jumps.*

Short Jump.   Short jumps are called *relative jumps* because they can be moved anywhere in memory without a change. This is because an address is *not* stored with the opcode. Instead of an address, a distance or *displacement* follows the opcode. The short jump displacement is a *distance* represented by a 1-byte signed number whose value ranges between +127 and −128. The short jump instruction appears in Figure 5–2. When the 80286 executes a short jump, the displacement sign-extends and

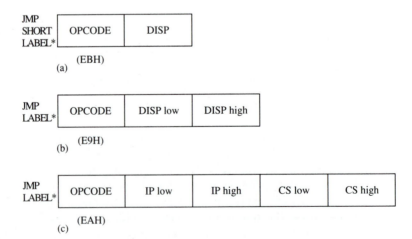

*Label in label field appears as LABEL:

FIGURE 5–1   The types of jump instructions. (a) Short JMP (2 bytes), (b) near JMP (3 bytes), and (c) far JMP (5 bytes).

FIGURE 5–2 A short JMP to four memory locations beyond the address of the next instruction. (Note that this will skip the next 4 bytes of memory.)

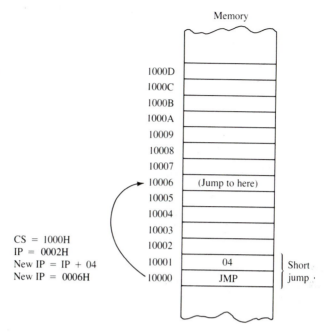

adds to the instruction pointer (IP) to generate the jump address within the current code segment. The short jump instruction branches to this new address for the next instruction in the program.

EXAMPLE 5–1

```
0000  33 DB                 XOR    BX,BX

0002  B8 0001    START:     MOV    AX,1
0005  03 C3                 ADD    AX,BX
0007  EB 17                 JMP    SHORT NEXT


0020  8B D8      NEXT:      MOV    BX,AX
0022  EB DE                 JMP    START
```

Example 5–1 shows how short jump instructions pass control from one part of the program to another. It also illustrates the use of a label with the jump instruction. Notice how one jump (JMP SHORT NEXT) uses the SHORT directive to force a short jump, while the other does not. The assembler chooses the best form of the jump instruction so the second (JMP START) jump instruction also assembles as a short jump. If we add the address of the next instruction (0009H) to the sign-extended displacement (0017H) of the first jump, the address of NEXT is location 0017H + 0009H or 0020H.

Whenever a jump instruction references an address, a *label* identifies the address. The JMP NEXT is an example, which jumps to label NEXT for the next

FIGURE 5–3 A near JMP, which adds the displacement to the contents of the IP register.

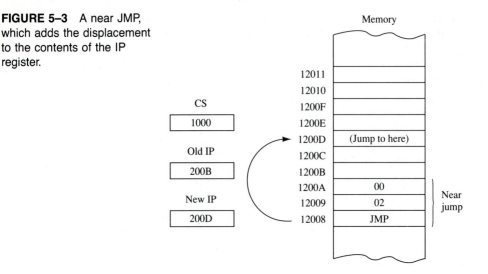

instruction. We never use an actual hexadecimal address with any jump instruction. The label NEXT must be followed by a colon (NEXT:) to allow an instruction to reference it for a jump. If a colon does not follow a label, you cannot jump to it.

Near Jump.   The near jump is similar to the short jump except the distance is farther. A near jump passes control to an instruction in the current code segment located within ±32K bytes from the near jump instruction. The near jump is a 3-byte instruction that contains an opcode followed by a signed 16-bit displacement. The signed displacement adds to the IP to generate the jump address. Because the signed displacement is in the range of ±32K, a near jump can jump to *any* memory location within the current code segment. Figure 5–3 illustrates the operation of the near jump instruction.

The near jump is also relocatable as was the short jump because it is also a *relative* jump. If the code segment moves to a new location in the memory, the distance between the jump instruction and the operand address remains the same. This allows a code segment to be relocated by moving it. This feature, with the relocatable data segments, makes the Intel family of microprocessors ideal for use in a general-purpose computer system. Software can be written and loaded anywhere in the memory and it functions without modification because of the relative jumps and relocatable data segments. This feature is true of very few other microprocessors.

EXAMPLE 5–2

```
0000 33 DB                    XOR    BX,BX

0002 B8 0001      START:      MOV    AX,1
0005 03 C3                    ADD    AX,BX
0007 E9 0200 R               JMP    NEXT

0200 8B D8        NEXT:       MOV    BX,AX
0202 E9 0002 R               JMP    START
```

Example 5–2 shows the same basic program that appeared in Example 5–1, except the jump distance is greater. The first jump (JMP NEXT) passes control to the instruction at memory location 0200H within the code segment. Notice that the instruction assembles as an E9 0200 R, the letter R denoting the relocatable jump address of 0200H. The relocatable address of 0200H is for the assembler's internal use only. The actual machine language instruction assembles as an E9 F6 01, which *does not* appear in the assembler listing. The actual displacement is a 01F6H for this jump instruction. The assembler lists the actual jump address as 0200 R so the address is easier to interpret as we develop software. If we were to view the linked execution file in hexadecimal, we would see this jump has assembled as an E9 F6 01.

Far Jump. Far jumps (see Figure 5–4) obtain a new segment and offset address to accomplish the jump. Bytes 2 and 3 of this 5-byte instruction contain the new offset address, and bytes 4 and 5 contain the new segment address.

EXAMPLE 5–3

```
                              EXTRN    UP:FAR

0000  33 DB                   XOR      BX,BX

0002  B8 0001       START:    MOV      AX,1
0005  03 C3                   ADD      AX,BX
0007  E9 0200 R               JMP      NEXT


0200  8B D8         NEXT:     MOV      BX,AX
0202  EA 0002 ---- R          JMP      FAR PTR START

0207  EA 0000 ---- E          JMP      UP
```

Example 5–3 lists a short program that uses a far jump instruction. The far jump instruction sometimes appears with the FAR PTR directive as illustrated. Another way to obtain a far jump is to define a label as a far label. A label is far only if it is external to the current code segment. The JMP UP instruction in the example references a far label. The label UP is defined as a far label by the EXTRN UP:FAR directive. External labels appear in programs that contain more than one program file.

When the program files are joined, the linker inserts the address for the UP label into the JMP UP instruction. It also inserts the segment address in the JMP START instruction. The segment address in JMP FAR PTR START is listed as ---- R for relocatable, and the segment address in JMP UP is listed as ---- E for external. In both cases the ---- is filled in by the linker when it links or joins the program files.

Jumps with Register Operands. The jump instruction also can specify a 16-bit register as an operand. This automatically sets up the instruction as an indirect jump. The address of the jump is in the register specified by the jump instruction. Unlike the

TABLE 5–1   Conditional jump instructions

Instruction	Condition Tested	Comment
JA	CF = 0 and ZF ≠ 0	Jump above
JAE	CF = 0	Jump above or equal to
JB	CF = 1	Jump below
JBE	CF = 1 or ZF = 1	Jump below or equal to
JC	CF = 1	Jump carry set
JE or JZ	ZF = 1	Jump equal to or jump zero
JG	ZF = 0 and SF = OF	Jump greater than
JGE	SF = OF	Jump greater than or equal to
JL	SF ≠ OF	Jump less than
JLE	ZF = 1 or SF ≠ OF	Jump less than or equal to
JNC	CF = 0	Jump carry cleared
JNE or JNZ	ZF = 0	Jump not equal to or jump not zero
JNO	OF = 0	Jump no overflow
JNS	SF = 0	Jump no sign
JNP/JPO	PF = 0	Jump no parity/jump parity odd
JO	OF = 1	Jump on overflow
JP/JPE	PF = 1	Jump on parity/jump parity even
JS	SF = 1	Jump on sign
JCXZ	CX = 0	Jump if CX = 0

Because we use both signed and unsigned numbers, and the order of these numbers is different, there are two sets of magnitude-comparison conditional jump instructions. Figure 5–5 shows the order of both signed and unsigned 8-bit numbers. The 16-bit numbers followed the same order as the 8-bit numbers except they are larger. Notice that an FFH is above the 00H in the set of unsigned numbers, but an FFH(-1) is less than 00H for signed numbers. Therefore, an unsigned FFH is *above* 00H, but a signed FFH is *less than* 00H.

FIGURE 5–5   Signed and unsigned numbers follow different orders.

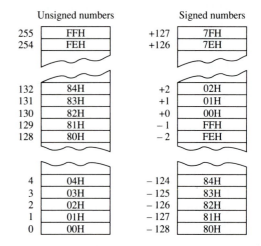

When we compare signed numbers, we use JG, JE, JGE, JLE, JE, and JNE. The terms *greater than* and *less than* refer to signed numbers. When we compare unsigned numbers, we use JA, JB, JAE, JBE, JE, and JNE. The terms *above* and *below* refer to unsigned numbers.

The remaining conditional jumps test individual flag bits such as overflow and parity. Notice that JE has an alternative opcode JZ. All instructions have alternates, but many aren't used in programming because they don't make much sense. (The alternates appear in Appendix B with the instruction set listing.) For example, the JA instruction (jump above) has the alternative JNBE (jump not below or equal). A JA functions exactly as a JNBE, but JNBE sounds and is awkward when compared to JA.

The most radical of the conditional jump instructions is JCXZ (jump if CX = 0). This is the only conditional jump instruction that does not test the flag bits. Instead, JCXZ directly tests the contents of the CX register without affecting the flag bits. If CX = 0, a jump occurs, and if CX ≠ 0, no jump occurs.

EXAMPLE 5–6

```
                    ;procedure that searches a table of 100 bytes
                    ;for a 0AH
                    ;
0000                SCAN    PROC  NEAR

0000 BE 0000 R              MOV   SI,OFFSET TABLE   ;address TABLE
0003 B9 0064                MOV   CX,100            ;load count
0006 B0 0A                  MOV   AL,0AH            ;load search data
0008 FC                     CLD
0009 F2/AE                  REPNE SCASB
000B E3 23                  JCXZ  NOT_FOUND
000D C3                     RET

000E                SCAN    ENDP
```

A program that uses JCXZ appears in Example 5–6. Here the SCASB instruction searches a table for a 0AH. Following the search, a JCXZ instruction tests CX to see if the count has become zero. If the count is zero, the 0AH is not found in the table. Another method used to test to see if the data are found is the JNE instruction. If JNE replaces JCXZ, it performs the same function. After the SCASB instruction executes, the flags indicate a not equal condition if the data was not found in the table.

LOOP

The LOOP instruction is a combination of a decrement CX and a conditional jump. It decrements CX and if CX ≠ 0, it jumps to the address indicated by the label. If CX becomes a 0, the next sequential instruction executes.

EXAMPLE 5-7

```
                                     ;procedure that adds word in BLOCK1 to BLOCK2
                                     ;
0000                     ADDS     PROC  NEAR

0000 B9 0064                       MOV   CX,100            ;load count
0003 BE 0064 R                     MOV   SI,OFFSET BLOCK1  ;address BLOCK1
0006 BF 0000 R                     MOV   DI,OFFSET BLOCK2  ;address BLOCK2

0009                     AGAIN:

0009 AD                            LODSW                   ;get BLOCK1 data
000A 26: 03 05                     ADD    AX,ES:[DI]       ;add BLOCK2 data
000D AB                            STOSW                   ;store in BLOCK2
000E E2 F9                         LOOP   AGAIN            ;repeat 100 times
0010 C3                            RET

0011                     ADDS     ENDP
```

Example 5–7 shows how data in one block of memory (BLOCK1) add to data in a second block of memory (BLOCK2) using LOOP to control how many numbers add. The LODSW and STOSW instructions access the data in BLOCK1 and BLOCK2. The ADD AX,ES:[DI] instruction accesses the data in BLOCK2 located in the extra segment. The only reason that BLOCK2 is in the extra segment is that DI addresses extra segment data for the STOSW instruction.

Conditional LOOPs.   As with REP, the LOOP instruction also has conditional forms: LOOPE and LOOPNE. The LOOPE (loop while equal) instruction jumps if CX ≠ 0 while an equal condition exists. It will exit the loop if the condition is not equal or if the CX register decrements to 0. The LOOPNE (loop while not equal) instruction jumps if CX ≠ 0 while a not equal condition exists. It will exit the loop if the condition is equal or if the CX register decrements to 0.

As with the conditional repeat instructions, alternates exist for LOOPE and LOOPNE. The LOOPE instruction is the same as LOOPZ and the LOOPNE is the same as LOOPNZ. In most programs only the LOOPE and LOOPNE apply.

5–2   PROCEDURES

The procedure or *subroutine* is an important part of any computer system's architecture. A *procedure* is a group of instructions that usually performs one task. A *procedure* is a reusable section of the software that is stored in memory once, but used as often as necessary. This saves memory space and makes it easier to develop software. The only disadvantage of a procedure is that it takes the computer a small amount of time to link to the procedure and return from it. The CALL instruction links to the procedure, and the RET instruction returns from the procedure.

The stack stores the return address whenever a procedure is called during the execution of a program. The CALL instruction pushes the address of the instruction following it on the stack. The RET instruction removes an address from the stack so the program returns to the instruction following the CALL.

EXAMPLE 5–8

```
0000                    SUMS    PROC  NEAR

0000  03 C3                     ADD   AX,BX
0002  03 C1                     ADD   AX,CX
0004  03 C2                     ADD   AX,DX
0006  C3                        RET

0007                    SUMS    ENDP

0007                    SUMS1   PROC  FAR

0007  03 C3                     ADD   AX,BX
0009  03 C1                     ADD   AX,CX
000B  03 C2                     ADD   AX,DX
000D  CB                        RET

000E                    SUMS1   ENDP
```

In the 80286 microprocessor's assembler, there are some finite rules for the storage of procedures. A procedure begins with the PROC directive and ends with the ENDP directive. Each directive appears with the name of the procedure. This structure makes it easy to locate the procedure in a program listing; for example, the PROC directive is followed by the type of procedure: NEAR or FAR. Example 5–8 shows how the assembler requires the definition of both a near (intrasegment) and far (intersegment) procedure.

When we compare these two procedures, the only difference is the opcode of the return instruction. The near return instruction uses opcode C3H and the far return uses opcode CBH. A near return removes a 16-bit number from the stack and places it into the instruction pointer. A far return removes 32 bits from the stack and places them into both IP and CS.

Most procedures that are to be used by all software (*global*) should be written as far procedures. Procedures that are used by a given task (*local*) are normally defined as near procedures.

CALL

The CALL instruction transfers the flow of the program to the procedure. The CALL instruction differs from the jump instruction because a CALL saves a return address on the stack. The return address returns control to the instruction that follows the CALL in a program when a RET instruction executes.

Near CALL. The near CALL instruction is 3 bytes long with the first byte containing the opcode and the second and third bytes containing the displacement or distance of ±32K. This is identical to the form of the near jump instruction. When the near

CALL executes, it first places the offset address of the next instruction on the stack. The offset address of the next instruction appears in the instruction pointer (IP). After saving this return address, it then adds the displacement from bytes 2 and 3 to the IP to transfer control to the procedure. There is no short CALL instruction.

Why save the IP on the stack? The instruction pointer always points to the next instruction in the program. For the CALL instruction, the contents of IP are pushed onto the stack so program control passes to the instruction following the CALL after a procedure ends. Figure 5–6 shows the return address (IP) stored on the stack, and the call to the procedure.

Far CALL.   The far CALL instruction is like a far jump because it can CALL a procedure stored in any memory location in the system. The far CALL is a 5-byte instruction that contains an opcode followed by the next value for the IP and CS registers. Bytes 2 and 3 contain the new contents of the IP and bytes 4 and 5 contain the new contents for CS.

The far CALL instruction places the contents of both IP and CS on the stack before jumping to the address indicated by bytes 2–5 of the instruction. This allows the far CALL to call a procedure located anywhere in the memory and return from that procedure.

Figure 5–7 shows how the far CALL instruction calls a far procedure. Here the contents of IP and CS are pushed onto the stack. Next the program branches to the procedure.

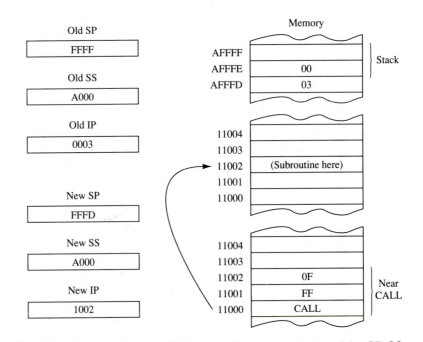

FIGURE 5–6   The effect of a near CALL instruction on the stack and the SP, SS, and IP registers. Notice how the old IP is stored on the stack.

FIGURE 5–7 The far CALL instruction.

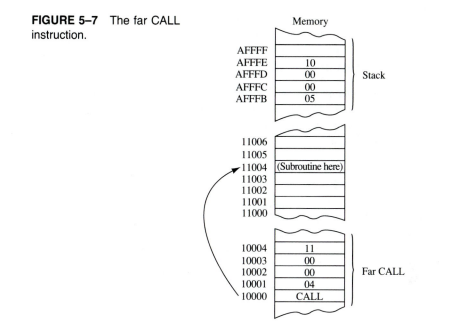

CALLs with Register Operands. Like jumps, CALLs can also contain a register operand. An example is the CALL BX instruction. This instruction pushes the contents of IP onto the stack. It then jumps to the offset address, located in register BX, in the current code segment. This type of CALL always uses a 16-bit offset address stored in any 16-bit register except the segment registers.

EXAMPLE 5–9

```
                        ;calling sequence
                        ;
0000  BE 0005 R                 MOV    SI,OFFSET COMP
0003  FF D6                     CALL   SI

                        ;
                        ;procedure COMP
                        ;
0005                    COMP     PROC   NEAR


0005  52                        PUSH   DX
0006  BA 03F8                   MOV    DX,03F8H
0009  EC                        IN     AL,DX
000A  42                        INC    DX
000B  EE                        OUT    DX,AL
000C  5A                        POP    DX
000D  C3                        RET


000E                    COMP     ENDP
```

Example 5–9 illustrates the use of the CALL register instruction to call a procedure that begins at offset address COMP. The OFFSET address COMP moves into the SI register, and then the CALL SI instruction calls the procedure beginning at address COMP.

CALLs with Indirect Memory Addresses.   The CALL with an indirect memory address is particularly useful whenever we need to choose different subroutines in a program. This selection process is often keyed with a number that addresses a CALL address in a lookup table.

EXAMPLE 5–10

```
                        ;lookup table
                        ;
0000  0100 R            TABLE   DW      ONE
0002  0200 R                    DW      TWO
0004  0300 R                    DW      THREE
                        ;
                        ;calling sequence
                        ;
0006  4B                        DEC     BX              ;scale BX
0007  03 DB                     ADD     BX,BX           ;double BX
0009  BF 0000 R                 MOV     DI,OFFSET TABLE ;address TABLE
000C  2E: FF 11                 CALL    CS:[BX+DI]
                        ;
                        ;procedures
                        ;
0100                    ONE     PROC    NEAR
                           .       .
                           .       .
0100                    ONE     ENDP

0200                    TWO     PROC    NEAR
                           .       .
                           .       .
0200                    TWO     ENDP

0300                    THREE   PROC    NEAR
                           .       .
                           .       .
0300                    THREE   ENDP
```

Example 5–10 shows three separate subroutines referenced by the numbers 1, 2, and 3 in AL. The calling sequence adjusts the value of AL and extends it to a 16-bit number before adding it to the location of the lookup table. This references one of the three subroutines using the CALL CS:[BX + DI] instruction. The CS: prefix appears before the CALL instruction's operand because the TABLE is in the code segment in this example.

The CALL instruction also can reference far pointers if the instruction appears as a CALL FAR PTR [SI]. This instruction retrieves a 32-bit address from the data segment memory location addressed by SI and uses it as the address of a far procedure.

RET

The return instruction (RET) removes either a 16-bit number (near return) from the stack and places it into IP or a 32-bit number (far return) and places it into IP and CS. The near and far return instructions are both defined in the procedure's PROC directive. This automatically selects the proper return instruction.

When IP or IP and CS are changed, the address of the next instruction is at a new memory location. This new location is the address of the instruction that immediately follows the most recent CALL to a procedure. Figure 5–8 shows how the CALL instruction links to a procedure and how the RET instruction returns.

There is one other form of the return instruction. This form adds a number to the contents of the stack pointer (SP) before the return. If the pushes must be deleted before a return, a 16-bit displacement adds to the SP before the return retrieves the return address from the stack. The effect of this is to delete stack data, or skip stack data.

EXAMPLE 5–11

```
0000                    TESTS     PROC  NEAR

0000 50                           PUSH  AX
0001 53                           PUSH  BX
                                  .     .
                                  .     .
0030 C2 0004                      RET   4

0033                    TESTS     ENDP
```

Example 5–11 shows how this type of return erases the data placed on the stack by a few pushes. The RET 4 adds a 4 to SP before removing the return address from

FIGURE 5–8 A short program and subroutine that illustrates the linkage between the program and the subroutine with the CALL and RET instructions.

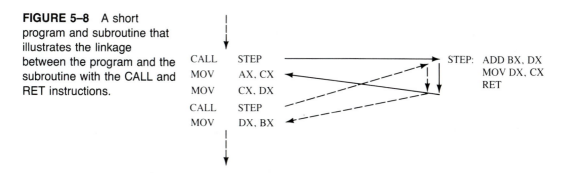

the stack. Since the PUSH AX and PUSH BX together place 4 bytes of data on the stack, this return effectively deletes AX and BX from the stack. This type of return appears rarely in programs.

5–3   INTRODUCTION TO INTERRUPTS

An *interrupt* is either a hardware-generated CALL (externally derived from a signal) or a software-generated CALL (internally derived from an instruction). Either will interrupt the program by calling an *interrupt service procedure* or *interrupt handler*.

We describe hardware interrupts in Chapter 10. This section explains software interrupts, which are special types of CALL instructions in the 80286 microprocessor. We cover the three types of software interrupt instructions (INT, INTO, and INT 3), provide a map of the interrupt vectors, and explain the purpose of the special interrupt return instruction (IRET).

Interrupt Vectors

An *interrupt vector* is a 4-byte number stored in the first 1,024 bytes of the memory (000000H–0003FFH). There are 256 different interrupt vectors, each of which contains the address of an *interrupt service procedure*—the procedure called by an interrupt. Table 5–2 lists the interrupt vectors with a brief description and the memory location of each vector. Each vector contains a value for IP and CS that forms the address of the interrupt service procedure. The first two bytes contain the IP and the last two bytes contain the CS.

Intel reserves the first 32 interrupt vectors for the 80286 and future products. The remaining interrupt vectors (32–255) are available for the user. Some reserved

TABLE 5–2   Interrupt vectors

Number	Address	Function
0	0H–3H	Divide error
1	4H–7H	Single step
2	8H–BH	NMI (hardware interrupt)
3	CH–FH	Breakpoint
4	10H–13H	Interrupt on overflow
5	14H–17H	BOUND interrupt
6	18H–1BH	Invalid opcode
7	1CH–1FH	Coprocessor emulation interrupt
8–15	20H–3FH	Reserved*
16	40H–43H	Coprocessor error
17–31	44H–7FH	Reserved*
32–255	80H–3FFH	User interrupts

*Some of these interrupts appear on newer versions of the 80286, such as the 80386 and 80486.

vectors are for errors that occur during the execution of software such as the divide error interrupt. Some vectors are reserved for the coprocessor. Still others occur for normal events in the system.

Interrupt Instructions

The 80286 has three different interrupt instructions available to the programmer: INT, INTO, and INT 3. Each of these instructions fetches a vector from the vector table and then calls the procedure stored at the location addressed by the vector. The interrupt call is similar to a far CALL instruction because it places the return address (IP and CS) on the stack. The difference is that it also places a copy of the flag register on the stack.

INTs. There are 256 different software interrupt instructions (INT) available to the programmer. Each INT instruction has a numeric operand whose range is 0 to 255 (00H–FFH). For example, the INT 100 uses interrupt vector 100, which appears at memory address 190H–193H. We calculate the address of the interrupt vector by multiplying the interrupt-type number times four. For example, the INT 10H instruction calls the interrupt service procedure whose address is stored beginning at memory location 40H (10H × 4).

Each INT instruction is two bytes in length. The first byte contains the opcode, and the second byte contains the vector-type number. The only exception to this is INT 3, a 1-byte special software interrupt used for breakpoints.

Whenever a software interrupt instruction executes, it (1) pushes the flags onto the stack, (2) clears the TF and IF flag bits, (3) pushes CS onto the stack, (4) fetches the new value for CS from the vector, (5) pushes IP onto the stack, (6) fetches the new value for IP from the vector, and (7) jumps to the new location addressed by CS and IP. The INT instruction performs as a far CALL except that it not only pushes CS and IP onto the stack, but it also pushes the flags onto the stack. The INT instruction is a combination PUSHF and far CALL instruction.

Notice that when the INT instruction executes, it clears the interrupt flag (IF), which controls the external hardware interrupt input pin INTR (interrupt request). When IF = 0, the microprocessor disables the INTR pin, and when IF = 1, the microprocessor enables the INTR pin. We discuss the purpose of the TF flag bit in Chapter 9.

Software interrupts are most commonly used to call system procedures. The system procedures are common to all system and application software. The interrupts often control printers, video displays, and disk drives. The INT instruction replaces a far CALL because the INT instruction is 2 bytes in length, where the far CALL is 5 bytes. Each time that the INT instruction replaces a far CALL it saves 3 bytes of memory in a program. This can amount to a sizable savings if the INT instruction appears often in a program.

IRET. The interrupt return instruction (IRET) is used only with software or hardware interrupt service procedures. Unlike a simple return instruction (RET), the IRET instruction will (1) pop stack data back into the IP, (2) pop stack data back into CS, and (3) pop stack data back into the flag register. The IRET instruction accomplishes the same tasks as the POPF and RET instructions.

Whenever an IRET instruction executes it restores the contents of IF and TF from the stack. This is important because it preserves the state of these flag bits. If interrupts were enabled before an interrupt service procedure, they are *automatically* reenabled by the IRET instruction because it restores the flag register.

INT 3.   An INT 3 instruction is a special software interrupt designed to be used as a breakpoint. The difference between it and the other software interrupts is that INT 3 is a 1-byte instruction, while the others are 2-byte instructions.

It is common to insert an INT 3 instruction in software to interrupt or break the flow of the software. This function is called a *breakpoint*. A breakpoint occurs for any software interrupt, but because INT 3 is 1 byte long, it is easier to use for this function. Breakpoints help to debug software.

INTO.   Interrupt on overflow (INTO) is a conditional software interrupt that tests the overflow flag (OF). If OF = 0, the INTO instruction performs no operation, but if OF = 1 and an INTO instruction executes, an interrupt occurs via vector-type number 4.

The INTO instruction appears in software that adds or subtracts signed binary numbers. With these operations it is possible to have an overflow. Either the JO instruction or INTO instruction detects the overflow condition.

An Interrupt Service Procedure.   Suppose that, in a particular system, we must add the contents of DI, SI, BP, and BX and save the sum in AX. Because this is a common task in this system, it is worthwhile to develop the task as a software interrupt. Example 5–12 shows this software interrupt. The main difference between this procedure and a normal far procedure is that it ends with the IRET instruction instead of the RET instruction.

EXAMPLE 5–12

```
0000                    INTS      PROC  FAR

0000  03 C3                       ADD   AX,BX
0002  03 C5                       ADD   AX,BP
0004  03 C7                       ADD   AX,DI
0006  03 C6                       ADD   AX,SI
0008  CF                          IRET

0009                    INTS      ENDP
```

Interrupt Control

Although this section does not explain hardware interrupts, we introduce two instructions that control the INTR pin. The set interrupt flag instruction (STI) places a 1 into IF, which enables the INTR pin. The clear interrupt flag instruction (CLI) places a 0 into IF, which disables the INTR pin. The STI instruction enables INTR and the CLI instruction disables INTR.

| 5–4 | ## MACHINE CONTROL AND MISCELLANEOUS INSTRUCTIONS |

The last category of real mode instructions found in the 80286 microprocessor is the machine control and miscellaneous instructions group. These instructions provide control of the carry bit, sample the $\overline{\text{BUSY}}$ pin, and perform various other functions. Because most of these instructions are used in hardware control, they need only be explained briefly at this point. We cover most of these instructions in more detail in later chapters that deal with the hardware.

Controlling the Carry Flag Bit

The carry flag (CF) propagates the carry or borrow in multiple-word addition and subtraction. It also indicates errors in procedures. There are three instructions that control the contents of the carry flag: STC (*set carry*), CLC (*clear carry*), and CMC (*complement carry*).

Because the carry flag is seldom used, except with multiple-word addition and subtraction, it is available for other uses. The most common task for the carry flag is to indicate error upon return from a procedure. Suppose that a procedure reads data from a disk memory file. This operation can be successful or an error can occur such as file-not-found. Upon return from this procedure, if CF = 1, an error has occurred, and if CF = 0, no error has occurred.

WAIT

The WAIT instruction monitors the hardware $\overline{\text{BUSY}}$ pin. If the WAIT instruction executes while the $\overline{\text{BUSY}}$ pin = 0, nothing happens and the next instruction executes. If the $\overline{\text{BUSY}}$ pin = 1 when the WAIT instruction executes, the microprocessor waits for the $\overline{\text{BUSY}}$ pin to return to a logic 0.

The $\overline{\text{BUSY}}$ pin of the 80286 is most often connected to the $\overline{\text{BUSY}}$ pin of the 80287 numeric coprocessor. This connection, with the WAIT instruction, allows the 80286 to wait until the coprocessor finishes a task.

HLT

The halt instruction (HLT) stops the execution of software. There are only three ways to exit a halt: by an interrupt, by a hardware reset, or during a DMA operation. This instruction normally appears in a program to wait for an interrupt. It often synchronizes external hardware interrupts with the software system.

NOP

When the 80286 microprocessor encounters a no operation instruction (NOP), it takes three clocking periods to execute. A NOP performs absolutely no operation and often pads software with space for future machine language instructions. If you are developing machine language programs, we recommend that you place NOPs into your program at 50-byte intervals. This is done in case you need to add instructions at some future point. A NOP also finds application in time delays to waste three clocking periods.

LOCK Prefix

The LOCK prefix appends an instruction and causes the $\overline{\text{LOCK}}$ pin to become a logic 0. The $\overline{\text{LOCK}}$ pin often disables external bus masters or other system components. The LOCK prefix causes the lock pin to activate for the duration of a locked instruction. If we lock more than one sequential instruction, the $\overline{\text{LOCK}}$ pin remains a logic 0 for the duration of the sequence of locked instruction. The LOCK:MOV AL,[SI] instruction is an example of a locked instruction.

ESC

The escape (ESC) instruction passes information to the 80287 coprocessor. Whenever an ESC instruction executes, the 80286 microprocessor addresses memory, if required, but otherwise performs a NOP. The 80287 uses 6 bits of the ESC instruction to obtain its opcode and begin executing a coprocessor instruction.

The ESC opcode never appears in a program. In its place are a set of coprocessor instructions (FLD, FST, FMUL, etc.) that assemble as ESC instructions for the coprocessor. We provide more details in the chapter that discusses the 80287 coprocessor.

BOUND

The BOUND instruction is a compare instruction that can cause an interrupt (vector-type number 5) to occur. This instruction compares the contents of any 16-bit register against the contents of two words of memory: an upper and a lower boundary. If the value in the register compared with memory is *not* within the upper and lower boundary, a type-5 interrupt follows. If it is within the boundary, the next instruction in the program executes.

If the BOUND SI,DATA instruction executes, word-sized location DATA contains the lower boundary and word-sized location DATA + 2 contains the upper boundary. If the number contained in SI is less than memory location DATA or greater than memory location DATA + 2, a type-5 interrupt occurs. Note that when this interrupt occurs the return address points to the BOUND instruction, not the instruction following BOUND.

ENTER and LEAVE

The ENTER and LEAVE instructions are used with stack frames. A stack frame is a mechanism used to pass parameters to a procedure through the stack memory. The stack frame also holds local memory variables for the procedure. Stack frames provide dynamic areas of memory for procedures.

The ENTER instruction creates a stack frame by pushing BP onto the stack and then loading BP with the uppermost address of the stack frame. This allows stack frame variables to be accessed through the BP register. The ENTER instruction contains two operands: the number of bytes to reserve for variables on the stack frame and the level of the procedure.

Suppose that an ENTER 8,0 instruction executes. This instruction reserves 8 bytes of memory for the stack frame, where the zero specifies level 0. Figure 5–9

FIGURE 5–9 A stack frame generated by the ENTER 8,0 instruction. The BP register is stored beginning at the top of the stack frame. This is followed by an 8-byte area called a stack frame.

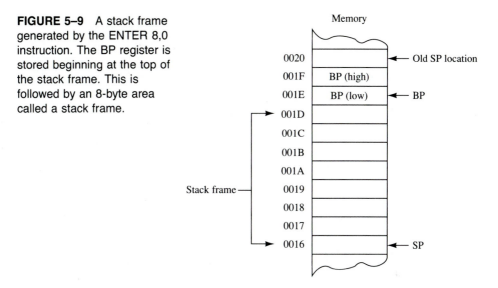

shows the stack frame set up for this instruction. Note that this instruction stores BP onto the top of the stack. It then subtracts 8 from the stack pointer, leaving 8 bytes of memory space for temporary data storage. The uppermost location of this 8-byte temporary storage area is addressed by BP. The LEAVE instruction reverses this process by reloading both SP and BP with their prior values.

EXAMPLE 5–13

```
                          ;sequence used to call system software that
                          ;uses paramters stored in a stack frame
                          ;
0000  C8 0004 00          ENTER  4,0           ;create 4 byte frame

0004  A1 00C8 R           MOV    AX,DATA1
0007  89 46 FC            MOV    [BP-4],AX      ;save para 1
000A  A1 00CA R           MOV    AX,DATA2
000D  89 46 FE            MOV    [BP-2],AX      ;save para 2

0010  E8 0100 R           CALL   SYS            ;call subroutine

0013  8B 46 FC            MOV    AX,[BP-4]      ;get result 1
0016  A3 00C8 R           MOV    DATA1,AX       ;save result 1
0019  8B 46 FE            MOV    AX,[BP-2]      ;get result 2
001C  A3 00CA R           MOV    DATA2,AX       ;save result 2

001F  C9                  LEAVE
                            .      .
                            .      .
```

```
                              (other software continues here)
                                  .        .
                                      .        .
                              ;system subroutine that uses the stack frame parameters
                              ;
0100                  SYS     PROC  NEAR

0100 60                       PUSHA

0101 8B 46 FC                 MOV   AX,[BP-4]          ;get para 1
0104 8B 5E FE                 MOV   BX,[BP-2]          ;get para 2
                                  .
                                  .        .
                              (software that uses the parameters)
                                  .        .
                                  .        .
0130 89 46 FC                 MOV   [BP-4],AX          ;save result 1
0133 89 5E FE                 MOV   [BP-2],BX          ;save result 2

0136 61                       POPA
0137 C3                       RET

0138                  SYS     ENDP
```

Example 5–13 shows how the ENTER instruction creates a stack frame so two 16-bit parameters can be passed to a system level procedure. Notice how the ENTER and LEAVE instructions appear in this program, and how the parameters pass through the stack frame to and from the procedure. This procedure uses two parameters that pass to it and return two results through the stack frame.

5–5   80286 PROTECTED MODE OPERATION AND CONTROL

The 80286 operates in protected mode to access memory above location 0FFFFFH (the first 1M byte of memory). Protected mode operation also provides a scheme for protecting and limiting access to the entire memory system. This section completely describes access and control of the protected memory system afforded by protected mode operation.

Protected Mode Registers

Early in this text (Section 1–4) we briefly introduced protected mode operation and the machine status word (MSW). Although this was adequate for an understanding of protected mode operation and access to the upper 15M bytes of memory, it did not illustrate the instructions associated with protected mode or any of the registers.

Figure 5–10 illustrates the program-invisible portions of the segment registers used during protected mode operation and the program-invisible base and limit registers. In protected mode operation, each segment register contains a program-invisible

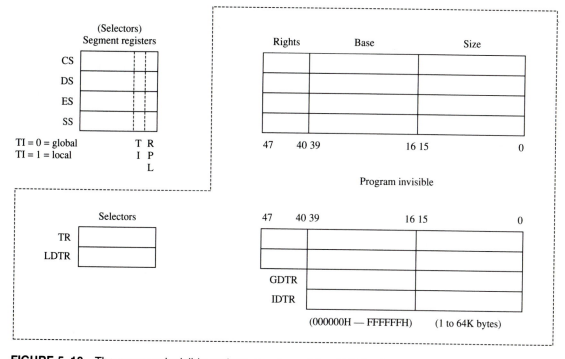

FIGURE 5–10 The program-invisible register structure of the 80286 microprocessor.

descriptor register that contains the size of the protected mode memory segment (1 to 64K bytes), location or base address (000000H–FFFFFFH), and access rights for the segment. This information is loaded from a descriptor table each time the selector located in the segment register changes. This means that the descriptor table is accessed only once each time the contents of the segment (selector) register changes.

Another set of program-invisible registers exists to address the global, local, and interrupt descriptor tables. Whenever the number in a segment register changes, the global or local descriptor registers locate the descriptor tables in the memory. Whenever an interrupt occurs, the microprocessor accesses the interrupt descriptor table to locate the interrupt service procedure, instead of the bottom 1K bytes of memory. This is different from real mode interrupts. This interrupt allows the operating system to completely control access to memory—for code, data, and the stack—and the system interrupts.

Suppose that a system operates in the protected mode and that the DS register changes to a 0008H. This uses the GDTR (global descriptor table register) to access descriptor number 1. In real mode, this number accesses memory location 00080H–1007FH. In the protected mode, the area of memory accessed by the 0008H in DS is determined by the descriptor in the GDT (global descriptor table) at descriptor number 1. The instant that DS loads with the 0008H, the microprocessor accesses the GDT and removes (in this case) descriptor 1 and places it into the program-invisible access rights, base address, and size section of the DS register as illustrated in Figure 5–10. The DS register now accesses the area of memory dictated by the descriptor. This can be at any area of the memory from location 000000H–FFFFFFH with any segment size from 1 byte to 64K bytes.

Placing Descriptors into the Global, Local, and Interrupt Descriptor Tables

Before we can switch to protected mode operation, the global (GDT), local (LDT), and interrupt (IDT) descriptor tables must be initialized. Both the global and local tables are each up to 64K bytes in length, while the interrupt descriptor table is 2K bytes in length. The local and global tables each contain up to 8K descriptors that are each 8 bytes in length. The interrupt descriptor table contains 256 descriptors, one for each interrupt type, that is each 8 bytes in length.

A series of three instructions load the descriptor table registers, which address the descriptor tables: LGDT (*load global descriptor table register*), LLDT (*load local descriptor table register*), and LIDT (*load interrupt descriptor table register*). These three instructions initialize the registers used to access each of these descriptor tables. Instructions that read these registers and store their contents in memory if required are SGDT, SLDT, and SIDT.

All 256 descriptors must be allocated for the interrupt descriptor table, while the global and local tables contain the number of descriptors required by a particular operating system or application. If all descriptors are allocated, then an overhead of 130K bytes of memory is required for the three tables and their descriptors. This memory overhead is needed if only one local descriptor table appears in the system. The 80286 allows up to 8K different local descriptor tables, with one local descriptor table active at a time.

The Data Structure.   Descriptors are often defined using the *data structure* available to the 80286 through the assembler program. We define the data structure by using the STRUC directive. The data structure is a template for storing memory data. A data structure makes it easier to set up a descriptor table entry for any of the different descriptor tables. A structure begins with the STRUC directive and ends with the ENDS directive. Associated with the STRUC directive is the name of the structure.

EXAMPLE 5–14

```
                       DES      STRUC                      ;structure for descriptor

0000 0000              LIM      DW      ?                  ;limit (size)
0002 0000              BASL     DW      ?                  ;Base B0—B15
0004 00                BASH     DB      ?                  ;base B16—B23
0005 00                RI       DB      ?                  ;access rights
0006 0000                       DW      0                  ;0000H

0008                   DES      ENDS
```

Example 5–14 shows a data structure template of any descriptor for the 80286 microprocessor. Here we call the structure DES for descriptor, which consists of DW directives that define the descriptor limit and descriptor base address. The DB directives follow, which define the remainder of the descriptor base and the access rights byte. The last DW defines the uppermost word of the descriptor as 0000H. This last word must be 0000H for upward compatibility with the 80386 and 80486 descriptors that use this word. A structure is used by the assembler to set up a template that is used to define an area of memory. The structure definition itself does not store data in the memory.

EXAMPLE 5–15

```
                    DES     STRUC                   ;structure for descriptor

0000 0000           LIM     DW      ?               ;limit (size)
0002 0000           BASL    DW      ?               ;Base B0—B15
0004 00             BASH    DB      ?               ;base B16—B23
0005 00             RI      DB      ?               ;access rights
0006 0000                   DW      0               ;0000H

0008                DES     ENDS

0000                DAT     SEGMENT                 ;data segment

0000 0000           LOC0    DES     <0,0,0,0,0>     ;descriptor 0
0002 0000
0004 00
0005 00
0006 0000

0008 0000           LOC1    DES     <0,0,0,0,0>     ;descriptor 1
000A 0000
000C 00
000D 00
000E 0000

0010 0000           LOC2    DES     <0,0,0,0,0>     ;descriptor 2
0012 0000
0014 00
0015 00
0016 0000

0020                DAT     ENDS
```

Example 5–15 shows how the structure sets up several descriptors in a section of the memory called LOCAL. Notice that the assembler uses the opcode DES to access the structure defined as DES. This sets up descriptors in the section of memory called LOCAL. The operand for a structure is always placed in <> symbols.

In this example, the first descriptor is defined with a LOC0 DES <0,0,0,0,0> statement. These five pieces of information <0,0,0,0,0> load the five DW and DB statements with data in the data segment (DAT). In this example all descriptor data initialize to 0.

EXAMPLE 5–16

```
                         DES       STRUC                    ;structure for descriptor

0000 0000                LIM       DW    ?                  ;limit (size)
0002 0000                BASL      DW    ?                  ;Base B0—B15
0004 00                  BASH      DB    ?                  ;base B16—B23
0005 00                  RI        DB    ?                  ;access rights
0006 0000                          DW    0                  ;0000H

0008                     DES       ENDS

0000                     DAT       SEGMENT                  ;data segment

0000 0000                LOC0      DES   <0,0,0,0,0>        ;descriptor 0
0002 0000
0004 00
0005 00
0006 0000

0008 0000                LOC1      DES   <0,0,0,0,0>        ;descriptor 1
000A 0000
000C 00
000D 00
000E 0000

0010 0000                LOC2      DES   <0,0,0,0,0>        ;descriptor 2
0012 0000
0014 00
0015 00
0016 0000

0020                     DAT       ENDS

0000                     CODE      SEGMENT

                                   ASSUME   CS:CODE,DS:DAT

0000                     MAIN      PROC  FAR

0000 C7 06 0008 R FFFF             MOV   LOC1.LIM,0FFFFH    ;load limit
0006 C7 06 000A R 0000             MOV   LOC1.BASL,0        ;load base low
000C C6 06 000C R 20               MOV   LOC1.BASH,20H      ;load base high
0011 B0 FC 90                      MOV   AL,ACC             ;load access rights
0014 A2 000D R                     MOV   LOC1.RI,AL

0017                     MAIN      ENDP

0017                     CODE      ENDS

                                   END   MAIN
```

Suppose the program that uses these descriptors must load them with different base, access rights, and limit information. How do we address these different fields within the structures? Example 5–16 shows how a new addressing mode (one that only applies to structures) initializes LOC1 with a limit or 0FFFFH (64K byte segment), an address of 200000H (for the start of the segment), and an access rights byte of ACC, defined elsewhere.

We address data in a structure by using the name of the structure followed by a period followed by the field we wish to address. In the example, the base address (low-order part) BASL of descriptor LOC1 is addressed as LOC1.BASL. Likewise the high part of the LOC1 descriptor is addressed as LOC1.BASH.

Descriptors and Gates

Before we can set up a protected mode operating system, the format of the descriptors and gates must be known. The 80286 contains descriptors that define code, data, and stack segments, and for system control. The system control descriptors are often called *descriptor gates* or just *gates*.

Code, Data, and Stack Descriptors.   These descriptors define memory segments that hold code, general data, and stack data. The general format for this descriptor appears in Figure 5–11. This is the same basic descriptor as defined in Section 1–4. Anytime that the segment registers access code, data, or the stack, we use this format of the descriptor to define the segment.

The limit is a 16-bit number that defines the last location of the segment and can indicate a segment with a length of 1 to 64K bytes. The base address is a 24-bit address broken into a 16-bit part (B0–B15) and an 8-bit part (B16–B23). The reserved word must contain a 0000H to be compatible with the 80386 and 80486 microprocessors. The access rights byte contains a P (present) bit, a DPL (descriptor

FIGURE 5–11   (a) The code, data, and stack descriptor. (b) The access rights byte.

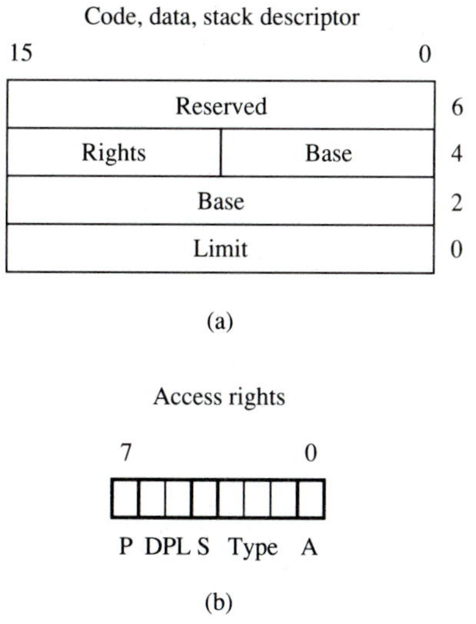

Code, data, stack descriptor

15		0	
Reserved			6
Rights		Base	4
Base			2
Limit			0

(a)

Access rights

7   0

P DPL S   Type   A

(b)

privilege level) field, an S (segment) bit, a type field, and an A (accessed) bit. These bits and fields function in the code, data, and stack descriptors as follows:

P (present): This bit indicates that the segment exists in the physical memory when a 1. If P = 0, the segment described by the descriptor does not exist in the memory system.

DPL (descriptor privilege level): This field contains a 00 for highest privilege level through 11 for the lowest privilege level. If the requested privilege level is lower than the DPL bits indicate, a type-13 interrupt occurs. For example, if DPL contains a 01, then the requested privilege levels 10 and 11 cause an interrupt, while levels 01 and 00 are allowed access to the descriptor.

S (segment): This bit must be a logic 1 for a code, data, or stack segment.

Type: This field indicates the type of code, data, or stack segment. Table 5–3 indicates the type of field definitions for this descriptor. Note that a conforming code segment is one that can be accessed by the same or any higher privilege level task. A nonconforming code segment is one that can only execute at the level defined by the DPL bits.

A (accessed): A 0 indicates that the segment has not been accessed, while a 1 indicates it has been accessed.

The typical data segment is type 001, which grows upward in the memory and can be written. This segment type is often referenced through the DS and ES selectors. The typical stack segment is type 011, which grows downward in the memory and can be written. This type is often referenced through the SS selector. Code segments are often type 110, which may not be read and conforms so the same or higher privilege levels can gain access. Code segments are usually referenced through the CS selector. Figure 5–12 shows how a few descriptors appear for various segment types.

With the data and code segments, the base address defines the start of the segment and the limit defines the last location of the segment. With the stack segment, the base address defines the start of the segment, but the limit defines the *bottom* location of the stack segment. If the base address for a stack segment is 200000H,

TABLE 5–3 Code, data, and stack segment descriptor-type field

Type	Function
000	Data segment type; grows upward; may not be written
001	Data segment type; grows upward; may be written
010	Data segment type; grows downward; may not be written
011	Data segment type; grows downward; may be written
100	Code segment type; may not be read
101	Code segment type; may be read
110	Code segment type; conforms; may not be read
111	Code segment type; conforms; may be read

FIGURE 5–12 (a) A data
segment located at
060700H–060A00H. (b) A
stack segment located at
060A00H–0706FFH. (c) A
code segment located at
02007DH–020823H.

Data segment descriptor

0 0 0 0
9 2 0 6
0 7 0 0
0 3 0 0

(a)

Stack segment descriptor

0 0 0 0
9 6 0 6
0 7 0 0
0 3 0 0

(b)

Code segment descriptor

0 0 0 0
9 E 0 2
0 0 7 D
0 7 A 6

(c)

the segment range is 200000H–20FFFFH. If the limit is 7000H, the top of the stack
is location 20FFFFH and the bottom is 207000H.

System Descriptors.   System descriptors and gate descriptors are indicated when the
S bit of the access rights byte is a zero. Other than this change in the access rights
byte, the A bit disappears and becomes part of a 4-bit type number. The format of
the access rights byte for the system descriptor appears in Figure 5–13. Refer to
Table 5–4 for a definition of each valid 80286 system descriptor type.

There are two basic types of system descriptor: one describes either a task state
segment (TSS) or a local descriptor table descriptor, and the other describes a gate.
The task state segment holds the entire environment of the 80286 microprocessor,
including all the internal registers and the linkage required to pass control from one
task to another. The TSS descriptor describes the memory area that applies to the
TSS and whether the TSS is busy or available. Figure 5–14 illustrates the TSS and
the placement of the 80286 environment within it.

The TSS contains three major areas: (1) the current task state, (2) the initial
stacks for current privilege levels (CPL) 0–2, and (3) the back-link entry selector
to TSS. The back-link entry selector contains the selector number for the old TSS

FIGURE 5–13 The access
rights byte for a system
descriptor.

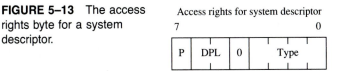

Access rights for system descriptor

7   0

P	DPL	0	Type

TABLE 5–4 Valid 80286 system descriptor types

Type	Function
0001	Available task state segment
0010	Local descriptor table descriptor
0011	Busy task state segment
0100	Call gate
0101	Task gate
0110	Interrupt gate
0111	Trap gate

Note: The remaining types 0000 and 1000–1111 are reserved for use in the 80386 and 80486 microprocessors.

FIGURE 5–14 The task state segment (TSS) for the 80286 microprocessor.

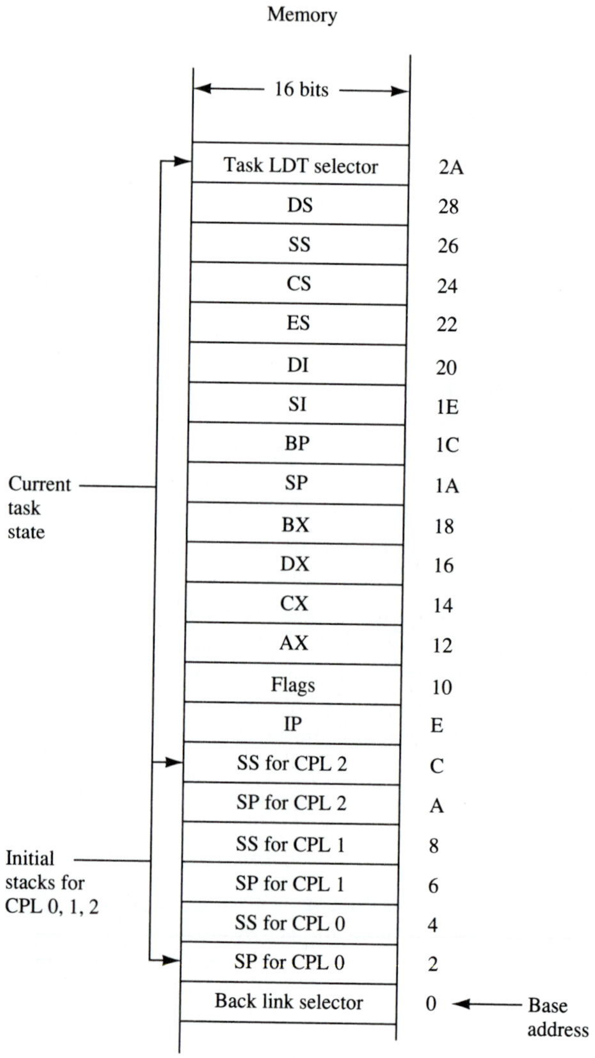

Memory

Current task state		
	Task LDT selector	2A
	DS	28
	SS	26
	CS	24
	ES	22
	DI	20
	SI	1E
	BP	1C
	SP	1A
	BX	18
	DX	16
	CX	14
	AX	12
	Flags	10
	IP	E
	SS for CPL 2	C
	SP for CPL 2	A
	SS for CPL 1	8
	SP for CPL 1	6
	SS for CPL 0	4
	SP for CPL 0	2
	Back link selector	0

16 bits

Initial stacks for CPL 0, 1, 2

Base address

FIGURE 5–15 The system segment descriptor that describes a busy or available TSS or a local descriptor table.

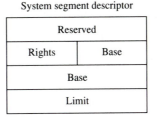

System segment descriptor

Reserved	
Rights	Base
Base	
Limit	

after a CALL or an interrupt. The back link allows the return to the prior TSS after a procedure using a RET or after an interrupt using an IRET. The back link operates as a return address. The initial stacks for current privilege levels 0–2 are used whenever a JMP or CALL switches to a new privilege level. The initial values load into SP and SS from the TSS and the prior contents of SP and SS are pushed onto the new stack. The current task state contains the internal environment of the 80286 microprocessor. A new TSS is obtained whenever a JMP, CALL, or interrupt occurs in protected mode.

The descriptor used for a valid and busy TSS and the local descriptor table descriptor appears in Figure 5–15. This descriptor is identical with the segment descriptors described in Figure 5–11 except the access rights byte is different, as depicted in Figure 5–13. The base address locates the beginning of the TSS or local descriptor table. The limit defines the last location in either the TSS or local descriptor table. Note that the TSS limit is usually 002BH and the limit for the local descriptor table is defined by the length of the table.

The format for the gate descriptors is different from the format of the other descriptors. A *gate descriptor* appears whenever a program calls a procedure, jumps to a new task, performs an interrupt, or performs a trap. Figure 5–16 illustrates the gate descriptor, which uses the same access rights byte as the system segment descriptor.

This descriptor does not contain a base address or a limit because it does not describe a memory segment. The gate descriptor describes the location (entry point) of a task. The gate descriptor contains the selector number and offset address of the task. It also contains a word count that can be 0–31. Only the call gate uses the word count, which indicates how many words are to be transferred from the old stack (caller's stack) to the new stack (procedures stack). This is useful for transferring data to the procedure from the calling program.

FIGURE 5–16 The gate descriptor used with JMP, CALL, interrupts, and traps.

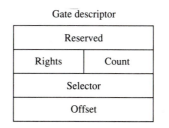

Gate descriptor

Reserved	
Rights	Count
Selector	
Offset	

5–6   PLACING THE 80286 INTO PROTECTED MODE

Now that we understand the descriptors, descriptor tables, and TSS, we place the 80286 into protected mode operation. Before protected mode can be entered, the descriptor tables must be initialized and a valid TSS must be defined.

Defining the GDT, LDT, and IDT

The data structure defines the GDT, LDT, and IDT. These tables must be defined before the switch from real to protected mode can occur.

The Global Descriptor Table (GDT). The *global descriptor table* (GDT) contains descriptors that are available to all tasks. The only type of descriptors that it may not contain are the interrupt and trap gates that must reside in the IDT. The very first entry in the GDT contains a *null descriptor* that must be zero. This descriptor is not used and is not available for use. The GDT, at a minimum, must contain descriptors that describe a code segment, a data segment, and a stack segment. A system that is described in this manner will have no local descriptor table and can perform no tasks except a main program.

A system that performs tasks for operation in multiuser systems will include additional global descriptors that describe the TSS and local descriptors that define local descriptor tables used by various applications. The local descriptor table is defined in the global table.

EXAMPLE 5–17

```
                          DES     STRUC                   ;structure for descriptor
0000 0000                 LIM     DW     ?                ;limit (size)
0002 0000                 BASL    DW     ?                ;Base B0—B15
0004 00                   BASH    DB     ?                ;base B16—B23
0005 00                   RI      DB     ?                ;access rights
0006 0000                         DW     0                ;0000H
0008                      DES     ENDS

0000                      DAT     SEGMENT

                          ;global descriptor table

0000 0000                 GD0     DES    <0,0,0,0,0>      ;null descriptor
0002 0000
0004 00
0005 00
0006 0000

0008 0000                 GD1     DES    <0,0,0,96H,0>    ;stack (0008H)
000A 0000
000C 00
000D 96
000E 0000
```

```
0010 FFFF          GD2     DES     <0FFFFH,0,1,9EH,0>      ;code (0010H)
0012 0000
0014 01
0015 9E
0016 0000

0018 FFFF          GD3     DES     <0FFFFH,0,2,9EH,0>      ;code (0018H)
001A 0000
001C 02
001D 9E
001E 0000

0020 FFFF          GD4     DES     <0FFFFH,0,10H,92H,0>    ;data (0020H)
0022 0000
0024 10
0025 92
0026 0000

0028 FFFF          GD5     DES     <0FFFFH,0,11H,92H,0>    ;data (0028H)
002A 0000
002C 11
002D 92
002E 0000

0030               DAT     ENDS
```

Example 5–17 shows the software required to initialize a global descriptor table for a system that has two code segments stored in memory locations 010000H–02FFFFH, two data segments stored in memory locations 100000H–11FFFFH, and a single stack segment stored at location 000000H–00FFFFH. It also requires a read-only memory at location FF000FH–FFFFFFH, which is the top of the memory system where the machine expects to find the reset software. The tables and initialization software must also exist at this top section of the memory system.

The contents of the segment register select an entry in the global descriptor table. In this example, the code segments are specified by selectors (segment register numbers) 0010H and 0018H, the stack is selector 0008H, and the data segments are selectors 0020H and 0028H.

The Interrupt Descriptor Table (IDT). The interrupt descriptor table (IDT) contains gates for interrupts and traps. The difference between an interrupt gate and a trap gate is that the interrupt gate clears the IF (interrupt flag) while the trap gate does not. The minimum IDT must contain the interrupt gates for the Intel reserved interrupt type 0–31. This requires that the IDT be at least 256 bytes (32×8) in length for these 32 gates. Because most systems also use the user interrupts, (types 32–255), the remainder of the IDT is normally defined. A complete IDT requires 2K bytes of memory to store all 256 eight-byte interrupt/trap gates.

EXAMPLE 5–18

	IG	STRUC		;structure for interrupt gate
0000 0000	OFFI	DW	?	;offset addres
0002 0000	SELI	DW	?	;selector
0004 00		DB	0	
0005 86		DB	86H	;interrupt gate
0006 0000		DW	0	;0000H
0008	IG	ENDS		
	TG	STRUC		;structure for trap gate
0000 0000	OFFT	DW	?	;offset addres
0002 0000	SELT	DW	?	;selector
0004 00		DB	0	
0005 87		DB	87H	;trap gate
0006 0000		DW	0	;0000H
0008	TG	ENDS		

In many systems the Intel reserved interrupt types use an interrupt gate, while the many remaining interrupt types often use the trap gate. Example 5–18 shows the data structures used to initialize both the interrupt gate (IG) and the trap gate (TP). This software does not initialize the IDT because each gate requires the address (selector and offset) of the procedures associated with the gates. These addresses are not available until we develop software for them. Note that the only difference in the descriptors for the trap and interrupt gates is the access rights byte, an 87H for the trap gate and an 86H for the interrupt gate. Either a hardware interrupt or the INT and INTO instructions access each type of gate.

EXAMPLE 5–19

0000		DAT	SEGMENT		
0000 0400[		IDT	DW	1024 dup (?)	
????					
]					
0800 0004[		GDT	DW	4 dup (?)	;null descriptor
????					
]					
0808 0000			DW	0H	;end of table
080A 4000[			DW	4000H dup (?)	
????					
]					
880A		DAT	ENDS		

```
0000                          CODE    SEGMENT

                              ASSUME  CS:CODE,DS:DAT

0000                          SETI    PROC FAR

0000 B8 0000                          MOV     AX,0
0003 8E C0                            MOV     ES,AX                   ;address vector table
0005 BF 0000                          MOV     DI,0
0008 B8 ---- R                        MOV     AX,DAT                  ;address IDT
000B 8E D8                            MOV     DS,AX
000D BE 0000 R                        MOV     SI,OFFSET IDT
0010 B9 0100                          MOV     CX,256                  ;load count

0013                          SETI1:

0013 26: 8B 05                        MOV     AX,ES:[DI]      ;get offset
0016 89 04                            MOV     [SI],AX                 ;save offset in IDT
0018 C7 44 04 8600                    MOV     WORD PTR [SI+4],8600H   ;save gate
001D C7 44 06 0000                    MOV     WORD PTR [SI+6],0       ;save reserved

0022 E8 0031 R                        CALL    GDTS                    ;save offset in GDT
                                                                      ;return with selector in AX
0025 89 44 02                         MOV     [SI+2],AX               ;save selector
0028 83 C6 08                         ADD     SI,8                    ;address next IDT
002B 83 C7 04                         ADD     DI,4                    ;address next vector
002E E2 E3                            LOOP    SETI1                   ;repeat 256 times
0030 CB                               RET

0031                          SETI    ENDP

0031                          GDTS    PROC NEAR                       ;save offset address in GDT
                                                                      ;return with selector in AX
0031 26: 8B 45 02                     MOV     AX,ES:[DI+2]            ;get segment address
0035 BB 0804 R                        MOV     BX,OFFSET GDT+4         ;address GDT
0038 BA 0008                          MOV     DX,0008H                ;load first selector

003B                          GDTS1:

003B 83 3F 00                         CMP     WORD PTR [BX],0         ;end of GDT?
003E 74 10                            JE      GDTS3                   ;if end GDT
0040 39 47 02                         CMP     [BX+2],AX               ;check for match
0043 74 08                            JE      GDTS2                   ;if match
0045 83 C2 08                         ADD     DX,8                    ;adjust selector
0048 83 C3 08                         ADD     BX,8                    ;adjust GDT pointer
004B EB EE                            JMP     GDTS1                   ;keep looking

004D                          GDTS2:

004D 8B C2                            MOV     AX,DX                   ;get selector
004F C3                               RET
```

```
0050                                        GDTS3:

0050  C7 07 FFFF              MOV    [BX],0FFFFH          ;save 64 K size
0054  89 47 02                MOV    [BX+2],AX            ;save segment address
0057  C7 47 04 9E00           MOV    WORD PTR [BX+4],9E00H ;save code segment
005C  C7 47 06 0000           MOV    WORD PTR [BX+6],0     ;save reserved
0061  C7 47 08 0000           MOV    WORD PTR [BX+8],0     ;end table
0066  8B C2                   MOV    AX,DX                ;get selector
0068  C3                      RET

0069            GDTS    ENDP

0069            CODE    ENDS

                        END
```

Example 5–19 illustrates software that can be used to take the addresses of the 256 DOS interrupt vectors (locations 00000H–003FFH) and load them into interrupt gates in an interrupt descriptor table. This software assumes that all interrupt vectors are defined and allows a full 64K-byte segment for each. This software also loads global descriptors for code segments each time a new area of memory is addressed for an interrupt vector. The first global descriptor created is descriptor 1, which uses selector 0008H. Notice that each new segment address from the vector programs a new descriptor in the GDT and a new selector number. Although this may be wasteful, it is a method of developing the descriptor table for the DOS interrupt vectors.

The Local Descriptor Table (LTD).   The local descriptor table (LDT) contains descriptors that define a particular task. These descriptors are not available to other tasks. The LDT contains segment descriptors and task and call gates. The LDT is a method of isolating a given task from the rest of the operating system. Each time a task executes at the global level, its TSS contains a task LDT selector. This local descriptor table selector references the local descriptor table descriptor (LDTD) that resides in the global descriptor table, and this LDTD locates the LDT for the task. Once the LDT is located, it is addressed through the selector when the TI bit of the selector is a logic one. This procedure allows any application to address 8K local and 8K global descriptors.

The Switch to Protected Mode

The switch to protected mode requires that at least the GDT and IDT exist before software loads the global descriptor table register (GDTR) and the interrupt descriptor table register (IDTR). If the system lacks local tasks, the switch is made by initializing the GDTR and the IDTR before loading the machine status word (MSW) to set the PE (protected entry) bit.

EXAMPLE 5–20

```
0000                    DAT     SEGMENT

0000 0800               IDTX    DW    2048              ;limit
0002 00000000                   DD    0                 ;base address

0006 4000               GDTX    DW    4000H             ;limit
0008 000007EC                   DD    2028              ;base address

000C                    DAT     ENDS

0000                    CODE    SEGMENT

                                ASSUME   CS:CODE,DS:DAT

0000                    SWITCH  PROC FAR

0000 B8 ---- R                  MOV   AX,DAT
0003 8E D8                      MOV   DS,AX

0005 0F 01 1E 0000 R            LIDT  FWORD PTR IDTX    ;address IDT
000A 0F 01 16 0006 R            LGDT  FWORD PTR GDTX    ;address GDT

000F 0F 01 E0                   SMSW  AX                ;get MSW
0012 0D 0001                    OR    AX,1              ;set PE bit
0015 0F 01 F0                   LMSW  AX                ;set protected

0018 EB 01 90                   JMP   NEXT              ;clear queue

001B                    NEXT:                           ;in protected mode


001B                    SWITCH  ENDP

001B                    CODE    ENDS

                                END
```

The software that switches to protected mode appears in Example 5–20. This example does not show the descriptor table GDT and IDT, but assumes that they are already loaded elsewhere. This software loads the GDTR and IDTR before placing a 1 in the PE bit of the MSW. After setting the PE bit, you must execute an intrasegment jump to clear the instruction cache.

Once operating in protected mode, you must use selectors to address different sections of the memory. The selectors are loaded after the intrasegment jump. To pass control to a task, the TSS must be set up in memory and a jump using a selector (far

TABLE 5–5 Global descriptor table for the INT 15H switch to protected mode

Entry	Function
0	Null, must be set to zeros
1	Global descriptor table
2	Interrupt descriptor table
3	User data segment
4	User extra segment
5	User stack segment
6	User code segment
7	BIOS code segment (initialized by BIOS)

jump) that refers to the TSS executed. This loads the task register and the general internal state of the machine.

Switching to protected mode is also accomplished by a BIOS interrupt. Except for the PS/2 Models 25 and 30, BIOS interrupt 15H is used to enter protected mode operation on any personal computer system. To use INT 15H, the AH register is loaded with 89H to access the switch to protected mode operation. Other registers loaded prior to the INT 15H instruction are BH = interrupt number for IRQ0 (usually 08H), BL = interrupt number for IRQ8 (usually 70H), and ES:SI = segment and offset address of the global descriptor table.

To properly switch to protected mode using INT 15H, a global descriptor table must be stored in memory. This table must contain the descriptors illustrated in Table 5–5.

On exit from INT 15H, carry is cleared to indicate a successful switch to protected mode. If the switch fails, DOS remains in real mode and carry is set to indicate the error.

5–7   SUMMARY

1. There are three types of unconditional jump instructions: short, near, and far. The short jump allows a branch to within +127 and −128 bytes. The near jump (using a displacement or ±32K) allows a jump to anywhere in the current code segment (intrasegment). The far jump allows a jump to any location in the memory (intersegment).
2. Whenever a label appears with a JMP instruction, the label must be followed by a colon (LABEL:).
3. The displacement that follows a short or near jump is the distance from the next instruction to the jump location.
4. Indirect jumps are available in two forms: (1) jump to the location stored in a register, and (2) jump to the location stored in a memory word (near indirect) or double word (far indirect).

5. Conditional jumps are all short jumps that test one or more of the flag bits: CF, ZF, OF, PF, or SF. If the condition is true, a jump occurs; if the condition is false, the next sequential instruction executes.

6. A special conditional jump instruction (LOOP) decrements CX and jumps to the label when CX is not 0. Other forms of loop include LOOPE, LOOPNE, LOOPZ, and LOOPNZ. The LOOPE instruction jumps if CX is not 0, and if an equal condition exists.

7. Procedures are groups of instructions that perform one task and are used from any point in a program. The CALL instruction links to a procedure and the RET instruction returns from a procedure. In assembly language, the PROC directive defines the name and type of procedure. The ENDP directive declares the end of the procedure.

8. The CALL instruction is a combination of a PUSH and a JMP instruction. When CALL executes, it pushes the return address on the stack and then jumps to the procedure. A near CALL places the contents of IP on the stack and a far CALL places both IP and CS on the stack.

9. The RET instruction returns from a procedure by removing the return address from the stack and placing it into IP (near return) or IP and CS (far return).

10. Interrupts are either software instructions similar to CALL or hardware signals used to call procedures. This process interrupts the current program and calls a procedure. After the procedure, an IRET instruction returns control to the interrupted software.

11. Interrupt vectors are 4 bytes in length and contain the address (IP and CS) of the interrupt service procedure. The 80286 microprocessor contains 256 interrupt vectors in the first 1K byte of memory. The first 32 bytes are defined by Intel, the remaining 224 are user interrupts.

12. Whenever an interrupt is accepted by the microprocessor, the flags, IP and CS, are pushed on the stack. Besides pushing the flags, the TF and IF flag bits are cleared to disable both the trace function and the INTR pin. The final event that occurs for the interrupt is that the interrupt vector is fetched from the vector table and a jump to the interrupt service procedure occurs.

13. Software interrupt instructions (INT) often replace system calls. Software interrupts save 3 bytes of memory each time they replace CALL instructions.

14. A special return instruction (IRET) must be used to return from an interrupt service procedure. The IRET instruction not only removes IP and CS from the stack, it also removes the flags from the stack.

15. Interrupt on an overflow (INTO) is a conditional interrupt that calls an interrupt service procedure if the overflow flag (OF) = 1.

16. The interrupt enable flag (IF) controls the INTR pin connection on the microprocessor. If the STI instruction executes, it sets IF to enable the INTR pin. If the CLI instruction executes, it clears IF to disable the INTR pin.

17. The carry flag bit (CF) is clear, set, and complemented by the CLC, STC, and CMC instructions.

18. The WAIT instruction tests the condition of the $\overline{\text{BUSY}}$ pin on the 80286 microprocessor. If $\overline{\text{BUSY}} = 0$, WAIT does not wait, but if $\overline{\text{BUSY}} = 1$, WAIT continues testing the $\overline{\text{BUSY}}$ pin until it becomes a logic 0.

19. The LOCK prefix causes the $\overline{\text{LOCK}}$ pin to become a logic 0 for the duration of the locked instruction. The ESC instruction passes instruction to the 80287 numeric coprocessor.

20. The BOUND instruction compares the contents of any 16-bit register against the contents of two words of memory: an upper and a lower boundary. If the value in the register compared with memory is *not* within the upper and lower boundary, a type-5 interrupt ensues.

21. The ENTER and LEAVE instructions are used with stack frames. A stack frame is a mechanism used to pass parameters to a procedure through the stack memory. The stack frame also holds local memory variables for the procedure. The ENTER instruction creates the stack frame, and the LEAVE instruction removes the stack frame from the stack. The BP register addresses stack frame data.

22. The global descriptor table, addressed by the global descriptor table registers, contains descriptors that define (1) data, code, and stack memory segment, (2) system descriptors that define the location of the TSS, and (3) gates that enter procedures and tasks.

23. The local descriptor table, addressed by a descriptor in the global descriptor table, contains descriptors that define the local data, code, and stack memory segments and the gates used to enter local procedures and tasks.

24. The interrupt descriptor table, addressed by the interrupt descriptor table register, contains either interrupt or trap gates. An interrupt gate disables the INTR pin and a trap gate does not.

25. The STRUC directive develops a data structure used to save coding time when many areas of memory require the same structure.

26. The switch to protected mode occurs after the global and interrupt descriptor tables are initialized. The act of placing a logic 1 in the PE bit of the MSW causes the machine to enter protected mode. After entrance to protected mode, an intrasegment jump instruction must occur to flush the 80286 instruction cache.

5–8   QUESTIONS AND PROBLEMS

1. What is a short JMP?
2. What type of JMP is used when jumping anywhere in a segment?
3. Which JMP instruction allows the program to continue execution at any memory location in the system?
4. What JMP instruction is 5 bytes long?
5. What can be said about a label that is followed by a colon?
6. The near jump modifies the program address by changing which register or registers?
7. The far jump modifies the program address by changing which register or registers?
8. Explain what the JMP AX instruction accomplishes. Also identify it as a near or a far jump instruction.
9. Contrast the operation of a JMP DI with a JMP [DI].

10. Contrast the operation of a JMP [DI] with a JMP FAR PTR [DI].
11. List the five flag bits tested by the conditional jump instructions.
12. Describe how the JA instruction operates.
13. When will the JO instruction jump?
14. What conditional jump instructions follow the comparison of signed numbers?
15. What conditional jump instructions follow the comparison of unsigned numbers?
16. Which conditional jump instructions test both the ZF and CF flag bits?
17. When does the JCXZ instruction jump?
18. The LOOP instruction decrements register _____ and tests it for a 0 to decide if a jump occurs.
19. Explain how the LOOPE instruction operates.
20. Develop a short sequence of instructions that stores a 00H into 150H bytes of memory beginning at extra segment memory location DATA. You must use the LOOP instruction to help perform this task.
21. Develop a sequence of instructions that searches through a block of 100H bytes of memory. This program must count all the unsigned numbers that are above 42H and all that are below 42H. Byte-sized memory location UP must contain the count of numbers above 42H, and location DOWN must contain the count of numbers below 42H.
22. What is a procedure?
23. Explain how the near and far CALL instructions function.
24. How does the near RET instruction function?
25. The last executable instruction in a procedure must be a _____.
26. What directive identifies the start of a procedure?
27. How is a procedure identified as near or far?
28. Explain what the RET 6 instruction accomplishes.
29. Write a near procedure that cubes the contents of the CX register. This procedure may not affect any register except CX.
30. Write a procedure that multiplies DI by SI and then divides the result by 100H. Make sure that the result is left in AX upon returning from the procedure. This procedure may not change any register except AX.
31. What is an interrupt?
32. What software instructions call an interrupt service procedure?
33. How many different interrupt types are available in the 80286 microprocessor?
34. What is the purpose of interrupt vector type number 0?
35. Illustrate the contents of an interrupt vector and explain the purpose of each part.
36. How does the IRET instruction differ from the RET instruction?
37. The INTO instruction only interrupts the program for what condition?
38. The interrupt vector for an INT 40H instruction is stored at what memory locations?
39. What instructions control the function of the INTR pin?
40. What instruction tests the $\overline{BUSY}$ pin?
41. When will the BOUND instruction interrupt a program?
42. An ENTER 16,0 instruction creates a stack frame that contains _____ bytes.
43. What register moves to the stack when an ENTER instruction executes?

44. Which instruction passes opcodes to the 80287 numeric coprocessor?
45. The first descriptor in the global descriptor table is called a _____ descriptor.
46. Which instruction loads the global descriptor table register?
47. The selector accesses the local descriptor table when the TI bit = _____.
48. Develop a data structure statement that defines a call gate. Name this structure CGATE.
49. When does the program-invisible portion of a selector (segment register) load with a new base address, limit, and access rights byte?
50. How many of the interrupt descriptor table descriptors must be defined for any protected mode operating system?
51. How is a local descriptor table defined?
52. The TSS contains what information?
53. What instruction is actually used to switch the 80286 into the protected mode?
54. What must follow the switch to protected mode?

CHAPTER 6

Programming the 80286 Microprocessor

INTRODUCTION

This chapter develops programs and programming techniques using the MASM macro assembler program, the DOS function calls, and the BIOS function calls. Some of the DOS function calls and BIOS function calls are used in this chapter, but all are explained in complete detail in Appendix A. Please review the function calls as required as you read this chapter. The MASM assembler has already been explained and demonstrated in prior chapters, yet there are still more features to learn at this point.

This chapter is meant as an introduction to programming, yet it provides valuable programming techniques that provide a wealth of background so that programs can be easily developed for the personal computer using either PC-DOS or MS-DOS as a springboard. Some of the programming techniques explained in this chapter include macro sequences, keyboard and display manipulation, program modules, library files, and interrupt hooks.

OBJECTIVES

Upon completion of this chapter, you will be able to:

1. Use the MASM assembler and linker program to create programs that contain more than one module.
2. Explain the use of EXTRN and PUBLIC as they apply to modular programming.
3. Set up a library file that contains commonly used subroutines.
4. Write and use MACRO and ENDM to develop macro sequences used with linear programming.
5. Show how both sequential and random access files are developed for use in a system.

6. Develop programs using DOS function calls.
7. Differentiate a DOS function call from a BIOS function call.
8. Show how to hook into interrupts using DOS function calls.

6–1   MODULAR PROGRAMMING

Most programs are too large to be developed by one person. This means that programs are often developed by teams of programmers. The linker program is provided with MS-DOS or PC-DOS so programming modules can be linked together into a complete program. This section describes the linker, the linking task, library files, EXTRN, and PUBLIC as they apply to program modules and modular programming.

The Assembler and Linker

The *assembler program* converts a symbolic source module (file) into a hexadecimal object file. We have seen many examples of symbolic source files in prior chapters. Example 6–1 shows the assembler dialog that appears as a source module named FILE.ASM is assembled. Whenever you create a source file it must have an extension of ASM. Note that the extension is not typed into the assembler prompt when assembling a file. Source files are created using the editor that comes with the assembler or by almost any other assembler or wordprocessor that is capable of generating an ASCII file.

EXAMPLE 6–1

A>>MASM

Microsoft (R) Macro Assembler Version 5.10
Copyright (C) Microsoft Corp 1981, 1989. All rights reserved.

Source filename [.ASM]: FILE
Object filename [FILE.OBJ]: FILE
Source listing [NUL.LST]: FILE
Cross reference [NUL.CRF]: FILE

The assembler program (MASM) asks for the source file name, the object file name, the list file name, and a cross-reference file name. In most cases the name for each of these will be the same as the source file. The object file (.OBJ) is not executable, but is designed as an input file to the linker. The source listing file (.LST) contains the assembled version of the source file and its hexadecimal machine language equivalent. The cross-reference file (.CRF) lists all labels and pertinent information required for cross-referencing.

The *linker program* reads the object files, created by the assembler program, and links them together into a single execution file. An *execution file* is created with the file name extension EXE. Execution files are executed by typing the file name at the DOS prompt (A>). An example execution file is FROG.EXE, which is executed by typing FROG at the DOS command prompt.

If a file is short enough, less than 64K bytes in length, it can be converted from an execution file to a *command file* (.COM). The command file is slightly different from an execution file in that the program must be originated at location 100H before it can execute. The program EXE2BIN is used for converting an execution file into a command file. The main advantage of a command file is that it loads off the disk into the computer much more quickly than an execution file. It also requires slightly less disk storage space than the execution file.

EXAMPLE 6–2

A>LINK

Microsoft (R) Overlay Linker Version 3.64
Copyright (C) Microsoft Corp 1983-1988. All rights reserved.

Object Modules [.OBJ]: FROG+WHAT+DONUT
Run File [FROG.EXE]: FROG
List File [NUL.MAP]: FROG
Libraries [.LIB]: LIBS

Example 6–2 shows the protocol involved to use the linker program to link the files FROG, WHAT, and DONUT. The linker also links the library files (LIBS) so the procedures located within LIBS can be used with the linked execution file. To invoke the linker, type LINK at the DOS command prompt as illustrated in Example 6–2. Note that before files can be linked, they must first be assembled and they must be *error free*.

In this example, after typing LINK, the linker program asks for the Object Modules, which are created by the assembler. In this example, we have three object modules: FROG, WHAT, and DONUT. If more than one object files exists, the main program file (FROG in this example) is typed first, followed by any other supporting modules. (We use a plus sign to separate module names.)

After the program module names are typed, the linker suggests that the execution (run-time) file name is FROG.EXE. This file may be selected by typing the same name or if desired by typing the enter key. It may also be changed to any other name at this point.

The list file is where a map of the program segments appears as created by the linking. If enter is typed, no list file is created, but if a name is typed, the list file appears on the disk.

Library files are entered in the last line. In this example we entered library file name LIBS. This library contains procedures used by the other program modules.

PUBLIC and EXTRN

The PUBLIC and EXTRN directives are very important to modular programming. We use PUBLIC to declare that labels of code, data, or entire segments are available to other program modules. We use EXTRN (external) to declare that labels are external to a module. Without these statements, we could not link modules together to create a program using modular programming techniques.

EXAMPLE 6–3

```
                        DAT1    SEGMENT  PUBLIC          ;declare entire segment public

                                PUBLIC  DATA1            ;declare DATA1, DATA2 public
                                PUBLIC  DATA2

0000 0064[              DATA1   DB      100 DUP (?)      ;global
        ??
                ]
0064 0064[              DATA2   DB      100 DUP (?)      ;global
        ??
                ]

00C8                    DAT1    ENDS

0000                    CODES   SEGMENT

                                ASSUME  CS:CODES,DS:DAT1

                                PUBLIC  READ             ;declare READ public

0000                    READ    PROC  FAR

0000 B4 06                      MOV     AH,6             ;read keyboard
0002 B2 FF                      MOV     DL,0FFH          ;no echo
0004 CD 21                      INT     21H
0006 74 F8                      JE      READ
0008 CB                         RET

0009                    READ    ENDP

0009                    CODES   ENDS

                                END
```

The PUBLIC directive is normally placed in the opcode field of an assembly language statement to define a label as public so it can be used by other modules. This label can be a jump address, a data address, or an entire segment can be made public. Example 6–3 shows the PUBLIC statement used to define some labels public to other modules. When segments are made public they are combined with other public segments that contain data with the same segment name.

EXAMPLE 6–4

```
0000                    DAT1    SEGMENT  PUBLIC                     ;declare entire segment public

                                EXTRN  DATA1:BYTE
                                EXTRN  DATA2:BYTE
                                EXTRN  DATA3:WORD
                                EXTRN  DATA4:DWORD

0000                    DAT1    ENDS

0000                    CODES   SEGMENT

                                ASSUME  CS:CODES,ES:DAT1

                                EXTRN  READ:FAR

0000                    MAIN    PROC  FAR

0000 B8 ---- R                  MOV     AX,DAT1
0003 8E C0                      MOV     ES,AX

0005 BF 0000 E                  MOV     DI,OFFSET DATA1
0008 B9 000A                    MOV     CX,10

000B                    MAIN1:

000B 9A 0000 ---- E             CALL    READ
0010 AA                         STOSB
0011 E2 F8                      LOOP    MAIN1
0013 CB                         RET

0014                    MAIN    ENDP

0014                    CODES   ENDS

                                END     MAIN
```

The EXTRN statement appears in both data and code segments to define labels as external to the segment. If data are defined as external, their size must be represented as BYTE, WORD, or DWORD. If a jump or call address is external, it must be represented as NEAR or FAR. Example 6–4 shows how the external statement is used to indicate that several labels are external to the program listed. Notice in this example that any external address or data is defined with the letter E in the hexadecimal assembled listing.

Libraries

Library files are collections of procedures that can be used by many different programs. These procedures are assembled and compiled into a library file by the LIB program that accompanies the MASM assembler program. Libraries allow common procedures to be collected into one place so they can be used by many different applications. The library file (FILENAME.LIB) is invoked when a program is linked with the linker program.

Why bother with library files? A library file is a good place to store a collection of related procedures. When the library file is linked with a program, only the procedures required by the program are removed from the library file and added to the program. If any amount of assembly language programming is to be accomplished efficiently, a good set of library files is essential.

Creating a Library File.   A library file is created with the LIB command typed at the DOS prompt. A library file is a collection of assembled .OBJ files that each perform one procedure. Example 6–5 shows two separate files (READ_KEY and ECHO) that will be used to structure a library file. Please notice that the name of the procedure must be declared PUBLIC in a library file and does not necessarily need to match the file name, although it does in this example.

EXAMPLE 6–5

```
                    ;The first library module is called READ_KEY.
                    ;This procedure reads a key from the keyboard
                    ;and returns with the ASCII character in AL.
                    ;
0000                LIB        SEGMENT

                               ASSUME  CS:LIB

                               PUBLIC  READ_KEY

0000                READ_KEY       PROC        FAR

0000 52                            PUSH        DX

0001                READ_KEY1:
0001 B4 06                         MOV         AH,6
0003 B2 0F                         MOV         DL,0FH
0005 CD 21                         INT         21H
0007 74 F8                         JE          READ_KEY1
0009 5A                            POP         DX
000A CB                            RET
000B                READ_KEY       ENDP

000B                LIB        ENDS

                               END
```

```
                        ;
                        ;This second library module is called ECHO
                        ;This procedure displays the ASCII character
                        ;in AL on the CRT screen.
                        ;
0000            LIB        SEGMENT

                           ASSUME  CS:LIB

                           PUBLIC  ECHO

0000            ECHO        PROC    FAR
0000 52                     PUSH    DX
0001 B4 06                  MOV     AH,6
0003 8A D0                  MOV     DL,AL
0005 CD 21                  INT     21H
0007 5A                     POP     DX
0008 CB                     RET
0009            ECHO        ENDP

0009            LIB     ENDS

                        END
```

After each file is assembled, the LIB program is used to combine them into a library file. The LIB program prompts for information as illustrated in Example 6–6 where these files are combined to form the library IO.

EXAMPLE 6–6

A>>LIB

Microsoft (R) Library Manager Version 3.10
Copyright (C) Microsoft Corp 1983-1988. All rights reserved.

Library name:IO
Library file does not exist. Create? Y
Operations:READ_KEY+ECHO
List file:IO

The LIB program begins with the copyright message from Microsoft, followed by the prompt *Library name:*. The library name chosen is IO for the IO.LIB file. Because this is a new file, the library program asks if we wish to create the library file. The *Operations:* prompt is where the library module names are typed. In this case we created a library using two procedure files (READ_KEY and ECHO). The list file shows the contents of the library and is illustrated for this library in Example 6–7. The list file shows the size and names of the files used to create the library and also the public label (procedure name) that is used in the library file.

EXAMPLE 6–7

ECHO..............ECHO   READ_KEY..........READ_KEY

READ_KEY   Offset: 00000010H Code and data size: BH
  READ_KEY

ECHO   Offset: 00000070H Code and data size: 9H
  ECHO

    If you must add additional library modules at a later time, type the name of the library file after invoking LIB. At the *Operations:* type the new module name preceded with a *plus sign* to add a new procedure. If you must delete a library module, use a *minus sign* before the operation file name.

    Once the library file is linked to your program file only the library procedures actually used by your program are placed in the execution file. Don't forget to use the label EXTRN when specifying library calls from your program module.

Macros

A macro is a group of instructions that performs one task, just as a procedure performs one task. The difference is that a procedure is accessed via a CALL instruction, while a macro is inserted in the program as a new opcode containing a sequence of instructions. A *macro* is a new opcode that you create. Macro sequences execute faster than procedures because there is no CALL and RET instruction to execute. The instructions of the macro are placed in your program at the point they are invoked.

    The MACRO and ENDM directives are used to delineate a macro sequence. The first statement of a macro is the MACRO statement that contains the name of the macro and any parameters associated with it. An example is MOVE MACRO A,B that defines the macro as MOVE. This new *opcode* uses two parameters A and B. The last statement of a macro is the ENDM instruction on a line by itself.

EXAMPLE 6–8

```
                    MOVE      MACRO    A,B              ;;moves word from B to A

                              PUSH     AX
                              MOV      AX,B
                              MOV      A,AX
                              POP      AX

                              ENDM

                    MOVE      VAR1,VAR2                 ;use macro MOVE

0000 50          1            PUSH     AX
0001 A1 0002 R   1            MOV      AX,VAR2
0004 A3 0000 R   1            MOV      VAR1,AX
0007 58          1            POP      AX
```

			MOVE	VAR3,VAR4	;use macro MOVE
0008	50	1	PUSH	AX	
0009	A1 0006 R	1	MOV	AX,VAR4	
000C	A3 0004 R	1	MOV	VAR3,AX	
000F	58	1	POP	AX	

Example 6–8 shows how a macro is created and used in a program. This macro moves the word-sized contents of memory location B into word-sized memory location A. After the macro is defined in the example, it is used twice. The macro is *expanded* in this example so that you can see how it assembles to generate the moves. A hexadecimal machine language statement followed by a 1 is a macro expansion statement. The expansion statement was not typed in the source program. Notice that the comment in the macro is preceded with a ;; instead of ; as is customary.

Local Variable in a Macro. Sometimes macros must contain local variables. A *local variable* is one that appears in the macro, but is not available outside the macro. To define a local variable we use the LOCAL directive. Example 6–9 shows how a local variable, used as a jump address, appears in a macro definition. If this jump address is not defined as local, the assembler will flag it with errors on the second and subsequent attempts to use the macro.

EXAMPLE 6–9

			READ	MACRO	A	;;reads keyboard
				LOCAL	READ1	;;define READ1 as local
				PUSH	DX	
			READ1:			
				MOV	AH,6	
				MOV	DL,0FFH	
				INT	21H	
				JE	READ1	
				MOV	A,AL	
				POP	DX	
				ENDM		
				READ	VAR5	;read key
0000	52	1		PUSH	DX	
0001		1	??0000:			
0001	B4 06	1		MOV	AH,6	
0003	B2 FF	1		MOV	DL,0FFH	
0005	CD 21	1		INT	21H	
0007	74 F8	1		JE	??0000	
0009	A2 0008 R	1		MOV	VAR5,AL	
000C	5A	1		POP	DX	

```
                              READ     VAR6                      ;read key

000D 52            1          PUSH     DX
000E               1   ??0001:
000E B4 06         1          MOV      AH,6
0010 B2 FF         1          MOV      DL,0FFH
0012 CD 21         1          INT      21H
0014 74 F8         1          JE       ??0001
0016 A2 0009 R     1          MOV      VAR6,AL
0019 5A            1          POP      DX
```

This example reads a character from the keyboard and stores into the byte-sized memory location indicated as a parameter with the macro. Notice how the local label READ1 is treated in the expanded macros.

The LOCAL directive must always immediately follow the MACRO directive without any intervening spaces or comments. If a comment or space appears between MACRO and LOCAL, the assembler indicates an error and will not accept the variable as local.

Placing MACRO Definitions in Their Own Module.   Macro definitions can be placed in the program file as shown, or can be placed in their own macro module. A file can be created that contains only macros that are to be included with other program files. We use the INCLUDE directive to indicate that a program file will include a module that contains external macro definitions. Although this is not a library file, it for all practical purposes functions as a library of macro sequences.

When macro sequences are placed in a file (often with the extension INC or MAC), they do not contain PUBLIC statements. If a file called MACRO.MAC contains macro sequences, the included statement is placed in the program file as INCLUDE C:\ASSM\MACRO.MAC. Notice that the macro file is on drive C, sub-directory ASSM in this example. The INCLUDE statement includes these macros just as if they had been typed into the file. No EXTRN statement is needed to access the macro statements that have been included.

The Modular Programming Approach

The modular programming approach often involves a team of people assigned different programming tasks. This allows the team manager to assign portions of the program to different team members. Often the team manager develops the system flowchart or shell and then divides it into modules for team members.

A team member might be assigned the task of developing a macro definition file. This file might contain macro definitions that handle the I/O operations for the system. Another team member might be assigned the task of developing the procedures used for the system. In most cases the procedures are organized as a library file that is linked to the program modules. Finally, several program files or modules might be used for the final system, each developed by different team members.

This approach requires good documentation and considerable communications between team members. Documentation is the key so that modules interface correctly, but communications between members also plays a key role in this approach.

6–2   USING THE KEYBOARD AND VIDEO DISPLAY

Today there are very few programs that don't make use of the keyboard and video display. This section of the text explains how to use the keyboard and video display connected to the IBM PC or compatible computer running under either MS-DOS or PC-DOS.

Reading the Keyboard with DOS Functions

The keyboard in the personal computer is read via a DOS function call. A complete listing of the DOS function calls appears in Appendix A. This section uses INT 21H with various DOS function calls to read the keyboard. Data read from the keyboard is either in ASCII-coded form or in extended ASCII-coded form.

The ASCII-coded data appear as outlined in Table 1–5 in Section 1–5. Notice that these codes correspond to most of the keys on the keyboard. Also available through the keyboard are extended ASCII-coded keyboard data. Table 6–1 lists most of the extended ASCII codes obtained with various keys and key combinations. Notice that most keys on the keyboard have alternative key codes. The function keys have four sets of codes selected by the function keys, the shift function keys, alternate function keys, and the control function keys.

There are three ways to read the keyboard. The first method reads a key and echoes (or displays) the key on the video screen. A second way just tests to see if a key is pressed, and if it is, it reads the key; otherwise, it returns without any key. The third way allows an entire character line to be read from the keyboard.

Reading a Key with an Echo.   Example 6–10 shows how a key is read from the keyboard and *echoed* (sent) back out to the video display. Although this is the easiest way to read a key, it is also the most limited because it always echoes the character to the screen even if it is an unwanted character. The DOS function number 01H also responds to the control C key and exits to DOS if it is typed.

EXAMPLE 6–10

```
0000                 KEY    PROC    FAR

0000 B4 01                  MOV     AH,1              ;function 01H
0002 CD 21                  INT     21H               ;read key
0004 0A C0                  OR      AL,AL             ;test for 00H
0006 75 03                  JNZ     KEY1
0008 CD 21                  INT     21H               ;get extended
000A F9                     STC                       ;indicate extended

000B                 KEY1:

000B CB                     RET

000C                 KEY    ENDP
```

TABLE 6–1 Extended ASCII-coded keyboard data

Second	First								
	0	1	2	3	4	5	6	7	8
0	—	aQ	aD	aB	—	down arrow	cF3	aF9	a9
1	aESC	aW	aF	aN	—	page down	cF4	aF10	a0
2	—	aE	aG	aM	—	insert	cF5	—	a-
3	c2	aR	aH	a,	—	delete	cF6	—	a=
4	—	aT	aJ	a.	—	sF1	cF7	—	.
5	—	aY	aK	a/	—	sF2	cF8	—	F11
6	—	aU	aL	—	—	sF3	cF9	—	F12
7	—	aI	a;	a*	home	sF4	cF10	—	sF11
8	—	aO	a'	—	up arrow	sF5	aF1	a1	sF12
9	—	aP	a`	a-	page up	sF6	aF2	a2	cF11
A	—	a[	—	—	—	sF7	aF3	a3	cF12
B	—	a]	a\	—	left arrow	sF8	aF4	a4	aF11
C	—	aENT	aZ	—	—	sF9	aF5	a5	aF12
D	—	—	aX	—	right arrows	F10	aF6	a6	—
E	aBS	aA	aC	—	a+	cF1	aF7	a7	—
F	sTAB	aS	—	—	end key	cF2	aF8	a8	—

Notes: a = alternate key, c = control key, and s = shift key.

To read and echo a character, the AH register is loaded with DOS function number 01H. This is followed by the INT 21H instruction. Upon return from the INT 21H, the AL register contains the ASCII character typed, and the video displays also shows the typed character. If AL = 0 after the return, the INT 21H instruction must again be executed to obtain the extended ASCII-coded character. This procedure returns with carry set (1) to indicate an extended ASCII character and carry cleared (0) to indicate a normal ASCII character.

Reading a Key with No Echo.   The best single-character key-reading function is function number 06H. This function reads a key without an echo to the screen. It also returns with extended ASCII characters and *does not* respond to the control C key. This function uses AH for the function number (06H) and DL = 0FFH to indicate that the function call (INT 21H) will read the keyboard without an echo.

EXAMPLE 6–11

```
0000                    KEYS    PROC    FAR

0000 B4 06                      MOV     AH,6        ;function 01H
0002 B2 FF                      MOV     DL,0FFH
0004 CD 21                      INT     21H         ;read key
0006 74 F8                      JE      KEYS        ;if no key
0008 0A C0                      OR      AL,AL       ;test for 00H
000A 75 03                      JNE     KEYS1
000C CD 21                      INT     21H         ;get extended
000E F9                         STC                 ;indicate extended

000F                    KEYS1:

000F CB                         RET

0010                    KEYS    ENDP
```

Example 6–11 shows a procedure that uses function number 06H to read the keyboard. This performs as Example 6–10 except that no character is echoed to the video display.

If you examine the procedure, there is one other difference. Function call number 06H returns from the INT 21H even if no key is typed, while function call 01H waits for a key to be typed. This is an important difference that should be noted. This feature allows software to perform other tasks between checking the keyboard for a character.

Read an Entire Line with Echo.   Sometimes it is advantageous to read an entire line of data with one function call. Function call number 0AH reads an entire line of information—up to 255 characters—from the keyboard. It continues to acquire keyboard data until the enter key (0DH) is typed. This function requires that AH = 0AH and DS:DX addresses the keyboard buffer (a memory area where the ASCII data are stored). The first byte of the buffer area must contain the maximum number of keyboard characters read by this function. If the number typed exceeds this maximum number, the function returns just as if the enter key were typed. The second byte of the buffer contains the count of the actual number of characters typed and the remaining locations in the buffer contain the ASCII keyboard data.

EXAMPLE 6–12

```
0000                    COD     SEGMENT

                        ASSUME  CS:COD,DS:COD

0000 0101[              BUF1    DB      257 DUP (?)
        ????
             ]
0102 0101[              BUF2    DB      257 DUP (?)
        ????
             ]

0204                    MAIN    PROC    FAR

0204 8C C8                      MOV     AX,CS
0206 8E D8                      MOV     DS,AX

0208 BA 0000 R                  MOV     DX,OFFSET BUF1      ;address buffer 1
020B C7 06 0000 R 00FF          MOV     BUF1,255           ;maximum count
0211 E8 0221 R                  CALL    LINE               ;read first line

0214 BA 0102 R                  MOV     DX,OFFSET BUF2      ;address buffer 2
0217 C7 06 0102 R 00FF          MOV     BUF2,255           ;maximum count
021D E8 0221 R                  CALL    LINE               ;read second line

0220 CB                         RET

0221                    MAIN    ENDP

0221                    LINE    PROC    NEAR

0221 B4 0A                      MOV     AH,0AH             ;function 0AH
0223 CD 21                      INT     21H
0225 C3                         RET

0226                    LINE    ENDP

0226                    COD     ENDS

                        END     MAIN
```

Example 6–12 shows how this function reads two lines of information into two memory buffers (BUF1 and BUF2). Before the call to the DOS function through procedure LINE, the first byte of the buffer is loaded with a 255, so up to 255 characters can be typed. If you assemble and execute this program, the first line is accepted and so is the second. The only problem is that the second line appears on top of the first line. The next section of the text explains how to output characters to the video display to solve this problem.

Writing to the Video Display with DOS Functions

For almost any program written, data must be displayed on the video display. Video data can be displayed in a number of different ways with DOS function calls. We use function 02H or 06H for displaying one character at a time or function 09H for displaying an entire string of characters. Because function 02H and 06H are identical, we tend to use function 06H because it is also used to read a key.

Displaying One ASCII Character. Both DOS functions 02H and 06H are explained together because they are identical for displaying ASCII data. Example 6–13 shows how this function is used to display a carriage return (0DH) and a line feed (0AH). Here a macro, called DISP (display), is used to display the carriage return and line feed. The combination of a carriage return and a line feed moves the cursor to the next line at the left margin of the video screen. This two-step process can be used to correct the problem that occurred between the lines typed through the keyboard in Example 6–12.

EXAMPLE 6–13

```
                        DISP    MACRO   A               ;display A

                                MOV     AH,06H
                                MOV     DL,A
                                INT     21H

                                ENDM

                        DISP    0DH             ;carriage return

0000 B4 06      1               MOV     AH,06H
0002 B2 0D      1               MOV     DL,0DH
0004 CD 21      1               INT     21H

                        DISP    0AH             ;line feed

0006 B4 06      1               MOV     AH,06H
0008 B2 0A      1               MOV     DL,0AH
000A CD 21      1               INT     21H
```

Displaying a Character String. A character string is a series of ASCII-coded characters that end with a $ (24H) when used with DOS function call number 09H. Example 6–14 shows how a message is displayed at the current cursor position on the video display. Function call number 09H requires that DS:DX addresses the character string before executing the INT 21H.

EXAMPLE 6–14

```
0000                    COD     SEGMENT

                                ASSUME  CS:COD,DS:COD

0000 0D 0A 0A 54 68 69  MES     DB      0DH,0AH,0AH,'This is a test line','$'
     73 20 69 73 20 61
     20 74 65 73 74 20
     6C 69 6E 65 24

0017                    MAIN    PROC    FAR

0017 8C C8                      MOV     AX,CS                   ;load DS
0019 8E D8                      MOV     DS,AX

001B B4 09                      MOV     AH,09H                  ;function 09H
001D BA 0000 R                  MOV     DX,OFFSET MES
0020 CD 21                      INT     21H

0022 B4 4C                      MOV     AH,4CH                  ;function 4CH
0024 CD 21                      INT     21H

0026                    MAIN    ENDP


0026                    COD     ENDS

                                END     MAIN
```

This example program can be entered into the assembler, linked, and executed to produce "This is a test line" on the video display. Notice that an additional DOS function call is appended to the end of this program. Function call 4CH returns the system to the DOS prompt at the end of the program. We often use function number 4CH to return to DOS.

Consolidated Read Key and Echo Library Procedures.   Example 6–15 illustrates two procedures that could be assembled, linked, and added to a library file. The READ procedure reads a keyboard character and returns with either the ASCII or extended ASCII character in AL. If carry is set, AL contains the extended ASCII code, and if carry is cleared, it contains the standard ASCII code. The ECHO procedure displays the ASCII-coded character located in AL at the current cursor position.

EXAMPLE 6–15

```
0000                    LIB     SEGMENT

                                ASSUME  CS:LIB

                                PUBLIC  READ
                                PUBLIC  ECHO
```

```
                        ;procedure that reads a key from the keyboard (no echo)
                        ;if CF = 0, AL = standard ASCII character
                        ;if CF = 1, AL = extended ASCII character
                        ;
0000            READ    PROC    FAR

0000 52                 PUSH    DX              ;save DX
0001 B4 06              MOV     AH,6            ;DOS function 06H
0003 B2 FF              MOV     DL,0FFH

0005            READ1:

0005 CD 21              INT     21H
0007 74 FC              JE      READ1           ;if no key
0009 0A C0              OR      AL,AL           ;test for extended
000B 75 03              JNZ     READ2           ;if standard ASCII

000D CD 21              INT     21H             ;get extended
000F F9                 STC                     ;set carry

0010            READ2:

0010 5A                 POP     DX
0011 CB                 RET

0012            READ    ENDP
                        ;
                        ;procedure that displays the ASCII character in AL
                        ;
0012            ECHO    PROC    FAR

0012 52                 PUSH    DX
0013 B4 06              MOV     AH,6            ;DOS function 06H
0015 8A D0              MOV     DL,AL           ;AL to DL
0017 CD 21              INT     21H
0019 5A                 POP     DX
001A CB                 RET

001B            ECHO    ENDP

001B            LIB     ENDS

                        END
```

Using BIOS Video Function Calls

In addition to the DOS function call INT 21H, we also have BIOS (*basic I/O system*) function calls at INT 10H. The DOS function calls allow a key to be read and a character to be displayed with ease, but the cursor is difficult to position at the desired screen location. The BIOS function calls allow more control over the video

TABLE 6–2 BIOS function INT 10H

AH	Description	Parameters
02H	Sets cursor position	DH = Row DL = Column BH = Page number
03H	Reads cursor position	BH = Page number DH = Row DL = Column

display than do the DOS function calls. The BIOS function calls also require less time to execute than the DOS function calls.

Cursor Position.   Before any information is placed on the video screen, the position of the cursor should be known. This allows the screen to be cleared and started at any location that is desired. Function number 03H allows the cursor position to be read from the video interface. Function number 02H allows the cursor to be placed at any screen position. Table 6–2 shows the contents of various registers for both function 02H and 03H.

The page number in register BH should be 0 before setting the cursor position. Most software does not normally access the other pages (1–7) for the display. The page number is often ignored after a cursor read. The 0 page is available in the CGA (*color graphics adaptor*), EGA (*enhanced graphics adapter*), and VGA (*variable graphics array*) text modes of operation.

The cursor position assumes that the left-hand page column is column 0 progressing across a line to column 79. The row number corresponds to the character line number on the screen. Row 0 is the uppermost line, while row 24 is the last line on the screen. This assumes that the text mode selected for the video adapter is 80 characters per line by 25 lines. Other text modes are available, such as 40 × 24 and 96 × 43.

EXAMPLE 6–16

```
0000                CODE    SEGMENT

                            ASSUME  CS:CODE

0000                MAIN    PROC    FAR

                    HOME    MACRO

                            MOV     AH,2        ;;set cursor position
                            MOV     BH,0        ;;page 0
                            MOV     DX,0        ;;row 0, column 0
                            INT     10H

                            ENDM

                    HOME
```

```
0000 B4 02      1              MOV     AH,2
0002 B7 00      1              MOV     BH,0
0004 BA 0000    1              MOV     DX,0
0007 CD 10      1              INT     10H

0009 B9 0780                   MOV     CX,1920
000C B4 06                     MOV     AH,6
000E B2 20                     MOV     DL,' '          ;space

0010                  MAIN1:

0010 CD 21                     INT     21H             ;display space
0012 E2 FC                     LOOP    MAIN1           ;repeat 1920 times


                               HOME
0014 B4 02      1              MOV     AH,2
0016 B7 00      1              MOV     BH,0
0018 BA 0000    1              MOV     DX,0
001B CD 10      1              INT     10H

001D B4 4C                     MOV     AH,4CH          ;exit to DOS
001F CD 21                     INT     21H

0021                  MAIN     ENDP

0021                  CODE     ENDS

                               END     MAIN
```

Example 6–16 shows how the INT 10H, BIOS function call is used to clear the video screen. This is just one method of clearing the screen. Notice that the first function call positions the cursor to row 0 and column 0, which is called the *home* position. Next we use the DOS function call to write 1920 (80 characters per line × 24 character lines) blank spaces (20H) on the video display, after which we again home the cursor.

If this example is assembled, linked, and executed, a problem surfaces. This program is far too slow to be useful in most cases. To correct this situation another BIOS function call is used. We can use the scroll function (06H) to clear the screen at a much higher speed.

EXAMPLE 6–17

```
0000                  CODE     SEGMENT

                               ASSUME  CS:CODE

0000                  MAIN     PROC     FAR

                      HOME     MACRO
```

```
                              MOV     AH,2          ;;set cursor position
                              MOV     BH,0          ;;page 0
                              MOV     DX,0          ;;row 0, column 0
                              INT     10H

                              ENDM

0000  32 FF                   XOR     BH,BH         ;page 0
0002  B4 08                   MOV     AH,8          ;read attributes
0004  CD 10                   INT     10H

0006  8A DF                   MOV     BL,BH
0008  8A FC                   MOV     BH,AH
000A  2B C9                   SUB     CX,CX
000C  BA 184F                 MOV     DX,184FH
000F  B8 0600                 MOV     AX,0600H      ;clear page 0
0012  CD 10                   INT     10H

                              HOME
0014  B4 02        1          MOV     AH,2
0016  B7 00        1          MOV     BH,0
0018  BA 0000      1          MOV     DX,0
001B  CD 10        1          INT     10H

001D  B4 4C                   MOV     AH,4CH        ;exit to DOS
001F  CD 21                   INT     21H

0021            MAIN          ENDP

0021            CODE          ENDS

                              END     MAIN
```

Function 06H is used with a 00H in AL to blank the entire screen. This allows Example 6–16 to be rewritten so that the screen clears at a much higher speed. See Example 6–17 for a better clear and home cursor program. Here function call number 08H reads the character attributes for blanking the screen. Next, they are positioned in the correct registers and DX is loaded with the screen size, 4FH (79) and 18H (24). If this program is assembled, linked, executed, and compared with Example 6–16, there is a big difference in the speed at which the screen is cleared. Please refer to Appendix A for other BIOS INT 10H function calls that may prove useful in your applications. Also contained in Appendix A is a complete listing of all the INT functions available in most computers.

6–3   DATA CONVERSIONS

In computer systems, data are seldom in the correct form, so one main task of the system is to convert data from one form to another. This section of the chapter describes conversions between binary and ASCII. Binary data are removed from a register or memory and converted to ASCII for the video display. In many cases, ASCII data are converted to binary as they are typed on the keyboard. We also explain converting between ASCII and hexadecimal data.

Converting from Binary to ASCII

Conversion from binary to ASCII is accomplished in two ways: (1) by the AAM instruction if the number is less than 100, or (2) by a series of decimal divisions (divide by 10). Both techniques are presented in this section.

The AAM instruction converts the value in AX into a two-digit unpacked BCD number in AX. If the number in AX is 0062H (98 decimal) before AAM executes, AX contains a 0908H after AAM executes. This is not ASCII code, but it is converted to ASCII code by adding a 3030H to AX. Example 6–18 illustrates a procedure that processes the binary value in AL (0–99) and displays it on the video screen as decimal. This procedure blanks a leading zero, which occurs for the numbers 0–9, with an ASCII space code.

EXAMPLE 6–18

```
0000                    DISP    PROC    FAR

0000 52                         PUSH    DX              ;save DX
0001 32 E4                      XOR     AH,AH           ;blank AH
0003 D4 0A                      AAM                     ;convert to BCD
0005 80 C4 20                   ADD     AH,20H          ;add 20H
0008 80 FC 20                   CMP     AH,20H          ;test for leading zero
000B 74 03                      JE      DISP1           ;if leading zero
000D 80 C4 10                   ADD     AH,10H          ;convert to ASCII

0010                    DISP1:

0010 50                         PUSH    AX
0011 8A D4                      MOV     DL,AH           ;display first digit
0013 B4 06                      MOV     AH,6
0015 CD 21                      INT     21H
0017 58                         POP     AX
0018 04 30                      ADD     AL,30H          ;convert to ASCII
001A 8A D0                      MOV     DL,AL
001C B4 06                      MOV     AH,6            ;display second digit
001E CD 21                      INT     21H
0020 5A                         POP     DX              ;restore DX
0021 CB                         RET

0022                    DISP    ENDP
```

The reason that AAM converts any number between 0 and 99 to a two-digit unpacked BCD number is because it divides AX by 10. The result is left in AX so AH contains the quotient and AL the remainder. This same scheme of dividing by 10 can be expanded to convert any whole number from binary to an ASCII-coded character string that can be displayed on the video screen. The algorithm for converting from binary to ASCII is as follows:

1. Divide by 10 and save the remainder on the stack as a significant BCD digit.
2. Repeat step 2 until the quotient is a 0.
3. Retrieve each remainder and add a 30H to convert to ASCII before displaying or printing.

Example 6–19 shows how the unsigned 16-bit contents of AX are converted to ASCII and displayed on the video screen. Here we divide AX by 10 and save the remainder on the stack after each division for later conversion to ASCII. After all the digits have been converted, the result is displayed on the video screen by removing the remainders from the stack and converting them to ASCII code. This procedure also blanks any leading zeros that occur.

EXAMPLE 6–19

```
0000                    DISPX    PROC     FAR

0000 52                          PUSH     DX          ;save BX, CX, and DX
0001 51                          PUSH     CX
0002 53                          PUSH     BX

0003 33 C9                       XOR      CX,CX       ;clear CX
0005 BB 000A                     MOV      BX,10       ;load 10

0008                    DISPX1:

0008 33 D2                       XOR      DX,DX       ;clear DX
000A F7 F3                       DIV      BX
000C 52                          PUSH     DX          ;save remainder
000D 41                          INC      CX          ;count remainder
000E 0B C0                       OR       AX,AX       ;test quotient
0010 75 F6                       JNZ      DISPX1      ;if not zero

0012                    DISPX2:

0012 5A                          POP      DX          ;display number
0013 B4 06                       MOV      AH,6
0015 80 C2 30                    ADD      DL,30H      ;convert to ASCII
0018 CD 21                       INT      21H
001A E2 F6                       LOOP     DISPX2      ;repeat

001C 5B                          POP      BX          ;restore BX, CX, and DX
001D 59                          POP      CX
001E 5A                          POP      DX
001F CB                          RET

0020                    DISPX    ENDP
```

Converting from ASCII to Binary

Conversions from ASCII to binary usually start with keyboard entry. If a single key is typed, the conversion occurs when a 30H is subtracted from the number. If more than one key is typed, conversion from ASCII to binary still requires that 30H be subtracted, but there is one additional step. After subtracting 30H, the number is added to the result after the prior result is first multiplied by a 10. The algorithm for converting from ASCII to binary is as follows:

1. Begin with a binary result of 0.
2. Subtract 30H from the character typed on the keyboard to convert it to BCD.
3. Multiply the result by 10 and add the new BCD digit.
4. Repeat steps 2 and 3 until the character typed is not an ASCII-coded number.

EXAMPLE 6–20

```
0000                    READN   PROC    FAR

0000 53                         PUSH    BX              ;save BX and CX
0001 51                         PUSH    CX
0002 B9 000A                    MOV     CX,10           ;load 10
0005 33 DB                      XOR     BX,BX           ;clear result

0007                    READN1:

0007 B4 06                      MOV     AH,6            ;read key
0009 B2 FF                      MOV     DL,0FFH
000B CD 21                      INT     21H
000D 74 F8                      JE      READN1          ;wait for key

000F 3C 30                      CMP     AL,'0'          ;test against 0
0011 72 18                      JB      READN2          ;if below 0
0013 3C 39                      CMP     AL,'9'          ;test against 9
0015 77 14                      JA      READN2          ;if above 9

0017 8A D0                      MOV     DL,AL           ;echo key
0019 CD 21                      INT     21H

001B 2C 30                      SUB     AL,'0'          ;convert to BCD

001D 50                         PUSH    AX
001E 8B C3                      MOV     AX,BX           ;multiply by 10
0020 F7 E1                      MUL     CX
0022 8B D8                      MOV     BX,AX           ;save product
0024 58                         POP     AX
0025 32 E4                      XOR     AH,AH
0027 03 D8                      ADD     BX,AX           ;add BCD to product
0029 EB DC                      JMP     READN1          ;repeat

002B                    READN2:
```

```
002B  8B C3                    MOV     AX,BX          ;move binary to AX
002D  59                       POP     CX             ;restore BX and CX
002E  5B                       POP     BX
002F  CB                       RET

0030              READN        ENDP
```

Example 6–20 illustrates a procedure that implements this algorithm. Here the binary number returns in the AX register as a 16-bit result. If a larger result is required, the procedure must be reworked for 32-bit addition. Each time this procedure is called, it reads a number from the keyboard until any key other than 0 through 9 is typed.

Displaying and Reading Hexadecimal Data

Hexadecimal data are easier to read from the keyboard and display than decimal data. This type of data is not used at the applications level, but at the system level. System-level data are often hexadecimal and must be either displayed in hexadecimal form or read from the keyboard as hexadecimal data.

Reading Hexadecimal Data. Hexadecimal data appear as 0 to 9 and A to F. The ASCII codes obtained from the keyboard for hexadecimal data are 30H to 39H for the numbers 0 through 9 and 41H to 46H (A–F) or 61H to 66H (a–f) for the letters. To be useful, a procedure that reads hexadecimal data must be able to accept both lowercase and uppercase letters.

EXAMPLE 6–21

```
0000              CONV     PROC    NEAR

0000  3C 39                CMP     AL,'9'
0002  76 08                JBE     CONV2          ;if a number
0004  3C 61                CMP     AL,'a'
0006  72 02                JB      CONV1          ;if uppercase
0008  2C 20                SUB     AL,20H

000A              CONV1:

000A  2C 07                SUB     AL,7

000C              CONV2:

000C  2C 30                SUB     AL,'0'
000E  C3                   RET

000F              CONV     ENDP

000F              READH    PROC    FAR

000F  51                   PUSH    CX             ;save BX and CX
0010  53                   PUSH    BX
```

```
0011  B9 0004              MOV     CX,4          ;load shift count
0014  8B F1                MOV     SI,CX         ;load count
0016  33 DB                XOR     BX,BX         ;clear result

0018            READH1:

0018  B4 06                MOV     AH,6          ;read key
001A  B2 FF                MOV     DL,0FFH
001C  CD 21                INT     21H
001E  74 F8                JE      READH1        ;wait for key
0020  8A D0                MOV     DL,AL         ;echo
0022  CD 21                INT     21H
0024  E8 0000 R            CALL    CONV          ;convert to hexadecimal
0027  D3 E3                SHL     BX,CL         ;shift result
0029  02 D8                ADD     BL,AL         ;add AL to result
002B  4E                   DEC     SI
002C  75 EA                JNZ     READH1        ;repeat 4 times
002E  5B                   POP     BX            ;restore BX and CX
002F  59                   POP     CX
0030  CB                   RET

0031            READH   ENDP
```

Example 6–21 shows two procedures: one converts the contents of the data in AL from ASCII code to a single hexadecimal digit while the other reads a 4-digit hexadecimal number from the keyboard and returns with it in register AX. This procedure can be modified to read any size hexadecimal number from the keyboard.

Displaying Hexadecimal Data. To display hexadecimal data, a number must be divided into 4-bit segments that are converted into hexadecimal digits. Conversion is accomplished by adding a 30H to the numbers 0 to 9 and a 37H to the letters A to F.

EXAMPLE 6–22

```
0000             DISPH   PROC    FAR

0000  51                 PUSH    CX            ;save CX and DX
0001  52                 PUSH    DX
0002  B1 04              MOV     CL,4          ;load rotate count
0004  B5 04              MOV     CH,4          ;load digit count

0006            DISPH1:

0006  D3 C0              ROL     AX,CL         ;position number
0008  50                 PUSH    AX            ;save it
0009  24 0F              AND     AL,0FH        ;get hex digit
000B  04 30              ADD     AL,30H        ;adjust it
000D  3C 39              CMP     AL,'9'        ;test against 9
000F  76 02              JBE     DISPH2        ;if 0 -- 9
0011  04 07              ADD     AL,7          ;adjust it

0013            DISPH2:
```

```
0013 B4 06                          MOV    AH,6
0015 8A D0                          MOV    DL,AL
0017 CD 21                          INT    21H            ;display digit
0019 58                             POP    AX             ;restore AX
001A FE CD                          DEC    CH
001C 75 E8                          JNZ    DISPH1         ;repeat

001E 5A                             POP    DX             ;restore CX and DX
001F 59                             POP    CX
0020 CB                             RET

0021               DISPH    ENDP
```

A procedure that displays the contents of the AX register on the video display appears in Example 6–22. Here the number is rotated left so the leftmost digit is displayed first. Because AX contains a 4-digit hexadecimal number, the procedure displays four hexadecimal digits.

Using Lookup Tables for Data Conversions

Lookup tables are often used to convert from one data form to another. A lookup table is formed in the memory as a list of data that is referenced by a procedure to perform conversions. In the case of many lookup tables, the XLAT instruction can often be used to look up data in a table, provided the table contains 8-bit-wide data and its length is less than or equal to 256 bytes.

EXAMPLE 6–23

```
0000               SEG7     PROC    FAR

0000 53                     PUSH    BX
0001 BB 0008 R              MOV     BX,OFFSET TABLE
0004 2E: D7                 XLAT    CS:TABLE        ;see text
0006 5B                     POP     BX
0007 CB                     RET

0008 3F            TABLE    DB      3FH             ;0
0009 06                     DB      6               ;1
000A 5B                     DB      5BH             ;2
000B 4F                     DB      4FH             ;3
000C 66                     DB      66H             ;4
000D 6D                     DB      6DH             ;5
000E 7D                     DB      7DH             ;6
000F 07                     DB      7               ;7
0010 7F                     DB      7FH             ;8
0011 6F                     DB      6FH             ;9

0012               SEG7     ENDP
```

Converting from BCD to 7-Segment Code. One simple application that uses a lookup table is the conversion of BCD to 7-segment code. Example 6–23 illustrates a lookup table that contains the 7-segment codes for the numbers 0 to 9. These codes are used with the 7-segment display pictured in Figure 6–1. This 7-segment display uses active high (logic 1) inputs to light a segment. The code is arranged so that the *a* segment is in bit position 0 and the *g* segment is in bit position 6. Bit position seven is zero in this example, but can be used for displaying a decimal point.

The procedure that performs the conversion contains only two instructions and assumes that AL contains the BCD digit to be converted to 7-segment code. One of the instructions addresses the lookup table by loading its address into BX and the other performs the conversion and returns the 7-segment code in AL.

Because the lookup table is located in the code segment, and the XLAT instruction accesses the data segment by default, the XLAT instruction includes a segment override. Notice that a dummy operand (TABLE) is added to the XLAT instruction so the (CS:) code segment override prefix can be added to the instruction. Normally XLAT does not contain an operand unless its default segment must be overridden. The LODS and MOVS instructions are also overridden in the same manner as XLAT by using a dummy operand.

Using a Lookup Table to Access ASCII Data. Some programming techniques require that numeric codes be converted to ASCII character strings. For example, if you need to display the days of the week for a calendar program, some type of lookup table must be used to reference the ASCII-coded days of the week, because the number of ASCII characters in each day is different.

Example 6–24 shows a table that references ASCII-coded character strings located in the code segment. Each character string contains an ASCII-coded day of the week. The table references each day of the week, and the procedure that accesses them uses the AL register and the numbers 0 to 6 to refer to Sunday through Saturday. If AL contains a 2 when this procedure is called, the word "Tuesday" is displayed on the video screen.

This procedure first addresses the table by loading its address into the SI register. Next the number in AL is converted into a 16-bit number and doubled because the table contains 2 bytes for each entry. This index is then added to SI to address the correct entry in the lookup table. The address of the ASCII character string is now loaded into DX by the MOV DX,CS:[SI] instruction.

FIGURE 6–1 The 7-segment display.

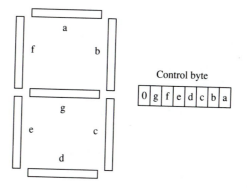

EXAMPLE 6–24

```
0000                    DAYS    PROC    FAR

0000 52                 PUSH    DX                      ;save DX and SI
0001 56                 PUSH    SI
0002 BE 001B R          MOV     SI,OFFSET DTAB          ;address DTAB
0005 32 E4              XOR     AH,AH                   ;clear AH
0007 03 C0              ADD     AX,AX                   ;double AX
0009 03 F0              ADD     SI,AX                   ;modify table address
000B 2E: 8B 14          MOV     DX,CS:[SI]              ;get string address
000E 8C C8              MOV     AX,CS                   ;change data segment
0010 1E                 PUSH    DS
0011 8E D8              MOV     DS,AX
0013 B4 09              MOV     AH,9
0015 CD 21              INT     21H                     ;display string
0017 1F                 POP     DS
0018 5E                 POP     SI                      ;restore DX and SI
0019 5A                 POP     DX
001A CB                 RET

001B 0029 R 0031 R      DTAB    DW      SUN,MON,TUE,WED,THU,FRI,SAT
     0039 R 0042 R
     004D R 0057 R
     005F R

0029 53 75 6E 64 61     SUN     DB      'Sunday $'
     79 20 24

0031 4D 6F 6E 64 61     MON     DB      'Monday $'
     79 20 24

0039 54 75 65 73 64     TUE     DB      'Tuesday $'
     61 79 20 24

0042 57 65 64 6E 65     WED     DB      'Wednesday $'
     73 64 61 79 20 24

004D 54 68 75 72 73     THU     DB      'Thursday $'
     64 61 79 20 24

0057 46 72 69 64 61     FRI     DB      'Friday $'
     79 20 24

005F 53 61 74 75 72     SAT     DB      'Saturday $'
     64 61 79 20 24

0069                    DAYS    ENDP
```

Before the INT 21H DOS function is called, the DS register is placed on the stack and loaded with the segment address of CS. This allows DOS function number

EXAMPLE 6–25

0000		STAC	SEGMENT STACK	

0000 0100[
    ????
        ]
		DW	256 DUP (?)	;set up stack

0200		STAC	ENDS	
0000		DAT	SEGMENT	
0000 0026 R 002F R 0038 R 0042 R 004E R 0059 R 0062 R	DAY	DW	SUN,MON,TUE,WED,THU,FRI,SAT	
000E 006D R 0076 R 0080 R 0087 R 008E R 0093 R 0099 R 009F R 00A7 R 00B2 R 00BB R 00C5 R	MONT	DW	JAN,FEB,MAR,APR,MAY,JUN,JUL,AUG,SEP,OCT,NOV,DCE	
0026 53 75 6E 64 61 79 2C 20 24	SUN	DB	'Sunday, $'	
002F 4D 6F 6E 64 61 79 2C 20 24	MON	DB	'Monday, $'	
0038 54 75 65 73 64 61 79 2C 20 24	TUE	DB	'Tuesday, $'	
0042 57 65 64 6E 65 73 64 61 79 2C 20 24	WE	DB	'Wednesday, $'	
004E 54 68 75 72 73 64 61 79 2C 20 24	THU	DB	'Thursday, $'	
0059 46 72 69 64 61 79 2C 20 24	FRI	DB	'Friday, $'	
0062 53 61 74 75 72 64 61 79 2C 20 24	SAT	DB	'Saturday, $'	
006D 4A 61 6E 75 61 72 79 20 24	JAN	DB	'January $'	
0076 46 65 62 72 75 61 72 79 20 24	FEB	DB	'February $'	
0080 4D 61 72 63 68 20 24	MAR	DB	'March $'	
0087 41 70 72 69 6C 20 24	APR	DB	'April $'	
008E 4D 61 79 20 24	MAY	DB	'May $'	
0093 4A 75 6E 65 20 24	JUN	DB	'June $'	
0099 4A 75 6C 79 20 24	JUL	DB	'July $'	
009F 41 75 67 75 73 74 20 24	AUG	DB	'August $'	
00A7 53 65 70 74 65 6D 62 65 72 20 24	SEP	DB	'September $'	
00B2 4F 63 74 6F 62 65 72 20 24	OCT	DB	'October $'	

```
00BB  4E 6F 76 65 6D 62        NOV     DB      'November $'
      65 72 20 24
00C5  44 65 63 65 6D 62        DCE     DB      'December $'
      65 72 20 24

00CF  0D 0A 24                 CRLF    DB      13,10,'$'
00D2  2E 4D 2E 20 20 24        MES1    DB      '.M. $'
00D8  2C 20 31 39 24           MES2    DB      ', 19$'
00DD  2C 20 32 30 24           MES3    DB      ', 20$'

00E2                  DAT      ENDS

0000                  COD      SEGMENT

                               ASSUME  CS:COD,DS:DAT,SS:STAC

0000                  MAIN     PROC    FAR                ;main program

0000  B8 ---- R                MOV     AX,DAT             ;load DS
0003  8E D8                    MOV     DS,AX

0005  BA 00CF R                MOV     DX,OFFSET CRLF     ;get new line
0008  B4 09                    MOV     AH,9
000A  CD 21                    INT     21H

000C  E8 001D R                CALL    TIMES              ;display time
000F  E8 007E R                CALL    DATES              ;display date

0012  BA 00CF R                MOV     DX,OFFSET CRLF     ;get new line
0015  B4 09                    MOV     AH,9
0017  CD 21                    INT     21H

0019  B4 4C                    MOV     AH,4CH             ;exit to DOS
001B  CD 21                    INT     21H

001D                  MAIN     ENDP

001D                  TIMES    PROC    NEAR               ;display time XX:XX A.M.

001D  B4 2C                    MOV     AH,2CH             ;get time
001F  CD 21                    INT     21H

0021  B7 41                    MOV     BH,'A'             ;set AM

0023  80 FD 0C                 CMP     CH,12              ;test against 12
0026  72 05                    JB      TIMES1             ;if AM

0028  B7 50                    MOV     BH,'P'             ;set PM
002A  80 ED 0C                 SUB     CH,12              ;adjust time
```

```
002D                    TIMES1:

002D  0A ED                     OR       CH,CH                ;test for 0 hours
002F  75 02                     JNE      TIMES2               ;if not 0 hours
0031  B5 0C                     MOV      CH,12                ;replace with 12 hours

0033                    TIMES2:

0033  8A C5                     MOV      AL,CH                ;get hours
0035  32 E4                     XOR      AH,AH                ;clear AH
0037  D4 0A                     AAM                           ;convert to BCD
0039  0A E4                     OR       AH,AH                ;test tens of hours
003B  74 09                     JZ       TIMES3               ;if no tens of hours
003D  50                        PUSH     AX
003E  8A C4                     MOV      AL,AH
0040  04 30                     ADD      AL,'0'               ;convert to ASCII
0042  E8 0075 R                 CALL     DISP                 ;display tens of hours
0045  58                        POP      AX

0046                    TIMES3:

0046  04 30                     ADD      AL,'0'               ;convert to ASCII
0048  E8 0075 R                 CALL     DISP                 ;display units of hours
004B  B0 3A                     MOV      AL,':'               ;display colon
004D  E8 0075 R                 CALL     DISP

0050  8A C1                     MOV      AL,CL                ;get minutes
0052  32 E4                     XOR      AH,AH                ;clear AH
0054  D4 0A                     AAM                           ;convert to BCD

0056  05 3030                   ADD      AX,3030H             ;convert to ASCII
0059  50                        PUSH     AX
005A  8A C4                     MOV      AL,AH
005C  E8 0075 R                 CALL     DISP                 ;display tens of minutes
005F  58                        POP      AX
0060  E8 0075 R                 CALL     DISP                 ;display units of minutes

0063  B0 20                     MOV      AL,' '               ;display space
0065  E8 0075 R                 CALL     DISP

0068  8A C7                     MOV      AL,BH                ;display A or P
006A  E8 0075 R                 CALL     DISP

006D  BA 00D2 R                 MOV      DX,OFFSET MES1       ;display .M.
0070  B4 09                     MOV      AH,9
0072  CD 21                     INT      21H
0074  C3                        RET

0075                    TIMES    ENDP
```

0075		DISP	PROC	NEAR	;display ASCII

0075 50		PUSH	AX	
0076 B4 06		MOV	AH,6	
0078 8A D0		MOV	DL,AL	
007A CD 21		INT	21H	
007C 58		POP	AX	
007D C3		RET		

007E		DISP	ENDP

007E		DATES	PROC	NEAR	;display date

007E B4 2A		MOV	AH,2AH	;get date
0080 CD 21		INT	21H	
0082 52		PUSH	DX	;save month and day

0083 32 E4		XOR	AH,AH	;clear AH
0085 03 C0		ADD	AX,AX	;double AX
0087 BE 0000 R		MOV	SI,OFFSET DAY	;address day table
008A 03 F0		ADD	SI,AX	
008C 8B 14		MOV	DX,[SI]	;get string address
008E B4 09		MOV	AH,9	
0090 CD 21		INT	21H	;display day

0092 5A		POP	DX	
0093 52		PUSH	DX	
0094 8A C6		MOV	AL,DH	;get month
0096 FE C8		DEC	AL	
0098 32 E4		XOR	AH,AH	
009A 03 C0		ADD	AX,AX	
009C BE 000E R		MOV	SI,OFFSET MONT	;address month table
009F 03 F0		ADD	SI,AX	
00A1 8B 14		MOV	DX,[SI]	;get string address
00A3 B4 09		MOV	AH,9	
00A5 CD 21		INT	21H	;display month

00A7 5A		POP	DX	;get day
00A8 8A C2		MOV	AL,DL	
00AA 32 E4		XOR	AH,AH	;clear AH
00AC D4 0A		AAM		;convert to BCD
00AE 0A E4		OR	AH,AH	;test tens of day
00B0 74 09		JZ	DATES1	;if zero
00B2 50		PUSH	AX	
00B3 8A C4		MOV	AL,AH	
00B5 04 30		ADD	AL,'0'	;convert to ASCII
00B7 E8 0075 R		CALL	DISP	;display tens of day
00BA 58		POP	AX	

00BB		DATES1:

```
00BB  04 30                ADD     AL,'0'              ;convert to ASCII
00BD  E8 0075 R            CALL    DISP                ;display units of day
00C0  BA 00D8 R            MOV     DX,OFFSET MES2
00C3  81 F9 07D0           CMP     CX,2000             ;test for year 2000
00C7  72 06                JB      DATES2              ;if year 19XX
00C9  83 E9 64             SUB     CX,100
00CC  BA 00DD R            MOV     DX,OFFSET MES3

00CF               DATES2:

00CF  B4 09                MOV     AH,9                ;display 19 or 20
00D1  CD 21                INT     21H
00D3  81 E9 076C           SUB     CX,1900             ;adjust year
00D7  8B C1                MOV     AX,CX
00D9  D4 0A                AAM                         ;convert to BCD
00DB  05 3030              ADD     AX,3030H            ;convert to ASCII
00DE  50                   PUSH    AX
00DF  8A C4                MOV     AL,AH
00E1  E8 0075 R            CALL    DISP                ;display tens of year
00E4  58                   POP     AX
00E5  E8 0075 R            CALL    DISP                ;display units of year
00E8  C3                   RET

00E9               DATES    ENDP

00E9               COD      ENDS

                            END     MAIN
```

09H (display a string) to be used to display the day of the week. This procedure converts the numbers 0 to 6 to the days of the week.

An Example Program Using Data Conversions

A program example is required to combine some of the data conversion DOS functions. Suppose that you must display the time and date on the video screen. This example program (see Example 6–25) displays the time as 10:45 P.M. and the date as Tuesday, May 14, 1991. The program is short because it calls one procedure that displays the time and another that displays the date.

The time is available from DOS using an INT 21H function call number 2C. This returns with the hours in CH and minutes in CL. Also available are seconds in DH and hundredths of seconds in DL. The date is available using the INT 21H function call number 2AH. This leaves the day of the week in AL, the year in CX, the day of the month in DH, and the month in DL.

This procedure uses two ASCII lookup tables that convert the day and month to ASCII character strings. It also uses the AAM instruction to convert from binary to BCD for the time and date. The displaying of data is handled in two ways: by character string (function 09H) and by single character (function 06H).

The memory consists of three segments: stack (STAC), data (DAT), and code (COD). The data segment contains the character strings used with the procedures that display time and date. The code segment contains MAIN, TIMES, DATES, and DISP procedures. The MAIN procedure is a FAR procedure because it is the program or main module. The other procedures are NEAR or local procedures used by MAIN.

6–4   DISK FILES

Data are found stored on the disk in the form of files. The disk itself is organized in four main parts: the boot sector, the file-allocation table (FAT), the root directory, and the data storage areas. The first sector on the disk is the boot sector. The boot sector is used to load the disk operating system (DOS) from the disk into the memory when power is applied to the computer. The FAT is where the names of files/subdirectories and their locations on the disk are stored by DOS. All references to any disk file are handled through the FAT. The root directory is where all other subdirectories and files are referenced. The disk files are all considered sequential access files, meaning that they are accessed a byte at a time from the beginning of the file toward the end.

Disk Organization

Figure 6–2 illustrates the organization of sectors and tracks on the surface of the disk. This organization applies to both floppy and hard disk memory systems. The outer track is always track 0 and the inner track is 39 (double density) or 79 (high density) on floppy disks. The inner track on a hard disk is determined by the disk size and could be 10,000 or higher for very large hard disks.

Figure 6–3 shows the organization of data on a disk. The length of the FAT is determined by the size of the disk. Likewise the length of the root directory is determined by the number of files and subdirectories located within it. The boot sector is always a single *512-byte*-long sector located in the outer track at sector 0, the first sector.

The boot sector contains a *bootstrap loader* program that is read into RAM when the system is powered. The bootstrap loader then executes and loads the IO.SYS* and MSDOS.SYS† programs into RAM. Next the bootstrap loader passes control to the MS-DOS control program, which puts the computer under the control of the DOS command processor.

The FAT indicates which sectors are free, which are corrupted (unusable), and which contain data. The FAT table is referenced each time that DOS writes data to the disk so that it can find a free sector. Each free cluster is indicated by a 0000H

---

*IO.SYS is an I/O control program provided by Microsoft Corporation with Microsoft DOS.
†MSDOS.SYS is the Microsoft Disk Operating System.

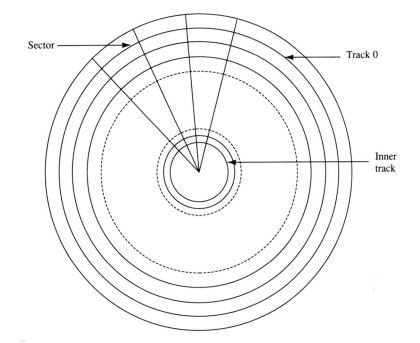

FIGURE 6–2 The disk memory showing tracks and sectors.

in the FAT and each occupied sector is indicated by the cluster number. A *cluster* can be anything from one sector to any number of sectors in length. Many hard disk memory systems use four sectors per cluster, which means the smallest file is 512 × 4 or 2048 bytes in length.

Figure 6–4 shows the format of each directory entry in the root or any other directory or subdirectory. Each entry contains the name, extension, attribute, time, date, location, and length. The length of the file is stored as a 32-bit number. This means that a file can have a maximum length of 4G bytes. The location is the starting cluster number.

FIGURE 6–3 The main data storage areas on a disk.

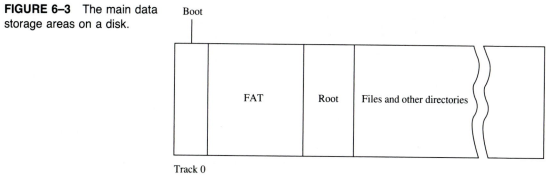

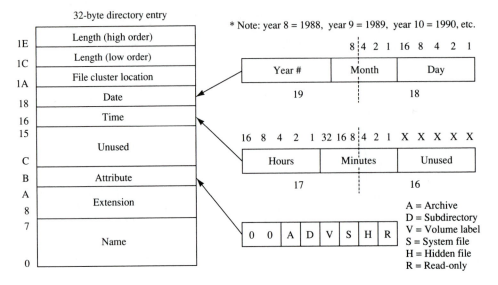

FIGURE 6–4   The format for any directory or subdirectory entry.

EXAMPLE 6–26

```
0000 49 4F 20 20 20 20 20 20 53 59 53 07 00 00 00 00    IO        SYS
0010 00 00 00 00 00 00 00 00 93 11 02 00 39 82 00 00

0020 4D 53 44 4F 53 20 20 20 53 59 53 07 00 00 00 00    MSDOS     SYS
0030 00 00 00 00 00 00 C0 44 93 12 13 00 92 00 00 00

0040 43 4F 4D 4D 41 4E 44 20 43 4F 4D 00 00 00 00 00    COMMAND   COM
0050 00 00 00 00 00 00 00 00 93 11 26 00 B5 92 00 00

0060 42 41 52 52 59 20 42 52 45 59 20 28 00 00 00 00    BARRY BREY
0070 00 00 00 00 00 00 E0 AD 6A 13 00 00 00 00 00 00

0080 50 43 54 4F 4F 4C 53 20 20 20 20 10 00 00 00 00    PCTOOLS
0090 00 00 00 00 00 00 80 AE 6A 13 5C 00 00 00 00 00

00A0 44 4F 53 20 20 20 20 20 20 20 20 10 00 00 00 00    DOS
00B0 00 00 00 00 00 00 E0 B0 6A 13 4E 00 00 00 00 00

00C0 52 55 4E 5F 46 57 20 20 42 41 54 00 00 00 00 00    FUN_FW    BAT
00D0 00 00 00 00 00 00 40 BD 6A 13 97 0F 4A 00 00 00

00E0 46 4F 4E 54 57 41 52 45 20 20 20 10 00 00 00 00    FONTWARE
00F0 00 00 00 00 00 00 60 BD 6A 13 6E 00 00 00 00 00
```

Example 6–26 shows how part of the root directory appears in a hexadecimal
dump. Try to identify the date, time, location, and length of each entry. Also identify

the attribute for each entry. The listing shows hexadecimal data and also ASCII data, as is customary for most computer dumps.

Files are usually accessed through DOS INT 21H function calls. There are two ways to access a file using INT 21H. One way uses a file control block, and the other uses a file handle. Today, all software accesses files via a file handle, so this text also uses file handles for file access. File-control blocks are a carryover from an earlier operating system called CPM (control program micro) that was used with 8-bit computer systems based on the Z80 or 8080 microprocessor.

Sequential File Access

All DOS files are sequential files. A sequential file is stored and accessed from the beginning of the file toward the end—the first byte and all bytes between it and the last must be accessed to read the last byte. Fortunately, files are read and written with the DOS INT 21H function calls (refer to Appendix A), which makes their access and manipulation easy. This section of the text describes how to create, read, write, delete, and rename a sequential access file.

File Creation. Before a file can be used, it must exist on the disk. A file is *created* by the INT 21H function call number 3CH. The file name must be stored at a location addressed by DS:DX before calling the function, and CX must contain the attribute of the file (or subdirectory) created.

EXAMPLE 6–27

0000		DAT	SEGMENT		
0000	44 4F 47 2E 54 58 54 00	FILE1	DB	'DOG.TXT',0	;file name DOG.TXT
0008	43 3A 44 41 54 41 2E 44 4F 43 00	FILE2	DB	'C:DATA.DOC',0	;file C:DATA.DOC
0013	43 3A 5C 44 52 45 41 44 5C 45 52 52 4F 52 2E 46 49 4C 00	FILE3	DB	'C:\DREAD\ERROR.FIL',0	;file C:\DREAD\ERROR.FIL
0026		DAT	ENDS		

A *file name* is always stored as an ASCII-Z string and may contain the drive and directory path(s) if needed. Example 6–27 shows several ASCII-Z string file names stored in a data segment for access by the file utilities. An *ASCII-Z string* is a character string that ends with a 00H or a null character.

Suppose that you have filled a 256 memory buffer area with data that must be stored in a new file called DATA.NEW on the default disk drive. Before data can be written to this new file, it must first be created. Example 6–28 lists a short procedure that creates this new file on the disk.

EXAMPLE 6–28

```
0000                     DAT      SEGMENT

0000 44 41 54 41 2E 4E   FILE1    DB      'DATA.NEW',0      ;file name DATA.NEW
     45 57 00
0009 0100[               BUFFER   DB      256 DUP (?)       ;data buffer
          ??
        ]

0109                     DAT      ENDS

0000                     COD      SEGMENT
                                  ASSUME  CS:COD,DS:DAT

0000 B8 ---- R           MOV      AX,DAT
0003 8E D8               MOV      DS,AX                     ;load DS

0005 B4 3C               MOV      AH,3CH                    ;load create function
0007 33 C9               XOR      CX,CX                     ;00H = attribute
0009 BA 0000 R           MOV      DX,OFFSET FILE1           ;address ASCII-Z name
000C CD 21               INT      21H                       ;create DATA.NEW

000E 72 20               JC       ERROR                     ;on creation error
                          .        .
                          .        .
                          .        .
0030                     COD      ENDS

                                  END
```

Whenever a file is created, the CX register must contain the attributes or characteristics of the file. Table 6–3 lists the attribute bit positions and defines them. A logic one in a bit selects the attribute, while a logic zero does not.

After returning from the INT 21H, the carry flag indicates whether an error occurred (CF = 1) during the creation of the file. Some errors that can occur, which are obtained if needed by INT 21H function call number 59H, are path not found, no file handles available, or media error. If carry is cleared, no error has occurred and the AX register contains a file handle. The *file handle* is a number that is used to refer to the file after it is created or opened. The file handle allows a file to be accessed without using the ASCII-Z string name of the file to speed the operation.

Writing to a File.   Now that we have created a new file, called FILE.NEW, data can be written to it. Before writing to a file it must have been created or opened. When a file is created or opened, the file handle returns in the AX register. The file handle is used to refer to the file whenever data are written to it.

TABLE 6–3 File attribute definitions

Bit Position	Attribute	Function
0	Read-only	A read-only file or subdirectory
1	Hidden	Prevents the file or subdirectory name from appearing in the directory when a DIR is used from the DOS command line
2	System	Specifies a file as a system file
3	Volume	Specifies the disk volume label
4	Subdirectory	Specifies a subdirectory name
5	Archive	Indicates that a file has been changed and that it should be archived

Function number 40H is used to write data to an opened or newly created file. In addition to loading a 40H into AH, we must load BX = the file handle, CX = the number of bytes to be written, and DS:DX = the address of the area to be written to the disk.

EXAMPLE 6–29

```
                    .        .
                    .        .
                    .        .
0010 8B D8          MOV      BX,AX              ;move handle to BX
0012 B4 40          MOV      AH,40H             ;load write function
0014 B9 0100        MOV      CX,256             ;load count
0017 BA 0009 R      MOV      DX,OFFSET BUFFER   ;address BUFFER
001A CD 21          INT      21H                ;write 256 bytes from BUFFER

001C 72 32          JC       ERROR1             ;on write error
```

Suppose that we must write all 256 bytes of BUFFER to the file. This is accomplished as illustrated in Example 6–29 using function 40H. If an error occurs during a write operation, the carry flag is set. If no error occurs, the carry flag is cleared and the number of bytes written to the file is returned in the AX register. Errors that occur for writes usually indicate that the disk is full or that there is some type of media error.

Opening, Reading, and Closing a File. To read a file, it must be opened first. When a file is opened, DOS checks the directory to determine if the file exists and returns the DOS file handle in register AX. The DOS file handle must be used for reading, writing, and closing a file.

EXAMPLE 6–30

```
0000                    READ    PROC    NEAR

0000 B4 3D                      MOV     AH,3DH              ;load open function
0002 B0 00                      MOV     AL,0                ;select read
0004 BA 0000 R                  MOV     DX,OFFSET FILE1     ;address file name
0007 CD 21                      INT     21H                 ;open file

0009 72 15                      JC      ERROR               ;on error

000B 8B D8                      MOV     BX,AX               ;move file handle to BX

000D B4 3F                      MOV     AH,3FH              ;load read function
000F B9 0100                    MOV     CX,256              ;number of bytes
0012 BA 0009 R                  MOV     DX,OFFSET BUFFER    ;address BUFFER
0015 CD 21                      INT     21H                 ;read 256 bytes

0017 72 07                      JC      ERROR               ;on error

0019 B4 3E                      MOV     AH,3EH              ;load close function
001B CD 21                      INT     21H                 ;close file

001D 72 01                      JC      ERROR               ;on error

001F C3                         RET

0020                    READ    ENDP
```

Example 6–30 shows a sequence of instructions that opens a file, reads 256 bytes from the file into memory area BUFFER, and then closes the file. When a file is opened (AH = 3DH), the AL register specifies the type of operation allowed for the opened file. If AL = 00H, the file is opened for a read; if AL = 01H, the file is opened for a write; and if AL = 02H, the file is opened for a read or a write.

Function number 3FH causes a file to be read. As with the write function, BX contains the file handle, CX the number of bytes to be read, and DS:DX the location of a memory area where the data are stored. As with all disk functions, the carry flag indicates an error when a logic 1 occurs. If a logic 0 occurs, the AX register indicates the number of bytes read from the file.

Closing a file is very important. If a file is left open, some serious problems can occur that can actually destroy the disk and all its data. If a file is written and not closed, the FAT can become corrupted, making it difficult or impossible to retrieve data from the disk. Always be certain to close a file after it is read or written.

The File Pointer. When a file is opened, written, or read, the file pointer addresses the current location in the sequential file. When a file is opened, the file pointer always addresses the first byte of the file. If a file is 1,024 bytes in length, and a read function reads 1,023 bytes, the file pointer addresses the last byte of the file, but not the end of the file.

The *file pointer* is a 32-bit number that addresses any byte in a file. Once a file is opened, the file pointer can be changed with the move file-pointer function number 42H. A file pointer can be moved from the start of the file (AL = 00H), from the current location (AL = 01H), or from the end of the file (AL = 02H). In practice all three directions of the move are used to access different parts of the file. The distance moved by the file pointer is specified by registers CX and DX. The DX register holds the least-significant part and CX the most-significant part of the distance. Register BX must contain the file handle before using function 42H to move the file pointer.

Suppose that a file exists on the disk and that you must append the file with 256 bytes of new information. When the file is opened, the file pointer addresses the first byte of the file. If you attempt to write without moving the file pointer to the end of the file, the new data will overwrite the first 256 bytes of the file. Example 6–31 shows a procedure that opens a file, moves the file pointer to the end of the file, writes 256 bytes of data, and then closes the file. This *appends* the file with 256 new bytes of data.

EXAMPLE 6–31

```
0000                    APPEND  PROC    NEAR

0000 B4 3D                      MOV     AH,3DH          ;load open function
0002 B0 01                      MOV     AL,1            ;select write
0004 BA 0000 R                  MOV     DX,OFFSET FILE1 ;address file name
0007 CD 21                      INT     21H             ;open file

0009 72 21                      JC      ERROR           ;on error

000B 8B D8                      MOV     BX,AX           ;move file handle to BX

000D B4 42                      MOV     AH,42H          ;load move file pointer function
000F B0 02                      MOV     AL,02H          ;move from end
0011 33 C9                      XOR     CX,CX           ;move 0 bytes from end
0013 33 D2                      XOR     DX,DX
0015 CD 21                      INT     21H             ;move pointer to end

0017 72 13                      JC      ERROR           ;on error

0019 B4 40                      MOV     AH,40H          ;load write function
001B B9 0100                    MOV     CX,256          ;number of bytes
001E BA 0009 R                  MOV     DX,OFFSET BUFFER ;address BUFFER
0021 CD 21                      INT     21H             ;write 256 bytes

0023 72 07                      JC      ERROR           ;on error

0025 B4 3E                      MOV     AH,3EH          ;load close function
0027 CD 21                      INT     21H             ;close file

0029 72 01                      JC      ERROR           ;on error

002B C3                         RET

002C                    APPEND  ENDP
```

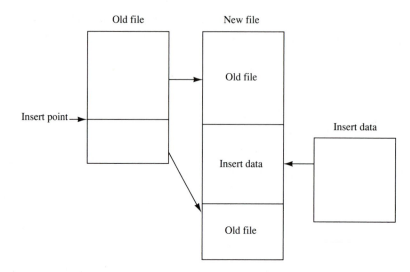

FIGURE 6–5 Inserting new data within an old file.

One of the more difficult file maneuvers is inserting new data in the middle of the file. Figure 6–5 shows how this is accomplished by creating a second file. Notice that the part of the file before the insertion point is copied into the new file. This is followed by the new information before the remainder of the file is appended after the insertion in the new file. Once the new file is complete, the old file is deleted and the new file is renamed to the old file name.

Example 6–32 shows a procedure that inserts new data, up to 64K bytes in length, into an old file. This procedure requires some input parameters to make it a general-purpose procedure. The first parameter is the old file name that is passed to the procedure through the DS:DX register. The second parameter (register CX) is the number of new bytes of information to write to the new file. The third parameter is the location (ES:SI) of the new data to be inserted in the file. The final parameter is the insertion point located in registers BP and DI, where BP contains the most-significant insert point and DI the least.

This procedure uses two new INT 21H function calls, delete and rename, to delete the old file before the temporary file is renamed to the old file name.

EXAMPLE 6–32

```
0000                        DATA    SEGMENT  PUBLIC

0000 0100[                  BUFFER  DB      256 DUP (?)      ;buffer
        ??
     ]
0100 0000                   TEMP    DW      ?                ;temporary data
0102 0000                   TEMP1   DW      ?                ;temporary data
0104 0000                   OLD_HAN DW      ?                ;old handle
0106 0000                   NEW_HAN DW      ?                ;temp handle
0108 54 45 4D 50 2E 24      TEMPS   DB      'TEMP.$$$',0     ;temp file
     24 24 00
```

```
0111                    DATA    ENDS

0000                    CODE    SEGMENT

                                ASSUME  CS:CODE,DS:DATA

0000                    INSERT  PROC    FAR

0000 89 16 0100 R               MOV     TEMP,DX              ;save old file address
0004 89 0E 0102 R               MOV     TEMP1,CX             ;save count

0008 B8 3D02                    MOV     AX,3D02H             ;open old file
000B CD 21                      INT     21H
000D A3 0104 R                  MOV     OLD_HAN,AX           ;save old file handle
0010 73 05                      JNC     INSERT1              ;if no error

0012 E8 009F R                  CALL    C_OLD                ;close old file
0015 F9                         STC                          ;indicate error
0016 CB                         RET

0017                    INSERT1:

0017 B4 3C                      MOV     AH,3CH               ;create temp file
0019 33 C9                      XOR     CX,CX
001B BA 0108 R                  MOV     DX,OFFSET TEMPS
001E CD 21                      INT     21H
0020 A3 0106 R                  MOV     NEW_HAN,AX           ;save temp file handle
0023 73 08                      JNC     INSERT2

0025                    EXIT:

0025 E8 00A8 R                  CALL    C_TEMP               ;close temp file
0028 E8 009F R                  CALL    C_OLD                ;close old file
002B F9                         STC                          ;indicate error
002C CB                         RET

002D                    INSERT2:

002D 81 FF 0100                 CMP     DI,256               ;test insert point
0031 77 07                      JA      INSERT3              ;if greater than 256
0033 0B ED                      OR      BP,BP
0035 75 03                      JNE     INSERT3              ;if greater than 256
0037 EB 17 90                   JMP     INSERT4              ;if less than 256

003A                    INSERT3:

003A B9 0100                    MOV     CX,256
003D E8 00B1 R                  CALL    R_OLD                ;read old file
0040 72 E3                      JC      EXIT                 ;on error
0042 E8 00BD R                  CALL    W_TEMP               ;write temp file
0045 72 DE                      JC      EXIT                 ;on error
```

```
0047  81 EF 0100          SUB     DI,256              ;decrement BP-DI by 256
004B  83 DD 00            SBB     BP,0
004E  EB DD               JMP     INSERT2

0050                INSERT4:

0050  8B CF               MOV     CX,DI               ;get count
0052  E8 00B1 R           CALL    R_OLD               ;read old file
0055  72 CE               JC      EXIT                ;on error
0057  E8 00BD R           CALL    W_TEMP              ;write temp file
005A  72 C9               JC      EXIT                ;on error

005C  8B 0E 0102 R        MOV     CX,TEMP1            ;get insert count
0060  1E                  PUSH    DS                  ;save data segment
0061  8C C0               MOV     AX,ES
0063  8E D8               MOV     DS,AX               ;load DS with ES

0065  8B D6               MOV     DX,SI               ;get address
0067  B4 40               MOV     AH,40H              ;write insert data
0069  CD 21               INT     21H
006B  1F                  POP     DS                  ;restore DS
006C  72 B7               JC      EXIT                ;on error

006E                INSERT5:

006E  B9 0100             MOV     CX,256              ;write remainder of file
0071  E8 00B1 R           CALL    R_OLD               ;read old file
0074  72 AF               JC      EXIT                ;on error
0076  0B C0               OR      AX,AX               ;test for end of file
0078  74 05               JE      INSERT6             ;if end file
007A  E8 00BD R           CALL    W_TEMP              ;write temp file
007D  EB EF               JMP     INSERT5             ;repeat until end

007F                INSERT6:

007F  E8 009F R           CALL    C_OLD               ;close old file
0082  E8 00A8 R           CALL    C_TEMP              ;close temp file
0085  8B 16 0100 R        MOV     DX,TEMP             ;delete old file
0089  B4 41               MOV     AH,41H
008B  CD 21               INT     21H

008D  06                  PUSH    ES                  ;save ES
008E  8C D8               MOV     AX,DS
0090  8E C0               MOV     ES,AX               ;load ES with DS

0092  8B 3E 0100 R        MOV     DI,TEMP             ;get old file name
0096  BA 0108 R           MOV     DX,OFFSET TEMPS
0099  B4 56               MOV     AH,56H              ;rename file
009B  CD 21               INT     21H
009D  07                  POP     ES
009E  CB                  RET
```

```
009F                    INSERT   ENDP

009F                    C_OLD    PROC    NEAR

009F  8B 1E 0104 R               MOV     BX,OLD_HAN              ;close old file
00A3  B4 3E                      MOV     AH,3EH
00A5  CD 21                      INT     21H
00A7  C3                         RET

00A8                    C_OLD    ENDP

00A8                    C_TEMP   PROC    NEAR                    ;close temp file

00A8  8B 1E 0106 R               MOV     BX,NEW_HAN
00AC  B4 3E                      MOV     AH,3EH
00AE  CD 21                      INT     21H
00B0  C3                         RET

00B1                    C_TEMP   ENDP

00B1                    R_OLD    PROC    NEAR

00B1  8B 1E 0104 R               MOV     BX,OLD_HAN
00B5  BA 0000 R                  MOV     DX,OFFSET BUFFER
00B8  B4 3F                      MOV     AH,3FH
00BA  CD 21                      INT     21H
00BC  C3                         RET

00BD                    R_OLD    ENDP

00BD                    W_TEMP   PROC    NEAR

00BD  8B C8                      MOV     CX,AX
00BF  8B 1E 0106 R               MOV     BX,NEW_HAN
00C3  BA 0000 R                  MOV     DX,OFFSET BUFFER
00C6  B4 40                      MOV     AH,40H
00C8  CD 21                      INT     21H
00CA  C3                         RET

00CB                    W_TEMP   ENDP

00CB                    CODE     ENDS

                                 END
```

Random Access Files

Random access files are developed through software using sequential access files. A random access file is addressed by a record number rather than by going through the file searching for data. The move pointer function call becomes very important when random access files are created. Random access files are much easier to use for large volumes of data.

Creating a Random Access File.   Planning ahead is paramount in creating a random access file system. Suppose that a random access file is required for storing the names of customers. Each customer record requires 16 bytes for the last name, 16 bytes for the first name, and 1 byte for the middle initial. Each customer record contains two street address lines of 32 bytes each, a city line of 16 bytes, 2 bytes for the state code, and 9 bytes for the ZIP code. Just the basic customer information requires 105 bytes. Additional information expands the record to 256 bytes in length. Because the business is growing, provisions are made for 5,000 customers. This means that the total random access file is 1,280,000 bytes in length.

EXAMPLE 6–33

```
0000                    DATA    SEGMENT

0000 0100[              BUFFER  DB      256 DUP (0)     ;buffer of 00H
         00
       ]
0100 41 3A 43 55 53 54  FILE    DB      'A:CUST.FIL',0  ;file name
     2E 46 49 4C 00

010B                    DATA    ENDS

0000                    CODE    SEGMENT

                        ASSUME  CS:CODE,DS:DATA

0000                    MAKE    PROC    FAR

0000 B8 ---- R                  MOV     AX,DATA         ;load DS
0003 8E D8                      MOV     DS,AX

0005 B4 3C                      MOV     AH,3CH          ;create CUST.FIL
0007 33 C9                      XOR     CX,CX
0009 BA 0100 R                  MOV     DX,OFFSET FILE
000C CD 21                      INT     21H

000E 8B D8                      MOV     BX,AX           ;handle to BX

0010 BF 1388                    MOV     DI,5000         ;load record count

0013                    MAKE1:

0013 B4 40                      MOV     AH,40H          ;write a record of 00H
0015 B9 0100                    MOV     CX,256
0018 BA 0000 R                  MOV     DX,OFFSET BUFFER
001B CD 21                      INT     21H
001D 4F                         DEC     DI
001E 75 F3                      JNZ     MAKE1           ;repeat 5000 times
```

```
0020 B4 3E              MOV    AH,3EH              ;close file
0022 CD 21              INT    21H

0024 B4 4C              MOV    AH,4CH              ;exit to DOS
0026 CD 21              INT    21H

0028              MAKE   ENDP

0028              CODE   ENDS

                        END    MAKE
```

Example 6–33 illustrates a short program that created a file called CUST.FIL and inserts 5,000 blank records of 256 bytes each. A blank record contains 00H in each byte. This appears to be a large file, but it fits on a single high-density 5-1/4″ or 3-1/2″ floppy disk drive; in fact, this program assumes that the disk is in drive A.

Reading and Writing a Record. Whenever a record must be read, the record number is loaded into the BP register and the procedure listed in Example 6–34 is called. This procedure assumes that FIL contains the handle number and that the CUST.FIL remains open at all times.

EXAMPLE 6–34

```
0000              READ   PROC   FAR

0000 8B 1E 0100 R        MOV    BX,FIL              ;get handle
0004 B8 0100             MOV    AX,256              ;multiple by 256
0007 F7 E5               MUL    BP
0009 8B CA               MOV    CX,DX
000B 8B D0               MOV    DX,AX
000D B8 4200             MOV    AX,4200H            ;move pointer
0010 CD 21               INT    21H

0012 B4 3F               MOV    AH,3FH              ;read record
0014 B9 0100             MOV    CX,256
0017 BA 0000 R           MOV    DX,OFFSET BUFFER
001A CD 21               INT    21H
001C CB                  RET

001D              READ   ENDP
```

Notice how the record number is multiplied by 256 to obtain a count for the move pointer function. In each case the file pointer is moved from the start of the file to the desired record before it is read into the memory area BUFFER. Although not shown, writing a record is performed in the same manner as reading one.

6–5   EXAMPLE PROGRAMS

Now that the basic programming building blocks have been discussed we present some example application programs. Although these example programs may seem trivial, they present some additional programming techniques and illustrate programming styles for the 80286 microprocessor.

Calculator Program

This program demonstrates how data conversion plays an important part in many application programs. Example 6–35 illustrates a program that accepts two numbers and adds, subtracts, multiplies, or divides them. To limit the complexity of the program, the numbers are limited to 2-digit numbers. For example, if you type a 12 + 24 = , the program will calculate the result and display a 36 as an answer. To further simplify the program, the numbers 0–9 must be entered as 2-digit numbers 00–99.

EXAMPLE 6–35

```
0000                 STAC    SEGMENT STACK

0000 0400[                   DW      1024 DUP (?)        ;set stack
            ????
        ]

0800                 STAC    ENDS

0000                 DATA    SEGMENT

0000 0D 0A 24        MES1    DB      13,10,'$'

0003                 DATA    ENDS

0000                 CODE    SEGMENT

                             ASSUME  CS:CODE,DS:DATA,SS:STAC

0000                 MAIN    PROC    FAR

0000 B8 ---- R               MOV     AX,DATA             ;load DS
0003 8E D8                   MOV     DS,AX

0005                 MAIN1:

0005 E8 0069 R               CALL    NEW                 ;get new line

0008 E8 0071 R               CALL    READ                ;get first number

000B                 MAIN2:
```

```
000B  E8 0097 R            CALL    KEY             ;get operation
000E  3C 2D                CMP     AL,'-'
0010  74 0C                JE      MAIN3           ;op ok
0012  3C 2B                CMP     AL,'+'
0014  74 08                JE      MAIN3           ;op ok
0016  3C 2F                CMP     AL,'/'
0018  74 04                JE      MAIN3           ;op ok
001A  3C 2A                CMP     AL,'*'
001C  75 ED                JNE     MAIN2           ;invalid op

001E          MAIN3:

001E  8A D0                MOV     DL,AL           ;echo op
0020  CD 21                INT     21H

0022  8A D8                MOV     BL,AL           ;save operation
0024  8B F5                MOV     SI,BP           ;save first number

0026  E8 00A0 R            CALL    SPACE
0029  E8 0071 R            CALL    READ            ;get second number

002C          MAIN4:

002C  E8 0097 R            CALL    KEY             ;get equal
002F  3C 3D                CMP     AL,'='
0031  75 F9                JNE     MAIN4           ;if not equal

0033  8A D0                MOV     DL,AL           ;echo equal
0035  CD 21                INT     21H
0037  E8 00A0 R            CALL    SPACE

003A  80 FB 2B             CMP     BL,'+'          ;test for +
003D  74 11                JE      PLUS
003F  80 FB 2D             CMP     BL,'-'          ;test for -
0042  74 13                JE      MIN
0044  80 FB 2F             CMP     BL,'/'          ;test for /
0047  74 15                JE      DIVS

0049  8B C5                MOV     AX,BP           ;multiply
004B  F7 E6                MUL     SI
004D  EB 15 90             JMP     MAIN5           ;display product

0050          PLUS:

0050  8B C5                MOV     AX,BP           ;add
0052  03 C6                ADD     AX,SI
0054  EB 0E 90             JMP     MAIN5           ;display sum

0057          MIN:

0057  8B C6                MOV     AX,SI           ;subtract
```

```
0059 2B C5                    SUB     AX,BP
005B EB 07 90                 JMP     MAIN5                   ;display difference

005E              DIVS:

005E 33 D2                    XOR     DX,DX                   ;divide
0060 8B C6                    MOV     AX,SI
0062 F7 F5                    DIV     BP                      ;display quotient

0064              MAIN5:

0064 E8 00A7 R                CALL    DISP                    ;display result
0067 EB 9C                    JMP     MAIN1                   ;repeat forever

0069              MAIN         ENDP

0069              NEW          PROC    NEAR

0069 B4 09                    MOV     AH,9                    ;display new line
006B BA 0000 R                MOV     DX,OFFSET MES1
006E CD 21                    INT     21H
0070 C3                       RET

0071              NEW          ENDP

0071              READ         PROC    NEAR

0071 33 ED                    XOR     BP,BP                   ;clear number
0073 B9 0002                  MOV     CX,2                    ;load count
0076 B7 0A                    MOV     BH,10                   ;load 10

0078              READ1:

0078 E8 0097 R                CALL    KEY                     ;read key
007B 3C 30                    CMP     AL,'0'                  ;test for number
007D 72 F9                    JB      READ1                   ;if not a number
007F 3C 39                    CMP     AL,'9'
0081 77 F5                    JA      READ1                   ;if not a number

0083 8A D0                    MOV     DL,AL                   ;echo to video
0085 CD 21                    INT     21H

0087 32 E4                    XOR     AH,AH
0089 2C 30                    SUB     AL,'0'

008B 95                       XCHG    BP,AX                   ;form number
008C F6 E7                    MUL     BH
008E 95                       XCHG    BP,AX
008F 03 E8                    ADD     BP,AX

0091 E2 E5                    LOOP    READ1                   ;repeat twice
```

```
0093  E8 00A0 R              CALL     SPACE              ;display space
0096  C3                     RET

0097            READ         ENDP

0097            KEY          PROC     NEAR

0097  B4 06                  MOV      AH,6               ;read key
0099  B2 FF                  MOV      DL,0FFH
009B  CD 21                  INT      21H
009D  74 F8                  JE       KEY
009F  C3                     RET

00A0            KEY          ENDP

00A0            SPACE        PROC     NEAR

00A0  B4 06                  MOV      AH,6               ;display space
00A2  B2 20                  MOV      DL,' '
00A4  CD 21                  INT      21H
00A6  C3                     RET

00A7            SPACE        ENDP


00A7            DISP         PROC     NEAR

00A7  33 C9                  XOR      CX,CX              ;clear count
00A9  BB 000A                MOV      BX,10              ;load 10
00AC  3D 8000                CMP      AX,8000H           ;test for negative
00AF  72 0A                  JB       DISP1              ;if positive
00B1  F7 D8                  NEG      AX                 ;make positive
00B3  50                     PUSH     AX
00B4  B2 2D                  MOV      DL,'-'             ;display -
00B6  B4 06                  MOV      AH,6
00B8  CD 21                  INT      21H
00BA  58                     POP      AX

00BB            DISP1:

00BB  33 D2                  XOR      DX,DX
00BD  F7 F3                  DIV      BX                 ;divide by 10
00BF  52                     PUSH     DX                 ;save remainder
00C0  41                     INC      CX                 ;count digit
00C1  0B C0                  OR       AX,AX              ;test quotient
00C3  75 F6                  JNE      DISP1              ;repeat until 0

00C5  B4 06                  MOV      AH,6

00C7            DISP2:
```

```
00C7 5A                    POP     DX              ;display digit
00C8 80 C2 30              ADD     DL,'0'
00CB CD 21                 INT     21H
00CD E2 F8                 LOOP    DISP2           ;repeat
00CF C3                    RET

00D0            DISP       ENDP

00D0            CODE       ENDS

                           END     MAIN
```

Note that this program is an infinite loop. When you have tested it and found that it functions, the control and alternate keys are held down then the delete key is pressed to reboot the computer and DOS. If you wish you can place an exit function in the software. This program does not support a backspace to correct an erroneous entry. No attempt has been made to recover from any errors.

Numeric Sort Program

At times numbers must be sorted into numeric order. This is often accomplished with a bubble sort. Figure 6–6 shows five numbers that are sorted with a bubble sort. Notice that the set of five numbers is tested four times with four passes. For each pass two consecutive numbers are compared and sometimes exchanged. Also notice that during the first pass, there are four comparisons, during the second three, and so forth.

Example 6–36 illustrates a program that accepts 10 numbers from the keyboard (0–65535). After these 16-bit numbers are accepted and stored in memory section ARRAY, they are sorted using the bubble sorting technique. This bubble sort uses a flag to determine if any numbers were exchanged in a pass. If no numbers were exchanged, the numbers are in order and the sort terminates.

FIGURE 6–6 A bubble sort showing data as they are sorted. *Note:* Sorting five numbers may require four passes.

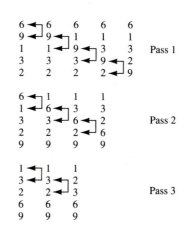

EXAMPLE 6–36

```
0000                    STAC    SEGMENT STACK

0000 0400[              DW      1024 DUP (?)                ;set stack
        ????
      ]

0800                    STAC    ENDS

0000                    DATA    SEGMENT

0000 000A[              ARRAY   DW      10 DUP (?)          ;space for numbers
        ????
      ]
0014 0D 0A 24           MES1    DB      13,10,'$'
0017 0D 0A 45 6E 74 65  MES2    DB      13,10,'Enter 10 numbers:',13,10,'$'
     72 20 31 30 20 6E
     75 6D 62 65 72 73
     3A 0D 0A 24

002D 0D 0A 53 6F 72 74  MES3    DB      13,10,'Sorted Data:',13,10,'$'
     65 64 20 44 61 74
     61 3A 0D 0A 24

003E                    DATA    ENDS

0000                    CODE    SEGMENT

                                ASSUME  CS:CODE,DS:DATA,SS:STAC

0000                    MAIN    PROC    FAR

0000 B8 ---- R                  MOV     AX,DATA             ;load DS
0003 8E D8                      MOV     DS,AX
0005 8E C0                      MOV     ES,AX               ;load ES

0007 B4 09                      MOV     AH,9                ;display MES2
0009 BA 0017 R                  MOV     DX,OFFSET MES2
000C CD 21                      INT     21H

000E FC                         CLD                         ;select auto-increment
000F BF 0000 R                  MOV     DI,OFFSET ARRAY     ;address ARRAY
0012 B9 000A                    MOV     CX,10               ;load count

0015                    MAIN1:

0015 E8 0039 R                  CALL    READ                ;read number
0018 E2 FB                      LOOP    MAIN1               ;repeat 10 times

001A BF 0000 R                  MOV     DI,OFFSET ARRAY     ;address ARRAY
001D B9 000A                    MOV     CX,10               ;load count
0020 E8 007A R                  CALL    SORT                ;sort numbers
```

```
0023 B4 09                    MOV      AH,9                   ;display MES3
0025 BA 002D R                MOV      DX,OFFSET MES3
0028 CD 21                    INT      21H

002A B9 000A                  MOV      CX,10                  ;load count
002D BE 0000 R                MOV      SI,OFFSET ARRAY        ;address ARRAY

0030               MAIN2:

0030 E8 009A R                CALL     DISP                   ;display number
0033 E2 FB                    LOOP     MAIN2

0035 B4 4C                    MOV      AH,4CH                 ;return to DOS
0037 CD 21                    INT      21H

0039               MAIN       ENDP

0039               READ       PROC     NEAR

0039 33 ED                    XOR      BP,BP                  ;clear result
003B BB 000A                  MOV      BX,10                  ;load 10

003E               READ1:

003E B4 06                    MOV      AH,6                   ;read key
0040 B2 FF                    MOV      DL,0FFH
0042 CD 21                    INT      21H
0044 74 F8                    JE       READ1                  ;if no key
0046 3C 0D                    CMP      AL,13
0048 74 25                    JE       READ2                  ;if enter key
004A 3C 30                    CMP      AL,'0'
004C 72 F0                    JB       READ1                  ;if not a number
004E 3C 39                    CMP      AL,'9'
0050 77 EC                    JA       READ1                  ;if not a number

0052 50                       PUSH     AX
0053 8B C5                    MOV      AX,BP                  ;multiply by 10
0055 F7 E3                    MUL      BX
0057 0B D2                    OR       DX,DX                  ;test for too big
0059 5A                       POP      DX
005A 75 E2                    JNZ      READ1                  ;too big
005C 52                       PUSH     DX
005D 32 F6                    XOR      DH,DH
005F 80 EA 30                 SUB      DL,'0'                 ;make BCD
0062 03 C2                    ADD      AX,DX                  ;form number
0064 5A                       POP      DX
0065 72 D7                    JC       READ1                  ;if too big
0067 8B E8                    MOV      BP,AX                  ;save number

0069 B4 06                    MOV      AH,6                   ;echo
006B CD 21                    INT      21H
006D EB CF                    JMP      READ1
```

```
006F                    READ2:

006F  8B C5                     MOV     AX,BP
0071  AB                        STOSW
0072  B4 09                     MOV     AH,9              ;get new line
0074  BA 0014 R                 MOV     DX,OFFSET MES1
0077  CD 21                     INT     21H
0079  C3                        RET


007A                    READ    ENDP

007A                    SORT    PROC    NEAR

007A  49                        DEC     CX                ;adjust count

007B                    SORT1:

007B  8B F7                     MOV     SI,DI             ;duplicate address
007D  8B D9                     MOV     BX,CX             ;duplicate count
007F  33 ED                     XOR     BP,BP             ;clear swap flag

0081                    SORT2:

0081  AD                        LODSW                     ;get data
0082  3B 04                     CMP     AX,[SI]
0084  72 0A                     JB      SORT3             ;no swap
0086  8B 14                     MOV     DX,[SI]           ;swap
0088  89 04                     MOV     [SI],AX
008A  89 54 FE                  MOV     [SI-2],DX
008D  BD 0001                   MOV     BP,1              ;indicate swap

0090                    SORT3:

0090  4B                        DEC     BX
0091  75 EE                     JNE     SORT2             ;repeat
0093  0B ED                     OR      BP,BP
0095  74 02                     JE      SORT4             ;done
0097  E2 E2                     LOOP    SORT1             ;repeat

0099                    SORT4:

0099  C3                        RET

009A                    SORT    ENDP

009A                    DISP    PROC    NEAR

009A  51                        PUSH    CX                ;save external count
009B  33 C9                     XOR     CX,CX             ;clear count
009D  BB 000A                   MOV     BX,10             ;load 10
00A0  AD                        LODSW                     ;get number
```

```
00A1                    DISP1:

00A1 33 D2                      XOR     DX,DX               ;clear DX
00A3 F7 F3                      DIV     BX                  ;divide by 10
00A5 52                         PUSH    DX                  ;save remainder
00A6 41                         INC     CX
00A7 0B C0                      OR      AX,AX               ;test quotient
00A9 75 F6                      JNZ     DISP1               ;repeat
00AB B4 06                      MOV     AH,6


00AD                    DISP2:

00AD 5A                         POP     DX                  ;get digit
00AE 80 C2 30                   ADD     DL,'0'              ;make ASCII
00B1 CD 21                      INT     21H                 ;display it
00B3 E2 F8                      LOOP    DISP2               ;repeat

00B5 B4 09                      MOV     AH,9                ;get new line
00B7 BA 0014 R                  MOV     DX,OFFSET MES1
00BA CD 21                      INT     21H

00BC 59                         POP     CX                  ;restore CX
00BD C3                         RET

00BE            DISP    ENDP

00BE            CODE    ENDS

                        END     MAIN
```

Once the numbers are sorted, they are displayed on the video screen in ascending numeric order. No provision is made for errors as each number is typed. The program terminates after sorting one set of 10 numbers and must be invoked again to sort 10 new numbers.

Hexadecimal File Dump

An example program that displays a file in hexadecimal format allows us to practice disk memory access. It also gives us the opportunity to read a parameter (the file name) from the DOS command line.

Whenever a command (program name) is typed at the DOS command line, any parameters that follow are placed in a *program segment prefix*. The program segment prefix (PSP) is listed in Appendix A, Figure A–6. Notice that the length of the command line and the command line parameters appear in the PSP along with other information. Upon execution of a program, the DS segment register addresses the PSP so an offset address of 80H is used to access the length (byte-sized) of the command line. After obtaining the length, the command line and its parameters can be accessed.

EXAMPLE 6–37

```
0000                    STAC      SEGMENT STACK

0000 0400[                        DW        1024 DUP (?)              ;set stack
           ????
                    ]

0800                    STAC      ENDS

0000                    DATA      SEGMENT

0000 0100[                        BUFFER    DB      256 DUP (?)
           ??
                    ]
0100 0040[                        FILE      DB      64 DUP (?)
           ??
                    ]

0140 0D 0A 2A 2A 2A 20            MES1      DB      13,10,'*** You enter file name      ***',13,10,'$'
     59 6F 75 20 65 6E
     74 65 72 20 66 69
     6C 65 20 6E 61 6D
     65 20 2A 2A 2A 0D
     0A 24
0160 0D 0A 2A 2A 2A 20            MES2      DB      13,10,'*** File not found ***',13,10,'$'
     46 69 6C 65 20 6E
     6F 74 20 66 6F 75
     6E 64 20 2A 2A 2A
     0D 0A 24
017B 0D 0A 2A 2A 2A 20            MES3      DB      13,10,'*** File corrupt ***',13,10,'$'
     46 69 6C 65 20 63
     6F 72 72 75 70 74
     20 2A 2A 2A 0D 0A
     24
0194 0D 0A 53 65 63 74            MES4      DB      13,10,'Section: $'
     69 6F 6E 3A 20 24
01A0 0D 0A 24                     MES5      DB      13,10,'$'
01A3 00                          SECT      DB      ?

01A4                    DATA      ENDS

0000                    CODE      SEGMENT

                                  ASSUME  CS:CODE,DS:DATA,SS:STAC

0000                    MAIN      PROC      FAR

0000 B8 ---- R                    MOV       AX,DATA              ;load ES
0003 8E C0                        MOV       ES,AX

0005 BE 0082                      MOV       SI,82H               ;address length
0008 80 7C FE 00                  CMP       BYTE PTR [SI-2],0
```

```
000C 75 0D                 JNE       MAIN2                ;if file name

000E 8E D8                 MOV       DS,AX                ;load DS
0010 BA 0140 R             MOV       DX,OFFSET MES1       ;display error

0013               MAIN1:

0013 B4 09                 MOV       AH,9
0015 CD 21                 INT       21H

0017 B4 4C                 MOV       AH,4CH               ;return to DOS
0019 CD 21                 INT       21H

001B               MAIN2:

001B 8A 4C FE              MOV       CL,[SI-2]            ;get length
001E 32 ED                 XOR       CH,CH                ;make 16-bits
0020 49                    DEC       CX                   ;adjust count
0021 BF 0100 R             MOV       DI,OFFSET FILE       ;address file name
0024 F3/ A4                REP MOVSB                      ;save file name
0026 C6 05 00              MOV       BYTE PTR [DI],0      ;make ASCII-Z string

0029 8C C0                 MOV       AX,ES                ;load DS
002B 8E D8                 MOV       DS,AX

002D B8 3D02               MOV       AX,3D02H             ;open file
0030 BA 0100 R             MOV       DX,OFFSET FILE
0033 CD 21                 INT       21H
0035 73 05                 JNC       MAIN3                ;if file found
0037 BA 0160 R             MOV       DX,OFFSET MES2       ;display file not found
003A EB D7                 JMP       MAIN1

003C               MAIN3:

003C 8B D8                 MOV       BX,AX                ;get file handle
003E C6 06 01A3 R FF       MOV       SECT,-1              ;set first section

0043               MAIN4:

0043 FE 06 01A3 R          INC       SECT
0047 B4 3F                 MOV       AH,3FH               ;read 256 bytes
0049 B9 0100               MOV       CX,256
004C BA 0000 R             MOV       DX,OFFSET BUFFER
004F CD 21                 INT       21H
0051 73 05                 JNC       MAIN5                ;if read good
0053 BA 017B R             MOV       DX,OFFSET MES3       ;display file corrupt
0056 EB BB                 JMP       MAIN1

0058               MAIN5:

0058 3D 0000               CMP       AX,0                 ;test for end of file
005B 75 0B                 JNE       MAIN6                ;not end
```

```
005D  B4 3E                    MOV     AH,3EH              ;close file
005F  CD 21                    INT     21H

0061  E8 00BF R                CALL    NEW

0064  B4 4C                    MOV     AH,4CH              ;exit to DOS
0066  CD 21                    INT     21H

0068               MAIN6:

0068  E8 006D R                CALL    DUMP                ;display 256 byte section
006B  EB D6                    JMP     MAIN4               ;repeat

006D               MAIN        ENDP

006D               DUMP        PROC    NEAR                ;display 256 byte section

006D  8B C8                    MOV     CX,AX               ;save count
006F  B4 09                    MOV     AH,9                ;display header
0071  BA 0194 R                MOV     DX,OFFSET MES4
0074  CD 21                    INT     21H

0076  A0 01A3 R                MOV     AL,SECT             ;display number
0079  E8 009C R                CALL    DISP

007C  BE 0000 R                MOV     SI,OFFSET BUFFER

007F               DUMP1:

007F  E8 00C7 R    CALL     DISPA                          ;display address

0082               DUMP1A:

0082  E8 00FA R                CALL    DISPN               ;display number
0085  49                       DEC     CX
0086  74 08                    JE      DUMP2
0088  8B C6                    MOV     AX,SI
008A  24 0F                    AND     AL,0FH              ;test address
008C  74 F1                    JZ      DUMP1
008E  EB F2                    JMP     DUMP1A

0090               DUMP2:

0090  B4 06                    MOV     AH,6                ;get a key
0092  B2 FF                    MOV     DL,0FFH
0094  CD 21                    INT     21H
0096  74 F8                    JE      DUMP2
0098  E8 00BF R                CALL    NEW
009B  C3                       RET

009C               DUMP        ENDP
```

```
009C                    DISP    PROC    NEAR            ;display decimal

009C 51                         PUSH    CX              ;save CX
009D 53                         PUSH    BX              ;save BX
009E 32 E4                      XOR     AH,AH
00A0 BB 000A                    MOV     BX,10           ;load 10
00A3 33 C9                      XOR     CX,CX           ;clear count

00A5                    DISP1:

00A5 33 D2                      XOR     DX,DX
00A7 F7 F3                      DIV     BX              ;divide by 10
00A9 52                         PUSH    DX              ;save remainder
00AA 41                         INC     CX              ;count remainder
00AB 0B C0                      OR      AX,AX           ;test quotient
00AD 75 F6                      JNE     DISP1           ;repeat
00AF B4 06                      MOV     AH,6

00B1                    DISP2:

00B1 5A                         POP     DX              ;get digit
00B2 80 C2 30                   ADD     DL,'0'          ;convert to ASCII
00B5 CD 21                      INT     21H
00B7 E2 F8                      LOOP    DISP2           ;repeat
00B9 E8 00BF R                  CALL    NEW             ;get new line
00BC 5B                         POP     BX
00BD 59                         POP     CX
00BE C3                         RET

00BF                    DISP    ENDP

00BF                    NEW     PROC    NEAR            ;display new line

00BF B4 09                      MOV     AH,9
00C1 BA 01A0 R                  MOV     DX,OFFSET MES5
00C4 CD 21                      INT     21H
00C6 C3                         RET

00C7                    NEW     ENDP

00C7                    DISPA   PROC    NEAR            ;display address

00C7 E8 00BF R                  CALL    NEW             ;get new line
00CA 8B C6                      MOV     AX,SI           ;get address
00CC E8 00DF R                  CALL    DIG             ;display digit
00CF E8 00DF R                  CALL    DIG
00D2 E8 00DF R                  CALL    DIG
00D5 E8 00DF R                  CALL    DIG

00D8 B4 06                      MOV     AH,6            ;display space
00DA B2 20                      MOV     DL,' '
00DC CD 21                      INT     21H
```

```
00DE C3                      RET

00DF              DISPA      ENDP

00DF              DIG        PROC    NEAR          ;display hex digit

00DF D1 C0                   ROL     AX,1          ;position digit
00E1 D1 C0                   ROL     AX,1
00E3 D1 C0                   ROL     AX,1
00E5 D1 C0                   ROL     AX,1
00E7 50                      PUSH    AX
00E8 24 0F                   AND     AL,0FH        ;mask
00EA 04 30                   ADD     AL,'0'        ;convert to ASCII
00EC 3C 39                   CMP     AL,'9'
00EE 76 02                   JBE     DIG1
00F0 04 07                   ADD     AL,7

00F2              DIG1:

00F2 8A D0                   MOV     DL,AL         ;display digit
00F4 B4 06                   MOV     AH,6
00F6 CD 21                   INT     21H
00F8 58                      POP     AX
00F9 C3                      RET

00FA              DIG        ENDP

00FA              DISPN      PROC    NEAR          ;display number

00FA AC                      LODSB                 ;get number
00FB 8A E0                   MOV     AH,AL
00FD E8 00DF R               CALL    DIG           ;display digit
0100 E8 00DF R               CALL    DIG

0103 B4 06                   MOV     AH,6
0105 B2 20                   MOV     DL,' '        ;display space
0107 CD 21                   INT     21H

0109 C3                      RET

010A              DISPN      ENDP

010A              CODE       ENDS

                             END     MAIN
```

Example 6–37 lists a program that obtains a file name from the command line and then displays the file in a hexadecimal listing. This program is useful for debugging faulty programs and also as practice with disk file access and conversions. The parameter following the command always starts with a space (20H) at offset address 81H and always ends with a carriage return (0DH). The length of the parameter is always one greater. For example, if DUMPS FROG is typed at the command line and DUMPS is the name of the program, the parameter FROG is stored beginning with a 20H at offset 81H, and the length is 5.

6–6   HOOKS

Hooks are used to tap into the interrupt structure of the microprocessor. For example, we might hook into the keyboard interrupt so we can detect a special keystroke called a *hot key*. Whenever the hot key is typed, we can access a terminate and stay resident (TSR) program that performs a special task. Some example hot key software are pop-up calculators, pop-up clocks, and so forth.

Tapping into an Interrupt

In order to tap into an interrupt, we must use a DOS function call that reads the current address from the interrupt vector. The DOS function call number 35H is used to read the current interrupt vector, and DOS function call number 25H is used to change the address of the current vector. In both DOS function calls, AL indicates the vector type number (00H–FFH) and AH indicates the DOS function call number.

When the vector is read using function 35H, the offset address is returned in register BX and the segment address is in register ES. These two registers are saved so they can be re-stored when the interrupt hook is removed from memory. When the vector is set, it is set to the address stored at the memory location addressed by DS:DX.

EXAMPLE 6–38

```
                    ORG      100H                        ;origin for a COM program

0100                START:

0100 EB 04                   JMP      MAIN

0102 00000000       ADDRESS DD       ?                   ;old interrupt vector

0106                MAIN:

0106 8C C8                   MOV      AX,CS              ;address CS with DS
0108 8E D8                   MOV      DS,AX

            ;get vector 0 address

010A B8 3500                 MOV      AX,3500H
010D CD 21                   INT      21H

        ;save vector address
```

```
010F  2E: 89 1E 0102 R          MOV     WORD PTR ADDRESS,BX
0114  2E: 8C 06 0104 R          MOV     WORD PTR ADDRESS+2,ES

                      ;install new interrupt vector 0 address

0119  B8 2500                   MOV     AX,2500H
011C  BA 0300 R                 MOV     DX,OFFSET NEW
011F  CD 21                     INT     21H
```

The process of installing an interrupt handler through a hook is illustrated in Example 6–38. This procedure reads the current interrupt vector address and stores it into a double-word memory location for access by the new interrupt service procedure. Next, the address of the new interrupt service procedure, stored in DS:DX, is placed into the vector using DOS function call number 25H.

Example TSR Alarm Clock

A fairly simple example showing an interrupt hook and TSR causes a beep on the speaker after a set amount of time elapses. The amount of time is specified in 10 second intervals as defined by an equate statement found in this software. For example, if the amount of the time interval specified is 60, a beep will occur after 10 minutes once this program is installed. The timing interval of the beep can be adjusted by changing the number stored with the equate statement.

EXAMPLE 6–39

```
0000                   CODES    SEGMENT  'CODE'

                                ASSUME   CS:CODES

                                ORG      5DH

005D 0000              COUNTS   DW       ?                ;timer interval

                                ORG      100H             ;origin for a COM program

0100                   START:

0100  E9 0091                   JMP      MAIN

0103 00000000          ADDR1    DD       ?                ;old interrupt vector
0107 B6                SEC10    DB       182              ;10 second counter
0108 00                ACTIVE   DB       0                ;timer flag

= 000A                 ALARM    EQU      10               ;alarm times 10 seconds
= 0320                 TONE     EQU      800              ;frequency in Hertz
= 0006                 LENG     EQU      6                ;duration = leng/18.2

0109                   BEEP     PROC     NEAR
```

```
0109 50                          PUSH      AX                    ;save registers
010A 53                          PUSH      BX
010B 51                          PUSH      CX
010C 52                          PUSH      DX
010D 06                          PUSH      ES
010E B0 B6                       MOV       AL,0B6H               ;initialize timer 2
0110 E6 43                       OUT       43H,AL

0112 BA 0012                     MOV       DX,12H                ;calculate count
0115 B8 34DC                     MOV       AX,34DCH
0118 BB 0320                     MOV       BX,TONE
011B F7 F3                       DIV       BX

011D E6 42                       OUT       42H,AL                ;program timer 2
011F 8A C4                       MOV       AL,AH
0121 E6 42                       OUT       42H,AL

0123 E4 61                       IN        AL,61H                ;speaker on
0125 0C 03                       OR        AL,3
0127 E6 61                       OUT       61H,AL

0129 BA 0006                     MOV       DX,LENG
012C 2B C9                       SUB       CX,CX
012E 8E C1                       MOV       ES,CX
0130 26: 03 16 046C              ADD       DX,ES:[46CH]
0135 26: 13 0E 046E              ADC       CX,ES:[46EH]
013A              BEEPS:

013A 26: 8B 1E 046C              MOV       BX,ES:[46CH]          ;wait leng clock ticks
013F 26: A1 046E                 MOV       AX,ES:[46EH]
0143 2B DA                       SUB       BX,DX
0145 1B C1                       SBB       AX,CX
0147 72 F1                       JC        BEEPS
0149 E4 61                       IN        AL,61H                ;speaker off
014B 34 03                       XOR       AL,3
014D E6 61                       OUT       61H,AL

014F 07                          POP       ES                    ;restore registers
0150 5A                          POP       DX
0151 59                          POP       CX
0152 5B                          POP       BX
0153 58                          POP       AX
0154 C3                          RET

0155              BEEP           ENDP

0155              TIMES          PROC      FAR                   ;new interrupt

0155 2E: 80 3E 0108 R            CMP       ACTIVE,0              ;test active
     00
015B 74 05                       JZ        TIMES1                ;if armed
015D 2E: FF 2E 0103 R            JMP       ADDR1                 ;do original interrupt
```

```
0162                    TIMES1:
0162  2E: FE 06 0108 R        INC     ACTIVE              ;set active
0167  9C                      PUSHF                       ;simulate interrupt
0168  2E: FF 1E 0103 R        CALL    ADDR1               ;do interrupt
016D  FB                      STI                         ;enable INTR
016E  1E                      PUSH    DS                  ;save registers
016F  0E                      PUSH    CS
0170  1F                      POP     DS                  ;get current code segment
0171  2E: FE 0E 0107 R        DEC     SEC10               ;decrement counter
0176  75 15                   JNZ     TIMES2              ;if not 10 seconds
0178  2E: C6 06 0107 R        MOV     SEC10,182           ;reload SEC10
      B6
017E  2E: FF 0E 005D R        DEC     COUNTS              ;decrement counter
0183  75 08                   JNZ     TIMES2              ;if no alarm
0185  E8 FF81                 CALL    BEEP                ;sound alarm
0188  2E: FE 06 0108 R        INC     ACTIVE

018D                    TIMES2:
018D  2E: FE 0E 0108 R        DEC     ACTIVE              ;decrement active
0192  1F                      POP     DS
0193  CF                      IRET

0194                    TIMES   ENDP

0194                    MAIN:
0194  8C C8                   MOV     AX,CS
0196  8E D8                   MOV     DS,AX

0198  B8 000A                 MOV     AX,ALARM
019B  2E: A3 005D R           MOV     COUNTS,AX           ;save alarm interval
019F  B8 3508                 MOV     AX,3508H            ;get vector 8
01A2  CD 21                   INT     21H
01A4  2E: 89 1E 0103 R        MOV     WORD PTR ADDR1,BX   ;save address
01A9  2E: 8C 06 0105 R        MOV     WORD PTR ADDR1+2,ES
01AE  B8 2508                 MOV     AX,2508H            ;install new interrupt
01B1  BA 0155 R               MOV     DX,OFFSET TIMES
01B4  CD 21                   INT     21H
01B6  BA 0194 R               MOV     DX,OFFSET MAIN      ;set length
01B9  B1 04                   MOV     CL,4
01BB  D3 EA                   SHR     DX,CL
01BD  42                      INC     DX
01BE  B8 3100                 MOV     AX,3100H            ;TSR
01C1  CD 21                   INT     21H

01C3                    CODES   ENDS

                        END     START
```

The beep is caused by using timer 2 of the timer found inside the PC so it generates an audio tone at the speaker. (Refer to Section 9–5 for a discussion of the timer and see Figure 6–7 for its connection in the computer.) Programming timer 2 with a particular beep frequency or tone is accomplished by programming timer 2

FIGURE 6–7 The speaker circuit connected to the timer inside the personal computer. (The 8255 is at I/O ports 60H–63H and the 8253 timer is at I/O ports 40H–43H.)

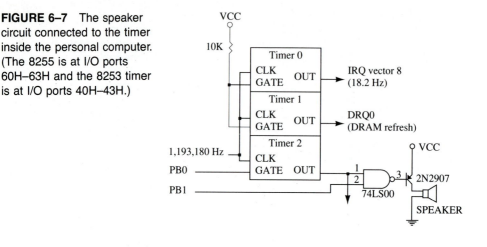

with 1,193,180 divided by the desired tone. For example, if we divide 1,193,180 by 800, the speaker generates an 800-Hz audio tone. Refer to the BEEP procedure (see Example 6–39) for programming the timer and turning the speaker on and off after a short wait determined by the number of clock ticks. This procedure uses six clock ticks that produces a beep of about a third of a second duration. Note that each clock tick occurs about 18.2 times a second (the actual time is 18.2064819336). This tick frequency is accomplished by using the user wait timer locations in the first segment of the memory. The user wait timer is updated 18.2 times per second by the computer so it can be used to time events.

The MAIN program utilizes the alarm counter with a 10, causing a 100-second delay before the speaker beeps. After initializing the alarm delay, the address of the original timer interrupt vector (type 8) is obtained by using DOS function call number 35H. The interrupt vector is then stored in memory location ADDR1. After obtaining the original interrupt vector, DOS function call 25H is used to store the address of TIMES (the new interrupt service procedure) into vector number 8. The very last few instructions of MAIN are used to make the interrupt service procedure and BEEP memory resident. This is accomplished by first calculating the length of these procedures. Note that the length is given as the number of 16-byte paragraphs. When DOS function call 31H is executed, the new interrupt service procedure and BEEP become memory resident. There is no provision for removing this memory resident software from the system once it is installed. All that happens after the alarm goes off is that the interrupt service procedure deactivates itself.

The program is assembled and linked as any other program, but in this example it is converted from an .EXE file into a .COM file. Conversion is accomplished by using the EXE2BIN program. All .COM files must begin executing software at location 100H and may not exceed 64K bytes in length. A .COM file is used in place of an .EXE file because it requires less memory to store. This is important for memory-resident software, but not an absolute requirement.

This example remains resident even after the alarm has sounded. If it is desirable to remove the program, it must terminate with DOS function call 4CH, just as we terminate most other software instead of with an interrupt return. This DOS function call removes the program from the memory and returns to DOS when activated. If you wish to terminate with DOS function 4CH, make sure that you replace the original interrupt vector into vector 8 before executing the DOS function 4CH call.

Example Hot Key Program

Hot keys are keystrokes that invoke programs that are terminated and stay resident. For example, an ALT C key could be defined as a hot key that calls a program that displays the time. Note that the hot key is located inside most applications, but not at the DOS command line, where if used, it may lock up the system. To detect a hot key we usually hook into interrupt vector 9, which is the keyboard interrupt that occurs if any key is typed. This allows us to test the keyboard and detect a hot key before the normal interrupt processes the keystroke.

EXAMPLE 6–40

```
0108 00000000        OLD9    DD    ?                 ;original vector address
010C 00              CODE    DB    ?                 ;scan code of hot key
010D 00              MASKS   DB    ?                 ;shift/alternate mask
010E 00              HOT     DB    ?                 ;correct hot shift/alternare
010F 00              FLAG    DB    0                 ;TSR flag

0200 FB        VEC9:    STI                          ;interrupt on
0201 50                 PUSH    AX
0202 E4 60              IN      AL,60H               ;get scan code
0204 2E: 3A 06 010C R   CMP     AL,CODE              ;check for hot key scan code
0209 75 2E              JNE     VEC91                ;if not hot key
020B 06                 PUSH    ES
020C 2B C0              SUB     AX,AX
020E 8E C0              MOV     ES,AX
0210 26: A0 0417        MOV     AL,ES:[417H]         ;get shift/alternate status
0214 2E: 22 06 010D R   AND     AL,MASKS             ;isolate bit(s)
0219 2E: 3A 06 010E R   CMP     AL,HOT               ;test for shift/alternate
021E 07                 POP     ES
021F 75 18              JNE     VEC91                ;if not hot key

               ;HOT KEY pressed

0221 FA                 CLI                          ;interrupt off
0222 E4 61              IN      AL,61H               ;throw away keystroke
0224 0C 80              OR      AL,80H               ;clear keyboard
0226 E6 61              OUT     61H,AL
0228 24 7F              AND     AL,7FH               ;signal break
022A E6 61              OUT     61H,AL
022C B0 20              MOV     AL,20H               ;reset interrupt controller
022E E6 20              OUT     20H,AL
0230 FB                 STI                          ;interrupts on
0231 58                 POP     AX
0232 2E: C6 06 010F R   MOV     FLAG,1               ;indicate hot key
     01
0238 CF                 IRET                         ;exit handler
```

```
                    ;HOT KEY NOT pressed

0239                     VEC91:

0239 58                      POP     AX
023A FA                      CLI                    ;interrupts off
023B 9C                      PUSHF                  ;simulate interrupt
023C 2E: FF 1E 0108 R        CALL    OLD9           ;call original keyboard interrupt
0241 CF                      IRET
```

Example 6–40 shows a short replacement interrupt service procedure that tests for a hot key and sets a flag if it is detected. This example does not illustrate the software used to install this replacement procedure. The CODE variable is the scan code (see Figure 6–8) of the hot key to be detected, the MASKS are the mask bits to extract the shift key or alternate key from the memory at location 0000:0417 (see Appendix A for details), and the HOT code is the desired combination of shift/alternate keys for the hot key. The procedure detects a hot key, and if it is active, the procedure places a 01H into the FLAG byte. The FLAG byte is usually detected by a replacement clock tick interrupt at vector 8.

Example 6–41 shows a program that hooks into interrupt vectors 9 and 8. Interrupt vector 9 is captured to access a hot key, and interrupt vector 8 is captured to execute a TSR program that is activated by the hot key. In this example, we use the hot key A that accesses a TSR program to display the time of day on the video screen. The time is displayed until the escape key is typed on the keyboard. When escape is typed, the original data are redisplayed over the time. This program only functions if the display adapter is in text mode.

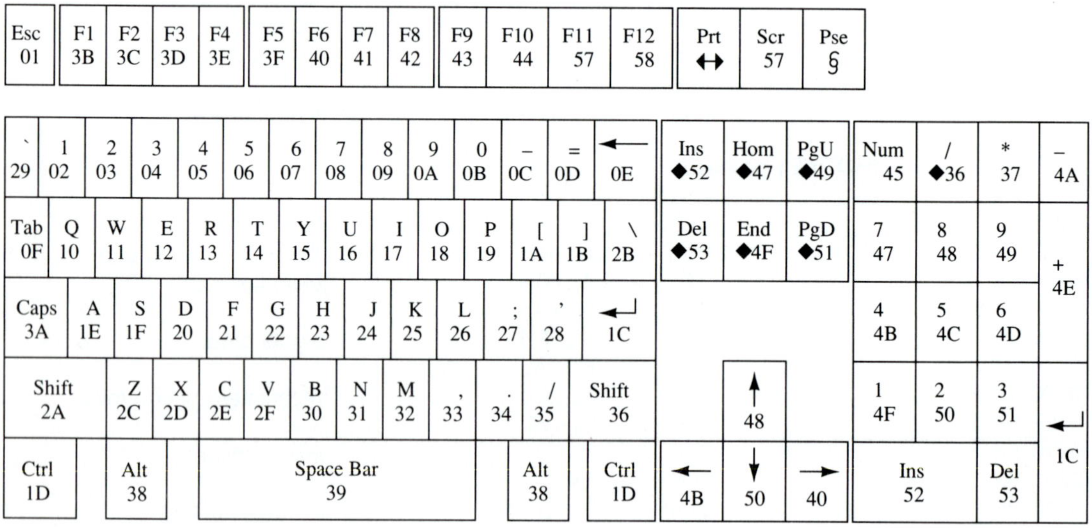

Esc 01	F1 3B	F2 3C	F3 3D	F4 3E	F5 3F	F6 40	F7 41	F8 42	F9 43	F10 44	F11 57	F12 58	Prt ↔	Scr 57	Pse §

| ` 29 | 1 02 | 2 03 | 3 04 | 4 05 | 5 06 | 6 07 | 7 08 | 8 09 | 9 0A | 0 0B | – 0C | = 0D | ← 0E | Ins ◆52 | Hom ◆47 | PgU ◆49 | Num 45 | / ◆36 | * 37 | – 4A |

| Tab 0F | Q 10 | W 11 | E 12 | R 13 | T 14 | Y 15 | U 16 | I 17 | O 18 | P 19 | [1A |] 1B | \ 2B | Del ◆53 | End ◆4F | PgD ◆51 | 7 47 | 8 48 | 9 49 | + 4E |

| Caps 3A | A 1E | S 1F | D 20 | F 21 | G 22 | H 23 | J 24 | K 25 | L 26 | ; 27 | ' 28 | ↵ 1C | | | | 4 4B | 5 4C | 6 4D | |

| Shift 2A | | Z 2C | X 2D | C 2E | V 2F | B 30 | N 31 | M 32 | , 33 | . 34 | / 35 | Shift 36 | ↑ 48 | | 1 4F | 2 50 | 3 51 | ↵ 1C |

| Ctrl 1D | | Alt 38 | | Space Bar 39 | | | | | Alt 38 | Ctrl 1D | ← 4B | ↓ 50 | → 40 | Ins 52 | Del 53 | |

FIGURE 6–8   Keyboard scan codes.

EXAMPLE 6–41

```
                        .286
                        ;
                        ;This program displays the time when hot-key ALT T is typed.
                        ;This program is set up as a .COM file with ORG 100H
                        ;
0000                    CODE    SEGMENT

                        ASSUME  CS:CODE

                        ORG     100H

0100  E9 0962           BEGIN:  JMP     START

0103  00000000          VEC8    DD      ?                       ;original vector 8 address
0107  00000000          VEC9    DD      ?                       ;original vector 9 address
010B  00000000          STPT    DD      ?                       ;original stack pointer
010F  00                H_FLAG  DB      0                       ;hot-key flag
0110  14                H_CODE  DB      14H                     ;scan code of hot key 'T'
0111  08                MASKS   DB      8                       ;alternate mask
0112  08                HOT     DB      8                       ;correct hot shift/alternate
0113  00                COL     DB      0                       ;display column
0114  00                ROW     DB      0                       ;display row
0115  00                T_ROW   DB      ?                       ;temp row
0116  00                T_COL   DB      ?                       ;temp column
0117  0005 [            BUF     DB      5 DUP (?)               ;old display data
         00
         ]
011C  24                        DB      '$'
011D  0005 [            BUF1    DB      5 DUP (?)               ;time buffer
         00
         ]
0122  24                        DB      '$'
0123  0000              TEMP    DW      ?
0125  0400 [                    DW      400H DUP (?)
         0000
         ]
0925 = 0925             STAC    EQU     THIS WORD


                        ;keyboard hot key intercept

0925                    KEY     PROC    FAR

0925  FB                        STI                             ;interrupts on
0926  50                        PUSH    AX
0927  E4 60                     IN      AL,60H                  ;get scan code
0929  2E: 3A 06 0110 R          CMP     AL,H_CODE               ;test for hot scan code
092E  75 2E                     JNE     KEY1                    ;if not hot key
0930  06                        PUSH    ES
0931  2B C0                     SUB     AX,AX
```

```
0933 8E C0                          MOV      ES,AX
0935 26: A0 0417                    MOV      AL,ES:[417H]        ;get shift/alternate status
0939 2E: 22 06 0111 R               AND      AL,MASKS            ;isolate alternate
093E 2E: 3A 06 0112 R               CMP      AL,HOT              ;test for alternate
0943 07                             POP      ES
0944 75 18                          JNE      KEY1                ;if not hot key

                     ;if HOT KEY detected

0946 FA                             CLI                          ;interrupts off
0947 E4 61                          IN       AL,61H              ;throw away keystroke
0949 0C 80                          OR       AL,80H              ;clear keyboard
094B E6 61                          OUT      61H,AL
094D 24 7F                          AND      AL,7FH              ;signal break
094F E6 61                          OUT      61H,AL
0951 B0 20                          MOV      AL,20H              ;reset interrupt controller
0953 E6 20                          OUT      20H,AL
0955 FB                             STI                          ;interrupts on
0956 58                             POP      AX
0957 2E: C6 06 010F R               MOV      H_FLAG,0FFH         ;indicate hot key
     FF
095D CF                             IRET

                     ;if HOT KEY not detected

095E                 KEY1:

095E 58                             POP      AX
095F FA                             CLI                          ;interrupts off
0960 9C                             PUSHF                        ;simulate interrupt
0961 2E: FF 1E 0107 R               CALL     CS:VEC9
0966 CF                             IRET

0967                 KEY      ENDP

                     ;clock tick interrupt TICK

0967                 TICK     PROC     FAR

0967 2E: 80 3E 010F R               CMP      H_FLAG,0            ;test for HOT KEY
     00
096D 75 05                          JNZ      TICK1               ;if HOT KEY active
096F 2E: FF 2E 0103 R               JMP      CS:VEC8             ;do normal interrupt

                     ;if HOT KEY ACTIVE

0974                 TICK1:

0974 2E: C6 06 010F R               MOV      H_FLAG,0            ;clear HOT KEY request
     00
```

```
097A 9C                          PUSHF                                ;do clock tick interrupt
097B 2E: FF 1E 0103 R            CALL       CS:VEC8

0980 FA                          CLI
0981 2E: A3 0123 R               MOV        TEMP,AX                   ;save old stack area
0985 8C D0                       MOV        AX,SS
0987 2E: A3 010D R               MOV        WORD PTR STPT+2,AX
098B 2E: 89 26 010B R            MOV        WORD PTR STPT,SP

0990 BC 0925 R                   MOV        SP,OFFSET STAC            ;get new stack area
0993 8C C8                       MOV        AX,CS
0995 8E D0                       MOV        SS,AX
0997 FB                          STI

0998 E8 0012                     CALL       CLOCK                     ;display time until any key

099B FA                          CLI
099C 2E: A1 010D R               MOV        AX,WORD PTR STPT+2   ;address old stack area
09A0 8E D0                       MOV        SS,AX
09A2 2E: 8B 26 010B R            MOV        SP,WORD PTR STPT
09A7 2E: A1 0123 R               MOV        AX,TEMP
09AB FB                          STI

09AC CF                          IRET

09AD                  TICK       ENDP

                      ;CLOCK procedure to display the time at COL, ROW

09AD                  CLOCK      PROC       NEAR

09AD 50                          PUSH       AX                        ;save registers
09AE 53                          PUSH       BX
09AF 51                          PUSH       CX
09B0 52                          PUSH       DX
09B1 57                          PUSH       DI
09B2 1E                          PUSH       DS

09B3 8C C8                       MOV        AX,CS
09B5 8E D8                       MOV        DS,AX

09B7 B4 03                       MOV        AH,3                      ;get current cursor position
09B9 B7 00                       MOV        BH,0
09BB CD 10                       INT        10H
09BD 2E: 88 36 0115 R            MOV        T_ROW,DH                  ;save row and column
09C2 2E: 88 16 0116 R            MOV        T_COL,DL
09C7 B4 02                       MOV        AH,2                      ;move cursor
09C9 2E: 8A 36 0114 R            MOV        DH,ROW
09CE 2E: 8A 16 0113 R            MOV        DL,COL
```

```
09D3  B7 00                        MOV      BH,0
09D5  CD 10                        INT      10H

09D7  BF 0117 R                    MOV      DI,OFFSET BUF        ;save current screen
09DA  B9 0005                      MOV      CX,5

09DD              CLOCK1:

09DD  B4 08                        MOV      AH,8                 ;read character
09DF  B7 00                        MOV      BH,0
09E1  CD 10                        INT      10H
09E3  88 05                        MOV      [DI],AL
09E5  47                           INC      DI
09E6  FE C2                        INC      DL                   ;next column
09E8  B4 02                        MOV      AH,2
09EA  CD 10                        INT      10H
09EC  E2 EF                        LOOP     CLOCK1

09EE  B4 02                        MOV      AH,2                 ;reposition cursor
09F0  80 EA 05                     SUB      DL,5
09F3  CD 10                        INT      10H

09F5  BF 011D R                    MOV      DI,OFFSET BUF1

09F8  B4 2C                        MOV      AH,2CH               ;get time
09FA  CD 21                        INT      21H
09FC  8A C5                        MOV      AL,CH
09FE  32 E4                        XOR      AH,AH
0A00  D4 0A                        AAM                           ;convert tens of hours
0A02  80 C4 20                     ADD      AH,20H
0A05  80 FC 20                     CMP      AH,20H
0A08  74 03                        JE       CLOCK2
0A0A  80 C4 10                     ADD      AH,10H

0A0D              CLOCK2:

0A0D  88 25                        MOV      [DI],AH
0A0F  04 30                        ADD      AL,30H
0A11  88 45 01                     MOV      [DI+1],AL
0A14  2E: C6 45 02 3A              MOV      BYTE PTR CS:[DI+2],":"
0A19  8A C1                        MOV      AL,CL                ;convert units of hours
0A1B  32 E4                        XOR      AH,AH
0A1D  D4 0A                        AAM
0A1F  05 3030                      ADD      AX,3030H
0A22  88 65 03                     MOV      [DI+3],AH
0A25  88 45 04                     MOV      [DI+4],AL
0A28  BA 011D R                    MOV      DX,OFFSET BUF1
0A2B  B4 09                        MOV      AH,9                 ;display time
0A2D  CD 21                        INT      21H

0A2F              CLOCK3:
```

```
0A2F B4 06                      MOV     AH,6                    ;test any key
0A31 B2 FF                      MOV     DL,0FFH
0A33 CD 21                      INT     21H
0A35 74 F8                      JZ      CLOCK3

0A37 B4 02                      MOV     AH,2
0A39 2E: 8A 36 0114 R           MOV     DH,ROW
0A3E 2E: 8A 16 0113 R           MOV     DL,COL
0A43 B7 00                      MOV     BH,0
0A45 CD 10                      INT     10H

0A47 B4 09                      MOV     AH,9
0A49 BA 0117 R                  MOV     DX,OFFSET BUF
0A4C CD 21                      INT     21H

0A4E B4 02                      MOV     AH,2
0A50 2E: 8A 36 0115 R           MOV     DH,T_ROW
0A55 2E: 8A 16 0116 R           MOV     DL,T_COL
0A5A B7 00                      MOV     BH,0
0A5C CD 10                      INT     10H

0A5E 1F                         POP     DS
0A5F 5F                         POP     DI
0A60 5A                         POP     DX
0A61 59                         POP     CX
0A62 5B                         POP     BX
0A63 58                         POP     AX
0A64 C3                         RET

0A65                    CLOCK   ENDP

                        ;install interrupt procedure 8 and 9

0A65                    START:

0A65 8C C8                      MOV     AX,CS
0A67 8E D8                      MOV     DS,AX

0A69 B8 3508                    MOV     AX,3508H                ;get vector 8
0A6C CD 21                      INT     21H
0A6E 2E: 89 1E 0103 R           MOV     WORD PTR VEC8,BX
0A73 2E: 8C 06 0105 R           MOV     WORD PTR VEC8+2,ES

0A78 B8 3509                    MOV     AX,3509H                ;get vector 9
0A7B CD 21                      INT     21H
0A7D 2E: 89 1E 0107 R           MOV     WORD PTR VEC9,BX
0A82 2E: 8C 06 0109 R           MOV     WORD PTR VEC9+2,ES

0A87 B8 2508                    MOV     AX,2508H                ;install TICK as 8
0A8A BA 0967 R                  MOV     DX,OFFSET TICK
0A8D CD 21                      INT     21H
```

```
0A8F  B8 2509                MOV     AX,2509H
0A92  BA 0925 R              MOV     DX,OFFSET KEY        ;install KEY as 9
0A95  CD 21                  INT     21H

0A97  BA 0A65 R              MOV     DX,OFFSET START      ;make resident
0A9A  C1 EA 04               SHR     DX,4
0A9D  42                     INC     DX
0A9E  B8 3100                MOV     AX,3100H
0AA1  CD 21                  INT     21H

0AA3           CODE          ENDS

               END           BEGIN
```

6–7   SUMMARY

1. The assembler program assembles modules that contain PUBLIC variables and segments plus EXTRN (external) variables. The linker program links modules and library files to create a run-time program executed from the DOS command line. The run-time program usually has the extension EXE.
2. The MACRO and ENDM directives create a new opcode for use in programs. These macros are similar to procedures, except there is no call or return. In place of them, the assembler inserts the code of the macro sequence into a program each time it is invoked. Macros can include variables that pass information and data to the macro sequence.
3. The DOS INT 21H function call provides a method of using the keyboard and video display. Function number 06H, placed into register AH, provides an interface to the keyboard and display. If DL = 0FFH, this function tests the keyboard for a keystroke. IF no keystroke is detected, it returns equal. If a keystroke is detected, the standard ASCII character returns in AL. If an extended ASCII character is typed, it returns with AL = 00H, where the function must again be called to return with the extended ASCII character in AL. To display a character, DL is loaded with the character and AH with 06H before the INT 21H is used in a program.
4. Character strings are displayed using function number 09H. The DS:DX register combination addresses the character string, which must end with a $.
5. The INT 10H instruction accesses BIOS (basic I/O system) procedures that control the video display and keyboard. The BIOS functions are independent of DOS and function with any operating system.
6. Data conversion from binary to BCD is accomplished with the AAM instruction for numbers that are less than 100 or by repeated division by 10 for larger numbers. Once converted to BCD, a 30H is added to convert each digit to ASCII code for the video display.

7. When converting from an ASCII number to BCD, a 30H is subtracted from each digit. To obtain the binary equivalent, we multiply by 10.

8. Lookup tables are used for code conversion with the XLAT instruction if the code is an 8-bit code. If the code is wider than 8-bits, then a short procedure that accesses a lookup table provides the conversion. Lookup tables are also used to hold addresses so that different parts of a program or different procedures can be selected.

9. The disk memory system contains tracks that hold information stored in sectors. Many disk systems store 512 bytes of information per sector. Data on the disk is organized in a boot sector, file-allocation table (FAT), root directory, and a data storage area. The boot sector loads the DOS system from the disk into the computer memory system. The FAT indicates which sectors are present and whether they contain data. The root directory contains file names and subdirectories, through which all disk files are accessed. The data storage area contains all subdirectories and data files.

10. Files are manipulated with the DOS INT 21H function call. To read a disk file, the file must be opened, read, and then closed. To write to a disk file, it must be opened, written, and then closed. When a file is opened, the file pointer addresses the first byte of the file. To access data at other locations, the file pointer is moved before data are read or written.

11. A sequential access file is a file that is accessed sequentially from the beginning to the end. A random access file is a file that is accessed at any point. Although all disk files are sequential, they can be treated as random access files by using software procedures.

12. The program segment prefix (PSP) contains information about a program. One important part of the PSP is the command line parameters.

13. Interrupt hooks allows application software to gain access to or intercept an interrupt. We often hook into the timer clock interrupt (vector 8) or the keyboard interrupt (vector 9).

14. A terminate and stay resident (TSR) program is a program that remains in the memory that is often accessed through a hooked interrupt using either the timer clock or a hot key.

15. A hot key is a key that activates a terminate and stay resident program through the keyboard interrupt hook.

6–8   QUESTIONS AND PROBLEMS

1. The assembler converts a source file to an _____ file.

2. What files are generated from the source file TEST.ASM as it is processed by MASM?

3. The linker program links object files and _____ files to create an execution file.

4. What does the PUBLIC directive indicate when placed in a program module?
5. What does the EXTRN directive indicate when placed in a program module?
6. What directives appear with labels defined external?
7. Describe how a library file works when it is linked to other object files by the linker program.
8. What assembler language directives delineate a macro sequence?
9. What is a macro sequence?
10. How are parameters transferred to a macro sequence?
11. Develop a macro called ADD32 that adds the 32-bit contents of DX–CX to the 32-bit contents of BX–AX.
12. How is the LOCAL directive used within a macro sequence?
13. Develop a macro called ADDLIST PARA1,PARA2 that adds the contents of PARA1 to PARA2. Each of these parameters represents an area of memory. The number of bytes added are indicated by register CX before the macro is invoked.
14. Develop a macro that sums a list of byte-sized data invoked by the macro ADDM LIST,LENGTH. The label LIST is the starting address of the data block, and LENGTH is the number of data added. The result must be a 16-bit sum found in AX at the end of the macro sequence.
15. What is the purpose of the INCLUDE directive?
16. Develop a procedure called RANDOM. This procedure must return an 8-bit random number in program CL at the end of the subroutine. (One way to generate a random number is to increment CL each time the DOS function 06H tests the keyboard and finds *no* keystroke. In this way a random number is generated.)
17. Develop a procedure that displays a character string that ends with a 00H. Your procedure must use the DS:DX register to address the start of the character string.
18. Develop a procedure that reads a key and displays the hexadecimal value of an extended ASCII-coded keyboard character if it is typed. If a normal character is typed, ignore it.
19. Use BIOS INT 10H to develop a procedure that positions the cursor at line 3, column 6.
20. When a number is converted from binary to BCD, the _____ instruction accomplishes the conversion provided the number is less than 100 decimal.
21. How is a large number (over 100 decimal) converted from binary to BCD?
22. A BCD digit is converted to ASCII code by adding a _____.
23. An ASCII-coded number is converted to BCD by subtracting _____.
24. Develop a procedure that reads an ASCII number from the keyboard and stores it as a BCD number into memory array DATA. The number ends when anything other than a number is typed.
25. Explain how a 3-digit ASCII-coded number is converted to binary.
26. Develop a procedure that converts all lowercase ASCII-coded letters into uppercase ASCII-coded letters. Your procedure may not change any other character except the letters a–z.
27. Develop a lookup table that converts hexadecimal data 00H–0FH into the ASCII-coded characters that represent the hexadecimal digits. Make sure to show the lookup table and any software required for the conversion.

28. Develop a program sequence that jumps to memory location ONE if AL = 6, TWO if AL = 7, and THREE if AL = 8.
29. Show how to use the XLAT instruction to access a lookup table called LOOK that is located in the stack segment.
30. Explain the purpose of a boot sector, FAT, and root directory.
31. The surface of a disk is divided into tracks that are further subdivided into _____.
32. What is a bootstrap loader and where is it found?
33. What is a cluster?
34. A directory entry contains an attribute byte. This byte indicates what information about the entry?
35. A directory entry contains the length of the disk file or subdirectory stored in _____ bytes of memory.
36. What is the maximum length of a file?
37. Develop a procedure that opens a file called TEST.LST, reads 512 bytes from the file into data segment memory area ARRAY, and closes the file.
38. Develop a procedure that renames file TEST.LST, TEST.LIS.
39. Write a program that reads any decimal number between 0 and 65,535 and displays the 16-bit binary version on the video display.
40. Write a program that displays the binary powers of two (in decimal) on the video screen for the powers 0 through 7. Your display shows 2^n = value for each power of 2.
41. Using the technique learned in Question 16, develop a program that displays random numbers between 1 and 47 (or whatever) for your state's lottery.
42. Develop a program that displays the hexadecimal contents of a block of 256 bytes of memory. Your software must be able to accept the starting address as a hexadecimal number between 00000H and FFF00H.
43. Develop a program that hooks into interrupt vector 0 to display the following message on a divide error: "Oops, you have attempted to divide by 0."

CHAPTER 7

80286 Hardware Specifications

INTRODUCTION

In this chapter, we describe the function of each pin of the 80286 microprocessor and provide details on the following hardware topics: clock generation, bus buffering, the bus controller, timing diagrams, and wait states.

Before it is possible to connect or interface anything to the microprocessor, it is necessary to understand the function of each pin and also the interaction of the microprocessor and its timing. Thus the information in this chapter is essential to a complete understanding of memory and I/O interfacing, which we cover in the remainder of the text.

OBJECTIVES

Upon completion of this chapter, you will be able to:

1. Describe the function of each 80286 pin connection.
2. Understand the DC characteristics and indicate the fanout to common logic families.
3. Use the 82284 clock generator to provide the clock signal.
4. Connect buffers to the 80286 to form a buffered system.
5. Interpret the timing diagrams and calculate memory access time.
6. Describe wait states and explain how to cause them.
7. Explain the operation of the 82288 bus controller.

7–1 PINOUT AND PIN FUNCTIONS

In this section we explain the function of each pin connection on the 80286 microprocessor. We also discuss the DC characteristics to provide a basis for interfacing and buffering.

The Pinout

Figure 7–1 shows the pinout of the 80286 microprocessor. This microprocessor is available as either an LCC (*leadless chip carrier*) or PGA (*pin grid array*). Because of the high cost of an LCC socket, most applications use the PGA version of this device. Figure 7–2 shows the outlines of both the LCC package (68 contacts) and the PGA package (68 pins). One additional package exists called a PLCC or *plastic leadless chip carrier,* but it is not illustrated because its pinout and basic shape is identical to the LCC.

Upon close inspection, the pinout reveals that there are 24 address connections (A_0–A_{23}), used to address 16M bytes of memory and 16 data connections (D_0–D_{15}) that access a word or byte of memory data. The remaining pin connections provide timing, power supply, and control signal connections between the microprocessor and system. The 80286 microprocessor is available with a clock speed of 8, 10, or 12.5 MHz from Intel, while other vendors have a 16-MHz version. On occasion the 16-MHz version is pushed to 20 MHz by adding a heat sink to the integrated circuit.

FIGURE 7–1 The pinout of the 80286 microprocessor.

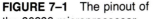

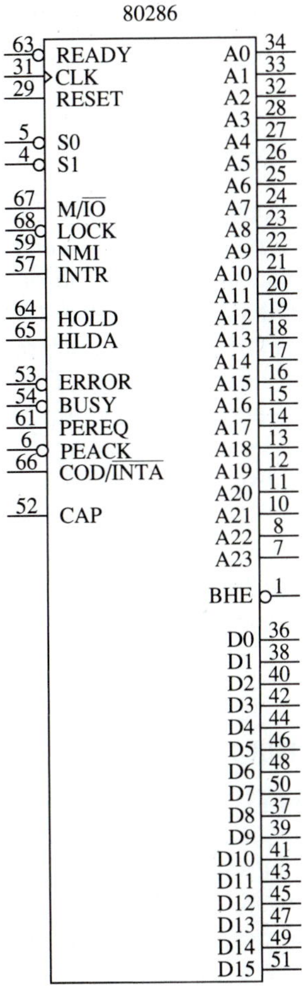

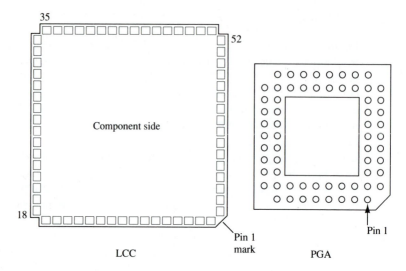

FIGURE 7–2   The leadless chip carrier (LCC) and pin grid array (PGA).

This pushes the microprocessor too far and can cause early failures due to excessive heat.

Power Supply Connections

The 80286 microprocessor requires a +5.0-V power supply with a supply voltage tolerance of ±5 percent. The power supply must be capable of providing 600 mA of current for the proper operation of the 80286. The 80286 is designed to operate at temperatures that range between 0° C and +70° C. (Note that 0° C is 32° F and +70° C is +158° F.) If these temperatures or voltage ratings are exceeded, there is no guarantee of proper operation. This temperature range is too narrow to function at outdoor temperatures unless we use the CMOS version. The 80C286 microprocessor has an extended temperature range of −40° C (−40° F) to +125° C (+257° F). The CMOS version also requires much less power (about 15 mA) for operation than the NMOS version. The CMOS version is also ideal for battery-powered applications.

In addition to the power supply connections, a pin is provided for a capacitor. The CAP pin must be connected to a 0.047-μF, ±20 percent, 12-V filter capacitor. This capacitor is used by an internal substrate bias pump as a filter capacitor. The purpose of the bias pump is to develop a bias voltage for the internal MOSFET circuitry.

DC Characteristics

It is impractical to connect anything to the pins of the microprocessor without first knowing its DC characteristics. We must know the input current requirement for an input pin and the output drive characteristics for an output pin. This information allows the hardware designer to select the proper interface components for use with the 80286 microprocessor. Without this information, the loading characteristics can be exceeded, causing a failure.

TABLE 7–1 Input characteristics of the 80286 microprocessor

Logic Level	Voltage	Current
0	0.8 V (max)	$\pm 10\ \mu A$ (max)
1	2.0 V (min)	$\pm 10\ \mu A$ (max)

Input Characteristics. The input capacitance of the 80286 is compatible (10 pF) with other logic families. Table 7–1 depicts the input characteristics, including the voltage and current levels. These characteristics apply to all 80286 input pin connections. These input currents are very small because of the high impedance of the gate region of the MOSFET input circuitry, and represent a small current load. This small load, along with the voltage levels, makes the 80286 compatible with other digital logic components.

Output Characteristics. Table 7–2 lists the output characteristics of all 80286 output pins. The logic 1 output voltage level is compatible with most standard logic families, but the logic 0 level is not. Standard logic circuits have a maximum logic 0 voltage of 0.4 V, and the 80286 has a maximum logic 0 voltage of 0.45 V. This is a difference of 0.05 V.

   The difference in logic 0 output voltage causes the noise immunity to be reduced from the standard 400-mV level (0.8 − 0.4 V) of most logic families to 350 mV (0.8 − 0.45 V). (*Noise immunity* is the difference between the logic 0 output voltage and the logic 0 input voltage.) This reduced noise immunity may result in problems with long wire connections and too many loads. It is therefore recommended that no more than 10 loads of any type or combination be connected to an output pin without buffering. If this loading is exceeded, noise will begin to take its toll as timing problems. Another consideration is capacitance of the load, which should never exceed 150 pF.

   Table 7–3 lists some common logic families and the recommended fanout from the 80286. The best choice of component types for the 80286 are the 74LSXXX, 74ALSXXX, 74ASXXX, 74FXXX, or 74HCXXX series.

Pin Functions

The following list specifies the function and purpose of each of the 80286 pin connections:

1. $A_{23}-A_0$ (Address Bus): Provides the memory with a 24-bit physical address so 16M bytes of memory are accessible. It also provides I/O with a 16-bit I/O device address ($A_{15}-A_0$) or an 8-bit I/O device address (A_7-A_0). Note that

TABLE 7–2 Output characteristics for the 80286 microprocessor

Logic Level	Voltage	Current
0	0.45 V (max)	2.0 mA (max)
1	2.4 V (min)	$-400\ \mu A$ (max)

TABLE 7–3 Fanout from the 80286 microprocessor

Family	Fanout	Sink Current	Source Current (μA)
TTL(74XXX)	1	−1.6 mA	40
TTL(74LSXXX)	5	−0.4 mA	20
TTL(74SXXX)	1	−2.0 mA	50
TTL(74ALSXXX)	10	−0.1 mA	20
TTL(74ASXXX)	4	−0.5 mA	25
TTL(74FXXX)	4	−0.5 mA	25
CMOS(74HCXXX)	10	−1.0 μA	1.0
CMOS(CD4XXX)	10	−1.0 μA	1.0
NMOS	10	−10 μA	10

A_{23}–A_{16} are low during all I/O operations and that A_{15}–A_8 are low during 8-bit I/O device addresses.

2. *BHE* (Bus High Enable): Activates the high portion (D_{15}–D_8) of the data bus during a memory or I/O transfer. The $\overline{BHE}$ and A_0 signals are used to control the activity on the data bus. Table 7–4 shows the function of the $\overline{BHE}$ and A_0 signals. We normally use $\overline{BHE}$ to activate the high part of the bus, and A_0 activates the low portion.

3. *BUSY* (Busy Input): A numeric coprocessor connection tested by the WAIT instruction to determine whether the coprocessor is busy. If a coprocessor is not connected, this pin can be used for other purposes in the system.

4. *CAP* (Capacitor): Connects to a 0.047-μF, ±20 percent, 12-V filter capacitor that is placed between this pin and ground.

5. *CLK* (Clock): Supplies the 80286 microprocessor with its basic timing signal. This input provides the microprocessor with a two-phase clock that is internally divided by 2 to generate the internal processor clock. If the CLK frequency is 20 MHz, the microprocessor operates at a basic clock frequency of 10 MHz.

6. *COD/$\overline{INTA}$* (Code/Interrupt Acknowledge): Indicates an instruction fetch or memory read/write. It also indicates an interrupt acknowledge or an I/O read/write.

7. *D_{15}–D_0* (Data Bus): Transfers data between the microprocessor and its memory and I/O system. Data transfer occurs as a 16-bit word or as an 8-bit byte operation on either half of the data bus (D_{15}–D_8 or D_7–D_0).

8. *$\overline{ERROR}$* (Error Input): Indicates an error to the microprocessor when the numeric coprocessor executes a WAIT or ESC instruction and the $\overline{ERROR}$ pin is a logic 0. This signal is generated directly by the numeric coprocessor. A processor

TABLE 7–4 Bus activity due to $\overline{BHE}$ and A_0

$\overline{BHE}$	A_0	Bus Activity
0	0	16-bit word transfer (D_{15}–D_0)
0	1	8-bit byte transfer (D_{15}–D_8)
1	0	8-bit byte transfer (D_7–D_0)
1	1	No transfer; bus idle

extension interrupt (vector number type 16) occurs in response to this input. If this pin is not used, no connection is required because it is internally pulled up to a logic 1 level.

9. *HLDA* (Hold Acknowledge): Becomes a logic 1 whenever the microprocessor places its address, data, and control buses at their high impedance state during a direct memory access hold operation.

10. *HOLD* (Hold Request): Activated (logic 1) to request the use of the system buses address, data, and control by another device. Once the request is granted through the HLDA pin, the microprocessor allows another device to gain access to its memory and I/O space.

11. *INTR* (Interrupt Request): An input that is placed at a logic 1 level to request an interrupt. This pin is masked by the interrupt flag bit (IF) in the flag register. Once the INTR input is noticed by the microprocessor, it sends the $\overline{INTA}$ to the external circuitry to cause the application of the interrupt vector type number to data bus connections (D_7–D_0).

12. $\overline{LOCK}$ (Bus Lock): Goes low whenever an instruction, prefixed by a $\overline{LOCK}$ prefix, is executed by the 80286 microprocessor. The purpose of the $\overline{LOCK}$ signal is to prevent other devices from gaining access to the microprocessor buses through the HOLD input.

13. $M/\overline{IO}$ (Memory–I/O Select): Dictates a memory (logic 1) or I/O (logic 0) access. This signal is used with the status signals ($\overline{S}_1$ and $\overline{S}_0$) to generate memory read, memory write, I/O read, and I/O write signals.

14. *NMI* (Nonmaskable Interrupt Input): Requests an interrupt type-2 vector. This input cannot be masked off as the INTR input.

15. $\overline{PEACK}$ (Processor Extension Operand Acknowledge): Used to show the processor extension (numeric coprocessor) that the microprocessor has transferred the requested operand.

16. $\overline{PEREQ}$ (Processor Extension Operand Request): Signals the microprocessor to perform a data transfer for the processor extension.

17. $\overline{READY}$ (Ready Input): Terminates a bus transfer when it becomes a logic 0. The READY input is used to insert extra clocking periods in the 80286 timing for slower memory and I/O components.

18. *RESET* (Reset System): Causes the 80286 to initialize itself. This input must be activated for at least 16 system clocking periods (38 when power is first applied) for a reset to take effect. Resetting the microprocessor causes it to enter the real mode of operation and fetch the first instruction from memory location FFFFF0H. Table 7–5 lists the internal changes that occur to the 80286 during a reset operation. Note that the reset address is FFFFF0H, which is 16 bytes from the top of its 16M-byte memory address range. As soon as a far jump occurs, the first 4 address bits (A_{23}–A_{20}) are cleared to zero for normal real mode memory addressing in the first 1M byte of memory.

19. $\overline{S}_1$ and $\overline{S}_0$ (Status Bits): Generate the system control signals when combined with $COD/\overline{INTA}$ and $M/\overline{IO}$. Table 7–6 lists the logical combination found on these four control signals and their function in the system.

20. V_{cc} (System Power): Supplies the microprocessor with its operating voltage of +5.0 V at ±5 percent.

21. V_{ss} (System Ground): Connects to the system ground bus.

TABLE 7–5 Internal changes to the 80286 after a reset

Register	Contents	Register	Contents
CS	F000H	DS Limit	FFFFH
DS	0000H	ES Limit	FFFFH
ES	0000H	SS Limit	FFFFH
SS	0000H	IDT Base	000000H
CS Base	FF0000H	IDT Limit	FFFFH
DS Base	000000H	IP	FFF0H
ES Base	000000H	MSW	FFF0H
SS Base	000000H	Flags	00002H
CS Limit	FFFFH		

TABLE 7–6 Control bus definitions

$\overline{S}_1$	$\overline{S}_0$	M/$\overline{IO}$	COD/$\overline{INTA}$	Cycle Type
0	0	0	0	Interrupt acknowledge
0	0	0	1	—
0	0	1	0	If A_1 = 1, then halt, else shut down
0	0	1	1	—
0	1	0	0	—
0	1	0	1	I/O read
0	1	1	0	Memory read
0	1	1	1	Opcode fetch
1	0	0	0	—
1	0	0	1	I/O write
1	0	1	0	Memory write
1	0	1	1	—
1	1	0	0	—
1	1	0	1	—
1	1	1	0	—
1	1	1	1	—

7–2   THE 82284 CLOCK GENERATOR

This section describes the operation of the 82284 clock generator used with the 80286 microprocessor. The *clock generator* provides the microprocessor with its clock, reset, and ready signals. Although the 82284 is not required for the operation of the 80286 microprocessor, it makes the task of generating the clock, reset, and ready much easier.

Pinout and Pin Functions

The 82284 is an ancillary component to the 80286 microprocessor. Without the clock generator, many additional circuits are required to generate the clock (CLK) and other signals in an 80286 system. The 82284 provides the following basic functions: clock generation for the 80286, RESET synchronization, $\overline{\text{READY}}$ synchronization, and a

TTL-level peripheral clock signal (PCLK). Figure 7–3 illustrates the pinout of the 82284 clock generator.

Pin Functions. The 82284 clock generator is an 18-pin integrated circuit designed specifically to support the 80286 microprocessor. The following is a list of each pin and its function:

1. $\overline{ARDY}$ (Asynchronous Ready): Provides the system with an asynchronous ready input signal used to cause wait states for slower memory components.
2. $\overline{ARDYEN}$ (Asynchronous Ready Enable): Enables the $\overline{ARDY}$ input when placed at a logic 0 level.
3. *CLK* (Clock Output): Provides a timing signal to the clock input (CLK) of the 80286 microprocessor. This signal is generated from an internal oscillator that uses an external crystal as a timing source or from an external frequency input (EFI). In any case, the CLK output is at the same frequency as either EFI or the crystal.
4. *EFI* (External Frequency Input): Provides system timing if the $F/\overline{C}$ input is placed at a logic 1 level. Note that CLK is the same frequency as this input signal.
5. $F/\overline{C}$ (Frequency/Crystal): Selects the external frequency input (EFI) when a logic 1 is applied, or selects the crystal oscillator when a logic 0 is applied to this pin.
6. *PCLK* (Peripheral Clock): Provides a timing signal at one-half the frequency of the CLK signal for peripheral components.
7. $\overline{READY}$ (Ready Output): Connects to the microprocessor $\overline{READY}$ input pin to supply the ready signal.
8. $\overline{RES}$ (Reset Input): Causes the RESET output pin to activate and reset the microprocessor and peripheral components.
9. *RESET* (Reset Output): Provides a reset signal to the microprocessor RESET input pin and also to peripheral components.
10. $\overline{S}_1$ *and* $\overline{S}_0$ (Status Inputs): Must be connected to the microprocessor status outputs to supply synchronization for the PCLK signal.
11. $\overline{SRDY}$ (Synchronized Ready Input): Provides the system with a ready input. This input must be synchronized externally to the system clock signal for proper function.

FIGURE 7–3 The pinout of the 82284 clock generator.

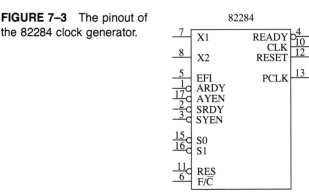

12. $\overline{SRDYEN}$ (Synchronous Ready Enable): Enables the synchronous ready input pin when placed at a logic 0 level.
13. X_2 *and* X_1 (Crystal Connections): Attach to the crystal to provide a timing source for an internal linear Pierce oscillator. The crystal must be a parallel resonant crystal.
14. V_{cc} (Power Supply): Connects to a power supply that provides +5.0 V with a tolerance of ±10 percent.
15. V_{ss} (Ground): Connects to the system ground bus.

Operation of the 82284

The clock generator's internal structure is illustrated in Figure 7–4. This device appears as three parts. The top portion contains the clock generator, the middle por-

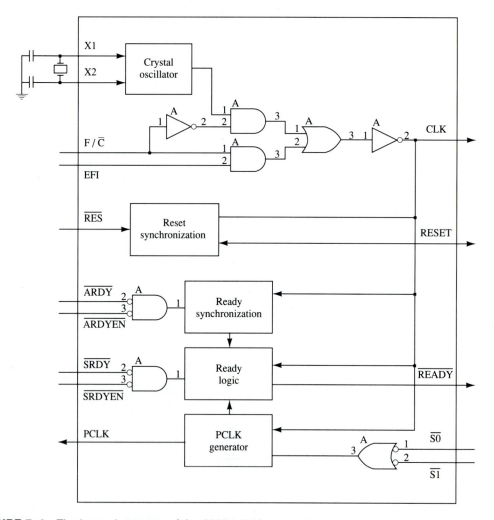

FIGURE 7–4   The internal structure of the 82284 clock generator.

tion contains the reset circuitry, and the bottom contains the wait state generator. The wait state section is explained in a later section of this chapter.

Operation of the Clock Section. The upper part of the internal structure of the 82284 and the very bottom part comprise the clock-generating circuitry. The quartz crystal is attached to the X_1 and X_2 pins to provide a timing element to an internal crystal-controlled oscillator. The oscillator generates the same frequency signal as the crystal and applies it to an AND–OR multiplexer. The multiplexer allows the crystal oscillator output or the external frequency input (EFI) to pass through to an inverting buffer and on to the CLK pin. It also provides timing for the reset circuit, ready circuit, and PCLK circuit.

Two capacitors are required with the parallel resonant crystal attached to X_1 and X_2. These capacitors are 25 pF for the one connected to X_1 and 15 pF for the one connected to X_2. These values function properly with a crystal frequency of 8–20 MHz. If a higher frequency crystal is specified, then the capacitors are both 15 pF.

The crystal or EFI input frequency is selected by the $F/\overline{C}$ pin. If a crystal is used as a timing source, $F/\overline{C}$ must be a logic 0, and if EFI provides timing, $F/\overline{C}$ must be a logic 1. The EFI or crystal frequency is passed through the AND–OR gate network and an inverting buffer to the CLK output pin. The frequency of the CLK pin is determined by the desired operating frequency of the 80286 where CLK generates the 80286 operating frequency. An 80286 that is to operate at a frequency of 12 MHz must have a CLK frequency of 24 MHz because the CLK input is internally divided by two by the 80286 to generate its timing. Here, a crystal frequency of 24 MHz is also selected (see Figure 7–5).

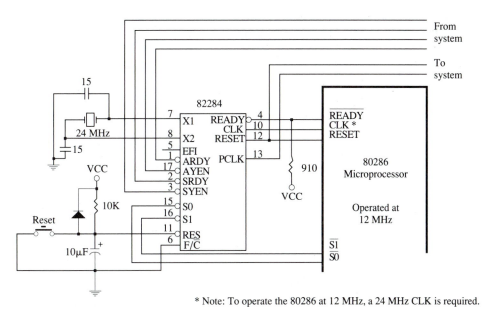

* Note: To operate the 80286 at 12 MHz, a 24 MHz CLK is required.

FIGURE 7–5 The 82284 interfaced to the 80286 so it operates at a 12-MHz rate.

The CLK signal also provides a timing input to the PCLK (peripheral clock) pin on the 82284. The PCLK frequency is the TTL square wave found on this pin that is one-half the CLK frequency. In the case of a 24-MHz crystal, PCLK is 12 MHz. PCLK is always the same frequency as the basic 80286 microprocessor operating frequency.

Operation of the Reset Section.   The reset section of the 82284 has an active low reset input and synchronization that generates an active high reset output signal for the microprocessor and the peripherals attached to the system. Figure 7–5, which illustrates the 82284 connected to the 80286, depicts the circuit normally connected to the $\overline{\text{RES}}$ input pin of the 82284.

When DC power is applied to the system, the capacitor is initially discharged to 0 V. This places a logic 0 on the $\overline{\text{RES}}$ input and generates a logic 1 on the RESET output connection to the 80286, resetting the microprocessor. As time passes, the capacitor charges toward +5.0 V through the 10-KΩ resister. After a short period, the voltage applied to the $\overline{\text{RES}}$ input goes above the logic 1 threshold. This causes the RESET signal to the microprocessor to become a logic 0, allowing the microprocessor to start executing software at memory location FFFFF0H.

If the push-button switch is closed, it discharges the capacitor and resets the microprocessor. An additional circuit, not shown in Figure 7–5, can be attached to the $\overline{\text{RES}}$ input so the microprocessor can reset itself with software. This is usually a flip-flop that is cleared by an out instruction and set by the RESET output pin. This returns the 80286 to the real-mode of operation and is used in some systems for this purpose.

7–3   THE 82288 SYSTEM BUS CONTROLLER

The status and M/$\overline{\text{IO}}$ signals indicate the bus cycle currently executing in the 80286 microprocessor. The memory and I/O system require control signals that select them for a read or a write operation. In order to provide these control signals, another component is often connected to the 80286—the 82288 *system bus controller*. The memory control signals provided by the 82288 are $\overline{\text{MRDC}}$ (*memory read control*) and $\overline{\text{MWTC}}$ (*memory write control*), and the I/O control signal are $\overline{\text{IORC}}$ (*I/O read control*) and $\overline{\text{IOWC}}$ (*I/O write control*). These control signals must be used to time transfers between the microprocessor and its memory and I/O system.

Pinout and Pin Functions

Figure 7–6 shows the pinout of the 82288 system bus controller. The system bus controller obtains its input information from the microprocessor and the 82284 clock generator. The microprocessor provides it with $\overline{\text{S}}_0$, $\overline{\text{S}}_1$, and M/$\overline{\text{IO}}$, and the clock generator provides CLK and $\overline{\text{READY}}$. From these five input signals, the 82288 generates the memory and I/O control signals, as well as signals that control a data bus buffer and generate an interrupt acknowledge signal.

FIGURE 7–6 The pinout of the 82288 bus controller.

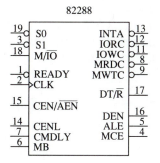

82288 Pin Functions. The system bus controller (82288) is essential to a working 80286-based system. Before it can be incorporated in the system, the function of each of its pins must be understood. The following list provides a description of each 82288 pin connection:

1. *ALE* (Address Latch Enable): Causes the address to be latched into an external address latch in some system connections for the 80286 microprocessor.
2. *CEN/AEN* (Command Enable/Address Enable): Operates the 82288 in two different ways. If MB = 0, this pin functions as the command enable input. A logic 1 on CEN allows the command signals generated by the 82288 to become active. A logic 0 on CEN disables the command signals. If MB = 1, this pin functions as an address enable input. The AEN pin is used when the 80286 is interfaced to the MULTIBUS* system.
3. *CENL* (Command Latch Enable): Connected to a logic 1 in systems that have a single system bus controller. In systems with multiple system bus controllers, this input is placed at a logic 1 by external logic that selects the active controller for an address range.
4. *CLK* (Clock Input): Connects to the system CLK signal that is generated by the 82284.
5. *CMDLY* (Command Delay): Causes the 82288 to extend the time allowed for reads and writes.
6. *DEN* (Data Bus Enable): Enables the data bus buffers connected to a buffered 80286 microprocessor.
7. *DT/R̄* (Data Transmit/Receive): Controls the direction of data flow through external bus buffers in a buffered 80286 system.
8. *INTA* (Interrupt Acknowledge): Acknowledges an interrupt request applied to the INTR pin on the microprocessor. This signal usually applies a vector type number to the data bus (D_7–D_0) to access one of the 256 different interrupt vectors.
9. *IORC* (I/O Read Control): Enables an I/O device for a read operation. This signal causes the I/O device to apply input data to the data bus where it is captured by the microprocessor.

---

*MULTIBUS is a registered trademark of Intel Corporation.

10. $\overline{IOWC}$ (I/O Write Control): Causes an I/O device to accept data during the execution of an OUT instruction.

11. $M/\overline{IO}$ (Memory–I/O): Activates memory when a logic 1 and I/O when a logic 0.

12. *MB* (Multibus Select): Selects multibus operation when placed at a logic 1 level. If placed at a logic 0 level, a single 82288 system bus controller exists in a system.

13. *MCE* (Master Cascade Enable): Enables other 82288 system bus controllers connected to a multibus system.

14. $\overline{MRDC}$ (Memory Read Control): Activates a memory device so data are read from memory into the microprocessor. This signal usually connects to the memory component's $\overline{OE}$ (output enable) pin.

15. $\overline{MWTC}$ (Memory Write Control): Causes a memory device to write data bus data into a selected memory location. This signal is usually attached to the $\overline{WE}$ (write enable) pin on a memory device.

16. $\overline{S}_0$ *and* $\overline{S}_1$ (Status Input Bits): Generate the control signals presented to the memory and I/O system. Table 7–6 in Section 7–1 lists the various encoded data found on these input pins.

17. V_{cc} (Supply Voltage): Connects to the system +5.0-V, $\pm$ 10 percent power supply.

18. V_{ss} (Ground): Connects to the system ground bus.

Connection of the 82288

The system bus controller provides the system with its memory and I/O control signals. It also provides signals that are used to control the data bus buffers and latch the address bus.

Figure 7–7 illustrates the interconnection of an 80286 microprocessor, an 82284 clock generator, and an 82288 system bus controller. Notice that no additional logic circuitry is required to interconnect these components that form the nucleus of an 80286-based computer system. The microprocessor provides the address and data bus connections; the clock generator provides the system ready signals, clock signal, and master reset signal; and the bus controller provides the memory and I/O control signals.

This is not the only way to connect the 82288 system bus controller to a system, as is discussed in Chapter 11, which explains DMA and multibus interfacing. The model shown at this point for the 80286, 82284, and 82288 is used for many systems that contain only a local bus (one microprocessor). The next section of this chapter explains how to buffer the system using the signals available at the 82288 system bus controller.

7–4   BUS BUFFERING AND ADDRESS LATCHING

In most systems based on the 80286 microprocessor, buffers are required because of the large number of components often attached to the microprocessor. This section of the chapter details buffering and address latching, which are often required with the 80286 microprocessor. Recall that because the drive current is low (2 mA) from

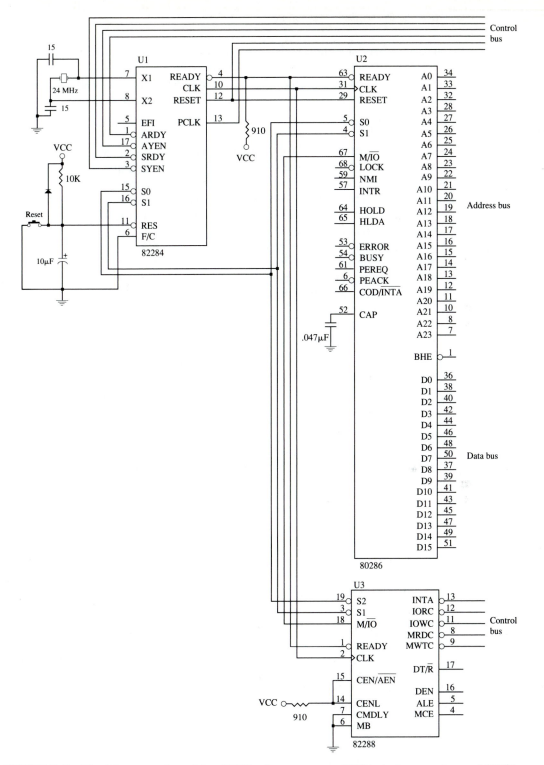

FIGURE 7-7 The interconnection of the 80286 microprocessor, 82284 clock generator, and 82288 system bus controller.

the microprocessor, a system with more than about 10 components requires buffers. The buffers used in this section of the text provide 32 mA of logic 0 current and −5.2 mA of logic 1 current. These buffers are designed to drive a fairly large system that contains capacitive loads such as MOSFET memory devices.

Buffering the Data Bus

The data bus is buffered with bidirectional bus buffers such as the 74LS245 or 74LS645. (The 74LS645 is preferred because of its short propagation delay time.) Both devices are octal bidirectional bus buffers that are controlled by an enable pin ($\overline{G}$) and a direction pin (DIR). The enable pin places the buffer at its high-impedance state when placed at logic 1 and enables the buffer when at logic 0. The direction pin controls the direction of flow. If DIR = 1, data flow from the A bus to the B bus, and if DIR = 0, data flow from the B bus to the A bus.

Figure 7–8 shows the data bus buffered by a pair of 74LS645 bidirectional data bus buffers. Notice that the A bus connections are attached to the microprocessor data bus connections and the B bus connections are attached to the buffered system data bus connections.

The control signals for the data bus buffer are generated by the 82288 system bus controller. The system bus controller provides a DEN signal that becomes a logic 1 to enable the data bus. This is a logic mismatch between the buffer and the 82288, a mismatch that is corrected by a NAND gate that functions as an inverter. The NAND gate also disables the data bus buffers in a system that contains an 80287 numeric coprocessor. The $\overline{DIS}$ signal and the 80287 are discussed in Chapter 12, which deals with numeric coprocessors. The DIR signal for the buffer comes from the 82288 DT/$\overline{R}$ pin. When the microprocessor writes data to memory or I/O,

FIGURE 7–8 The buffered 80286 data bus using 74LS645 bidirectional bus buffers.

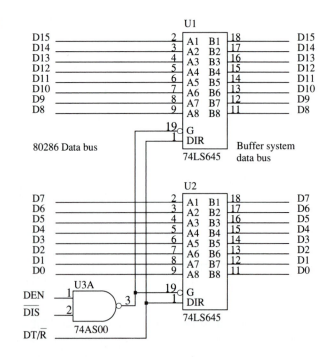

the DT/$\overline{R}$ pin becomes a logic 0. This causes the buffer to transfer data from the A bus to the B bus. During a memory read or I/O read, DT/$\overline{R}$ = 1, which causes the buffer to transfer data from the B bus to the A bus and into the microprocessor.

Buffering the Address Bus

The address bus is buffered with unidirectional buffers instead of bidirectional buffers because data only flow in one direction on the address bus. The address connections in the 80286 system are buffered by using latches. Address bus latches are required to present a stable memory address or I/O address to the memory and I/O devices in a system. We often use the 74LS373 or 74AS533 octal latch for this purpose. (The 74AS533 is preferred because its propagation delay time is shorter than that of the 74LS373.)

Figure 7–9 shows a series of three 74AS533 latches, which are identical in function to the 74LS373 latches, used to capture the address bus information whenever

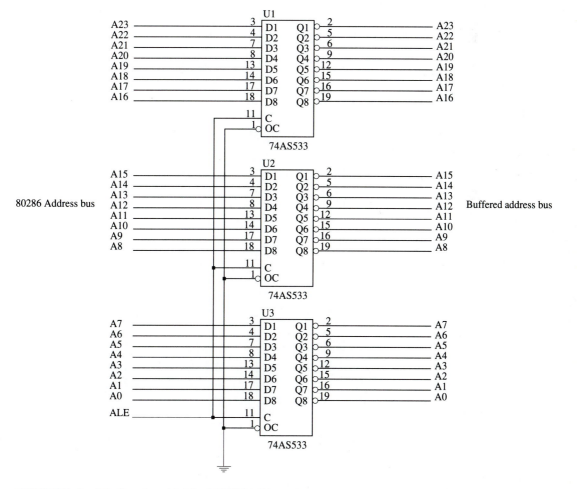

FIGURE 7–9 A buffered and latched 80286 address bus.

the ALE signal changes from a one to a zero. These latches are called transparent latches because they pass information when the clock input (C) is a logic 1 and capture information when it returns to a logic 0. The ALE signal, developed by the system controller, applies a clock pulse to the C inputs of the latches to capture the address information. The $\overline{OE}$ connections are grounded so the outputs, which are buffered address signals, are present at all times. The $\overline{OE}$ connection is placed at a logic 1 in systems that use direct memory access (DMA).

A Complete 80286 Buffered System

Figure 7–10 shows a buffered system containing the 80286, 82284, and 82288. This circuit incorporates the data bus buffers and address bus latches explained earlier

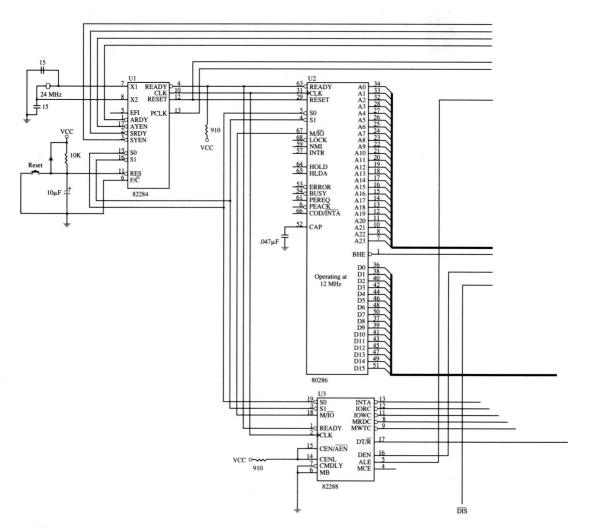

FIGURE 7–10   A buffered 80286 system.

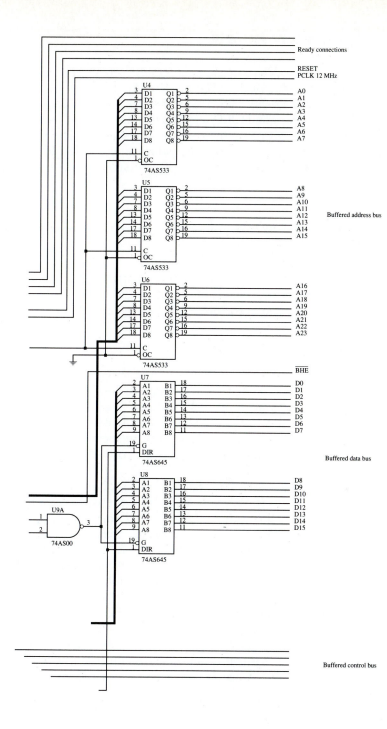

FIGURE 7–10 *(continued)*

in this section. The 82288 internally buffers the control bus connections. Some of the microprocessor pins, such as HOLD, HLDA, NMI, and INTR, are also control signals, but are not usually buffered because they seldom connect to more than a few external devices. The HOLD and HLDA pins are used for DMA actions, and the NMI and INTR pins are used for interrupt requests. The $\overline{\text{BUSY}}$ and $\overline{\text{ERROR}}$ pins are not connected and are internally pulled up to a logic 1 level. These two pins attach to the 80287 numeric coprocessor if it is present in the system.

7–5   BUS TIMING

The bus timing diagrams and definitions are important to I/O and memory interface. Without a complete understanding of timing, interfacing is impossible. This section provides insight into the operation of the bus signals and the basic timing of the 80286 microprocessor.

Basic Bus Timing

The three buses of the 80286 microprocessor—address, data, and control—function to control the selection and access of a memory or an I/O device. The address bus provides an address to the memory or I/O device and selects a unique memory or I/O location; the data bus conveys the information between the microprocessor and memory or I/O, and the control bus selects memory or I/O and causes a read or a write to occur.

Figure 7–11 illustrates the simplified timing diagram for a read and a write operation when the 80286, 82284, and 82288 are used to form the basic system. The 80286 system reads or writes data in two clocking periods composed of T_s and T_c. The combination of Ts and Tc form one *bus cycle*.

During T_s (*send–status*) the 80286 outputs the status signals, address signals, M/$\overline{\text{IO}}$, and COD/$\overline{\text{INTA}}$. These signals, aside from the address, are used by the 82288 to generate ALE, DEN, DT/$\overline{\text{R}}$, and the other control bus signals.

The T_c (*command*) state is where the actual data are transferred between the microprocessor and its memory and I/O devices. This data transfer occurs at the end of T_c. Notice that the address information disappears from the address connection in the middle of the T_c clocking period. This is the main reason that a latch is required on the address bus connections. The latch maintains a stable address on the address bus for the I/O and memory devices connected to the system. Without this stable address, most memory devices would fail to read or write data to the selected memory location.

The timing diagram also illustrates two clocking waveforms: CLK and PCLK. Although PCLK is not connected to the microprocessor and not available on the microprocessor, it is internally generated where it dictates the operation of the microprocessor.

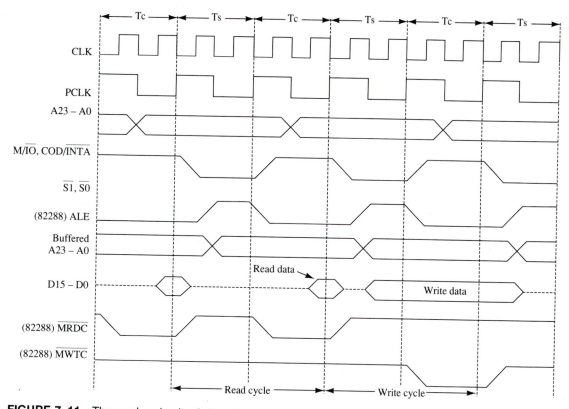

FIGURE 7–11 The read and write timing diagram for the 80286 and 82288.

Other timing states also appear, but are not shown in Figure 7–11. One is the T_i state, or *idle state*. This state occurs if the microprocessor is not accessing memory or I/O or one clock before the T_h (*hold*) state. The hold state is discussed in more detail in Chapter 11, which explains DMA operation.

Memory Access Time

One of the most important timing considerations in any microprocessor is the memory access time. *Memory access time* is the time that the microprocessor allows the memory to look up data for a read operation. Figure 7–12 illustrates the major cycle timing for the 80286, 82284, and 82288. The access time for a microprocessor spans the time beginning from where it sends the address to the memory or I/O device until the time where it samples the data from the memory or I/O device.

In the 80286 system, the access time starts when ALE becomes a logic 1, and runs until the data bus is sampled or read at the end of T_c. If you look closely at the timing diagram, you will find that ALE goes to a logic 1 just after (time 16) the center of T_s. Data are sampled at the end of T_c, but there is a setup time requirement

WAVEFORMS

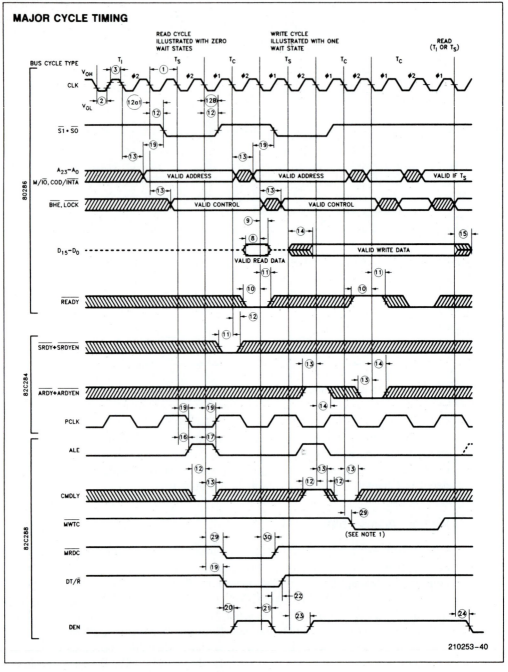

NOTE:
1. The modified timing is due to the $\overline{\text{CMDLY}}$ signal being active.

FIGURE 7–12   The timing diagram of the 80286.

(time 8) before the end of T_c. (Refer to Figure 7–13 for the AC characteristics of the 80286.) For this microprocessor, access time is 3 CLKs minus the sum of times 16 and 8. (This result ignores any delay time through the address latch that buffers the address bus and through the data bus buffers that buffer the data bus.) If the 80286 operates at a rate of 8 MHz (PCLK), the CLK signal is 16 MHz or has a period of 62.5 ns. Three clocking periods (CLKs) are equal to 187.5 ns. Time 8 is 10 ns for the 8-MHz version of the 80286, and time 16 is between 3 and 20 ns. Using the worst cases, the access time allowed to the memory is 187.5 ns − 10 ns − 20 ns or 157.5 ns. This, of course, assumes no delay in the address latch or data bus buffers. To be fair, the delays in the address latch (11.5 ns) and data bus buffers (7.5 ns) should also be included, so the actual access time allowed memory is 138.5 ns. With this amount of access time, memory components rated at an access time of 120 ns (industry standard DRAM) are used with the system. This allows 18.5 ns for bus propagation delay times and memory address decoder delay times.

Suppose that the 80286 is operated at 12 MHz. A clocking period (CLK = 1/24 MHz) at this frequency is 41.67 ns. Three clocks are 125 ns. The access time is 125 ns (3 CLKs) − 5 ns (time 8) − 16 ns (time 16) − 11.5 (address latch) − 7.5 ns (data bus buffers) or 85 ns. This system requires memory components that have an access time of 70 ns allowing 15 ns for propagation delay and address decoding. These devices are very expensive and have just started to become commonly available. Note that some of the newer memory components have access times of as little as 60 ns. If shorter access times are required, either static RAM, with an access time of as little as 20 ns, or ECL (*emitter-coupled logic*) memory can be used, with an access time of as little as 2 ns.

Two ways exist to handle this speed problem. One method uses wait states to slow the microprocessor down whenever memory is accessed; the other changes the way that memory is accessed and is called *memory interleaving*. Both techniques are described in subsequent subsections of this chapter.

Wait States

Wait states are introduced into the timing to delay T_c so that additional clocking periods are inserted between T_s and T_c. These additional clocking states are also called T_c, but function as wait states because no data are sampled during these additional T_c states. The $\overline{READY}$ signal controls the insertion of wait states into the normal timing. A single wait state expands the access time by two CLK periods or one PCLK period. In a system running at 12 MHz, allowing 85 ns of memory access time, a single wait state expands the access time by 83.3 ns to 168.3 ns.

The $\overline{READY}$ pin (refer to Figure 7–12) is sampled at the end of T_c. If $\overline{READY}$ is a logic 0 when sampled, no wait states follow and the data bus is read by the microprocessor. If $\overline{READY}$ is a logic 1 at the end of T_c, the data are not sampled and another T_c clocking period follows. By controlling the $\overline{READY}$ pin, any number of wait states can be inserted into the timing.

The 82284 clock generator has two wait state control pins called $\overline{SRDY}$ (synchronous ready) and $\overline{ARDY}$ (asynchronous ready). Each of these wait state control pins is qualified by an enable pin called $\overline{SRDYEN}$ and $\overline{ARDYEN}$. The enable pins allow either $\overline{ARDY}$ or $\overline{SRDY}$ to be selected. To insert a wait state both $\overline{ARDY}$ and

A.C. CHARACTERISTICS (V_{CC} = 5V ±5%, T_{CASE} = 0°C to +85°C)*

AC timings are referenced to 0.8V and 2.0V points of signals as illustrated in datasheet waveforms, unless otherwise noted.

Symbol	Parameter	8 MHz		10 MHz		12.5 MHz		Unit	Test Condition
		-8 Min	-8 Max	-10 Min	-10 Max	-12 Min	-12 Max		
1	System Clock (CLK) Period	62	250	50	250	40	250	ns	
2	System Clock (CLK) LOW Time	15	225	12	232	11	237	ns	at 1.0V
3	System Clock (CLK) HIGH Time	25	235	16	239	13	239	ns	at 3.6V
17	System Clock (CLK) Rise Time		10		8	—	8	ns	1.0V to 3.6V, (Note 7)
18	System Clock (CLK) Fall Time		10		8	—	8	ns	3.6V to 1.0V, (Note 7)
4	Asynch. Inputs Setup Time	20		20		15		ns	(Note 1)
5	Asynch. Inputs Hold Time	20		20		15		ns	(Note 1)
6	RESET Setup Time	28		23		18		ns	
7	RESET Hold Time	5		5		5		ns	
8	Read Data Setup Time	10		8		5		ns	
9	Read Data Hold Time	8		8		6		ns	
10	$\overline{READY}$ Setup Time	38		26		22		ns	
11	$\overline{READY}$ Hold Time	25		25		20		ns	
12	Status/$\overline{PEACK}$ Valid Delay	1	40	—	—	—	—	ns	(Notes 2, 3)
12a1	Status Active Delay	—	—	1	22	3	18	ns	(Notes 2, 3)
12a2	$\overline{PEACK}$ Active Delay	—	—	1	22	3	20	ns	(Notes 2, 3)
12b	Status/$\overline{PEACK}$ Inactive Delay	—	—	1	30	3	22	ns	(Notes 2, 3)
13	Address Valid Delay	1	60	1	35	1	32	ns	(Notes 2, 3)
14	Write Data Valid Delay	0	50	0	30	0	30	ns	(Notes 2, 3)
15	Address/Status/Data Float Delay	0	50	0	47	0	32	ns	(Notes 2, 4, 7)
16	HLDA Valid Delay	0	50	0	47	0	27	ns	(Notes 2, 3)
19	Address Valid To Status Valid Setup Time	38		27		22		ns	(Notes 3, 5, 6, 7)

*T_A is guaranteed from 0°C to +55°C as long as T_{CASE} is not exceeded.

NOTES:
1. Asynchronous inputs are INTR, NMI, HOLD, PEREQ, $\overline{ERROR}$, and $\overline{BUSY}$. This specification is given only for testing purposes, to assure recognition at a specific CLK edge.
2. Delay from 1.0V on the CLK, to 0.8V or 2.0V or float on the output as appropriate for valid or floating condition.
3. Output load: C_L = 100 pF.
4. Float condition occurs when output current is less than I_{LO} in magnitude.
5. Delay measured from address either reaching 0.8V or 2.0V (valid) to status going active reaching 2.0V or status going inactive reaching 0.8V.
6. For load capacitance of 10 pF or more on STATUS/$\overline{PEACK}$ lines, subtract typically 7 ns.
7. These are not tested. They are guaranteed by design characterization.

FIGURE 7–13   The AC characteristics of the 80286, 82284, and 82288. (Courtesy of Intel Corporation)

$\overline{SRDY}$ must be inactive (logic 1) or disabled. The difference between $\overline{ARDY}$ and $\overline{SRDY}$ is where these two signals are sampled by the 82284 clock generator (refer to Figure 7–12). The $\overline{SRDY}$ input is sampled in the middle of T_c, while the $\overline{ARDY}$ pin is sample at the start of Tc. The $\overline{SRDY}$ input allows the external logic additional time to decide if a wait state is needed.

A.C. CHARACTERISTICS (Continued)

82C284 Timing Requirements

Symbol	Parameter	82C284-8		82C284-10		82C284-12		Units	Test Conditions
		Min	Max	Min	Max	Min	Max		
11	SRDY/SRDYEN Setup Time	20		18		18		ns	
12	SRDY/SRDYEN Hold Time	0		2		2		ns	
13	ARDY/ARDYEN Setup Time	0		0		0		ns	(Note 1)
14	ARDY/ARDYEN Hold Time	30		30		25		ns	(Note 1)
19	PCLK Delay	0	45	0	35	0	23	ns	C_L = 75 pF I_{OL} = 5 mA I_{OH} = −1 mA

NOTE 1:
These times are given for testing purposes to assure a predetermined action.

82C288 Timing Requirements

Symbol	Parameter		82C288-8		82C288-10		82C288-12		Units	Test Conditions
			Min	Max	Min	Max	Min	Max		
12	CMDLY Setup Time		20		15		15		ns	
13	CMDLY Hold Time		1		1		1		ns	
30	Command Delay from CLK	Command Inactive	5	20	5	20	5	20	ns	C_L = 300 pF max I_{OL} = 32 mA max I_{OH} = −5 mA max
29		Command Active	3	25	3	21	3	21		
16	ALE Active Delay		3	20	3	16	3	16	ns	
17	ALE Inactive Delay			25		19		19	ns	
19	DT/R Read Active Delay			25		23		23	ns	C_L = 150 pF I_{OL} = 16 mA max I_{OH} = −1 mA max
22	DT/R Read Inactive Delay		5	35	5	20	5	18	ns	
20	DEN Read Active Delay		5	35	5	21	5	21	ns	
21	DEN Read Inactive Delay		3	35	3	21	3	19	ns	
23	DEN Write Active Delay			30		23		23	ns	
24	DEN Write Inactive Delay		3	30	3	19	3	19	ns	

FIGURE 7–13 (*continued*)

Figure 7–14 shows a simple circuit that generates and inserts different numbers of waits states. Here a shift register is used to develop the waveform applied to the SRDY input of the 82284 clock generator. Notice that ALE is shifted through the shift register to generate the desired number of wait states when one of the Wait inputs is placed at a logic 1. The Wait inputs allow a specific number of wait states to be inserted as dictated by a range of memory locations. Wait 2 might be connected to an EPROM chip select circuitry to insert 2 waits for an EPROM access, while the RAM chip select circuitry might insert 0 waits.

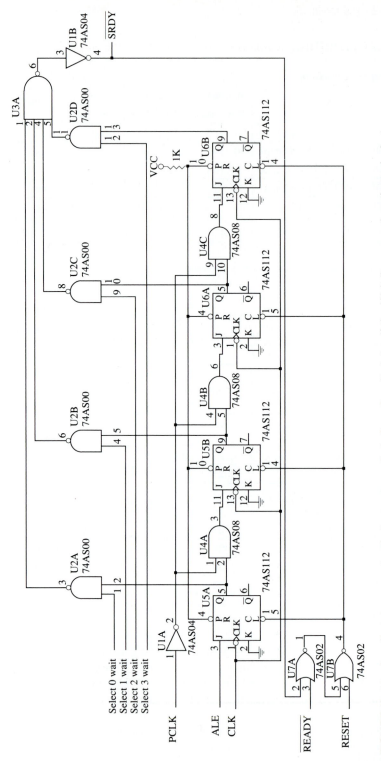

FIGURE 7–14 A wait state generator that can cause 0, 1, 2, or 3 wait states if the Wait lines are placed at a logic 1.

The timing diagram for the wait state generator is illustrated in Figure 7–15. In this diagram only the timing for 3 wait states is illustrated. Other timing diagrams can be developed to show how 0, 1, or 2 waits are inserted into the timing.

Interleaved Memory

Interleaved memory systems increase the amount of access time allowed for the memory. In an interleaved memory system there are usually two memory banks that store data. Banks are accessed alternately, which increases the amount of access time for the memory from the microprocessor. Earlier we found that an 8-MHz 80286 allowed 138.5 ns of access time to the memory. An 8-MHz interleaved memory system allows 223.5 ns of access time. The 12.5-MHz 80286 allows 85 ns for memory access, while the interleaved 12.5-MHz system allows 144 ns. This increase in access time means that slower memory components can be used at the same clock frequency.

Interleaved memory is not perfect. An interleaved memory system saves time when the addresses are sequential, as they are when most software executes. Because we access one location after another, the memory control logic can automatically provide the next address to the alternate memory bank, thereby increasing memory speed. There are cases where consecutive access to the same bank occur. If the same bank is accessed twice in a row (*back-to-back*), then a wait state must be introduced. The occurrence of a back-to-back hit is about 7 percent for a typical software application. According to tests, this results in about a 4 percent longer execution time.

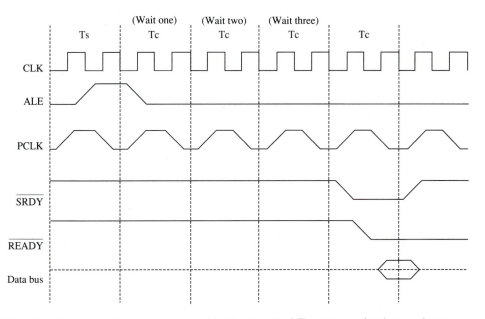

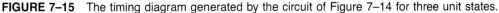

FIGURE 7–15   The timing diagram generated by the circuit of Figure 7–14 for three unit states.

While one bank of an interleaved memory system is accessed, the other bank receives its address and begins to access data. The addresses are generated by the control logic in the interleaved memory system. This allows each bank more time to access memory. The next chapter contains more detail and an interface for an interleaved memory system.

7–6   SUMMARY

1. The 80286 microprocessor is available in an 8-, 10-, and 12.5-MHz version from Intel, while other vendors can supply a 16-MHz version. The device is packaged in either an LCC or PGA that has 68 pin connections. The 80286 requires about 600 mA of current from a +5.0-V power supply that has a voltage tolerance of ±5 percent.

2. The input pin characteristics of the 80286 are compatible with standard TTL and other logic families, and draw only ±10 μA of current. The output pins can sink 2.0 mA of current and source −400 μA. The logic 1 output is TTL compatible, but the logic 0 output is degraded by 0.05 V, which reduces the system noise margin from the standard 400 mV to 350 mV.

3. The 80286 contains a 24-bit address bus that allows it to access 16M bytes of memory. It also contains a 16-bit data bus that allows it to access bytes or words of memory. Delineation between a byte access (upper or lower bank) and a word access is provided by the $\overline{\text{BHE}}$ and A0 signals.

4. The 82284 clock generator chip performs three functions in the 80286 system: it generates the clock, provides the $\overline{\text{READY}}$ signal, and provides the RESET signal. There are two timing signals used as outputs from the 82284 clock generator. One supplies the CLK signal to the microprocessor, while the other provides the PCLK (peripheral) clock signal. The CLK signal is at the same frequency as the crystal attached to the 82284 and the PCLK signal is one-half the crystal frequency.

5. The 82288 system bus controller provides the system with its control bus. The control bus contains memory read ($\overline{\text{MRDC}}$) and write ($\overline{\text{MWTC}}$) control signals and I/O read ($\overline{\text{IORC}}$) and write ($\overline{\text{IOWC}}$) signals. In addition to these four main control signals it also provides $\overline{\text{INTA}}$ (interrupt acknowledge), ALE (address latch enable), DT/$\overline{\text{R}}$ (data transmit/receive), and DEN (data bus enable) signals.

6. The 80286 microprocessor is buffered using latches to buffer the address connections and bidirectional data bus buffers to buffer the data bus. In any case, these buffers provide 32 mA of sink current and −5.2 mA of source current. These buffers are designed to drive the high-capacitance loads often found in memory components.

7. The 80286 microprocessor timing consists of four different timing periods called T states. The two main T states are T_s (status) and T_c (command). During the T_s state the microprocessor sends the system address and other status bits, and during T_c the microprocessor either reads or writes data. The idle state (T_i) appears occasionally when the microprocessor is not accessing the bus system.

The hold state (T_h) occurs during a hold cycle used for direct memory access operations (DMA).

8. The amount of time the microprocessor allows the memory to read information is called the memory access time. This time is calculated from the timing diagram provided for the microprocessor. Access time equals 3 CLK periods minus time 16 and time 8. This is the access time at the inputs of the buffers and not the memory. For the actual access time, also subtract 19 ns for these buffers. Actual access time is therefore 3 CLK periods minus time 16, time 8, and 19 ns for the buffers.

9. Wait states (extra T_c periods) are inserted by controlling the $\overline{READY}$ line. If $\overline{READY}$ = 0, no wait states are inserted, and if $\overline{READY}$ = 1, wait states are inserted. A wait state delays the point at which data are sampled during a read or written during a write. The 82288 system bus controller provides two inputs that cause wait states. The $\overline{SRDY}$ input allows the external logic more time to decide if a wait state is required than the other input, $\overline{ARDY}$.

10. Additional access time can be achieved by using an interleaved memory system. In the interleaved system, while one bank of memory is accessed, the other bank receives its address and begins to access data. This allows additional access time to the memory, which allows slower memory components to be used in the system. An interleaved memory system requires about 4 percent more time to execute software than a noninterleaved system that uses more costly higher speed memory.

7–7 QUESTIONS AND PROBLEMS

1. The 80286 is packaged in either an LCC, PLCC, or a _____.
2. The 80286 contains _____ address pins.
3. Power supply current is about _____ mA for the 80286 microprocessor.
4. A _____-V power supply with a tolerance of ±5 percent is required to operate the 80286.
5. What is the purpose of the CAP pin on the 80286 microprocessor?
6. What is the noise immunity of the 80286 in millivolts?
7. How many CD4XXX devices can be connected to any 80286 output pin connection?
8. How many 74ALSXXX devices can be connected to any 80286 output pin connection?
9. What 80286 control signal selects the high data bus (D_{15}–D_8)?
10. What 80286 signal selects the low data bus (D_7–D_0)?
11. If the CLK frequency applied to the 80286 is 14 MHz, the 80286 operates at what internal clock frequency?
12. What is the purpose of the $M/\overline{IO}$ signal?
13. Whenever the 80286 is reset, it fetches its first instruction from which memory location?
14. What is the purpose of the status bits $\overline{S}_1$ and $\overline{S}_0$?

15. What major system signals are provided by the 82284 clock generator?
16. If a 12-MHz crystal is attached to the X_1 and X_2 pins of the 82284, what frequency signals are found at the CLK pin and the PCLK pin?
17. If a crystal is used as a timing element for the 82284, the $F/\overline{C}$ pin is connected to a logic _____.
18. What is the purpose of the EFI input to the 82284 clock generator?
19. What function is performed by the $\overline{S}_1$ and $\overline{S}_0$ inputs to the 82284?
20. Explain how the reset circuit (refer to Figure 7–5) resets the microprocessor whenever power is applied.
21. What is the purpose of the 82288 system bus controller?
22. The system bus controller provides which two memory control signals?
23. The system bus controller provides which two I/O control signals?
24. Bus buffers provide _____ mA of logic 0 current.
25. If the DIR pin of the 74LS645 is connected to a logic 1, data flow from the _____ bus to the _____ bus.
26. If the $\overline{G}$ pin on the 74LS645 is a logic 1, what happens to the buffer?
27. Which 82288 signal is attached to the 74LS645 DIR pin?
28. What devices are used to buffer the address bus?
29. What is the purpose of the system bus controller ALE signal?
30. A transparent latch passes information when its clock input is a logic _____ level.
31. The main clocking periods in the timing diagram of the 80286 are T_s and _____.
32. What events occur during the 80286 send–states clocking period?
33. What events occur during the 80286 command clocking period?
34. Memory access time is the amount of time the microprocessor allows the _____ to access data.
35. When is the data bus sampled by the 80286 microprocessor during a read operation?
36. If the 80286 operates with a CLK signal of 20 MHz, the access time is _____.
37. If the 80286 operates with a PLCK signal of 9 MHz, the access time is _____.
38. Wait states are inserted into the 80286 timing by which pin?
39. A wait state is an extra _____ clocking period.
40. When is the $\overline{READY}$ sampled by the 80286 microprocessor?
41. Explain the operation of the wait state generator of Figure 7–14.
42. Interleaved memory allows additional access time because of _____.
43. Interleaved memory requires about _____ percent more time than noninterleaved memory to execute software.

CHAPTER 8

Memory Interface

INTRODUCTION

Whether simple or complex, every microprocessor has a memory system. The 80286 microprocessor is no different from any other microprocessor or computer system in this respect.

Almost all systems contains two main types of memory: (1) the read-only memory (ROM) that stores permanent system data, and (2) the random access memory (RAM) or read/write memory that stores temporary data. This chapter explains how to interface these main memory types to the microprocessor. It also explains the different types of memory components available and several ways to decode or select memory for an 80286-based system.

OBJECTIVES

Upon completion of this chapter, you will be able to:

1. Use an integrated circuit decoder, a PROM decoder, and a PAL decoder to decode and select memory.
2. Explain how to interface both ROM and RAM to the 80286.
3. Explain how parity detects memory errors.
4. Interface memory as both noninterleaved and interleaved to the 80286 microprocessor.
5. Explain the operation of a dynamic RAM controller and interface memory to the microprocessor using it.

8–1   MEMORY DEVICES

Before memory can be interfaced to the microprocessor, the operation of memory devices must be understood. This section provides a description of the operation of common memory types. These types include read-only memory (ROM), static random access memory (SRAM), and dynamic random access memory (DRAM).

Memory Device Connections

All memory devices have address inputs, data outputs or data input/outputs, and control connections. The control connections allow the memory component to be selected and cause a read or write operation. Figure 8–1 illustrates the basic pin connections for a ROM and RAM pseudomemory component. Note that only the RAM contains the $\overline{WE}$ pin connection; otherwise the components are the same.

Address Connections.   All memory devices have address inputs used to select a memory location within the memory device. The number of address pins is determined by the number of memory locations found within the memory device.

Today more common memory devices have between 1K (1,024) and 4M memory locations, with 16M memory devices imminent. A 1K memory device has 10 address pins. A 10-bit memory address (1,024 combinations) is therefore required to access a single location within the 1K memory device. If a memory device has 11 address connections, it contains 2K (2,048) memory locations. The number of memory locations can thus be extrapolated from the number of address connections found on a memory device. For example, a 4K memory device has 12 address connections, an 8K device has 13, and so forth. Another important address pin count to remember is that a 1M memory device has a 20-bit address. This too can be extrapolated to larger devices such as a 4M device that contains 22 address connections.

Data Connections.   All memory devices have data outputs or input/output connections that transfer data between the memory device and the microprocessor's data bus connections. The device illustrated in Figure 8–1 has a set of common input/output (I/O) connections.

The data connections are the points at which data enter or leave a memory device. In the illustration there are 8 data connections, which means that the memory device can store 8 bits of data in each of its memory locations. An 8-bit wide memory device is often called a *byte-wide memory.* Not all memory devices are 8 bits wide. Some memory devices have 4, 2, or even a single data connection.

FIGURE 8–1   A pseudomemory component illustrating the address, data, and control connections.

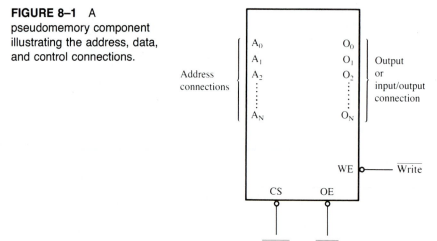

Catalog listings of memory components often refer to the total number of memory locations *times* the number of bits in each memory location. For example, a memory device with 1K locations that are each 8 bits wide is often listed as either a 1K × 8 or as an 8K device. A memory listed as a 16K device can be organized as a 16K × 1, a 4K × 4, or a 2K × 8 device. The actual organization depends on how the manufacturer has decided to connect the data I/O connections.

Selection Connections.   Each memory device has an input—sometimes more than one—that selects or enables the memory. This kind of input is most often called either a *chip select* ($\overline{CS}$) or *chip enable* ($\overline{CE}$) input. The RAM (read/write) memory usually has at least one $\overline{CS}$ input, while the ROM (read-only) memory usually has a $\overline{CE}$ connection. If the $\overline{CS}$ or $\overline{CE}$ input is active (a logic 0), the memory device can do a read or a write. If the $\overline{CS}$ or $\overline{CE}$ pin is inactive (logic 1), the memory device disconnects itself from its data connections. When the device is disabled, it presents a high-impedance path to the data connections so they do not interfere with other data on the microprocessor data bus connections. If a device has more than one $\overline{CS}$ or $\overline{CE}$ connection, they must all be active to select or enable the device. For example, suppose that a memory device has a $\overline{CS_1}$ and CS_2 connection. Here $\overline{CS_1}$ is an active low connection and CS_2 is active high. This means that $\overline{CS_1} = 0$ and $CS_2 = 1$ to activate the memory component.

Control Connections.   All memory devices must be controlled so they perform a read or a write operation. A ROM usually has only one control input, while a RAM often has two control inputs.

The control input found on a ROM is the *output enable* ($\overline{OE}$) or the *output control* ($\overline{OC}$) connection. If $\overline{OE}$ or $\overline{OC}$ is a logic 0 and the memory device is selected with the $\overline{CS}$ or $\overline{CE}$ connection, the output is enabled and the device performs a read operation. If $\overline{OE}$ or $\overline{OC}$ is a logic 1, then no read operation is performed even though the $\overline{CS}$ or $\overline{CE}$ connection may be active. Inside the memory device the OE/OC connection is logically combined with CS/CE to enable a set of three-state output buffers.

The RAM (read/write) memory device often contains two control inputs in addition to the select input. If a RAM contains only one control input, it is labeled R/$\overline{W}$ for read/write. The R/$\overline{W}$ pin selects a read operation if a logic 1 and a write operation if a logic 0 provided the device is selected with $\overline{CS}$. If the RAM has two control inputs, they are often labeled $\overline{WE}$ (*write enable*) and $\overline{OE}$ (*output enable*). If the RAM is selected, $\overline{WE}$ is placed at a logic 0 to cause a write, and $\overline{OE}$ is placed at a logic 0 to cause a read. These pins must never both be placed at logic 0 levels. If both $\overline{WE}$ and $\overline{OE}$ are logic 1s, no read or write occurs and the data connections are at their high-impedance state.

ROM Memory

The read-only memory (ROM) permanently stores programs and data. This form of storage is used to store programs and data that must remain resident to a system after power is removed. The BIOS (basic I/O system) in a personal computer is an example of a software that must stay resident after power is removed. Recall that the BIOS provided the computer with a set of basic I/O procedures that make

FIGURE 8–2 The 2764 EPROM. Note that the $\overline{PGM}$ and VPP pins are used for programming and under normal operation are connected to +5.0 V.

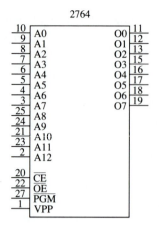

it compatible with other computer systems. The BIOS also contains the software required to load the disk operating system (DOS) so it can perform tasks.

The ROM device is available in many different forms today. The *mask programmed ROM* is purchased in mass quantities from the manufacturer, where it is programmed during its fabrication at the factory. A mask programmed ROM is only economical in large quantities because there is a one-time mask setup charge of $10,000. If you buy one device, it will cost $10,001 — $10,000 for the mask and $1 for the device.

The EPROM (*erasable programmable ROM*) is programmed in the field on a device called an *EPROM programmer*. The EPROM is programmed in a few minutes, but erasure often takes anywhere from 6 to 30 minutes. An EPROM is removed from the system and erased by a high-intensity ultraviolet lamp. The EPROM memory device is probably the most common form of read-only memory. It is economical unless more than 1,000 identical read-only memory devices are required.

The PROM (*programmable ROM*) is also field-programmable, but it cannot be erased. Most PROM devices are bipolar devices with access times of 25 ns or less. The EPROM is a MOSFET device with access times of 100 ns and longer. A PROM is programmed by burning open tiny Nichrome or silicon oxide fuses. Once a fuse is blown, it cannot be connected again; this is why these devices cannot be erased. The PROM memory finds some application as a memory or I/O address decoder.

The EEPROM (*electrically erasable programmable ROM* or *FLASH RAM**) can be programmed and erased electrically without removing it from the system. The EPROM must be removed from the system for both programming and erasing. The only disadvantage of the EEPROM is that it can only be erased up to 10,000 times before it fails. In many applications, this presents no problem because this is more erasures than are required for the application. At this time it is probably more cost efficient to use a battery-backed-up memory system than to use an EEPROM. The personal computer system uses a battery-backed-up memory, called a *CMOS memory,* to store setup information for the computer. A CMOS memory is a standard static RAM constructed from CMOS technology.

---

*FLASH RAM is a registered trademark of Intel Corporation.

Figure 8–2 shows the pinout of the 2764 EPROM. This device contains 13 address connections and 8 data outputs. The 2764 is an 8K × 8 memory device. The 27XXX series of EPROMs contains the following part numbers: 2704 (512 × 8), 2708 (1K × 8), 2716 (2K × 8), 2732 (4K × 8), 2764 (8K × 8), 27128 (16K × 8), 27256 (32K × 8), and 27512 (64K × 8). There is even a 256K × 8 (272001) EPROM. Each of these standard components contains address connections, 8 data output connections, one chip selection pin ($\overline{CE}$), and one output enable pin ($\overline{OE}$).

Figure 8–3 depicts the timing diagram for the 27512 EPROM and also the AC characteristics. Data only appear at the output connection after a logic 0 is placed on both the $\overline{CE}$ and $\overline{OE}$ pins. If $\overline{CE}$ and $\overline{OE}$ are not both logic 0s, the data output connections remain at their high-impedance or off state.

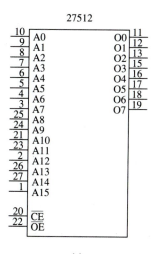

(a)

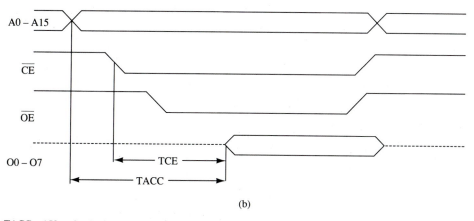

(b)

TACC = 150 ns for the 27512–15 and 200 ns for the 27512–20

TCE = 150 ns for the 27512–15 and 200 ns for the 27512–20

FIGURE 8–3 The pinout (a) and timing diagram (b) for the 27512 EPROM.

One important piece of information is provided by the timing diagram and AC characteristics—the *memory access time*. Memory access time is the time it takes the EPROM to present data at the data connections after the address is applied and the device is selected. As Figure 8–3 shows, the memory access time (T_{acc}) is measured from the application of the address until the data appear at the data connections. This measurement is based upon the assumption that the $\overline{CE}$ pin goes low at the same time that the address is applied. It also assumes that $\overline{OE}$ is also a logic 0 so data can appear.

The basic speed for all EPROM memory is 450 ns, with higher speed devices available. The manufacturer guarantees that the data are found at the output connects within 450 ns for this speed device. In many cases the EPROM memory requires the insertion of wait states into the timing each time that it is accessed by the 80286 system.

Static RAM (SRAM) Memory

Static RAM (SRAM) memory devices retain data for as long as DC power is applied. Because no special action is required to retain data, this device is called a *static memory*. The main difference between a ROM and RAM is that RAM is written into under normal operation, while the ROM is not normally written while in the system. The EEPROM is an exception, but it is only written under special circumstances and is often dubbed an RMM (*read-mostly memory*). The SRAM stores temporary data and is often used when the memory system size is less than 512K bytes. If a system is larger than this, we normally use dynamic RAM memory.

Figure 8–4 illustrates the pinouts of the 6116, 6164, and 62256—three different-size SRAM devices. All three devices have the same control structure, and they all use at least one $\overline{CS}$ connection for chip selection, an $\overline{OE}$ connection to cause a read, and a $\overline{WE}$ connection to cause a write. The 6164 has two chip selection inputs

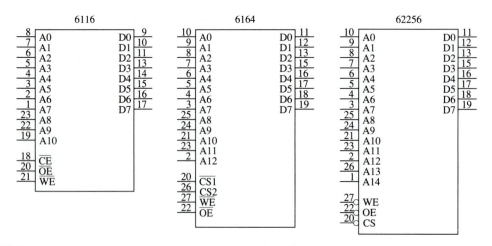

FIGURE 8–4   The pinouts of the 6116 (2K × 8), 6164 (8K × 8), and 62256 (32K × 8) static RAM devices.

($\overline{CS}_1$ and CS_2) that must both be active in order to read or write memory data. The standard speed version (access time) of the SRAM is 250 ns. Higher speed versions are available that access data at 125 ns. If still higher speed SRAM is required, there are high-speed static RAMs available with access times that are as little as 25 ns, but these devices are fairly expensive. In most cases 25-ns memory devices are found in cache memory systems.

Figure 8–5 illustrates the pinout of the 6287 64K × 1 SRAM. This device is different from the other SRAM devices presented in Figure 8–4. Its access time is 25 ns instead of 250 ns for the SRAMs illustrated earlier. It also has a different control pin structure. It contains only two control pins, chip select ($\overline{CS}$) and write enable ($\overline{WE}$). When selected, a logic 1 on $\overline{WE}$ causes a read, while a logic 0 causes a write. The data connections are also different. So far all SRAM devices had common I/O connections that are used to both read and write data. This device has separate I/O connections, one an input to write data, and the other an output to read data.

Dynamic RAM (DRAM) Memory

About the largest static RAM commonly available is the 62256 32K × 8. Dynamic RAM (DRAM) is available in sizes of up to 4M bytes. In most other respects DRAM is similar to SRAM except that it only retains data for 2–4 ms. In order to retain data for extended periods of time, the DRAM must be periodically refreshed. A refresh occurs when data are read and rewritten. A refresh automatically occurs internally for any read or write operation. The reason that the DRAM only retains data for such a short time is that data are stored internally on integrated gate capacitors. These capacitors lose their charge after a short period, so they must be rewritten or refreshed.

Instead of requiring the almost impossible task of reading the contents of each memory location with a program, the manufacturer has internally constructed the DRAM so fewer reads are required to refresh the device. Figure 8–6 illustrates the

FIGURE 8–5 The 6287 (64K × 1) high-speed static RAM that has an access time of 25 ns.

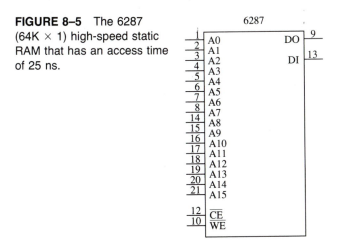

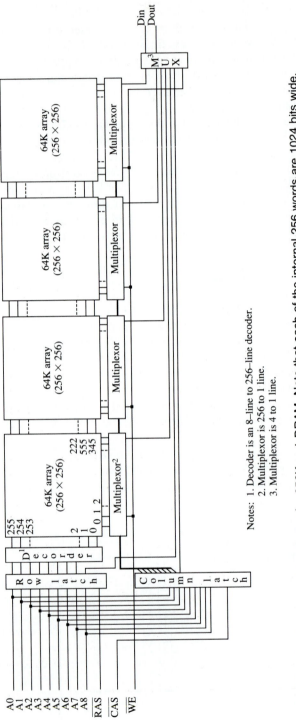

FIGURE 8–6 The internal structure of a 256K × 1 DRAM. Note that each of the internal 256 words are 1024 bits wide.

FIGURE 8–7 The pinouts of the 41256 (256K × 1) and 511000 (1M × 1) dynamic RAMs.

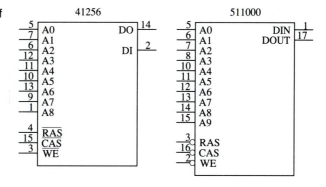

internal structure of a 256K × 1 dynamic RAM. This device can be refreshed in 256 reads because it is internally constructed with 256 words that are each 1,024 bits wide. In order to refresh this device, 256 reads — one from each internal word or row — must occur in 4 ms. Whenever a row is addressed, the entire 1,024 bits located in the row are automatically read and rewritten or refreshed.

The address for a location within the DRAM is applied through nine address connections. The 18-bit address is sent through these nine connections, nine bits at a time. Two control signals $\overline{RAS}$ (row address strobe) and $\overline{CAS}$ (column address strobe) clock each half of the address into internal latches. One, the row latch, uses 8 of its 9 bits to access one of the 256 rows. The other, the column latch, uses 8 of its 9 bits to access one column in each 64K-bit array. The remaining two bits of the address connect to a multiplexer that selects one bit from one of the four internal memory arrays.

The pinout of the 41256 DRAM (256K × 1) and the 511000 (1M × 1) DRAM appears in Figure 8–7. Notice the 41256 has nine address connections (A_0–A_8) and the 511000 (TMX4C1024)* has ten address connections (A_0–A_9). Through these connections, either 18 microprocessor address bits (41256) or 20 address bits (511000) are entered into these memory devices to access either 256K or 1M bits of memory. More details on DRAM memory devices and their interface to the microprocessor appear in Section 8–4.

In addition to the DRAM memory devices presented in Figure 8–7 we also find memory in the form of the SIMM† (*single in-line memory modules*). These are available in sizes of 256K × 9 through 4M × 9. The pinout of a 1M × 9 bit SIMM (421000C9) is illustrated in Figure 8–8. Internally, the SIMM is constructed from standard DRAM memory parts that have been assembled into memory modules. The 421000C9 contains an 8-bit wide memory that uses D_1–D_8 as its I/O connection and a ninth bit used for parity that contains a separate data input and data output pin.

---

*The TMX4C1024 is a Texas Instruments, Inc. part number for the 1M × 1 DRAM.

†SIMM® is a registered trademark of Wang Laboratories.

FIGURE 8–8   The pinout of the 421000C9 1M × 9 SIMM dynamic memory module.

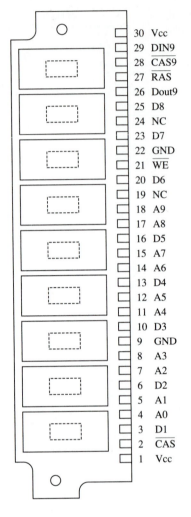

30	Vcc
29	DIN9
28	$\overline{CAS9}$
27	$\overline{RAS}$
26	Dout9
25	D8
24	NC
23	D7
22	GND
21	$\overline{WE}$
20	D6
19	NC
18	A9
17	A8
16	D5
15	A7
14	A6
13	D4
12	A5
11	A4
10	D3
9	GND
8	A3
7	A2
6	D2
5	A1
4	A0
3	D1
2	$\overline{CAS}$
1	Vcc

This device also contains 10 address connections for the 20-bit multiplexed address. The $\overline{CAS}$ input selects the data memory, and $\overline{CAS}_9$ selects the ninth parity bit. This device is also available as a 1M × 8 memory module, the 421000C8. The pins used on the 421000C9 for the ninth bit are not connected on the 421000C8.

8–2   MEMORY ADDRESS DECODERS

In order to attach a memory device to a microprocessor, it is necessary to decode the memory address. When the address is decoded, it selects the memory device for a unique section of the memory map. Without a memory address decoder, only one memory device can be attached to the microprocessor—making the system useless.

In this section, we describe a few of the more common address-decoding techniques as well as the decoders that are found in many memory systems.

Why Decode Memory?

As a comparison of the 80286 microprocessor and the 2764 EPROM reveals, the EPROM had 13 address connections while the microprocessor contains 24. This means that the microprocessor sends out a 24-bit address whenever it reads or writes data. Since the EPROM contains only 13 address connections, there is a mismatch that must somehow be corrected. If only 13 of the 24 microprocessor address connections are attached to memory, the 80286 will see only 8K bytes of data instead of the 16M bytes it expects the memory to contain. The decoder selects the memory device for an 8K-byte address range instead of a 16M-byte range. The decoder usually uses all of the address connections except the 13 connected to the memory component.

The 80286 Memory System

The memory map of the 80286 microprocessor appears in Figure 8–9. This memory system is constructed with two 8-bit memory banks that each contain 8M bytes of memory. Before memory can be decoded or interfaced to the microprocessor, its structure must be understood. Each memory bank is a separate entity that can be read and written independently of the other memory bank. The high bank, connected to the high half of the data bus (D_{15}–D_8), contains all of the odd-numbered bytes of memory. The low bank, connected to the low half of the data bus (D_7–D_0), contains all of the even-numbered bytes of memory.

Data are transferred between the 80286 and the memory as either bytes or words. Table 8–1 illustrates how the A_0 and $\overline{BHE}$ signals indicate which memory bank is currently active for the microprocessor. If a word is transferred between the

FIGURE 8–9 The structure of the 80286 memory system.

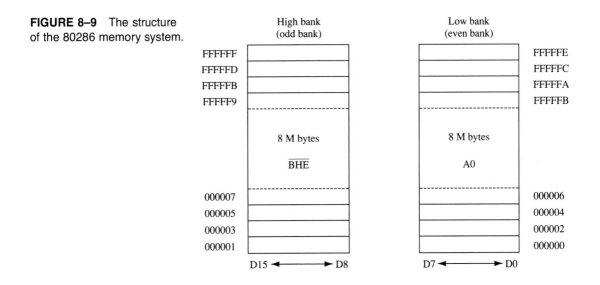

TABLE 8–1   Truth table of $\overline{BHE}$ and A_0

$\overline{BHE}$	A_0	Function
0	0	16-bit transfer using both banks (D_{15}–D_0)
0	1	8-bit transfer using the high bank (D_{15}–D_8)
1	0	8-bit transfer using the low bank (D_7–D_0)
1	1	No transfer

microprocessor and memory, both banks are active. If a byte is transferred, only one of the two banks is active. The A_0 and $\overline{BHE}$ enable signals must be used to activate the appropriate memory banks for each transfer.

Simple NAND Date Decoder

Address connections A_0–A_{12} appear on the 2764 EPROM. One would think that they were connected to microprocessor address connections A_0–A_{12}, but they are not. Instead memory connections A_0–A_{12} are connected to microprocessor connections A_1–A_{13}. The reason for this connection is that the A_0 address pin from the microprocessor is used to select a memory bank, not a location within the memory device. If $A_0 = 0$, the low bank is enabled, and if $A_0 = 1$, the low bank is disabled. Although this pin is labeled A_0 it does not function as other address connections, but as a $\overline{BLE}$ (bus low enable) signal.

If the memory is located in the low bank and we connect A_0 to A_0, only memory locations within the memory device that use a logic 0 on A_0 will function. If the memory is located in the high bank and we connect A_0 to A_0, then only memory locations that use a logic 1 on A_0 will function. This erroneous connection uses only half the available locations in the memory device.

Figure 8–10 illustrates two 2764s connected to the 80286 to function at memory locations FFC000H–FFFFFFH. This is an address range of 16K bytes (4000H). Each 2764 EPROM contains 8K bytes of memory for a total of 16K bytes. One EPROM activates for all the even locations between FFC000H and FFFFFFH, and the other for all the odd locations.

Example 8–1 illustrates the range of addresses converted to binary for this section of memory. The rightmost 14 bits of the address change from every combination from all zeroes to all ones. These bits are considered don't cares (X) as far as the decoder is concerned. Bits A_1–A_{13} are decoded by the EPROMs, and bit A_0 is used to select the low memory bank. The remaining address bits (A_{14}–A_{23}) are all logic 1s for this 16K-byte section of the memory.

EXAMPLE 8–1

```
1111  1111  1100  0000  0000  0000 = FFC000H
              to
1111  1111  1111  1111  1111  1111 = FFFFFFH
              or
1111  1111  11XX  XXXX  XXXX  XXXX
```

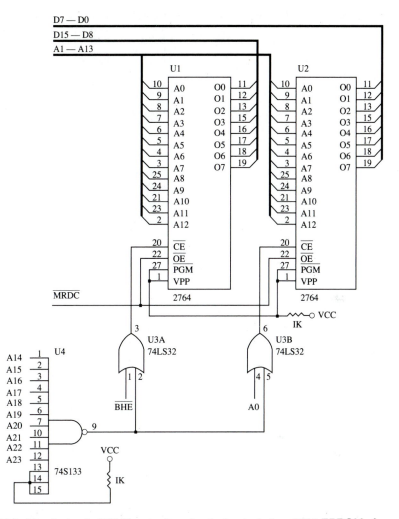

FIGURE 8–10 A simple NAND gate decoder that selects two 2764 EPROMs for memory address range FFC000H–FFFFFFH.

Notice how the don't cares (X) are used to represent the bits that are decoded by the memory and also bit position A_0. Bits A_0–A_{13} are represented as Xs and the remaining bits, because of the address range, are represented as logic 1s. The 74133 NAND gate is used to logically combine address connections A_{14}–A_{23} so if they are all logic 1s, the output of the NAND gate becomes a logic 0. Two OR gates combine the NAND gate's output with the $\overline{BHE}$ and A_0 signals to enable either or both memory components for address range FFC000H–FFFFFFH.

If the address is changed to location FFBFFFH (1111 1111 10XX XXXX XXXX), just one location below FFC000H, the output of the NAND gate becomes a logic 1, disabling both memory components. Likewise if the address changes to one location above FFFFFFH or 000000H (0000 0000 00XX XXXX XXXX), the

FIGURE 8–11 The 74ALS138 3-to-8 line decoder.

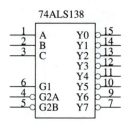

output of the NAND gate also becomes a logic 1, disabling the memory. This NAND gate decodes a unique 16K-byte range of memory.

The EPROM memory contains a $\overline{CE}$ pin that connects to the OR gate to select the EPROM. The $\overline{OE}$ pin connects directly to the $\overline{MRDC}$ (memory read) control signal. Both the V_{pp} and $\overline{PGM}$ pins are pulled up to +5.0 V through a 1-KΩ pull-up resister for normal memory operation. These two pins are used during programming, which is not discussed here.

The 3-to-8 Line Decoder (74ALS138)

One of the more common integrated decoders found in many microprocessor-based systems is the 74ALS138 3-to-8 line decoder. Figure 8–11 illustrates this decoder and Table 8–2 illustrates its truth table.

The truth table shows that only one of the eight outputs ever goes low at any time. For any output to go low, the three enable inputs—G_1, $\overline{G_2A}$, and $\overline{G_2B}$—must all be active. To be active, both $\overline{G_2A}$ and $\overline{G_2B}$ must be low (logic 0) and G_1 must be high (logic 1).

TABLE 8–2 The truth table for the 74ALS138 3-to-8 line decoder

Inputs						Outputs							
Enable			Select										
G_1	$\overline{G_2A}$	$\overline{G_2B}$	C	B	A	$\overline{0}$	$\overline{1}$	$\overline{2}$	$\overline{3}$	$\overline{4}$	$\overline{5}$	$\overline{6}$	$\overline{7}$
0	X	X	X	X	X	1 1 1 1 1 1 1 1							
X	1	X	X	X	X	1 1 1 1 1 1 1 1							
X	X	1	X	X	X	1 1 1 1 1 1 1 1							
1	0	0	0	0	0	0 1 1 1 1 1 1 1							
1	0	0	0	0	1	1 0 1 1 1 1 1 1							
1	0	0	0	1	0	1 1 0 1 1 1 1 1							
1	0	0	0	1	1	1 1 1 0 1 1 1 1							
1	0	0	1	0	0	1 1 1 1 0 1 1 1							
1	0	0	1	0	1	1 1 1 1 1 0 1 1							
1	0	0	1	1	0	1 1 1 1 1 1 0 1							
1	0	0	1	1	1	1 1 1 1 1 1 1 0							

Once the 74ALS138 is enabled, the select inputs (C, B, and A) choose the output that becomes a logic 0. Imagine eight EPROM memory components attached to the eight output connections of this decoder. This is a very powerful device because it can select up to eight different memory components.

A Sample Low Bank Decoder Circuit. The outputs of the decoder, illustrated in Figure 8–12, are connected to eight different 27512 64K-byte EPROMs. This decoder selects 64K-byte blocks of memory for a total of 512K bytes. This decoder selects only low bank memory. To select high bank memory A_0 is removed, and in its place we

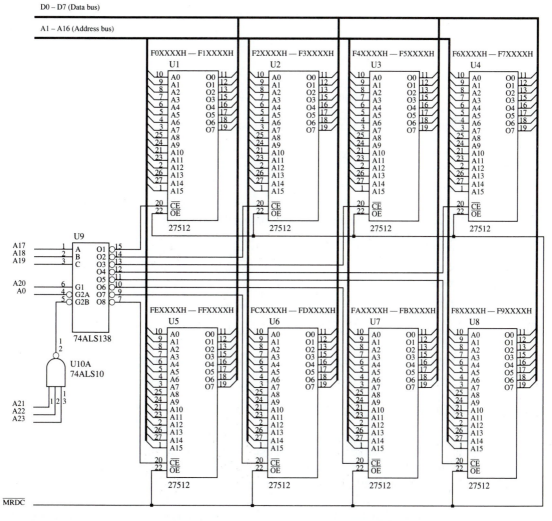

FIGURE 8–12 A single 74ALS138 decoder that selects eight 27512 EPROM devices. The decoder selects these devices for the low memory bank at addresses F00000H–FFFFFFH.

connect the $\overline{BHE}$ signal and we change the data bus connection to D_8–D_{15} from D_0–D_7.

The decode selects memory for any address between locations F00000H and FFFFFFH, a 1M-byte address range. Only 512K locations are active because the decoder only enables when $A_0 = 0$. This means that only the even-numbered memory locations between F000000H and FFFFFFH are stored in this memory array. In order to store the entire 1M byte of memory a second decoder and eight additional EPROM devices are required.

Example 8–2 shows the address range decoded (even addresses only) at output number $\overline{2}$ of the decoder. For output $\overline{2}$ to become a logic zero, $G_1 = 1$, $\overline{G_2A} = 0$, $\overline{G_2B} = 0$, and a 010 is applied to the C, B, and A inputs. This series of inputs is generated whenever even memory addresses between F40000H and F5FFFEH are output on the 80286 address bus.

EXAMPLE 8–2

```
1111  0010  0000  0000  0000  000X  = F20000H
                      to
1111  0011  1111  1111  1111  111X  = F3FFFEH
                      or
1111  001X  XXXX  XXXX  XXXX  XXXX  = F2XXXXH—F3XXXXH
```

Example 8–3 illustrates the range of addresses decoded at output number $\overline{5}$ of the 72ALS138 of Figure 8–12. This output decodes even memory addresses FA0000H through FBFFFEH.

EXAMPLE 8–3

```
1111  1010  0000  0000  0000  000X  = FA0000H
                      to
1111  1011  1111  1111  1111  111X  = FBFFFEH
                      or
1111  101X  XXXX  XXXX  XXXX  XXXX  = FAXXXXH—FBXXXXH
```

PROM Address Decoder

Another common address decoder is the PROM (programmable read-only memory). Figure 8–13 illustrates a PROM decoder in place of the 74ALS138 decoder presented in Figure 8–12. Notice that because the PROM decoder has additional inputs (the 74ALS138 only had six), it is better suited to decoding memory in a microprocessor-based system like the 80286.

The PROM used in this circuit is the 5349 that is a 512×8 memory device. The 5349 contains nine address connections (A_0–A_8) and an enable input ($\overline{CE}$). The eight output connections are used as enable inputs to the eight EPROM memory devices in

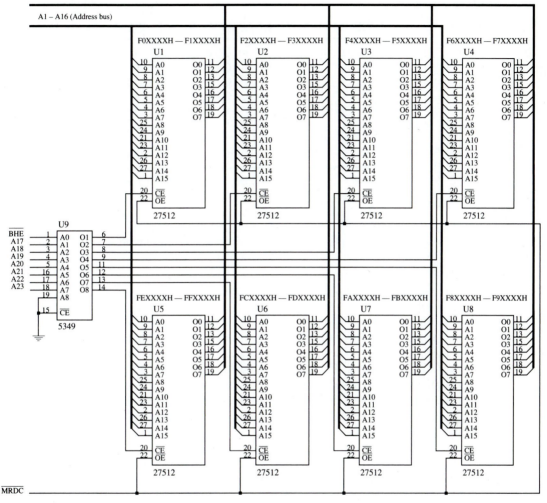

FIGURE 8–13 A single PROM decoder that selects eight 27512 EPROM memory devices. The decoder selects these devices for odd-numbered addresses between locations F00001H and FFFFFFH.

this interface. The difference between the decoder and the PROM is that the PROM uses programmed logic. We program the PROM to select the memory devices for any range of addresses desired. Table 8–3 shows the bit pattern programmed into the 5349 of Figure 8–13. This PROM selects the same memory address ranges as the decoder except that this example uses $\overline{\text{BHE}}$ to select the EPROM for the high bank of memory instead of the low bank as in Figure 8–12.

Whenever a PROM is purchased all locations contain 1111 1111. In this example, only 8 of the 512 locations are programmed, so programming time and cost is kept to a minimum. Also note that the access time of most PROM memory devices

TABLE 8–3 The program for the PROM of Figure 8–12

	Inputs										Outputs							
$\overline{CE}$	A_8	A_0	A_7	A_6	A_5	A_4	A_3	A_2	A_1		O1	O2	O3	O4	O5	O6	O7	O8
0	0	0	1	1	1	1	0	0	0		0	1	1	1	1	1	1	1
0	0	0	1	1	1	1	0	0	1		1	0	1	1	1	1	1	1
0	0	0	1	1	1	1	0	1	0		1	1	0	1	1	1	1	1
0	0	0	1	1	1	1	0	1	1		1	1	1	0	1	1	1	1
0	0	0	1	1	1	1	1	0	0		1	1	1	1	0	1	1	1
0	0	0	1	1	1	1	1	0	1		1	1	1	1	1	0	1	1
0	0	0	1	1	1	1	1	1	0		1	1	1	1	1	1	0	1
0	0	0	1	1	1	1	1	1	1		1	1	1	1	1	1	1	0

Note: All other PROM locations are programmed with 1111 1111.

is equivalent to the access time of the decoder, so no alteration in memory access time is required when using a PROM in place of a decoder.

PAL Address Decoder

This section of the text explains the use of the programmable logic device or PLD as a decoder. Recently, the PAL* has replaced PROM address decoders in the latest memory interfaces. There are three devices that function in the same manner, but have different names: PLA (programmable logic array), PAL (programmable array logic), and GAL† (gated array logic). Although these devices have been in existence since the mid-1970s, they have recently begun appearing in memory systems and digital designs. The PAL and the PLA are fuse programmed, as is the PROM, and some of the GALs are erasable devices, as are EPROMs. In essence, all three devices are arrays of logic elements that are programmable.

Combinatorial Programmable Logic Arrays.   One of the two basic types of PALs is the combinatorial programmable logic array. This device is internally structured as a programmable array of combinational logic circuits. Figure 8–14 illustrates the internal structure of the PAL 16L8 that is constructed with AND/OR gate logic. This device has 10 fixed inputs, 2 fixed outputs, and 6 pins that are programmable as inputs or outputs. Each output pin is generated from a 7-input OR gate that has an AND gate attached to each input. The outputs of the OR gates pass through a three state inverter that defines each out as an AND/NOR function. Initially all of the fuses connect all of the vertical/horizontal connections illustrated in this figure. Programming is accomplished by blowing fuses to connect various inputs to the

---

*PAL® is a registered trademark of Advanced Micro Devices, Inc.

†GAL® is a registered trademark of LATTICE Semiconductors, Inc.

Logic Diagram   16L8

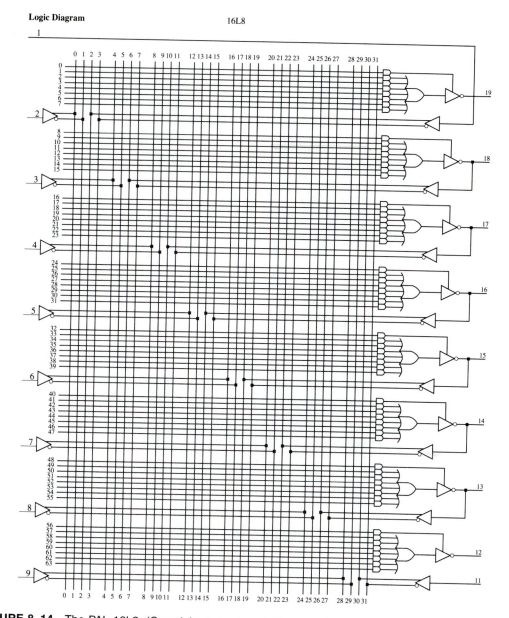

FIGURE 8–14 The PAL 16L8. (Copyright © Advanced Micro Devices, Inc., 1988. Reprinted with permission of copyright owner. All rights reserved.)

OR gate array. The wired AND function is performed at each input connection that allows a product term of up to 16 inputs. A logic expression using the PAL 16L8 can have 7 product terms with 16 inputs NORed together to generate the output expression. This device is ideal as a memory address decoder because of its structure.

Fortunately, we don't have to choose the fuses by number for programming. We program the PAL using a software package called PALASM* (PAL assembler), version 2. The PALASM program and its syntax are an industry standard for programming PAL devices. Example 8–4 shows a program that decodes the same areas of memory as are decoded in Figures 8–12 and 8–13.

EXAMPLE 8–4

TITLE	Address Decoder
PATTERN	Test 1
REVISION	A
AUTHOR	Barry B. Brey
COMPANY	Symbiotic Systems
DATE	1/23/92
CHIP	Decoder1 PAL16L8

```
;pins 1    2    3    4    5    6    7    8    9   10
      BHE  A17  A18  A19  A20  A21  A22  A23  NC  GND

;pins 11  12  13  14  15  16  17  18  19  20
      NC  O8  O7  O6  O5  O4  O3  O2  O1  VCC
```

EQUATIONS

/O1 = /BHE * A23 * A22 * A21 * A20 * /A19 * /A18 * /A17
/O2 = /BHE * A23 * A22 * A21 * A20 * /A19 * /A18 * A17
/O3 = /BHE * A23 * A22 * A21 * A20 * /A19 * A18 * /A17
/O4 = /BHE * A23 * A22 * A21 * A20 * /A19 * A18 * A17
/O5 = /BHE * A23 * A22 * A21 * A20 * A19 * /A18 * /A17
/O6 = /BHE * A23 * A22 * A21 * A20 * A19 * /A18 * A17
/O7 = /BHE * A23 * A22 * A21 * A20 * A19 * A18 * /A17
/O8 = /BHE * A23 * A22 * A21 * A20 * A19 * A18 * A17

The first eight lines of the program illustrated in Example 8–4 identify the program title, pattern, revision, author, company, date, and chip type with the program name. Here the chip type is a 16L8 and the program is called decoder. After the program is identified, a comment statement (;pins) identifies the pin numbers. The pins as defined for this application appear below this comment state. Once all the pins are defined, we use the EQUATIONS statement to indicate that the equations for this application follow. In this example, the equations define the 8-chip enable outputs for the 8 EPROM memory devices. Refer to Figure 8–15 for the complete schematic diagram of this PAL decoder.

---

*PALASM® is a registered trademark of Advanced Micro Devices, Inc.

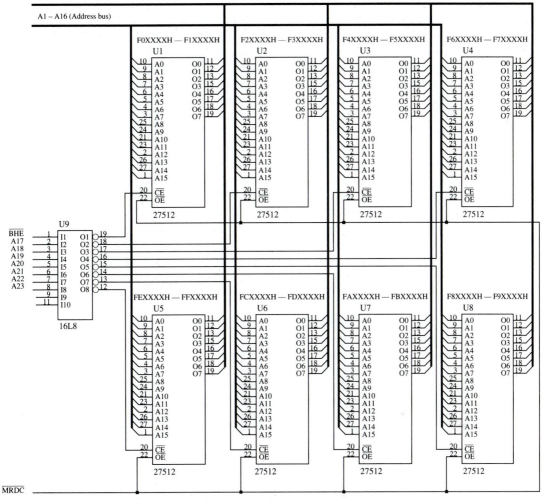

FIGURE 8–15 A PAL (16L8) used to select eight EPROM memory devices.

8–3   80286 MEMORY INTERFACE

This section describes memory interfacing so the skills required to connect memory to the 80286 can be understood. Here we examine the memory interface to both RAM and ROM. We also explain parity checking, which is commonplace in many microprocessor-based systems. We also briefly mention error correction schemes used in some memory systems.

Basic Memory Interface

As mentioned, the 80286 microprocessor contains a 16-bit data bus and a 24-bit address bus. For the 80286 to function correctly with the memory, the memory system must decode an address to properly select a memory device, and it must use the $\overline{MRDC}$ (memory read) and $\overline{MWTC}$ (memory write) control signals provided by the 82288 system bus controller. The basic memory interface assumes that the system contains the 82288 system bus controller or an equivalent that generates the $\overline{MRDC}$ and $\overline{MWTC}$ control signals. It also assumes that the address is latched as described in Chapter 7–4.

We connect memory to the microprocessor using a memory decoder that decodes a 16-bit-wide memory and applies separate write strobes to each of the memory banks. In the last section, we decoded 16-bit-wide memory and used the $\overline{BHE}$ or A_0 signal to enable the high or low memory bank.

Figure 8–16 illustrates the simple circuit used to generate separate write strobe signals called $\overline{HWR}$ (high bank write) and $\overline{LWR}$ (low bank write). When we select 16-bit-wide memory we enable both banks for every read operation with the $\overline{MRDC}$ signals and the high, low, or high and low banks for a write operation. We can always enable both memory banks for a read operation because the microprocessor will only read the bank or banks that it needs to read.

Interfacing EPROM to the 80286.   You will find this section very similar to Section 8–2 on decoders. The main difference is that in this section we discuss waits states and decoding two memory banks instead of one.

Figure 8–17 illustrates the 80286 system interfaced to four 27256 EPROM memory devices. These memory devices contain 32K bytes of memory accessed through 15 address connections (A_0–A_{14}). This system decodes this 128K-byte section of memory at locations 010000H through 02FFFFH. Because of the number of address connections to be decoded, A_{16}–A_{23}, we use a PAL 16L8 as a decoder.

The PAL selects memory devices U_1 and U_3 together as a 16-bit-wide section of memory, and it selects U_2 and U_4 together as another 16-bit-wide section of memory. Because each memory device is a 32K-byte device and two devices are selected at a time, the PAL decodes a 64K-byte block of memory at each of its outputs. Output $\overline{O_2}$ selects U_1 and U_3 for memory locations 010000H–01FFFFH, and $\overline{O_3}$ selects U_2 and U_4 for locations 020000H–02FFFFH. Example 8–5 shows the program for the PAL 16L8 used to select both the memory components and to

FIGURE 8–16   The memory bank write selection inputs signals $\overline{HWR}$ (high bank write) and $\overline{LWR}$ (low bank write).

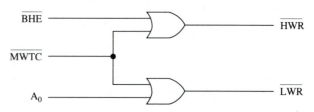
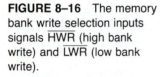

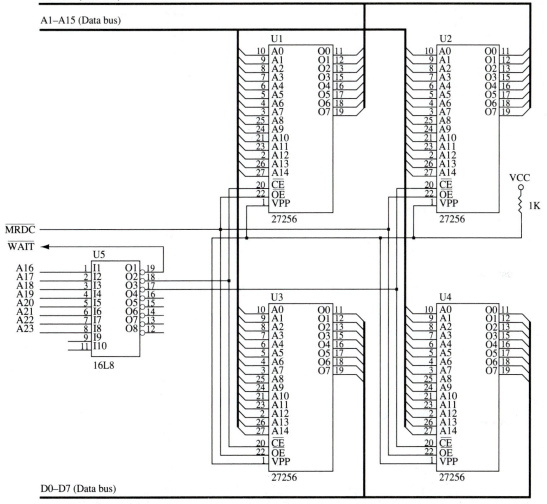

FIGURE 8–17 A 128K-byte EPROM memory system interfaced at locations 010000H–02FFFFH. Note the output signal for the wait state generator.

generate a signal called $\overline{\text{WAIT}}$ for the wait state generator (not pictured) whenever a location between 010000H and 02FFFFH is accessed.

Because most EPROM requires more access time than often provided by the microprocessor, the PAL also generates the $\overline{\text{WAIT}}$ output signal. This causes the correct number of wait states to be inserted into the 80286 timing for the memory. Suppose that the 8-MHz version of the 80286 is connected. It allows the memory system 138.5 ns of access time. In order to allow a 250-ns EPROM to function, one wait state of 125 ns is inserted into the timing. The wait state is generated as described in Chapter 7.

EXAMPLE 8–5

TITLE	EPROM System
PATTERN	Test 2
REVISION	C
AUTHOR	Barry B. Brey
COMPANY	Symbiotic Systems
DATE	1/24/92
CHIP	Decoder2 PAL16L8

```
;pins 1   2    3    4    5    6    7    8    9   10
      A16 A17 A18 A19 A20 A21 A22 A23  NC  GND

;pins 11 12 13 14 15 16 17 18 19  20
      NC NC NC NC NC NC O3 O2 WAIT VCC
```

EQUATIONS

/WAIT = /A23 * /A22 * /A21 * /A20 * /A19 * /A18 * /A17 * A16
      + /A23 * /A22 * /A21 * /A20 * /A19 * /A18 * A17 * /A16

/O3 = /A23 * /A22 * /A21 * /A20 * /A19 * /A18 * A17 * /A16
/O2 = /A23 * /A22 * /A21 * /A20 * /A19 * /A18 * /A17 * A16

Interfacing RAM to the 80286.   A RAM memory component is interfaced in the same manner as an EPROM except for one small difference. Because a RAM can both read and write data, the memory system must be controlled by both the $\overline{\text{MRDC}}$ and $\overline{\text{MWTC}}$ signals.

Figure 8–18 shows a small RAM memory system that is decoded at memory locations 110000H–13FFFFH. This memory system contains 192K bytes of RAM. The type of RAM used for this interface is the 62256 SRAM that stores 32K bytes of data. Because six 62256 SRAMs are interfaced, the total memory system contains 192K bytes.

The PAL 16L8 (see Example 8–6) generates the high and low bank memory write signals and also selects the three sections of memory for address ranges: 110000H–11FFFFH, 120000H–12FFFFH, and 130000H–13FFFFH. As mentioned earlier, the two bank write signals are used to write to the high bank, low bank, or both banks. Note that pin 13 ($\overline{\text{MTWC}}$) is a programmable I/O pin on the PAL 16L8. If an equation is provided for this pin, it becomes an output connection. If no equations (as in Example 8–6) are provided, this pin is an input pin. No special instructions are required for programming this I/O pin.

EXAMPLE 8–6

TITLE	SRAM System
PATTERN	Test 3
REVISION	B
AUTHOR	Barry B. Brey
COMPANY	Symbiotic Systems
DATE	1/25/92
CHIP	Decoder3 PAL16L8

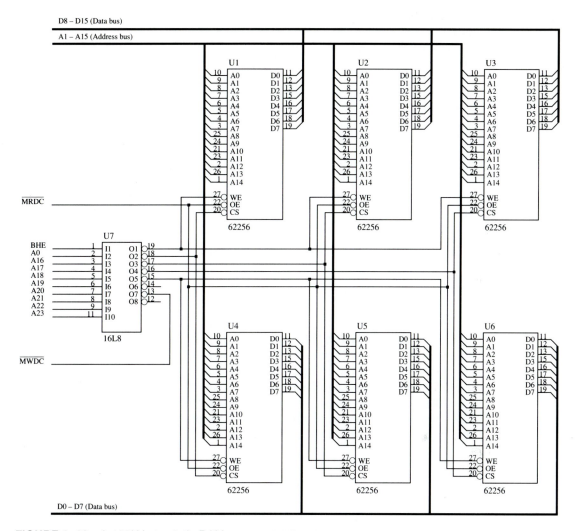

FIGURE 8–18 A 192K-byte static RAM memory system.

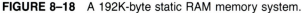

```
;pins  1    2    3    4    5    6    7    8    9    10
      BHE  A0  A16  A17  A18  A19  A20  A21  A22  GND

;pins 11   12   13        14   15   16   17   18   19   20
      A23  NC  MWTC       NC  LWR  O4   O3   O2  HWR  VCC
```

EQUATIONS

```
/HWR = /BHE * /MWTC
/LWR = /A0 * /MWTC
/O2  = /A23 * /A22 * /A21 * A20 * /A19 * /A18 * /A17 * A16
/O3  = /A23 * /A22 * /A21 * A20 * /A19 * /A18 * A17 * /A16
/O4  = /A23 * /A22 * /A21 * A20 * /A19 * /A18 * A17 * A16
```

FIGURE 8–19 An example memory map containing an area of EPROM and an area of RAM.

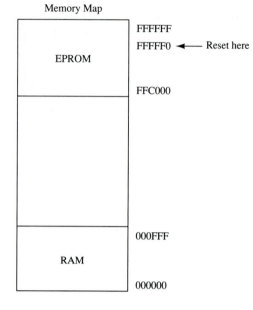

Memory Map

EPROM

RAM

FFFFFF
FFFFF0 ◄─── Reset here

FFC000

000FFF

000000

An Example Memory System Interface. The memory map for an example memory system appears in Figure 8–19. This memory map is designed for a small microprocessor-based system that requires a small area of RAM and a larger area of EPROM for its memory requirements. Because the 80286 resets to memory location FFFFF0H, the EPROM must be placed at the top of memory. The RAM in most 80286 systems is placed beginning at the bottom of memory because of a series of interrupt vectors that are situated in the first 1K byte of memory.

The memory map illustrated shows that the EPROM begins at memory location FFC000H and ends at location FFFFFFH for a memory size of 16K bytes. Two 2764 EPROMs (the 2764 is an 8K-byte EPROM) are chosen to provide the EPROM area of memory for the system. The RAM area on the memory map begins at location 000000H and ends at location 000FFFH for a memory size of 4K bytes. Two 6116 RAMs (the 6116 is a 2K-byte RAM) are chosen to provide this RAM area of memory. The entire memory system is illustrated in Figure 8–20. The decoder used for this interface is a PAL 16L8. The program for the PAL, which also generates WAIT signals, appears in Example 8–7. Because not enough pins are found on the PAL, a 74AS32 OR gate is used to generate the high and low bank write signals for this circuit.

EXAMPLE 8–7

TITLE	Example System
PATTERN	Test 4
REVISION	A
AUTHOR	Barry B. Brey
COMPANY	Symbiotic Systems
DATE	1/26/92
CHIP	Decoder4 PAL16L8

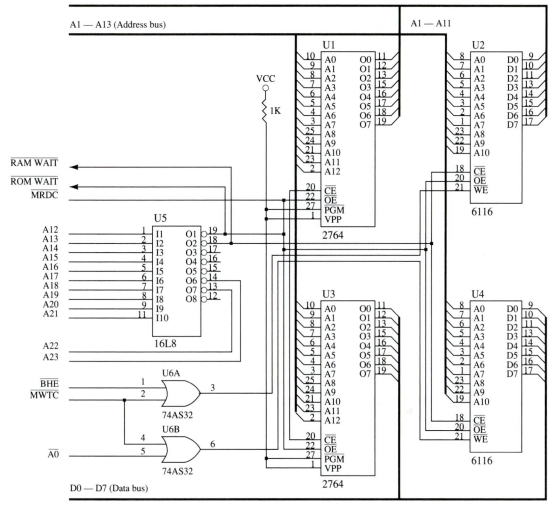

FIGURE 8–20 The EPROM and RAM interface that implements the memory map of Figure 8–19.

```
;pins  1    2    3    4    5    6    7    8    9    10
       A12  A13  A14  A15  A16  A17  A18  A19  A20  GND

;pins  11   12   13   14   15   16   17   18   19   20
       A21  NC   A22  A23  NC   NC   NC   O2   O1   VCC

EQUATIONS

/O1 = A23 * A22 * A21 * A20 * A19 * A18 * A17 * A16 * A15 * A14
/O2 = /A23 * /A22 * /A21 * /A20 * /A19 * /A18 * /A17 * /A16 * /A15 * /A14 * /A13 * /A12
```

FIGURE 8–21 The pinout of the 74AS280 parity generator/detector.

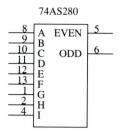

Parity for Memory Error Detection

Because large memory systems are available today, and because circuit costs are minimal, many memory board manufacturers have added parity checking to their memory systems. Parity checks the number of 1s in data and indicates if they contain an even or an odd number of 1s. If data are always stored with even parity, a 1-bit change (error) can be detected.

Figure 8–21 illustrates the 74AS280 parity generator/detector. This device has nine input pins and generates either even or odd parity for the 9-bit number placed on its inputs. It also checks the parity of the 9-bit number placed on its inputs.

Figure 8–22 illustrates a 128K-byte RAM memory system that uses the 74AS280 to both generate and store parity each time that data are stored and to check parity each time data are read. Notice that each memory bank contains 8-bit-wide memory components and also a ninth bit of memory for parity storage. Checking parity requires that an additional memory device be added to store the parity bit in each memory bank. This means that a 16-bit-wide memory system requires two additional bits for parity storage. See Example 8–8 that lists the program for the PAL decoder. This decoder selects memory for locations 600000H–61FFFFH.

Whenever data are written to a memory bank, the 8-bit data are also sent to a 74AS280 parity generator to generate the ninth parity bit. The extra input to the parity generator is grounded. In the example circuit, the parity generator is used to generate a 1 for an even number of 1s and a 0 for an odd number of 1s.

EXAMPLE 8–8

```
    TITLE        Memory with Parity
    PATTERN      Test 5
    REVISION     A
    AUTHOR       Barry B. Brey
    COMPANY      Symbiotic Systems
    DATE         1/27/92
    CHIP         Decoder5  PAL16L8

;pins 1    2    3    4    5    6    7    8    9    10
      BHE  A0  A16  A17  A18  A19  A20  A21  A22  GND
```

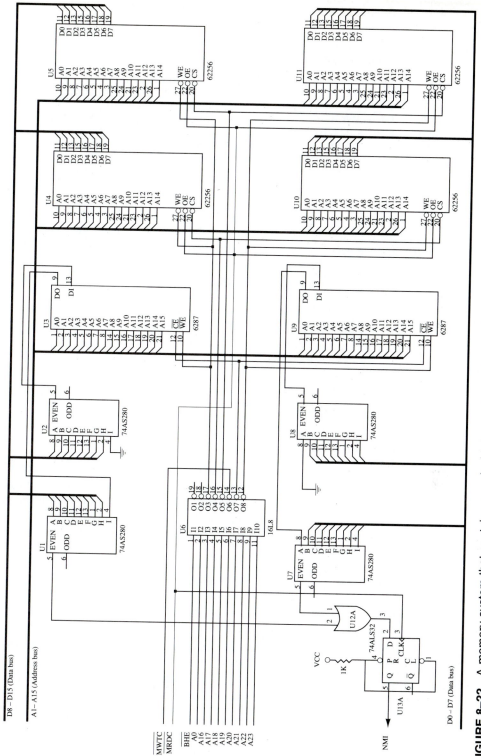

FIGURE 8–22 A memory system that contains a parity bit for each memory bank.

```
;pins 11   12    13  14      15   16   17    18  19   20
       A23  LWR  CP  MWTC   CS1  CS2  HWR   NC  NC   VCC
```

EQUATIONS

```
/LWR = /A0 + /MWTC
/HWR = /BHE + /MWTC
/CP  = /A23 * A22 * A21 * /A20 * /A19 * /A18 * /A17
/CS1 = /A23 * A22 * A21 * /A20 * /A19 * /A18 * /A17 * /A16
/CS2 = /A23 * A22 * A21 * /A20 * /A19 * /A18 * /A17 * A16
```

When data are read from memory they pass through another 74AS280 that functions as a parity checker or detector. The detector is connected with all eight data bits and the parity bit as an input. If a parity error is detected in this circuit, the 74AS280's even output pin becomes a logic 1. This pin is ORed with the opposite memory bank parity output that connects, through a flip-flop, to the NMI input of the 80286 microprocessor.

The NMI input is a special nonmaskable interrupt input. If a logic 1 appears on the NMI pin, the microprocessor interrupts its program and calls a procedure that indicates a parity error. More details on interrupts is provided in Chapter 10. The application of a parity error, if detected, is timed by a flip-flop. Notice that the clock signal for the flip-flop is provided by the $\overline{MRDC}$ signal. At the end of the read cycle, $\overline{MRDC}$ returns to a logic 1, clocking the output of the parity detectors that are ORed together onto the NMI pin.

Error Correction

Error correction schemes have been around for a long time, but integrated circuit manufacturers have only recently started to produce error correction circuits. Error correction uses a Hamming code that predicts which bit is in error. A *Hamming code* detects and corrects an error by storing check bits with data bits. A device that uses a Hamming code to detect and correct a 1-bit error is the 74LS636. This device also detects a 2-bit error.

The device corrects and detects errors by storing five parity bits with each 8-bit byte of data. Although this does increase the amount of memory required for an application, it allows the memory system to automatically correct any 1-bit error. It also detects a 2-bit error. If more than a 2-bit error occurs, this circuit may not detect it. Fortunately a 2 or more bit error is rare, making the effort to correct more than a 1-bit error futile. Whenever a memory component fails, the circuit flags the microprocessor with a multiple-bit error.

Figure 8–23 depicts the pinout of the 74LS636. The 74LS636 has eight data I/O connections, five check bit I/O pins, two control inputs (S_0 and S_1), and two error outputs. The error outputs indicate a single-bit error (SEF) and a double-bit error (DEF). The control inputs select the operation performed (see Table 8–4 for a listing).

FIGURE 8–23 The pinout of
the 74LS636 8-bit error
correction and detection
circuit.

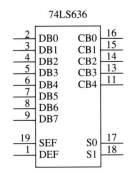

When data are written to memory, the 74LS636 generates the check word so it can be written to the check word memory area. In order for the device to generate a check word, the S_0 and S_1 pins must contain a 00. When data are read from memory, the 74LS636 must be placed in mode 10 so that the data and check word may be read into the device. By placing an 11 on the S_0 and S_1 inputs, the 74LS636 indicates an error on the SEF and DEF pins. If the error is to be corrected, the S_0 and S_1 inputs are next switched to a 01 to generate the corrected code on a single-bit error.

Figure 8–24 illustrates the 74LS636 connected to correct an error if a single-bit error is detected, or to cause an NMI interrupt if a double-bit error is detected. This schematic illustrates a 32K-byte section of the memory and can represent the high or low memory bank in a system. Notice that U_2 stores the data and U_3 stores the 5-bit check bits.

This circuit reads data from the memory (both the data and check bits) except when a read or a write occurs. When data are written both S_1 and S_0 become 00 and the write occurs. When the read occurs, the S_0 and S_1 pins switch to an 11 and cause the 74LS636 to latch the read data and indicate an error if one occurs. If no error occurs SEF and DEF are both low and the microprocessor can continue. If a single-error occurs, SEF becomes a logic 1, causing a WAIT and also causing S_0 and S_1 to become a 01 and correct the error. As soon as the error is corrected by this device, SEF returns to a 0 and the WAIT is released, allowing the system to continue.

TABLE 8–4 The 74LS636
control bits

S_0	S_1	Function
0	0	Generate check word (write)
0	1	Correct data word
1	0	Read data and check word
1	1	Latch data and errors

FIGURE 8–24 An error detection and correction circuit using the 74LS636.

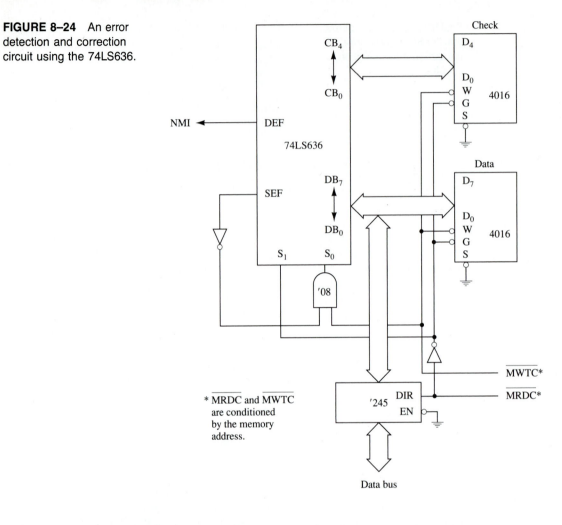

DYNAMIC RAM

Because RAM memory in the 80286 system is often very large, it requires many SRAM devices at a great cost, or just a few DRAMs (dynamic RAMs) at a much reduced cost. The DRAM memory, as briefly described in Section 8–1, is fairly complex because it requires address multiplexing and refreshing. Luckily, the integrated circuit manufacturers provide dynamic RAM controllers that include the address multiplexers and all the timing necessary for refreshing. This section of the text presents the DRAM memory device and the DRAM controller.

DRAM Revisited

As mentioned in Section 8–1, a DRAM retains data for only 2–4 ms and requires an address multiplexer. Some recent DRAM memory retains data for 8 ms. The address connections on the DRAM require an external multiplexer to strobe both the row and column addresses into the memory device. Figure 8–25 illustrates a simple address multiplexer used with a device such as the 41256, 256K × 1 DRAM. This device contains nine address connections where we apply the 18-bit memory address a half at a time.

This address multiplexer uses 74AS257 quad 2 line to 1 line multiplexers to send either A_1–A_9 or A_{10}–A_{18} to the address input pin of the 41256 DRAM. The $\overline{RAS}$ signal switches the outputs of the multiplexer from the A inputs (when $\overline{RAS}$ = 0) to the B inputs (when $\overline{RAS}$ = 1). When the $\overline{RAS}$ signal changes from a 1 to a 0, the outputs of the decoder still contain address signals A_{10}–A_{18}. The row address for the connection in Figure 8–24 is A_{10}–A_{18}. Shortly after the $\overline{RAS}$ signal

FIGURE 8–25 The address multiplexer used to send an 18-bit address (A1–A18) into the 41256 DRAM.

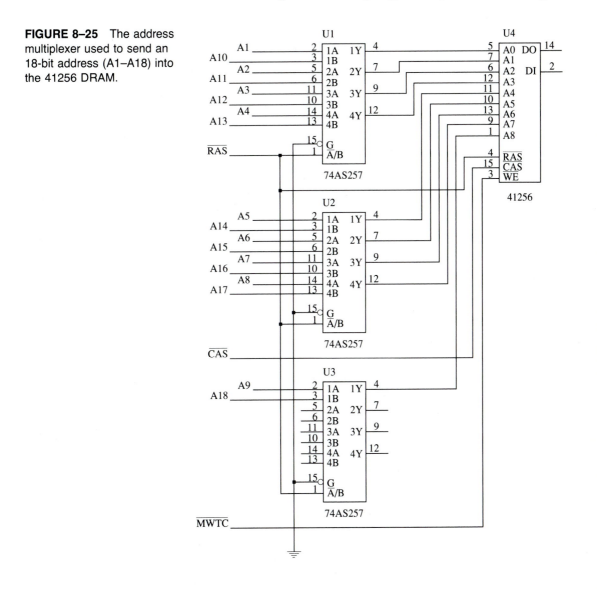

becomes a logic 0, the outputs of the multiplexer switch to the A inputs so that the $\overline{\text{CAS}}$ signal can capture A_1–A_9. In practice this multiplexer circuit is built into the DRAM controller.

In order to truly understand the operation of the DRAM, the timing diagram of Figure 8–26 describes the interaction of all the DRAM pin connections. Notice that the row address is captured as $\overline{\text{RAS}}$ changes to a logic 0, and the column address is captured when $\overline{\text{CAS}}$ changes to a logic 0. The most critical part of the DRAM timing diagram is the distance between the $\overline{\text{RAS}}$ and $\overline{\text{CAS}}$ signals. This time is often only 25–40 ns. Access times for dynamic RAM varies from a current low of 70 ns to 150 ns for older DRAMs.

Periodically DRAM must be refreshed to retain data. This is accomplished by reading or writing to a memory location that refreshes the entire row. The row size varies with the size of the DRAM. In order to refresh the entire DRAM, all rows must be read or written in 2 or 4 ms. For example, suppose that a DRAM has 128 rows and a refresh time of 2 ms. This device must have all 128 rows read in 2 ms, or we must make certain to read a row every 15.625 μs. Other DRAM devices, with 256 rows, allow a refresh time of 4 ms. This still means that a row must be refreshed at least each 15.625 μs.

One of the simplest ways to refresh the dynamic RAM is to cause an interrupt every 2, 4, or 8 ms. Recall from Chapter 7 that an interrupt calls a procedure that services the interrupt, and then control is returned to the program that was interrupted. The interrupt service procedure could read all of the rows each time that the program is interrupted. This satisfies the requirement that the DRAM be refreshed in 2, 4, or 8 ms. As a rule if a DRAM contains 128 rows, it requires a refresh every 2 ms, if it has 256 rows, it requires a refresh every 4 ms, and if it contains 512 rows, it requires a refresh every 8 ms.

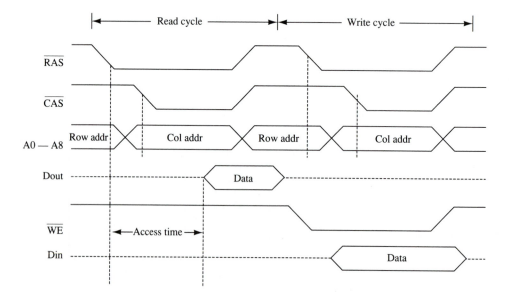

FIGURE 8–26   The read and write timing for the DRAM memory device.

EXAMPLE 8–9

```
                    ;(??c) = clock periods

0000               FRESH    PROC    FAR              ;(23c)

0000  51                    PUSH    CX               ;save registers (3c)
0001  56                    PUSH    SI               ;(3c)
0002  50                    PUSH    AX               ;(3c)

0003  B9 0080               MOV     CX,128           ;load count (2c)
0006  BE 0000               MOV     SI,0             ;load row 0 address (2c)

0009               BACK:

0009  AC                    LODSB                    ;read byte (5c)
000A  E2 FD                 LOOP    BACK             ;repeat 128 times (9c)

000C  58                    POP     AX               ;restore registers (5c)
000D  5E                    POP     SI               ;(5c)
000E  59                    POP     CX               ;(5c)

000F  CF                    IRET                     ;return from interrupt (17c)

0010               FRESH    ENDP
```

Example 8–9 lists a short interrupt service procedure that refreshes a DRAM memory device that contains 128 rows. Here we assume that the row address is the least significant 7 bits of the memory address. Notice that the procedure reads all 128 rows of the DRAM before returning to the program that was interrupted. If the interrupt occurs once every 2 ms, the DRAM will be properly refreshed. This procedure requires 460 clocking periods to execute. At a clock frequency of 8 MHz it takes 57.5 μs to execute this procedure. In other words, every 2,000 μs (2 ms) it requires 57.5 μs to (execute the procedure) refresh the DRAM in the system. We sacrifice about 2.9 percent of the microprocessor's active software execution time for refreshing the memory system in this manner.

Another way to refresh the DRAM is to periodically cause the microprocessor to wait and allow hardware to refresh the DRAM. By using this technique, we reduce the amount of time required to refresh the DRAM from 57.5 μs to 16 μs. This assumes that it requires one clocking period to refresh a memory location. The hardware refresh system therefore uses 0.8 percent of the microprocessor's execution time—a savings over the interrupt method.

Still another, far more costly method would be to develop hardware that re-members which location is read or written during a 2-ms interval. Then during the wait, the hardware only refreshes the locations not read or written. As mentioned, this technique is far more costly, but can be implemented for the most savings. The average amount of time used to refresh memory using this system of course varies with the software, but in most applications the refresh time is much less than 0.5 percent. A memory, called a CAM (contents-addressable memory), is used to store the addresses used to access memory. Then, during the refresh wait period, the contents-addressable memory is used to access only the rows that need to be refreshed.

DRAM Controller

In most systems, a DRAM controller integrated circuit performs the task of address multiplexing and the generation of the DRAM control signals. A typical DRAM controller is the Intel 82C08, which controls up to two banks of 256K × 16 DRAM memory. With the 80286 microprocessor, this can be up to 1M byte of memory.

The 82C08 contains an address multiplexer that multiplexes an 18-bit address onto nine address connections for 256K memory devices. Figure 8–27 shows the pinout of the DRAM controller. The address inputs are labeled AL_0–AL_8 and AH_0–AH_8. The address outputs to the DRAM are labeled AO_0–AO_8. The 82C08 contains circuitry that generates the $\overline{CAS}$ and $\overline{RAS}$ signals for the DRAM. These signals are developed by the CLK, S_0, and S_1 status signals. The $\overline{AA/XA}$ signal is an acknowledge output that is usually connected to the 82284 clock generator $\overline{SRDY}$ input for wait state generation.

Figure 8–28 illustrates this device connected to a series of four 256K × 8 bit SIMM memory modules (41256A8) that comprise a 1M-byte memory system for the 80286 microprocessor. Memory parts U_3 and U_5 from the high memory bank and parts U_4 and U_6 from the low bank. The PAL 16L8 combines the WE signal from the 82C08 with A_0 to generate the bank write signal for U_4 and U_6, and it combines WE with $\overline{BHE}$ to generate a bank write signal for U_3 and U_5. The PAL also develops the controller selection signal ($\overline{PE}$) by combining $M/\overline{IO}$ with address lines A_{20}–A_{23}

FIGURE 8–27 The 82C08 DRAM controller that controls two banks of memory.

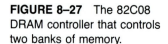

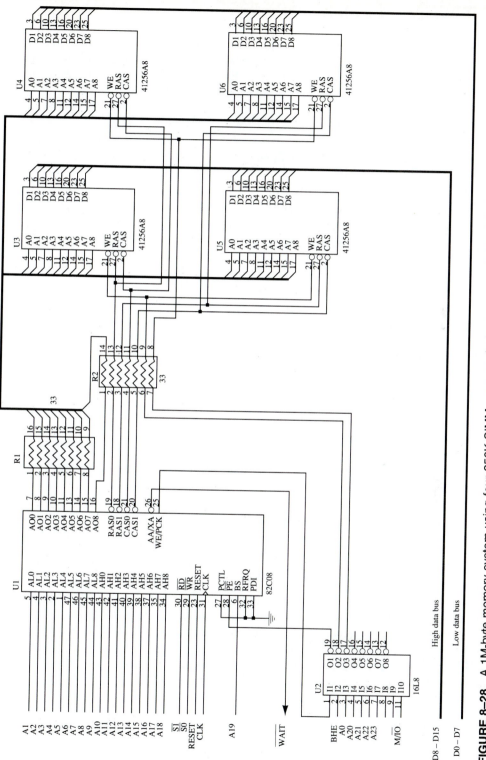

FIGURE 8–28 A 1M-byte memory system using four 256K SIMM memory devices and the 82C08 DRAM controller. This section of memory is decoded at locations 000000H–0FFFFFH by the PAL 16L8.

to decode the memory at locations 000000H–0FFFFFH. The A_{19} signal selects the upper bank (U_3 and U_4) or the lower bank (U_5 and U_6) through the BS (bank select) input to the 82C08 DRAM controller. Example 8–10 lists the program for the PAL 16L8 used for bank and memory selection.

EXAMPLE 8–10

TITLE	DRAM Memory System
PATTERN	Test 5A
REVISION	A
AUTHOR	Barry B. Brey
COMPANY	Symbiotic Systems
DATE	1/27/92
CHIP	Decode5A PAL16L8

```
;pins 1   2    3   4    5    6    7    8   9   10
      WE  BHE  A0  A20  A21  A22  A23  NC  NC  GND

;pins 11  12  13  14  15  16  17   18   19  20
      MIO NC  NC  NC  NC  NC  HWR  LWR  PE  VCC
```

EQUATIONS

```
/HWR = /BHE * /WE
/LWR = /A0 * /WE
/PE  = /A20 * /A21 * /A22 * /A23 * MIO
```

8–5   **INTERLEAVED MEMORY INTERFACE**

Interleaved memory systems are found so memory access times can be lengthened without the need for wait states. An interleaved memory system requires two complete sets of address buses and a controller that provides addresses for each bus.

Operation of Interleaved Memory

An interleaved memory is divided into two parts. For the 80286 microprocessor, one part contains 16-bit addresses 000000H–000001H, 000004H–000005H, and so forth, while the other part contains addresses 000002–000003, 000006H–000007H, and so forth. While the microprocessor accesses locations 000000H–000001H, the interleave control logic is generating address strobe signals for locations 000002H–000003H. This process is continued as the microprocessor addresses consecutive memory locations. This process lengthens the amount of access time provided to the memory, because the address is generated before the memory can actually use it. This is because the microprocessor pipelines memory addresses, sending the next address out before the data are read from the last address.

The problem with interleaving, although not major, is that the memory addresses must be accessed so each section is addressed alternately. This does not always happen as a program executes. Under normal program execution, the microprocessor alternately addresses memory approximately 93 percent of the time. During the remaining 7 percent, the microprocessor addresses data in the same memory section, which means that in this 7 percent of the memory accesses, the memory system must cause wait states because of the reduced access time. The access time is reduced because the memory must wait until the previous data are transferred before it can obtain their address. This leaves it with less access time; therefore, a wait state is required for accesses in the same memory bank.

Refer to Figure 8–29 for the timing diagram of the address as it appears at the microprocessor address pins. This timing diagram shows how the next address is output before the current data are accessed. It also shows how access time is increased using interleaved memory addresses for each section of memory compared to a noninterleaved access, which requires a wait state.

The Interleave Controller

Figure 8–30 pictures the interleave controller. Admittedly, this is a fairly complex logic circuit that needs some explanation. First, if the SEL input (used to select this section of the memory) is inactive (logic 0), then the $\overline{\text{WAIT}}$ signal is a logic 1. Also,

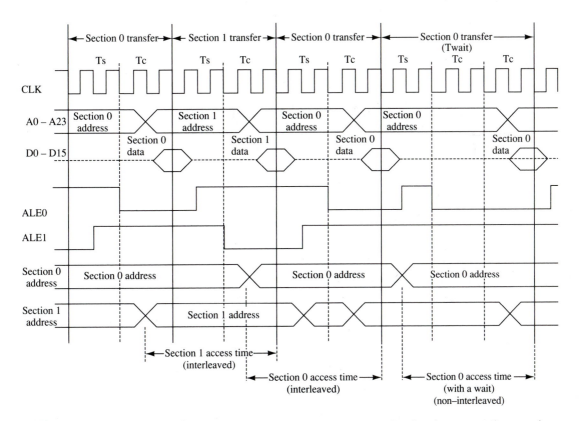

FIGURE 8–29 The timing diagram of an interleaved memory system showing the access times and address signals for both sections of memory.

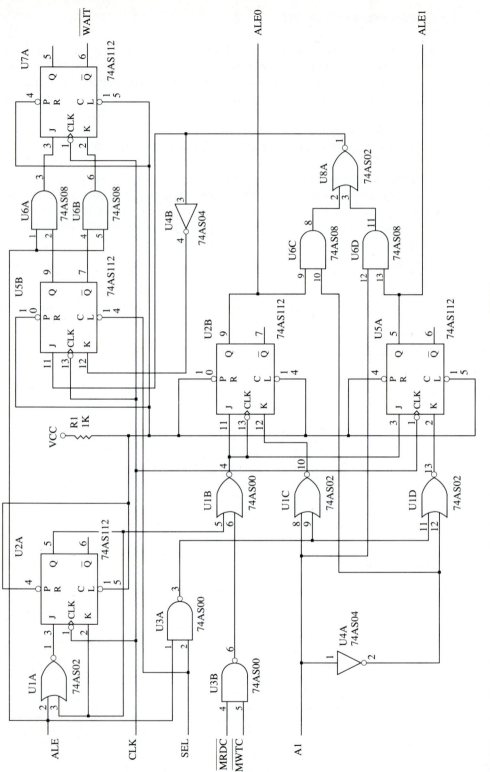

FIGURE 8–30 The interleave control logic that generates separate ALE signals and a $\overline{\text{WAIT}}$ signal used to control interleaved memory.

both ALE_0 and ALE_1, used to strobe the address to the memory sections, are both logic 1s, which means the latches connected to them become transparent.

As soon as the SEL input becomes a logic 1, this circuit begins to function. The A_1 input is used to determine which latch (U_2B or U_5A) becomes a logic 0 selecting a section of the memory. Also the ALE pin that becomes a logic 0 is compared with the previous state of the ALE pins. If the same section of memory is accessed a second time, the $\overline{WAIT}$ signal becomes a logic 0 requesting a wait state.

An Interleaved Memory System

Figure 8–31 illustrates an interleaved memory system that uses the circuit of Figure 8–30. Notice how the ALE_0 and ALE_1 signals are used to capture the address for either section of memory. The memory in each bank is 16 bits wide. If accesses to memory require 8-bit data, then in most cases the system causes wait states. As a program executes, the 80286 fetches instruction 16 bits at a time from normally

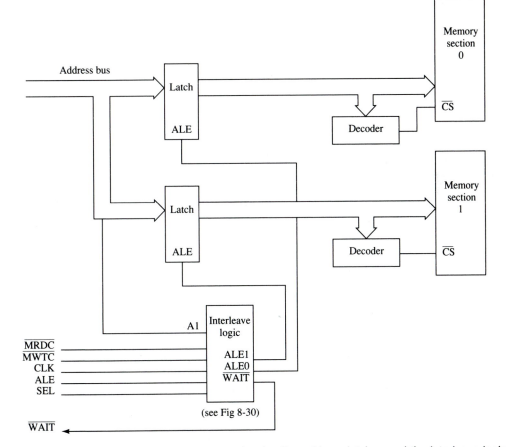

FIGURE 8–31 An interleaved memory system showing the address latches and the interleave logic circuit.

sequential memory locations. Program execution uses interleaving in most cases. If a system is going to access mostly 8-bit data, it is doubtful that memory interleaving will reduce the number of wait states.

The access time allowed by an interleaved system such as the one shown in Figure 8–31 is increased to 223.5 ns from 138.5 ns using an 8-MHz system clock. (If a wait system is inserted, access time with an 8-MHz clock is 263.5 ns, which means an interleaved system performs at about the same rate as a system with one wait state.) If the clock is increased to 12.5 MHz, the interleaved memory requires 144 ns, while standard memory interfaces allow 80 ns for memory access. At this higher clock rate a 120-ns DRAM functions properly, without wait states when the memory addresses are interleaved. If an access to the same section occurs, then a wait state is inserted because the microprocessor only allows 80 ns without any wait states in this case.

8–6   SUMMARY

1. All memory components have common features, such as address connections, data connections, and control connections. The address connections select a memory location whose contents are written or read through the data connection. The control connections enable the memory device so a read or write is performed. Control connections found on memory components include $\overline{CE}$ and $\overline{CS}$, used to enable the device; $\overline{OE}$, used to cause a read; and $\overline{WE}$, used to cause a write.

2. Memory types appear as read-only memory (ROM, PROM, EPROM, and EEPROM) or as read/write memory (SRAM and DRAM). Read-only memory devices store long-term data, while RAM stores transitory data.

3. Memory access time is the time that the memory device requires to access data. This elapsed time for a memory access is from the point where the address is applied to the memory component to where the data appear at the output connections.

4. A memory-address decoder selects a memory device for a unique range of a memory address. Memory address decoders can be NAND gates, TTL decoders, or PAL devices.

5. The 80286 memory system consists of two memory banks that are each 8 bits in width and hold up to 8M bytes of data. This allows the 80286 to address 16M bytes of memory. The low bank (even bank) holds all even-addressed bytes of data, while the high bank (odd bank) holds all odd-addressed bytes. Because of this organization, the 80286 can read/write any memory byte or any (16-bit) memory word. The high bank is selected by the $\overline{BHE}$ (bus high enable) signal and the low bank is selected by A_0.

6. Memory devices are interfaced to the 80286 by connecting its 24-bit address bus, 16-bit control bus, and two memory-selection signals ($\overline{MRDC}$ and $\overline{MWTC}$) to the address decoder and memory components. The address decoder selects the memory device for a unique range of addresses, and the control signals cause

either a read ($\overline{\text{MRDC}}$) or a write ($\overline{\text{MWTC}}$). In many cases, we develop separate write signals for each memory bank called high bank write ($\overline{\text{HWR}}$) and low bank write ($\overline{\text{LWR}}$).

7. Parity is often used to check memory data as they are read. Parity is a count of the number of ones expressed as even or odd. If data are always written with even parity, they can be tested when read by testing for even parity. If data are read with odd parity, as in this situation, they are invalid.

8. Error correction is accomplished by using an integrated error checker. This device will correct a single-bit error and detect a 2-bit error. The only disadvantage of correcting an erroneous bit is that it requires an extra 5 bits of memory per byte to store the error correction codes.

9. Dynamic RAM must be refreshed every 2–4 ms. Refreshing is accomplished by reading/writing each memory row in this time interval. Dynamic RAM also requires that the address sent to the DRAM is multiplexed. An external multiplexer must send half the address to a row address latch and the other half to a column address latch. The row address is entered into the DRAM by the $\overline{\text{RAS}}$ signal, and the column address is entered with the $\overline{\text{CAS}}$ signal.

10. A DRAM controller is a device that contains an address multiplexer, selection logic to enable more than one bank of memory, and logic that generates the system control signals $\overline{\text{RAS}}$ and $\overline{\text{CAS}}$. Some DRAM controllers also enable and execute the refresh function.

11. An interleaved memory system is organized in two sections. Alternate sections of the memory are accessed, allowing an increase in access time to the memory components in a section. If sections are accessed sequentially, then a wait state is inserted. An interleaved system allows almost as much access time as a noninterleaved system with one wait state.

8–7 QUESTIONS AND PROBLEMS

1. Explain the general purpose of the following memory connections:
   a. address inputs
   b. data connections
   c. $\overline{\text{CE}}$ or $\overline{\text{CS}}$ pins
   d. $\overline{\text{OE}}$ connection
   e. $\overline{\text{WE}}$ pin

2. List the number of address connections found on the following memory components:
   a. 1K × 8
   b. 4K × 8
   c. 64K × 1
   d. 256K × 4
   e. 1M × 1

3. Using (a)–(e) of Question 2, list how many data connections are found on each of these memory devices.

4. A memory device is enabled if CE_1 = _____, $\overline{CE_2}$ = _____, and CE_3 = _____.
5. Define memory access time as it applies to a memory component.
6. What is the difference between a ROM and an EPROM?
7. Which read-only memory types of devices are erasable?
8. What is a static RAM and why is it called static?
9. What is a dynamic RAM and why is it called dynamic?
10. How often must a DRAM be refreshed?
11. When is a DRAM refreshed?
12. What is a row address and how is it entered into a DRAM?
13. What is a column address and how is it entered into a DRAM?
14. A SRAM memory device with 10 address pin connections (A_0–A_9) addresses how many memory locations?
15. A DRAM memory device with 10 address pin connections (A_0–A_9) addresses how many memory locations?
16. Why is it necessary to decode a memory address?
17. The 80286 high memory bank connects to data bus connections _____ through _____.
18. Which 80286 memory bank contains all even-addressed bytes of data?
19. What 80286 control signal enables the high memory bank?
20. What 80286 pin enables the low memory bank?
21. How many memory bytes are addressable in the 80286 memory system?
22. How many memory words (16 bits) are addressable in the 80286 memory system?
23. Memory address connection A_0 is generally connected to which 80286 address connection?
24. Develop a NAND gate decoder that enables a memory device for address 800000H–81FFFFH.
25. Develop a NAND gate decoder that enables a memory device for addresses C40000H–C7FFFFH.
26. Develop a memory address decoder that uses the 74ALS138 to decode a block of memory beginning at location 380000H and ending at location 39FFFFH. Each output of the decoder must become active for a 16K-byte block of memory.
27. Develop a memory address decoder that uses the 74ALS138 to decode a block of memory beginning at location A40000H and ending at location A5FFFFH. Each output of the decoder must become active for a 16K-byte block of memory.
28. Develop a memory address decoder that uses a PAL to decode a block of memory beginning at location BC0000H and ending at location BFFFFFH. Each of the eight outputs must become active for a 32K-byte block of memory.
29. Develop a memory address decoder that uses a PAL to decode a block of memory beginning at location 340000H and ending at location 37FFFFH. Each of the eight outputs must become active for a 32K-byte block of memory.
30. Develop a 16-bit EPROM memory system for the 80286 microprocessor beginning at location 400000H and ending at location 43FFFFH. Show both memory banks, all control signals, and use a PAL to perform all decoding.
31. Develop a 16-bit EPROM memory system for the 80286 microprocessor beginning at location 780000H and ending at location 7BFFFFH. Show both memory banks, all control signals, and use a PAL to perform all decoding.

32. Develop a 16-bit SRAM memory system for the 80286 microprocessor beginning at location 840000H and ending at location 85FFFFH. Show both memory banks, all control signals, and use a PAL to perform all decoding.
33. Develop a 16-bit SRAM memory system for the 80286 microprocessor beginning at location 960000H and ending at location 97FFFFH. Show both memory banks, all control signals, and use a PAL to perform all decoding.
34. Develop a memory system for the 80286 that contains EPROM at location FFC000H–FFFFFFH and SRAM at locations 000000H–000FFFH and 200000H–21FFFFH. Show both memory banks, all control signals, and use a PAL to perform decoding.
35. Develop a memory system for the 80286 that contains EPROM at location FF8000H–FFFFFFH and SRAM at locations 000000H–000FFFH and 440000H–47FFFFH. Show both memory banks, all control signals, and use a PAL to perform decoding.
36. What is parity?
37. How can a parity bit help detect errors in a memory system?
38. If a single bit error is to be detected in a byte of data, how many check bits are required?
39. Describe the operation of the address multiplexer in Figure 8–24.
40. Is software a viable approach to refreshing a DRAM memory system?
41. What functions are performed in a DRAM memory system by the DRAM controller?
42. Develop a DRAM memory system that appears at memory locations 100000H–1FFFFFH.
43. Develop a DRAM memory system that appears at memory locations 400000H–4FFFFFH.
44. Explain what happens to the $\overline{\text{WAIT}}$ signal in the circuit of Figure 8–29 when SEL = 0.
45. In an interleaved memory system, when is a wait state requested?
46. Compare the access times allowed the memory for an interleaved memory system and a standard memory system.

CHAPTER 9

Basic I/O Interface

INTRODUCTION

A microprocessor is great at solving problems, but if it can't communicate with the outside world, it is of little worth. This chapter outlines some of the basic methods of communication, both serial and parallel, between humans or machines and the microprocessor.

In this chapter, we will first introduce the basic I/O interface and discuss decoding for I/O devices. Then we will provide details on parallel and serial interfacing, both of which have a wide variety of applications. As applications, we connect analog-to-digital and digital-to-analog converters as well as both DC and stepper motors to the microprocessor.

OBJECTIVES

Upon completion of this chapter, you will be able to:

1. Explain the operation of the basic input and output interfaces.
2. Decode an 8-bit and a 16-bit I/O device so it can be used at any I/O port address.
3. Define handshaking and explain how to use it with I/O devices.
4. Interface and program the 8255-5 programmable parallel interface.
5. Interface and program the 8279-5 programmable keyboard/display controller.
6. Interface and program the 8251A serial communications interface adapter.
7. Interface and program the 8254-2 programmable interval timer.
8. Interface an analog-to-digital converter and a digital-to-analog converter to the 80286 microprocessor.
9. Interface both DC and stepper motors to the 80286 microprocessor.

9–1   INTRODUCTION TO I/O INTERFACE

In this section of the text, we explain the operation of the I/O instructions (IN, INS, OUT, and OUTS). We also explain the concept of *isolated* (sometimes called direct or I/O mapped I/O) and *memory-mapped I/O,* the basic input and output interfaces, and *handshaking.* A working knowledge of these topics will make it easier to understand the connection and operation of the programmable interface components and I/O techniques presented in the remainder of this chapter and text.

I/O Instructions

The 80286 instruction set contains one type of instruction that transfers information to an I/O device (OUT) and another type to read information from an I/O device (IN). Instructions (INS and OUTS) are also provided to transfer strings of data between the memory and an I/O device. Four different versions of each of the IN and OUT instructions are available and two different versions of each of the INS and OUTS instructions are available. Table 9–1 lists all versions of each instruction found in the 80286 microprocessor's instruction set.

TABLE 9–1   80286 input/output instructions

Instruction	Data Width	Comment
IN AL,p8	8	Read a byte from I/O address p8 into AL
IN AL,DX	8	Read a byte from the I/O address indexed by DX into AL
IN AX,p8	16	Read a word from I/O address p8 into AX
IN AX,DX	16	Read a word from the I/O address indexed by DX into AX
INSB	8	Read a byte from the I/O address indexed by DX and store it in the location indexed by ES:DI, then increment/decrement DI by 1
INSW	16	Read a word from the I/O address indexed by DX and store it in the location indexed by ES:DI, then increment/decrement DI by 2
OUT p8,AL	8	Write a byte from AL into I/O address p8
OUT DX,AL	8	Write a byte from AL into the I/O address indexed by DX
OUT p8,AX	16	Write a word from AX into I/O address p8
OUT DX,AX	16	Write a word from AX into the I/O address indexed by DX
OUTSB	8	Write a byte from the memory location indexed by DS:SI into the I/O address indexed by DX, then increment/decrement SI by 1
OUTSW	16	Write a word from the memory location indexed by DS:SI into the I/O address indexed by DX, then increment/decrement SI by 2

Both the IN and OUT instructions transfer data between an I/O device and the microprocessor's accumulator (AL or AX). The I/O address is stored in register DX as a 16-bit I/O address or in the byte (p8) immediately following the opcode as an 8-bit I/O address. Intel calls the 8-bit form (p8) a *fixed address* because it is stored with the instruction, usually in a ROM. The 16-bit I/O address in DX is called a *variable address* because it is stored in a register, which can be varied. Both the INS and OUTS instructions use a variable I/O address contained in the DX register.

Whenever data are transferred using the IN or OUT instruction, the I/O address, often called a *port number,* appears on the address bus. The external I/O interface decodes it in the same manner that it decodes a memory address. The 8-bit fixed-port number (p8) appears on address bus connections A_7–A_0 with bits A_{15}–$A_8 = 0000$ 0000. Address connections A_{23}–A_{16} are undefined for an I/O instruction. The 16-bit variable-port number (DX) appears on address connections A_{15}–A_0. This means that the first 256 I/O port addresses (00H–FFH) can be accessed by both the fixed and variable I/O instructions, but any I/O address from 0100H–FFFFH can only be accessed by the variable I/O address. In many dedicated-task systems only the rightmost 8 bits of the address are decoded, because this reduces the amount of circuitry required for decoding. In a PC, all 16 address bus bits are decoded with location 00XXH, 02XXH, or 03XXH being used for most I/O in the PC.

The INS and OUTS instructions address the I/O device using the DX register, but do not transfer data between the accumulator and the I/O device as IN and OUT. Instead these instructions transfer data between memory and the I/O device. The memory address is located by ES:DI for the INS instruction and DS:SI for the OUTS instruction. As with other string instructions, the contents of the pointers are incremented or decremented as dictated by the state of the direction flag (DF). Both INS and OUTS can also be prefixed with the REP prefix allowing more than one byte or word to be transferred between I/O and memory.

Isolated and Memory-Mapped I/O

There are two completely different methods of interfacing I/O to the 80286 microprocessor: *isolated I/O* and *memory-mapped I/O*. In isolated I/O the IN, INS, OUT, and OUTS instructions transfer data between the microprocessor accumulator or memory and the I/O device. In memory-mapped I/O, any instruction that references memory can accomplish the transfer. Both isolated and memory mapped I/O are in use, so both are discussed in this text.

Isolated I/O.   The most common I/O transfer technique used in the 80286 system is isolated I/O. The term *isolated* describes how the I/O locations are isolated from the memory system in a separate I/O address space. (Figure 9–1 illustrates both the isolated and memory-mapped address spaces.) The addresses for isolated I/O devices, called *ports,* are separate from the memory. As a result, the user can expand the memory to a full 16M bytes without using any of this space for I/O devices. A disadvantage of isolated I/O is that the data transferred between I/O and the 80286 must be accessed by the IN, INS, OUT, and OUTS instructions. Separate control signals for the I/O space, which indicate an I/O read (IORC) or an I/O write (IOWC) operation, are developed by the 82288 system bus controller. These signals indicate that an I/O port address appears on the address bus that is used to select the I/O

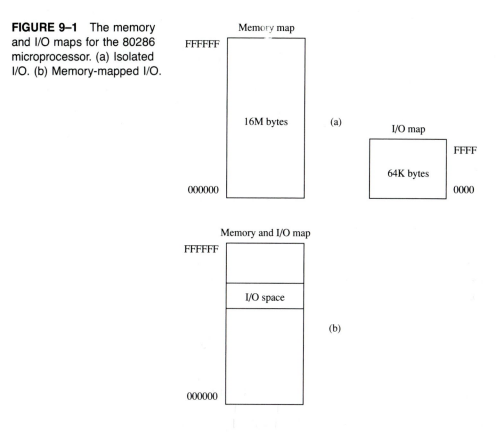

FIGURE 9–1 The memory and I/O maps for the 80286 microprocessor. (a) Isolated I/O. (b) Memory-mapped I/O.

device. In the personal computer, isolated I/O ports are used for controlling peripheral devices. As a rule, an 8-bit port address is used to access devices located on the system board, such as the timer and keyboard interface, and a 16-bit port is used to access serial and parallel ports as well as video and disk drive systems.

Memory-Mapped I/O. Unlike isolated I/O, memory-mapped I/O does not use the IN, INS, OUT, or OUTS instructions. Instead, it uses any instruction that transfers data between the microprocessor and memory. A memory-mapped I/O device is treated as a memory location in the memory map. The main advantage of memory-mapped I/O is that any memory transfer instruction can be used to access the I/O device. The main disadvantage is that a portion of the memory system is used as the I/O map. This reduces the amount of memory available to applications. Another advantage is that the (IORC) and (IOWC) signals have no function in a memory-mapped I/O system, which reduces the amount of circuitry required for decoding.

Basic Input and Output Interfaces

The basic input device is a set of 8 or 16 three-state buffers. The basic output device is a set of 8 or 16 data latches. The term *IN* refers to moving data from an I/O device into the microprocessor, and the term *OUT* refers to moving data out of the microprocessor to an I/O device.

The Basic Input Interface. Eight three-state buffers are used to construct the 8-bit input port depicted in Figure 9–2. Notice that the external TTL data (simple toggle switches in this example) are connected to the inputs of the buffers. The outputs of the buffers connect to the 80286 data bus (either D_{15}–D_8 or D_7–D_0). This connection allows the microprocessor to read the contents of the eight switches that connect to the data bus when the select signals $\overline{SEL}$ becomes a logic 0.

When the 80286 executes an IN instruction, the I/O port address is decoded to generate the logic 0 on $\overline{SEL}$. A 0 placed on the output control inputs ($\overline{1G}$ and $\overline{2G}$) of the 74ALS244 buffer causes the data input connections (A) to be connected to the data output (Y) connections. If a logic 1 is placed on the output control inputs of the 74ALS244 buffer, the device enters the three-state high-impedance mode that effectively disconnects the switches from the data bus.

This basic input circuit is not optional and must appear any time that input data are interfaced to the microprocessor. Sometimes this input circuit appears as a discrete part of the circuit, as in Figure 9–2, and sometimes it is built into a programmable I/O device.

Sixteen-bit data can also be interfaced to the 80286, but this is not nearly as common as 8-bit data. To interface 16-bits of data, the circuit in Figure 9–2 is doubled to include two 74ALS244 buffers that connect 16-bits of input data to the 16-bit data bus.

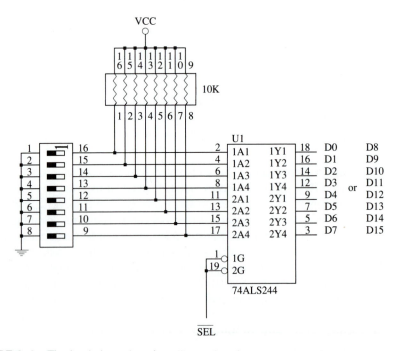

FIGURE 9–2   The basic input interface illustrating the connection of eight switches. Note that the 74ALS244 is a three-state buffer that controls the application of the switch data to the data bus.

The Basic Output Interface. The basic output interface receives data from the 80286 and must usually hold it for some external device. Its latches, like the buffers found in the input device, are often built into the I/O device.

Figure 9–3 shows how eight simple light-emitting diodes (LEDs) connect to the microprocessor through a set of eight data latches. The latch captures the output data from the 80286 which allows the display of any 8-bit binary number on the LEDs. Latches are needed to hold the data because when the 80286 executes an OUT instruction, the data are only present on the data bus for less than $1.0 \mu s$. Without a latch, the viewer would never see the LEDs illuminate.

When the OUT instruction is executed, the data from either AL or AX are transferred to the latch via the data bus (D_{15}–D_8 and/or D_7–D_0). Here the D inputs of a 74ALS374 octal latch are connected to the data bus to capture that output data, and the Q outputs of the latch are attached to the LEDs. When a Q output becomes logic 0, the $\overline{LED}$ attached to it illuminates. Each time that the OUT instruction executes, the $\overline{SEL}$ signal to the latch activates, capturing the data output to the latch from the data bus. The data are held until the next OUT instruction executes.

Handshaking

Many I/O devices accept or release information at a much slower rate than the microprocessor; therefore, a method of I/O control, called *handshaking* or *polling*,

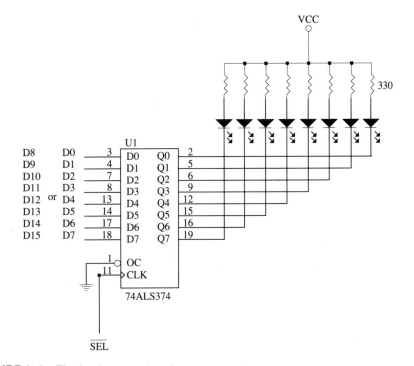

FIGURE 9–3 The basic output interface connected to a set of LED displays.

is used to synchronize the I/O device with the microprocessor. An example device that requires handshaking is a printer that prints 100 characters per second (CPS). It is obvious that the 80286 can definitely send more than 100 CPS to the printer, so a way to slow the microprocessor down to match speeds with the printer must be used.

Figure 9–4 illustrates the typical input and output connections found on a printer. Here data are transferred through a series of data connections (D_7–D_0), BUSY indicates that the printer is busy, and $\overline{STB}$ is a clock pulse used to send data into the printer for printing.

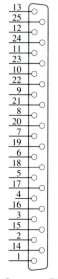

Connector DB25

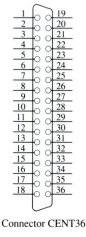

Connector CENT36

DB25 Pin number	CENT36 Pin number	Function	DB25 Pin number	CENT36 Pin number	Function
1	1	Data Strobe ($\overline{STB}$)	12	12	Paper empty
2	2	Data 0 (D0)	13	13	Select
3	3	Data 1 (D1)	14	14	$\overline{Afd}$
4	4	Data 2 (D2)	15	32	$\overline{Error}$
5	5	Data 3 (D3)	16	—	$\overline{RESET}$
6	6	Data 4 (D4)	17	31	$\overline{Select\ in}$
7	7	Data 5 (D5)	18—25	19—30	Ground
8	8	Data 6 (D6)	—	17	Frame ground
9	9	Data 7 (D7)	—	16	Ground
10	10	$\overline{Ack}$	—	33	Ground
11	11	Busy			

FIGURE 9–4   The DB25 connector found on computers and the Centronics 36-pin connector found on printers for the Centronics parallel printer interface.

The ASCII data to be printed by the printer are placed on D_7–D_0 and a pulse is applied to the $\overline{STB}$ connection. The strobe signals send the data into the printer so they can be printed. As soon as the printer receives the data, it places a logic 1 on the BUSY pin, indicating that it is busy printing data. The microprocessor polls or tests the BUSY pin to decide if the printer is busy. If the printer is busy, the microprocessor waits; if it is not busy, the microprocessor sends another ASCII character to the printer. The process of *interrogating* the printer is called *handshaking* or *polling*. Example 9–1 illustrates a simple procedure that tests the printer BUSY flag and sends data to the printer if it is not busy. The PRINT procedure prints the ASCII-coded contents of BL only if the BUSY flag is a logic 0, indicating the printer is not busy.

EXAMPLE 9–1

```
                    ;procedure that prints the contents of BL
                    ;
0000                PRINT   PROC    FAR

0000 E4 4B                  IN      AL,BUSY         ;get BUSY flag
0002 A8 04                  TEST    AL,BUSY_BIT     ;test BUSY
0004 75 FA                  JNE     PRINT           ;if busy = 1
0006 8A C3                  MOV     AL,BL           ;print character
0008 E6 4A                  OUT     PRINTER,AL
000A CB                     RET

000B                PRINT   ENDP
```

<hr>

9–2   I/O PORT ADDRESS DECODING

I/O port address decoding is very similar to memory address decoding, especially for memory-mapped I/O devices. In fact, we do not discuss memory-mapped I/O decoding because it is treated exactly the same as memory, except that the $\overline{IORC}$ and $\overline{IOWC}$ are not used, since there is no IN or OUT instruction. The decision to use memory-mapped I/O is often determined by the size of the memory system and the placement of the I/O devices in the system.

The main difference between memory decoding and isolated I/O decoding is the number of address pins. We decode A_{23}–A_0 for memory and A_{15}–A_0 for isolated I/O. Sometimes, if the I/O devices use only fixed I/O addressing, we use A_7–A_0. Another difference is that we use the $\overline{IORC}$ and $\overline{IOWC}$ to activate I/O devices for a read or a write operation.

Decoding 8-Bit I/O Addresses

As mentioned, the fixed I/O instructions use an 8-bit I/O port address that appears on A_{15}–A_0 as 0000H–00FFH. If a system contains less than 256 I/O devices, we often decode only address connections A_7–A_0 for an 8-bit I/O port address. Please note that the DX register can also be used to address I/O ports 00H–FFH. Also note

FIGURE 9–5   A port decoder that decodes 8-bit I/O ports. This decoder generates active low outputs for ports F0H–F7H.

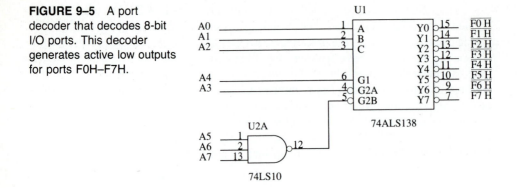

that if the address is decoded as an 8-bit address, then we can never include I/O devices that use a 16-bit I/O address.

Figure 9–5 illustrates a 74ALS138 decoder that decodes 8-bit I/O ports F0H through F7H. This decoder is identical to a memory address decoder except we only connect address bits A_7–A_0 to the inputs of the decoder. Figure 9–6 shows the PAL version of this decoder. Notice that this is a better decoder circuit because the number of integrated circuits has been reduced to one device, the PAL. The program for the PAL appears in Example 9–2.

EXAMPLE 9–2

TITLE	8-bit I/O Port Decoder
PATTERN	Test 6
REVISION	A
AUTHOR	Barry B. Brey
COMPANY	Symbiotic Systems
DATE	1/28/92
CHIP	Decoder6 PAL16L8

```
;pins 1   2   3   4   5   6   7   8   9   10
      A0  A1  A2  A3  A4  A5  A6  A7  NC  GND

;pins 11  12  13  14  15  16  17  18  19  20
      NC  F7  F6  F5  F4  F3  F2  F1  F0  VCC
```

EQUATIONS

```
/F0 = A7 * A6 * A5 * A4 * /A3 * /A2 * /A1 * /A0
/F1 = A7 * A6 * A5 * A4 * /A3 * /A2 * /A1 * A0
/F2 = A7 * A6 * A5 * A4 * /A3 * /A2 * A1 * /A0
/F3 = A7 * A6 * A5 * A4 * /A3 * /A2 * A1 * A0
/F4 = A7 * A6 * A5 * A4 * /A3 * A2 * /A1 * /A0
/F5 = A7 * A6 * A5 * A4 * /A3 * A2 * /A1 * A0
/F6 = A7 * A6 * A5 * A4 * /A3 * A2 * A1 * /A0
/F7 = A7 * A6 * A5 * A4 * /A3 * A2 * A1 * A0
```

FIGURE 9–6 A PAL16L8 decoder that generates I/O port signals for ports F0H–F7H.

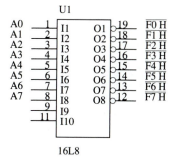

Decoding 16-Bit I/O Addresses

We also decode 16-bit I/O addresses, especially in a personal computer system. The main difference between decoding an 8-bit I/O address and a 16-bit I/O address is that eight additional address lines (A_{15}–A_8) must be decoded. Figure 9–7 illustrates a circuit that contains 2 PAL16L8s used to decode I/O ports 3F8H–3FFH. These are common I/O port assignments in a PC.

The first PAL16L8 (U_1) decodes the first 8 bits of the I/O port address (A_{15}–A_8) so it generates a signal to enable the second PAL16L8 (U_2) for any I/O address between 0300H and 03FFH. The second PAL16L8 further decodes the I/O address to produce 8 active low output strobes $\overline{\text{3F8H}}$–$\overline{\text{3FFH}}$. The programs for both PAL16L8 devices, U_1 and U_2, appear in Examples 9–3 and 9–4.

FIGURE 9–7 A PAL16L8 circuit that decodes 16-bit I/O ports $\overline{\text{3F8H}}$–$\overline{\text{3FFH}}$.

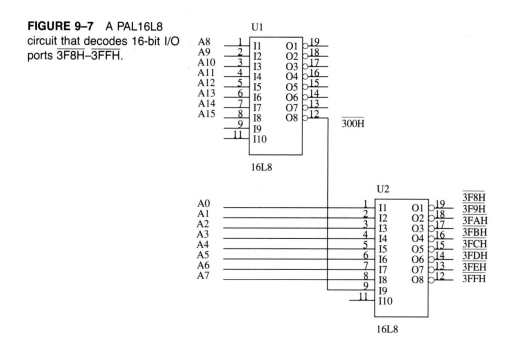

EXAMPLE 9–3

TITLE   U1 decoder
PATTERN   Test 7
REVISION   A
AUTHOR   Barry B. Brey
COMPANY   Symbiotic Systems
DATE   1/29/92
CHIP   Decoder7 PAL16L8

;pins 1   2   3   4   5   6   7   8   9   10
      A8 A9 A10 A11 A12 A13 A14 A15 NC GND

;pins 11 12   13 14 15 16 17 18 19   20
      NC 300H NC NC NC NC NC NC NC VCC

EQUATIONS

/300H = /A15 * /A14 * /A13 * /A12 * /A11 * /A10 * A9 * A8

EXAMPLE 9–4

TITLE   U2 decoder
PATTERN   Test 8
REVISION   A
AUTHOR   Barry B. Brey
COMPANY   Symbiotic Systems
DATE   1/30/92
CHIP   Decoder8 PAL16L8

;pins 1   2   3   4   5   6   7   8   9   10
      A0 A1 A2 A3 A4 A5 A6 A7 300H GND

;pins 11 12 13 14 15 16 17 18 19   20
      NC O7 O6 O5 O4 O3 O2 O1 O0 VCC

EQUATIONS

/O0 = /300H * A7 * A6 * A5 * A4 * A3 * /A2 * /A1 * /A0
/O1 = /300H * A7 * A6 * A5 * A4 * A3 * /A2 * /A1 * A0
/O2 = /300H * A7 * A6 * A5 * A4 * A3 * /A2 * A1 * /A0
/O3 = /300H * A7 * A6 * A5 * A4 * A3 * /A2 * A1 * A0
/O4 = /300H * A7 * A6 * A5 * A4 * A3 * A2 * /A1 * /A0
/O5 = /300H * A7 * A6 * A5 * A4 * A3 * A2 * /A1 * A0
/O6 = /300H * A7 * A6 * A5 * A4 * A3 * A2 * A1 * /A0
/O7 = /300H * A7 * A6 * A5 * A4 * A3 * A2 * A1 * A0

8-Bit and 16-Bit I/O Ports

Now that we understand that decoding the I/O port address is probably simpler than decoding a memory address (because of the number of bits), we explain how data are transferred between the microprocessor and 8- or 16-bit I/O devices. Data transferred to an 8-bit I/O device exists in one of the I/O banks of the 80286. I/O as memory contains two 8-bit memory banks. This is illustrated in Figure 9–8, which shows the separate I/O banks found in the 80286 system.

Because two I/O banks exist, any 8-bit I/O write requires a separate write strobe to function correctly. I/O reads do not require separate read strobes because, as with memory, the microprocessor only reads the byte it expects and ignores the other byte. The only time that a read can cause problems is when the I/O device responds incorrectly to a read operation. In the case of an I/O device that responds to a read from the wrong bank, we may need to include separate read signals discussed later in this chapter.

Figure 9–9 illustrates a system that contains two different 8-bit output devices located at 8-bit I/O addresses 40H and 41H. Because these are 8-bit devices and because they appear in different I/O banks, we generate separate I/O write signals. The program for the PAL16L8 decoder used in Figure 9–9 is illustrated in Example 9–5.

EXAMPLE 9–5

TITLE	Output Port Decoder
PATTERN	Test 9
REVISION	A
AUTHOR	Barry B. Brey
COMPANY	Symbiotic Systems
DATE	1/31/92
CHIP	Decoder9 PAL16L8

```
;pins 1    2    3  4  5  6  7  8  9  10
      BHE IOWC A0 A1 A2 A3 A4 A5 A6 GND

;pins 11 12  13 14 15  16 17  18  19  20
      A7 NC  NC NC NC  NC NC  O40 O41 VCC
```

EQUATIONS

$$/O40 = /A0 * /IOWC * /A7 * A6 * /A5 * /A4 * /A3 * /A2 * /A1$$
$$/O41 = /BHE * /IOWC * /A7 * A6 * /A5 * /A4 * /A3 * /A2 * /A1$$

When selecting 16-bit-wide I/O devices, the A_0 and $\overline{BHE}$ pins have no function because both I/O banks are selected together. Although 16-bit I/O devices are relatively rare, a few do exist for analog-to-digital and digital-to-analog converters, as well as for some video and disk memory interfaces.

Figure 9–10 illustrates a 16-bit input device connected to function at 8-bit I/O addresses 64H and 65H. Notice that the PAL16L8 decoder does not have a connection for address bit A_0 and $\overline{BHE}$ because these signals do not apply to 16-bit-wide I/O devices. The program for the PAL16L8 is illustrated in Example 9–6 to show how the enable signals are generated for the three-state buffers (74ALS244) used as input devices.

FIGURE 9–8   The I/O banks found in the 80286 microprocessor-based system.

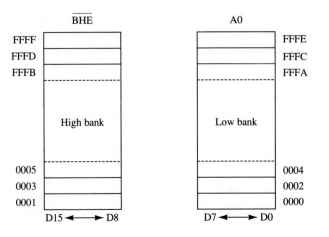

FIGURE 9–9   An I/O port decoder that selects ports 40H and 41H for output data.

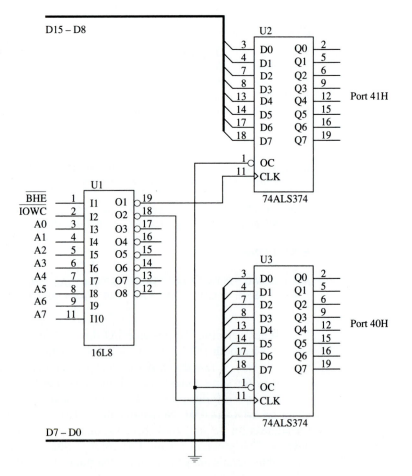

FIGURE 9–10   A 16-bit I/O
port decoded at I/O
addresses 64H and 65H.

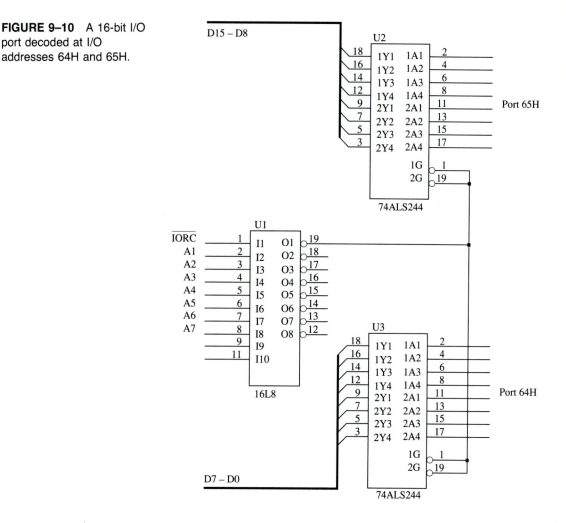

EXAMPLE 9–6

TITLE	Input Port Decoder
PATTERN	Test 10
REVISION	A
AUTHOR	Barry B. Brey
COMPANY	Symbiotic Systems
DATE	1/31/92
CHIP	DecoderA PAL16L8

```
;pins 1    2   3   4   5   6   7   8   9    10
      IORC A1  A2  A3  A4  A5  A6  A7  NC   GND

;pins 11  12  13  14  15  16  17  18  19   20
      NC  NC  NC  NC  NC  NC  NC  NC  O6X  VCC
```

EQUATIONS

/O6X = /IORC * /A7 * A6 * A5 * /A4 * /A3 * A2 * /A1

9–3   ## THE 8255A-5 PROGRAMMABLE PERIPHERAL INTERFACE

The 8255A-5 *programmable peripheral interface* (PPI) is a very popular low-cost interfacing component found in many applications. The PPI has 24 pins for I/O, programmable in groups of 12, that are used in three separate modes of operation. The 8255A-5 can interface any TTL-compatible I/O device to the 80286 microprocessor. The 8255-5 requires the insertion of two wait states (for an 8-MHz 80286) whenever it is activated by an IN or an OUT command. Because I/O devices are inherently slow anyway, wait states used during I/O transfers do not impact upon the speed of the system. The 8255-5 still finds application (compatible for programming, although it may not appear in the system) even in the latest 80486-based computer system. The 8255-5 is used for interface to the keyboard and the parallel printer port in these personal computers.

Basic Description of the 8255A-5

Figure 9–11 illustrates the pinout diagram of the 8255A-5. Its three I/O ports (labeled A, B, and C) are programmed in groups of 12 pins. Group A connections consist of Port A (PA_7–PA_0) and the upper half of port C (PC_7–PC_4), and group B consists of port B (PB_7–PB_0) and the lower half of port C (PC_3–PC_0). The 8255A-5 is selected by its $\overline{CS}$ pin for programming and for reading or writing to a port. Register selection is accomplished through the A_1 and A_0 pins that select an internal register

FIGURE 9–11 The pinout of the 8255A peripheral interface adapter (PPI).

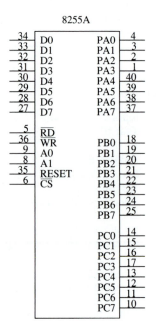

TABLE 9–2 I/O port assignments for the 8255A-5

A_1	A_2	Function
0	0	Port A
0	1	Port B
1	0	Port C
1	1	Command register

for programming or operation. Table 9–2 shows the I/O port assignments used for programming and access to the I/O ports. In the personal computer an 8255A or its equivalent is decoded at I/O ports 60H–63H.

The 8255A-5 is a fairly simple device to interface to the 80286 and program. For the 8255A-5 to be read or written, the $\overline{CS}$ input must be a logic 0 and the correct I/O address must be applied to the A_1 and A_0 pins. The remaining port address pins are don't cares and are externally decoded to select the 8255A-5.

Figure 9–12 shows an 8255A-5 connected to the 80286 so it functions at 8-bit I/O port addresses C0H (port A), C2H (port B), C4H (port C), and C6H (command register). This interface uses the low bank of the 80286 I/O map. Notice from this interface that all the 8255A-5 pins are direct connections to the 80286 except for the $\overline{CS}$ pin. The $\overline{CS}$ pin is decoded and selected by a 74ALS138 decoder.

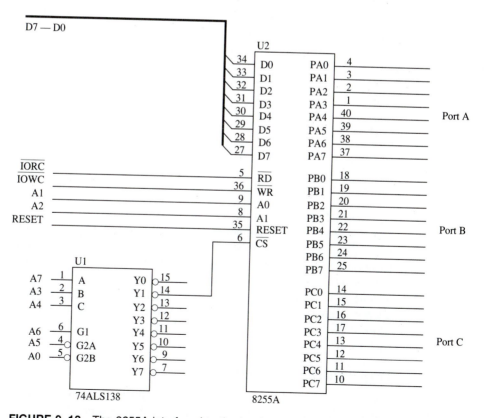

FIGURE 9–12 The 8255A interfaced to the low bank of the 80286 microprocessor.

FIGURE 9–13 The command byte of the command register in the 8255A. (a) Programs ports A, B, and C.

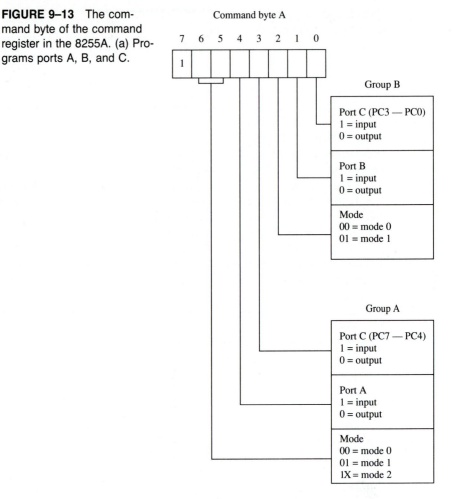

(a)

The RESET input to the 8255A-5 initializes the device whenever the microprocessor is reset. A RESET input to the 8255A-5 causes all ports to be set up as simple ports using mode 0 operation. Because the port pins are internally programmed as input pins on a reset, this setup prevents damage when the power is first applied to the system. After a RESET no other commands are needed to program the 8255A-5 as long as it must be programmed as an input device at all three ports. Note that an 8255-5 is interfaced to the personal computer at port addresses 60H–63H for keyboard control and also for controlling the speaker, timer, and other internal devices such as memory expansion.

Programming the 8255A-5

The 8255A-5 is easy to program because it only contains two internal command registers as illustrated in Figure 9–13. Notice that bit position 7 selects either command

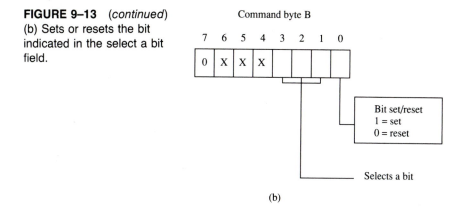

FIGURE 9–13 (*continued*) (b) Sets or resets the bit indicated in the select a bit field.

(b)

byte A or command byte B. Command byte A programs the function of group A and B, while command byte B sets (1) or resets (0) bits of port C only if the 8255A-5 is programmed in mode 1 or 2.

Group B pins (port B and the lower part of port C) are programmed as either input or output pins. Group B can operate in either mode 0 or mode 1. Mode 0 is the basic I/O mode that allows the pins of group B to be programmed as simple input and latched output connections. Mode 1 operation is the strobed operation for group B connections where data are transferred through port B, and port C provides handshaking signals.

Group A pins (port A and the upper part of port C) are also programmed as either input or output pins. The difference is that group A can operate in modes 0, 1, and 2. Mode 2 operation is a bidirectional mode of operation for port A.

If a 0 is place in bit position 7 of the command byte, command byte B is selected. This command allows any bit of port C to be set (1) or reset (0) if the 8255A-5 is operated in either mode 1 or 2; otherwise, this command byte is not used for programming. We often use the bit set/reset function in control systems to set or clear a control bit at port C.

Mode 0 Operation

Mode 0 operation causes the 8255A-5 to function as either a buffered input or as a latched output. These are the same as the basic input and output circuits discussed in the first section of the chapter.

Figure 9–14 shows the 8255A-5 connected to a set of eight 7-segment LED displays. In this circuit, both ports A and B are programmed as (mode 0) simple latched output ports. Port A provides the segment data output to the display and port B provides a means of selecting a display position at a time for multiplexing the displays. The 8255A-5 is interfaced to the 80286 through a PAL16L8 so it functions on the low data bus (D_0–D_7) at I/O port number 0700H–0703H. The program for the PAL16L8 is listed in Example 9–7. The PAL decodes the I/O address and also develops the lower write strobe for the $\overline{WR}$ pin of the 8255A-5.

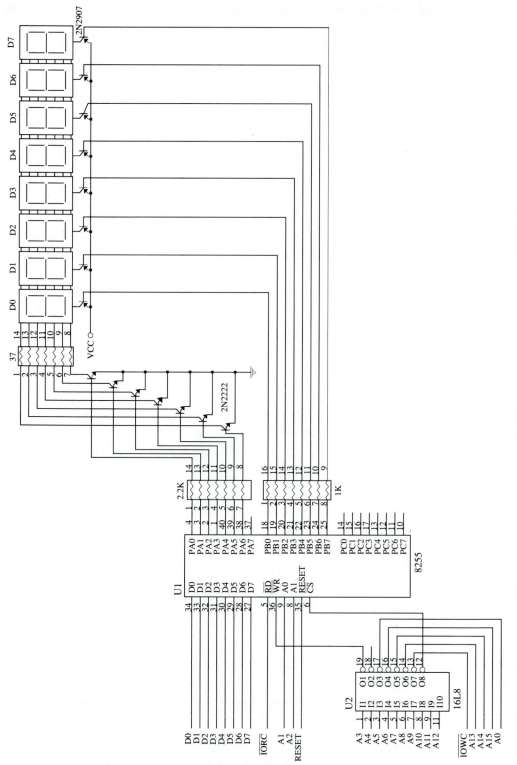

FIGURE 9–14 An eight-digit LED display interfaced to the 80286 microprocessor through an 8255A PIA.

EXAMPLE 9–7

TITLE	Mode 0, Display Interface
PATTERN	Test 11
REVISION	A
AUTHOR	Barry B. Brey
COMPANY	Symbiotic Systems
DATE	2/1/92
CHIP	DecoderB PAL16L8

```
;pins 1  2   3   4   5   6   7   8   9    10
      A3 A4  A5  A6  A7  A8  A9  A10 A11  GND

;pins 11  12 13    14   15   16  17 18 19  20
      A12 CS IOWC  A13  A14  A15 A0 NC WR  VCC
```

EQUATIONS

/WR = /A0 * /IOWC
/CS = /A15*/A14*/A13*/A12*/A11*/A10*A9*A8*/A7*/A6*/A5*/A4*/A2

The resistor values are chosen in Figure 9–14 so the segment current is 80 mA. This current is required to produce an average current of 10 mA per segment as the displays are multiplexed. In this type of display system, only one of the eight display positions is on at any given instant. The peak anode current is 560 mA, but the average anode current is 70 mA. Whenever displays are multiplexed, we increase the segment current from 10 mA to a value equal to the number of display positions times 10 mA. This means that a 4-digit display uses 40 mA per segment, a 5-digit display uses 50 mA, and so forth.

Before software to operate the display is examined, we must first program the 8255A-5. This is accomplished with the short sequence of instructions listed in Example 9–8. Here ports A and B are both programmed as outputs.

EXAMPLE 9–8

```
                ;software to program the 8255A
                ;
0000 B0 80          MOV    AL,10000000B      ;set up command
0002 BA 0703        MOV    DX,COMMAND        ;address command register
0005 EE             OUT    DX,AL             ;program the 8255A
```

The procedure to drive these displays is listed in Example 9–9. For this display system to function correctly, we must call this procedure often. Notice that the procedure calls another procedure (DELAY) that causes a 1-ms time delay. This time delay is not illustrated in this example, but is used to allow time for each display position to turn on. It is recommended by the manufacturers of LED displays that the display flash be between 100 Hz and 1,500 Hz. Using a 1-ms time delay we light each digit for 1 ms for a total display flash rate of 1,000 Hz / 8 or 125.

EXAMPLE 9–9

```
                    ;procedure to scan the 8 digits of the multiplexed LED display.
                    ;This procedure must be called continuously from a program to
                    ;display the 7-segment coded information in area MEMORY.
                    ;
0006                DISP    PROC    NEAR

0006 9C                     PUSHF                                   ;save registers
0007 50                     PUSH    AX
0008 53                     PUSH    BX
0009 52                     PUSH    DX
000A 56                     PUSH    SI

                    ;set up register for display

000B BB 0008                MOV     BX,8                            ;load count
000E B4 7F                  MOV     AH,7FH                          ;load select pattern
0010 BE FFFF R              MOV     SI,OFFSET MEMORY-1              ;address display RAM
0013 BA 0701                MOV     DX,PORTB                        ;address port B

                    ;display eight digits

0016                DISP1:

0016 8A C4                  MOV     AL,AH                           ;select digit
0018 EE                     OUT     DX,AL
0019 4A                     DEC     DX                              ;address port A
001A 8A 00                  MOV     AL,[BX+SI]                      ;get data
001C EE                     OUT     DX,AL                           ;display data

001D E8 029A R              CALL    DELAY                           ;wait 1 ms

0020 D0 CC                  ROR     AH,1                            ;adjust selection code
0022 42                     INC     DX                              ;address port B
0023 4B                     DEC     BX                              ;adjust count
0024 75 F0                  JNZ     DISP1                           ;repeat 8 times

0026 5E                     POP     SI                              ;restore registers
0027 5A                     POP     DX
0028 5B                     POP     BX
0029 58                     POP     AX
002A 9D                     POPF
002B C3                     RET

002C                DISP    ENDP
```

The display procedure addresses an area of memory where the data, in 7-segment code, is stored for the eight display digits. The AH register is loaded with a code (7FH) that initially addresses the most significant display position. Once this position is selected, the contents of memory location MEMORY+7 is addressed and sent to the most significant digit. The selection code is then adjusted to select the next display digit, as is the address. This process repeats eight times to display the contents of location MEMORY through MEMORY+7 on the 8 display digits.

Mode 1 Strobed Input

Mode 1 operation causes port A and/or port B to function as latching input devices. This allows external data to be stored into the port until the microprocessor is ready to retrieve it. Port C is also used in mode 1 operation, not for data, but for control or handshaking signals that help operate either or both port A and port B as strobed input ports. Figure 9–15 shows both the timing diagram and how both ports are structured for mode 1 strobed input operation.

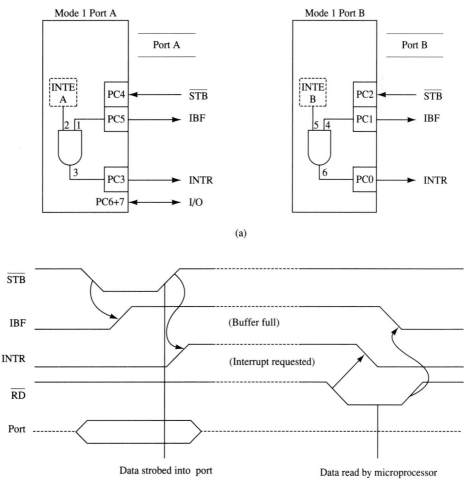

FIGURE 9–15   Strobed input operation (mode 1) of the 8255A. (a) Internal structure. (b) Timing diagram.

The strobed input port captures data from the port pins when the strobe ($\overline{STB}$) is activated. Note that the strobe captures the port data on the 0-to-1 transition. The $\overline{STB}$ signal causes data to be captured in the port and it also activates the IBF (input buffer full) and INTR (interrupt request) signals. Once the microprocessor, through software (IBF) or hardware (INTR) notices that data are strobed into the port, it executes an IN instruction to read the port ($\overline{RD}$). The act of reading the port restores both IBF and INTR to their inactive states until the next datum is strobed into the port.

Signal Definitions for Mode 1 Strobed Input

1. $\overline{STB}$—Strobe: an input used to load data into the port latch, which holds the information until it is input to the microprocessor via the IN instruction.
2. IBF—Input Buffer Full: an output that indicates that the input latch contains information.
3. INTR—Interrupt Request: an output that requests an interrupt. The INTR pin becomes a logic 1 when the $\overline{STB}$ input returns to a logic 1 and is cleared when the data are input from the port by the microprocessor.
4. INTE—Interrupt Enable: neither an input nor an output, but an internal bit programmed via the port PC_4 (port A) or PC_2 (port B) bit position.
5. PC_7, PC_6—Port Pins 7 and 6: general-purpose I/O pins that are available for any purpose.

Strobe Input Example.

A keyboard is an excellent example of a strobed input device. The keyboard encoder debounces the keyswitches and provides a strobe signal whenever a key is a depressed, and the data output contain the ASCII-coded keycode. Figure 9–16 illustrates a keyboard connected to strobed input port A. Here $\overline{DAV}$ (data available) is activated for 1 μs each time that a key is typed on the keyboard. This causes data to be strobed into port A because $\overline{DAV}$ is connected to the $\overline{STB}$ input of port A. So each time a key is typed, it is stored into port A of the 8255A-5. The $\overline{STB}$ input also activates the IBF signal, indicating that data are in port A.

FIGURE 9–16 Using the 8255A for strobed input operation of a keyboard.

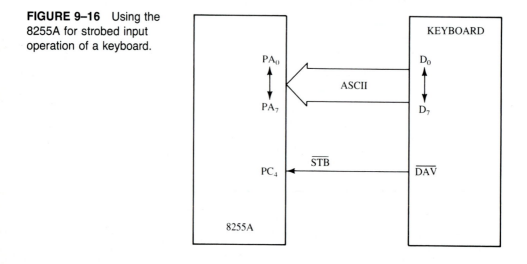

Example 9–10 shows a procedure that reads data from the keyboard each time a key is typed. This procedure reads the key from port A and returns with the ASCII code in AL. To detect a key, port C is read and the IBF bit (bit position PC_5) is tested to see if the buffer is full. If the buffer is empty (IBF = 0), then the procedure keeps testing this bit, waiting for a character to be typed on the keyboard.

EXAMPLE 9–10

```
                    ;procedure that reads the keyboard encoder and returns
                    ;with the ASCII character in AL
                    ;
= 0020              BIT5     EQU     20H

0000                READ     PROC    NEAR

0000 E4 22                   IN      AL,PORTC            ;read port C
0002 A8 20                   TEST    AL,BIT5             ;test IBF
0004 74 FA                   JZ      READ                ;if IBF = 0

0006 E4 20                   IN      AL,PORTA            ;read ASCII code
0008 C3                      RET

0009                READ     ENDP
```

Mode 1 Strobed Output

Figure 9–17 illustrates the internal configuration and timing diagram of the 8255A-5 when it is operated as a strobed output device under mode 1. Strobed output operation is similar to mode 0 output except that control signals are included to provide handshaking.

Whenever data are written to a port programmed as a strobed output port, the $\overline{OBF}$ (output buffer full) signal becomes a logic 0 to indicate that data are present in the port latch. This signal indicates that data are available to an external I/O device that removes the data by strobing the $\overline{ACK}$ (acknowledge) input to the port. The $\overline{ACK}$ signal returns the $\overline{OBF}$ signal to a logic 1, indicating that the buffer is not full.

Signal Definitions for Mode 1 Strobed Output

1. $\overline{OBF}$—Output Buffer Full: an output that goes low whenever data are output (OUT) to the port A or port B latch. This signal is set to a logic 1 whenever the $\overline{ACK}$ pulse returns from the external device.
2. $\overline{ACK}$—Acknowledge: a signal that causes the $\overline{OBF}$ pin to return to a logic 1 level. The $\overline{ACK}$ is a response from an external device that indicates it has received the data from the 8255A-5 port.
3. INTR—Interrupt Request: a signal that interrupts the microprocessor when the external device receives the data via the $\overline{ACK}$ signal. This pin is qualified by the internal INTE (interrupt enable) bit.

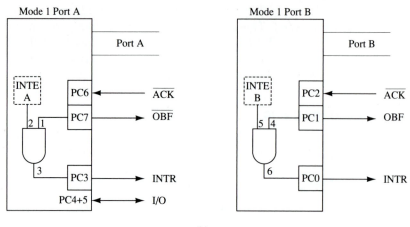

(a)

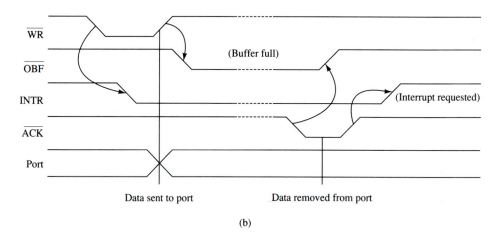

(b)

FIGURE 9–17   Strobed output operation (mode 1) of the 8255A. (a) Internal structure. (b) Timing diagram.

4. INTE—Interrupt Enable: neither an input nor an output, but an internal bit programmed to enable or disable the INTR pin. The INTE A bit is programmed as PC_6 and INTE B is PC_2.

5. PC_5, PC_4—Port C bits 5 and 4 are general-purpose I/O pins: the bit set and reset command may be used to set or reset these two pins.

Strobed Output Example.   The printer interface discussed in Section 9–1 is used here to demonstrate how to achieve strobed output synchronization between the printer and the 8255A-5. Figure 9–18 illustrates port B connected to a parallel printer with eight data inputs for receiving ASCII-coded data, a $\overline{DS}$ (data strobe) input to strobe data into the printer, and an $\overline{ACK}$ output to acknowledge the receipt of the ASCII character.

FIGURE 9–18 The 8255A connected to a parallel printer interface that illustrates the strobed output mode of operation for the 8255A.

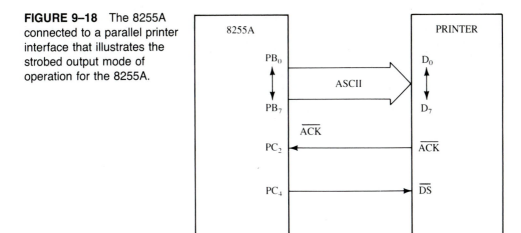

In this circuit there is no signal to generate the $\overline{DS}$ signal to the printer, so PC_4 is used with software that generates the $\overline{DS}$ signal. The $\overline{ACK}$ signal that is returned from the printer acknowledges the receipt of the data and is connected to the $\overline{ACK}$ input of the 8255A-5.

Example 9–11 lists the software that sends the ASCII-coded character in AH to the printer. The procedure first tests $\overline{OBF}$ to decide if the printer has removed the data from port B. If it has not ($\overline{OBF} = 0$), the procedure waits for the $\overline{ACK}$ signal to return from the printer. If $\overline{OBF} = 1$, then the procedure sends the contents of AH to the printer through port B and also sends the $\overline{DS}$ signal.

EXAMPLE 9–11

```
                    ;Procedure that transfers the ASCII-coded character from AH
                    ;to the printer via port B
                    ;
= 0002              BIT1    EQU     2H

0000                PRINT   PROC    NEAR

                    ;check for printer ready

0000 E4 62                  IN      AL,PORTC        ;get OBF
0002 A8 02                  TEST    AL,BIT1         ;test OBF
0004 74 FA                  JZ      PRINT           ;if OBF = 0

                    ;send character to printer via port B

0006 8A C4                  MOV     AL,AH           ;get character
0008 E6 61                  OUT     PORTB,AL        ;send it
```

;send DS to printer

```
000A B0 08              MOV     AL,8            ;clear DS
000C E6 63              OUT     COMMAND,AL
000E B0 09              MOV     AL,9            ;set DS
0010 E6 63              OUT     COMMAND,AL
0012 C3                 RET

0013           PRINT    ENDP
```

Mode 2 Bidirectional Operation

In mode 2, which is allowed only for group A, port A becomes bidirectional, allowing data to be transmitted and received over the same eight wires. Bidirectional bused data are useful when interfacing two computers. They are also used for the IEEE-488 parallel high-speed (general-purpose instrumentation bus GPIB*) interface standard. Figure 9–19 shows the internal structure and timing diagram for mode 2 bidirectional operation.

Signal Definitions for Bidirectional Mode 2

1. INTR—Interrupt Request: an output used to interrupt the microprocessor for both input and output conditions.
2. $\overline{OBF}$—Output Buffer Full: an output that indicates that the output buffer contains data for the bidirectional bus.
3. $\overline{ACK}$—Acknowledge: an input that enables the three-state buffers so data can appear on port A. If $\overline{ACK}$ is a logic 1, the output buffers of port A are at their high-impedance state.
4. $\overline{STB}$—Strobe: an input used to load the port A input latch with external data from the bidirectional port A bus.
5. IBF—Input Buffer Full: an output used to signal that the input buffer contains data for the external bidirectional bus.
6. INTE—Interrupt Enable: internal bits (INTE1 and INTE2) that enable the INTR pin. The state of the INTR pin is controlled through port C bits PC_6 (INTE1) and PC_4 (INTE2).
7. PC_2, PC_1, and PC_0—General-purpose I/O pins in mode 2 controlled by the bit set and reset command.

The Bidirectional Bus.   The bidirectional bus is used by referencing port A with the IN and OUT instructions. To transmit data through the bidirectional bus, the program first tests the $\overline{OBF}$ signal to determine whether the output buffer is empty. If it is, then data are sent to the output buffer via the OUT instruction. The external circuitry also

---

*GPIB (general-purpose instrumentation bus) is a registered trademark of Hewlett-Packard Corporation.

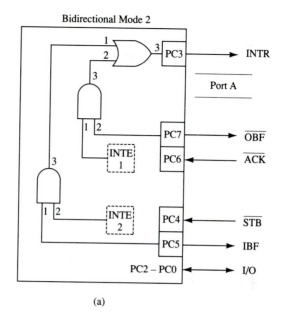

(a)

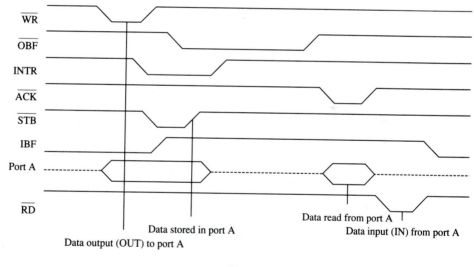

(b)

FIGURE 9–19 Mode 2 operation of the 8255A. (a) Internal structure (b) Timing diagram.

monitors the $\overline{\text{OBF}}$ signal to decide if the microprocessor has sent data to the bus. As soon as the output circuitry sees a logic 0 on $\overline{\text{OBF}}$, it sends back the $\overline{\text{ACK}}$ signal to remove it from the output buffer. The $\overline{\text{ACK}}$ signal sets the $\overline{\text{OBF}}$ bit and also enables the three-state output buffers so data may be read. Example 9–12 lists a procedure that transmits the contents of the AH register through bidirectional port A.

EXAMPLE 9–12

```
                        ;Procedure that transmits AH through the bidirectional
                        ;bus of port A
                        ;
= 0080                  BIT7      EQU       80H

0000                    TRANS     PROC      NEAR

                        ;test OBF

0000 E4 62                        IN        AL,PORTC            ;get OBF
0002 A8 80                        TEST      AL,BIT7             ;test OBF
0004 74 FA                        JZ        TRANS               ;if OBF = 0

                        ;send data

0006 8A C4                        MOV       AL,AH               ;get data
0008 E6 60                        OUT       PORTA,AL
000A C3                           RET

000B                    TRANS     ENDP
```

To receive data through the bidirectional port A bus, the IBF bit is tested with software to decide if data have been strobed into the port. If IBF = 1, then data are input using the IN instruction. The external interface sends data into the port using the $\overline{STB}$ signal. When $\overline{STB}$ is activated, the IBF signal becomes a logic 1, and the data at port A are held inside the port in a latch. When the IN instruction executes, the IBF bit is cleared and the data in the port are moved into AL. Example 9–13 lists a procedure that reads data from the port.

EXAMPLE 9–13

```
                        ;Procedure that inputs data from the bidirectional
                        ;bus and returns with it in AL
                        ;
= 0020                  BIT5      EQU       20H

0000                    READ      PROC      NEAR

                        ;test IBF

0000 E4 62                        IN        AL,PORTC            ;get IBF
0002 A8 20                        TEST      AL,BIT5             ;test IBF
0004 74 FA                        JZ        READ                ;if IBF = 0

                        ;read data

0006 E4 60                        IN        AL,PORTA
0008 C3                           RET

0009                    READ      ENDP
```

FIGURE 9–20 A summary of the port connections for the 8255A PIA.

		Mode 0		Mode 1		Mode 2
Port A		IN	OUT	IN	OUT	I/O
Port B		IN	OUT	IN	OUT	Not used
Port C	0	IN	OUT	$INTR_B$	$INTR_B$	I/O
	1			IBF_B	$\overline{OBF_B}$	I/O
	2			$\overline{STB_B}$	$\overline{ACK_B}$	I/O
	3			$INTR_A$	$INTR_A$	INTR
	4			$\overline{STB_A}$	I/O	$\overline{STB}$
	5			IBF_A	I/O	IBF
	6			I/O	$\overline{ACK_A}$	$\overline{ACK}$
	7			I/O	$\overline{OBF_A}$	$\overline{OBF}$

The INTR (interrupt request) pin can be activated from both directions of data flow through the bus. If INTR is enabled by both INTE bits, then the output and input buffers both cause interrupt requests. This occurs when data are strobed into the buffer using $\overline{STB}$ or when data are written using OUT.

8255A-5 Mode Summary

Figure 9–20 shows a graphical summary of the three modes of operation for the 8255A-5. Mode 0 provides simple I/O, mode 1 provides strobed I/O, and mode 2 provides bidirectional I/O. As mentioned earlier, these modes are selected through the command register of the 8255A-5.

9–4   THE 8279-5 PROGRAMMABLE KEYBOARD/DISPLAY INTERFACE

The 8279-5 is a programmable keyboard and display interfacing component that can scan and encode up to a 64-key keyboard and up to a 16-digit numerical display. The keyboard interface has a built-in first-in, first-out (FIFO) buffer that allows it to store up to eight keystrokes before the microprocessor must retrieve a character. The display section can scan up to 16 numeric displays from an internal 16×8 RAM, which stores the coded display information.

Basic Description of the 8279-5

As we shall see, the 8279-5 is designed for ease of interfacing with the 80286 or any other microprocessor. Figure 9–21 illustrates the pinout of this device. The definition of each pin connection follows.

Pin Definition for the 8279-5

1. A_0 — Address Input: a pin that selects data or control for reads and writes between the microprocessor and the 8279-5. A logic 0 selects data and a logic 1 selects control/status.

FIGURE 9–21 The pinout of the 8279 keyboard/display controller produced by Intel.

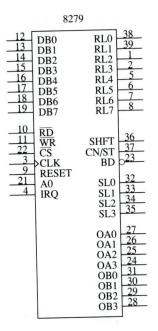

2. $\overline{BD}$—Blank: an output used to blank the displays.
3. CLK—Clock: an input used to generate internal timing for the 8279-5. The maximum allowable frequency on the CLK pin is 3.125 MHz.
4. CN/ST—Control/Strobe: an input normally connected to the control key on a keyboard.
5. $\overline{CS}$—Chip Select: an input used to enable the 8279-5 for programming, reading the keyboard and status information, and writing control and display data.
6. DB_7–DB_0—Data Bus: bidirectional pins that connect to the upper or lower half of the data bus on the 80286 microprocessor.
7. IRQ—Interrupt Request: an output that becomes a logic 1 whenever a key is pressed on the keyboard. This signal indicates that keyboard data are available for the microprocessor.
8. $OUTA_3$–$OUTA_0$—Outputs: used to send data to the displays (most significant).
9. $OUTB_3$–$OUTB_0$—Outputs: used to send data to the displays (least significant).
10. $\overline{RD}$—Read: an input directly connected to the $\overline{IORC}$ signal from the 82288 system bus controller. The $\overline{RD}$ input causes, when $\overline{CS}$ is a logic 0, a read from the data registers or status register.
11. RESET—Reset: an input that connects to the RESET output pin of the 82284 clock generator.
12. RL_7–RL_0—Return Lines: inputs used to sense any key depression in the keyboard matrix.
13. SHIFT—-Shift: an input normally connected to the shift key on a keyboard.
14. SL_3–SL_0—Scan Lines: outputs used to scan both the keyboard and the displays.
15. $\overline{WR}$—Write: an input that connects to either the upper write or lower write strobe signals that are developed with external logic. The $\overline{WR}$ inputs causes data to be written to either the data registers or control registers within the 8279-5.

16. V_{cc}—Supply: a pin connected to the system +5.0-V bus.
17. V_{ss}—Ground: a pin connected to the system ground.

Interfacing the 8279-5 to the 80286

In Figure 9–22, the 8279 is connected to the 80286 microprocessor. The 8279-5 is decoded to function at 8-bit I/O addresses 10H and 12H, where port 10H is the data port and 12H is the control port. This circuit uses PAL16L8 (see Example 9–14) to decode the I/O address as well as to generate the low bank I/O write signal for the 8279-5. Address bus bit A1 is used to select either the data or control port. Notice that the $\overline{CS}$ signal selects the 8279-5 and also provides a signal called $\overline{WAIT2}$ that is used to cause 2 wait states so that this device functions with an 8-MHz 80286.

EXAMPLE 9–14

TITLE	8279-5 Interface
PATTERN	Test 12
REVISION	A
AUTHOR	Barry B. Brey
COMPANY	Symbiotic Systems
DATE	2/2/92
CHIP	DecoderC PAL16L8

;pins 1 2   3   4   5   6   7   8   9   10
      A0 A2 A3 A4 A5 A6 A7 NC IOWC GND

;pins 11 12 13 14 15 16 17 18 19 20
      NC NC NC NC NC NC NC CS WE VCC

EQUATIONS

/CS = /A7 * /A6 * /A5 * A4 * /A3 * /A2
/WR = /A0 * /IOWC

The only signal not connected is the IRQ output. This is an interrupt request pin and is beyond the scope of this section of the text. The next chapter explains interrupts, where their operation and function in a system are explained.

Keyboard Interface

Suppose that a 64-key keyboard (with no numeric displays) is connected through the 8279-5 to the 80286 microprocessor. Figure 9–23 shows this connection as well as the keyboard. With the 8279-5, the keyboard matrix is any size between 2 × 2 (4 keys) to 8 × 8 (64 keys). (Note that each crossover point in the matrix contains a normally open push-button switch that connects one vertical column with one horizontal row when a key is pressed.)

The I/O port number decoded is the same as that decoded for Figure 9–22. I/O port number 10H is the data port and 12H is the control port for this circuit.

The 74ALS138 decoder generates eight active low column strobes for the keyboard. The selection pins SL_2–SL_0 sequentially scan each column of the keyboard,

FIGURE 9–22 The 8279-5 interfaced to the 80286 microprocessor to function at 8-bit I/O ports 10H and 12H.

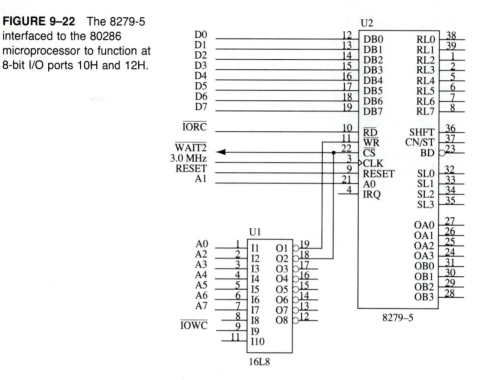

and the internal circuitry of the 8279-5 scans the RL pins, searching for a key switch closure. Pullup resisters, normally found on input lines of a keyboard, are not required because the 8279-5 contains internal pullups on the RL inputs.

Programming the Keyboard Interface.   Before any keystroke can be detected, the 8279-5 must be programmed, a more involved procedure than with the 8255A-5. The 8279-5 has eight control words to consider before is programmed. This first three bits of the number sent to the control port (12H in this example) select one of the eight different control words. Table 9–3 lists all eight control words and briefly describes them.

Control Word Descriptions.   Following is a list of the control words so they can be used to program the 8279-5. Note that the first three bits are the control register numbers, which are followed by other binary bits of information as they apply to each control.

1. 000DDKKK—Mode Set: a command with an opcode of 000 and two fields programmed to select the mode of operation for the 8279-5. The DD field selects the mode of operation for the displays (see Table 9–4), and the KKK fields selects the mode of operation for the keyboard (see Table 9–5).

      The DD field selects either an 8- or 16-digit display and determines whether new data are entered to the rightmost or leftmost display position. The KKK field is quite a bit more complex. It provides encoded, decoded, or strobed keyboard operation.

      In encoded mode, the SL outputs are active-high and follow the binary bit pattern 0 through 7 or 0 through 15, depending whether 8- or 16-digit displays

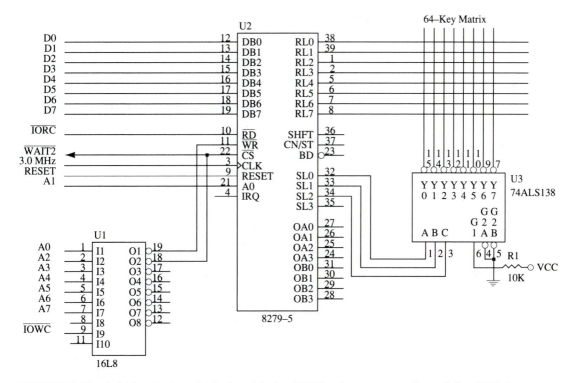

FIGURE 9–23 A 64-key keyboard interfaced to the 80286 microprocessor through the 8279-5.

TABLE 9–3 The 8279-5 control word summary

D_7	D_6	D_5	Function	Purpose
0	0	0	Mode set	Selects the number of display positions, left or right entry, and type of keyboard scan
0	0	1	Clock	Programs the internal clock
0	1	0	Read FIFO	Selects the type of FIFO read and the address to be read
0	1	1	Read display	Selects the type of display read and the address of the display position
1	0	0	Write display	Selects the type of display write and the address of the display position
1	0	1	Display write inhibit	Allows half-byte to be blanked or inhibited
1	1	0	Clear	Allows the display or FIFO to be cleared
1	1	1	End interrupt	Clears the IRQ pin at the end of an interrupt service procedure

TABLE 9–4 Binary bit assignment for DD of the mode set control word

D	D	Function
0	0	8-character display with left entry
0	1	16-character display with left entry
1	0	8-character display with right entry
1	1	16-character display with right entry

are selected. In decoded mode, the SL outputs are active-low, and only one of the four outputs is low at any given instant. The decoded outputs repeat the pattern: 1110, 1101, 1011, and 0111. In strobed mode, an active-high pulse on the CN/ST input pin strobes data from the RL pins into an internal FIFO, where they are held for the microprocessor.

It is also possible to select either 2-key lockout or *N*-key rollover. Two-key lockout prevents two keys from being recognized if pressed simultaneously, while *N*-key rollover will accept all keys pressed simultaneously, from first to last.

2. 001PPPPP—Clock: a command word that programs the internal clock divider. The code PPPPP is a prescaler that divides the clock input pin (CLK) to achieve the desired operating frequency, or approximately 100 KHz. An input clock of 1 MHz thus requires a prescaler of 01010_2 for PPPPP.

3. 010Z0AAA—Read FIFO: a control word that selects the address of a keystroke from the internal FIFO buffer. Bit positions AAA select the desired FIFO location from 000 to 111, and Z selects auto-increment for the address. Under normal operation, this control word is used only with the sensor matrix operation of the 8279-5.

4. 011ZAAAA—Display Read: a control word that selects the read address of one of the display RAM positions for reading through the data port. AAAA is the address of the position to be read, and Z selects auto-increment mode. This command is used if the information stored in the display RAM must be read.

5. 100ZAAAA—Write Display: a control word that selects the write address of one of the displays. AAAA addresses the position to be written to through the data port and Z selects auto-increment, so subsequent writes through the data port are to subsequent display positions.

TABLE 9–5 Binary bit assignment for KKK of the mode set control word

K	K	K	Function
0	0	0	Encoded keyboard with 2-key lockout
0	0	1	Decoded keyboard with 2-key lockout
0	1	0	Encoded keyboard with *N*-key rollover
0	1	1	Decoded keyboard with *N*-key rollover
1	0	0	Encoded sensor matrix
1	0	1	Decoded sensor matrix
1	1	0	Strobed keyboard, encoded display scan
1	1	1	Strobed keyboard, decoded display scan

6. 1010WWBB—Display Write Inhibit: a control word that inhibits writing to either half of each display RAM location. The leftmost W inhibits writing to the leftmost four bits of the display RAM location, and the rightmost W inhibits the rightmost four bits. The BB field functions in a like manner, except they blank (turn off) either half of the output pins.

7. 1100CCFA—Clear: a control word that clears the display, the FIFO, or both the display and FIFO. Bit F clears the FIFO, the display RAM status, and sets the address pointer to 000. If the CC bits are 00 or 01, all the display RAM locations become 0000000, if CC = 10, all locations become 00100000, and if CC = 11, all locations become 11111111.

8. 111E000—End Interrupt: a control word that is issued to clear the IRQ pin to zero in the sensor matrix mode.

The large number of control words make programming the keyboard interface appear complex. Before anything can be programmed, the clock divider rate must be determined. In the circuit illustrated in Figure 9–23, we used a 3.0-MHz clock input signal. To program the prescaler to generate a 100-KHz internal rate we program PPPPP of the clock control word with a 30 or 11110_2.

The next step involves programming the keyboard type. In the example keyboard of Figure 9–23, we have an encoded keyboard. Notice that the circuit includes an external decoder that converts the encoded data from the SL pins into decoded column-selection signals. We are free in this example to choose either 2-key lockout or N-key rollover, but most applications use 2-key lockout.

Finally, we program the operation of the FIFO. Once the FIFO is programmed, it never needs to be reprogrammed unless we need to read prior keyboard codes. Each time a key is typed, the data are stored in the FIFO. If the data are read from the FIFO before the FIFO is full (eight characters), then the data from the FIFO follows the same order as the typed data. Example 9–15 provides the software required to initialize the 8279-5 to control the keyboard illustrated in Figure 9–23.

EXAMPLE 9–15

```
                         ;Initialization dialog for the keyboard interface
                         ;
                         ;program clock

0000 B0 3E                      MOV     AL,00111110B
0002 E6 12                      OUT     CNTR,AL

                         ;program mode set

0004 B0 00                      MOV     AL,0
0006 E6 12                      OUT     CNTR,AL

                         ;program to read FIFO and keyboard

0008 B0 50                      MOV     AL,01010000B
000A E6 12                      OUT     CNTR,AL
```

FIGURE 9–24   The 8279-5 FIFO status register.

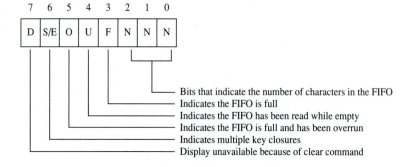

        The data that indicate the number of characters in the FIFO
        Indicates the FIFO is full
        Indicates the FIFO has been read while empty
        Indicates the FIFO is full and has been overrun
        Indicates multiple key closures
        Display unavailable because of clear command

Once the 8279-5 is initialized, a procedure is required that reads data from the keyboard. We determine if a character is typed in the keyboard by looking at the FIFO status register. If the control port is addressed by the IN instruction, the contents of the FIFO status word are copied into the AL register. Figure 9–24 shows the contents of the FIFO status register and defines the purpose of each status bit.

The procedure listed in Example 9–16 first tests the FIFO status register to see if it contains any data. If NNN is 000, the FIFO is empty. Upon determining that the FIFO is not empty, the procedure inputs data to AL and returns with the keyboard code in AL.

EXAMPLE 9–16

```
                    ;Procedure that reads data from the FIFO and returns
                    ;with it in AL
                    ;
= 0007              MASKS    EQU      7

0000                READ     PROC     FAR

                    ;test FIFO status

0000 E4 12                   IN       AL,STATUS        ;get status
0002 A8 07                   TEST     AL,MASKS         ;test NNN
0004 74 FA                   JZ       READ             ;if NNN = 000

                    ;read FIFO

0006 E4 10                   IN       AL,DATA          ;get data
0008 CB                      RET

0009                READ     ENDP
```

The data found in AL upon returning from the subroutine contain raw data from the keyboard. Figure 9–25 shows the format of these data for both the scanned and strobed modes of operation. The scanned code is returned from our keyboard interface and is converted to ASCII code by using the XLAT instruction with an ASCII code lookup table. The scanned code is returned with the row and column number occupying the rightmost six bits. The SH shows the state of the shift pin,

FIGURE 9–25 The (a) scanned keyboard code and (b) strobed keyboard code for the 8279-5 FIFO.

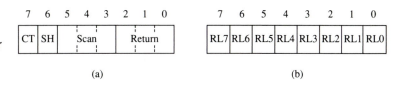

(a)   (b)

and the CT bit shows the state of the control pin. In the strobed mode, the contents of the eight RL inputs appear as they are sampled by placing a logic 1 on the strobe input pin to the 8279-5.

Six-Digit Display Interface

Figure 9–26 depicts the 8279-5 connected to the 80286 microprocessor and a 6-digit numeric display. This interface uses a PAL16L8 (program not shown) to decode the 8279-5 at I/O ports 21H (data) and 23H (control/status). The segment data are supplied to the displays through the OUTA and OUTB pins of the 8279-5. These bits are buffered by a segment driver (ULN2003A) to drive the segment inputs to the display.

A 74ALS138 3-to-8 line decoder enables the anode switches of each display position. The SL_2–SL_0 pins supply the decoder with the encoded display position from the 8279-5. Notice that the left-hand display is at position 0101 and the right-hand display is at position 0000. These are the addresses of the display positions as indicated in control words for the 8279-5.

It is necessary to choose resistor values that allow 60 mA of current flow per segment. In this circuit we use 47-Ω resistors. If we allow 60 mA of segment current, then the average segment current is 10 mA, or one-sixth of 60 mA because current flows for only one-sixth of the time through a segment. The anode switches must supply the current for all seven segments plus the decimal point. Here the total anode current is 8×60 mA or 480 mA.

Example 9–17 lists the initialization dialog for programming the 8279-5 to function with this 6-digit display. This software programs the display and clears the display RAM.

EXAMPLE 9–17

```
                              ;Initialization dialog for the 6-digit display
                              ;
                              ;program the clock

0000  B0 3E                        MOV     AL,00111110B
0002  E6 23                        OUT     CNTR,AL

                              ;program mode set

0004  B0 00                        MOV     AL,0
0006  E6 23                        OUT     CNTR,AL

                              ;clear display

0008  B0 C1                        MOV     AL,11000001B
000A  E6 23                        OUT     CNTR,AL
```

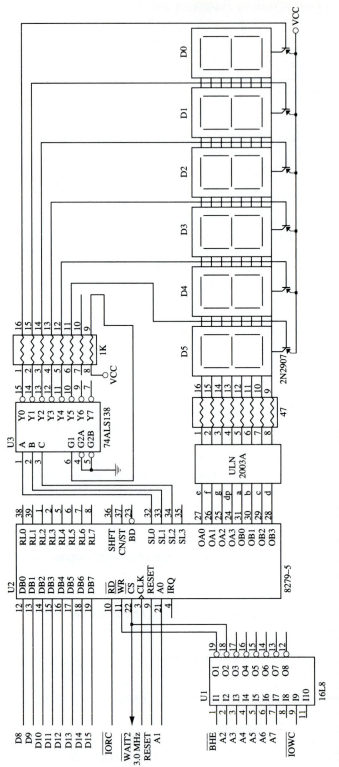

FIGURE 9–26 A 6-digit numeric display interfaced to the 8279-5.

Example 9–18 lists a procedure for displaying information on the displays. Data are transferred to the procedure through the AX register. AH contains the 7-segment display code and AL contains the address of the display.

EXAMPLE 9–18

```
                    ;Procedure to display AH on the display position
                    ;addressed by AL
                    ;
= 0080              MASKS    EQU       80H

000C                DISP     PROC      NEAR

000C 50                      PUSH      AX              ;save data
000D 0C 80                   OR        AL,MASKS        ;select display
000F E6 23                   OUT       CNTR,AL

                    ;display data

0011 8A C4                   MOV       AL,AH
0013 E6 21                   OUT       DATA,AL
0015 58                      POP       AX
0016 C3                      RET

0017                DISP     ENDP
```

9–5   8254-2 PROGRAMMABLE INTERVAL TIMER

The 8254-2 programmable interval timer consists of three independent 16-bit programmable counters. Each counter is capable of counting in binary or binary-coded decimal (BCD). The allowable input frequency to any counter is 10 MHz. This device is useful wherever the microprocessor must control real-time events. Some examples of usage include real-time clock, events counter, and motor speed and direction control. This timer also appears in the personal computer decoded at ports 40H–43H to (1) generate a basic timer interrupt that occurs at approximately 18.2 Hz, (2) cause the DRAM memory system to be refreshed, and (3) provide a timing source to the internal speaker and other devices.

8254-2 Functional Description

Figure 9–27 shows both the pinout of the 8254-2, which is a higher speed version of the 8253, and a diagram of one of the three counters. Each timer contains a CLK input, a gate input, and an output (OUT) connection. The CLK input provides the basic operating frequency to the timer, the gate pin controls the timer in some modes, and the OUT pin is where we obtain the output of the timer.

The signals that connect to the 80286 are the data bus pins (D_7–D_0), $\overline{RD}$, $\overline{WR}$, $\overline{CS}$, and address inputs A_1 and A_0. The address inputs are present to select

FIGURE 9–27 The (a) pinout of the 8254-2 timer and (b) the structure of a counter.

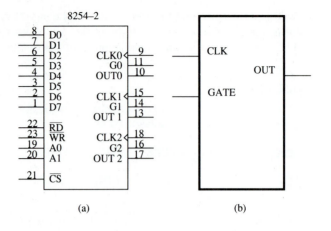

(a)   (b)

any of the four internal registers used for programming, reading, or writing to a counter. The personal computer contains an 8253 timer or its equivalent decoded at I/O ports 40H–43H. Timer zero is programmed to generate an 18.2-Hz signal that interrupts the microprocessor at interrupt vector 8 for a clock tick. The tick is often used to time programs and events. Timer 1 is programmed for a 15-μs output that is used on an XT personal computer to request a DMA action used to refresh the dynamic RAM. Timer 2 is programmed to generate tone on the personal computer speaker.

Pin Definitions

1. A_1–A_0—Address Inputs: select one of four internal registers within the 8254-2. These inputs are connected to A_2 and A_1 of the 80286 microprocessor. See Table 9–6 for the function of the A_1 and A_0 address bits.
2. CLK—Clock Input: used as a timing source for each of the internal counters. This input is often connected to the PCLK signal from the 82288 system bus controller.
3. $\overline{CS}$—Chip Select: enables the 8254-2 for programming and reading or writing a counter.
4. G—Gate Input: controls the operation of the counter in some modes of operation.
5. GND—Ground: connected to the system ground bus.
6. OUT—Counter Output: the output is where the waveform generated by the timer is available.
7. $\overline{RD}$—Read: reads data from the 8254-2 with the $\overline{IORC}$ signal from the 82288 system bus controller.
8. V_{cc}—Power: connected to the +5.0-V power supply.

TABLE 9–6 Address selection inputs to the 8254-2

A_1	A_0	Function
0	0	Counter 0
0	1	Counter 1
1	0	Counter 2
1	1	Control word

9. $\overline{WR}$—Write: writes data to the 8254-2 with the upper or lower bank write strobe from the 80286 system.

Programming the 8254-2

Each counter can be individually programmed by writing a control word followed by the initial count. Figure 9–28 lists the program control word for the 8254-2 and the function for each bit. The control word allows the programmer to select the counter, mode of operation, and type of operation (read/write). The control word is also used to select either a binary or BCD count. Each counter may be programmed with a count of 1 to FFFFH. A count of 0 is equal to FFFFH+1 (65,536), or 10,000 in BCD. The minimum count of 1 applies to all modes of operation except modes 2 and 3, which have a minimum count of 2. Timer 0 is used in the personal computer with a divide by count of 64K (FFFFH) to generate the 18.2-Hz interrupt clock tick.

The control word uses the BCD bit to select a BCD count (BCD = 1) or a binary count (BCD = 0). The M_2, M_1, and M_0 bits select one of the six different modes of operation (000–101) for the counter. The RW_1 and RW_0 bits determine how the data are read or written to the counter. The SC_1 and SC_0 bits select a counter or the special read-back mode of operation discussed later in this section.

Each counter has a program control word used to select the way the counter operates. If 2 bytes are programmed into a counter, then the first byte (LSB) will stop the count, and the second byte (MSB) will start the counter with the new count. The order of programming is important for each counter, but programming of different counters may be interleaved for better control. For example, the control word may be sent to each counter for individual programming. Example 9–19 shows a few ways to program counter 1 and 2. The first method programs both control words, then the LSB of the count for each counter, which stops them from counting. Finally,

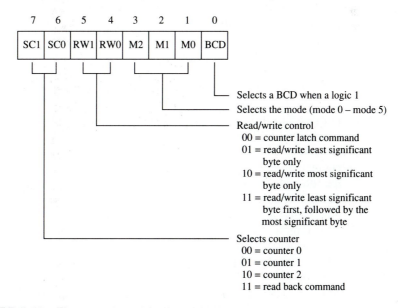

FIGURE 9–28 The control word for the 8254-2 timer.

the MSB portion of the count is programmed, starting both counters with the new count. The second example shows one counter programmed before the other.

EXAMPLE 9–19

PROGRAM CONTROL WORD 1	;set up counter 1
PROGRAM CONTROL WORD 2	;set up counter 2
PROGRAM LSB 1	;stop counter 1 and program LSB
PROGRAM LSB 2	;stop counter 2 and program LSB
PROGRAM MSB 1	;program MSB and start counter 1
PROGRAM MSB 2	;program MSB and start counter 2

or

PROGRAM CONTROL WORD 1	;set up counter 1
PROGRAM LSB 1	;stop counter 1 and program LSB
PROGRAM MSB 1	;program MSB and start counter 1
PROGRAM CONTROL WORD 2	;set up counter 2
PROGRAM LSB 2	;stop counter 2 and program LSB
PROGRAM MSB 2	;program MSB and start counter 2

Modes of Operation.   Six modes (mode 0–mode 5) of operation are available to each of the 8254-2 counters. Figure 9–29 shows how each of these modes functions with the CLK input, the gate (G) control signal, and OUT signal. A description of each mode follows:

1. *Mode 0* allows the 8254-2 counter to be used as an events counter. In this mode, the output becomes a logic 0 when the control word is written and remains there until N plus the number of programmed counts. For example, if a count of 5 is programmed, the output will remain a logic 0 for 6 counts beginning with N. Note that the gate (G) input must be a logic 1 to allow the counter to count. If G becomes a logic 0 in the middle of the count, the counter will stop until G again becomes a logic 1.
2. *Mode 1* causes the counter to function as a retriggerable monostable multivibrator (one-shot). In this mode the G input triggers the counter so that it develops a pulse at the OUT connection that becomes a logic 0 for the duration of the count. If the count is 10, then the OUT connection goes low for the 10 clocking periods when triggered. If the G input occurs within the duration of the output pulse, the counter is again reloaded with the count and the OUT connection continues for the total length of the count.
3. *Mode 2* allows the counter to generate a series of continuous pulses that are one clock pulse in width. The separation between pulses is determined by the count. For example, for a count of 10, the output is a logic 1 for nine clock periods and low for one clock period. This cycle is repeated until the counter is programmed with a new count or until the G pin is placed at a logic 0 level. The G input must be a logic 1 for this mode to generate a continuous series of pulses.
4. *Mode 3* generates a continuous square wave at the OUT connection, provided the G pin is a logic 1. If the count is even, the output is high for one-half the count

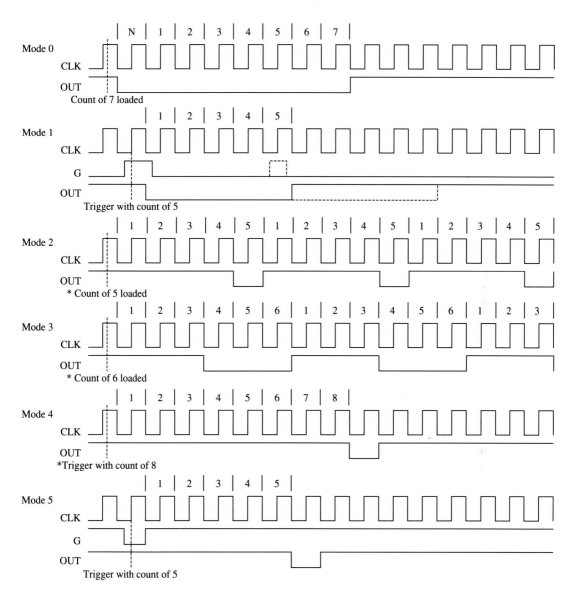

FIGURE 9–29 The six modes of operation for the 8254-2 programmable interval timer. *The G input stops the count when 0 in modes 2, 3, and 4.

and low for one-half the count. If the count is odd, the output is high for one clocking period longer than it is low. For example, if the counter is programmed for a count of five, the output is high for three clocks and low for two.

5. *Mode 4* allows the counter to produce a single pulse at the output. If the count is programmed as a 10, the output is high for 10 clocking periods and then low for one clocking period. The cycle does not begin until the counter is loaded with its complete count. This mode operates as a software triggered one-shot. As with

modes 2 and 3, this mode also uses the G input to enable the counter. The G input must be a logic 1 for the counter to operate for these three modes.

6. *Mode 5* is a hardware-triggered one-shot that functions as mode 4 except it is started by a trigger pulse on the G pin instead of by software. This mode is also similar to mode 1 because it is retriggerable.

Generating a Waveform with the 8254-2. Figure 9–30 shows an 8254-2 connected to functions at I/O ports 0700H, 0702H, 0704H, and 0706H. The addresses are decoded using a PAL16L8 that also generates a write strobe signal for the 8254-2, which is connected to the low-order data bus connections. The PAL also generate a wait signal for the microprocessor that causes two wait states when the 8254-2 is accessed. The program for the PAL is not illustrated here because it is basically the same as many of the other prior examples.

Example 9–20 lists the program that generates a 100-KHz square wave at OUT_0 and a 200-KHz continuous pulses at OUT_1. We use mode 3 for counter 0 and mode 2 for counter 1. The count programmed into counter 0 is 80, and the count for counter 1 is 40. These counts generate the desired output frequencies with an 8-MHz input clock.

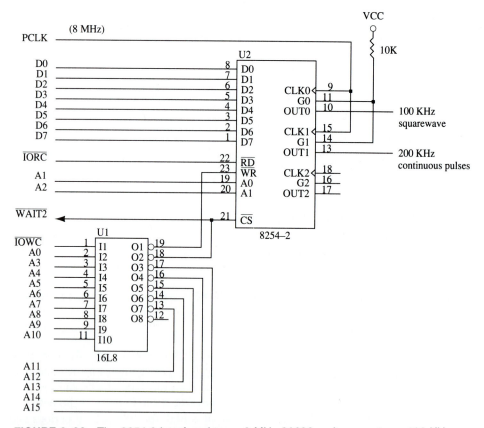

FIGURE 9–30   The 8254-2 interfaced to an 8-MHz 80286 so it generates a 100-KHz square wave at OUT_0 and a 200-KHz continuous pulse at OUT_1.

EXAMPLE 9–20

```
                          ;Procedure that programs the 8254-2 timer to
                          ;function as indicated in Figure 9-30
                          ;
0000                 TIME      PROC      NEAR

0000 50                        PUSH      AX               ;save registers
0001 52                        PUSH      DX

0002 BA 0706                   MOV       DX,706H          ;address control word
0005 B0 36                     MOV       AL,00110110B     ;mode 3
0007 EE                        OUT       DX,AL            ;program control for 0
0008 B0 74                     MOV       AL,01110100B     ;mode 2
000A EE                        OUT       DX,AL            ;program control for 1

000B BA 0700                   MOV       DX,700H          ;address counter 0
000E B0 50                     MOV       AL,80            ;load count of 80
0010 EE                        OUT       DX,AL
0011 32 C0                     XOR       AL,AL
0013 EE                        OUT       DX,AL

0014 BA 0702                   MOV       DX,702H          ;address counter 1
0017 B0 28                     MOV       AL,40            ;load count of 40
0019 EE                        OUT       DX,AL
001A 32 C0                     XOR       AL,AL
001C EE                        OUT       DX,AL

001D 5A                        POP       DX               ;restore registers
001E 58                        POP       AX
001F C3                        RET

0020                 TIME      ENDP
```

Reading a Counter. Each counter has an internal latch that is read with the read counter port operation. These latches will normally follow the count. If the contents of the counter are needed at a particular time, then the latch can remember the count by programming the counter latch control word (see Figure 9–31), which causes the

FIGURE 9–31 The 8254-2 counter latch control word.

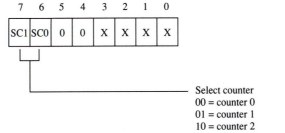

FIGURE 9–32 The 8254-2 read-back control word.

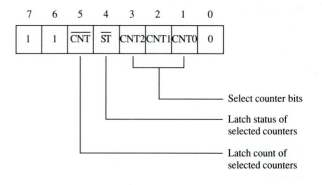

contents of the counter to be held in a latch until it is read. Whenever a read from the latch or the counter is programmed, the latch tracks the contents of the counter.

When it is necessary for the contents of more than one counter to be read at the same time, we use the read-back control word illustrated in Figure 9–32. With the read-back control word, the $\overline{CNT}$ bit is a logic 0 used to cause the counters selected by CNT_0, CNT_1, and CNT_2 to be latched. If the status register is to be latched, the $\overline{ST}$ bit is placed at a logic 0. Figure 9–33 shows the status register, which shows the state of the output pin, whether the counter is at its null state (0), and how the counter is programmed.

Motor Speed and Direction Control

One application for the 8242-2 timer is motor speed control for a DC motor. Figure 9–34 shows the schematic diagram of the motor and its associated driver circuitry. It also illustrates the interconnection of the 8254-2, a flip-flop, and the motor and its driver.

The operation of the motor driver circuitry is fairly straightforward. If the Q output of the 74ALS112 is a logic 1, the base Q_2 is pulled up to +12 V through the base pullup resistor, and the base of Q_2 is open-circuited. This means that Q_1 is off and Q_2 is on, with ground applied to the positive lead of the motor. The bases of both Q_3 and Q_4 are pulled low to ground through the inverters. This causes Q_3 to conduction, or turn on, and Q_4 to turn off, applying ground to the negative lead of the motor. The logic 1 at the Q output of the flip-flop therefore connects +12 V to the positive lead of the motor and ground to the negative lead. This connection causes

FIGURE 9–33 The 8254-2 status register.

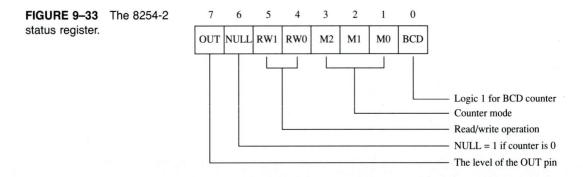

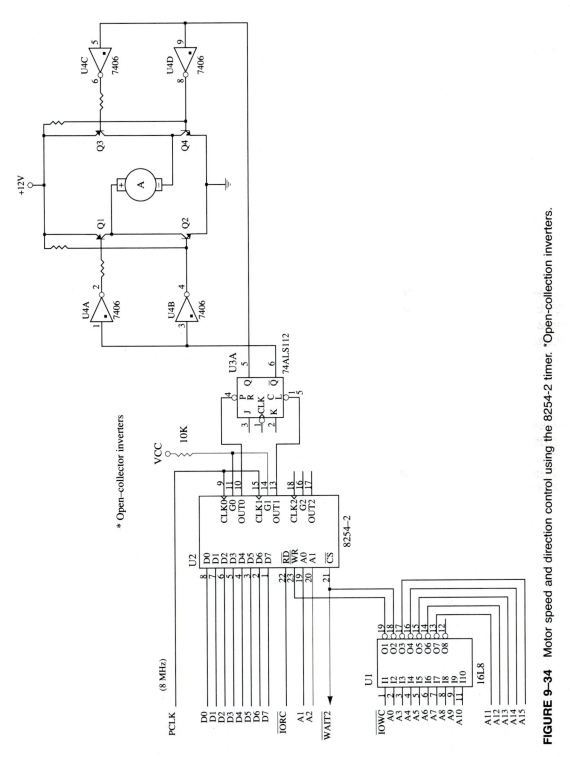

FIGURE 9–34 Motor speed and direction control using the 8254-2 timer. *Open-collection inverters.

377

the motor to spin in its forward direction. If the state of the Q output of the flip-flop becomes a logic 0, then the conditions of the transistors are reversed and +12 V is attached to the negative lead of the motor with ground attached to the positive lead. This causes the motor to spin in the reverse direction.

If the output of the flip-flop is alternated between a logic 1 and 0, the motor spins in either direction at various speeds. If the duty cycle of the Q output is 50 percent, the motor will not spin at all and exhibits some holding torque because current flows through it. Figure 9–35 shows some timing diagrams and their effects

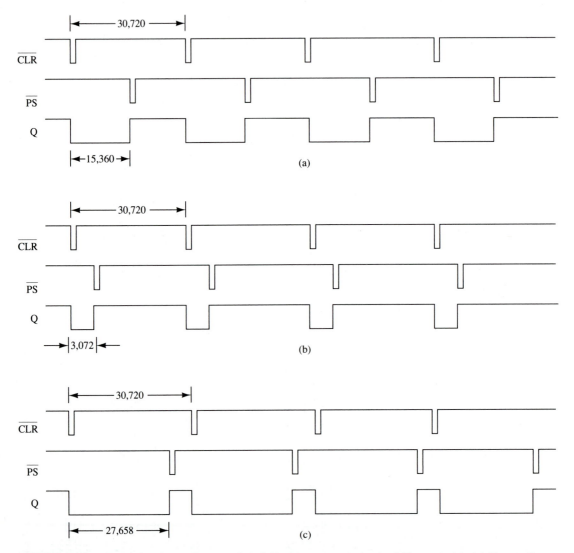

FIGURE 9–35 Timing for the motor speed and direction control circuit of Figure 9–34. (a) No rotation. (b) High-speed rotation in the reverse direction. (c) High-speed rotation in the forward direction.

on the speed and direction of the motor. Notice how each counter generates pulses at different positions to vary the duty cycle at the Q output of the flip-flop. This output is also called pulse-width modulation.

To generate these waveforms, counters 0 and 1 are both programmed to divide the input clock (PCLK) by 30,720. We change the duty cycle of Q by changing the point at which counter 1 is started in relationship to counter 0. This changes the direction and speed of the motor. But why divide the 8-MHz clock by 30,720? The divide rate of 30,720 is divisible by 256, so we can develop a short program that allows 256 different speeds. This program also produces a basic operating frequency to power the motor. It is important to keep this operating frequency below 1,000 Hz, but above 60 Hz.

Example 9–21 lists a procedure that controls the speed and direction of the motor. The speed is controlled by the value of AH when this procedure is called. Because we have an 8-bit number to represent speed, a 50 percent duty cycle for a stopped motor is a count of 128. By changing the value in AH when the procedure is called, we can adjust the motor speed. As the value in AH approaches 00H, the motor begins to increase its speed in the reverse direction. As the value of AH approaches FFH, the motor increases its speed in the forward direction.

EXAMPLE 9–21

```
                    ;Procedure that controls the duty cycle of Q and
                    ;therefore the speed and direction of the motor.
                    ;
                    ;AH contains a number between 00H and FFH that
                    ;selects both direction and speed of the motor.
                    ;
= 0706              CNTR    EQU     706H              ;control port
= 0700              CNT0    EQU     700H              ;counter 0 port
= 0702              CNT1    EQU     702H              ;counter 1 port
= 7800              COUNT   EQU     30720             ;count of 30,720

0000                SPEED   PROC    NEAR

0000 50                     PUSH    AX                ;save registers
0001 52                     PUSH    DX
0002 53                     PUSH    BX

                    ;calculate count

0003 8A DC                  MOV     BL,AH
0005 B8 0078                MOV     AX,120
0008 F6 E3                  MUL     BL
000A 8B D8                  MOV     BX,AX
000C B8 7800                MOV     AX,COUNT
000F 2B C3                  SUB     AX,BX
0011 8B D8                  MOV     BX,AX
```

```
                          ;program counter control words

0013  BA 0706             MOV     DX,CNTR            ;load port address of control
0016  B0 34               MOV     AL,00110100B       ;control for CNT0
0018  EE                  OUT     DX,AL
0019  B0 74               MOV     AL,01110100B       ;control for CNT1
001B  EE                  OUT     DX,AL

                          ;start counter 1 to generate clear

001C  BA 0702             MOV     DX,CNT1            ;address counter 1
001F  B8 7800             MOV     AX,COUNT           ;get count
0022  EE                  OUT     DX,AL              ;stop counter 1
0023  8A C4               MOV     AL,AH
0025  EE                  OUT     DX,AL              ;start counter 1

                          ;wait for counter 1 to reach calculated count

0026              SPE:

0026  EC                  IN      AL,DX              ;get count
0027  86 C4               XCHG    AL,AH
0029  EC                  IN      AL,DX

002A  86 C4               XCHG    AL,AH
002C  3B C3               CMP     AX,BX              ;test count
002E  72 F6               JB      SPE                ;if CNT1 below count

                          ;start counter 0 to generate set

0030  BA 0700             MOV     DX,CNT0            ;address counter 0
0033  B8 7800             MOV     AX,COUNT           ;get count
0036  EE                  OUT     DX,AL              ;stop counter 0
0037  8A C4               MOV     AL,AH
0039  EE                  OUT     DX,AL              ;start counter 1

003A  5B                  POP     BX                 ;restore registers
003B  5A                  POP     DX
003C  58                  POP     AX
003D  C3                  RET

003E              SPEED   ENDP
```

The procedure adjusts the waveform at Q by first calculating the count that counter 0 is to start at in relationship to counter 1. This is accomplished by multiplying AH by 120 and then subtracting it from 30,720. This calculation is required because the counters are down-counters that count from the programmed count to 0 before restarting. Next counter 1 is programmed with a count of 30,720 and started to generate the clear waveform for the flip-flop. After counter 1 is started it is read and compared with the calculated count. Once it reaches this count, counter 0 is started with a count of 30,720. From this point forward, both counters continue generating the clear and set waveforms until the procedure is again called to adjust the speed and direction of the motor.

9–6   8251A PROGRAMMABLE COMMUNICATIONS INTERFACE

The 8251A is a programmable communications interface designed to connect to virtually any type of serial interface. The 8251A is a *universal synchronous/asynchronous receiver/transmitter* (USART) that is fully compatible with the Intel 80286 microprocessor provided that two wait states are inserted if the 80286 operates at 8 MHz. The 8251A is capable of operating at 0–64 Kbaud (Bd) (bits per second) in the synchronous mode and 0–19.2 KBd in the asynchronous mode. *Baud rate* is the number of bits transferred per second, including start, stop, data, and parity. The programmer of the 8251A selects the number of data bits, number of stop bits, type of parity (even or odd), and the clock rate in the asynchronous mode. In the synchronous mode, the programmer selects the number of data bits, parity, and the number of synchronization characters (one or two).

Asynchronous Serial Data

Asynchronous serial data are information that is transmitted and received without a clock or timing signal. Figure 9–36 illustrates two frames of asynchronous serial data. Each frame contains a start bit, seven data bits, parity, and one stop bit. In this figure, a frame, which contains one ASCII character, has 10 bits. Most communications systems use 10 bits for asynchronous serial data with even parity.

Synchronous Serial Data

Figure 9–37 shows the format of synchronous serial data. Notice that this information contains no start or stop bits, only data and parity. Also notice that the data are referenced or synchronized to a clock or timing element. Instead of using the start

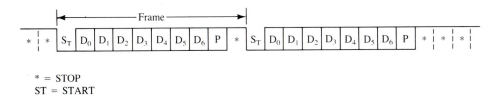

* = STOP
ST = START

FIGURE 9–36 Asynchronous serial data.

FIGURE 9–37 Synchronous serial data.

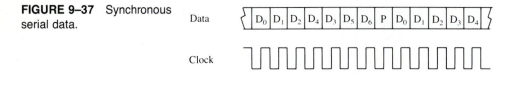

and stop bits for synchronizing each character, synchronous data uses a sync character or characters to synchronize blocks of data. A sync character or characters are sent and then followed by a block of data in a synchronous system. If we use two sync characters, the system is called *bi-sync,* and is the most common. The advantage of the synchronous system is that more bits of information are transferred per second, but the disadvantage is that the clock signal must also be transmitted with the data.

8251A Functional Description

Figure 9–38 illustrates the pinout of the 8251A USART. Two completely separate sections are responsible for data communications: the receiver and the transmitter. Because each of these sections is independent of the other, the 8251A is able to function in *simplex, half-duplex,* or *full-duplex* modes.

An example simplex system is where the transmitter or receiver is used by itself such as in an FM (frequency modulation) radio station. An example of a half-duplex system is a CB (citizens band) radio, where we transmit and receive, but not both at the same time. The full-duplex system allows transmission and reception in both directions simultaneously. An example full-duplex system is the telephone.

The 8251A can control a *modem* (modulator/demodulator), which is a device that converts TTL levels of serial data into audio tones that can pass through the telephone system. Four pins on the 8251A are devoted to modem control: $\overline{\text{DSR}}$ (data set ready), $\overline{\text{DTR}}$ (data terminal ready), $\overline{\text{CTS}}$ (clear-to-send), and $\overline{\text{RTS}}$ (request-to-send). The modem is referred to as the *data set,* and the 8251A is referred to as the *data terminal.*

FIGURE 9–38 The pinout of the 8251A universal synchronous/asynchronous receiver/transmitter (USART).

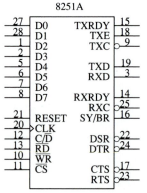

Pin Functions

1. C/$\overline{D}$—Command/Data Input: selects either the command/status register or data for the transmitter or from the receiver. This pin is a logic 1 to access the command/status register and a logic 0 to access data.
2. CLK—Clock Input: provides the 8251A with its timing source. The frequency of the clock signal must be 3.125 MHz or less. This input does not determine the transmission rate of the digital data, but it must be at least 16 times higher than the transmit or receive clocks.
3. $\overline{CS}$—Chip Select: enables the 8251A when a logic 0.
4. $\overline{CTS}$—Clear-to-Send: a return signal from the modem that indicates it is ready to begin sending information. Note that this pin must be grounded in order to transmit data.
5. D_7–D_0—Data Bus: pins that connect to the upper or lower data bus half in the 80286 system.
6. $\overline{DSR}$—Data Set Ready: an inverting input used to test the $\overline{DSR}$ signal from the modem (data set). The $\overline{DSR}$ input indicates that the data set is ready to begin transferring information.
7. $\overline{DTR}$—Data Terminal Ready: an inverting output that signals the data set that the data terminal (8251A) is ready to transfer information.
8. RESET—Reset Input: clears the internal circuitry of the 8251A selecting the synchronous mode of operation. This input is connected to the RESET pin on the 82284 clock generator.
9. $\overline{RD}$—Read Input: used to read data from the receiver or to read the status register.
10. $\overline{RTS}$—Request-to-Send: an inverting output that signals the data set that the 8251A is requesting that the line be turned around for transmission. This signal is used in the half-duplex mode of operation.
11. $\overline{RxC}$—Receiver Clock: provides a timing signal for the receiver.
12. $\overline{RxD}$—Receiver Data: accepts serial data for the receiver.
13. RxRDY—Receiver Ready: shows that the receiver has received a serial datum that is ready for transfer, in parallel, for the microprocessor from the 8251A.
14. SY/BD—Sync Detect/Break Detect: an output that indicates either synchronization in the synchronous mode or the receipt of a break character in the asynchronous mode. A break character is two complete frames of start pulses and is often used to break communications.
15. $\overline{TxC}$—Transmitter Clock: provides the 8251A transmitter with its baud rate determining clock frequency. This input can be scaled by factors of 1, 16, or 64 in the asynchronous mode, and represents the actual baud rate for synchronous operation.
16. TxD—Transmit Data: serial data output connection.
17. TxEMPTY—Transmitter Empty: indicates that the transmitter, within the 8251A, has finished transmitting all data.
18. TxRDY—Transmitter Ready: a signal that indicates that the transmitter within the 8251A is ready to receive another character for transmission.
19. $\overline{WR}$—Write Input: strobes data into the internal command register for programming.

Programming the 8251A

Programming the 8251A is simple when compared to some of the other programmable interfaces described in this chapter. Programming is a two-part process that includes initialization dialog and operational dialog.

Initialization dialog, which occurs after a hardware or software reset, consists of two parts: reset and mode. Because of an apparent design flaw, the 8251A does not reset properly from the RESET input pin. Instead, it must be reset by a series of instructions that send the command register three 00H's followed by a 40H (the software reset command).

Once the 8251A is reset, it may be programmed with the mode word, which directs the 8251A to function as either an asynchronous or synchronous device. Figure 9–39 shows both the synchronous and asynchronous mode command words. Both words specify the number of data bits and parity. In the asynchronous mode, the number of stop bits and clock divider are programmed, and in the synchronous mode, the number of sync characters and the function of SY are programmed. The SY pin is programmed as either an input that indicates synchronization, or as an output that indicates the sync characters have been received.

In the asynchronous mode, once the mode instruction is programmed, the initialization programming is complete. In the synchronous mode, the one or two sync characters are programmed following the mode command to complete initialization programming.

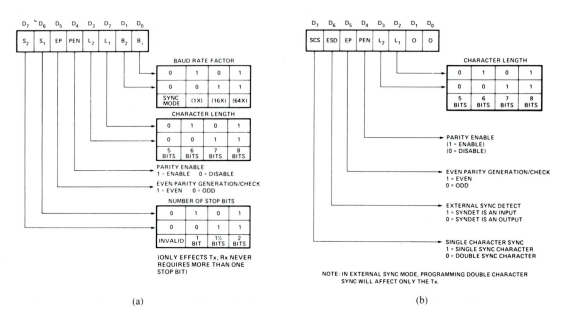

(a)   (b)

FIGURE 9–39   8251A mode instruction words. (a) Asynchronous. (b) Synchronous. (Courtesy of Intel Corporation)

Suppose that an asynchronous system requires seven data bits, odd parity, a clock divider of 64, and one stop bit. Example 9–22 lists a procedure that initializes the 8251A to function in this manner. Figure 9–40 shows the interface to the 80286 microprocessor using a PAL 16L8 to decode the 8-bit port addresses FDH and FFH. Here port FDH accesses the data register and FFH the command register. Notice that the baud clock input is 76,800 Hz, and that the transmitted and received serial data are at 1200 Bd. The reason is that the baud rate multiplier is programmed to divide the input clock by a factor of 64 in this example.

EXAMPLE 9–22

```
                        ;Initialization procedure for the 8251A used in
                        ;asynchronous operation.
                        ;
= 00FF                  CNTR    EQU     0FFH            ;command port
= 0040                  RESET   EQU     40H             ;reset code

0000                    PROG    PROC    NEAR

0000 50                         PUSH    AX              ;save AX

                        ;reset the 8251A

0001 32 C0                      XOR     AL,AL
0003 E6 FF                      OUT     CNTR,AL
0005 E6 FF                      OUT     CNTR,AL
0007 E6 FF                      OUT     CNTR,AL
0009 B0 40                      MOV     AL,RESET
000B E6 FF                      OUT     CNTR,AL

                        ;program mode

000D B0 5B                      MOV     AL,01011011B
000F E6 FF                      OUT     CNTR,AL

                        ;enable receiver and trasnmitter

0011 B0 15                      MOV     AL,00010101B
0013 E6 FF                      OUT     CNTR,AL

0015 58                         POP     AX              ;restore AX
0016 C3                         RET

0017                    PROG    ENDP
```

If the 8251A is operated in synchronous mode, the programming sequence is very similar except that one or two sync characters are also programmed. Example

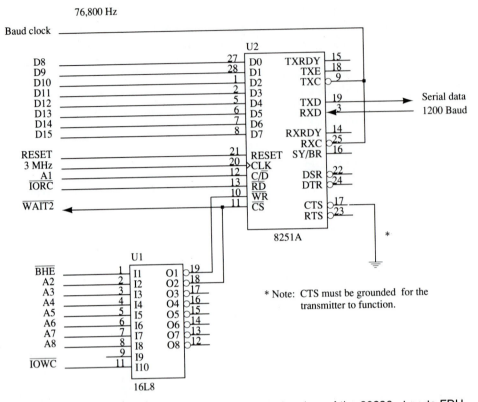

FIGURE 9–40   The 8251A interfaced to the upper data bus of the 80286 at ports FDH and FFH.

9–23 lists a procedure that programs the 8251A for synchronous operation, using seven data bits, even parity, SY as an output, and two sync characters.

EXAMPLE 9–23

```
                    ;Initialization procedure for the 8251A used in
                    ;synchronous operation.
                    ;
= 00FF              CNTR      EQU      0FFH              ;command port
= 0040              RESET     EQU      40H               ;reset code
= 007F              SYNC1     EQU      7FH               ;sync code 1
= 007E              SYNC2     EQU      7EH               ;sync code 2

0000                PROGS     PROC     NEAR

0000  50                     PUSH     AX                ;save AX
```

```
                                    ;reset the 8251A

0001 32 C0                          XOR        AL,AL
0003 E6 FF                          OUT        CNTR,AL
0005 E6 FF                          OUT        CNTR,AL
0007 E6 FF                          OUT        CNTR,AL
0009 B0 40                          MOV        AL,RESET
000B E6 FF                          OUT        CNTR,AL

                            ;program mode

000D B0 B8                          MOV        AL,10111000B
000F E6 FF                          OUT        CNTR,AL

                            ;program sync characters

0011 B0 7F                          MOV        AL,SYNC1
0013 E6 FF                          OUT        CNTR,AL
0015 B0 7E                          MOV        AL,SYNC2
0017 E6 FF                          OUT        CNTR,AL

                            ;enable receiver and trasnmitter

0019 B0 15                          MOV        AL,00010101B
001B E6 FF                          OUT        CNTR,AL

001D 58                             POP        AX                    ;restore AX
001E C3                             RET

001F                    PROGS    ENDP
```

After the mode instruction is programmed into the 8251A, it is still not ready to function. After programming the mode in asynchronous operation, and after programming the mode and sync characters in synchronous operation, we still must program the command register. Figure 9–41 illustrates the command word for the 8251A. The command word enables the transmitter and receiver, controls DTR and RTS, sends a break character in asynchronous mode, resets errors, resets the 8251A, and enters the hunt mode for synchronous operation. Refer to example command words as programmed in Examples 9–22 and 9–23.

Before it is possible to write software to send or receive serial data through the 8251A, we need to know the function of the status register (see Figure 9–42). The status word contains information about error conditions, the states of DSR, SY/BD, TxEMPTY, RxRDY, and TxRDY.

Suppose that a procedure (see Example 9–24) is written to transmit the contents of AH to 8251A and out through its serial data pin (TxD). The TxRDY bit is polled by

FIGURE 9–41 The 8251A command word. (Courtesy of Intel Corporation)

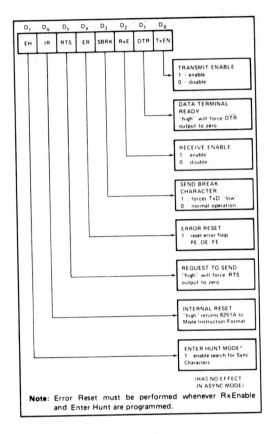

software to determine whether the transmitter is ready to receive data. This procedure uses the circuit of Figure 9–40.

EXAMPLE 9–24

```
                      ;Procedure that transmits the contents of AH
                      ;
= 00FF                CNTR    EQU     0FFH              ;command port
= 00FD                DATA    EQU     0FDH              ;data port

0000                  SEND    PROC    NEAR

0000 50                       PUSH    AX                ;save AX

                      ;test TxRDY

0001                  SEND1:

0001 E4 FF                    IN      AL,CNTR           ;read status
0003 D0 C8                    ROR     AL,1              ;rotate TxRDY to CF
0005 73 FA                    JNC     SEND1             ;if not ready
```

FIGURE 9–42 The 8251A status word. (Courtesy of Intel Corporation)

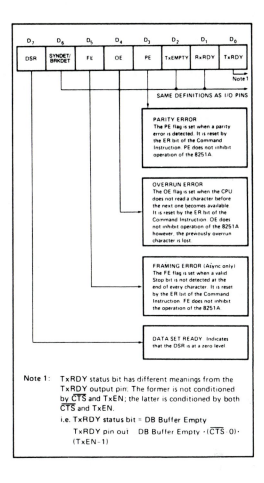

```
                                          ;transmit data

0007 8A C4                        MOV     AL,AH
0009 E6 FD                        OUT     DATA,AL

000B 58                           POP     AX                    ;restore AX
000C C3                           RET

000D                      SEND     ENDP
```

To read received information from the 8251A we test the RxRDY bit of the status register. Example 9–25 lists a procedure that tests the RxRDY bit to decide if the 8251A has received data. Upon reception of data, the procedure tests for errors. If an error is detected, the procedure returns with AL = ?. If no error has occurred, then the procedure returns with AL equal to the received character.

EXAMPLE 9–25

```
                         ;Procedure that receives data from the 8251A
                         ;
= 00FF          CNTR     EQU      0FFH                ;command port
= 00FD          DATA     EQU      0FDH                ;data port
= 0004          MASKS    EQU      4                   ;RxRDY mask
= 0038          ERROR    EQU      38H                 ;error mask
= 0015          E_RES    EQU      15H                 ;error reset
= 003F          QUES     EQU      '?'                 ;question mark

0000            RECV     PROC     NEAR

                ;test RxRDY

0000            RECV1:

0000 E4 FF               IN       AL,CNTR             ;read status
0002 A8 04               TEST     AL,MASKS            ;test RxRDY
0004 74 FA               JZ       RECV1               ;if not ready

                ;test for errors

0006 A8 38               TEST     AL,ERROR
0008 75 03               JNZ      ERR                 ;if an error

                ;read data

000A E4 FD               IN       AL,DATA
000C C3                  RET

                ;error

000D            ERR:

000D B0 15               MOV      AL,E_RES            ;reset error
000F E6 FF               OUT      CNTR,AL
0011 B0 3F               MOV      AL,QUES             ;get ?
0013 C3                  RET

0014            RECV     ENDP
```

The types of errors detected by the 8251A are: parity error, framing error, and overrun error. A parity error indicates that the received data contains the wrong parity, a framing error indicates that the start and stop bits are not in their proper places, and an overrun error indicates that data have overrun the internal receiver buffer. These errors should not occur during normal operation. If a parity error occurs, it indicates that noise was encountered during reception. A framing error occurs if the receiver is receiving data at an incorrect baud rate, and an overrun error only occurs if the software fails to read the data from the USART.

9–7   ANALOG-TO-DIGITAL AND DIGITAL-TO-ANALOG CONVERTERS

Analog-to-digital (ADC) and digital-to-analog (DAC) converters are used to interface the microprocessor to the analog world. Many events that are monitored and controlled by the microprocessor are analog events. These often include monitoring all forms of events, from speech to the control of motors and like devices. In order to interface the microprocessor to these events, we must have an understanding of the interface and control of the ADC and DAC, which convert between analog and digital data.

The DAC0830 Digital-to-Analog Converter

A fairly common and low-cost digital-to-analog converter is the DAC0830.* This device is an 8-bit converter that transforms an 8-bit binary number into an analog voltage. Other converters are available that convert from 10-, 12-, or 16-bits into analog voltages. The number of voltage steps generated by the converter is equal to the number of binary input combinations. Therefore an 8-bit converter generates 256 different voltage levels, a 10-bit converter generates 1,024 levels, and so forth. The DAC0830 is a medium-speed converter that transforms a digital input to an analog output in approximately 1.0 μs.

Figure 9–43 illustrates the pinout of the DAC0830. This device has a set of eight data bus connections for the application of the digital input code and a pair of analog outputs labeled I_{out1} and I_{out2} that are designed as inputs to an external operational amplifier. Because this is an 8-bit converter, its output step voltage is defined as $-V_{ref}$ (reference voltage) divided by 255. For example, if the reference voltage is -5.0 V, its output step voltage is $+0.0196078431373$ V. Note that the output voltage is the opposite polarity of the reference voltage. If an input of 1001 0010 is applied to the device, the output voltage will be the step voltage times 1001 0010, or in this case $+2.86274509804$ V. By changing the reference voltage to -5.1 V the step voltage becomes $+0.02$ V. The step voltage is also often called the resolution of the converter.

Internal Structure of the DAC0830. Figure 9–44 illustrates the internal structure of the DAC0830. Notice that this device contains two internal registers. The first is a holding register, while the second connects to the R-2R internal ladder converter. The two latches allow one byte to be held while another is converted. In many cases we disable the first latch and only use the second for entering data into the converter. This process is accomplished by connecting a logic 1 to ILE and a logic 0 to $\overline{CS}$ (chip select).

Both latches within the DAC0830 are transparent latches. When the G input to the latch is a logic 1, data pass through the latch, but when the G input becomes a logic 0, data are latched or held. The converter has a reference input pin (V_{ref}) that

---

*The DAC0830 is a product of National Semiconductor Corporation.

FIGURE 9–43 The pinout of the DAC0830 digital-to-analog converter.

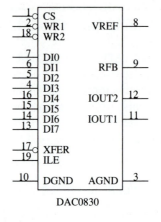

DAC0830

establishes the full-scale output voltage. If -10 V is placed on V_{ref}, the full-scale (1111 1111) voltage is $+10$ V. The output of the R-2R ladder within the converter appears at I_{out1} and I_{out2}. These outputs are designed to be applied to an operational amplifier, such as a 741 or similar device.

Connecting the DAC0830 to the Microprocessor. The DAC0830 is connected to the microprocessor as illustrated in Figure 9–45. Here a PAL16L8 is used to decode the DAC0830 at 8-bit I/O port address 20H. Whenever an OUT 20H,AL instruction is executed, the contents of data bus connection AD_0–AD_7 are passed to the converter within the DAC0830. The 741 operational amplifier along with the -12-V Zener reference voltage causes the full-scale output voltage to equal $+12$ V. The output

FIGURE 9–44 The internal structure of the DAC0830.

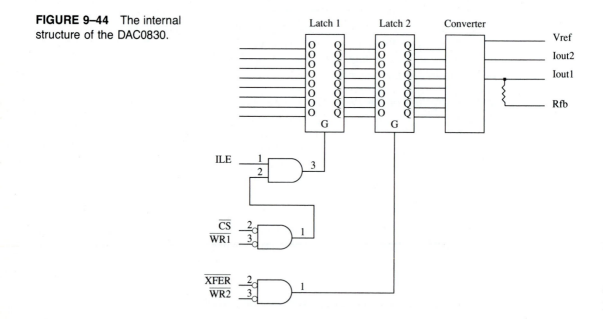

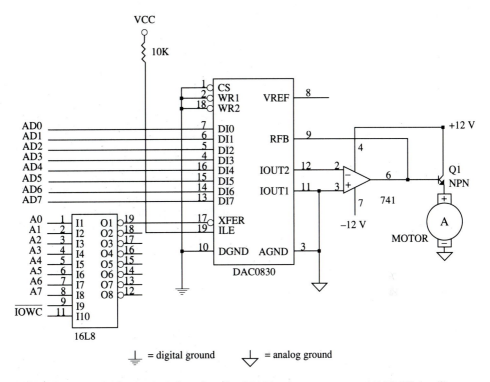

FIGURE 9–45 DAC0830 interfaced to the 80286 microprocessor at 8-bit I/O location 20H.

of the operational amplifier feeds a driver that powers a 12-V DC motor. This driver is a Darlington amplifier for large motors. This example shows the converter driving a motor, but other devices could be used as an output.

The ADC0804 Analog-to-Digital Converter

A common low-cost ADC is the ADC0804, which belongs to a family of converters that are all identical except for accuracy. This device is compatible with a wide range of microprocessors such as the 80286. There are faster ADCs available and some with more resolution than 8 bits, but this device is ideal for many applications that do not require a high degree of accuracy. The ADC0804 requires up to 100 μs to convert an analog input voltage into a digital output code.

Figure 9–46 shows the pinout of the ADC0804* converter. To operate the converter, the $\overline{WR}$ pin is pulsed with $\overline{CS}$ grounded to start the conversion process. Because this converter requires a considerable amount of time for the conversion, a pin labeled INTR signals the end of the conversion. Refer to Figure 9–47 for a

---

*The ADC0804 is a product of National Semiconductor Corporation.

FIGURE 9–46 The pinout of the ADC0804 analog-to-digital converter.

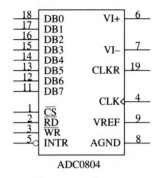

timing diagram that shows the interaction of the control signals. As can be seen, we start the converter with the $\overline{\text{WR}}$ pulse, we wait for INTR to return to a logic 0 level, and then we read the data from the converter. If a time delay is used that allows at least 100 μs of time, then we don't need to test the INTR pin. Another option is to connect the INTR pin to an interrupt input so when the conversion is complete, an interrupt occurs.

The Analog Input Signal.   Before the ADC0804 can be connected to the microprocessor its analog inputs must be understood. There are two analog inputs to the ADC0804: V_{in} (+) and V_{in} (−). These inputs are connected to an internal operational amplifier and are differential inputs as shown in Figure 9–48. The differential inputs are summed by the operational amplifier to produce a signal for the internal analog-to-digital converter. Figure 9–48 shows a few ways to use these differential inputs. The first way (Figure 9–48[a]) uses a single input that can vary between 0 V and +5.0 V. The second (Figure 9–48[b]) shows a variable voltage applied to the V_{in} (−) pin so the zero reference for V_{in} (+) can be adjusted.

Generating the Clock Signal.   The ADC0804 requires a clock source for operation. The clock can be an external clock applied to the CLK IN pin or it can be generated with an RC circuit. The permissible range of clock frequencies is between 100 KHz and 1460 KHz. It is desirable to use a frequency that is as close as possible to 1460 KHz so conversion time is kept to a minimum.

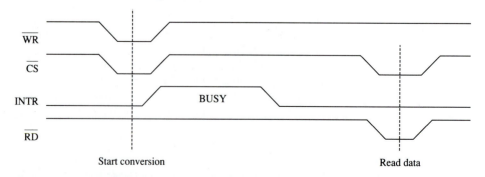

FIGURE 9–47 The timing for the ADC0804 analog-to-digital converter.

FIGURE 9–48 The analog inputs to the ADC0804 converter. (a) To sense a 0- to +5.0-V input. (b) To sense an input offset from ground.

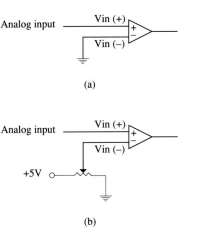

If the clock is generated with an RC circuit, we use the CLK IN and CLK R pins connected to an RC circuit as illustrated in Figure 9–49. When this connection is in use, the clock frequency is calculated by the following equation:

$$F_{CLK} = \frac{1}{1.1RC}$$

Connecting the ADC0804 to the Microprocessor. The ADC0804 is interfaced to the 80286 microprocessor as illustrated in Figure 9–50. Note the V_{ref} signal is not attached to anything, which is normal. Suppose that the ADC0804 is decoded at 8-bit I/O port address 40H for the data and port address 42H for the INTR signal and a procedure is required to start and read the data from the ADC. This procedure is listed in Example 9–26. Notice that the INTR bit is polled and if it becomes a logic 0, the procedure ends with AL containing the converted digital code.

EXAMPLE 9–26

```
                    ;Procedure that reads data from the ADC and returns
                    ;with it in AL
                    ;
0000                ADCX    PROC    NEAR
```

FIGURE 9–49 Connecting the RC circuit to the CLK IN and CLK R pins on the ADC0804.

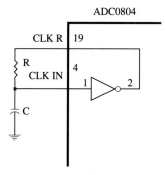

```
0000 E6 40                        OUT       40H,AL                    ;start conversion

0002                   ADCX1:

0002 E4 42                        IN        AL,42H                    ;read INTR
0004 A8 80                        TEST      AL,80H                    ;test INTR
0006 75 FA                        JNZ       ADCX1                     ;repeat until INTR = 0

0008 E4 40                        IN        AL,40H                    ;get data from ADC
000A C3                           RET

000B                   ADCX      ENDP
```

Using the ADC0804 and the DAC0830

This section of the text illustrates an example using both the ADC0804 and the DAC0830 to capture and replay audio signals or speech. In the past we often used a speech synthesizer to generate speech, but the quality of the speech was poor. For

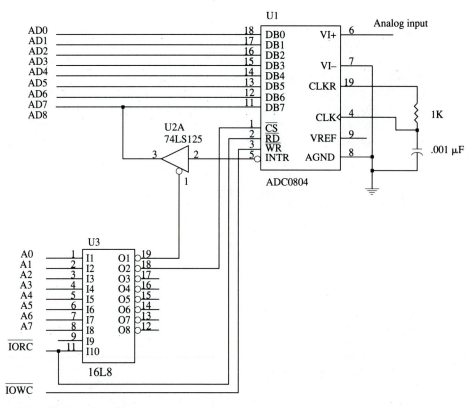

FIGURE 9–50   The ADC0804 interfaced to the microprocessor.

human-quality speech we can use the ADC0804 to capture an audio signal and store it in memory for later playback through the DAC0830.

Figure 9–51 illustrates the circuitry required to connect the ADC0804 at 16-bit I/O ports 0700H and 0702H. The DAC0830 is interfaced at I/O port 704H. The software used to run this converter is given in Example 9–27. This software reads a

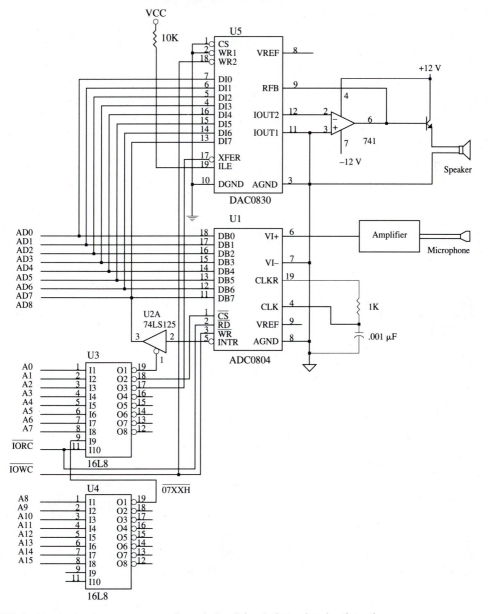

FIGURE 9–51 A circuit to store speech and play it back through a loudspeaker.

1-second burst of speech and then plays it back 10 times. This process repeats until the system is turned off.

EXAMPLE 9–27

```
                         ;Software that records a 1 second passage of speech and
                         ;plays it back 10 times before recording the next 1 second
                         ;of speech.
                         ;
                         ;Assumes that the clock is 8 MHz
                         ;
0000                     STAC     SEGMENT STACK

0000 0800 [                       DW       2048 DUP (?)           ;stack space
        0000
             ]

1000                     STAC     ENDS

0000                     DATA1    SEGMENT 'DATA'

0000 03E8 [              WORDS    DB       1000 DUP (?)           ;space for 1 second of speech
        00
             ]

03E8                     DATA1    ENDS

0000                     CODE1    SEGMENT 'CODE'

                                  ASSUME      CS:CODE1,DS:DATA1,SS:STAC

0000                     START    PROC     FAR

0000 B8 ---- R                    MOV      AX,DATA1              ;load DS
0003 8E D8                        MOV      DS,AX
0005 33 C0                        XOR      AX,AX                 ;load ES
0007 8E C0                        MOV      ES,AX

0009 E8 000A                      CALL     READ                 ;read speech

000C B9 000A                      MOV      CX,10

000F                     START1:

000F E8 0023                      CALL     WRITE                ;talk
0012 E2 FB                        LOOP     START1               ;repeat 10 times

0014 EB EA                        JMP      START                ;redo all

0016                     START    ENDP
```

```
0016              READ      PROC    NEAR

0016 BF 0000 R             MOV     DI,OFFSET WORDS    ;address data
0019 B9 03E8               MOV     CX,1000            ;load count
001C BA 0700               MOV     DX,0700H           ;address port

001F              READ1:

001F EE                    OUT     DX,AL              ;start converter
0020 83 C2 02              ADD     DX,2

0023              READ2:

0023 EC                    IN      AL,DX              ;get INTR
0024 A8 80                 TEST    AL,80H             ;test INTR
0026 75 FB                 JNZ     READ2              ;wait for INTR = 0

0028 83 EA 02              SUB     DX,2
002B EC                    IN      AL,DX              ;get data
002C 88 05                 MOV     [DI],AL            ;save data
002E 47                    INC     DI

002F E8 0018               CALL    DELAY              ;wait 1/1000 second

0032 E2 EB                 LOOP    READ1              ;repeat 1024 times
0034 C3                    RET

0035              READ      ENDP

0035              WRITE     PROC    NEAR

0035 51                    PUSH    CX
0036 BF 0000 R             MOV     DI,OFFSET WORDS    ;address data
0039 B9 03E8               MOV     CX,1000            ;load count
003C BA 0704               MOV     DX,0704H           ;address port

003F              WRITE1:

003F 8A 05                 MOV     AL,[DI]            ;get data
0041 EE                    OUT     DX,AL              ;output data
0042 47                    INC     DI

0043 E8 0004               CALL    DELAY              ;wait 1/1000 second

0046 E2 F7                 LOOP    WRITE1
0048 59                    POP     CX
0049 C3                    RET

004A              WRITE     ENDP

004A              DELAY     PROC    NEAR
```

```
                    ;wait 1/1000 second

004A 51                              PUSH    CX
004B B9 03E8                         MOV     CX,1000

004E                 DELAY1:

004E E2 FE                           LOOP    DELAY1
0050 59                              POP     CX
0051 C3                              RET

0052                 DELAY   ENDP

0052                 CODE1   ENDS

                             END     START
```

9–8   SUMMARY

1. The 80286 has two basic types of I/O instructions: IN and OUT. The IN instruction inputs data from an external I/O device into either the AL (8-bit) or AX (16-bit) register. The IN instruction is available as a fixed-port instruction, a variable-port instruction, or as a string instruction INSB or INSW. The OUT instruction outputs data from AL or AX to an external I/O device and is also available as a fixed, variable, or string instruction OUTSB or OUTSW. The fixed-port instruction uses an 8-bit I/O port address, while the variable and string I/O instructions use a 16-bit port number found in the DX register.

2. Isolated I/O, sometimes called direct I/O, uses a separate map for the I/O space, freeing the entire memory for use by the program. Isolated I/O uses the IN and OUT instructions to transfer data between the I/O device and the 80286. The control structure of the I/O map uses $\overline{IORC}$ (I/O read control) and $\overline{IOWC}$ (I/O write control) plus the bank selection signals $\overline{BHE}$ and A_0 to effect the I/O transfer.

3. Memory-mapped I/O uses a portion of the memory space for I/O transfers. This reduces the amount of memory available, but it negates the need to use the $\overline{IORC}$ and $\overline{IOWC}$ signals for I/O transfers. In addition, any instruction that addresses a memory location using any addressing mode can be used to transfer data between the microprocessor and the I/O device using memory-mapped I/O.

4. All input devices are buffered so the I/O data are only connected to the data bus during the execution of the IN instruction. The buffer is either built into a programmable peripheral or located separately.

5. All output devices use a latch to capture output data during the execution of the OUT instruction. This is necessary because data appear on the data bus for less than 100 ns for an out instruction, and most output devices require the data for a longer time. In many cases the latch is built into the peripheral.

6. Handshaking or polling is the act of two independent devices synchronizing with a few control lines. For example, the computer asks a printer if it is busy by

inputting the BUSY signal from the printer. If it isn't busy, the computer outputs data to the printer and informs the printer that data are available with a data strobe ($\overline{DS}$) signal.

7. The I/O port number appears on address bus connections A_7–A_0 for a fixed-port I/O instruction and on A_{15}–A_0 for a variable-port I/O instruction. In both cases, address bits A_{23}–A_{16} are 00000000. The 8-bit I/O address found on A_7–A_0 also contains logic 0s on address connections A_{15}–A_8.

8. Because the 80286 contains a 16-bit data bus and the I/O addresses reference byte-sized I/O locations, the I/O space is also organized in banks as is the memory system. In order to interface an 8-bit I/O device to the 80286 we often require separate write strobes, an upper and a lower, for I/O write operations.

9. The I/O port decoder is much like the memory address decoder except instead of decoding a 24-bit address, the I/O port decoder decodes only a 16-bit address for variable-port instructions and often an 8-bit port number for fixed I/O instructions.

10. The 8255A-5 is a programmable peripheral interface (PIA) that has 24 I/O pins that are programmable in two groups of 12 pins each (group A and group B). The 8255A-5 operates in three modes: simple I/O (mode 0), strobed I/O (mode 1), and bidirectional I/O (mode 2). When the 8255A-5 is interfaced to the 80286, we insert two wait states because the speed of the microprocessor is faster than the 8255A-5 can handle.

11. The 8279-5 is a programmable keyboard/display controller that can control a 64-key keyboard and a 16-digit numeric display.

12. The 8254-2 is a programmable interval timer that contains three 16-bit counters that count in binary or binary-coded decimal (BCD). Each counter is independent of each other, and operates in six different modes. The six modes of the counter are (1) events counter, (2) retriggerable monostable multivibrator, (3) pulse generator, (4) square-wave generator, (5) software-triggered pulse generator, and (6) hardware-triggered pulse generator.

13. The 8251A-5 is a programmable communications interface capable of receiving and transmitting either asynchronous or synchronous serial data.

14. The DAC0830 is an 8-bit digital-to-analog converter that converts a digital signal to an analog voltage within 1 μs.

15. The ADC0804 is an 8-bit analog-to-digital converter that converts an analog signal into a digital signal within 100 μs.

9–9   QUESTIONS AND PROBLEMS

1. Explain which way the data flow for an IN and an OUT instruction.
2. Where is the I/O port number stored for a fixed I/O instruction?
3. Where is the I/O port number stored for a variable I/O instruction?
4. Where is the I/O port number stored for a string I/O instruction?
5. To which register are data input to by the 16-bit IN instruction?
6. Describe the operation of the OUTSB instruction.
7. Describe the operation of the INSW instruction.

8. Contrast a memory-mapped I/O system with an isolated I/O system.

9. What is the basic input interface?

10. What is the basic output interface?

11. Explain the term *handshaking* as it applies to computer I/O systems.

12. An even-numbered I/O port address is found in the _____ I/O bank in the 80286 microprocessor.

13. Show the circuitry required to generate the upper and lower I/O write strobes.

14. Develop an I/O port decoder, using a 74ALS138, that generates low-bank I/O strobes for the 8-bit I/O port addresses: 10H, 12H, 14H, 16H, 18H, 1AH, 1CH, and 1EH.

15. Develop an I/O port decoder, using a 74ALS138, that generates high-bank I/O strobes for the 8-bit I/O port addresses: 11H, 13H, 15H, 17H, 19H, 1BH, 1DH, and 1FH.

16. Develop an I/O port decoder, using a PAL16L8, that generates 16-bit I/O strobes for the 16-bit I/O port addresses: 1000H–1001H, 1002H–1003H, 1004H–1005H, 1006H–1007H, 1008H–1009H, 100AH–100BH, 100CH–100DH, and 100EH–100FH.

17. Develop an I/O port decoder, using the PAL16L8, that generates the following low-bank I/O strobes: 00A8H, 00B6H, and 00EEH.

18. Develop an I/O port decoder, using the PAL16L8, that generates the following high-bank I/O strobes: 300DH, 300BH, 1005H, and 1007H.

19. Why are both $\overline{BHE}$ and A_0 ignored in a 16-bit port address decoder?

20. An 8-bit I/O device, located at I/O port address 0010H, is connected to which data bus connections?

21. An 8-bit I/O device located at I/O port address 100DH is connected to which data bus connections?

22. The 8255A-5 has how many programmable I/O pin connections?

23. List the pins that belong to group A and to group B in the 8255A-5.

24. What two 8255A-5 pins accomplish internal I/O port address selection?

25. The $\overline{RD}$ connection on the 8255A-5 is attached to which 80286 system control bus connection?

26. Using a PAL16L8, interface an 8255A-5 to the 80286 microprocessor so it functions at I/O locations 0380H, 0382H, 0384H, and 0386H.

27. When the 8255A-5 is reset, its I/O ports are all initialized as _____ .

28. What three modes of operation are available to the 8255A-5?

29. What is the purpose of the $\overline{STB}$ signal in strobed input operation of the 8255A-5?

30. What sets the IBF pin in strobed input operation of the 8255A-5?

31. Write the software that places a logic 1 on the PC_7 pin of the 8255A-5 during strobed input operation.

32. How is the interrupt request pin (INTR) enabled in the strobed input mode of operation of the 8255A-5?

33. In strobed output operation of the 8255A-5, what is the purpose of the $\overline{ACK}$ signal?

34. What clears the $\overline{OBF}$ signal in strobed output operation of the 8255A-5?

35. Write the software required to decide if PC_4 is a logic 1 when the 8255A-5 is operated in the strobed output mode.

36. Which group of pins is used during bidirectional operation of the 8255A-5?

37. What pins are general-purpose I/O pins during mode 2 operation of the 8255A-5?
38. What is normally connected to the CLK pin of the 8279-5?
39. How many wait states are required to interface the 8279-5 to the 80286 microprocessor operating with an 8-MHz clock?
40. If the 8279-5 CLK pin is connected to a 3.0-MHz clock, program the internal clock.
41. What is an overrun error in the 8279-5?
42. What is the difference between encoded and decoded as defined for the 8279-5?
43. Interface the 8279-5 so it functions at 8-bit I/O ports 40H–7FH. Use the 74ALS138 as a decoder and use either the upper or lower data bus.
44. Interface a 16-key keyboard and an 8-digit numeric display to the 8279-5.
45. The 8254-2 interval timer functions from DC to _____ Hz.
46. Each counter in 8254-2 function in how many different modes?
47. Interface an 8254-2 to function at I/O port addresses XX10H, XX12H, XX14H, and XX16H. Write the software required to cause counter 2 to generate an 80-KHz square wave if the CLK input to counter 2 is 8 MHz.
48. What number is programmed in an 8254-2 counter to count 300 events?
49. If a 16-bit count is programmed into the 8254-2, which byte of the count is programmed first?
50. Explain how the read-back control word functions in the 8254-2.
51. Program counter 1 of the 8254-2 so it generates a continuous series of pulses that have a high time of 100 μs and a low time of 1 μs. Make sure to indicate the CLK frequency required to accomplish this task.
52. Why does a 50 percent duty cycle cause the motor to stand still in the motor speed and direction control circuit presented in this chapter?
53. What is asynchronous serial data?
54. What is synchronous serial data?
55. What is baud rate?
56. Program the 8251A for asynchronous operation using six data bits, even parity, one stop bit, and a baud rate divider of 1. (Assume that the I/O ports are numbered 20H and 22H.)
57. If the 8251A is to generate an asynchronous serial signal at a baud rate of 2400 Bd, and the divider is programmed for 16, what is the frequency of the signal attached to the TxC pin?
58. Describe the following terms: simplex, half-duplex, and full-duplex.
59. How is the 8251A reset?
60. The DAC0830 converts an 8-bit digital input to an analog output in approximately _____ .
61. What is the step voltage at the output of the DAC0830 if the reference voltage is −2.55 V?
62. Interface a DAC0830 to the 80286 so it operates at I/O port 400H.
63. Develop a program for the interface of Question 62 so the DAC0830 generates a triangular voltage waveform. The frequency of this wave form must be approximately 100 Hz.
64. The ADC080X requires approximately _____ to convert an analog voltage into a digital code.
65. What is the purpose of the INTR pin on the ADC080X?

66. The $\overline{\text{WR}}$ pin on the ADC080X is used for what purpose?
67. Interface an ADC080X at I/O port 0260H for data and 0270H to test the INTR pin.
68. Develop a program for the ADC080X in Question 67 so it reads an input voltage once per 100 ms and stores the results in a memory array that is 100H bytes in length.

CHAPTER 10

Interrupts

INTRODUCTION

In this chapter, we expand our coverage of basic I/O and programmable peripheral interfaces by examining a technique called interrupt-processed I/O. An interrupt is a hardware-initialed procedure that interrupts whatever program is currently executing.

This chapter provides examples and a detailed explanation of the interrupt structure of the 80286 microprocessor.

OBJECTIVES

Upon completion of this chapter, you will be able to:

1. Explain the interrupt structure of the 80286 microprocessor.
2. Explain the operation of software interrupt instructions INT, INTO, INT 3, and BOUND.
3. Explain how the interrupt enable flag bit (IF) modifies the interrupt structure.
4. Describe the function of the trap interrupt flag bit (TF) and the operation of trap-generated tracing.
5. Develop interrupt service procedures that control lower speed external peripheral devices.
6. Expand the interrupt structure of the 80286 using the 8259A programmable interrupt controller and other techniques.
7. Explain the purpose and operation of a real-time clock.

10–1 BASIC INTERRUPT PROCESSING

In this section, we discuss the function of an interrupt in a microprocessor-based system and the structure and features of interrupts available in the 80286 microprocessor.

The Purpose of Interrupts

Interrupts are particularly useful when interfacing I/O devices that provide or require data at relatively low data transfer rates. In Chapter 9, for instance, we saw a keyboard example using strobed input operation of the 8255A-5. In that example, software polled the 8255A-5 and its IBF bit to decide if data were available from the keyboard. If the person using the keyboard typed one character per second, the software for the 8255A-5 waited an entire second between each keystroke for the person to type another key. This process is such a tremendous waste of time that designers have developed another process called *interrupt processing* to handle this situation.

Unlike the polling technique, interrupt processing allows the microprocessor to execute other software while the keyboard operator is thinking about what key to type next. As soon as a key is pressed, the keyboard encoder debounces the switch and puts out one pulse that interrupts the microprocessor. In this way, the microprocessor executes other software until the key is actually pressed, when it reads a key and returns to the program that was interrupted. As a result, the microprocessor can print reports or complete any other task while the operator is typing a document and thinking about what to type next.

Figure 10–1 shows a time line that indicates a typist typing data on a keyboard, a printer removing data from the memory, and a program executing. The program is the main program that is interrupted for each keystroke and each character that is to print on the printer. Note that the keyboard interrupt service procedure, called by the keyboard interrupt, and the printer interrupt service procedure each take little time to execute.

80286 Interrupts

The interrupts of the 80286 microprocessor include two hardware pins that are used to request interrupts (INTR and NMI) and one hardware pin ($\overline{\text{INTA}}$) that acknowledges an interrupt requested through INTR. In addition to the pins, the microprocessor also has software interrupts INT, INTO, INT 3, and BOUND. Two flag bits, IF (interrupt flag) and TF (trap flag) are also used with the interrupt structure and a special return instruction IRET.

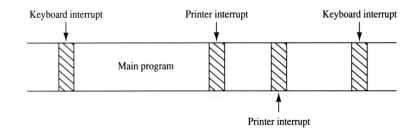
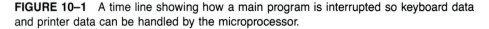

FIGURE 10–1 A time line showing how a main program is interrupted so keyboard data and printer data can be handled by the microprocessor.

Interrupt Vectors. The interrupt vectors and vector table are crucial to an understanding of hardware and software interrupts. The *interrupt vector table* is located in the first 1,024 bytes of memory at addresses 000000H–0003FFH. It contains 256 different 4-byte interrupt vectors. An *interrupt vector* contains the address (segment and offset) of the interrupt service procedure.

Figure 10–2 illustrates the interrupt vector table for the 80286 microprocessor. The first five interrupt vectors are identical in all Intel microprocessor family members, from the 8086 to the 80486. Other interrupt vectors exist for the 80286 that are upward compatible to the 80386 and 80486, but not downward compatible to the 8086 or 8088. Intel reserves the first 32 interrupt vectors for their use in various microprocessor family members. The last 224 vectors are available as user interrupt vectors. Each vector is 4 bytes in length and contains the starting address of the interrupt service procedure. The first two bytes of the vector contain the offset address, and the last two bytes contain the segment address.

The following list describes the function of each dedicated interrupt in the 80286 microprocessor:

1. Type 0—Divide Error: occurs whenever the result of a division overflows or whenever an attempt is made to divide by zero.
2. Type 1—Single-Step or Trap: occurs after the execution of each instruction if the trap flag bit (TF) is set. Upon accepting this interrupt, the TF bit is cleared so the interrupt service procedure executes at full speed. More detail is provided about this interrupt later in this section.
3. Type 2—Nonmaskable Hardware Interrupt: a result of placing a logic 1 on the NMI input pin to the 80286 microprocessor. This input is nonmaskable, which means that it cannot be disabled.
4. Type 3—One-Byte Interrupt: is a special 1-byte instruction (INT 3) that uses this vector to access its interrupt service procedure. The INT 3 instruction is often used to store a breakpoint in a program for debugging.
5. Type 4—Overflow: is a special vector used with the INTO instruction. The INTO instruction interrupts the program if an overflow condition exists, as reflected by the overflow flag (OF).
6. Type 5—BOUND: is an instruction that compares a register with boundaries stored in the memory. If the contents of the register are greater than or equal to the first word in memory and less than or equal to the second word, no interrupt occurs because the contents of the register are within bounds. If the contents of the register are out of bounds, a type-5 interrupt ensues.
7. Type 6—Invalid Opcode: occurs whenever an undefined opcode is encountered in a program.
8. Type 7—Coprocessor Not Available: occurs when a coprocessor is not found in the system as dictated by the machine status word (MSW) coprocessor control bits. If an ESC or WAIT instruction executes and the coprocessor is not found, a type-7 exception or interrupt occurs.
9. Type 8—Double Fault: is activated whenever two separate interrupts occur during the same instruction.
10. Type 9—Coprocessor Segment Overrun: occurs if the ESC instruction (coprocessor opcode) memory operand extends beyond offset address FFFFH.

FIGURE 10–2 (a) The interrupt vector table for the 80286 microprocessor. (b) The contents of an interrupt vector.

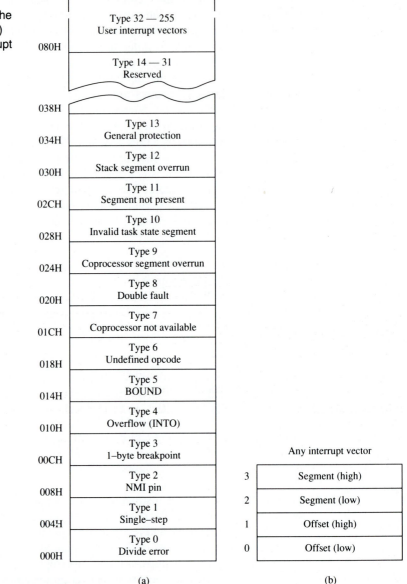

	Type 32 — 255 User interrupt vectors
080H	
	Type 14 — 31 Reserved
038H	
	Type 13 General protection
034H	
	Type 12 Stack segment overrun
030H	
	Type 11 Segment not present
02CH	
	Type 10 Invalid task state segment
028H	
	Type 9 Coprocessor segment overrun
024H	
	Type 8 Double fault
020H	
	Type 7 Coprocessor not available
01CH	
	Type 6 Undefined opcode
018H	
	Type 5 BOUND
014H	
	Type 4 Overflow (INTO)
010H	
	Type 3 1–byte breakpoint
00CH	
	Type 2 NMI pin
008H	
	Type 1 Single–step
004H	
	Type 0 Divide error
000H	

(a)

Any interrupt vector

3	Segment (high)
2	Segment (low)
1	Offset (high)
0	Offset (low)

(b)

11. Type 10—Invalid Task State Segment: occurs if the TSS is invalid because the segment limit field is not 002BH or higher. In most cases this condition is caused because the TSS is not initialized.

12. Type 11—Segment not Present: interrupts occur when the P bit (P = 0) in a descriptor indicates that the segment is not present or not valid.

13. Type 12—Stack Segment Overrun: occurs if the stack segment is not present (P = 0) or if the limit of the stack segment is exceeded.

14. Type 13—General Protection: occurs for most protection violation in the 80286 protected-mode system. A list of these protection violations follows:
    a. descriptor table limit exceeded
    b. privilege rules violated
    c. invalid descriptor segment type loaded
    d. write to code segment that is protected
    e. read from execute-only code segment
    f. write to read-only data segment
    g. segment limit exceeded
    h. CPL ≠ 0 when executing CTS, HLT, LGDT, LIDT, LLDT, LMSW, or LTR
    i. CPL > IOPL when executing CLI, IN, INS, LOCK, OUT, OUTS, and STI

Interrupt Instructions: BOUND, INTO, INT, INT 3, and IRET

Of the five software interrupt instructions available to the 80286 microprocessor, INT and INT 3 are very similar, BOUND and INTO are conditional, and IRET is a special interrupt return instruction.

The BOUND instruction, which has two operands, compares a register with two words of memory data. For example, if the instruction BOUND AX,DATA is executed, AX is compared with the contents of DATA and DATA+1 and also with DATA+2 and DATA+3. If AX is less than the contents of DATA and DATA+1, a type-5 interrupt occurs. If AX is greater than DATA+2 and DATA+3, a type-5 interrupt occurs. If AX is within the bounds of these two memory words, no interrupt occurs.

The INTO instruction checks the overflow flag (OF). If OF = 1, the INTO instruction calls the procedure whose address is stored in interrupt vector type number 4. If OF = 0, then the INTO instruction performs a NOP and the next sequential instruction in the program executes.

The INT *n* instruction calls the interrupt service procedure that begins at the address represented in vector number *n*. For example, an INT 80H or INT 128 calls the interrupt service procedure whose address is stored in vector type number 80H (000200H–000203H). To determine the vector address, just multiply the vector type number (*n*) by 4. This gives the beginning address of the 4-byte-long interrupt vector. For example, an INT 5 = 4 × 5 or 20 (14H). The vector for INT 5 begins at address 000014H and continues to 000017H. Each INT instruction is stored in two bytes of memory, with the first byte containing the opcode and the second the interrupt-type number. The only exception to this is the INT 3 instruction, a 1-byte instruction. The INT 3 instruction is often used as a breakpoint interrupt because it is easy to insert a 1-byte instruction into a program. Break points are often used to debug faulty software.

The IRET instruction is a special return instruction used to return for both software and hardware interrupts. The IRET instruction is much like a normal far RET because it retrieves the return address from the stack. It is unlike the normal return because it also retrieves a copy of the flag register from the stack. An IRET instruction removes six bytes from the stack, two for the IP, two for the CS, and two for the flags.

The Operation of an Interrupt

When the 80286 completes executing the current instruction, it determines whether an interrupt is active by checking (1) instruction executions, (2) single-step, (3) NMI, (4) coprocessor segment overrun, (5) INTR, and (6) INT instruction in the order presented. If one or more of these interrupt conditions are present, the following sequence of events occurs:

1. The contents of the flag register are pushed onto the stack.
2. Both the interrupt (IF) and trap (TF) are cleared. This disables the INTR pin and also the trap or single-step feature.
3. The contents of the code segment register (CS) are pushed onto the stack.
4. The contents of the instruction pointer (IP) are pushed onto the stack.
5. The interrupt vector contents are fetched and placed into both IP and CS so the next instruction executes at the interrupt service procedure addressed by the vector.

Whenever an interrupt is accepted, the microprocessor stacks the contents of the flag register, CS and IP; clears both IF and TF; and jumps to the procedure addressed by the interrupt vector. After the flags are pushed onto the stack, IF and TF are cleared. These flags are retuned to the state prior to the interrupt, when the IRET instruction is encountered at the end of the interrupt service procedure. Therefore, if interrupts were enabled prior to the interrupt service procedure, they are automatically reenabled by the IRET instruction at the end of the procedure.

The return address (in CS and IP) is pushed onto the stack during the interrupt. Sometimes the return address points to the next instruction in the program and sometimes it points to the instruction or point in the program where the interrupt occurred. Interrupt-type numbers 0, 5, 6, 7, 8, 10, 11, 12, and 13 push a return address that points to the offending instruction instead of the next instruction in the program. This allows the interrupt service procedure to possibly retry the instruction in certain error cases.

Some of the protected mode interrupts (types 8, 10, 11, 12, and 13) place an error code on the stack following the return address. The error code identifies the selector that caused the interrupt. In cases where no selector is involved, the error code is a 0.

Interrupt Flag Bits

The interrupt flag (IF) and the trap flag (TF) are both cleared after the contents of the flag register are stacked during an interrupt. Figure 10–3 illustrates the contents of the flag register and the location of IF and TF. When the IF bit is set, it allows the INTR pin to cause an interrupt; when the IF bit is cleared, it prevents the INTR pin from causing an interrupt. When TF = 1, it causes a trap interrupt (type number 1)

FIGURE 10–3 The 80286 flag register. (Courtesy of Intel Corporation)

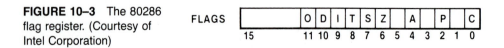

to occur after each instruction executes. This is why we often call trap a single-step. When TF = 0, normal program execution occurs.

The interrupt flag is set and cleared by the STI and CLI instructions, respectively. There are no special instructions that set or clear the trap flag. Example 10–1 shows an interrupt service procedure that turns tracing on by setting the trap flag bit on the stack from inside the procedure. Example 10–2 shows an interrupt service procedure that turns tracing off by clearing the trap flag on the stack from within the procedure.

EXAMPLE 10–1

```
                  ;Procedure that sets TF to enable trap
                  ;
0000              TRON    PROC    FAR

0000 50                   PUSH    AX              ;save registers
0001 55                   PUSH    BP

0002 8B EC                MOV     BP,SP           ;get SP
0004 8B 46 08             MOV     AX,[BP+8]       ;get flags
0007 80 CC 01             OR      AH,1            ;set TF
000A 89 46 08             MOV     [BP+8],AX       ;save flags

000D 5D                   POP     BP              ;restore registers
000E 58                   POP     AX
000F CF                   IRET

0010              TRON    ENDP
```

EXAMPLE 10–2

```
                  ;Procedure that clears TF to disable trap
                  ;
0010              TROFF   PROC    FAR

0010 50                   PUSH    AX              ;save registers
0011 55                   PUSH    BP

0012 8B EC                MOV     BP,SP           ;get SP
0014 8B 46 08             MOV     AX,[BP+8]       ;get flags
0017 80 E4 FE             AND     AH,0FEH         ;clear TF
001A 89 46 08             MOV     [BP+8],AX       ;save flags

001D 5D                   POP     BP              ;restore registers
001E 58                   POP     AX
001F CF                   IRET

0020              TROFF   ENDP
```

In both examples, the flag register is retrieved from the stack by using the BP register, which by default addresses the stack segment. After the flags are retrieved, the TF bit is either set (TRON) or clears (TROFF) before returning from the interrupt service procedure. The IRET instruction restores the flag register with the new state of the trap flag.

Trace Procedure.   Assuming that TRON is accessed by an INT 40H instruction and TROFF is accessed by an INT 41H instruction, Example 10–3 traces through a program immediately following the INT 40H instruction. The interrupt service procedure illustrated in Example 10–3, responds to interrupt type number 1 or a trap interrupt. Each time that this occurs—after each instruction executes following INT 40H—the TRACE procedure displays the contents of all the 80286 registers in the CRT screen. This display provides a register trace of all the instructions between the INT 40H (TRON) and INT 41H (TROFF).

EXAMPLE 10–3

```
                    ;Procedure that displays all the registers and their contents
                    ;on the video screen in response to a trap interrupt.
                    ;
0000                TRACE   PROC    FAR

0000 50                     PUSH    AX                  ;save registers
0001 55                     PUSH    BP
0002 53                     PUSH    BX

0003 BB 0054 R              MOV     BX,OFFSET NAMES     ;address register names

                    ;display registers

0006 E8 009A R              CALL    CRLF                ;get new display line
0009 E8 00A9 R              CALL    DISP                ;display AX
000C 8B C3                  MOV     AX,BX
000E E8 00A9 R              CALL    DISP                ;display BX
0011 8B C1                  MOV     AX,CX
0013 E8 00A9 R              CALL    DISP                ;display CX
0016 8B C2                  MOV     AX,DX
0018 E8 00A9 R              CALL    DISP                ;display DX
001B 8B C4                  MOV     AX,SP
001D 05 000C                ADD     AX,12
0020 E8 00A9 R              CALL    DISP                ;display SP
0023 8B C5                  MOV     AX,BP
0025 E8 00A9 R              CALL    DISP                ;display BP
0028 8B C6                  MOV     AX,SI
002A E8 00A9 R              CALL    DISP                ;display SI
002D 8B EC                  MOV     BP,SP               ;address stack with BP
002F 8B 46 06               MOV     AX,[BP+6]
0032 E8 00A9 R              CALL    DISP                ;display IP
0035 8B 46 0A               MOV     AX,[BP+10]
0038 E8 00A9 R              CALL    DISP                ;display flags
003B 8B 46 08               MOV     AX,[BP+8]
003E E8 00A9 R              CALL    DISP                ;display CS
0041 8C D8                  MOV     AX,DS
```

```
0043  E8 00A9 R              CALL    DISP          ;display DS
0046  8C C0                  MOV     AX,ES
0048  E8 00A9 R              CALL    DISP          ;display ES
004B  8C D0                  MOV     AX,SS
004D  E8 00A9 R              CALL    DISP          ;display SS

0050  5B                     POP     BX            ;restore registers
0051  5D                     POP     BP
0052  58                     POP     AX
0053  CF                     IRET

0054           TRACE         ENDP

0054  41 58 20 3D 20  NAMES  DB      'AX = '
0059  42 58 20 3D 20         DB      'BX = '
005E  43 58 20 3D 20         DB      'CX = '
0063  44 58 20 3D 20         DB      'DX = '
0068  53 50 20 3D 20         DB      'SP = '
006D  42 50 20 3D 20         DB      'BP = '
0072  53 49 20 3D 20         DB      'SI = '
0077  44 49 20 3D 20         DB      'DI = '
007C  49 50 20 3D 20         DB      'IP = '
0081  46 4C 20 3D 20         DB      'FL = '
0086  43 53 20 3D 20         DB      'CS = '
008B  44 53 20 3D 20         DB      'DS = '
0090  45 53 20 3D 20         DB      'ES = '
0095  53 53 20 3D 20         DB      'SS = '

009A           CRLF          PROC    NEAR

009A  50                     PUSH    AX            ;save registers
009B  52                     PUSH    DX

009C  B4 06                  MOV     AH,6
009E  B2 0D                  MOV     DL,13
00A0  CD 21                  INT     21H           ;display CR
00A2  B2 0A                  MOV     DL,10
00A4  CD 21                  INT     21H           ;display LF

00A6  5A                     POP     DX            ;restore registers
00A7  58                     POP     AX
00A8  C3                     RET

00A9           CRLF          ENDP

00A9           DISP          PROC    NEAR

00A9  52                     PUSH    DX            ;save registers
00AA  57                     PUSH    DI
00AB  51                     PUSH    CX
00AC  50                     PUSH    AX
```

```
00AD  B4 06                    MOV       AH,6
00AF  B9 0005                  MOV       CX,5

00B2                 DISP1:

00B2  2E: 8A 17                MOV       DL,CS:[BX]         ;display name
00B5  CD 21                    INT       21H
00B7  43                       INC       BX
00B8  E2 F8                    LOOP      DISP1

00BA  5F                       POP       DI                 ;get numeric value
00BB  57                       PUSH      DI
00BC  B6 04                    MOV       DH,4               ;set count

00BE                 DISP2:

00BE  B9 0004                  MOV       CX,4
00C1  D3 C7                    ROL       DI,CL
00C3  8B C7                    MOV       AX,DI
00C5  B4 06                    MOV       AH,6
00C7  8A D0                    MOV       DL,AL
00C9  80 E2 0F                 AND       DL,15
00CC  80 C2 30                 ADD       DL,30H             ;convert to ASCII
00CF  80 FA 39                 CMP       DL,39H
00D2  76 03                    JBE       DISP3
00D4  80 C2 07                 ADD       DL,7

00D7                 DISP3:

00D7  CD 21                    INT       21H
00D9  FE CE                    DEC       DH
00DB  75 E1                    JNZ       DISP2              ;repeat for 4 digits

00DD  B4 06                    MOV       AH,6
00DF  B2 20                    MOV       DL,' '             ;display space
00E1  CD 21                    INT       21H

00E3  58                       POP       AX                 ;restore registers
00E4  59                       POP       CX
00E5  5F                       POP       DI
00E6  5A                       POP       DX
00E7  C3                       RET

00E8                 DISP    ENDP
```

Storing an Interrupt Vector in the Vector Table

In order to install an interrupt vector—sometimes called a *hook*—the assembler must address absolute memory. Example 10–4 shows how a new vector is added to the interrupt vector table by using the assembler and a DOS function call. Here INT 21H function call number 25H initializes the interrupt vector. Notice that the first thing done in this procedure is the saving of the old interrupt vector number by using DOS INT 21H function call number 35H to read the current vector. Refer to Appendix A for more details on DOS function calls.

EXAMPLE 10–4

```
                        ;Procedure that installs a new interrupt vector at interrupt
                        ;type number 40H
                        ;
0000 0000       OLDOFF  DW       ?
0002 0000       OLDSEG  DW       ?
= 0004          NEWOFF  EQU      THIS WORD
= 0006          NEWSEG  EQU      THIS WORD+2
0004 0200 ---- R NEW    DD       FAR PTR TRON

0008            IN_40H  PROC     NEAR

0008 06                 PUSH     ES                    ;save registers
0009 1E                 PUSH     DS
000A 50                 PUSH     AX
000B 53                 PUSH     BX
000C 52                 PUSH     DX

000D B4 35              MOV      AH,35H                ;get current vector
000F B0 40              MOV      AL,40H                ;type number
0011 CD 21              INT      21H

0013 2E: 89 1E 0000 R   MOV      CS:OLDOFF,BX          ;save old offset
0018 8C C0              MOV      AX,ES
001A 2E: A3 0002 R      MOV      CS:OLDSEG,AX          ;save old segment

001E 2E: 8B 16 0004 R   MOV      DX,NEWOFF             ;get new offset
0023 2E: A1 0006 R      MOV      AX,NEWSEG             ;get new segment
0027 8E D8              MOV      DS,AX

0029 B4 25              MOV      AH,25H                ;install new vector
002B B0 40              MOV      AL,40H                ;type number
002D CD 21              INT      21H

002F 5A                 POP      DX                    ;restore registers
0030 5B                 POP      BX
0031 58                 POP      AX
0032 1F                 POP      DS
0033 07                 POP      ES
0034 C3                 RET

0035            IN_40H  ENDP
```

10–2   HARDWARE INTERRUPTS

The 80286 has two hardware interrupt inputs: nonmaskable interrupt (NMI) and interrupt request (INTR). Whenever the NMI input is activated, a type-2 interrupt occurs because NMI is internally decoded. The INTR input must be externally decoded to select a vector. Any interrupt vector can be chosen for the INTR pin, but we usually use an interrupt type number between 20H and FFH. The $\overline{\text{INTA}}$ signal is also an interrupt pin on the 80286, but it is an output that is used in response to the INTR input to apply a vector type number to the data bus connections D_7–D_0. Figure 10–4 shows the three interrupt connections on the 80286 microprocessor.

NMI

The nonmaskable interrupt (NMI) is an edge-triggered input that requests an interrupt on the positive edge (0-to-1 transition). After a positive edge, the NMI pin must remain a logic 1 until it is recognized by the 80286. Note that before the positive edge is recognized, the NMI pin must be a logic 0 for at least two clocking periods.

The NMI input is often used for parity errors and other major system faults, such as power failures. Power failures are easily detected by monitoring the AC power line and causing an NMI interrupt whenever AC power drops out. In response to this type of interrupt, the microprocessor stores all the internal register in a battery-backed-up memory or an EEPROM. Figure 10–5 shows a power-failure-detection circuit that provides a logic 1 to the NMI input whenever AC power is interrupted.

In this circuit, an optical isolator provides isolation from the AC power line. The output of the isolator is shaped by a Schmitt-trigger inverter that provides a 60-Hz pulse to the trigger input of the 74LS122 retriggerable monostable multivibrator. The values of R and C are chosen so that the 74LS122 has an active pulse width of 33 ms or 2 AC input periods. Because the 74LS122 is retriggerable as long as AC power is applied, the Q output remains triggered at a logic 1 and $\overline{\text{Q}}$ remains a logic 0.

If the AC power fails, the 74LS122 no longer receives trigger pulses from the 74ALS14, which means that Q returns to a logic 0 and $\overline{\text{Q}}$ returns to a logic 1, interrupting the microprocessor through the NMI pin. The interrupt service procedure, not shown here, stores the contents of all internal registers and other data into a battery-backed-up memory. This system assumes that the system power supply has a

FIGURE 10–4 The 80286 interrupt pins.

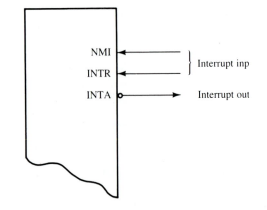

NMI   ⎫
INTR   ⎬ Interrupt inp
INTA   ⎭ Interrupt out

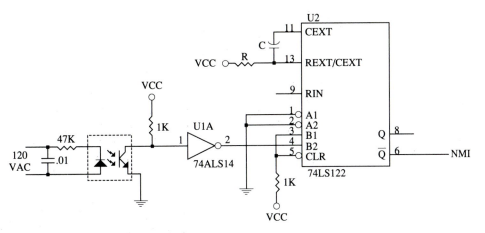

FIGURE 10–5 A power-failure detection circuit.

large enough filter capacitor to provide energy for at least 75 ms after the AC power ceases.

Figure 10–6 shows a circuit that supplies power to a memory after the DC power fails. Here diodes are used to switch supply voltages from the DC power supply to the battery. The diodes used are standard silicon diodes because the power supply to this memory circuit is elevated above +5.0 V to +5.7 V. Also notice that the resistor is used to trickle-charge the battery, which is either NiCAD, Lithium, or a gel cell.

When DC power fails, the battery provides a reduced voltage to the V_{cc} connection on the memory device. Most memory devices will retain data with V_{cc} voltages as low as 1.5 V so the battery voltage does not need to be +5.0 V. The $\overline{WR}$ pin is pulled to V_{cc} during a power outage so no data will be written to the memory.

INTR and $\overline{INTA}$

The interrupt request input (INTR) is level-sensitive, which means that it must be held at a logic 1 level until it is recognized. The INTR pin is set by an external event and cleared inside the interrupt service procedure. This input is automatically disabled

FIGURE 10–6 A battery-backed-up memory system using a NiCAD, lithium, or gel cell.

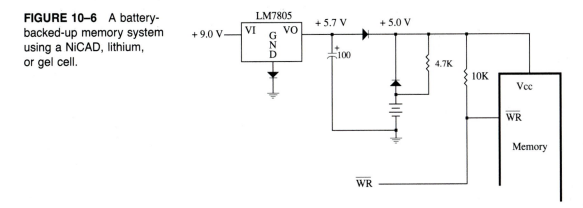

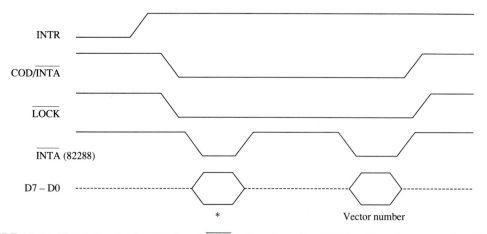

INTR

COD/$\overline{\text{INTA}}$

$\overline{\text{LOCK}}$

$\overline{\text{INTA}}$ (82288)

D7 – D0

      *   Vector number

FIGURE 10–7 The timing for the INTR and $\overline{\text{INTA}}$ pulses from the 82288 system bus controller. *Note:* This portion of the data bus is ignored and usually contains the vector type number.

once it is accepted by the microprocessor and reenabled by the IRET instruction at the end of the interrupt service procedure.

The 80286 responds to the INTR input by pulsing the $\overline{\text{INTA}}$ output in anticipation of receiving an interrupt vector type number on data bus connection D_7–D_0. Figure 10–7 shows the timing diagram for the INTR and $\overline{\text{INTA}}$ pins of the 80286. There are two $\overline{\text{INTA}}$ pulses generated by the 82288 system bus controller (we always use the output from the system bus controller as $\overline{\text{INTA}}$) that are used to insert the vector type number on the data bus.

Figure 10–8 illustrates a simple circuit that applies the interrupt vector types number FFH to the data bus in response to an INTR. Notice that the $\overline{\text{INTA}}$ pin is not

FIGURE 10–8 A simple method for generating interrupt vector type number FFH in response to INTR.

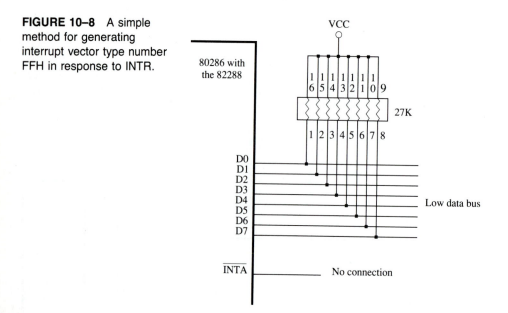

connected in this circuit. Because resistors are used to pull the data bus connections (D_0–D_7) high, the microprocessor automatically sees vector type number FFH in response to the INTR input. This is possibly the least expensive way to implement the INTR pin on the 80286 microprocessor.

Using a Three-State Buffer for $\overline{INTA}$. Figure 10–9 shows how interrupt vector type number 80H is applied to the data bus (D_0–D_7) in response to an INTR. In response to the INTR, the 80286 microprocessor outputs the $\overline{INTA}$ that is used to enable a 74ALS244 three-state octal buffer. The octal buffer applies the interrupt vector type number to the data bus in response to the $\overline{INTA}$ pulse. The vector type number is easily changed with the DIP switches that are shown in this illustration.

Making the INTR Input Edge-Triggered. Often we need an edge-triggered input instead of a level sensitive input. The INTR input can be converted to an edge-triggered

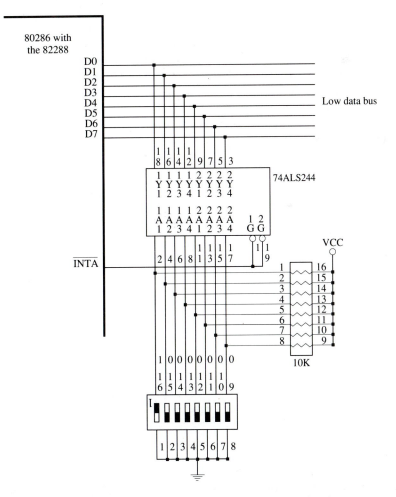

FIGURE 10–9 A circuit that applies any interrupt vector type number in response to $\overline{INTA}$. Here the circuit is applying type number 80H.

input by using a D-type flip-flop as illustrated in Figure 10–10. Here the clock input becomes an edge-triggered interrupt request input, and the clear input is used to clear the request when the $\overline{\text{INTA}}$ signal is output by the microprocessor. Also note that the RESET signal initially clears the flip-flop so no interrupt is requested when the system is first powered.

The 8255A-5 Keyboard Interrupt

The keyboard example presented in the previous chapter provides a simple example of the operation of the INTR input and an interrupt. Figure 10–11 illustrates the interconnection of the 8255A-5 with the 80286 microprocessor and the keyboard. It also shows how a 74ALS244 octal buffer is used to provide the 80286 with interrupt vector type number 40H in response to the keyboard interrupt during the $\overline{\text{INTA}}$ pulse.

The 8255A-5 is decoded at I/O port addresses 0500H, 0502H, 0504H, and 0506H by a PAL16L8 (the program is not illustrated). The 8255A-5 is operated in mode 1 (strobed input mode), so whenever a key is typed, the INTR output (PC$_3$) becomes a logic 1, requesting an interrupt through the INTR pin on the microprocessor. The INTR pin remains high until the ASCII data are read from port A. In other words, every time a key is typed, the 8255A-5 requests a type 40H interrupt through the INTR pin. The $\overline{\text{DAV}}$ signal from the keyboard causes data to be latched into port A and also causes INTR to become a logic 1.

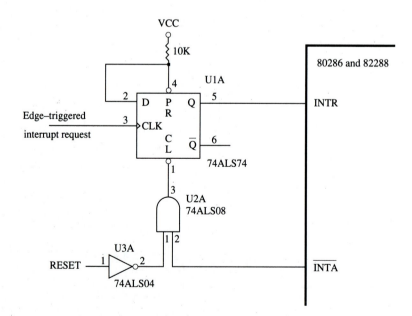

FIGURE 10–10 Converting INTR into an edge-triggered interrupt request input.

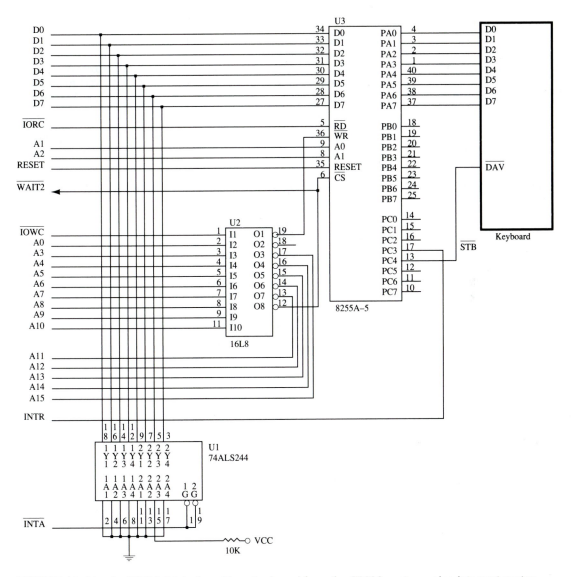

FIGURE 10–11 An 8255A-5 interfaced to a keyboard from the 80286 system using interrupt vector 40H.

Example 10–5 illustrates the interrupt service procedure for the keyboard. It is very important that all registers affected by an interrupt are saved before they are used. In the software required to initialize the 8255A-5 (not shown here), the FIFO is initialized so both pointers are equal, the INTR request pin is enabled through the INTE bit inside the 8255A-5, and the mode of operation is programmed.

EXAMPLE 10–5

```
                                 ;Interrupt service procedure that reads a key
                                 ;from the keyboard.
= 0500                  PORTA    EQU      500H                  ;port A
= 0506                  CNTR     EQU      506H                  ;control register
0000 0100[              FIFO     DB       256 DUP (?)           ;FIFO buffer
        ??
      ]
0100 0000               INP      DW       ?                     ;input pointer
0102 0000               OUTP     DW       ?                     ;output pointer

0104            KEY      PROC     FAR

0104 50                  PUSH     AX                            ;save registers
0105 53                  PUSH     BX
0106 57                  PUSH     DI
0107 52                  PUSH     DX

0108 2E: 8B 1E 0100 R    MOV      BX,INP                        ;address FIFO
010D 2E: 8B 3E 0102 R    MOV      DI,OUTP
0112 FE C3               INC      BL                            ;test for full
0114 3B DF               CMP      BX,DI
0116 74 11               JE       FULL                          ;if full

0118 FE CB               DEC      BL
011A BA 0500             MOV      DX,PORTA
011D EC                  IN       AL,DX                         ;get data
011E 2E: 88 07           MOV      CS:[BX],AL                    ;save data
0121 2E: FE 06 0100 R    INC      BYTE PTR INP
0126 EB 07 90            JMP      DONE

0129            FULL:

0129 B0 08               MOV      AL,8                          ;disable interrupts
012B BA 0506             MOV      DX,CNTR
012E EE                  OUT      DX,AL

012F            DONE:

012F 5A                  POP      DX                            ;restore registers
0130 5F                  POP      DI
0131 5B                  POP      BX
0132 58                  POP      AX
0133 CF                  IRET

0134            KEY      ENDP
```

The procedure is fairly short because the 80286 already knows that keyboard data are available when the procedure is called. Data are input from the keyboard and then stored in the FIFO buffer. Most keyboard interfaces contain a FIFO that is at least 16 bytes in depth. The FIFO in this example is 256 bytes, which is more than adequate for a keyboard interface.

This procedure first checks to see if the FIFO is full. A full condition is indicated when the input point (INP) is one byte below the output pointer (OUTP). If the FIFO is full, the interrupt is disabled with a bit set/reset command to the 8255A-5, and a return from the interrupt occurs. If the FIFO is not full, the data are input from port A, and the input pointer is incremented before a return occurs.

Example 10–6 shows the procedure that removes data from the FIFO. This procedure first determines whether the FIFO is empty by comparing the two pointers. If the pointers are equal, the FIFO is empty, and the software waits at the EMPTY loop where it continuously tests the pointers. The EMPTY loop is interrupted by the keyboard interrupt, which stores data into the FIFO so it is no longer empty. This procedure returns with the character in register AH.

EXAMPLE 10–6

```
                        ;Procedure that reads a key from the FIFO and
                        ;returns with it in AH
                        ;
0104                    READ     PROC     FAR

0104 53                          PUSH     BX               ;save registers
0105 57                          PUSH     DI
0106 52                          PUSH     DX

0107                    EMPTY:

0107 2E: 8B 1E 0100 R            MOV      BX,INP           ;address FIFO
010C 2E: 8B 3E 0102 R            MOV      DI,OUTP
0111 3B DF                       CMP      BX,DI            ;test for empty
0113 74 F2                       JE       EMPTY            ;if empty

0115 2E: 8A 25                   MOV      AH,CS:[DI]       ;get data

0118 B0 09                       MOV      AL,9             ;enable 8255A-5 interrupt
011A BA 0506                     MOV      DX,CNTR
011D EE                          OUT      DX,AL

011E 2E: FE 06 0102 R            INC      BYTE PTR OUTP    ;increment pointer

0123 5A                          POP      DX               ;restore registers
0124 5F                          POP      DI
0125 5B                          POP      BX
0126 CB                          RET

0127                    READ     ENDP
```

10–3   EXPANDING THE INTERRUPT STRUCTURE

This text covers three of the more common methods of expanding the interrupt structure of the 80286 microprocessor. In this section, we explain how, with software and some hardware modification of the circuit of Figure 10–9, it is possible to expand the INTR input so it accepts seven interrupt inputs. We also explain how to "daisy chain" interrupts by software polling. In the next section, we describe a third technique in which up to 63 interrupting inputs can be added by means of the 8259A programmable interrupt controller.

Using the 74ALS244 to Expand Interrupts

The modification shown in Figure 10–12 allows the circuit for Figure 10–9 to accommodate up to seven additional interrupt inputs. The only hardware change is the addition of an 8-input NAND gate, which provides the INTR signal to the microprocessor when any of the $\overline{\text{IR}}$ inputs becomes active.

Operation.   If any of the $\overline{\text{IR}}$ inputs become a logic 0, then the output of the NAND gate goes to a logic 1 and requests an interrupt through the INTR input. Which interrupt vector is fetched during the $\overline{\text{INTA}}$ pulse depends on which interrupt request

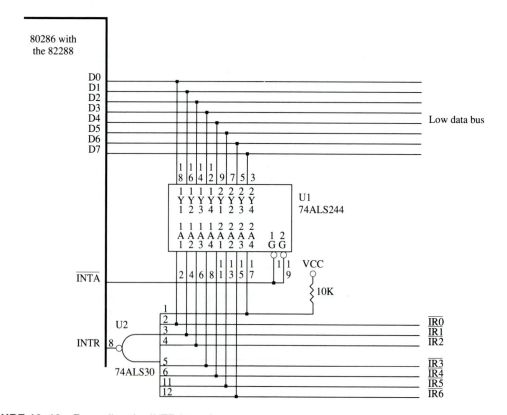

FIGURE 10–12   Expanding the INTR input from one to seven interrupt request lines.

TABLE 10–1 Single interrupt request for Figure 10–12

AD_7	IR_6	IR_5	IR_4	IR_3	IR_2	IR_1	IR_0	Vector
1	1	1	1	1	1	1	0	FEH (254)
1	1	1	1	1	1	0	1	FDH (253)
1	1	1	1	1	0	1	1	FBH (251)
1	1	1	1	0	1	1	1	F7H (247)
1	1	1	0	1	1	1	1	EFH (239)
1	1	0	1	1	1	1	1	DFH (223)
1	0	1	1	1	1	1	1	BFH (191)

line becomes active. Table 10–1 shows the interrupt vectors used by a single interrupt request input.

If two or more interrupt request inputs are simultaneously active, a new interrupt vector is generated. For example, if $\overline{IR_1}$ and $\overline{IR_0}$ are both active, the interrupt vector generated is FCH (252). Priority is resolved at this location. If the $\overline{IR_0}$ input is to have the higher priority, the vector address for $\overline{IR_0}$ is stored at vector location FCH. The entire top shelf of the vector table and its 128 interrupt vectors must be used to accommodate all possible conditions of these seven interrupt request inputs. This seems wasteful, but in many dedicated applications it is a cost-effective approach to interrupt expansion.

Daisy-Chained Interrupt

Expansion by means of a daisy-chained interrupt is in many ways better than using the 74ALS244 interrupt expansion because it requires only one interrupt vector. The task of determining priority is left to the interrupt service procedure. Setting priority for a daisy chain does require additional software execution time, but in general this is a much better approach to expanding the interrupt structure of the 80286 microprocessor.

Figure 10–13 illustrates a set of two 8255A-5 peripheral interfaces with their four INTR outputs daisy chained and connected to the single INTR input of the 80286 microprocessor. If any interrupt output becomes a logic 1, so does the INTR input to the 80286, causing an interrupt.

When a daisy chain is used to request an interrupt it is better to pull the data bus connections (D_0–D_7) high using pullup resistors so interrupt vector FFH is used for the chain. Actually any interrupt vector can be used to respond to a daisy chain. In the circuit, any of the four INTR outputs from the two 8255A-5s will cause the INTR pin on the microprocessor to go high requesting an interrupt.

When the INTR pin on the 80286 does go high with a daisy chain, the hardware gives no direct indication as to which 8255A-5 or which INTR output caused the interrupt. The task of locating which INTR output became active is up to the interrupt service procedure, which must poll the 8255A-5s to determine what caused the interrupt.

Example 10–7 illustrates the interrupt service procedure that responds to the daisy-chain interrupt request. This procedure polls each 8255A-5 and each INTR output to decide which interrupt service procedure to utilize.

FIGURE 10–13 Two 8255A-5 PIAs connected so the INTR outputs are daisy chained to produce an INTR signal for the 80286.

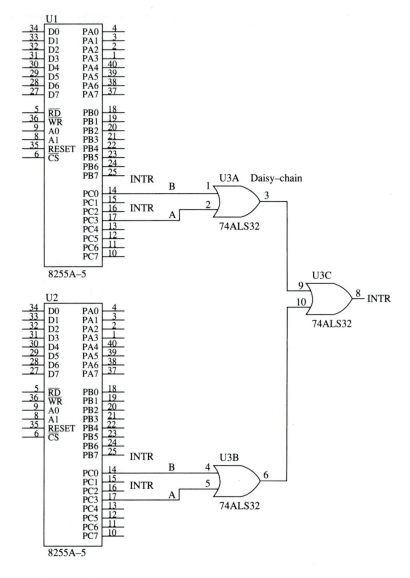

EXAMPLE 10–7

```
                    ;Procedure that services the daisy-chain interrupt
                    ;
= 0504      C1      EQU     504H                    ;first 8255A-5
= 0604      C2      EQU     604H                    ;second 8255A-5
= 0001      MASK1   EQU     1                       ;INTRB
= 0008      MASK2   EQU     8                       ;INTRA

0000        POLL    PROC    FAR

0000 50             PUSH    AX                      ;save registers
0001 52             PUSH    DX
```

```
0002  BA 0504                    MOV     DX,C1              ;address port C
0005  EC                         IN      AL,DX
0006  A8 01                      TEST    AL,MASK1
0008  75 0F                      JNZ     LEVEL_0            ;if INTRB of first 8255A-5

000A  A8 08                      TEST    AL,MASK2
000C  75 13                      JNZ     LEVEL_1            ;if INTRA of first 8255A-5

000E  BA 0604                    MOV     DX,C2              ;address port C
0011  EC                         IN      AL,DX
0012  A8 01                      TEST    AL,MASK1
0014  75 1B                      JNZ     LEVEL_2            ;if INTRB of second 8255A-5

0016  EB 29 90                   JMP     LEVEL_3            ;if INTRA of second 8255A-5

0019            POLL     ENDP
```

10–4   8259A PROGRAMMABLE INTERRUPT CONTROLLER

The 8259A programmable interrupt controller (PIC) adds eight vectored priority encoded interrupts to the 80286 microprocessor. This controller can be expanded without additional hardware to accept up to 64 interrupt request inputs. This expansion requires a master 8259A and eight 8259A slaves.

General Description of the 8259A

Figure 10–14 shows the pinout of the 8259A. The 8259A is easy to connect to the microprocessor because all of its pins are direct connections except the $\overline{CS}$ pin, which must be decoded, and the $\overline{WR}$ pin, which must have an I/O bank write pulse. Following is a description of each pin on the 8259A:

1. D_7–D_0—Bidirectional Data Connections: pins normally connected to either the upper or lower data bus on the 80286 microprocessor.

FIGURE 10–14 The pinout of the 8259A programmable interrupt controller (PIC).

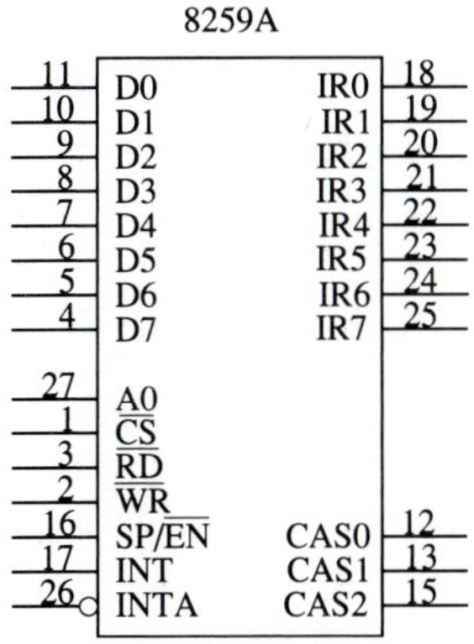

2. IR_7–IR_0—Interrupt Request Inputs: used to request an interrupt and to connect to a slave in a system with multiple 8259As.
3. $\overline{WR}$–Write: an input connected to either the lower or upper write strobe signal.
4. $\overline{RD}$—Read: an input connected to the $\overline{IORC}$ signal.
5. INT—Interrupt: an output connected to the INTR pin on the 80286 from the master, and connected to a master IR pin on a slave.
6. $\overline{INTA}$–Interrupt Acknowledge: an input connected to the $\overline{INTA}$ signal on the 82288 system bus controller. In a system with a master and slaves, only the master $\overline{INTA}$ signal is connected.
7. A_0—Address: an input that selects different command words within the 8259A.
8. $\overline{CS}$–Chip Select: used to enable the 8259A for program and control.
9. SP/$\overline{EN}$—Slave Program/Enable Buffer: a dual-function pin. When the 8259A is in buffered mode, this is an output that controls the data bus transceivers. When the 8259A is not in the buffered mode, this pin programs the device as a master (1) or a slave (0).
10. CAS_2–CAS_0—Cascade Lines: used as outputs from the master to the slaves for cascading multiple 8259As in a system.

Connecting a Single 8259A

Figure 10–15 shows a single 8259A connected to an 80286 system. Here the SP/$\overline{EN}$ pin is pulled high to indicate that it is a master. Also note that the 8259A is decoded at I/O ports 0400H and 0402H by the PAL16L8 (no program shown). Like other peripherals discussed in the prior chapter, the 8259A requires two wait states for it to function properly with the 8-MHz 80286.

Cascading Multiple 8259As

Figure 10–16 shows two 8259As connected to the 80286 microprocessor in a way that is often found in the AT-style computer, which has two 8259As for interrupts. The XT- or PC-style computer uses one 8259A at interrupt vectors 08H through 0FH. The AT-style computer uses interrupt vector 0AH as a cascade input from a second 8259A located at vectors 70H through 77H. Appendix A contains a table that lists the functions of all the interrupt vectors used in the PC-, XT-, and AT-style computers.

This circuit uses vectors 08H–0FH and I/O ports 0300H and 0302H for U_1, the master, and vectors 70H–77H and I/O ports 0304H and 0306H for U_2, the slave. Notice that we also include data bus buffers to illustrate the use of the SP/$\overline{EN}$ pin on the 8259A. These buffers are used only in very large systems that have many devices connected to their data bus connections. In practice, we seldom find these buffers.

Programming the 8259A

The 8259A is programmed by initialization and operation command words. *Initialization command words* (ICWs) are programmed before the 8259A is able to function in the system and dictate the basic operation of the 8259A. *Operation command words* (OCWs) are programmed during the normal course of operation and allow the 8259A to function properly.

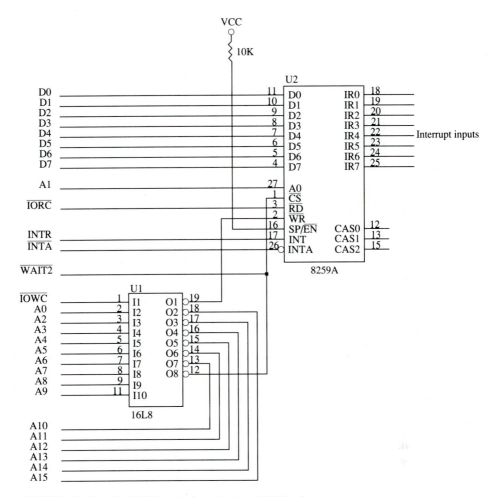

FIGURE 10–15   An 8295A interfaced to the 80286 microprocessor.

Initialization Command Words.   There are four initialization command words (ICWs) for the 8259A that are selected when the A_0 pin is a logic 1. When the 8259A is first powered up, it must be sent ICW_1, ICW_2, and ICW_4. If the 8259A is programmed in cascade mode by ICW_1, then we also must program ICW_3. So if a single 8259A is used in a system, ICW_1, ICW_2, and ICW_4 must be programmed. If cascade mode is used in a system, then all four ICWs must be programmed. Refer to Figure 10–17 for the format of all four ICWs. The following is a description of each ICW:

1. ICW_1 — programs the basic operation of the 8259A. To program this ICW for 80286 operation, we place a logic 1 in bit IC_4. Bits AD_1, A_7, A_6, and A_5 are don't cares for 80286 operation and only apply to the 8269A when used with an 8-bit 8085 microprocessor. This ICW selects single or cascade operation by programming the SNGL bit. If cascade operation is selected, we must also program ICW_3. The LTIM bit determines whether the interrupt request inputs are positive-edge triggered or level triggered.

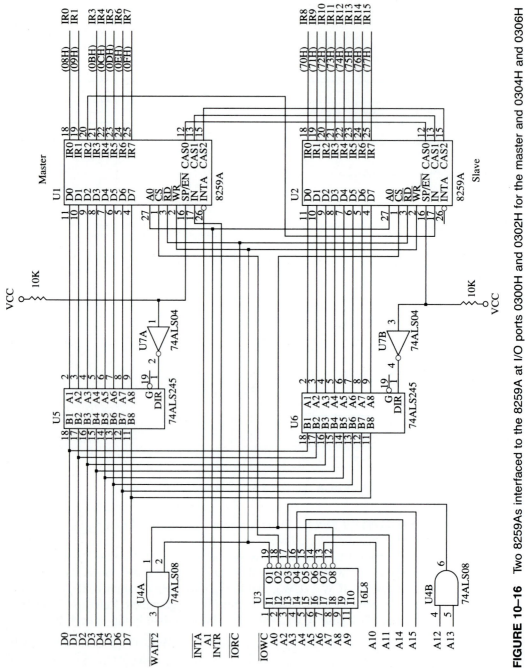

FIGURE 10–16 Two 8259As interfaced to the 8259A at I/O ports 0300H and 0302H for the master and 0304H and 0306H for the slave.

430

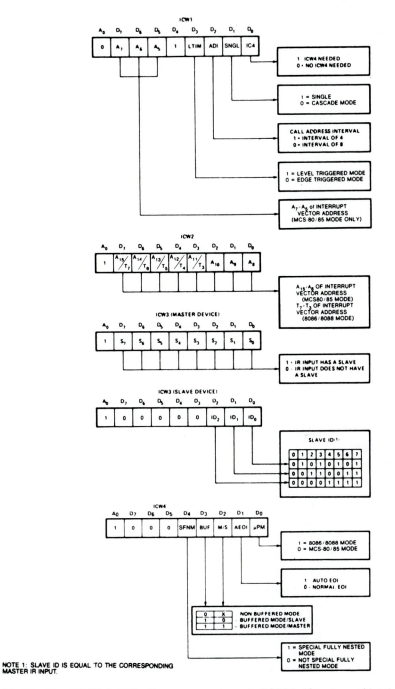

FIGURE 10–17 The 8259A initialization command words (ICWs). (Courtesy of Intel Corporation)

2. ICW_2—selects the vector number used with the interrupt request inputs. For example, if we decide to program the 8259A so it functions at vector locations 08H–0FH, we place a 08H into this command word. Likewise, if we decide to program the 8259A for vectors 70H–77H, we place a 70H in this ICW.
3. ICW3—only used when ICW_1 indicates that the system is operated in cascade mode. This ICW indicates where the slave is connected to the master. For example, in Figure 10–16 we connected a slave to IR_2. To program ICW_3 for this connection, in both master and slave, we place a 04H in ICW_3. Suppose we have two slaves connected to a master using IR_0 and IR_1. The master is programmed with an ICW_3 of 03H, and one slave is programmed with an ICW_3 of 01H and the other with an ICW_3 of 02H.
4. ICW4—programmed for use with the 80286 microprocessor. This ICW is not programmed in a system that functions with the 8085 microprocessor. The rightmost bit must be a logic 1 to select operation with the 80286 microprocessor, and the remaining bits are programmed as follows:
   a. SFNM—selects the special fully nested mode of operation for the 8259A if a logic 1 is placed in this bit. This allows the highest priority interrupt request from a slave to be recognized by the master while it is processing another interrupt from a slave. Normally only one interrupt request is processed at a time and others are ignored until the process is complete.
   b. BUF and M/S—buffer and master slave are used together to select buffered operation or nonbuffered operation for the 8259A as a master or a slave.
   c. AEOI—selects automatic or normal end of interrupt (discussed more fully under operation command words). The EOI commands of OCW_2 are only used if the AEOI mode is not selected by ICW_4. If AEOI is selected, the interrupt automatically resets the interrupt request bit and does not modify priority. This is the preferred mode of operation for the 8259A, and it reduces the length of the interrupt service procedure.

Operation Command Words.   The operation command words (OCWs) are used to direct the operation of the 8259A once it is programmed with the ICWs. The OCWs are selected when the A_0 pin is at a logic 0 level, except for OCW_1, which is selected when A_0 is a logic 1. Figure 10–18 lists the binary bit patterns for all three operation command words of the 8259A. Following is a list describing the function of each OCW:

1. OCW_1—used to set and read the interrupt mask register. When a mask bit is set, it will *turn off* (mask) the corresponding interrupt input. The mask register is read when OCW_1 is read. Because the state of the mask bits is unknown when the 8259A is first initialized, OCW_1 must be programmed after programming the ICWs upon initialization.
2. OCW_2—programmed only when the AEOI mode is not selected from the 8259A. In this case, this OCW selects how the 8259A responds to an interrupt. The modes are listed as follows:
   a. Nonspecific End-of-Interrupt—a command sent by the interrupt service procedure to signal the end of the interrupt. The 8259A automatically determines which interrupt level was active and resets the correct bit of the interrupt status

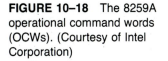

FIGURE 10–18 The 8259A operational command words (OCWs). (Courtesy of Intel Corporation)

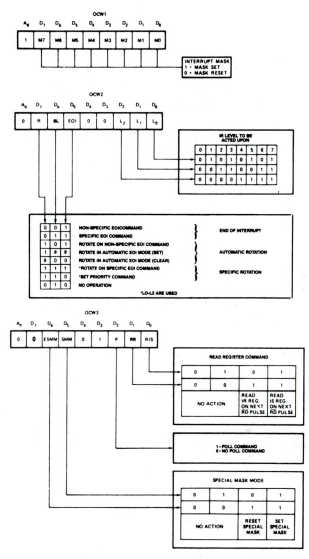

register. Resetting the status bit allows the interrupt to take action again or a lower priority interrupt to take effect.

b. Specific End-of-Interrupt—a command that allows a specific interrupt request to be reset. The exact position is determined with bits L_2–L_0 of OCW_2.

c. Rotate-on-Nonspecific EOI—a command that functions exactly like the non-specific end-of-interrupt command, except it rotates interrupt priorities after resetting the interrupt status register bit. The level reset by this command becomes the lowest priority interrupt. For example, if IR_4 was just serviced by this command, it becomes the lowest priority interrupt input and IR_5 becomes the highest priority.

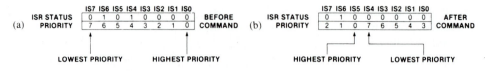

FIGURE 10–19 The 8259A in-service register (ISR). (a) Before IR$_4$ is accepted, and (b) after IR$_4$ is accepted. (Courtesy of Intel Corporation)

    d. Rotate-on-Automatic EOI—a command that selects automatic EOI with rotating priority. This command must only be sent to the 8259A once if this mode is desired. If this mode must be turned off, use the clear command.

    e. Rotate-on-Specific EOI—functions as the specific EOI, except that it selects rotating priority.

    f. Set priority—allows the programmer to set the lowest priority interrupt input using the L_2–L_0 bits.

3. OCW$_3$—selects the register to be read, the operation of the special mask register, and the poll command. If polling is selected, the P bit must be set and then output to the 8259A. The next read operation will read the poll word. The rightmost three bits of the poll word indicate the active interrupt request with the highest priority. The leftmost bit indicates whether there is an interrupt, and must be checked to determine whether the rightmost three bits contain valid information.

Status Register. Three status registers are readable in the 8259A: interrupt request register (IRR), in-service register (ISR), and interrupt mask register (IMR). (Refer to Figure 10–19 for all three status registers.) The IRR is an 8-bit register that indicates which interrupt request inputs are active. The ISR is an 8-bit register that contains the level of the interrupt being serviced. The IMR is an 8-bit register that contains the level of the interrupt being serviced. The IMR is an 8-bit register that holds the interrupt mask bits and indicates which interrupts are masked off.

    Both the IRR and ISR are read by programming OCW$_3$, and IMR is read through OCW$_2$. To read the IMR, $A_0 = 1$, and to read either IRR or ISR, $A_0 = 0$. Bit positions D_0 and D_1 of OCW$_3$ select which register (IRR or ISR) is read when $A_0 = 0$.

8259A Programming Example

Figure 10–20 illustrates the 8259A programmable interrupt controller connected to an 8251A programmable communications controller. In this circuit, three interrupt output pins from the 8251A (TxRDY, RxRDY, and SY/BR) are connected to the PICs interrupt request inputs IR$_0$, IR$_1$, and IR$_2$. An IR$_0$ occurs whenever the transmitter is ready to send another character. When the receiver has received a character for the 80286, IR$_1$ is active because of RxRDY. The IR$_2$ input is used for break detection. Notice that the 8251A is decoded at 8-bit I/O ports 40H and 42H, and the 8259A is decoded at 8-bit I/O ports 44H and 46H. Because A$_5$ is not connected to the decoder (partially decoded ports), the 8251A also functions at ports 60H and 62H and the 8259A functions at ports 64H and 66H. Both devices are interfaced to the lower data bus.

Initialization Software. The first portion of the software for this system must program both the 8251A and the 8259A and then enable the INTR pin on the 80286 so

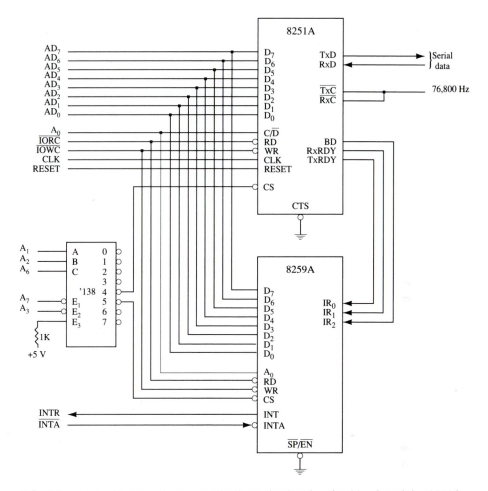

FIGURE 10–20 An example communications circuit using the 8251A and the 8259A.

interrupts can take effect. Example 10–8 lists the software required to program both
devices and enable INTR.

EXAMPLE 10–8

```
                    ;Initialization dialog for the 8251A and the 8259A
                    ;
= 0042              PCC_C    EQU      42H              ;8251A control register
= 0044              PIC_C1   EQU      44H              ;8259A control A0 = 0
= 0046              PIC_C2   EQU      46H              ;8259A control A0 = 1
= 0040              FORTY    EQU      40H              ;reset command for 8251A
= 007B              INST1    EQU      7BH              ;8251A mode word
= 0015              INST2    EQU      15H              ;8251A command word
= 001B              ICW1     EQU      1BH              ;8259A ICW1
= 0080              ICW2     EQU      80H              ;8259A ICW2
```

```
= 0003                ICW4    EQU    03H                    ;8259A ICW4
= 00F9                OCW1    EQU    0F9H                   ;8259A OCW1

0000                  START   PROC   FAR

                      ;set up the 8251A for 7 data bits, even parity, one stop bit,
                      ;and a clock divider of 64.
                      ;
                      ;program 8251A
                      ;
0000  32 C0                   XOR    AL,AL                  ;reset 8251A
0002  E6 42                   OUT    PCC_C,AL
0004  E6 42                   OUT    PCC_C,AL
0006  E6 42                   OUT    PCC_C,AL
0008  B0 40                   MOV    AL,FORTY
000A  E6 42                   OUT    PCC_C,AL

000C  B0 7B                   MOV    AL,INST1               ;program 8251A mode
000E  E6 42                   OUT    PCC_C,AL
0010  B0 15                   MOV    AL,INST2               ;program 8251A command
0012  E6 42                   OUT    PCC_C,AL

                      ;program 8259A

0014  B0 1B                   MOV    AL,ICW1                ;program ICW1
0016  E6 44                   OUT    PIC_C1,AL
0018  B0 80                   MOV    AL,ICW2                ;program ICW2
001A  E6 46                   OUT    PIC_C2,AL
001C  B0 03                   MOV    AL,ICW4                ;program ICW4
001E  E6 46                   OUT    PIC_C2,AL

0020  B0 F9                   MOV    AL,OCW1                ;program OCW1
0022  E6 46                   OUT    PIC_C2,AL

0024  FB                      STI                           ;enable INTR
0025  CB                      RET

0026                  START   ENDP
```

The first portion of the procedure (START) resets the 8251A and programs the mode and command words. The mode selects seven data bits, even parity, one stop bit, and a clock divider of 64 that causes the transmitter and receiver to transfer serial data at 1200 Bd. The command enables both the transmitter and receiver.

The second part of the procedure programs the 8259A with its three ICWs and its one OCW. The 8259A is set up so it functions at interrupt vectors 80H–87H and operates with automatic EOI. The ICW enables the break detection interrupt and the receiver interrupt, but not the transmitter interrupt. The transmitter interrupt is only enabled when there are data to transmit. The transmitter is periodically enabled and disabled during normal operation by reading OCW_1, modifying the mask bits, and then rewriting OCW_1.

The last thing that the START procedure does is enable the INTR pin so a receiver or break detection interrupt can take effect immediately.

Receiving Data from the 8251A. The data received by the 8251A are stored in a FIFO memory until the software in the main program can use them. The FIFO memory used for received data is 16K bytes in length, so many characters can easily be stored and received before any intervention from the 80286 is required to empty the receiver FIFO. The receiver FIFO is stored in the extra segment so string instructions, using the DI register, can be used to access it.

Receiving data from the 8251A requires two procedures: one reads the data register of the 8251A each time that the RxRDY pin requests an interrupt and stores it into the FIFO, and the other reads data from the FIFO from the main program.

Example 10–9 lists the procedure used to read data from the FIFO from the main program. This procedure assumes that the pointers (IIN and IOUT) are initialized in the initialization dialog for the system (not shown). The READ procedure returns with AL containing a character read from the FIFO. If the FIFO is empty, the procedure returns with the character FEH in AL. This means that FEH is not allowed as a character at the receiver.

EXAMPLE 10–9

```
                        ;Main procedure to read a character from the FIFO
                        ;AL is the characater upon return or FEH if FIFO is empty.
                        ;
= 0046                  OCW1      EQU     46H             ;address of OCW1
= 00FD                  MASK1     EQU     0FDH

0000                    READ      PROC    FAR

0000 53                           PUSH    BX              ;save registers
0001 57                           PUSH    DI

                        ;test for empty FIFO

0002 26: 8B 3E 4002 R             MOV     DI,IOUT         ;get output pointer
0007 26: 8B 1E 4000 R             MOV     BX,IIN          ;get input pointer

000C 3B DF                        CMP     BX,DI           ;test for empty
000E B0 FE                        MOV     AL,0FEH         ;indicate empty
0010 74 16                        JE      DONE            ;if empty

                        ;get character from FIFO

0012 26: 8A 05                    MOV     AL,ES:[DI]      ;get data

                        ;modify and save output pointer
```

```
0015 47                              INC     DI                              ;adjust pointer
0016 81 FF 4000 R                    CMP     DI,OFFSET FIFO+16*1024
001A 26: 89 3E 4002 R               MOV     IOUT,DI
001F 76 07                           JBE     DONE                            ;if within bounds
0021 26: C7 06 4002 R 0000 R        MOV     IOUT,OFFSET FIFO                ;point to FIFO start

                    ;enable RxRDY interrupt

0028                    DONE:

0028 50                              PUSH    AX
0029 E4 46                           IN      AL,OCW1
002B 24 FD                           AND     AL,MASK1
002D E6 46                           OUT     OCW1,AL

002F 58                              POP     AX                              ;restore registers
0030 5F                              POP     DI
0031 5B                              POP     BX
0032 CB                              RET

0033                    READ    ENDP
```

Example 10–10 lists the RxRDY interrupt service procedure that is called each time the 8251A receives a character for the 80286. In this example, this interrupt uses vector type number 81H, which must contain the address of the RxRDY interrupt service procedure. Each time this interrupt occurs, the RxRDY procedure reads a character from the 8251A and stores it in the FIFO. If the FIFO is full, the IR_1 input to the 8259A is disabled. This may result in lost data, but at least it will not cause the interrupt to overrun valid data already stored in the FIFO. Any error conditions detected by the 8251A store a ? (3FH) in the FIFO.

EXAMPLE 10–10

```
                    ;Interrupt service procedure for RxRDY (IR1)
                    ;
= 0040              DATA    EQU     40H                     ;8251A data port
= 0046              OCW1    EQU     46H                     ;8259A OCW1 port
= 0002              MASK2   EQU     02H                     ;turn off IR1 mask
= 0042              PCC_C   EQU     42H                     ;8251A command port
= 0038              MASK3   EQU     38H                     ;8251A error mask

0000                RXRDY   PROC    FAR

0000 50                     PUSH    AX                      ;save registers
0001 53                     PUSH    BX
0002 57                     PUSH    DI
0003 56                     PUSH    SI
0004 26: 8B 1E 4002 R      MOV     BX,IOUT                 ;load output pointer
0009 26: 8B 36 4000 R      MOV     SI,IIN                  ;load input pointer
```

```
                        ;is FIFO full?

000E  8B FE                         MOV     DI,SI
0010  46                            INC     SI
0011  81 FE 4000 R                  CMP     SI,OFFSET FIFO+16*1024
0015  76 03                         JBE     NEXT
0017  BE 0000 R                     MOV     SI,OFFSET FIFO

001A                   NEXT:

001A  3B DE                         CMP     BX,SI
001C  74 20                         JE      FULL

                        ;test for 8251A errors

001E  E4 42                         IN      AL,PCC_C        ;get 8251A status register
0020  24 38                         AND     AL,MASK3
0022  74 0F                         JZ      NEXT1           ;if no errors
0024  B0 10                         MOV     AL,10H          ;reset errors
0026  E6 42                         OUT     PCC_C,AL
0028  B0 3F                         MOV     AL,'?'
002A  AA                            STOSB
002B  26: 89 36 4000 R              MOV     IIN,SI
0030  EB 12 90                      JMP     DONE            ;if an error

                        ;read character

0033                   NEXT1:

0033  E4 40                         IN      AL,DATA         ;get 8251A data
0035  AA                            STOSB
0036  26: 89 36 4000 R              MOV     IIN,SI
003B  EB 07 90                      JMP     DONE

                        ;if full

003E                   FULL:

003E  E4 46                         IN      AL,OCW1         ;disable IR1
0040  0C 02                         OR      AL,MASK2
0042  E6 46                         OUT     OCW1,AL

0044                   DONE:

0044  5E                            POP     SI              ;restore registers
0045  5F                            POP     DI
0046  5B                            POP     BX
0047  58                            POP     AX
0048  CF                            IRET

0049                   RXRDY    ENDP
```

Transmitting Data to the 8251A.   Data are transmitted to the 8251A in much the same manner as they are received, except the interrupt service procedure removes transmit data from the second 16K-byte FIFO.

Example 10–11 lists the procedure that fills the output FIFO. It is similar to the procedure listed in Example 10–9, except it determines whether the FIFO is full instead of empty.

EXAMPLE 10–11

```
                    ;Procedure that places data into the output FIFO for
                    ;transmission by the transmitter interrupt service procedure.
                    ;AL = character to be transmitted.
                    ;
= 0046              OCW1    EQU     46H                 ;8259A OCW1 port
= 00FE              MASK4   EQU     0FEH                ;turn IR0 on

0000                TRANS   PROC    FAR

0000 53                     PUSH    BX                  ;save registers
0001 57                     PUSH    DI
0002 56                     PUSH    SI

                    ;check if FIFO is full

0003 26: 8B 36 8004 R       MOV     SI,OIN              ;get input pointer
0008 26: 8B 1E 8006 R       MOV     BX,OOUT             ;get output pointer
000D 8B FE                  MOV     DI,SI
000F 46                     INC     SI
0010 81 FE 8004 R           CMP     SI,OFFSET OFIFO+16*1024
0014 76 03                  JBE     NEXT
0016 BE 4004 R              MOV     SI,OFFSET OFIFO

0019                NEXT:

0019 3B DE                  CMP     BX,SI
001B 74 06                  JE      DONE                ;if full
001D AA                     STOSB
001E 26: 89 36 8004 R       MOV     OIN,SI

                    DONE:

0023 E4 46                  IN      AL,OCW1             ;enable transmitter interrupt
0025 24 FE                  AND     AL,MASK4
0027 E6 46                  OUT     OCW1,AL

0029 5E                     POP     SI                  ;restore registers
002A 5F                     POP     DI
002B 5B                     POP     BX
002C CB                     RET

002D                TRANS   ENDP
```

Example 10–12 lists the interrupt service subroutine for the 8251A transmitter, TxRDY, using interrupt vector number 80H. This procedure is similar to the RxRDY procedure of Example 10–10, except it determines whether the FIFO is empty rather than full. Note that we do not include an interrupt service procedure for the break interrupt.

EXAMPLE 10–12

```
                      ;Interrupt service procedure for the 8251A transmitter
                      ;
= 0040                DATA     EQU      40H              ;8251A data port
= 0001                MASK5    EQU      01H              ;turn IR0 off

002D                  TXRDY    PROC     FAR

002D 50                        PUSH     AX               ;save registers
002E 53                        PUSH     BX
002F 57                        PUSH     DI
0030 26: 8B 1E 8004 R          MOV      BX,OIN           ;load input pointer
0035 26: 8B 3E 8006 R          MOV      DI,OOUT          ;load output pointer

              ;is FIFO empty?

003A 3B DF                     CMP      BX,DI
003C 74 17                     JE       EMPTY            ;if empty

              ;write character

003E 26: 8A 05                 MOV      AL,ES:[DI]
0041 E6 40                     OUT      DATA,AL
0043 47                        INC      DI
0044 81 FF 8004 R              CMP      DI,OFFSET OFIFO+16*1024
0048 76 03                     JBE      NEXT1
004A BF 4004 R                 MOV      DI,OFFSET OFIFO

004D                  NEXT1:

004D 26: 89 3E 8006 R          MOV      OOUT,DI
0052 EB 07 90                  JMP      DONES

0055                  EMPTY:

0055 E4 46                     IN       AL,OCW1
0057 0C 01                     OR       AL,MASK5
0059 E6 46                     OUT      OCW1,AL

005B                  DONES:

005B 5F                        POP      DI               ;restore registers
005C 5B                        POP      BX
```

```
005D 58                      POP      AX
005E CF                      IRET


005F             TXRDY       ENDP
```

10–5   REAL-TIME CLOCK

This section of the text presents a real-time clock as an example use of an interrupt. A real-time clock keeps time in real time, that is, in hours and minutes. The example illustrated here keeps time in hours, minutes, seconds, and 1/60 second using four memory locations to hold the BCD time of day.

Figure 10–21 illustrates a simple circuit that uses the 60-Hz AC power line to generate a periodic interrupt request signal for the NMI interrupt input pin. Although we are using a signal from the AC power line, which varies slightly in frequency from time to time, it is accurate over a period of time. The circuit uses a signal from the 120-VAC power line that is conditioned by a Schmitt-trigger inverter before it is applied to the NMI interrupt input. Note that the power line ground must be connected to the system ground in this schematic. The power line ground (neutral) connection is the large flat pin on the power line; the narrow flat pin is the hot side or 120-VAC side of the line.

The software for the real-time clock contains an interrupt service procedure that is called 60 times per second and a procedure that updates the count located in four memory locations. Example 10–13 lists both procedures along with the four bytes of memory used to hold the BCD time of day.

EXAMPLE 10–13

```
0000 00          TIME       DB       ?          ;1/60 seconds counter
0001 00                     DB       ?          ;seconds counter
0002 00                     DB       ?          ;minutes counter
0003 00                     DB       ?          ;hours counter (24 hour clock)


                 ;Interrupt service procedure for NMI


0004             TIMES      PROC     FAR


0004 50                     PUSH     AX         ;save registers
0005 56                     PUSH     SI
```

FIGURE 10–21 Converting the AC power line to a 60-Hz TTL signal for the NMI input.

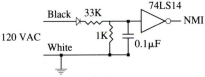

```
0006  B4 60                MOV      AH,60H              ;load modulus of counter
0008  BE 0000 R            MOV      SI,OFFSET TIME      ;address time
000B  E8 0022 R            CALL     UP                  ;adjust 1/60 counter
000E  75 0F               JNZ      DONE
0010  E8 0022 R            CALL     UP                  ;adjust seconds counter
0013  75 0A               JZ       DONE
0015  E8 0022 R            CALL     UP                  ;adjust minutes
0018  75 05               JZ       DONE
001A  B4 24               MOV      AH,24H              ;modulus 24
001C  E8 0022 R            CALL     UP

001F          DONE:

001F  5E                  POP      SI                  ;restore registers
0020  58                  POP      AX
0021  CF                  IRET

0022          TIMES       ENDP

0022          UP          PROC     NEAR

0022  2E: 8A 04           MOV      AL,CS:[SI]
0025  46                  INC      SI
0026  04 01               ADD      AL,1                ;increment counter
0028  27                  DAA
0029  2E: 88 44 FF        MOV      CS:[SI-1],AL
002D  2A C4               SUB      AL,AH
002F  75 04               JNZ      UP1
0031  2E: 88 44 FF        MOV      CS:[SI-1],AL

0035          UP1:

0035  C3                  RET

0036          UP          ENDP
```

10–6   SUMMARY

1. An interrupt is a hardware- or software-initiated call that interrupts the currently executing program at any point and calls a procedure. The procedure called by the interrupt is an interrupt service procedure.

2. Interrupts are useful when an I/O device needs to be serviced only occasionally at low data transfer rates.

3. The 80286 microprocessor has five instructions that apply to interrupts: BOUND, INT, INT 3, INTO, and IRET. The INT and INT 3 instructions call procedures with addresses stored in the interrupt vector whose type is indicated by the

instruction. The BOUND instruction is a conditional interrupt that uses interrupt vector type number 5. The INTO instruction is a conditional interrupt that only interrupts a program if the overflow flag is set. Finally, the IRET instruction is used to return from interrupt service procedures.

4. The 80286 has three pins that apply to its hardware interrupt structure: INTR, NMI, and COD/$\overline{\text{INTA}}$. The interrupt inputs are INTR and NMI, which are used to request interrupts, and COD/$\overline{\text{INTA}}$ is an output used to acknowledge the INTR interrupt request. In practice we use the $\overline{\text{INTA}}$ pin on the 82288 system bus controller to acknowledge the INTR interrupt request.

5. Interrupts are referenced through a vector table that occupies memory locations 000000H–0003FFH. Each interrupt vector is 4 bytes in length and contains the offset and segment addresses of the interrupt service procedure.

6. Two flag bits are used with the interrupt structure of the 80286 microprocessor: trap (TF) and interrupt enable (IF). The IF flag bit enables the INTR interrupt input, and the TF flag bit causes interrupts to occur after the execution of each instruction as long as TF is active.

7. The first 32 interrupt vector locations are reserved for Intel use, with many predefined in the 80286 microprocessor. The last 224 interrupt vectors are for user use and can perform any function desired.

8. Whenever an interrupt is detected, the following events occur: (1) the flags are pushed onto the stack, (2) the IF and TF flag bits are both cleared, (3) the IP and CS registers are both pushed onto the stack, and (4) the interrupt vector is fetched from the interrupt vector table and the interrupt service subroutine is accessed through the vector address.

9. Tracing or single-stepping is accomplished by setting the TF flag bit. This causes an interrupt to occur after the execution of each instruction for debugging.

10. The nonmaskable interrupt input (NMI) calls the procedure whose address is stored at interrupt vector type number 2. This input is positive-edge triggered.

11. The INTR pin is not internally decoded as is the NMI pin. Instead, $\overline{\text{INTA}}$ is used to apply the interrupt vector type number to data bus connections D_0–D_7 during the $\overline{\text{INTA}}$ pulse.

12. Methods of applying the interrupt vector type number to the data bus during $\overline{\text{INTA}}$ vary widely. One method uses resistors to apply interrupt type number FFH to the data bus, while another uses a three-state buffer to apply any vector type number.

13. The 8259A programmable interrupt controller (PIC) adds at least eight interrupt inputs to the 80286 microprocessor. If more interrupts are needed, this device can be cascaded to provide up to 64 interrupt inputs.

14. Programming the 8259A is a two-step process. First a series of initialization command words (ICWs) is sent to the 8259A, then a series of operation command words (OCWs) is sent.

15. The 8259A contains three status registers: IMR (interrupt mask register), ISR (in-service register), and IRR (interrupt request register).

16. A real-time clock is used to keep time in real time. In most cases time is stored in either binary or BCD form in several memory locations.

10–7   QUESTIONS AND PROBLEMS

1. What is interrupted by an interrupt?
2. Define the term *interrupt*.
3. What is called by an interrupt?
4. Why do interrupts free up time for the microprocessor?
5. List the interrupt pins found on the 80286 microprocessor.
6. List the five interrupt instructions for the 80286.
7. What is an interrupt vector?
8. Where are the interrupt vectors located in the 80286 memory?
9. How many different interrupt vectors are found in the interrupt vector table?
10. Which interrupt vectors are reserved by Intel?
11. Explain how a type-0 interrupt occurs.
12. Describe the operation of the BOUND instruction.
13. Describe the operation of the INTO instruction.
14. What memory locations contain the vector for the INT 44H instruction?
15. Explain the operation of the IRET instruction.
16. What is the purpose of interrupt vector type number 7?
17. List the events that occur when an interrupt becomes active.
18. Explain the purpose of the interrupt flag (IF).
19. Explain the purpose of the trap flag (TF).
20. How is IF cleared and set?
21. How is TF cleared and set?
22. The NMI interrupt input automatically vectors through which vector type number?
23. Does the $\overline{\text{INTA}}$ signal activate for the NMI pin?
24. The INTR input is _____-sensitive.
25. The $\overline{\text{NMI}}$ input is _____-sensitive.
26. When the $\overline{\text{INTA}}$ signal becomes a logic 0, it indicates that the 80286 is waiting for an interrupt _____ number to be placed on the data bus (D_0–D_7).
27. What is a FIFO?
28. Develop a circuit that places interrupt type number 86H on the data bus in response to the INTR input.
29. Develop a circuit that places interrupt type number CCH on the data bus in response to the INTR input.
30. Explain why pullup resistors on D_0–D_7 cause the 80286 to respond with interrupt vector type number FFH for the $\overline{\text{INTA}}$ pulse.
31. What is a daisy chain?
32. Why must interrupting devices be polled in a daisy-chained interrupt system?
33. What is the 8259A?
34. How many 8259As are required to have 64 interrupt inputs?
35. What is the purpose of the IR_0–IR_7 pins on the 8259A?
36. When are the CAS_2–CAS_0 pins used on the 8259A?
37. Where is a slave INT pin connected on the master 8259A in a cascaded system?

38. What is an ICW?
39. What is an OCW?
40. How many ICWs are needed to program the 8259A when operated as a single master in a system?
41. Where is the vector type number stored in the 8259A?
42. Where is the sensitivity of the IR pins programmed in the 8259A?
43. What is the purpose of ICW_1?
44. What is a nonspecific EOI?
45. Explain priority rotation in the 8259A.
46. What is the purpose of IRR in the 8259A?

CHAPTER 11

Direct Memory Access

INTRODUCTION

In previous chapters, we discussed basic and interrupt-processed I/O. Now we turn to the final form of I/O called *direct memory access* (DMA). The DMA I/O technique provides direct access to the memory while the microprocessor is temporarily disabled. This allows data to be transferred between memory and the I/O device at a rate that is limited only by the speed of the memory components in the system or the DMA controller. The DMA transfer speed can approach 10–12M-byte transfer rates with today's high-speed RAM memory components.

DMA transfers are used for many purposes, but more common are DRAM refresh, video displays for refreshing the screen, and disk memory system reads and writes. The DMA transfer is also used to do high-speed memory-to-memory transfers.

OBJECTIVES

Upon completion of this chapter, you will be able to:

1. Describe a DMA transfer.
2. Explain the operation of the 80286 HOLD and HLDA control signals.
3. Explain the function of the 82258 advanced DMA controller when used for DMA transfers.
4. Program the 82258 to accomplish DMA transfers.
5. Describe the disk standards found in personal computer systems.
6. Describe the various video interface standards that are found in the personal computer.

11–1   BASIC DMA OPERATION

Two control signals are used to request and acknowledge a direct memory access (DMA) transfer in the 80286-based system. The HOLD pin is used to request a DMA action and the HLDA pin acknowledges the DMA action. Figure 11–1 shows the timing that is typically found on these two DMA control pins.

Whenever the HOLD input is placed at a logic 1 level, a DMA action (hold) is requested. The 80286 responds, within a few clocks, by suspending the execution of the program and by placing its address, data, and control bus at their high-impedance states. The high-impedance state causes the 80286 to appear as if it has been removed from its socket. This state allows external I/O devices or other microprocessors to gain access to the system buses so memory can be accessed directly.

As the timing diagram indicates, HOLD is sampled in the middle of any clocking cycle. Thus the hold can take effect at any time during the operation of any instruction in the 80286 microprocessor. As soon as the microprocessor recognizes the hold, it stops executing software and enters hold cycles (T_c) after one idle cycle (T_i). Note that the HOLD input has a higher priority than the INTR or NMI interrupt inputs. Interrupts can only take effect at the end of an instruction, while a HOLD can take effect in the middle of an instruction. The only 80286 pin that has a higher priority than a HOLD is the RESET pin, but HOLD cannot be active during a RESET or reset is not guaranteed.

The HLDA signal becomes active to indicate that the 80286 has indeed placed its buses at their high-impedance state, as can be seen in the timing diagram. Note that there are a few clock cycles between the time that HOLD changes until the time that HLDA changes. The HLDA output is a signal to the external requesting device that the microprocessor has relinquished control of its memory and I/O space. You could call the HOLD input a DMA request input and the HLDA output a DMA grant signal.

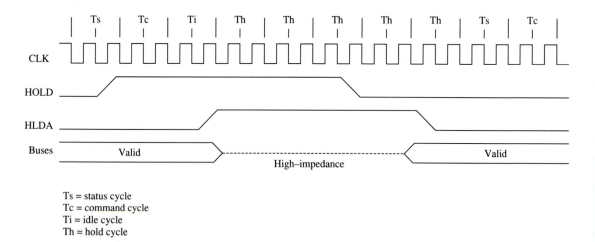

Ts = status cycle
Tc = command cycle
Ti = idle cycle
Th = hold cycle

FIGURE 11–1   Timing for the HOLD and HLDA pin of the 80286 microprocessor.

Basic DMA Definitions

Direct memory accesses normally occur between an I/O device and memory without the use of the microprocessor. A *DMA read* transfers data from the memory to the I/O device. A *DMA write* transfers data from an I/O device to memory. In both operations, the memory and I/O are controlled simultaneously, and that is why the system contains separate memory and I/O control signals. This control bus structure of the 80286 microprocessor allows DMA transfers. A DMA read causes the $\overline{MRDC}$ and $\overline{IOWC}$ signals to both activate transferring data from the memory to the I/O device. The DMA controller provides the memory with its address, and a signal from the controller ($\overline{DACK}$) selects the I/O device during the DMA transfer.

The data transfer speed is determined by the speed of the memory device or a DMA controller that often controls DMA transfers. If the memory speed is 100 ns, DMA transfers can occur at rates of up to 1/100 ns or 10M-bytes per second. If the DMA controller in a system functions at a maximum rate of 5 MHz and we still use 100-ns memory, the maximum transfer rate is 5 MHz, because the DMA controller is slower than the memory. In many cases the DMA controller slows the speed of the system when DMA transfers occur.

11–2   THE 82258 ADMA COPROCESSOR

The 82258 advanced direct memory access (ADMA) controller, actually a coprocessor, supplies memory and I/O with control signals and memory and I/O selection during the DMA transfer. This device performs the DMA transfers at rates of up to 8 M bytes per second when operated with an 8 MHz 80286 microprocessor. The 82258 is called a coprocessor because it does respond to instructions that are stored in a section of memory called a channel control block. The 82256 can translate data from one code to another as it transfers data, it can mask data, and it can compare data and make decisions based upon these comparisons. The translations, maskings, and comparisons are performed by instructions stored in the control block.

Pinout and Basic Description

Figure 11–2 shows the pinout of the 82258 ADMA. This device is designed to interface the 80286 or the older 8086/8088 to a direct memory access system. The ADMA is a four-channel device that allows up to four different DMA transfers to be programmed at a time. Each channel contains a 24-bit address register and a 24-bit byte counter that allow the ADMA to transfer up to 16M bytes of data between an I/O device and any memory location. The ADMA also allows memory-to-memory DMA transfers. Each channel has a source and destination address for memory-to-memory transfers. Expansion from the 4 basic channels to 32 additional subchannels is accomplished by connecting the ADMA via a multiplexed scheme to channel 3 of the master 82258. This allows almost any size DMA based I/O system.

Pin Definitions.   Following is a list of the pin connections on the 82258 and their functions when operated with the 80286 microprocessor:

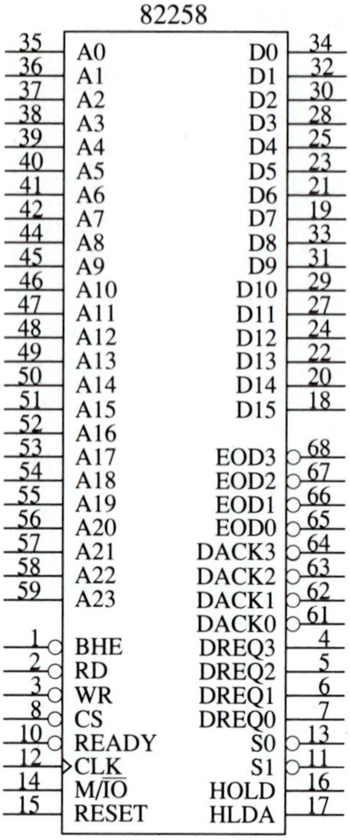

FIGURE 11–2 The 82258 advanced direct memory access (ADMA) controller.

1. A_7–A_0—Address I/O Connections: provide the lower eight bits of the address during a DMA transfer operation and are also used during programming to select one of the internal registers. There are 256 different internal registers on the 82258.
2. A_{23}–A_8—Address Outputs: provide the most significant 16 bits of the address during a DMA transfer operation.
3. $\overline{BHE}$—Bus High Enable: indicates the upper half of the data bus (D_7–D_0) contains data.
4. CLK—Clock Input: connected directly to the CLK output of the 82284 clock generator to provide the timing for the ADMA. The ADMA operates at one-half the frequency of the clock input pin, which allows the same clock signal to be used for both the microprocessor and the ADMA controller.
5. $\overline{CS}$—Chip Select: activated to select the ADMA for programming and also for reading various signal registers.
6. D_{15}–D_0—Data Bus Connections: used to pass information between the ADMA and the microprocessor and its memory and I/O system.
7. $\overline{DACK_3}$–$\overline{DACK_0}$—DMA Acknowledge Outputs: signal that the ADMA is responding to a request on the DMA request input pins.
8. $DREQ_3$–$DREQ_0$—DMA Request Inputs: used to request DMA transfers.
9. $\overline{EOD_3}$–$\overline{EOD_0}$—End of DMA: signal that the channel has completed a transfer or function as directed under program control. They can also function as inputs to

abort a DMA transfer. An application for these connections is to cause interrupts at the end of a DMA transfer.

10. HLDA—Hold Acknowledge Input: is placed at a logic 1 level to signal that the microprocessor has relinquished the system buses.
11. HOLD—Hold Output: becomes a logic 1 to request a DMA action from the microprocessor.
12. M/$\overline{\text{IO}}$—Memory/$\overline{\text{IO}}$ Select: generated by the ADMA to select either memory or I/O during a DMA transfer.
13. $\overline{\text{RD}}$—Read Input: allows an internal register to be read from the ADMA during programming.
14. $\overline{\text{READY}}$—Ready Input: used to terminate a bus cycle.
15. RESET—Reset Input: causes the ADMA to reset its initial state.
16. $\overline{S}_1, \overline{S}_0$—Status Connections: used by the ADMA as outputs to control the system during a DMA transfer and as inputs during programming.
17. $\overline{\text{WR}}$—Write Input: allows an internal register to be written during programming.
18. V_{cc}—System Power: connected to + 5.0 V.
19. V_{ss}—System Ground: connected to the system ground bus.

Connecting the 82258 ADMA

The 82258 is a coprocessor often connected to the 80286 microprocessor in the local bus configuration. This means that the ADMA is connected directly to the microprocessor before the system address latches and data bus transceivers. Figure 11–3 illustrates this interconnection to the 80286 microprocessor, plus the 82284 clock generator and 82288 system controller. Communications between the microprocessor and the ADMA are accomplished by the HOLD and HLDA connections. If the ADMA desires memory and I/O control, it places a logic 1 on the hold input to the microprocessor causing the 80286 to relinquish bus control to the ADMA. The HLDA signal informs the ADMA that the microprocessor has released the buses.

Notice how the 82258 is almost a parallel device to the 80286 with only a few of its pins attached to other components. The $\overline{\text{CS}}$ input is normally connected to a PAL decoder to select the ADMA for programming. This decoder is not illustrated in Figure 11–3. Also not illustrated are the address latches and data bus transceivers that connect the local address and data buses to the system address and data buses.

If a DMA access is requested by activating one of the DREQ inputs to the ADMA (or by software command), the ADMA responds by placing a logic 1 on the HOLD input to the 80286 microprocessor. In time, the 80286 recognizes the HOLD input and signals the ADMA, through the HLDA line, that it has stopped executing software and relinquished its buses. This allows the ADMA to take over the system memory and I/O buses through its connection to the local bus. The ADMA remains in control until it has completed its DMA transfer. At the end of the transfer, the ADMA places a logic 0 on the HOLD input to the microprocessor to signal the end of the DMA action. This allows the 80286 to again regain control of the system buses through its local bus connection. Notice how either the ADMA is in control or how the microprocessor is in control of the system.

When the 80286 Is in Control. When the 80286 is in control of the local buses, both the HOLD and HLDA pins are at logic 0 levels. During this time, the microprocessor

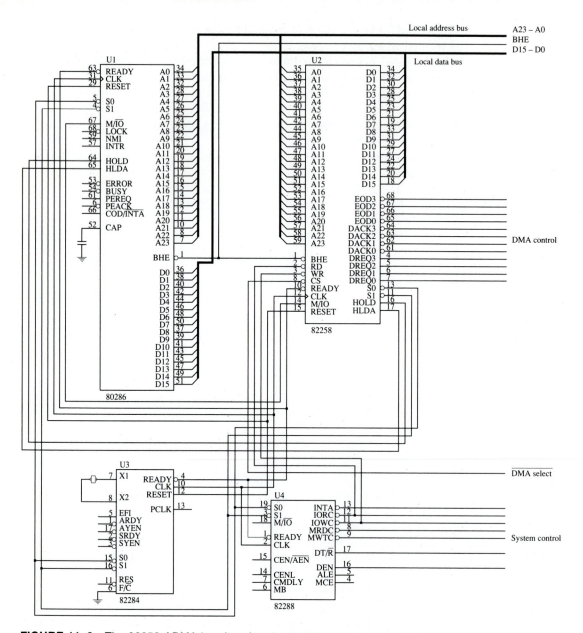

FIGURE 11–3   The 82258 ADMA interfaced to the 80286 as a local bus device.

is free to execute software that includes programming the 82258 ADMA. When the 80286 is in control of the system the 82258 appears as a programmable I/O device.

When the 82258 ADMA Is in Control.   When the 82258 ADMA is in control of the system, both the HOLD and HLDA pins are at logic 1 levels. During this time, the ADMA is free to transfer data, via the system buses, between memory and I/O or between memory locations. While the ADMA is in control of the system, the 80286 microprocessor is idle and remains passive and the ADMA provides memory address and control bus information.

Connecting Peripherals to the ADMA

Peripheral devices normally gain the attention of the 82258 through one of its DREQ inputs. There is one DREQ input for each of the four channels. If the ADMA is programmed to transfer data, a DREQ input is flagged for attention by the peripheral. The peripheral does this by placing a logic 1 on the DREQ input for the desired channel. Figure 11–4 shows how a simple Centronics printer interface is connected to the DREQ input of the 82258 to cause a request each time that the printer is no longer busy printing data. Here the $\overline{\text{DACK}}$ output signal, which activates when the channel has attention, becomes a logic 0 to select a data transfer to the Centronics printer port.

When the Centronics interface is busy its BUSY pin is at a logic 1 level, which does not request a DMA action through the DREQ input because of the inverter. When BUSY becomes a logic 0, indicating that the port is not busy, the DREQ pin is raised to a logic 1 level through the inverter. This requests a DMA action from the ADMA, which then places a logic 0 on the $\overline{\text{DACK}}$ pin.

The $\overline{\text{DACK}}$ pin allows the $\overline{\text{IOWC}}$ signal to pass to the clock (G) input pin of the latch, causing it to capture data bus information for the port. The circuit required to generate a data strobe $(\overline{\text{DS}})$ signal to the printer is not shown in this illustration.

Notice how the DREQ input requests a DMA transfer and how the $\overline{\text{DACK}}$ output pin selects the I/O device. The ADMA provides the memory with an address through its address bus, and the $\overline{\text{DACK}}$ signal selects the desired I/O device. This allows a memory location to be selected simultaneously with the I/O device for the DMA transfer.

FIGURE 11–4 A partial interface to a Centronics printer port illustrating how the port requests a DMA action and how it receives data from the ADMA.

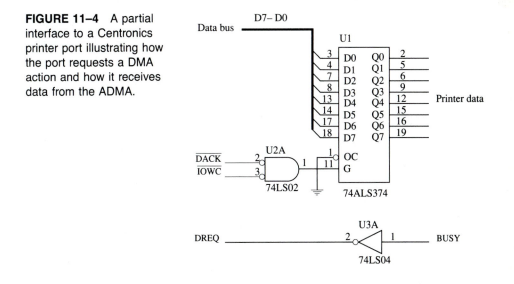

Programming the 82258 ADMA

Before the ADMA can be interfaced to an actual example I/O device, its internal register set and programming model must be understood. Figure 11–5 shows the internal programming model of the ADMA. Note that this device is a very sophisticated peripheral that contains many internal programmable I/O port locations used during the control of a DMA action. This map is used for all four channels, except that the illustration shows the port numbers for channel 0. The port numbers used

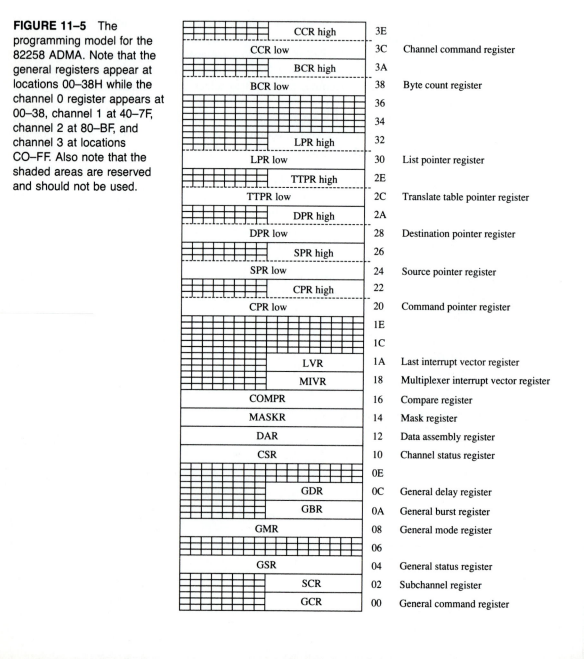

FIGURE 11–5 The programming model for the 82258 ADMA. Note that the general registers appear at locations 00–38H while the channel 0 register appears at 00–38, channel 1 at 40–7F, channel 2 at 80–BF, and channel 3 at locations CO–FF. Also note that the shaded areas are reserved and should not be used.

Register	Port	Description
CCR high	3E	
CCR low	3C	Channel command register
BCR high	3A	
BCR low	38	Byte count register
	36	
	34	
LPR high	32	
LPR low	30	List pointer register
TTPR high	2E	
TTPR low	2C	Translate table pointer register
DPR high	2A	
DPR low	28	Destination pointer register
SPR high	26	
SPR low	24	Source pointer register
CPR high	22	
CPR low	20	Command pointer register
	1E	
	1C	
LVR	1A	Last interrupt vector register
MIVR	18	Multiplexer interrupt vector register
COMPR	16	Compare register
MASKR	14	Mask register
DAR	12	Data assembly register
CSR	10	Channel status register
	0E	
GDR	0C	General delay register
GBR	0A	General burst register
GMR	08	General mode register
	06	
GSR	04	General status register
SCR	02	Subchannel register
GCR	00	General command register

for channel 1 are 40H–7FH, channel 2 uses 80H–BFH, and channel 3 uses ports COH–FFH. The general registers only appear in the channel 0 address space, and the MIVR and LIV registers only appear in the channel 3 address space.

General Registers. The general registers are used to control the general operation of the ADMA. General registers are programmed after a reset to initialize the operation of the 82258. The first register programmed after a reset is the general mode register (GMR) located at I/O port 08H. Figure 11–6 illustrates the binary bit pattern of this register.

The GMR allows the width of the I/O and memory buses to be set at 8- or 16-bits. This, for example, allows the memory width to be 16 bits and the I/O bus width to be 8 bits. The GMR also dictates how channel 3 is used in a system. If a single ADMA exists, channel 3 is a normal DMA channel, but if multiple ADMAs exist, then channel 3 is used to multiplex additional ADMAs into a system. If the 82258 is multiplexed through channel 3, we can connect up to 32 subchannels through channel 3. The local mode is used when the 82258 is connected as illustrated in Figure 11–3, and the remote mode is used when the 82258 is connected as a remote device to the system bus instead of the local bus.

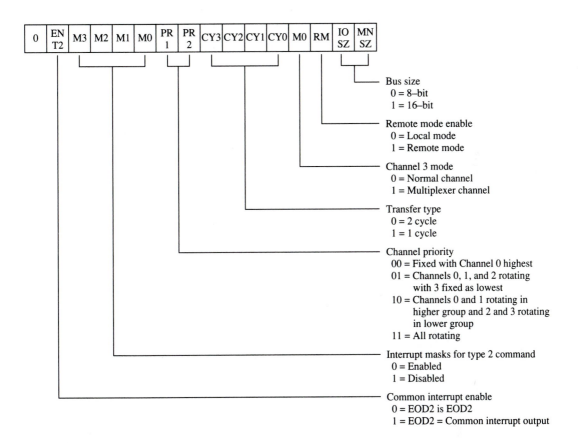

FIGURE 11–6 The general mode register (GMR) for the 82258 ADMA.

The transfer type is also selected by the GMR. In a one-cycle transfer, the ADMA provides the memory with its address and control signals, and it provides the I/O device with its control signals and the $\overline{\text{DACK}}$ signal for selection. In the one-cycle transfer system no subchannels are allowed and no memory-to-memory transfers can occur. The two-cycle transfer allows multiplexer operation for multiple subchannels and also memory-to-memory transfers. The two-cycle transfer uses the first cycle to provide the source address during a memory-to-memory transfer and also reads the source data. The second cycle provides the destination memory address and stores the data. Note that each channel is individually programmable for one or two cycles. The remaining bits in the GMR allow interrupts to be masked, select priority types, and program the function of the EOD pin.

Figure 11–7 illustrates the way that data are transferred using both the one-cycle transfer and the two-cycle transfer. Again note that the two-cycle transfer must be used whenever data are transferred from memory-to-memory, while I/O transfers usually use the one-cycle transfer. Two-cycle transfers actually store memory data within the ADMA during the first cycle, and during the second cycle, the stored data are returned to a different memory location.

Figure 11–8 shows the binary bit pattern of the general status register (GSR). The GSR provides status information for all channels when I/O port 04H is read. The GSR indicates the operational status of each channel, its interrupt status, and the control space location. When the 82258 is operated in the local mode, the control space can be on the memory address bus or the I/O bus. If the 82258 is operated in remote mode, the control space can be on the system bus or the resident bus.

Figure 11–9 illustrates the general command register (GCR) located at I/O port number 00H. The GCR is used to start or stop a channel. This command register can be used to control a single channel or multiple channels via the channel select bits.

The general burst register (GBR), located at I/O port 0AH, selects the maximum number of contiguous bus cycles. This register prevents the ADMA from continuously tying up the system with DMA transfers. For example, if the GBR is programmed with a 10, then 10 bus cycles maximum can occur before the ADMA must release the bus back to the microprocessor. If a 00H is loaded into the GBR, then the number of contiguous cycles is infinite.

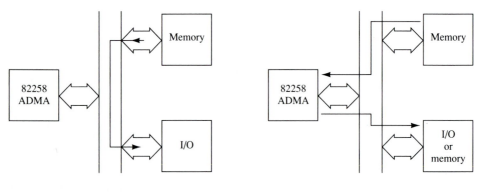

1 Cycle transfer   2 Cycle transfer

FIGURE 11–7   Note the difference between the one- and two-cycle transfers for the 82258 ADMA.

FIGURE 11–8 The general status register (GSR) for the 82258 ADMA.

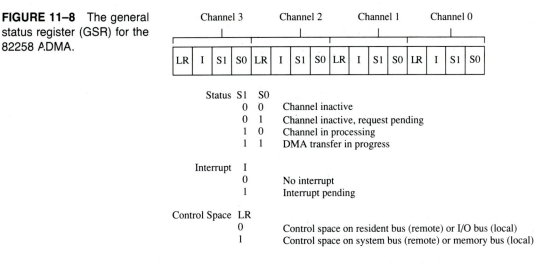

FIGURE 11–9 The general command register (GCR) for the 82258 ADMA.

The general delay register (GDR), located at I/O port 0CH, determines the maximum number of clocks between ADMA burst accesses. For example, if the GBR is programmed with a 10 and the GDR is programmed with a 20, the ADMA can access the system for 10 cycles and then must release the bus for 20 clocks before it can again do another DMA transfer. These registers control the percentage of clocks that can be used by the ADMA for DMA transfers. In a system that requires little DMA action, the GBR is programmed with a 00H.

Although not a general register, the multiplexer interrupt vector register (MIVR), located at I/O port D8H, is discussed in this section. This register is read to determine which channels are stopped and is illustrated in Figure 11–10. The 5-bit

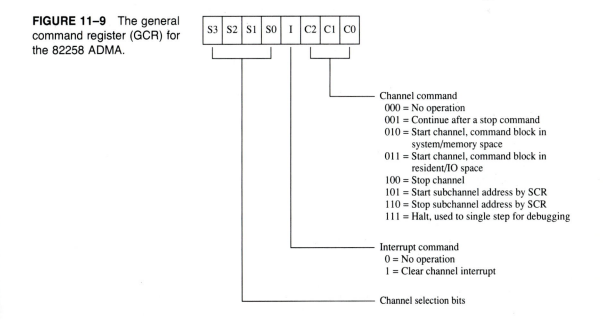

FIGURE 11–10 The multiplexer interrupt vector register (MIVR) for the 82258 ADMA.

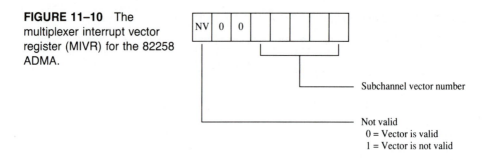

Subchannel vector number

Not valid
0 = Vector is valid
1 = Vector is not valid

vector returned by a register read indicates the highest priority subchannel stopped and not yet read.

The last interrupt vector register (LVR), located at I/O port DAH, indicates the last interrupt vector read by the 82258. This is used in the case of a fatal error stop of the channel 3 multiplexer register so the guilty subchannel can be detected.

Example 11–1 lists software used to program a single 82258 ADMA controller to operate in a system at I/O ports 1000H–10FFH. This single device is initialized for fixed priority, but the channels are not started and no commands are directed to the DMA channels. This software allows bursts of five cycles with a rest period between bursts of 10 clocks. In this example each channel is set up as a two-cycle channel so memory-to-memory DMA transfers can occur. In practice some channels may be programmed as one-cycle transfers if they normally transfer data between memory and I/O.

EXAMPLE 11–1

```
                          ;Procedure that initializes the 82258 ADMA

= 1008           GMR      EQU       1008H
= 100A           GBR      EQU       100AH
= 100C           GDR      EQU       100CH

0000             INIT     PROC      FAR

0000 BA 1008              MOV       DX,GMR
0003 B8 0001              MOV       AX,0001H          ;program mode
0006 EF                   OUT       DX,AX

0007 BA 100A              MOV       DX,GBR
000A B0 05                MOV       AL,5              ;program burst
000C EE                   OUT       DX,AL

000D BA 100C              MOV       DX,GDR
0010 B0 0A                MOV       AL,10             ;program delay
0012 EE                   OUT       DX,AL

0013 CB                   RET

0014             INIT     ENDP
```

Channel Registers and Control Blocks.   After the 82258 is initialized by programming the general registers, DMA actions are controlled through the channel registers and the general command register (GCR). The channel registers are loaded from a control block in the memory. This makes the 82258 easier to program than if all the channel registers would have to be programmed for each transfer with OUT instructions. Each DMA transfer requires a channel control block that is specified in the memory for each DMA channel and subchannel. Figure 11–11 illustrates the contents of the channel control block for a type 1 command. Type 1 commands are used to transfer data using DMA techniques. The 82258 accesses the channel control block through a linear memory address stored in the *command pointer register* (CPR). Each channel has its own CPR located at 20H–23H (channel 0), 60H–63H (channel 1), A0H–A3H (channel 2), and E0H–E3H (channel 3). Note that the command pointer register functions to access the program stored in the channel control block. You might call the CPR a program counter or instruction pointer for the 82258 ADMA controller.

Before the channel control block can be programmed, the contents of the type 1 and type 2 commands must be discussed. Figure 11–12 shows the contents of the type 1 command. The rightmost 8 bits are used to detail the operation of the source and destination addresses, and the leftmost 8 bits control the channel. The

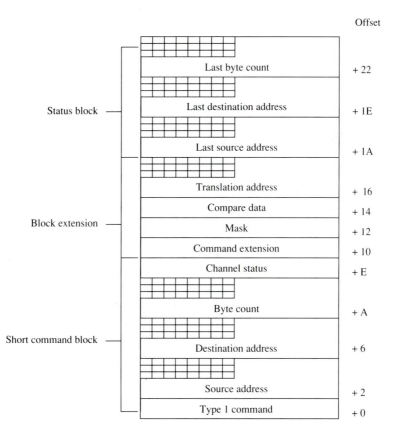

FIGURE 11–11   The command block for a type 1 command located in memory for the 82258 ADMA.

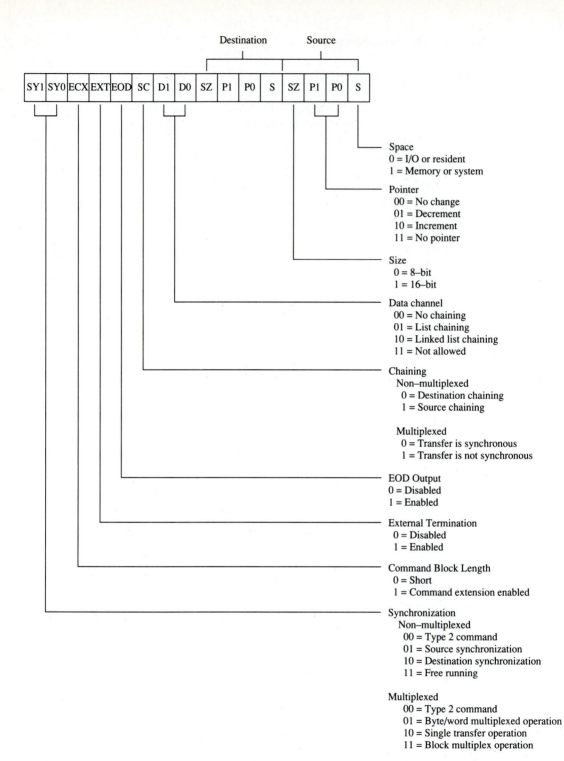

FIGURE 11–12 The type 1 channel command found in the channel command block for the 82258 ADMA.

460

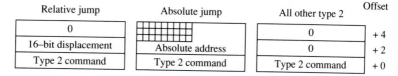

FIGURE 11–13 The type 2 command blocks for the 82258 ADMA.

type 1 command controls data transfer operations and it also selects the length of the channel control block as either short or extended. The short channel control block is used for most transfer unless data translation, masking, or comparison are to occur. When these operations are performed in addition to the transfer, the extended channel control block is selected.

The type 2 command allows conditional jumps and conditional stops. All channel programs consist of at least one type 1 command followed by one type 2 command. The type 1 command dictates the channel data transfer parameters, and the type 2 command either stops the channel program, repeats it, or progresses to another type 1 command block.

Figure 11–13 shows the binary bit pattern of the type 2 channel control block. Notice that the type 2 control block is 6 bytes in length instead of the many bytes required for a type 1 control block (see Figure 11–11). Notice that the type 2 command is followed by either a jump address (relative or absolute) or zero data.

Figure 11–14 depicts the binary bit pattern of the type 2 command. Conditions are established through the condition code bits of the type 2 command. For example, if

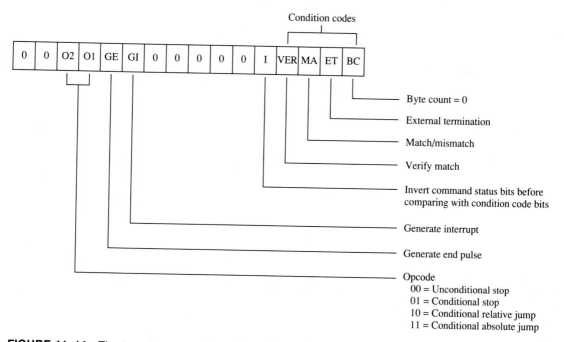

FIGURE 11–14 The type 2 command for the 82258 ADMA.

we wish to terminate a DMA action on a byte count of 0, we place a logic 1 in the BC bit position and a 01 in the opcode bits. If we wish to jump to another path we could use an opcode of 10 with a 1 in the BC bit to jump if the byte count reaches 0.

Figure 11–15 shows various structures that are often used to program a channel. The simplest of these structures is a type 1 control block followed by a type 2 control block that stops the channel. As can be imagined, the command structure for a channel could be extremely complex because of the conditional jump type 2 commands. These command structures are often called *chained commands* because one command leads to another in a chain. Notice how a single DMA transfer is performed and also how it can be changed to an automatically repeating sequence by changing the stop command to an unconditional jump command.

Example 11–2 shows the type 1 and type 2 channel control blocks and a procedure that causes the 82258 to perform a memory-to-memory DMA transfer. This application transfers 1,000H bytes of data from memory to locations 001000H–001FFFH into location 004000H–004FFH using channel 1 of the 82258. The source address, destination address, and byte count are all linear addresses and counts. A linear address or count is simply a 24-bit address or count. This software assumes that the ADMA has been initialized as illustrated in Example 11–1 and that it resides at I/O addresses 1000H–10FFH. Note that the leftmost two bits of the channel command determine the type of synchronization. Free-running starts the transfer via software through the GCR, and the transfers continue under control of the type 1 command until the byte count expires. The type 2 command is a simple unconditional channel stop command.

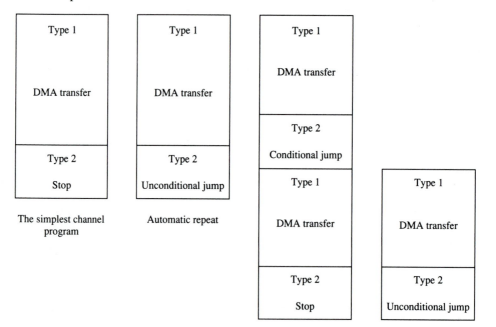

FIGURE 11–15 Some command paths for a DMA channel in the 82258 ADMA.

EXAMPLE 11–2

```
                        ;Procedure that transfers 1000H bytes of data from memory locations
                        ;001000H--001FFFH into locations 004000H--004FFFH using channel 1 of
                        ;the 82258 ADMA.

= 1000           GCR      EQU       1000H                    ;GCR port
= 1060           CPR1     EQU       1060H                    ;CPR1 port


0000             MEMT     PROC      FAR

0000 8C C8                MOV       AX,CS                    ;get linear address
0002 8B D8                MOV       BX,AX
0004 C1 E0 04             SHL       AX,4
0007 C1 EB 0C             SHR       BX,12
000A 05 0021 R            ADD       AX,OFFSET CB1            ;address control block
000D 83 D3 00             ADC       BX,0

0010 BA 1060             MOV       DX,CPR1                  ;address CPR1
0013 EF                   OUT       DX,AX
0014 83 C2 02             ADD       DX,2
0017 8B C3                MOV       AX,BX
0019 EF                   OUT       DX,AX

001A BA 1000             MOV       DX,GCR                   ;address GCR
001D B0 22                MOV       AL,22H                   ;start channel 1
001F EE                   OUT       DX,AL

0020 CB                   RET

0021             MEMT     ENDP

                        ;Type 1 command

0021             CB1:
0021 C0DD                 DW        0C0DDH                   ;type 1 command
0023 1000                 DW        1000H                    ;source address
0025 0000                 DW        0
0027 4000                 DW        4000H                    ;destination address
0029 0000                 DW        0
002B 1000                 DW        1000H                    ;byte count
002D 0000                 DW        0
002F 0000                 DW        0                        ;channel status

                        ;Type 2 STOP command

0031             CB2:
0031 0000                 DW        0000H                    ;STOP command
0033 0000                 DW        0
0035 0000                 DW        0
```

It is very important that the contents of the channel control block remain unchanged until the DMA action is completed by the 82258. The channel operational status is tested as defined in the general status register (GSR) before the channel control block may be changed. Example 11–3 illustrates a procedure that tests the status of channel 1. If the channel has completed a DMA transfer, the procedure returns with carry cleared to zero, and if the channel is busy, the carry flag is set before the return.

EXAMPLE 11–3

```
                    ;Procedure that performs a test to determine if the
                    ;channel 1 DMA action is complete.
                    ;
                    ;return carry = 1  (DMA action occurring)
                    ;
                    ;return carry = 0  (DMA action complete)


= 1004              GSR     EQU     1004H              ;address of CSR

0000                TEST1   PROC    FAR

0000 BA 1004                MOV     DX,GSR             ;address GSR
0003 ED                     IN      AX,DX              ;get status
0004 A9 0030                TEST    AX,30H             ;test channel 1 status
0007 74 01                  JZ      TEST1A             ;if transfer completed

0009 F9                     STC                        ;otherwise set carry

000A                TEST1A:

000A CB                     RET

000B                TEST1   ENDP
```

The channel control block can be extended to allow the use of some of the internal features of the 82258 as data are transferred. These features include mask and compare, which allows data to be tested as they are transferred. Also included is translate, which allows data to be modified as they are transferred. Translation is often used for converting data from one code to another. When 16-bit data are transferred and translated, each byte is translated via a translation table that is addressed by the translation table address in the extended control block. A translation table has up to 256 entries and functions as the XLAT instruction by converting the source data to the translation data code.

Suppose that a block of memory data contains ASCII-coded data that must be converted to EBCDIC data. (EBCDIC data are often used in mainframe computers systems and are extended binary coded decimal interchange code.) The procedure illustrated in Example 11–4 shows how the contents of memory location 001000H–002FFFH are converted from ASCII to EBCDIC code. Note that the contents of the EBCDIC code are not provided in this example because of the length. We also assume that the initiation software (see Figure 11–1) has been executed and that the I/O ports are 1000H–10FFH.

EXAMPLE 11–4

```
                        ;Procedure that performs data conversion using a translation
                        ;lookup table to convert a block of memory data from ASCII
                        ;to EBCDIC code.  This procedure uses channel 0

= 1020                  CPR0    EQU     1020H           ;control pointer register
= 1000                  GCR     EQU     1000H           ;general command register

0000                    TRANS   PROC    FAR

0000 8C C8                      MOV     AX,CS           ;get control block address
0002 8B D8                      MOV     BX,AX
0004 C1 E0 04                   SHL     AX,4
0007 C1 EB 0C                   SHR     BX,12
000A 50                         PUSH    AX
000B 53                         PUSH    BX
000C 05 0034 R                  ADD     AX,OFFSET CCB0
000F 83 D3 00                   ADC     BX,0
0012 BA 1020                    MOV     DX,CPR0         ;program control pointer
0015 EF                         OUT     DX,AX
0016 83 C2 02                   ADD     DX,2
0019 8B C3                      MOV     AX,BX
001B EF                         OUT     DX,AX
001C 5B                         POP     BX
001D 58                         POP     AX              ;store translation table address
001E 05 004E R                  ADD     AX,OFFSET TABLE
0021 83 D3 00                   ADC     BX,0
0024 2E: A3 004A R              MOV     TRAL,AX
0028 2E: 89 1E 004C R           MOV     TRAH,BX

002D BA 1000                    MOV     DX,GCR          ;start channel
0030 B0 12                      MOV     AL,12H
0032 EE                         OUT     DX,AL

0033 CB                         RET

0034            TRANS   ENDP

                ;Channel 0 control block

0034            CCB0:
```

```
0034 E0DD                    DW      0E0DDH              ;channel type 1 command
0036 1000                    DW      1000H               ;source address
0038 0000                    DW      0
003A 1000                    DW      1000H               ;destination address
003C 0000                    DW      0
003E 2000                    DW      2000H               ;count
0040 0000                    DW      0
0042 0000                    DW      0                   ;status
0044 0010                    DW      10H                 ;command extension
0046 0000                    DW      0                   ;mask
0048 0000                    DW      0                   ;compare data
004A 0000           TRAL     DW      ?                   ;translation table address
004C 0000           TRAH     DW      ?

                    ;STOP channel control block

004E                CB2:

004E 0000                    DW      0000H               ;stop command
0050 0000                    DW      0
0052 0000                    DW      0

                    ;Translation table location (Data to be defined)

0054                TABLE:

0054 0080 [                  DB      128 DUP (?)         ;EBCDIC conversion data
          00
     ]
```

Printer Spooler Using DMA Techniques

A common I/O channel using DMA techniques is a print spooler. The print spooler prints data from an area of memory or from a disk file using DMA transfer techniques. This example will use a standard Centronics printer interface port to bring data stored in memory on the system printer. Figure 11–16 illustrates the complete Centronics printer interface and its timing diagram. Note that the 82258 ADMA connects to the printer interface through its $DREQ_1$ and $\overline{DACK_1}$ pin connections. The BUSY signal requests a DMA transfer, and the $\overline{DACK_1}$ signal activates a one-shot that produces a data strobe signal to the printer. A latch is incorporated to capture and hold data for the printer.

Again assuming that the 82258 is interfaced to function at I/O space 1000H–10FFH, a program and control blocks are written to allow data to be sent to the printer. Once the 82258 is initialized as illustrated in Example 11–1 (except channel 0 is initialized as a one-cycle transfer), software to program the ADMA is provided

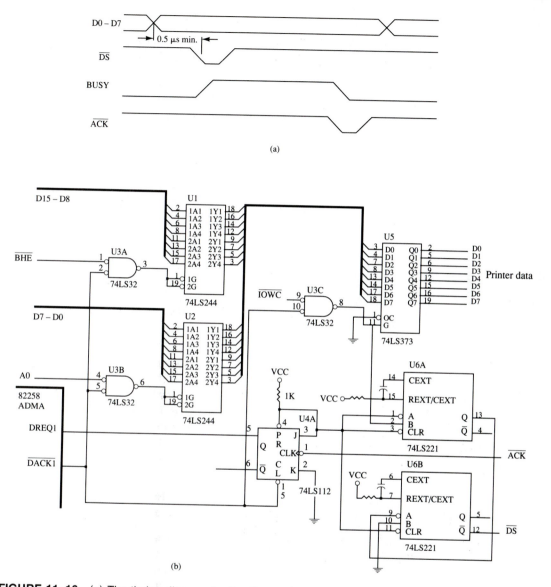

FIGURE 11–16 (a) The timing diagram for the Centronics parallel printer interface. (b) The Centronics printer interface.

to initialize the channel pointer register so the contents of a block of memory can be sent to the printer as controlled by a channel control block. A general procedure that prints the contents of the block of memory addressed by DS:SI is illustrated in Example 11–5. Here the value of CS determines the length of the printed block and DS:SI is the starting address.

EXAMPLE 11–5

```
= 1020                  CPR0    EQU     1020H            ;control pointer register
= 1000                  GCR     EQU     1000H            ;general command register

                        ;Procedure that performs data transfer to the printer using
                        ;channel 0 of the 82258.    Software assumes that the
                        ;channel is initialized for a 1 cycle transfer.

0000                    SEND    PROC    FAR

0000 8C C8                      MOV     AX,CS            ;get control block address
0002 8B D8                      MOV     BX,AX
0004 C1 E0 04                   SHL     AX,4
0007 C1 EB 0C                   SHR     BX,12
000A 05 003E R                  ADD     AX,OFFSET CCB0
000D 83 D3 00                   ADC     BX,0
0010 BA 1020                    MOV     DX,CPR0          ;program control pointer
0013 EF                         OUT     DX,AX
0014 83 C2 02                   ADD     DX,2
0017 8B C3                      MOV     AX,BX
0019 EF                         OUT     DX,AX

001A 2E: 89 0E 0048 R           MOV     COUNT,CX         ;store count

001F 8C D8                      MOV     AX,DS            ;form linear source address
0021 8B D8                      MOV     BX,AX
0023 C1 E0 04                   SHL     AX,4
0026 C1 EB 0C                   SHR     BX,12
0029 03 C6                      ADD     AX,SI
002B 83 D3 00                   ADC     BX,0
002E 2E: A3 0040 R              MOV     SOURL,AX
0032 2E: 89 1E 0042 R           MOV     SOURH,BX

0037 BA 1000                    MOV     DX,GCR           ;start channel
003A B0 12                      MOV     AL,12H
003C EE                         OUT     DX,AL

003D CB                         RET

003E                    SEND    ENDP

                        ;Channel 0 control block

003E                    CCB0:

003E E00D                       DW      0E00DH           ;channel type 1 command
0040 0000               SOURL   DW      0                ;source address
0042 0000               SOURH   DW      0
0044 0000                       DW      0
0046 0000                       DW      0
0048 0000               COUNT   DW      0                ;count
```

004A 0000		DW	0	
004C 0000		DW	0	;status

;Type 2 STOP command

004E 0000		DW	0000H	;unconditional channel stop
0050 0000		DW	0	
0052 0000		DW	0	

Suppose that a printer system is required that uses a double buffer for holding printed matter. Double buffers are commonly used when interfacing to printers so data may be placed in one buffer while the contents of another buffer are printed. Using the same hardware provided in Figure 11–16 as a basis for the printer interface, a program is written that fills and manages two separate printer buffers for data transfer to the printer.

Example 11–6 illustrates a procedure that fills two print buffers and controls the transfer of data to the printer using the 82258 ADMA. This procedure is accessed for each printed message, with DS:SI addressing the message. The procedure transfers the printed message into the buffers and continues to do so until the last character of printed data, which must be a 1AH (control Z), indicates the end of the printed data.

EXAMPLE 11–6

```
                        ;Procedure that uses a double-buffer for DMA data.
                        ;The DMA channel programs are not ilustrated.
                        ;
0000                    DATA    SEGMENT PUBLIC

                                EXTRN   COUNT0:WORD     ;external counter
                                EXTRN   COUNT1:WORD

0000                    DATA    ENDS

0000                    EXTRA   SEGMENT

0000 0000               COUNT   DW      ?
0002 0100 [             BUF1    DB      256 DUP (?)     ;channel 0 buffer
          00
        ]
0102 0100 [             BUF2    DB      256 DUP (?)     ;channel 1 buffer
          00
        ]
0202 00                 FLAG    DB      ?

0203                    EXTRA   ENDS
```

```
= 1004              GSR    EQU     1004H           ;general status register
= 0000              GCR    EQU     0               ;general command register

0000                CODE   SEGMENT

                           ASSUME CS:CODE,ES:EXTRA,DS:DATA

0000                FILL   PROC    FAR

0000 06                    PUSH    ES
0001 B8 ---- R             MOV     AX,EXTRA
0004 8E C0                 MOV     ES,AX
0006 FC                    CLD
0007 26: C6 06 0202 R      MOV     FLAG,0
     00

000D                FILL1:

000D B3 00                 MOV     BL,0
000F E8 0025               CALL    TESTS           ;test BUF1
0012 72 F9                 JC      FILL1           ;if busy

0014 BF 0002 R             MOV     DI,OFFSET BUF1
0017 E8 0036               CALL    LOAD            ;load BUF1

001A B3 00                 MOV     BL,0            ;send BUF1
001C E8 0054               CALL    SEND

001F 75 14                 JNZ     FILL_END

0021                FILL2:

0021 B3 01                 MOV     BL,1            ;test BUF2
0023 E8 0011               CALL    TESTS
0026 72 F9                 JC      FILL2           ;if busy

0028 BF 0102 R             MOV     DI,OFFSET BUF2
002B E8 0022               CALL    LOAD            ;load BUF2

002E B3 01                 MOV     BL,1            ;send BUF2
0030 E8 0040               CALL    SEND
0033 74 D8                 JZ      FILL1           ;repeat until done

0035                FILL_END:

0035 07                    POP     ES
0036 CB                    RET

0037                FILL   ENDP
```

```
0037                     TESTS    PROC    NEAR

0037 BA 1004                      MOV     DX,GSR         ;test for busy channel
003A ED                           IN      AX,DX
003B 80 FB 00                     CMP     BL,0
003E 75 08                        JNE     TEST1
0040 83 E0 03                     AND     AX,3
0043 83 F8 03                     CMP     AX,3
0046 F5                           CMC
0047 C3                           RET

0048                     TEST1:

0048 83 E0 30                     AND     AX,30H
004B 83 F8 30                     CMP     AX,30H
004E F5                           CMC
004F C3                           RET

0050                     TESTS    ENDP

0050                     LOAD     PROC    NEAR

0050 B9 0100                      MOV     CX,256

0053                     LOAD1:

0053 AC                           LODSB                  ;get data
0054 3C 1A                        CMP     AL,1AH
0056 74 0B                        JE      LOAD2          ;if finished
0058 AA                           STOSB
0059 E2 F8                        LOOP    LOAD1
005B 26: C7 06 0000 R             MOV     COUNT,256
     0100
0062 C3                           RET

0063                     LOAD2:

0063 26: C6 06 0202 R             MOV     FLAG,1         ;signal finished
     01
0069 B8 0100                      MOV     AX,256
006C 2B C1                        SUB     AX,CX
006E 26: A3 0000 R                MOV     COUNT,AX       ;save byte count
0072 C3                           RET

0073                     LOAD     ENDP

0073                     SEND     PROC    NEAR

0073 80 FB 00                     CMP     BL,0
0076 75 14                        JNE     SEND1
0078 26: A1 0000 R                MOV     AX,COUNT       ;set up count
```

```
007C A3 0000 E              MOV     COUNT0,AX
007F B0 02                  MOV     AL,02H              ;start channel 0
0081 BA 0000                MOV     DX,GCR
0084 EE                     OUT     DX,AL
0085 26: 80 3E 0202 R       CMP     FLAG,0              ;test finished
     00
008B C3                     RET

008C              SEND1:

008C 26: A1 0000 R          MOV     AX,COUNT
0090 A3 0000 E              MOV     COUNT1,AX
0093 B0 22                  MOV     AL,22H              ;start channel 1
0095 BA 0000                MOV     DX,GCR
0098 EE                     OUT     DX,AL
0099 26: 80 3E 0202 R       CMP     FLAG,0
     00
009F C3                     RET

00A0      SEND    ENDP

00A0      CODE    ENDS

          END
```

The procedure first fills the buffer 1 with 256 bytes of ASCII code before starting the DMA action that prints buffer 1. While buffer 1 is printing, additional characters are stored in buffer 2. If buffer 2 fills, the procedure waits for buffer 1 to complete printing action before it starts the transfer of data in buffer 2 to the printer. This action of filling and printing the two buffers continues until the control Z character is received by the procedure.

Chaining DMA Actions

Chaining allows complex DMA sequences to be performed by the 82258 ADMA. Command chaining occurs for a type 2 command block, while data, list, and linked-list chaining occur with a type 1 command block. In any case, chains are set up to allow the controller to accomplish complex DMA transfer operations on lists of DMA actions located in many control blocks that could be scattered through the memory system.

The command chain is a series of sequential commands stored in one control block following the next. There can be up to 64K bytes of command strung together to form a command chain. Control transfers from the first channel command to each subsequent command until a type 2 stop command is encountered. This form of channel control allows DMA operations to be stacked and executed sequentially. Figure 11–17 illustrates a string of commands strung together to form a command chain. Whenever commands are chained, they must all be one-cycle or two-cycle

FIGURE 11–17 A series of type 1 commands chained together to transfer three blocks of data.

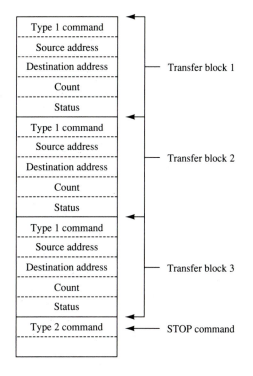

Type 1 command
Source address
Destination address
Count
Status
Type 1 command
Source address
Destination address
Count
Status
Type 1 command
Source address
Destination address
Count
Status
Type 2 command

Transfer block 1

Transfer block 2

Transfer block 3

STOP command

transfers, because the operation of the channel cannot be changed while the chain is executing. This means that DMA I/O actions cannot be interspersed with memory-to-memory transfers.

List chaining is efficient when several blocks of data scattered throughout the memory are to be transferred using DMA techniques. The destination address points to a data chain list that contains the counts and locations of the data to be transferred. Here, one type 1 command is issued, and the DMA controller proceeds to transfer blocks of data until it encounters an entry in the data chain list that contains a byte count of zero. Figure 11–18 shows a chained list using destination list chaining. Note that data chains may occur for a source or destination address, but may only occur using one cycle transfer.

In the illustration, the DMA action selected transfers data from an external I/O device into various destination blocks. After the first block is filled, the chaining continues to fill subsequent blocks until a byte count of zero is encountered. Also notice that commands can still be chained to the channel control block to form extremely complex channel control operations.

Another chaining sequence called the *linked list* is similar to data chaining except that the data chain block locations can also be scattered through the memory, as can the data blocks. Figure 11–19 illustrates a destination linked list that transfers data from an I/O device to various blocks in the memory. This technique is more suitable to most systems because the chain can be expanded as new data are to be transferred through the DMA controller.

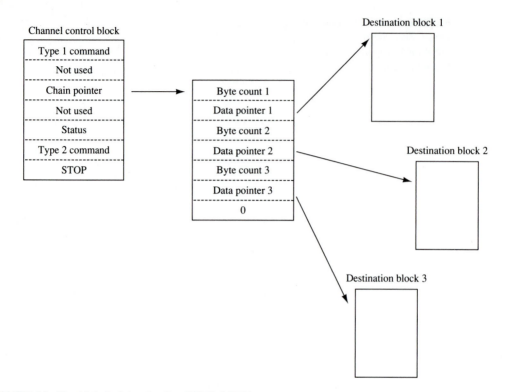

FIGURE 11–18   List chaining for the 82258 ADMA.

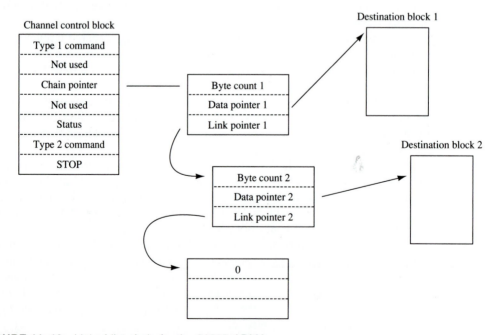

FIGURE 11–19   Linked list chain for the 82258 ADMA.

Multiplexing Subchannels to the 82258 ADMA

As mentioned earlier, expansion of the 82258 is possibly through channel 3. When using the multiplexed subchannel scheme, an 8259A programmable interrupt controller is used to request DMA actions through the channel 3 DREQ input of the 82258. The vector number provided by the 8259A, during the channel 3 $\overline{\text{DACK}}$ output, is used to access a subchannel multiplexer table located in the memory. The subchannel multiplexer table is addressed by the multiplexer table pointer register (MTPR) located within the 82258 at I/O ports E_0H–E_3H. Note that these ports also function as the channel 3 list pointer register (LPR), loaded during a channel operation, that uses a data list chain.

11–3 DISK MEMORY SYSTEMS

Disk memory is used to store long-term data. Many types of disk storage systems are available today. All disk memory systems use magnetic media except the optical disk memory, which stores data on a plastic disk. Optical disk memory is either a *CDROM* (compact disk/read-only memory) that is read, but never written, or a *WORM* (write once/read mostly) that is read most of the time, but can be written once by a laser beam. Also becoming available is optical disk memory that can be read and written many times, but there is still a limitation on the number of write operations allowed. This section of the chapter provides an introduction to disk memory systems so that they may be used with computer systems. It also provides details of their operation.

Floppy Disk Memory

The most common and the most basic form of disk memory is the floppy or flexible disk. This magnetic recording medium is available in three sizes: the 8" *standard*, 5¼" *minifloppy*, and the 3½" *microfloppy*. Today the 8" standard version has all but disappeared, giving way to the mini- and microfloppy disks. The 8" disk is too large and unwieldy to handle and store. To solve this problem, industry developed the 5¼" minifloppy disk. Today, the microfloppy disk is quickly replacing the minifloppy in newer systems because of its reduced size, ease of storage, and its durability.

All disks have several things in common. They are all organized so that data are stored in tracks. A *track* is a concentric ring of data that is stored on the surface of a disk. Figure 11–20 illustrates the surface of a 5¼" minifloppy disk showing a track that is divided into sectors. A *sector* is a common subdivision of a track that is designed to hold a reasonable amount of data. In many systems a sector often holds either 512 or 1,024 bytes of data. The size of a sector can be any size from 128 bytes to the length of one entire track.

Notice from the illustration that there is a hole through the disk that is labeled an index hole. The *index hole* is designed so the electronic system, which reads the disk, is able to find the beginning of a track and its first sector (00). Tracks are

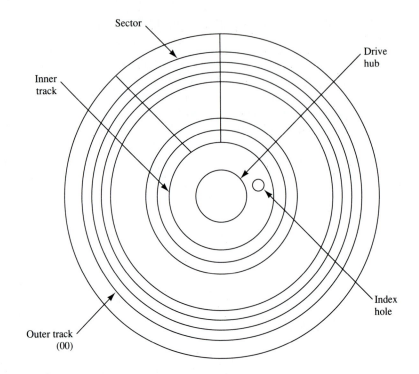

FIGURE 11–20   The format of a 5¼″ floppy disk.

numbered from track 00, the outermost track, in increasing value toward the center or innermost track. Sectors are often numbered from sector 00 on the outermost track, to whatever value is required to reach the innermost track and its last sector.

The 5¼″ Minifloppy Disk.   Today, the 5¼″ floppy is probably the most popular disk size used with older microcomputer systems. Figure 11–21 illustrates this minifloppy disk. The floppy disk is rotated 300 RPMs inside its semi-rigid plastic jacket. The head mechanism in a floppy disk drive makes physical contact with the surface of the disk, which eventually causes wear and damage to the disk. This could present a potential problem, but disks usually last many years before data are lost due to wear.

   Today most minifloppy disks are double-sided. This means that data are written on both the top and bottom surfaces of the disk. A set of tracks is called a *cylinder* and consists of one top and one bottom track. Cylinder 00, for example, consists of the outermost top and bottom tracks.

   Floppy disk data are stored in the double-density format, which uses a recording technique called *MFM* (modified frequency modulation) to store the information. Double-sided, double density (*DSDD*) disks are normally organized with 40 tracks of data on each side of the disk. A double-density disk track is typically divided into 9 sectors, with each sector containing 512 bytes of information. This means

FIGURE 11–21 The 5¼″ minifloppy disk.

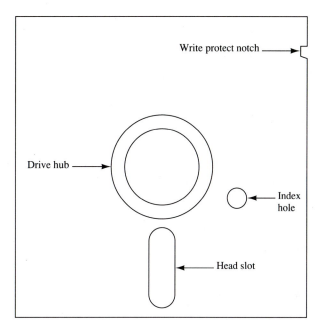

Write protect notch

Drive hub

Index hole

Head slot

that the total capacity of a double-density, double-sided disk is 40 tracks per side × 2 sides × 9 sectors per track × 512 bytes per sector, or 368,640 (360K) bytes of information.

Earlier disk memory systems used single-density and *FM* (frequency modulation) to store information in 40 tracks on one or two sides of the disk. Each of the 8 or 9 sectors on the single-density disk stored 256 bytes of data. This meant that a single-density disk stored 90K bytes or data per side. A single-density, double-sided disk stored 180K bytes of data.

Also common today are *high-density (HD)* minifloppy disks, which contain 80 tracks of information per side with 8 sectors per track. Each sector contains 1024 bytes of information. This gives the 5¼″ high-density minifloppy disk a total capacity of 80 tracks per side × 2 sides × 8 sectors per track × 1024 bytes per sector or 1,310,720 (1.2M) bytes of information.

The magnetic recording technique used to store data on the surface of the disk is called *nonreturn to zero* (NRZ) recording. With NRZ recording, magnetic flux placed on the surface of the disk never returns to zero. Figure 11–22 illustrates the information stored in a portion of a track. It also shows how the magnetic field encodes the data. Note that arrows are used in this illustration to show polarity of the magnetic field stored on the surface of the disk.

The main reason that this form of magnetic encoding was chosen is that it automatically erases old information when new information is recorded. If another technique were used, a separate erase head would be required. The mechanical alignment of a separate erase head and a separate read/write head is virtually impossible. The magnetic flux density of the NRZ signal is so intense that it completely satu-

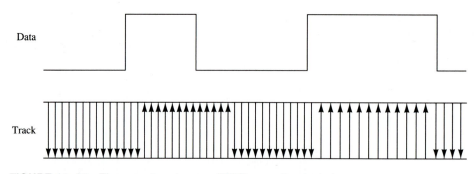

FIGURE 11–22 The nonreturn to zero (NRZ) recording technique.

rates (magnetizes) the surface of the disk, erasing all prior data. It also ensures that information will not be affected by noise because the amplitude of the magnetic field contains no information. The information is stored in the placement of the changes of magnetic field.

Data are stored in the form of MFM (modified frequency modulation) in modern floppy disk systems. The MFM recording technique stores data in the form illustrated in Figure 11–23. Notice that each bit time is $2\mu s$ in width on a double-density disk. This means that data are recorded at the rate of 500,000 bits per second. Each 2-μs bit time is divided into two parts. One part is designated to hold a clock pulse and the other holds a data pulse. If a clock pulse is present, it is 1 μs in width as is a data pulse. Clock and data pulses are never present at the same time in one bit period. (Note that high-density disk drives half these times so that a bit time is 1 μs and a clock or data pulse is 0.5 μs is width. This also doubles the transfer rate to 1 million bits per second.)

If a data pulse is present, the bit time represents a logic 1. If no data or no clock are present, the bit time represents a logic 0. If a clock pulse is present with no data pulse, the bit time also represents a logic 0. The rules followed when data are stored using MFM are

1. A data pulse is always stored for a logic 1.
2. No data and no clock are stored for the first logic 0 in a string of logic 0s.
3. The second and subsequent logic 0s in a row contain a clock pulse, but no data pulse.

The reason that a clock is inserted as the second and subsequent zero in a row is to maintain sychronization while data are read from the disk. The electronics

FIGURE 11–23 Modified frequency modulation (MFM) used with disk memory.

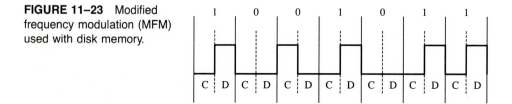

used to recapture the data from the disk drive use a phase-locked loop to generate a clock and a data window. The phase-locked loop needs a clock or data to maintain sychronized operation.

The 3½″ Microfloppy Disk. Another very popular disk size is the 3½″ microfloppy disk. Recently this size floppy disk has begun to sell very well and in the future promises to be the dominant-size floppy disk. The microfloppy is a much-improved version of the minifloppy described earlier. Figure 11–24 illustrates the 3½″ microfloppy disk.

Disk designers noticed several shortcomings in the minifloppy, a scaled-down version of the 8″ standard floppy, soon after it was released. Probably one of the biggest problems with the minifloppy is that it is packaged in a semirigid plastic cover that bends easily. The microfloppy is packaged in a rigid plastic jacket that will not bend easily. This rigidity provides a much greater degree of protection to the disk inside the jacket.

Another problem with the minifloppy is the head slot that continually exposes the surface of the disk to contaminants. This problem is also corrected on the microfloppy, because it is constructed with a spring-loaded sliding head door. The head door remains closed until the disk is inserted into the drive. Once inside the drive, the drive mechanism slides open the door, exposing the surface of the disk to the read/write heads. This provides a great deal of protection to the surface of the microfloppy disk.

Yet another improvement is the sliding plastic write protection mechanism on the microfloppy disk. On the minifloppy disk a piece of tape was placed over a notch on the side the jacket to prevent writing. This plastic tape easily became dislodged

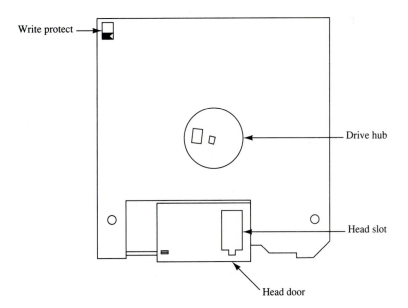

FIGURE 11–24 The 3½″ microfloppy disk.

inside disk drives, causing problems. On the microfloppy, an integrated plastic slide has replaced the tape write protection mechanism. To write protect (prevent writing) the microfloppy disk, the plastic slide is moved to *open* the hole through the disk jacket. This allows light to strike the sensor that inhibits writing.

Still another improvement is the replacement of the index hole with a different drive mechanism. The drive mechanism on the minifloppy allowed the disk drive to grab the disk at any point. This required the index hole so that the electronics could find the beginning of a track. The index hole was another trouble spot because it collected dirt and dust. The microfloppy has a drive mechanism that is keyed so that it only fits one way inside the disk drive. The index hole is no longer required because of this keyed drive mechanism. Because of the sliding head mechanism and the fact that no index hole exists, the microfloppy disk has no place to catch dust or dirt.

Two types of microfloppy disks are widely available: the double-sided, double-density (*DSDD*) and the high-density (*HD*). The double-sided, double-density microfloppy disk has 80 tracks per side with each track containing 9 sectors. Each sector contains 512 bytes of information. This allows 80 tracks per side $\times$ 2 sides $\times$ 9 sectors $\times$ 512 bytes per sector or 737,280 (720K) bytes of data to be stored on a double-density, double-sided floppy disk.

The high-density, double-sided microfloppy disk stores even more information. The high-density version has 80 tracks per side, but the number of sectors is doubled to 18 per track. This format still uses 512 bytes per sector, as did the double-density format. The total number of bytes on a high-density, double-sided microfloppy disk is 80 tracks per side $\times$ 2 sides $\times$ 18 sectors per track $\times$ 512 bytes per sector or 1,474,560 (1.44M) bytes of information.

Recently, a new size 3 ½″ floppy disk has been introduced, the EHD (extended high density) floppy disk. This new format stores 2.88M bytes of data on a single floppy disk. At this time this format is expensive and will take time to become common.

Hard Disk Memory

Larger disk memory is available in the form of the hard disk drive. The hard disk drive is often called a *fixed disk* because it is not removable like the floppy disk. A hard disk is also often called a *rigid disk,* as sometimes is the term *Winchester drive*. Hard disk memory has a much larger capacity than the floppy disk memory. Hard disk memory is available in sizes approaching 1G byte of data. Common, low-cost sizes are currently 65M bytes or 80M bytes.

There are several differences between the floppy disk and the hard disk memory. The hard disk memory uses a flying head to store and read data from the surface of the disk. A flying head, which is very small and light, does not touch the surface of the disk. It flies above the surface on a film of air that is carried with the surface of the disk as it spins, at typically 3,600 RPM, which is 12 times faster than the floppy disk. This higher rotational speed is what allows the head to fly (just as an airplane flies) just over the top of the surface of the disk, and is an important feature because there is no wear on the surface as there is with the floppy disk.

Problems can arise because of flying heads. One problem is a head crash. If the power is abruptly interrupted or the hard disk drive is jarred, the head can crash onto the disk surface. This can damage the disk surface or the head. To help prevent crashes, some drive manufacturers have included a system that automatically parks the head when power is interrupted. This type of disk drive has autoparking heads. When the heads are parked they are moved to a safe landing zone (unused track) when the power is disconnected. Some drives are not autoparking. This type of drive usually requires a program that parks the heads on the innermost track before power is disconnected. The innermost track is a safe landing area because it is the very last track filled by the disk drive. Parking is the responsibility of the operator in this type of disk drive.

Another difference between a floppy disk drive and a hard disk drive is the number of heads and disk surfaces. A floppy disk drive has two heads, one for the upper surface and one for the lower surface. The hard disk drive may have up to eight disk surfaces (four platters) with up to two heads per surface. Each time that a new cylinder is obtained by moving the head assembly, 16 new tracks are available under the heads. Refer to Figure 11–25, which illustrates a hard disk system.

Heads are moved from track to track using either a stepper motor or a voice coil. The stepper motor is slow and noisy, while the voice coil mechanism is quiet and quick. Moving the head assembly requires one step per cylinder in a system that uses a stepper motor to position the heads. In a system that uses a voice coil, the heads can be moved many cylinders with one sweeping motion. This makes the disk drive faster when seeking new cylinders.

Another advantage of the voice coil system is that a servomechanism can monitor the amplitude of the signal as it comes from the read head and make slight adjustments in the position of the heads. This is not possible with a stepper motor, which relies strictly on mechanics to position the head. Stepper-motor-type head

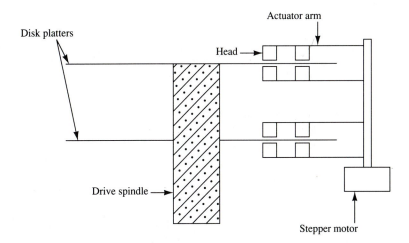

FIGURE 11–25 A hard disk drive that uses four heads per platter.

positioning mechanisms can often become misaligned with use, while the voice coil mechanism corrects for any misalignment.

Hard disk drives often store information in sectors that are 1,024 bytes in length. Data are addressed in *clusters* of four sectors, which contain 4,096 bytes on most hard drives. Hard disk drives use either MFM or RLL to store information. MFM is described with floppy disk drives. *Run-length limited* (RLL) is described here.

A typical MFM hard disk drive uses 18 sector per track so that 18K bytes of data are stored per track. If a hard disk drive has a capacity of 40M bytes, it contains approximately 2,280 tracks. If the disk drive has two heads, this means that it contains, 1,140 cylinders. If it contains four heads, then it has 570 cylinders. These specifications vary from disk drive to disk drive.

RLL Storage.   Run-length limited (RLL) disk drives use a different method for encoding the data than MFM. The term *RLL* means that the run of zeros (zeros in a row) is limited. A common RLL encoding scheme in use today is *RLL 2,7*. This means that the run of zeros is always between two and seven. Table 11–1 illustrates the coding used with standard RLL.

Data are first encoded using Table 11–1 before being sent to the drive electronics for storage on the disk surface. Because of this encoding technique, it is possible to achieve a 50 percent increase in data storage on a disk drive when compared to MFM. The main difference is that the RLL drive often contains 27 tracks instead of the 18 found on the MFM drive. (Some RLL drives also use 35 sectors per track.)

It is interesting to note that RLL encoding requires no change to the drive electronics or surface of the disk in most cases. The only difference is a slight decrease in the pulse width using RLL, which may require slightly finer oxide particles on the surface of the disk. Disk manufacturers test the surface of the disk and grade the disk drive as either an MFM-certified or an RLL-certified drive. Other than grading, there is no difference in the construction of the disk drive or the magnetic material that coats the surface of the disks.

Figure 11–26 shows a comparison of MFM data and RLL data. Notice that the amount of time (space) required to store RLL data is reduced when compared to MFM. Here a 101001011 is coded in both MFM and RLL so that these two standards can be compared. Notice that the width of the RLL signal has been reduced so that three pulses fit in the same space as a clock and a data pulse for MFM. A 40M-

TABLE 11–1   Standard RLL 2,7 coding

Input Data	RLL Output
000	000100
10	0100
010	100100
0010	00100100
11	1000
011	001000
0011	00001000

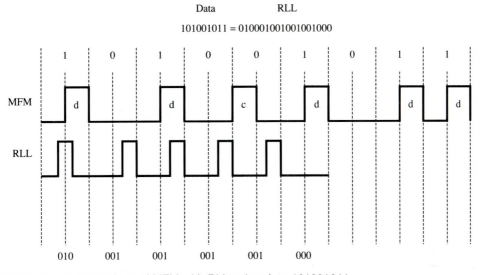

FIGURE 11–26 A comparison of MFM with RLL using data 101001011.

byte MFM disk can hold 60M bytes of RLL-encoded data. Besides holding more information, the RLL drive can be written and read at a higher rate.

All hard disk drives use either MFM or RLL encoding. There are a number of disk drive interfaces in use today. The oldest is the ST-506 interface, which uses either MFM or RLL data. A disk system using this interface is also called either an MFM or RLL disk system. Newer standards are also in use today. These include ESDI, SCSI, and IDE, all of which use RLL, even though they normally do not call attention to it. The main difference is the interface between the computer and the disk drive. The IDE system is becoming the standard hard disk memory interface.

The *enhanced small disk interface* (ESDI) system is capable of transferring data between itself and the computer at rates approaching 10M bytes per second. An ST-506 interface can approach a transfer rate of 860K bytes per second.

The *small computer system interface* (SCSI) system is also in use, because it allows up to seven different disk or other interfaces to be connected to the computer through the same interface controller. SCSI is found in some PC-type computers and also in the Apple Macintosh system. An improved version, SCSI-II, has started to appear in some systems.

The newest system is *integrated drive electronics* (IDE), which incorporates the disk controller in the disk drive, and attaches the disk drive to the host system through a small interface cable. This cable allows many disk drives to be connected to a system without worrying about bus conflicts or controllers conflicts. IDE drives are found in newer IBM PS-2 systems and many clones. The IDE interface is also capable of driving other I/O devices besides the hard disk. This interface also usually contains 32K bytes of cache memory for disk data. The cache speeds disk transfers. Common access times for an IDE drive are often less than 16 ms, where the access time for a floppy disk is about 200 ms.

Optical Disk Memory

Optical disk memory is commonly available in two forms: the *CDROM* (compact disk/read only memory) and the *WORM* (write once/read mostly). The CDROM is the lowest cost optical disk, but it suffers from lack of speed. Access times for a CDROM are typically 150 ms, about the same as a floppy disk. Hard disk magnetic memory can have access times of as little as 16 ms. The CDROM also suffers from lack of software applications at this time. The CDROM is available with large-volume data storage, such as the Bible, Encyclopedia, clip art, and magazine articles. None of these applications have wide appeal at the current prices. At some future date if access times decrease and more applications are introduced, the CDROM may become very popular. A CDROM stores 680M bytes of data or a combination of data and musical passages. As systems develop and become more visually active, the use of the CDROM drive will become more common.

The WORM drive sees far more commercial application than the CDROM. The problem is that its application is very specialized due to the nature of the WORM. Because data may only be written once, the main application is in the banking industry, insurance industry, and other massive data-storing organizations. The WORM is normally used to form an audit trail of transactions that are spooled onto the WORM and retrieved only during an audit. You might call the WORM an archiving device.

Many WORM and read/write optical disk memory systems are interfaced to the microprocessor using the SCSI or ESDI interface standards used with hard disk memory. The difference is that the current optical disk drives are no faster than most floppy drives. Some CDROM drives are interfaced to the microprocessor through proprietary interfaces that are not compatible with other disk drives.

The main advantage of the optical disk is its durability. Because a solid-state laser beam is used to read the data from the disk, and the focus point is below a protective plastic coating, the surface of the disk may contain small scratches and dirt particles and still be read correctly. This feature allows less care of the optical disk than a comparable floppy disk. About the only way to destroy data on an optical disk is to break it or deeply scar it.

Figure 11–27 illustrates the internal structure of a CDROM drive and the CDROM disk. The data are stored on the bottom side of a CDROM as a series of *pits* and *lands*. A pit represents a logic 0 and a land represents a logic 1. The series of pits and lands are stored in a spiral track, much like the track on a phonograph record, that is nearly 3 miles in length. A single CDROM can store a combination of music (70–80 minutes) and digital data (680M bytes).

Data are read from the CDROM by flooding the bottom of the disk with the light generated by an infrared laser diode. The laser beam is focused through a semitransparent mirror and a series of lenses onto the data track. If the laser beam strikes a land, most of the light is reflected back through the lens arrangement and semitransparent mirror, where it strikes a photodiode and produces an output voltage. If the laser beam strikes a pit, most of the light is diffused by the pit, so very little light strikes the photodiode and no output signal is produced.

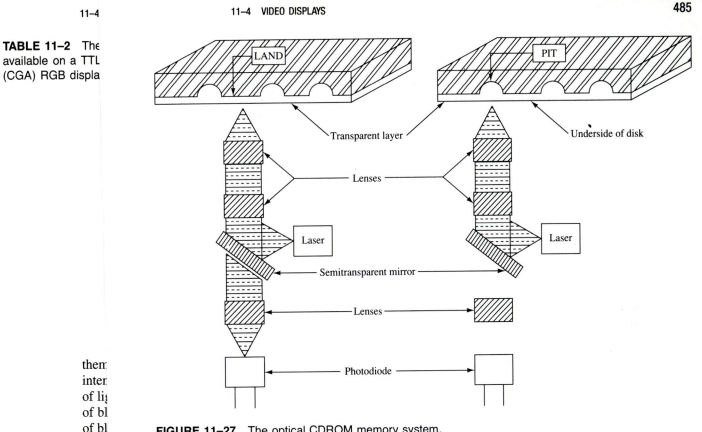

FIGURE 11–27 The optical CDROM memory system.

them
inter
of li;
of bl
of bl
(low·
colo:
low ;
of lit

itor ‹
Two
tion ‹

11–4 VIDEO DISPLAYS

Modern video displays are *OEM* (original equipment manufacturer) devices that are usually purchased and incorporated into a system. Today there are many different types of video displays available. Of the types available, either color or monochrome versions are found.

Monochrome versions usually display information using amber, green, or paper-white displays. The paper-white display is becoming extremely popular for many applications. The most common of these applications are desk-top publishing and computer-aided drafting (CAD).

The color displays are more diverse. Color display systems are available that accept information as a composite video signal much as your home television does, as TTL voltage level signals (0 or 5V), and as analog signals (0–0.7 V). Composite video displays are disappearing because the resolution available is too low. Today many applications require high-resolution graphics that cannot be displayed on a composite display such as a home television receiver. Early composite video displays were found with Commodore 64, Apple 2, and similar computer systems.

Vic

Fig
is
illu
the
bui
exi
in
dis
Co
tel

sep
mo
pul

syr
vid
the
col

Th

Th
use
to
dif
sys

string of zeros, and a clock pulse for the second and subsequent logic 0 in a string of zeros. The RLL scheme encodes data so 50 percent more information can be packaged onto the same disk area. Most modern disk memory systems use the RLL encoding scheme.

10. Video monitors are either TTL or analog. The TTL monitor uses two discrete voltage levels of 0 V and 5.0 V. The analog monitor uses an infinite number of voltage levels between 0.0 V and 0.7 V. Analog monitors can display an infinite number of video levels, while the TTL monitor is limited to two video levels.

11. The color TTL monitor displays 16 different colors. This variety is accomplished through three video signals (red, green, and blue) and an intensity input. The analog color monitor can display an infinite number of colors through its three video inputs. In practice, the most common form of color analog display system (VGA) can display 256K different colors.

12. The video standards found today include VGA (640×480), SVGA (800×600), and EVGA or XVGA (1024×768). In all three cases, the video information can be 256 colors out of a possible total of 256K colors.

11–6   QUESTIONS AND PROBLEMS

1. What 80286 pins are used to request and acknowledge a DMA transfer?
2. Explain what happens whenever a logic 1 is placed on the 80286 HOLD input pin.
3. A DMA read transfers data from _____ to _____.
4. A DMA write transfers data from _____ to _____.
5. The DMA controller selects the memory location used for a DMA transfer through what bus signals?
6. The DMA controller selects the I/O device used during a DMA transfer by which pin?
7. What is a memory-to-memory DMA transfer?
8. Describe the effect on the 80286 and DMA controller when the HOLD and HLDA pins are at their logic 1 levels.
9. Describe the effect on the 80286 and DMA controller when the HOLD and HLDA pins are at their logic 0 levels.
10. The 82258 ADMA is a _____ channel DMA controller.
11. True or false: Address connections A_0–A_7 are used to select internal registers during programming of the 82258 ADMA.
12. What is meant by the term *local bus*?
13. If the 82258 ADMA is decoded at I/O ports 2000H–20FFH, what ports are used to program channel 1?
14. Describe how the 82285 ADMA is programmed so it will not tie up the system with DMA transfers.
15. Describe the difference between a one-cycle and a two-cycle transfer using the 82258 ADMA.
16. A memory-to-memory transfer must be a _____ cycle transfer when using the 82258 ADMA.

FIGURE 11–28

17. Which register programs the 82258 for a one- or two-cycle transfer?
18. Which 82258 ADMA registers are programmed to initialize the controller?
19. Describe the purpose of the channel control block.
20. What is a type 1 command?
21. What is a type 2 command?
22. What determines whether a channel control block is short or extended?
23. If a DMA transfer occurs using memory location segment address 1000H and offset address 2000H, what address is placed in the channel control block?
24. How many bytes can be transferred by the 82258 ADMA?
25. Write a sequence of instructions that transfer data from memory location 10000H–100FFH to 20000H–200FFH using channel 2 of the 82258 ADMA. You must initialize the ADMA and use I/O ports 4000H–40FFH for this program.
26. Write a sequence of instructions that transfer data from memory to an external I/O device using channel 3 of the ADMA. The memory area to be transferred is at location 20000H–20FFFH and the ADMA is decoded at I/O ports 3000H–30FFH.
27. The $5 \frac{1}{4}''$ disk is known as a _____-floppy disk.
28. The $3 \frac{1}{2}''$ disk is known as a _____-floppy disk.
29. Data are recorded in concentric rings on the surface of a disk known as a _____.
30. A track is divided into sections of data called _____.
31. On a double-sided disk, the upper and lower tracks together are called a _____.
32. Why is NRZ recording used on a disk memory system?
33. Draw the timing diagram generated to write a 1001010000 using MFM encoding.
34. Draw the timing diagram generated to write a 1001010000 using RLL encoding.
35. What is a flying head?
36. Why must the heads on a hard disk be parked?
37. What is the difference between a voice coil head position mechanism and a stepper motor head positioning mechanism?
38. What is a WORM?
39. What is a CDROM?
40. What is the difference between a TTL monitor and an analog monitor?
41. What are the three primary colors of light?
42. What are the three secondary colors of light?
43. What is a pixel?
44. A video display with a resolution of 800 × 600 contains _____ lines of video information with each line divided into _____ pixels.
45. Explain how a TTL RGB monitor can display 16 different colors.
46. Explain how an analog RGB monitor can display an infinite number of colors.
47. If an analog RGB video system uses 7-bit DACs, it can generate _____ different colors.
48. Why does standard VGA only allow 256 different colors out of 256K colors to be displayed at one time?
49. If a video system uses a vertical frequency of 60 Hz and a horizontal frequency of 32,400 Hz, how many raster lines are generated?

CHAPTER 12

The Family of Arithmetic Coprocessors

INTRODUCTION

The Intel family of arithmetic coprocessors includes the 8087, 80287, 80387SX, 80387DX, 80487SX, and the 80486DX microprocessor that contains its own built-in arithmetic coprocessor. The instruction sets and programming for these devices are almost identical, the difference being that each coprocessor is designed to function with a different Intel microprocessor. This chapter provides details on the entire family, generically providing details on only the 80287–80286 interface.

    The family of coprocessors, which we label the 80X87, is able to multiply, divide, add, subtract, find the square root, partial tangent, partial arctangent, and logarithms. Data types include 16-, 32-, and 64-bit signed integers; 18-digit BCD data; and 32-, 64-, and 80-bit floating-point numbers. The operations performed by the 80X87 generally execute at about 100 times faster than equivalent operations written with the most efficient programs.

OBJECTIVES

Upon completion of this chapter, you will be able to:

1. Convert data between decimal and the data type allowed for the arithmetic coprocessor.
2. Explain the operation of the 80287 arithmetic coprocessor when interfaced to the 80286 microprocessor.
3. Interface an 80287 to an 80286.
4. Explain the operation and addressing modes for each arithmetic coprocessor instruction.
5. Develop software solving complex arithmetic problems using the arithmetic coprocessor.

12–1   DATA FORMATS FOR THE ARITHMETIC COPROCESSOR

This section of the text presents the types of data used with all family members (8087, 80287, 80387SX, 80387DX, 80487SX, and the 80486DX). These types include signed integer, BCD, and floating point. Each has a specific use in a system, and many systems require all three data types.

Signed Integers

The signed integers used with the coprocessor are basically the same as those described in Chapter 1. When used with the arithmetic coprocessor, signed integers are 16 (word), 32 (short integer), or 64 bits (long integer) in width. Conversion between decimal and signed-integer format is handled in exactly the same manner as it was for 8-bit signed integers described in Chapter 1. As you will recall, positive numbers are stored in true form with a leftmost sign-bit of 0, and negative numbers are stored in two's complement form with a leftmost sign-bit of 1.

The word integer ranges in value from $-32,768$ to $+32,767$, the short integer from -2×10^9 to $+2 \times 10^9$, and the long integer from -9×10^{18} to $+9 \times 10^{18}$. Integer data types are found in many applications that use the arithmetic coprocessor. Refer to Figure 12–1, which shows these three forms of signed-integer data.

Data are stored in memory using the same assembler directives described and used in earlier chapters. We use the DW directive to define words, DD to define short integers, and DQ to define long integers. Example 12–1 shows how several different sizes of signed integers are defined for use by the assembler.

EXAMPLE 12–1

0000 0002	DATA1	DW	+2 ;16-bit integer
0002 FFDE	DATA2	DW	-34 ;16-bit integer
0004 000004D2	DATA3	DD	+1234 ;short integer
0008 FFFFFF9C	DATA4	DD	-100 ;short integer
000C 0000000000005BA0	DATA5	DQ	+23456 ;long integer
0014 FFFFFFFFFFFFFF86	DATA6	DQ	-122 ;long integer

Binary-Coded Decimal

The binary-coded-decimal (BCD) form requires 80 bits of memory. Each number is stored as an 18-digit packed number in 9 bytes of memory as two digits per byte. The tenth byte contains only a sign bit for the 18-digit signed BCD number. Figure 12–2 shows the format of the BCD number used with the arithmetic coprocessor. Note that both positive and negative numbers are stored in true form and never in 10's complement form. The DT directive is used to store BCD data in the memory.

FIGURE 12–1　Integer forms of data for the 80287 family of numeric coprocessors. (a) Word, (b) short, and (c) long.

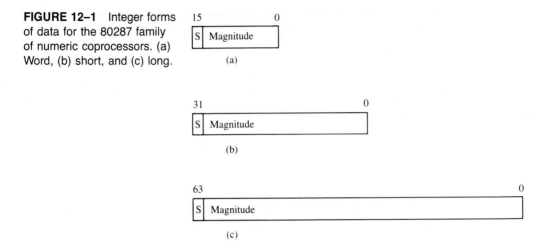

Floating Point

Floating-point numbers are often called *real numbers* because they hold integers, fractions, or mixed numbers. A floating-point number has three parts: a *sign-bit,* a *biased exponent,* and a *significand.* Floating-point numbers are written in *scientific binary notation.* The Intel family of arithmetic coprocessors supports three types of floating-point numbers: short (32 bits), long (64 bits), and temporary (80 bits). Refer to Figure 12–3 for examples of the three forms of the floating-point number. Please note that we also call the short form a *single-precision* number and the long form a *double-precision* number. Sometimes the 80-bit temporary form is called an *extended-precision* number. The floating-point numbers and the operations performed by the arithmetic coprocessor conform to the IEEE-754 standard as adopted by all major software producers.

Converting to Floating-Point Form.　Converting from decimal to floating-point form is a simple task that is accomplished by the following steps:

1. Convert the decimal number into binary.
2. Normalize the binary number.
3. Calculate the biased exponent.
4. Store the number in floating-point form.

These four steps are illustrated for the decimal number 100.25 in Example 12–2. Here the decimal number is converted to a single-precision floating-point number.

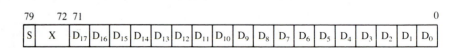

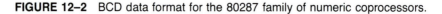

FIGURE 12–2　BCD data format for the 80287 family of numeric coprocessors.

EXAMPLE 12–2

Step	Result
1	$100.25 = 1100100.01$
2	$1100100.01 = 1.10010001 \times 2^6$
3	$110 = 110 + 0111111 = 10000101$

Step	S Exponent Significand
4	0 10000101 10010001000000000000000

In step three the biased exponent is the exponent, a +6 (110), plus a bias of 01111111 (7FH). All single-precision numbers use a bias of 7FH, double-precision numbers use a bias of 3FFH, and extended-precision numbers use a bias of 3FFFH.

Step 4 is where all the information is combined to generate the floating-point number. The leftmost bit is the sign-bit of the number. In this case, it is a 0 because the number was +100.25 The biased exponent follows the sign-bit. The significand is a 23-bit number with an implied one-bit. Note that the significand of a number 1.XXXXX is the XXXX portion. The 1 is an implied one-bit that is only stored in the extended-precision form of the floating-point number as an explicit one-bit.

Some special rules apply to a few numbers. The number 0, for example, is stored as all zeros except for the sign-bit, which can be a logic 1 to represent a negative zero. We also store plus and minus infinity as logic 1s in the exponent with a significand of all zeros and the sign-bit that represents plus or minus. A NAN (not-a-number) is an invalid floating-point result that has all ones in the exponent with a significand that is not all zeros.

FIGURE 12–3 Floating-point (real) numbers. (a) Short with a bias of 127 (7FH)and an implicit 1, (b) long with a bias of 1023 (3FFH) and an implicit 1, and (3) temporary with a bias of 16,383 (3FFFH) and a nonimplicit 1.

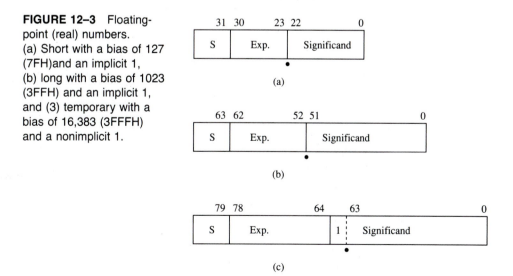

Converting from Floating-Point Form.   Conversion to a decimal number from a floating-point number is summarized in the following steps:

1. Separate the sign-bit, biased exponent, and significand.
2. Convert the biased exponent into a true exponent by subtracting the bias.
3. Write the number as a normalized binary number.
4. Convert it to a denormalized binary number.
5. Convert the denormalized binary number into decimal.

These five steps are used to convert a single-precision floating-point number to decimal form in Example 12–3. Notice how the sign-bit of 1 makes the decimal result negative. Also notice that the implied 1 bit is added to the normalized binary result in step 3.

EXAMPLE 12–3

Step	Result
1	1 100000011 10010010000000000000000
2	10000011 = 1000011 - 01111111 = 100
3	1.1001001×2^4
4	11001.001
5	- 25.125

Storing Floating-Point Data in Memory.   Floating-point numbers are stored with the assembler using the DD directive for single precision, DQ for double precision, and DT for extended precision. Some examples of floating-point data storage are shown in Example 12–4.

EXAMPLE 12–4

0000 C377999A	DATA7	DD	-247.6	;define single precision
0004 40000000	DATA8	DD	2.0	;define single precision
0008 486F4200	DATA9	DD	2.45E+5	;define single precision
000C 0000000000105940	DATA10	DQ	+100.25	;define double precision
0014 406A1327F73B54BF	DATA11	DQ	-.001235	;define double precision
001C 764F1E166A4DF3870440	DATA12	DT	+33.9876	;define extended precision

12–2   THE 80287 ARCHITECTURE

This section details the 80287 architecture, which is almost identical to the 8087 and 80387 architectures. The 80287 is designed to operate concurrently with the 80286 microprocessor, as is the 8087 with the 8086/8088 and the 80387 with the 80386.

Note that the 80486 microprocessor contains its own internal and fully compatible version of the 80387. The 80287 executes 68 different instructions with the 80286 microprocessor. The 80286 executes all normal instructions, and the 80287 executes arithmetic coprocessor instructions. Figure 12–4 shows the pinout of the Intel 80287 arithmetic coprocessor, which is sometimes called a *numeric coprocessor*.

80287 Pin Definitions

The following list describes all the pins on the 80287 arithmetic coprocessor:

1. CLK—Clock Input: provides the 80287 with its basic timing signal.
2. CLM—Clock Mode: selects whether the CLK input is divided by 3 or used directly. A logic 1 on this pin will cause the CLK input to be used as the internal clock signal.
3. CLK286—80286 Clock Input: connected to the 80286 CLK pin in most systems.
4. RESET—Reset Input: used to initialize the 80287.
5. D_{15}–D_0—Data Bus: used to capture data and commands from the system data bus and to transfer information to the system data bus.
6. $\overline{BUSY}$—Busy Output: a signal that indicates the 80287 is busy executing an arithmetic coprocessor instruction. This pin is connected to the $\overline{BUSY}$ pin on the 80286 microprocessor.
7. $\overline{ERROR}$—Error Output: a signal that indicates a unmasked error condition and is a direct reflection of the ES status bit.
8. PEREQ—Coprocessor Operand Data Transfer Request: signals that the 80287 is ready to transfer data through its data bus connection.
9. $\overline{PEACK}$—Coprocessor Operand Data Transfer Acknowledge: an input that indicates that the PEREQ signal has been recognized by the 80286 microprocessor.
10. $\overline{NPRD}$—Coprocessor Read: this input enables a data transfer from the 80287.
11. $\overline{NPWR}$—Coprocessor Write: this input writes data to the 80287.
12. $\overline{NPS_1}$, NPS_2—Coprocessor Select: these lines select the 80287 so it can perform arithmetic coprocessor operations.

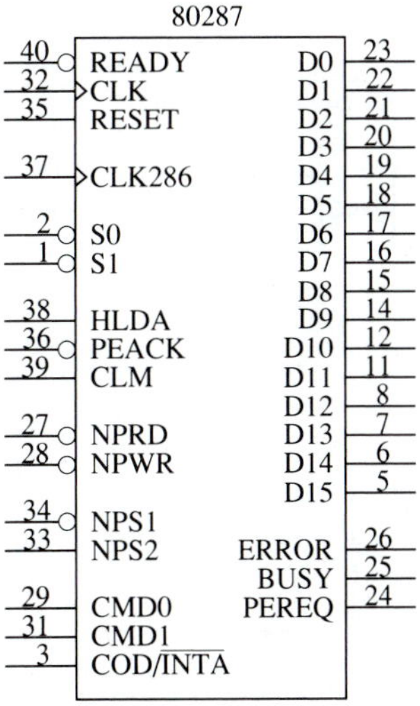

FIGURE 12–4 The 80287 arithmetic coprocessor.

13. CMD$_1$, CMD$_0$—Command Lines: direct the operation of the 80287. These pins normally connect to A$_2$ and A$_1$, respectively.
14. HLDA—Hold Acknowledge: connects directly to the HLDA pin on the 80286.
15. COD/$\overline{\text{INTA}}$—Code/Interrupt Acknowledge: connects to the same pin on the 80286.
16. V$_{cc}$—Power Supply: connected to the system +5.0-V power supply bus.
17. V$_{ss}$—Ground: connected to the system ground.

Internal Structure of the 80287

Figure 12–5 shows the internal structure of the 80287 arithmetic coprocessor. Notice that this device is divided into two major sections: the *control unit* and the *numeric execution unit*.

The control unit interfaces the 80287 to the 80286 microprocessor system data bus. Both the 80286 and 80287 monitor the instruction stream. If the instruction is an ESC (coprocessor) instruction, the 80287 executes, and if not, the 80286 executes it.

The numeric execution unit (NEU) is responsible for executing all 68 instructions. The NEU has an eight-register stack that holds operands for arithmetic instructions and for results of arithmetic instructions. Instructions either address data in specific stack data registers or use a push and pop mechanism to store and retrieve data. Other registers in the NEU are status, control, tag, and exception pointers.

The stack within the 80287 contains eight registers that are each 80 bits in width. These stack registers always contain an 80-bit extended-precision floating-

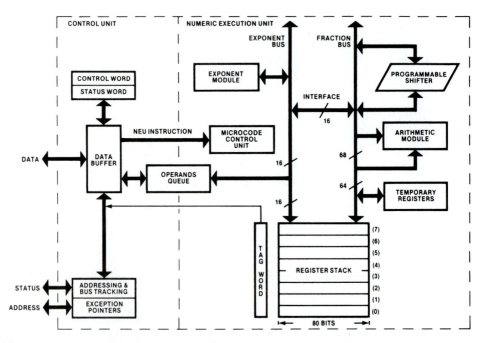

FIGURE 12–5   The internal structure of the 80287. (Courtesy of Intel Corporation)

point number. The only time data appear as any other form is when they are transferred between the coprocessor and the memory system.

Status Register. The status register (see Figure 12–6) reflects the overall operation of the 80287. The status register is accessed by executing the 80287 instruction (FSTSW) that stores the contents of the status register into a word of memory. The FSTSWAX instruction copies the status register directly to the AX register. Once status is stored in memory or AX, the bit positions of the status register can be examined by normal 80286 software.

Following is a list of the status bits and their application:

1. B—Busy: indicates that the 80287 is busy executing a task.
2. C_3–C_0—Condition Code Bits: refer to Table 12–1 for a complete listing of each combination of these bits and their function. Note that these bits have different meanings for different instructions.
3. TOP—Top-of-Stack: indicates the current register addressed as the top-of-the-stack.
4. ES—Error Summary: is set if any unmasked error bit (PE, UE, OE, ZE, DE, or IE) is set.
5. PE—Precision Error: results or operands exceed selected precision.
6. UE—Underflow Error: indicates a nonzero result that is too small to represent.
7. OE—Overflow Error: indicates a result that is too large to be represented. If this error is masked, the 80287 generates infinity.
8. ZE—Zero Error: indicates that the divisor was zero, while the dividend is a noninfinity, nonzero number.
9. DE—Denormalized Error: indicates that at least one of the operands is denormalized.
10. IE—Invalid Error: indicates a stack overflow or underflow, indeterminate form ($0/0$, ∞, $-\infty$, etc.), or the use of a NAN as an operand. This flag indicates errors such as those produced by taking the squareroot of a negative number.

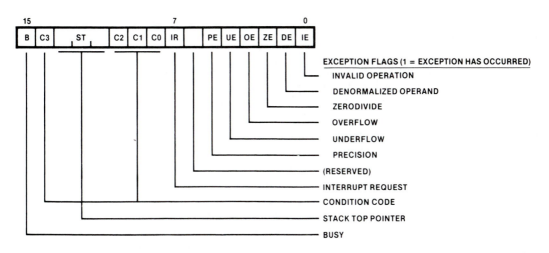

FIGURE 12–6 80287 family status word. (Courtesy of Intel Corporation)

TABLE 12–1 The 80287 status register condition code bits

Instruction	C_3	C_2	C_1	C_0	Function
FTST,FCOM	0	0	X	0	ST > Source or (0 FTST)
	0	0	X	1	ST < Source or (0 FTST)
	1	0	X	0	ST = Source or (0 FTST)
	1	1	X	1	ST is not comparable
FPREM	Q1	0	Q0	Q2	Rightmost 3 bits of quotient
	?	1	?	?	Incomplete
FXAM	0	0	0	0	+ Unnormal
	0	0	0	1	+ NAN
	0	0	1	0	− Unnormal
	0	0	1	1	− NAN
	0	1	0	0	+ Normal
	0	1	0	1	+ ∞
	0	1	1	0	− Normal
	0	1	1	1	− ∞
	1	0	0	0	+ 0
	1	0	0	1	Empty
	1	0	1	0	− 0
	1	0	1	1	Empty
	1	1	0	0	+ Denormal
	1	1	0	1	Empty
	1	1	1	0	− Denormal
	1	1	1	1	Empty

Notes: Unnormal = leading bits of the significand are zero; denormal = exponent at its most negative value; normal = standard floating-point form; and NAN (not-a-number) = an exponent of all ones and a significand not equal to zero.

Control Register.   The control register is pictured in Figure 12–7. The control word selects precision, rounding control, and infinity control. It also masks and unmasks the exception bits that correspond to the rightmost six bits of the status register. The FLDCW instruction is used to load a value into the control register.

    Following is a description of each bit or grouping of bits found in the control register:

1. IC—Infinity Control: selects either affine or projective infinity. Affine allows positive and negative affinity, while projective assumes infinity is unsigned.
2. RC—Rounding Control: selects the type of rounding as defined in Figure 12–7.
3. PC—Precision Control: selects the precision of the result as defined in Figure 12–7.
4. Exception Masks: determine whether the error indicated by the exception affects the error bit in the status register. If a logic 1 is placed in one of the exception control bits, the corresponding status register bit is masked off.

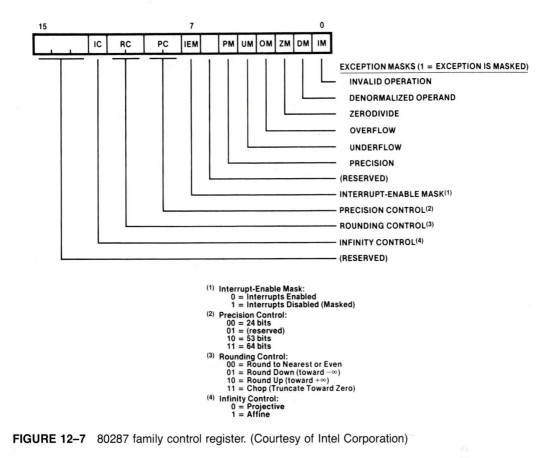

FIGURE 12–7 80287 family control register. (Courtesy of Intel Corporation)

Tag Register. The tag register indicates the contents of each location in the 80287 stack. Figure 12–8 illustrates the tag register and the status indicated by each tag. The tag indicates whether a register is valid, zero, invalid or infinity, or empty. The only way that a program can view the tag register is by storing the coprocessor environment using the FSTENV, FSAVE, or FRSTOR instructions. Each of these instructions stores the tag register along with other coprocessor data.

15							0
TAG (7)	TAG (6)	TAG (5)	TAG (4)	TAG (3)	TAG (2)	TAG (1)	TAG (0)

NOTE:
The index i of tag(i) is not top–relative. A program typically uses the "top" field of Status Word to determine which tag(i) field refers to logical top of stack.

TAG VALUES:
00 = VALID
01 = ZERO
10 = INVALID or INFINITY
11 = EMPTY

FIGURE 12–8 The TAG register and conditions held in each TAG. (Courtesy of Intel Corporation)

12–3 PROCESSOR INTERFACE

The interface of the 80287 and 80286 is much simpler when compared to most peripherals. Figure 12–9 illustrates the 80287 interfaced to a system that contains the 80286 microprocessor, the 82288 system bus controller, and the 82284 clock generator.

The interface to the 80286 system requires one additional circuit to decode I/O addresses 00F8H, 00FAH, and 00FCH, which are dedicated to the 80287 coprocessor. The microprocessor automatically generates these I/O port addresses during normal communications to the 80287.

FIGURE 12–9 The 80287 interfaced to the 80286, 82288, and 82284.

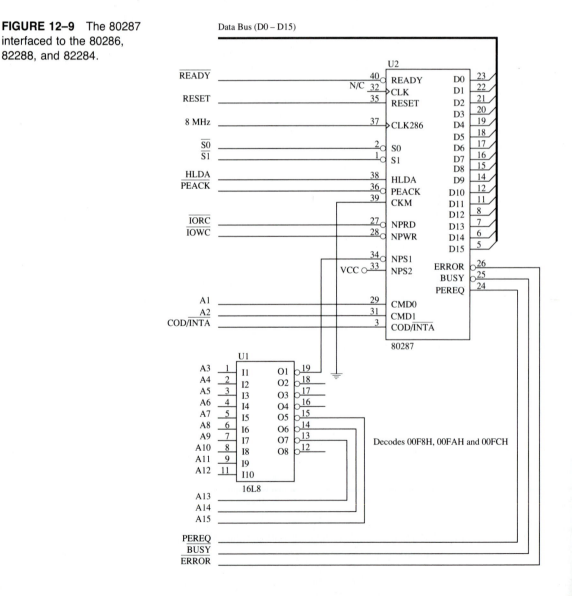

TABLE 12–2 Internal state of the 80287 after a RESET or FINIT

Field	Value	Condition
Infinity	0	Projective
Rounding	00	Round-to-nearest
Precision	11	64-bit
Error Masks	11111	Error bits disabled
Busy	0	Not busy
C_3–C_0	????	Unknown
TOP	000	Register 000
ES	0	No error
Error bits	00000	No errors
Tags	11	Empty
Registers	—	Not changed

The RESET pin initializes the 80287 whenever the microprocessor is reset. The 80287 responds to a reset input or to the software reset instruction, FINIT, in almost the same manner. The hardware reset forces the 80287 to operate in the real-mode and the FINIT instruction does not change the mode. Table 12–2 shows how the various internal sections of the 80287 respond to a reset. In all but special cases we normally operate the 80287 in the default reset mode of operation.

12–4   INSTRUCTION SET

The 80287 arithmetic coprocessor is able to execute 68 different instructions. Whenever a coprocessor instruction references the memory, the 80286 automatically generates the memory address for the instruction. The 80287 uses the data bus for data transfers during coprocessor instructions, and the 80286 uses it during normal 80286 instructions.

This section of the text describes the function of each instruction and lists its assembly language form. Because the 80287 uses the 80286 addressing modes, not all possible forms of each instruction are illustrated. Each time that the assembler encounters one of the 80287 mnemonic opcodes, it converts it into a machine language ESC instruction. The ESC instruction represents an opcode to the 80287.

Data Transfer Instructions

There are three basic data transfers: floating point, signed integer, and BCD. The only time that data ever appear in signed-integer or BCD form is in the memory. Inside the 80287, data are always stored as 80-bit extended-precision floating-point data.

Floating-Point Data Transfers. There are four floating-point data transfer instructions in the 80287 instruction set: FLD (load real), FST (store real), FSTP (store real and pop), and FXCH (exchange).

The FLD instruction loads memory data to the top of the internal 80287 stack. This instruction stores the data on the top of the stack and then decrements the stack pointer by one. Data loaded to the top of the stack are from any memory location or from another register. For example, an FLD ST(2) instruction copies the contents of register 2 to the stack top, which is ST. The top of the stack is register 0 when the 80287 is reset or initialized. Another example is the FLD DATA7 instruction that copies the contents of memory location DATA7 to the top of the stack. The size of the transfer is automatically determined by the assembler through the directives DD for single precision, DQ for double precision, and DT for extended precision.

The FST instruction stores a copy of the top of the stack into the memory location or 80287 register indicated by the operand. At the time of storage, the internal, extended-precision floating-point number is rounded to the size of the floating-point number indicated by the control register.

The FSTP instruction stores a copy of the top of the stack into memory or any 80287 register and then pops the data from the top of the stack. FST could be thought of as a *copy* instruction and FSTP as a *removal* instruction.

The FXCH instruction exchanges the register indicated by the operand with the top of the stack. For example, the FXCH ST(2) instruction, exchanges the top of the stack with register 2.

Integer Data Transfer Instructions.   The 80287 supports three integer data transfer instructions: FILD (load integer), FIST (store integer), and FISTP (store integer and pop). These three instructions function as did FLD, FST, and FSTP, except the data transferred are integer data. The 80287 automatically converts the internal extended-precision data to integer data. The size of the data is determined by the way that the label is defined with DW, DD, or DQ.

BCD Data Transfer Instructions.   Two instructions are used to load or store BCD data. The FBLD instructions loads the top of the stack with BCD memory data, and the FBSTP stores the top of the stack and does a pop.

Example 12–5 shows how the assembler automatically adjusts the FLD, FILD, and FBLD instructions for different size operands. (Look closely at the machine-coded forms of the instructions.) Note in this example, that it begins with the .286 and .287 directives that identify the microprocessor as an 80286 and the coprocessor as an 80287. The assembler by default assumes that the software is assembled for an 8086/8088 with an 8087 coprocessor.

EXAMPLE 12–5

```
                             .286
                             .287

0000                         DATAS    SEGMENT

0000  41F00000               DATA1    DD    30.0        ;single-precision
0004  0000000000003E40       DATA2    DQ    30.0        ;double-precision
000C  0000000000000F00340    DATA3    DT    30.0        ;extended-precision
```

```
0016 001E                              DATA4    DW      30          ;16-bit integer
0018 0000001E                          DATA5    DD      30          ;32-bit integer
001C 1E00000000000000                  DATA6    DQ      30          ;64-bit integer

0024 30000000000000000000              DATA7    DT      30H         ;BCD 30

002E                                   DATAS    ENDS

0000                                   CODE     SEGMENT

                                                ASSUME  CS:CODE,DS:DATAS

0000 D9 06 0000 R                               FLD     DATA1
0004 DD 06 0004 R                               FLD     DATA2
0008 DB 2E 000C R                               FLD     DATA3

000C DF 06 0016 R                               FILD    DATA4
0010 DB 06 0018 R                               FILD    DATA5
0014 DF 2E 001C R                               FILD    DATA6

0018 DF 26 0024 R                               FBLD    DATA7

001C                                   CODE     ENDS
                                                END
```

Arithmetic Instructions

Arithmetic instructions for the 80287 include addition, subtraction, multiplication, division, and square root. Arithmetic-related instructions include scaling, rounding, absolute value, and changing the sign.

Table 12–3 shows the basic addressing modes allowed for the arithmetic operations in the 80287. Each addressing mode is shown with an example using the FADD (real addition) instruction. All arithmetic operations are floating-point except in some cases when memory data are referenced as an operand.

The classic stack form of addressing operand data (stack addressing) uses the top of the stack as a source operand and the next to the top of the stack as a

TABLE 12–3 Arithmetic addressing mode for the 80287

Mode	Form	Examples
Stack	ST,ST(1)	FADD
Register	ST,ST(n)	FADD ST,ST(2)
	ST(n),ST	FADD ST(6),ST
Register pop	ST(n),ST	FADDP ST(3),ST
Memory	Operand	FADD DATA

Note: Stack addressing is fixed as ST,ST(1) and n = register number 0–7.

destination operand. Afterwards, the two original data are removed from the stack, leaving only the result remaining at the top of the stack. To use this addressing form the instruction is placed in the program without any operands such as FADD or FSUB. The FADD instruction adds ST and ST(1) and stores the answer at the top of the stack. It also removes the original two data from the stack by popping.

The register-addressing mode uses ST for the top of the stack and ST(n) for another location where n is the register number. With this form, one operand must be ST and the other ST(n). Note that to double the top of the stack we use the FADD ST,ST(0) instruction, where ST(0) addresses the top of the stack. One of the two operands in the register-addressing mode must be ST, while the other must be in the form ST(n), where n is a stack register 0–7.

The memory-addressing mode always uses a top-of-the-stack destination because the 80287 is a stack-oriented machine. For example, the FADD DATA instruction adds the real number contents of memory location data to the top of the stack.

Arithmetic Operations.   The letter P in an opcode specifies a register pop after the operation (FADDP compared to FADD). The letter R in an opcode (subtraction and division only) indicates reverse mode. The reverse mode is useful for memory data because normally memory data subtract from the top of the stack. A reversed subtract instruction subtracts the top of the stack from memory and stores the result in the top of the stack. For example, if the top of the stack contains a 10 and memory location DATA1 contains a 1, then the FSUB DATA1 instruction results in a +9 on the stack top and the FSUBR instruction results in a −9.

The letter I as a second letter in an opcode indicates that the memory operand is an integer. For example, the FADD DATA instruction is a floating-point addition, while the FIADD DATA is an integer addition that adds the integer at memory location DATA to the floating-point number at the top of the stack. The same rules apply to FADD, FSUB, FMUL, and FDIV instructions.

Arithmetic-Related Operations.   Other operations that are arithmetic in nature include FSQRT (square root), FSCALE (scale a number), FPREM (find partial remainder), FRNDINT (round to integer), FXTRACT (extract exponent and significand), FABS (find absolute value), and FCHG (change sign). These instructions and the functions they perform follow:

1. FSQRT—finds the square root of the top of the stack and leaves the resultant square root at the top of the stack. An invalid error occurs for the square root of a negative number. For this reason, the IE bit of the status register should be tested whenever an invalid result can occur.
2. FSCALE—adds the contents of ST(1) (interpreted as an integer) to the exponent at the top of the stack. FSCALE can multiply or divide rapidly by powers of two. The value in ST(1) must be between 2^{-15} and 2^{+15}.
3. FPREM—performs modulo division of ST by ST(1). The resultant remainder is found in the top of the stack and has the same sign as the original dividend.
4. FRNDINT—rounds the top of the stack to an integer.
5. FXTRACT—decomposes the number at the top of the stack into two separate numbers that represent the value of the exponent and the value of the significand.

The extracted significand is found at the top of the stack and the exponent at ST(1). We often use this instruction in converting a floating-point number into a form that can be printed.

6. FABS—changes the sign of the top of the stack to positive.
7. FCHS—changes any sign of the top of the stack from positive to negative or negative to positive.

Comparison Instructions

The comparison instructions all examine data at the top of the stack in relation to another element and return the result of the comparison in the status register condition code bits C_3–C_0. Comparisons that are allowed by the 80287 coprocessor are FCOM (floating-point compare), FCOMP (floating-point compare with a pop), FCOMPP (floating-point compare with 2 pops), FICOM (integer compare), FICOMP (integer compare and pop), FSTS (test), and FXAM (examine). Following is a list of these instructions with a description of their function:

1. FCOM—compares the floating-point data at the top of the stack with an operand, which may be any register or any memory operand. If the operand is not coded with the instruction, the next stack element ST(1) is compared with the stack top ST.
2. FCOMP and FCOMPP—both instructions perform as FCOM, but they also pop one or two registers from the stack.
3. FICOM and FICOMP—the top of the stack is compared with the integer stored at a memory operand. In addition to the compare, FICOMP also pops the top of the stack.
4. FTST—test the contents of the top of the stack against a zero. The result of the comparison is coded in the status register condition code bits, as illustrated in Table 12–1 with the status register.
5. FXAM—examines the stack top and modifies the condition code bits to indicate whether the contents are positive, negative, normalized, or what their function is. Refer back to the status register in Table 12–1.

Transcendental Operations

The transcendental instructions include FPTAN (partial tangent), FPATAM (partial arctangent), F2XM1 ($2^x - 1$), FYL2X ($Y \log_2 X$), and FYL2XP1 ($Y \log_2(X + 1)$). A list of these operations follows with a description of each transcendental operation:

1. FPTAN—finds the partial tangent of $Y/X = \tan \Theta$. The value of Θ is at the top of the stack and must be between 0 and $\pi/4$. The result is a ratio that is found as $ST = X$ and $ST(1) = Y$. If the value is outside of the allowable range, an invalid error occurs, as indicated by the status register.
2. FPATAN—finds the partial tangent at $\Theta = ARCTAN\ X/Y$. The value of X is at the top of the stack, and Y is at ST(1). The values of X and Y must be as follows: $0 \le Y < X < \infty$. The instruction pops the stack and leaves Θ at the top of the stack.
3. F2AM1—finds the function $2^x - 1$. The value of X is taken from the top of the stack and the result if returned to the top of the stack. To obtain 2^x, add one to

TABLE 12–4 Exponential functions

Function	Equation
10^x	$2^{x \log_2 10}$
e^x	$2^{x \log_2 e}$
y^x	$2^{x \log_2 y}$

the result at the top of the stack. This function can be used to derive the functions listed in Table 12–4. Note that the constants $\log_2 10$ and $\log_2 e$ are built in as standard values for the 80287.

4. FYL2X—finds $Y \log_2 X$. The value X is taken from the stack top, and Y is taken from ST(1). The result is found at the top of the stack after a pop. The value of X must range between 0 and ∞, and the value of Y must be between $-\infty$ and $+\infty$.

5. FYL2XP1—finds $Y \log_2(X + 1)$. The value of X is taken from the stack top and Y is taken from ST(1). The result is found at the top of the stack after a pop. The value of X must range between 0 and $1 - \sqrt{2/2}$, and the value of Y must be between $-\infty$ and $+\infty$.

Constant Operations

The 80287 instruction set includes opcodes that return constants to the top of the stack. A list of these instructions is given in Table 12–5.

80287 Control Instructions

The 80287 coprocessor has control instructions for initialization, exception handling, and task switching. The control instructions have two forms. For example, FINIT initializes the coprocessor and so does FNINIT. The difference is that FNINIT does not cause any wait states, while $\overline{\text{FINIT}}$ does cause waits. The 80286 will wait for the FINIT instruction by testing the $\overline{\text{BUSY}}$ pin on the coprocessor. All control instructions have these two forms. Following is a list of each control instructions with their functions:

1. FINIT/FNINIT—this instruction performs the same basic function as reset as described in Section 12–3. The 80287 operates with a closure of projective, rounds to the nearest, and uses a precision of 64 bits when reset or initialized.

TABLE 12–5 Constant operations

Instruction	Constant Pushed to ST
FLDZ	$+0.0$
FLD1	$+1.0$
FLDPI	π
FLDL2T	$\log_2 10$
FLDL2E	$\log_2 e$
FLDLG2	$\log_{10} 2$
FLDLN2	$\log_e 2$

2. FSETPM—changes the addressing mode of the 80287 to the protected addressing mode. This mode is used when the 80286 is also operated in the protected mode. As with the 80286, protected mode can only be exited by a hardware reset.

3. FLDCW—loads the control register with the word addressed by the operand.

4. FSTCW/FNSTCW—stores the control register into the word-sized memory operand.

5. FSTSW AX/FNSTSW AX—copies the contents of the control register to the AX register.

6. FCLEX/FNCLEX—clears the error flags in the status register and also the busy flag.

7. FSAVE/FNSAVE—writes the entire state of the machine to memory. Figure 12–10 shows the memory layout for this instruction.

FIGURE 12–10 Memory format when the 80287 registers are stored by the FSAVE instruction. (Courtesy of Intel Corporation)

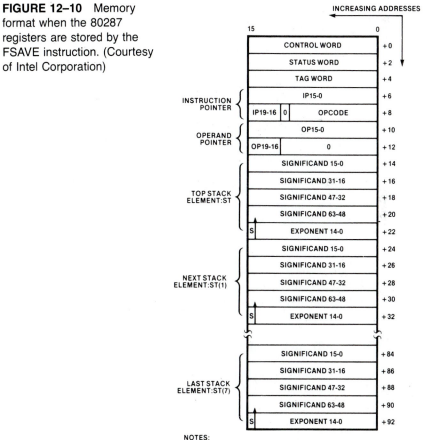

NOTES:
S = Sign
Bit 0 of each field is rightmost, least significant bit of corresponding register field.
Bit 63 of significand is integer bit (assumed binary point is immediately to the right).

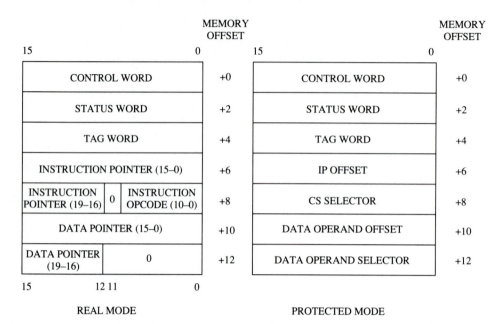

FIGURE 12–11   The memory format for the FSTENV instruction. (Courtesy of Intel Corporation)

8. FRSTOR—restores the state of the machine from memory. This instruction is used to restore the information saved by FSAVE/FNSAVE.
9. FSTENV/FNSTENV—stores the environment of the 80287 as shown in Figure 12–11.
10. FLDENV—reloads the environment saved by FSTENV/FNSTENV.
11. FINCST—increments the stack pointer.
12. FDECSTP—decrements the stack pointer.
13. FFREE—frees a register by changing the destination register's tag to empty. It does not affect the contents of the register.
14. FNOP—floating-point coprocessor NOP.
15. FWAIT—causes the microprocessor to wait for the coprocessor to finish an operation. FWAIT should be used before the microprocessor accesses memory data that are affected by the coprocessor.

80387/80487 Instructions

Although we have yet to talk about the 80386 microprocessor and its companion co-processor the 80387, the 80486DX and its built-in coprocessor, or the 80486SX and its companion coprocessor the 80487SX, we can discuss the instruction sets of these coprocessors and their differences with the 80287. These newer coprocessors contain the same basic instructions provided by the 80287, plus the following additional instructions: FCOS (cosine), FPREM1 (partial remainder), FSIN (sine), FSINCOS (sine and cosine), and FUCOM/FUCOMP/FUCOMPP (unordered compare). The sine and cosine instructions are the most significant addition to the instruction set, because in the 80287, we must calculate sine and cosine from the tangent.

Table 12–6 lists the instruction sets for all versions of the coprocessor. It also lists the number of clocking periods required to execute each instruction. Execution times are listed for the 8087, 80287, 80387, and 80486 or 80487. To determine the execution time of an instruction, the clock time is multiplied times the listed execution time. The FADD instruction requires 70–143 clocks for the 80287. Suppose we use an 8-MHz clock for the 80287, which has a clock period of 1/8 μs or 125 ns per clock. The FADD instruction requires between 8.75 and 17.875 μs to execute. Using a 25-MHz (40-ns) 80486, this instruction requires between 0.32 and 0.8 μs to execute.

Table 12–6 uses some shorthand notation to represent the displacement that may or may not be required for an instruction that uses a memory-addressing mode. It also uses the abbreviation oo to represent the mode, mmm to represent a register/memory addressing mode, and rrr to represent one of the floating-point coprocessor registers ST(0)–ST(7). The d bit that appears in some instruction opcodes defines the direction of the data flow, as in FADD ST,ST(2) or FADD ST(2),ST. The d bit is a logic 0 for flow toward ST as in FADD ST,ST(2), and a logic 1 for FADD ST(2),ST.

TABLE 12–6 The instruction set of the arithmetic coprocessor.

F2XM1 2ST - 1		
11011001 11110000		
Example		Clocks
F2XM1	8087	310—630
	80287	310—630
	80387	211—476
	80486/7	140—279

FABS Absolute value of ST		
11011001 11100001		
Example		Clocks
FABS	8087	10—17
	80287	10—17
	80387	22
	80486/7	3

TABLE 12–6 *(continued)*

FADD/FADDP/FIADD Addition

```
11011000  oo000mmm  disp     32-bit memory (FADD)
11011100  oo000mmm  disp     64-bit memory (FADD)
11011d00  11000rrr           FADD ST,ST(rrr)
11011110  11000rrr           FADDP ST,ST(rrr)
11011110  oo000mmm  disp     16-bit memory (FIADD)
11011010  oo000mmm  disp     32-bit memory (FIADD)
```

Format	Examples	Clocks	
FADD FADDP FIADD	FADD DATA FADD ST,ST(1) FADDP FIADD NUMBER FADD ST,ST(3) FADDP ST,ST(2) FADD ST(2),ST	8087	70—143
		80287	70—143
		80387	23—72
		80486/7	8—20

FCLEX/FNCLEX Clear errors

```
11011011  11100010
```

Example	Clocks	
FCLEX FNCLEX	8087	2—8
	80287	2—8
	80387	11
	80486/7	7

FCOM/FCOMP/FCOMPP/FICOM/FICOMP Compare

```
11011000  oo010mmm  disp     32-bit memory (FCOM)
11011100  oo010mmm  disp     64-bit memory (FCOM)
11011000  11010rrr           FCOM ST(rrr)
11011000  oo011mmm  disp     32-bit memory (FCOMP)
11011100  oo011mmm  disp     64-bit memory (FCOMP)
11011000  11011rrr           FCOMP ST(rrr)
11011110  11011001           FCOMPP
11011110  oo010mmm  disp     16-bit memory (FICOM)
11011010  oo010mmm  disp     32-bit memory (FICOM)
11011110  oo011mmm  disp     16-bit memory (FICOMP)
11011010  oo011mmm  disp     32-bit memory (FICOMP)
```

Format	Examples	Clocks	
FCOM FCOMP FCOMPP FICOM FICOMP	FCOM ST(2) FCOMP DATA FCOMPP FICOM NUMBER FICOMP DATA3	8087	40—93
		80287	40—93
		80387	24—63
		80486/7	15—20

TABLE 12–6 *(continued)*

FCOS   Cosine of ST

11011001 11111111

Example	Clocks	
FCOS	8087	—
	80287	—
	80387	123—772
	80486/7	193—279

FDECSTP   Decrement stack pointer

11011001 11110110

Example	Clocks	
FDECSTP	8087	6—12
	80287	6—12
	80387	22
	80486/7	3

FDISI/FNDISI   Disable interrupts

11011011 11100001
(ignored on the 80287, 80387, and 80486/7)

Example	Clocks	
FDISI	8087	2—8
FNDISI	80287	—
	80387	—
	80486/7	—

FDIV/FDIVP/FIDIV   Divison

```
11011000 oo110mmm  disp        32-bit memory (FDIV)
11011100 oo100mmm  disp        64-bit memory (FDIV)
11011d00 11111rrr              FDIV ST,ST(rrr)
11011110 11111rrr              FDIVP ST,ST(rrr)
11011110 oo110mmm  disp        16-bit memory (FIDIV)
11011010 oo110mmm  disp        32-bit memory (FIDIV)
```

Format	Examples	Clocks

TABLE 12–6 *(continued)*

FDIV FDIVP FIDIV	FDIV DATA FDIV ST,ST(3) FDIVP FIDIV NUMBER FDIV ST,ST(5) FDIVP ST,ST(2) FDIV ST(2),ST	8087	191—243
		80287	191—243
		80387	88—140
		80486/7	8—89

FDIVR/FDIVRP/FIDIVR   Divison reversed

```
11011000  oo111mmm  disp       32-bit memory (FDIVR)
11011100  oo111mmm  disp       64-bit memory (FDIVR)
11011d00  11110rrr             FDIVR ST,ST(rrr)
11011110  11110rrr             FDIVRP ST,ST(rrr)
11011110  oo111mmm  disp       16-bit memory (FIDIVR)
11011010  oo111mmm  disp       32-bit memory (FIDIVR)
```

Format	Examples		Clocks
FDIVR FDIVRP FIDIVR	FDIVR DATA FDIVR ST,ST(3) FDIVRP FIDIVR NUMBER FDIVR ST,ST(5) FDIVRP ST,ST(2) FDIVR ST(2),ST	8087	191—243
		80287	191—243
		80387	88—140
		80486/7	8—89

FENI/FNENI   Disable interrupts

```
11011011  11100000
```

(ignored on the 80287, 80387, and 80486/7)

Example		Clocks
FENI FNENI	8087	2—8
	80287	—
	80387	—
	80486/7	—

FFREE   Free register

```
11011101  11000rrr
```

Format	Examples		Clocks
FFREE	FFREE FFREE ST(1) FFREE ST(2)	8087	9—16
		80287	9—16
		80387	18
		80486/7	3

FINCSTP   Increment stack pointer

TABLE 12–6 *(continued)*

11011001 11110111

Example		Clocks
FINCSTP	8087	6—12
	80287	6—12
	80387	21
	80486/7	3

FINIT/FNINIT   Initialize coprocessor

11011001 11110110

Example		Clocks
FINIT FNINIT	8087	2—8
	80287	2—8
	80387	33
	80486/7	17

FLD/FILD/FBLD   Load data to ST(0)

11011001	oo000mmm disp	32-bit memory (FLD)
11011101	oo000mmm disp	64-bit memory (FLD)
11011011	oo101mmm disp	80-bit memory (FLD)
11011111	oo000mmm disp	16-bit memory (FILD)
11011011	oo000mmm disp	32-bit memory (FILD)
11011111	oo101mmm disp	64-bit memory (FILD)
11011111	oo100mmm disp	80-bit memory (FBLD)

Format	Examples		Clocks
FLD FILD FBLD	FLD DATA FILD DATA1 FBLD DEC_DATA	8087	17—310
		80287	17—310
		80387	14—275
		80486/7	3—103

FLD1   Load + 1.0 to ST(0)

11011001 11101000

Example		Clocks
FLD1	8087	15—21
	80287	15—21
	80387	24

TABLE 12–6 *(continued)*

	80486/7	4

FLDZ   Load + 0.0 to ST(0)

11011001 11101110

Example		Clocks
FLDZ	8087	11—17
	80287	11—17
	80387	20
	80486/7	4

FLDPI   Load π to ST(0)

11011001 11101011

Example		Clocks
FLDPI	8087	16—22
	80287	16—22
	80387	40
	80486/7	8

FLDL2E   Load $\log_2$ e to ST(0)

11011001 11101010

Example		Clocks
FLDL2E	8087	15—21
	80287	15—21
	80387	40
	80486/7	8

FLDL2T   Load $\log_2$ 10 to ST(0)

11011001 11101001

Example		Clocks
FLDL2T	8087	16—22
	80287	16—22

TABLE 12–6 (*continued*)

	80387	40
	80486/7	8

FLDLG2 Load $\log_{10} 2$ to ST(0)

11011001 11101000

Example		Clocks
FLDLG2	8087	18—24
	80287	18—24
	80387	41
	80486/7	8

FLDLN2 Load $\log_e 2$ to ST(0)

11011001 11101101

Example		Clocks
FLDLN2	8087	17—23
	80287	17—23
	80387	41
	80486/7	8

FLDCW Load control register

11011001 oo101mmm disp

Format	Examples		Clocks
FLDCW	FLDCW DATA FLDCW STATUS	8087	7—14
		80287	7—14
		80387	19
		80486/7	4

FLDENV Load environment

11011001 oo100mmm disp

Format	Examples		Clocks
FLDENV	FLDENV ENVIRON FLDENV DATA	8087	35—45
		80287	25—45

521

TABLE 12–6 *(continued)*

		80387	71
		80486/7	34—44

FMUL/FMULP/FIMUL   Multiplication

```
11011000  oo001mmm  disp      32-bit memory (FMUL)
11011100  oo001mmm  disp      64-bit memory (FMUL)
11011d00  11001rrr            FMUL ST,ST(rrr)
11011110  11001rrr            FMULP ST,ST(rrr)
11011110  oo001mmm  disp      16-bit memory (FIMUL)
11011010  oo001mmm  disp      32-bit memory (FIMUL)
```

Format	Examples		Clocks
FMUL	FMUL DATA	8087	110—168
FMULP	FMUL ST,ST(2)		
FIMUL	FMUL ST(2),ST	80287	110—168
	FMULP		
	FIMUL DATA3	80387	29—82
		80486/7	11—27

FNOP   No operation

```
11011001  11010000
```

Example		Clocks
FNOP	8087	10—16
	80287	10—16
	80387	12
	80486/7	3

FPATAN   Partial arctangent of ST(0)

```
11011001  11110011
```

Example		Clocks
FPATAN	8087	250—800
	80287	250—800
	80387	314—487
	80486/7	218—303

FPREM   Partial remainder

```
11011001  11111000
```

Example		Clocks

TABLE 12–6 *(continued)*

FPREM		8087	15—190
		80287	15—190
		80387	74—155
		80486/7	70—138

FPREM1 Partial remainder (IEEE)

11011001 11110101

Example			Clocks
FPREM1		8087	—
		80287	—
		80387	95—185
		80486/7	72—167

FPTAN Partial tangent of ST(0)

11011001 11110010

Example			Clocks
FPTAN		8087	30—450
		80287	30—450
		80387	191—497
		80486/7	200—273

FRNDINT Round ST(0) to an integer

11011001 11111100

Example			Clocks
FRNDINT		8087	16—50
		80287	16—50
		80387	66—80
		80486/7	21—30

FRSTOR Restore state

11011101 oo110mmm disp

Format	Examples		Clocks

TABLE 12–6 *(continued)*

FRSTOR	FRSTOR DATA FRSTOR STATE FRSTOR NACHINE	8087	197—207
		80287	197—207
		80387	308
		80486/7	120—131

FSAVE/FNSAVE   Save machine state

11011101 oo110mmm disp

Format	Examples		Clocks
FSAVE FNSAVE	FSAVE STATE FNSAVE STATUS FSAVE MACHINE	8087	197—207
		80287	197—207
		80387	375
		80486/7	143—154

FSCALE   Scale ST(0) by ST(1)

11011001 11111101

Example		Clocks
FSCALE	8087	32—38
	80287	32—38
	80387	67—86
	80486/7	30—32

FSETPM   Set protected mode

11011011 11100100

Example		Clocks
FSETPM	8087	—
	80287	2—18
	80387	12
	80486/7	—

FSIN   Sine of ST(0)

11011001 11111110

Example		Clocks

TABLE 12–6 *(continued)*

FSIN	8087	—
	80287	—
	80387	122—771
	80486/7	193—279

FSINCOS Find sine and cosine of ST(0)

11011001 11111011

Example		Clocks
FSINCOS	8087	—
	80287	—
	80387	194—809
	80486/7	243—329

FSQRT Square root of ST(0)

11011001 11111010

Example		Clocks
FSQRT	8087	180—186
	80287	180—186
	80387	122—129
	80486/7	83—87

FST/FSTP/FIST/FISTP/FBSTP Store

```
11011001  oo010mmm  disp      32-bit memory (FST)
11011101  oo010mmm  disp      64-bit memory (FST)
11011101  11010rrr            FST ST(rrr)
11011011  oo011mmm  disp      32-bit memory (FSTP)
11011101  oo011mmm  disp      64-bit memory (FSTP)
11011011  oo111mmm  disp      80-bit memory (FSTP)
11011101  11001rrr            FSTP ST(rrr)
11011111  oo010mmm  disp      16-bit memory (FIST)
11011011  oo010mmm  disp      32-bit memory (FIST)
11011111  oo011mmm  disp      16-bit memory (FISTP)
11011011  oo011mmm  disp      32-bit memory (FISTP)
11011111  oo111mmm  disp      64-bit memory (FISTP)
11011111  oo110mmm  disp      80-bit memory (FBSTP)
```

Format	Examples		Clocks
FST	FST DATA	8087	15—540
FSTP	FST ST(3)		
FIST	FST	80287	15—540
FISTP	FSTP		
FBSTP	FIST DATA2	80387	11—534
	FBSTP DATA6		

TABLE 12–6 *(continued)*

	FISTP DATA9	80486/7	3—176

FSTCW/FNSTCW   Store control register

11011001 oo111mmm disp

Format	Examples		Clocks
FSTCW FNSTCW	FSTCW CONTROL FNSTCW STATUS FSTCW MACHINE	8087	12—18
		80287	12—18
		80387	15
		80486/7	3

FSTENV/FNSTENV   Store environment

11011001 oo110mmm disp

Format	Examples		Clocks
FSTENV FNSTENV	FSTENV CONTROL FNSTENV STATUS FSTENV MACHINE	8087	40—50
		80287	40—50
		80387	103—104
		80486/7	58—67

FSTSW/FNSTSW   Store status register

11011101 oo111mmm disp

Format	Examples		Clocks
FSTSW FNSTSW	FSTSW CONTROL FNSTSW STATUS FSTSW MACHINE	8087	12—18
		80287	12—18
		80387	15
		80486/7	3

FSUB/FSUBP/FISUB   Subtraction

```
11011000  oo100mmm  disp      32-bit memory (FSUB)
11011100  oo100mmm  disp      64-bit memory (FSUB)
11011d00  11101rrr            FSUB ST,ST(rrr)
11011110  11101rrr            FSUBP ST,ST(rrr)
11011110  oo100mmm  disp      16-bit memory (FISUB)
11011010  oo100mmm  disp      32-bit memory (FISUB)
```

Format	Examples	Clocks

TABLE 12–6 *(continued)*

FSUB FSUBP FISUB	FSUB DATA FSUB ST,ST(2) FSUB ST(2),ST FSUBP FISUB DATA3	8087	70—143
		80287	70—143
		80387	29—82
		80486/7	8—35

FSUBR/FSUBRP/FISUBR Reverse subtraction

```
11011000 oo101mmm disp    32-bit memory (FSUBR)
11011100 oo101mmm disp    64-bit memory (FSUBR)
11011d00 11100rrr         FSUBR ST,ST(rrr)
11011110 11100rrr         FSUBRP ST,ST(rrr)
11011110 oo101mmm disp    16-bit memory (FISUBR)
11011010 oo101mmm disp    32-bit memory (FISUBR)
```

Format	Examples		Clocks
FSUBR FSUBRP FISUBR	FSUBR DATA FSUBR ST,ST(2) FSUBR ST(2),ST FSUBRP FISUBR DATA3	8087	70—143
		80287	70—143
		80387	29—82
		80486/7	8—35

FTST Compare ST(0) with + 0.0

```
11011001 11100100
```

Example		Clocks
FTST	8087	38—48
	80287	38—48
	80387	28
	80486/7	4

FUCOM/FUCOMP/FUCOMPP Unordered compare

```
11011101 11100rrr         FUCOM ST,ST(rrr)
11011101 11101rrr         FUCOMP ST,ST(rrr)
11011101 11101001         FUCOMPP
```

Format	Examples		Clocks
FUCOM FUCOMP FUCOMPP	FUCOM ST,ST(2) FUCOM FUCOMP ST,ST(3) FUCOMP FUCOMPP	8087	—
		80287	—
		80387	24—26
		80486/7	4—5

527

TABLE 12–6 *(continued)*

FWAIT   Wait

10011011

Example		Clocks
FWAIT	8087	4
	80287	3
	80387	6
	80486/7	1—3

FXAM   Examine ST(0)

11011001 11100101

Example		Clocks
FXAM	8087	12—23
	80287	12—23
	80387	30—38
	80486/7	8

FXCH   Exchange ST(0) with another register

11011001 11001rrr   FXCH ST,ST(rrr)

Format	Examples		Clocks
FXCH	FXCH ST,ST(1) FXCH FXCH ST,ST(4)	8087	10—15
		80287	10—15
		80387	18
		80486/7	4

FXTRACT   Extract components of ST(0)

11011001 11110100

Example		Clocks
FXTRACT	8087	27—55
	80287	27—55
	80387	70—76
	80486/7	16—20

TABLE 12–6 *(continued)*

FYL2X $ST(1) \times \log_2 ST(0)$		
11011001 11110001		
Example		Clocks
FYL2X	8087	900—1100
	80287	900—1100
	80387	120—538
	80486/7	196—329

FXL2XP1 $ST(1) \times \log_2 [ST(0) + 1.0]$		
11011001 11111001		
Example		Clocks
FXL2XP1	8087	700—1000
	80287	700—1000
	80387	257—547
	80486/7	171—326

Note: d = direction where d = 0 for ST as the destination and d = 1 for ST as the source, rrr = floating-point register number, oo = mode, mmm = r/m field, and disp = displacement.

12–5 PROGRAMMING WITH THE ARITHMETIC COPROCESSOR

This section of the chapter provides programming examples for the arithmetic co-processor. Each example is chosen to illustrate a programming technique for the coprocessor.

Calculating the Area of a Circle

This programming example provides a simple illustration of a method of addressing the 80287 stack. First recall that the equation for calculating the area of a circle is $A = \pi R^2$. A procedure that performs this calculation is listed in Example 12–6.

EXAMPLE 12–6

```
;Procedure that calculates the area of a circle.
;
;The radius must be stored at memory location RADIUS
```

```
                        ;before calling this procedure.  The result is found
                        ;in memory location AREA after the procedure.
                        ;
0000                    AREAS    PROC    FAR

0000 D9 06 0004 R                FLD     RADIUS            ;radius to ST
0004 D8 C8                       FMUL    ST,ST(0)          ;sqaure radius
0006 D9 EB                       FLDPI                     ;π to ST
0008 DE C9                       FMUL                      ;multiply ST = ST x ST(1)
000A D9 1E 0000 R                FSTP    AREA              ;save area
000E 9B                          FWAIT                     ;wait for coprocessor
000F CB                          RET

0010                    AREAS    ENDP
```

This is a rather simple procedure, but it does illustrate the operation of the stack. To provide a better understanding of the operation of the stack, Figure 12–12 shows the contents of the stack after each instruction of Example 12–6 executes.

The first instruction loads the contents of memory location RADIUS to the top of the stack. Next the FMUL ST,ST(0) instruction squares the radius on the

FIGURE 12–12 Operation of the 80287 stack with the procedure of Example 12–6. *Note:* Stack shown after the execution of the indicated instruction.

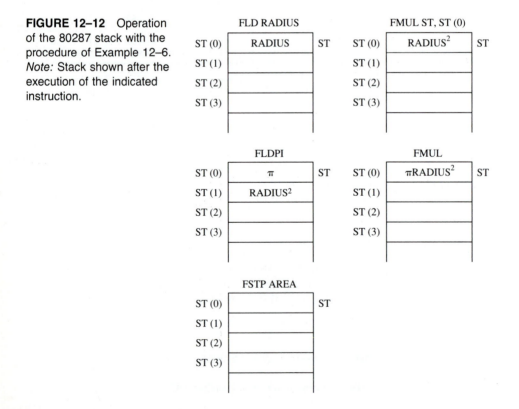

top of the stack, after which the FLDPI instruction loads π to the stack top. The FMUL instruction then uses the classic stack-addressing mode to multiply ST by ST(1). After the multiplication both prior values are removed from the stack and the product replaces them at the top of the stack. Finally, the FSTP instruction copies the top of the stack, the area, to memory location AREA and clears the stack.

The FWAIT instruction appears just before the return instruction in this example. The reason that we use the FWAIT instruction is to wait for the coprocessor to finish finding the area before returning. If we were not to wait, the main program might access memory location AREA before the coprocessor stores the result into location AREA.

Finding the Resonant Frequency

An equation commonly used in electronics is the formula for determining the resonant frequency of an *LC* circuit. The equation solved by the procedure illustrated in Example 12–7 is $F_r = 1/(2\pi\sqrt{LC})$.

EXAMPLE 12–7

```
0000                      DATAS    SEGMENT

0000 00000000             RESO     DD    ?           ;resonant frequency
0004 358637BD             L        DD    .000001     ;inducatance
0008 358637BD             C        DD    .000001     ;capacitance
000C 40000000             TWO      DD    2.0         ;constant

0010                      DATAS    ENDS

0000                      CODE     SEGMENT

                          ASSUME  CS:CODE,DS:DATAS

                 ;Procedure that finds the resonant frequecny.

0000                      FREQ     PROC    FAR

0000 D9 06 0004 R         FLD      L             ;get L
0004 D8 0E 0008 R         FMUL     C             ;find LC

0008 D9 FA                FSQRT                  ;find √LC

000A D8 0E 000C R         FMUL     TWO           ;find 2√LC

000E D9 EB                FLDPI                  ;get π
0010 DE C9                FMUL                   ;get 2π√LC

0012 D9 E8                FLD1                   ;get 1
0014 DE F1                FDIVR                  ;form 1/(2π√LC)

0016 D9 1E 0000 R         FSTP     RESO          ;save frequecny
```

001A 9B		FWAIT
001B CB		RET
001C	FREQ	ENDP
001C	CODE	ENDS
		END

Notice the straightforward manner in which the procedure solves this equation. Very little extra data manipulation is required because of the stack inside the 80287. Also notice how the constant TWO is defined for the program and how the DIVRP, using classic stack addressing, is used to form the reciprocal.

Finding the Roots Using the Quadratic Equation

This example illustrates how to find the roots of a polynomial expression $(ax^2 + \underline{bx} + c = 0)$ using the quadratic equation. The quadratic equation is $(b \pm \sqrt{b^2 - 4ac})/2a$. Example 12–8 illustrates a procedure that finds the roots (R1 and R2) for the quadratic equation. The constants are stored in memory locations A, B, and C.

EXAMPLE 12–8

		.286		
		.287		
0000		DATAS	SEGMENT	
0000 40000000		TWO	DD	2.0
0004 40800000		FOUR	DD	4.0
0008 3F800000		A	DD	1.0
000C C1800000		B	DD	-16.0
0010 421C0000		C	DD	+39.0
0014 00000000		R1	DD	?
0018 00000000		R2	DD	?
001C		DATAS	ENDS	
0000		CODE	SEGMENT	
		ASSUME CS:CODE,DS:DATAS		
		;Procedure that solves the quadratic equation.		
0000		ROOTS	PROC	FAR
0000 D9 06 0000 R		FLD	TWO	
0004 D8 0E 0008 R		FMUL	A	;form 2a
0008 D9 06 0004 R		FLD	FOUR	
000C D8 0E 0008 R		FMUL	A	
0010 D8 0E 0010 R		FMUL	C	;form 4ac
0014 D9 06 000C R		FLD	B	

```
0018  D8 0E 000C R          FMUL     B              ;form b²
001C  DE E1                 FSUBR                   ;form b² - 4ac
001E  D9 FA                 FSQRT                   ;form square root of b² - 4ac

0020  D9 06 000C R          FLD      B
0024  D8 E1                 FSUB     ST,ST(1)
0026  D8 F2                 FDIV     ST,ST(2)
0028  D9 1E 0014 R          FSTP     R1             ;save root1

002C  D9 06 000C R          FLD      B
0030  DE C1                 FADD
0032  DE F1                 FDIVR
0034  D9 1E 0018 R          FSTP     R2             ;save root2

0038  9B                    FWAIT
0039  CB                    RET

003A            ROOTS       ENDP

003A            CODE        ENDS

                            END
```

Displaying a Single-Precision Floating-Point Number

This section of the text shows how to take the floating-point contents of a 32-bit single-precision floating-point number and display them on the video display. The procedure displays the floating-point number as a mixed number with an integer part and a fractional part separated by a decimal point. In order to simplify the procedure we have placed a limit on the display size of the mixed number so the integer portion is a 32-bit binary number and the fraction is a 24-bit binary number. The procedure will not function properly for larger or smaller numbers.

EXAMPLE 12–9

```
                            .286
                            .287
0000                        DATAS    SEGMENT

0000  C50B0C00              NUMB     DD       -2224.75
0004  0000                  TEMP     DW       ?
0006  0000                  WHOLE    DW       ?
0008  00000000              FRACT    DD       ?

000C                        DATAS    ENDS

0000                        CODE     SEGMENT

                            ASSUME  CS:CODE,DS:DATAS

                            ;Main program that displays NUMB
                            ;
```

```
0000                      MAIN    PROC    FAR

0000 B8 ---- R                    MOV     AX,DATAS
0003 8E D8                        MOV     DS,AX
0005 E8 0013 R                    CALL    DISP            ;display NUMB
0008 B4 4C                        MOV     AH,4CH          ;exit to DOS
000A CD 21                        INT     21H

000C                      MAIN    ENDP

000C                      DISPS   PROC    NEAR

000C B4 06                        MOV     AH,6            ;display AL
000E 8A D0                        MOV     DL,AL
0010 CD 21                        INT     21H
0012 C3                           RET

0013                      DISPS   ENDP

0013                      DISP    PROC    NEAR

0013 9B D9 3E 0004 R             FSTCW   TEMP            ;set rounding to chop
0018 81 0E 0004 R 0C00           OR      TEMP,0C00H
001E 9B D9 2E 0004 R             FLDCW   TEMP

0023 D9 06 0000 R                FLD     NUMB            ;get NUMB
0027 D9 E4                       FTST                    ;test NUMB
0029 9B DF E0                    FSTSW   AX              ;status to AX
002C 25 4500                     AND     AX,4500H        ;get C3, C2, and C0
002F 3D 0100                     CMP     AX,0100H        ;test for -
0032 75 05                       JNE     DISP1           ;if positive
0034 B0 2D                       MOV     AL,'-'
0036 E8 000C R                   CALL    DISPS           ;display minus

0039                      DISP1:

0039 D9 E1                       FABS                    ;make ST positive
003B D9 FC                       FRNDINT                 ;get integer
003D DF 16 0006 R                FIST    WHOLE           ;store integer
0041 D9 06 0000 R                FLD     NUMB
0045 D9 E1                       FABS
0047 DE E9                       FSUB                    ;get fraction
0049 D9 E1                       FABS
004B D9 1E 0008 R                FSTP    FRACT           ;save fraction
004F 9B                          FWAIT

                         ;display integer part

0050 A1 0006 R                   MOV     AX,WHOLE
0053 B9 0000                     MOV     CX,0
0056 BB 000A                     MOV     BX,10
```

```
0059                        DISP2:

0059 41                            INC       CX
005A 33 D2                         XOR       DX,DX
005C F7 F3                         DIV       BX
005E 83 C2 30                      ADD       DX,'0'              ;convert to ASCII
0061 52                            PUSH      DX
0062 0B C0                         OR        AX,AX
0064 75 F3                         JNE       DISP2               ;if not zero

0066                        DISP3:

0066 58                            POP       AX
0067 E8 000C R                     CALL      DISPS               ;display it
006A E2 FA                         LOOP      DISP3
006C B0 2E                         MOV       AL,'.'              ;display decimal point
006E E8 000C R                     CALL      DISPS

                           ;display fractional part

0071 A1 0008 R                     MOV       AX,WORD PTR FRACT
0074 8B 16 000A R                  MOV       DX,WORD PTR FRACT+2
0078 B9 0008                       MOV       CX,8

007B                        DISP4:

007B D1 E0                         SHL       AX,1
007D D1 D2                         RCL       DX,1
007F E2 FA                         LOOP      DISP4
0081 81 CA 8000                    OR        DX,8000H            ;set implied bit

0085 92                            XCHG      AX,DX
0086 BB 000A                       MOV       BX,10

0089                        DISP5:

0089 F7 E3                         MUL       BX
008B 50                            PUSH      AX
008C 92                            XCHG      DX,AX
008D 04 30                         ADD       AL,'0'
008F E8 000C R                     CALL      DISPS               ;display digit
0092 58                            POP       AX
0093 0B C0                         OR        AX,AX
0095 75 F2                         JNZ       DISP5
0097 C3                            RET

0098                 DISP       ENDP

0098                 CODE       ENDS

                            END       MAIN
```

Example 12–9 lists the procedure for displaying the contents of memory location NUMB on the video display at the current cursor position. The procedure first tests the sign of the number and displays a space for a positive number and a minus sign for a negative number. After displaying the sign, the number is made positive by the FABS instruction. Next we divide the number into integer and fractional parts and store them at WHOLE and FRACT.

The last part of the procedure displays the whole number part followed by the fractional part. Note that since we have not adjusted the number to remove the rounding error that is inherent in floating-point fractional numbers, the fractional part may contain a rounding error for certain values.

Reading a Mixed Number from the Keyboard

If floating-point arithmetic is used in a program, we must have a method of reading the number from the keyboard and converting it to floating-point form. The procedure listed in Example 12–10 reads a signed mixed number from the keyboard and converts it to a floating-point number located at the top of the stack inside the coprocessor.

EXAMPLE 12–10

```
                       .287
                       .286
0000                   DATA    SEGMENT

0000 00                SIGN    DB      ?
0001 0000              TEMP1   DW      ?
0003 41200000          TEN     DD      10.0

0007                   DATA    ENDS

0000                   CODE    SEGMENT

                       ASSUME CS:CODE,DS:DATA

                       ;procedure that reads a mixed number from the keyboard
                       ;and leaves it at the top of the coprocessor stack.

0000                   READ    PROC    FAR

0000 B8 ---- R         MOV     AX,DATA           ;address data segment
0003 8E D8             MOV     DS,AX
0005 9B D9 EE          FLDZ                      ;clear ST
0008 C6 06 0000 R 00   MOV     SIGN,0            ;clear sign
000D E8 007C           CALL    GET               ;read a character
0010 3C 2D             CMP     AL,'-'            ;test for minus
0012 75 07             JNE     READ1             ;if not minus
0014 C6 06 0000 R FF   MOV     SIGN,0FFH         ;set sign for minus
0019 EB 0F             JMP     READ3             ;Get integer part

001B                   READ1:
```

```
001B 3C 2B              CMP     AL,'+'              ;test for plus
001D 74 0B              JE      READ3               ;get integer part
001F 3C 30              CMP     AL,'0'              ;test for number
0021 72 06              JB      READ2
0023 3C 39              CMP     AL,'9'
0025 77 02              JA      READ2
0027 EB 04              JMP     READ4               ;if a number

0029            READ2:

0029 CB                 RET

002A            READ3:

002A E8 005F             CALL    GET                ;read integer part

002D            READ4:

002D 3C 2E               CMP     AL,'.'             ;test for fraction

002F 74 27               JE      READ7              ;if fraction
0031 3C 30               CMP     AL,'0'             ;test for number
0033 72 17               JB      READ5
0035 3C 39               CMP     AL,'9'
0037 77 13               JA      READ5
0039 9B D8 0E 0003 R     FMUL    TEN                ;form integer
003E 32 E4               XOR     AH,AH
0040 2C 30               SUB     AL,'0'
0042 A3 0001 R           MOV     TEMP1,AX
0045 9B DE 06 0001 R     FIADD   TEMP1
004A EB DE               JMP     READ3

004C            READ5:

004C 80 3E 0000 R 00     CMP     SIGN,0             ;adjust sign
0051 75 01               JNE     READ6
0053 CB                  RET

0054            READ6:

0054 9B D9 E0            FCHS
0057 CB                  RET

0058            READ7:

0058 9B D9 E8            FLD1                        ;form fraction
005B 9B D8 36 0003 R     FDIV    TEN

0060            READ8:

0060 E8 0029             CALL    GET                ;read character
0063 3C 30               CMP     AL,'0'             ;test for number
```

```
0065  72 20                    JB       READ9
0067  3C 39                    CMP      AL,'9'
0069  77 1C                    JA       READ9
006B  32 E4                    XOR      AH,AH
006D  2C 30                    SUB      AL,'0'
006F  A3 0001 R                MOV      TEMP1,AX
0072  9B DF 06 0001 R          FILD     TEMP1              ;load number
0077  9B D8 C9                 FMUL     ST,ST(1)           ;form fraction
007A  9B DC C2                 FADD     ST(2),ST
007D  9B D8 D9                 FCOMP
0080  9B D8 36 0003 R          FDIV     TEN
0085  EB D9                    JMP      READ8

0087                  READ9:

0087  9B D8 D9                 FCOMP                       ;clear stack
008A  EB C0                    JMP      READ5

008C             READ      ENDP

008C             GET       PROC     NEAR

008C  B4 06                    MOV      AH,6               ;read character
008E  B2 FF                    MOV      DL,0FFH
0090  CD 21                    INT      21H
0092  74 F8                    JZ       GET
0094  C3                       RET

0095             GET       ENDP

0095             CODE      ENDS

                           END
```

Here the sign is first read from the keyboard, if present, and saved for later use in adjusting the sign of the resultant floating-point number. Next, the integer portion of the number is read. This portion terminates with a period, space, or carriage return. If a period is typed, then the procedure continues and reads a fractional part, but if a space or carriage return is entered, the number is converted to floating-point form.

12–6   SUMMARY

1. The 80287 arithmetic coprocessor functions in parallel with the 80286 micro-processor.
2. The data types manipulated by the 80287 include signed integer, floating point, and binary-coded decimal (BCD).

3. There are three forms of integers for the 80287: word (16 bits), short (32 bits), and long (64 bits). Each integer contains a signed number in true magnitude for positive numbers and two's complement form for negative numbers.

4. A BCD number is stored as an 18-digit number in 10 bytes of memory. The most significant byte contains the sign-bit, and the remaining 9 bytes contain an 18-digit-packed BCD number.

5. The 80287 supports three types of floating-point numbers: single precision (32 bits), double precision (64 bits), and extended precision (80 bits). A floating-point number is formed of three parts: the sign, biased exponent, and significand. In the 80287, the exponent is biased with a constant, and the integer bit of the normalized number is not stored in the significand except in the extended-precision form.

6. Decimal numbers are converted to floating-point numbers by converting the number to binary, normalizing the binary number, adding the bias to the exponent, and storing the number in floating-point form.

7. Floating-point numbers are converted to decimal by subtracting the bias from the exponent, unnormalizing the number, and then converting it to decimal.

8. The 80287 uses I/O space for the execution of some of its instructions. This space is invisible to the program and is used internally by the 80286/80287 system. These 16-bit I/O addresses are 00F8H, 00FAH, and 00FCH, but they must not be used for I/O data transfers in a system that contains an 80287.

9. The 80287 contains a status register that indicates busy, what conditions follow a compare or test, the location of the top of the stack, and the state of the error bits.

10. The control register of the 80287 contains control bits that select infinity, rounding, precision, and error masks.

11. The following directives are often used with the 80287 for storing data: DW (define word), DD (define double word), DQ (define quad word) and DT (define 10 bytes).

12. The 80287 uses a stack to transfer data between itself and the memory system. Generally data are loaded to the top of the stack or removed from the top of the stack for storage.

13. At internal 80287 data are always in the 80-bit extended-precision form. The only time that data are in any other form is when they are stored or loaded from the memory.

14. The 80287 addressing modes include the classic stack mode, register, register with a pop, and memory. Stack addressing is implied and the data at ST become the source, ST(1) the destination, and the result is found in ST after a pop. The other addressing modes are self-explanatory.

15. The 80287 arithmetic operations include addition, subtraction, multiplication, division, and square root.

16. There are transcendental functions in the 80287 instruction set. These functions find the partial tangent or arctangent, $2^x - 1$, $Y \log_2 X$, and $Y \log_2(X + 1)$.

17. Constants are stored inside the 80287 that provide: $+0.0$, $+1.0$, π, $\log_2 10$, $\log_2 e$, $\log_{10} 2$, and $\log_e 2$.

18. The 80387 functions with the 80386 microprocessor, and the 80487SX functions with the 80486SX microprocessor, but the 80486DX contains its own internal

arithmetic coprocessor. The instructions performed by the 80287 are available on these coprocessors. In addition to these instructions, the 80387 and 80486/7 can also find the sine and cosine.

12–7   QUESTIONS AND PROBLEMS

1. List the three types of data that are loaded or stored in memory by the 80287.
2. List the three integer data types, the range of the integers stored in them, and the number of bits allotted to each.
3. Explain how a BCD number is stored in memory by the 80287.
4. List the three types of floating-point numbers used with the 80287 and the number of binary bits assigned to each.
5. Convert the following decimal numbers into single-precision floating-point numbers:
   a. 28.75
   b. 624
   c. −0.615
   d. +0.0
   e. −1000.5
6. Convert the following single-precision floating-point numbers into decimals:
   a. 11000000   11110000   00000000   00000000
   b. 00111111   00010000   00000000   00000000
   c. 01000011   10011001   00000000   00000000
   d. 01000000   00000000   00000000   00000000
   e. 01000001   00100000   00000000   00000000
   f. 00000000   00000000   00000000   00000000
7. What is the purpose of the CLM pin on the 80287?
8. Where is the $\overline{\text{BUSY}}$ pin on the 80287 connected?
9. What is the purpose of $\overline{\text{NPRD}}$ and where does it connect?
10. Explain what the 80287 does when a normal 80286 instruction executes.
11. Explain what the 80286 does when an 80287 instruction executes.
12. What is the purpose of the C_3–C_0 bits in the status register?
13. How is the rounding mode selected in the 80287?
14. What 80287 instruction uses the 80286 AX register?
15. How are data stored inside the 80287?
16. Whenever the 80287 is reset, the top of the stack register is register number _____.
17. What does the term *chop* mean in the rounding control bits of the control register?
18. What is the difference between affine and projective infinity control?
19. What 80286 instruction forms the opcodes for the 80287?
20. Using assembler pseudo-opcodes, form statements that accomplish the following:
   a. Store a 23.44 into a double-precision floating-point memory location named FROG.

  b. Store a -123 into a 32-bit signed integer location named DATA3.

  c. Store a -23.8 into a single-precision floating-point memory location named DATA1.

  d. Reserve a double-precision memory location named DATA2.

21. Describe how the FST DATA instruction functions. Assume that DATA is defined as a 64-bit memory location.

22. What does the FILD DATA instruction accomplish?

23. Form an instruction that adds the contents of register 3 to the top of the stack.

24. Describe the operation of the FADD instruction.

25. Choose an instruction that subtracts the contents of register 2 from the top of the stack and stores the result in register 2.

26. What is the function of the FBSTP DATA instruction?

27. What is the difference between a forward and a reverse division?

28. What is the difference between the FTST instruction and FXAM?

29. Explain what the F2XM1 instruction calculates.

30. What instruction pushes π onto the top of the stack?

31. What will FFREE ST(2) accomplish when executed?

32. What instruction stores the environment?

33. What does the FSAVE instruction save?

34. Develop a procedure that finds the area of a rectangle ($A = L \times W$). Memory locations for this procedure are single-precision A, L, and W.

35. Write a procedure that finds the inductive reactance ($XL = 2\pi FL$). Memory locations for this procedure are single-precision XL, F, and L.

36. Develop a procedure that generates a table of square roots for the integers 2 through 10.

37. When is the FWAIT instruction used in a program?

38. Given the series/parallel circuit and the equation illustrated in Figure 12–13, develop a program using single-precision values for R1, R2, R3, and R4 that finds the total resistance and stores the result at single-precision location RT.

FIGURE 12–13

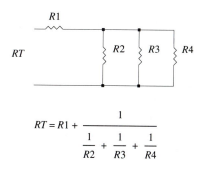

$$RT = R1 + \cfrac{1}{\cfrac{1}{R2} + \cfrac{1}{R3} + \cfrac{1}{R4}}$$

CHAPTER 13

The 80386 and 80486 Microprocessors

INTRODUCTION

The 80386 microprocessor is a full 32-bit version of the 80286 microprocessor. Besides this larger word size there are many improvements and additional features. The 80386 microprocessor features multitasking, memory management, virtual memory with or without paging, software protection, and a large memory system. All software written for the early 8086/8088 and the 80286 are upward compatible to the 80386 microprocessor. The amount of memory addressable by the 80386 is increased from the 1M byte found in the 8086/8088 and the 16M bytes found in the 80286 to 4G bytes in the 80386. The 80386 can switch between protected mode and real mode without resetting the microprocessor. Switching from protected mode to real mode was a problem on the 80286 microprocessor.

The 80486 microprocessor is an enhanced version of the 80386 microprocessor that executes many of its instructions in one clocking period. The 80486 microprocessor also contains an 8K byte cache memory and an improved 80387 numeric coprocessor. When the 80486 is operated at the same clock frequency as an 80386, it performs with about a 50 percent speed improvement.

OBJECTIVES

Upon completion of this chapter, you will be able to:

1. Contrast the 80386 microprocessor with the 80286.
2. Describe the organization and interface of the 32-bit 80386 memory system.
3. Describe the operation of the 80386 memory-management unit and paging unit.
4. Switch between protected mode and real mode.
5. Define the operation of additional 80386 instructions and addressing modes.
6. Explain the operation of a cache memory system.

7. Detail the interrupt structure and direct memory access structure of the 80386.
8. Contrast the 80486 with the 80386 and 80286 microprocessors.
9. Detail the operation of new 80486 instructions.
10. Explain the operation of the 80486 cache memory.

13–1   INTRODUCTION TO THE 80386 MICROPROCESSOR

Before this microprocessor can be used in a system, the function of each pin must be understood. This section of the chapter details the operation of each pin along with the internal register structure and external memory system and the I/O structures of the 80386.

Figure 13–1 illustrates the pinout of the 80386DX microprocessor that is packaged in a 132-pin PGA (pin grid array). Two versions of the 80386 are commonly available: the 80386DX, illustrated and described in this chapter, is the full version, and the 80386SX, which is a reduced bus version. A new version of the 80386, the 80386SL, which incorporates much of the AT bus system, is also available.

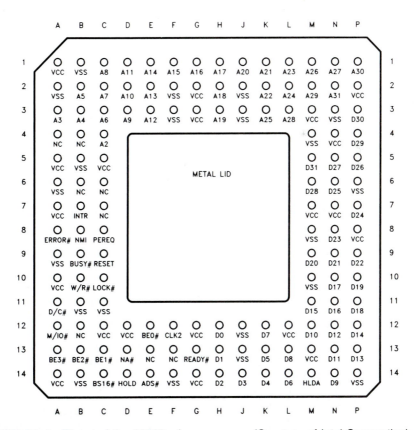

FIGURE 13–1 Pinout of the 80386 microprocessor. (Courtesy of Intel Corporation)

The 80386DX addresses 4G bytes of memory through its 32-bit data bus and 32-bit address. The 80386SX, more like the 80286, addresses 16M bytes of memory with its 24-bit address bus via its 16-bit data bus. The 80386SX was developed after the 80386DX for applications that didn't require the full 32-bit bus version. The 80386SX is found in many personal computers that use the same basic motherboard design as the 80286. At this time most applications require less than 16M bytes of memory, so the 80386SX is a fairly popular and less costly version of the 80386 microprocessor.

The 80286 requires a +5.0-V power supply, as does the 80386 microprocessor. The power supply current averages 550 mA for the 25-MHz version of the 80386, 500 mA for the 20-MHz version, and 450 mA for the 16-MHz version. Also available is a 33-MHz version that requires 600 mA of power supply current. Note that during some modes of normal operation, power supply current can surge to over 1.0 A. This means that the power supply and power distribution network must be capable of supplying these surges. This device contains multiple V_{cc} and V_{ss} connections that must all be connected to +5.0 V and ground for proper operation. Some of the pins are labeled N/C (no connection) and may not be connected.

Each 80386 output pin is capable of providing 4.0 mA (address and data connections) or 5.0 mA (other connections). This capability represents an increase in drive current compared to the 2.0 mA available at an 80286 output pin. Each input pin represents a small load requiring only $\pm 10 \mu A$ of current. In most systems, except the smallest, these current levels require bus buffers.

The function of each 80386 group of pins follows:

1. A_{31}–A_2—Address Bus Connections: used to address any of the 1G × 32 memory locations found in the 80386 memory system. Note that A_0 and A_1 are encoded in the bus enable ($\overline{BE_3}$–$\overline{BE_0}$) described elsewhere.
2. D_{31}–D_0—Data Bus Connections: used to transfer data between the microprocessor and its memory and I/O system.
3. $\overline{BE3}$–$\overline{BE0}$—Bank Enable Signals: used to access a byte, word, or double word of data. These signals are generated internally by the microprocessor from address bits A_1 and A_0.
4. M/$\overline{IO}$—Memory/IO: selects a memory device when a logic 1 or an I/O device when a logic 0. During the I/O operation the address bus contains a 16-bit I/O address.
5. W/$\overline{R}$—Write/Read: indicates that the current bus cycle is a write when a logic 1 and a read when a logic 0.
6. $\overline{ADS}$—Address Data Strobe: becomes active whenever the 80386 has issued a valid memory or I/O address. This signal is combined with the W/$\overline{R}$ signal to generate the separate read and write signals present in the 80286 system.
7. RESET—Reset: initializes the 80386, causing it to begin executing software from memory location FFFFFFF0H. The 80386 is reset to the real mode, and the leftmost 12 address connections remain logic 1s (FFFH) until a far jump or far call is executed.
8. CLK2—Clock Times 2: driven by a clock signal that is twice the operating frequency of the 80386. For example, to operate the 80386 at 16 MHz, we apply a 32-MHz clock to this pin.

9. $\overline{\text{READY}}$—Ready: used to control the number of wait states inserted into the timing to control memory accesses.
10. $\overline{\text{LOCK}}$—Lock: becomes a logic 0 whenever an instruction is prefixed with the LOCK: prefix. This is most often used during DMA accesses.
11. D/$\overline{\text{C}}$—Data/Control: indicates the data bus contains data for or from memory or I/O when a logic 1. If D/$\overline{\text{C}}$ is a logic 0, the microprocessor is halted or executing an interrupt acknowledge.
12. $\overline{\text{BS16}}$—Bus Size 16 Bits: selects either a 32-bit data bus ($\overline{\text{BS16}}$ = 1) or a 16-bit data bus ($\overline{\text{BS16}}$ = 0). In most cases, if an 80386 is operated on a 16-bit data bus, we use the 80386SX that has a 16-bit data bus.
13. $\overline{\text{NA}}$—Next Address: causes the 80386 to output the address of the next instruction or data in the current bus cycle. This pin is often used for pipelining the address.
14. HOLD—Hold: requests a DMA action as it did on the 80286.
15. HLDA—Hold Acknowledge: indicates that the 80386 is currently in a hold condition.
16. PEREQ—Coprocessor Request: asks the 80386 to relinquish control, and is a direct connection to the 80387 arithmetic coprocessor.
17. $\overline{\text{BUSY}}$—Busy: an input used by the WAIT or FWAIT instruction that waits for the coprocessor to become not busy. This is also a direct connection to the 80387 from the 80386.
18. $\overline{\text{ERROR}}$—Error: indicates to the microprocessor that an error is detected by the coprocessor.
19. INTR—Interrupt Request: is used by external circuitry to request an interrupt.
20. NMI—Nonmaskable Interrupt: requests a nonmaskable interrupt as it did on the 80286 microprocessor.

The Memory System

The physical memory system of the 80386DX is 4G bytes in size and can be addressed as such, or if virtual addressing is used, 64T bytes are mapped into the 4G bytes of physical space by the memory management unit. Figure 13–2 shows the organization of the 80386DX physical memory system.

The memory is divided into four 8-bit-wide memory banks, with each containing up to 1G bytes of memory. This 32-bit-wide memory organization allows bytes, words, or double words of memory data to be accessed directly. The 80386DX transfers up to a 32-bit-wide number in a single memory cycle, where the early 8088 required four cycles to accomplish the same transfer, and the 80286 required two cycles. Today, this data width is important, especially with single-precision floating-point numbers that are 32-bits in width. High-level software normally uses floating-point numbers for data storage, so 32-bit memory locations speed the execution of high-level software if it is written to take advantage of this wider memory.

Each memory byte is numbered in hexadecimal as it was in prior versions of the family. The difference is that the 80386DX uses a 32-bit-wide memory address with memory bytes numbered from location 00000000H through FFFFFFFFH.

The two memory banks in the 80286 system were accessed via A_0 and $\overline{\text{BHE}}$. In the 80386DX, the memory banks are accessed via four bank enable signals $\overline{\text{BE0}}$–

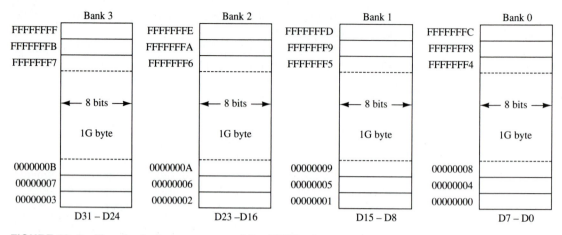

FIGURE 13–2　The physical memory map of the 80386 microprocessor.

$\overline{BE3}$. This arrangement allows a single byte to be accessed when one bank enable signal is activated by the microprocessor. It also allows a word to be addressed when two bank enable signals are activated. In most cases, a word is addressed in bank 0 and 1 or in bank 2 and 3. Memory location 00000000H is in bank 0, memory location 00000001H is in bank 1, 00000002H is in bank 2, and location 00000003H is in bank 3. The 80386DX does not contain address connections A_0 and A_1 because these have been decoded as the bank enable signals.

Buffered System.　Figure 13–3 shows the 80386DX connected to buffers that increase fanout from its address, data, and control connections. This microprocessor is operated at 25 MHz using a 50-MHz clock input signal that is generated by an integrated oscillator module. Oscillator modules are almost always used to provide a clock in modern microprocessor-based equipment. The HLDA signal is used to enable all buffers in a system that uses direct memory access. Otherwise, the buffer enable pins are connected to ground in a non-DMA system.

Pipelines and Caches.　The *cache memory* is a buffer that allows the 80386 to function more efficiently with lower DRAM speeds. A *pipeline* is a special way of handling memory accesses so the memory has additional time to access data. A 16-MHz 80386 allows memory devices with access times of 50 ns or less to operate at full speed. Obviously there are no DRAMs currently available with these access times. In fact, the fasted DRAMs currently in production have access times of 60 ns or longer. This means that some technique must be found to interface these, slower than the microprocessor, memory devices. Three techniques are available: interleaved memory, caching, and a pipeline. We discussed the interleaved memory system in Chapters 7 and 8 and we will not repeat it here. The 16-MHz 80386 operates using 100 ns DRAM in a system that uses interleaved memory.

　　The pipeline is the preferred means of interfacing memory because the microprocessor supports pipelined memory accesses. Pipelining in the 80386 allows

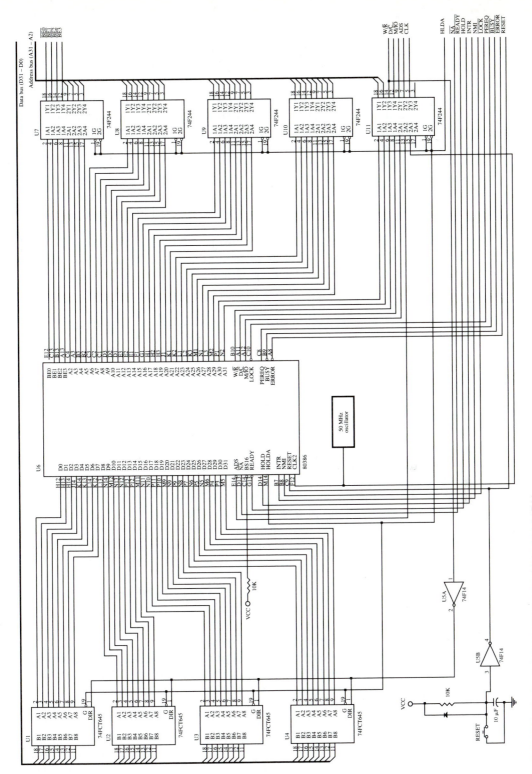

FIGURE 13-3 A fully buffered 25-MHz 80386DX.

547

memory an extra clocking period to access data. The extra clock extends the access time from 50 ns to 81 ns on an 80386 operating with a 16-MHz clock. The *pipe,* as it is often called, is set up by the microprocessor. When an instruction is fetched from memory, the microprocessor has extra time before the next instruction is fetched. During this extra time, the address of the next instruction is sent out the address bus ahead of time. This extra time (one clock period) is used to allow additional access time to slower memory components.

Not all memory references can take advantage of the pipe, which means that some memory cycles are not pipelined. These nonpipelined memory cycles request one wait state if the normal pipeline cycle requires no wait states. Overall, pipes are a cost-saving feature that reduces the access time required by the memory system in low-speed systems.

Not all systems can take advantage of the pipe. Those systems are typically ones that operate at 20, 25, or 33 MHz. In these higher speed systems, another technique must be used to increase the memory system speed. The *cache* memory system improves overall performance of the memory systems for data that are accessed more than once.

A cache is a high-speed memory system that is placed between the microprocessor and the DRAM memory system. Cache memory devices are usually TTL memory components with access times of less than 25 ns. In many cases we see cache memory systems of sizes between 32K bytes and 256K bytes. The size of the cache memory is determined more by the application than by the microprocessor. If a program is small and refers to little memory data, a small cache is beneficial. If a program is large and references large blocks of memory, the largest cache size possible is recommended. In many cases a 64K improves speed sufficiently.

The cache memory operates in the following fashion. Whenever the microprocessor accesses memory, the cache is first tested to see if the data are stored in the cache. If the data are in the cache, we have a cache *hit.* Whenever a hit occurs, the data are fetched from the cache without any wait states. If the data are not in the cache, we have a cache *miss.* When a miss occurs, the data are read from the DRAM and stored in the cache and read into the microprocessor. This of course requires wait states to slow the microprocessor to match speeds with the slow-speed DRAM memory.

When writing data to the memory we also write it to the cache. Although this causes normal DRAM wait states, if the data are read later, they are already in the cache, meaning zero wait state operation on subsequent reads of the same data. This method of writing is called *cache write through* operation.

In a cache memory system, data are organized into blocks of bytes. Blocks are from 2 to 16 bytes in length. Each time there is a cache miss, the microprocessor reads from 2 to 16 bytes of data from the memory into the cache. In the case of the 80386 microprocessor, we use a block size of 16 bytes or four 32-bit memory locations. When data are fetched from memory as four 32-bit memory locations, we call the transfer a *burst transfer.* The reason that the cache is organized this way is because most programs and data are sequential. By transferring four 32-bit double words from the memory into the cache for each miss, we are actually storing the next data or instructions used by the microprocessor in the cache. This method of filling the cache is called *cache lookahead*.

Figure 13–4 depicts a typical 32K-byte cache memory system. The cache is organized as an 8K × 49 memory. This means that there are 8K locations, with each location containing 49 bits. The 49-bit-wide memory is divided into two sections: one section is 32 bits wide and stores data, the other is 17 bits wide and stores a tag. The tag is a portion of the memory address (A_{32}–A_{15}). This means that there are 32K bytes (8K × 32) for data storage and 8K × 17 for tag information. Tag information is never included in the cache memory size, so this is a 32K-byte cache. The tags are stored inside the cache controller, and therefore no external memory is required for tag storage.

This is a direct-mapped cache because only the leftmost 17 bits of the address are stored in the tag field. The remaining 13 bits of the address (A_{14}–A_2) are used to address one of the 8K data locations (four bytes) and a location in the 8K tag memory. (See Figure 13–5 for the cache memory organization.)

Each time that the microprocessor sends an address to the memory system, the cache controller checks the tag (A_{31}–A_{15}) to determine whether the location addressed by A_{14}–A_2 is stored in the cache. The comparison tests the address stored in the tag field against address bits A_{31}–A_{15} to check for a match or hit. If the tag matches, the microprocessor fetches the data from the cache memory. If it doesn't match, the microprocessor reads the data from the main memory, stores it in the cache, and also stores the tag in the tag memory. To read data from the main memory may require up to four wait states, while a read from the cache requires no waits.

If data are written to the memory, the cache controller writes the data to a cache location and also to the tag memory. A write typically takes one wait state.

Suppose the microprocessor has just read data from memory location 01007FF0H. The data from this location are stored in the cache memory at location 111 1111 1111 00XX (least-significant 13 address bits). The tag that is stored in the tag memory for this access is 0000 0001 0000 0000 0. If this is the same address currently stored in the tag memory location, we have a hit.

If we have a hit in this example for location 01007FF0H and the microprocessor now attempts to read location 02007FF0H, we address the same location in the cache and also the same tag location. Because the leftmost 17 address bits do not match, we have a miss. Luckily memory accesses are normally sequential, so this type of miss rarely happens. More commonly, the next miss would occur when address 0100FFF0H is accessed. (Note that 0100FFF0H is 32K bytes above 01007FF0H.)

The I/O System

The I/O system of the 80386 is basically the same as that found in the 80286 microprocessor. There are 64K different bytes of I/O space available if isolated I/O is implemented. The I/O port address appears on address bus connections A_{15}–A_2, with $\overline{BE3}$–$\overline{BE0}$ used to select a byte, word, or double word of I/O data. If memory-mapped I/O is implemented, then the number of I/O locations can be any amount up to 4G bytes. Almost all 80386 systems use isolated I/O because of the I/O protection scheme used by the 80386 in protected mode.

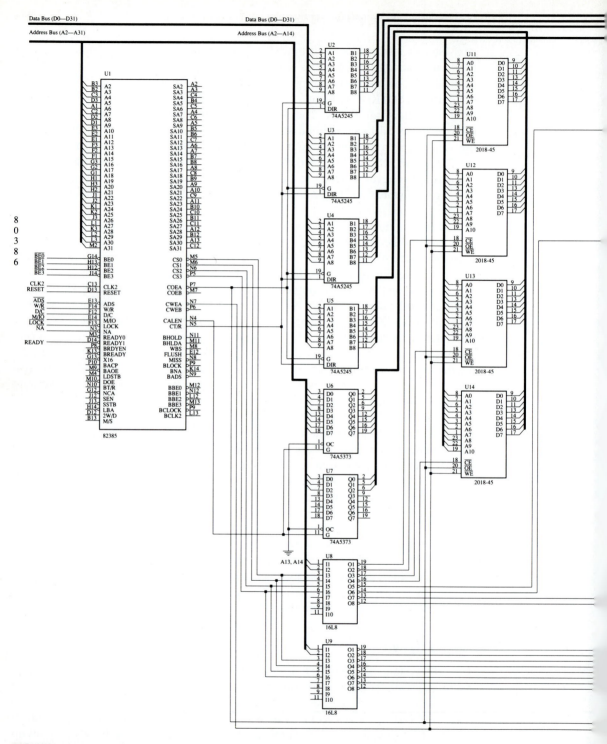

FIGURE 13–4 A 32K-byte cache memory system controlled by the 82385 cache controller. The memory consists of 2K × 8 high-speed static RAM that has an access time of 45 ns.

550

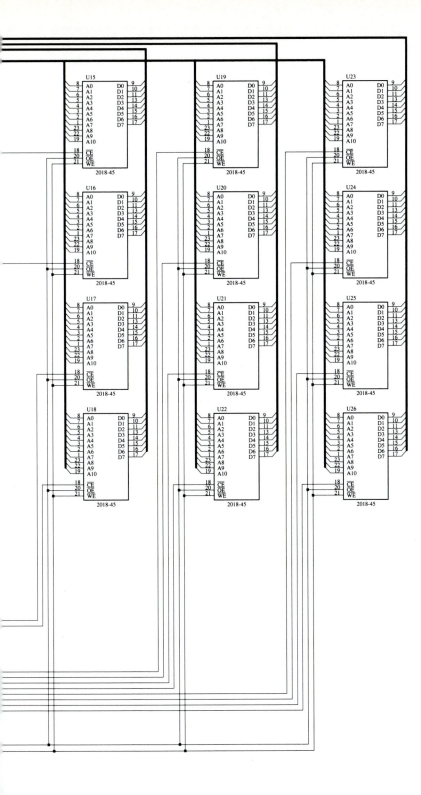

FIGURE 13–5 Organization of the direct-mapped 32K-byte cache memory.

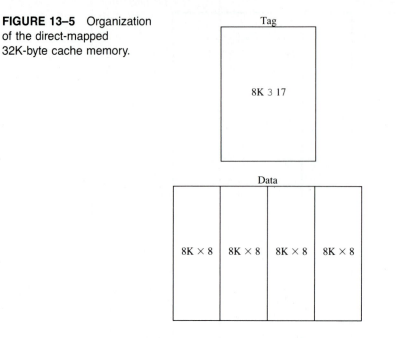

Figure 13–6 shows the I/O map for the 80386 microprocessor. Unlike the I/O map for the 80286, the 80386 uses a full 32-bit-wide I/O system divided into four banks just as the memory system is divided into four banks. Most I/O transfers are 8 bits wide because we often use ASCII code (a 7-bit code) for transferring alphanumeric data between the microprocessor and printers and keyboards. Recently, I/O devices that are 16 and even 32 bits wide have appeared for systems such as disk memory and video display interfaces. These wider I/O paths increase the data transfer rate between the microprocessor and the I/O device when compared to 8-bit transfers.

The I/O locations are numbered from 0000H through FFFFH. A portion of the I/O map is designated for the 80387 arithmetic coprocessor. Although the port numbers for the coprocessor are well above the normal I/O map, it is important that

FIGURE 13–6 The I/O map for the 80386 microprocessor showing all 64K I/O locations.

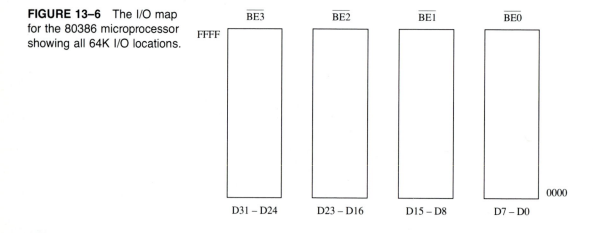

they be taken into account when decoding I/O space (overlaps). The coprocessor uses I/O location 800000F8H–800000FFH for communications between the 80387 and 80386. (Recall that the 80287 used I/O addresses 00F8H–00FDH for the same purpose.) Because we often only decode address connections A_{15}–A_2 to select an I/O device, be aware that the coprocessor will activate devices 00F8H–00FFH unless address line A_{31} is also decoded.

The only new feature that is added to the 80386 with respect to I/O is the I/O privilege information added to the tail end of the TSS when the 80386 is operated in protected mode. In the protected mode, as described in the section on 80386 memory management, an I/O location can be blocked or inhibited. If the blocked I/O location is addressed, an interrupt (type 13) is generated. This scheme is added so I/O access can be prohibited in a multiuser environment. Blocking is an extension of the protected mode operation as are privilege levels.

Memory and I/O Control Signals

As with the 80286, the memory and I/O are controlled with separate signals. The M/$\overline{\text{IO}}$ signal indicates whether the transfer is memory or I/O. In addition to M/IO, the memory and I/O systems must read or write data. The W/$\overline{\text{R}}$ signal is a logic 0 for a read operation, and a logic 1 for a write operation. The $\overline{\text{ADS}}$ signal is used to qualify these two control signals. This is a deviation from the 80286 system that used separate signals for memory read and write and I/O read and write.

Timing. Timing is important in understanding how to interface memory and I/O to the 80386 microprocessor. Figure 13–7 shows the timing diagram of a nonpipelined memory read cycle. Notice that the timing is referenced to the CLK2 input signal and that a bus cycle consists of four clocking periods.

FIGURE 13–7 The nonpipelined read timing for the 80386 microprocessor.

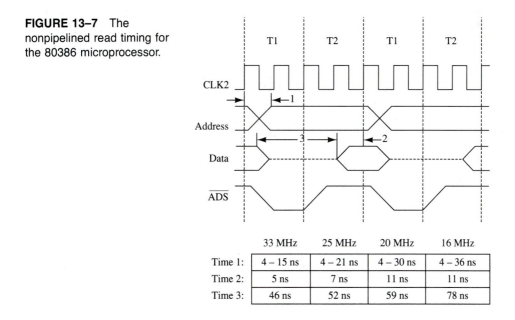

	33 MHz	25 MHz	20 MHz	16 MHz
Time 1:	4 – 15 ns	4 – 21 ns	4 – 30 ns	4 – 36 ns
Time 2:	5 ns	7 ns	11 ns	11 ns
Time 3:	46 ns	52 ns	59 ns	78 ns

Each bus cycle contains two clocking states, with each state (T_1 and T_2) containing two clocking periods. Notice in Figure 13–7 that the access time is listed as time number 3. The 16-MHz version allows memory an access time of 78 ns before wait states are inserted in this nonpipelined mode of operation. To select the nonpipelined mode, we place a logic 1 on the $\overline{NA}$ pin.

Figure 13–8 illustrates the read timing when the 80386 is operated in the pipelined mode. Notice that additional time is allowed the memory for accessing data because the address is sent out early. Pipelined mode is selected by placing a logic 0 on the $\overline{NA}$ pin and using address latches to capture the pipelined address. The clock pulse applied to the address latches is the $\overline{ADS}$ signal. Address latches must be used with a pipelined system as well as interleaved memory banks. The minimum number of interleaved banks is two, though four have been successfully used in some applications.

Notice that the pipelined address appears one complete clocking state before it normally appears with nonpipelined addressing. In the 16-MHz version of the 80386, this feature allows an additional 67.5 ns for memory access. In the nonpipelined system we had a memory access time of 78 ns, while in the pipelined system we have 145.5 ns. The advantages of the pipelined system are that no wait states (in many, but not all, bus cycles) are required and that lower speed memory devices can be connected to the microprocessor. The disadvantage is that we need to interleave memory to use a pipe, which requires additional circuitry and occasional wait states.

FIGURE 13–8 The pipelined read timing for the 80386 microprocessor.

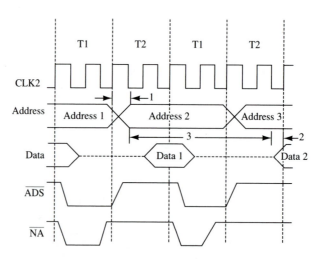

	33 MHz	25 MHz	20 MHz	16 MHz
Time 1:	4 – 15 ns	4 – 21 ns	4 – 30 ns	4 – 36 ns
Time 2:	5 ns	7 ns	11 ns	11 ns
Time 3:	80 ns	92 ns	109 ns	145.5 ns

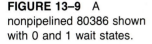

FIGURE 13–9 A nonpipelined 80386 shown with 0 and 1 wait states.

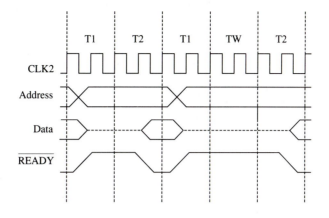

Wait States

Just as with the 80286, we need to introduce wait states if memory access times are long compared with the time allowed by the 80386 for memory access. In a nonpipelined 33-MHz system, access time is only 46 ns, but no DRAM memory exists that has an access time of 46 ns. This lack means that either wait states (1 wait for 70 ns DRAM) or an EPROM that has an access time of 100 ns (2 waits) must be introduced to access the DRAM.

The $\overline{READY}$ input controls whether or not waits states are inserted into the timing. The $\overline{READY}$ input on the 80386 is a dynamic input that must be activated during each bus cycle. Figure 13–9 shows a few bus cycles with one normal (0 wait) cycle and one that contains a single wait state. Notice how the $\overline{READY}$ is controlled to cause 0 or 1 wait.

The $\overline{READY}$ signal is sampled at the end of a bus cycle to determine if the clock cycle is T_2 or TW. If $\overline{READY} = 0$ at this time, it is the end of the bus cycle or T_2. If $\overline{READY}$ is 1 at the end of a clock cycle, the cycle is a TW and the microprocessor continues to test $\overline{READY}$, searching for a logic 0 and the end of the bus cycle.

In the nonpipelined system, whenever $\overline{ADS}$ becomes a logic 0, $\overline{READY} = 1$. After $\overline{ADS}$ returns to a logic 1, the positive edges of the clock are counted to generate the $\overline{READY}$ signal. The $\overline{READY}$ signal becomes a logic 0 after the first clock to insert zero waits states. If one wait state is inserted, the READY line must remain a logic 1 until at least two clocks have elapsed. If additional wait states are desired, then additional time must elapse before $\overline{READY}$ is cleared.

Figure 13–10 shows a circuit that inserts zero through three wait states for various memory addresses. In the example, one wait state is produced for a DRAM access and two waits for an EPROM access. The 74F164 clears whenever $\overline{ADS}$ is low and D/$\overline{C}$ is high. It begins to shift after $\overline{ADS}$ returns to a logic 1 level. As it shifts, the 00000000 in the shift register begins to fill with logic 1s from the QA connection toward the QH connection. The four different outputs are connected to an inverting multiplexer that generates the active low $\overline{READY}$ signal.

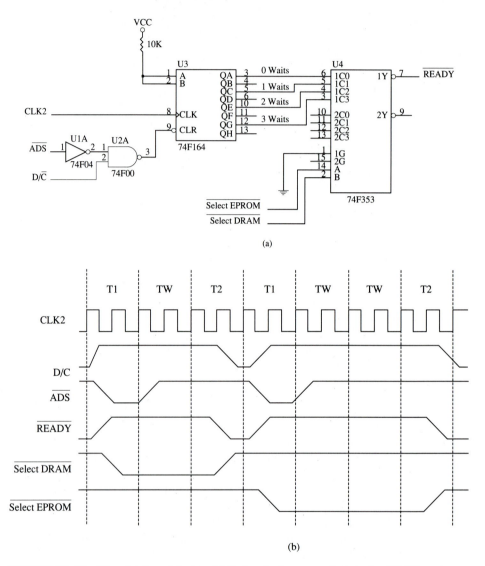

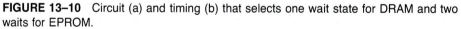

(b)

FIGURE 13–10 Circuit (a) and timing (b) that selects one wait state for DRAM and two waits for EPROM.

13–2 THE 80386 REGISTER STRUCTURE

The register structure of the 80386 is a much expanded version of the registers found in the 80286 microprocessor. Figure 13–11 shows the program-visible-register structure of the 80386 microprocessor. The registers are divided into three sections just as they are in the 80286: (1) *general purpose*, (2) *segment (selector) registers*, and (3) *housekeeping*.

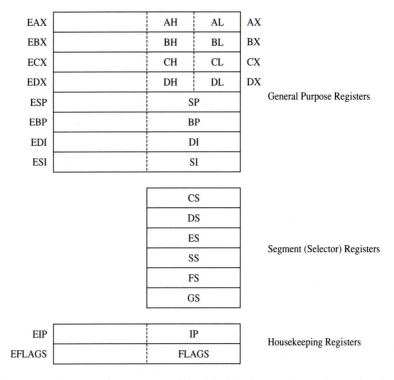

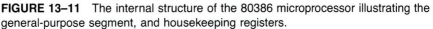

FIGURE 13–11 The internal structure of the 80386 microprocessor illustrating the general-purpose segment, and housekeeping registers.

The general-purpose registers are accessed through most instructions and are designed to hold, 8-, 16- or 32-bit data. The 80286 contains byte- and word-sized registers, while the 80386 also contains double-word-sized or extended registers. The 8- and 16-bit registers are addressed using the same names as with the 80286. The new 32-bit registers are addressed as extended registers, with the letter E augmenting the normal 16-bit designation. For example, EAX is the 32-bit extended version of AX.

The segment (selector) registers are similar to the 80286, except the 80386 contains two additional segment registers labeled FS and GS. In real mode operation, segment registers contain a segment address, and in protected mode operation, they contain a selector just as in the 80286 microprocessor. We use a prefix to address data using either FS or GS. For example, to use GS to address data in the GS segment we might find a MOV EAX,GS:DATA instruction. The prefix GS: or FS: is used to select these two new segment registers for any memory-addressing mode.

The housekeeping registers consist of a 32-bit instruction pointer (EIP) and a 32-bit flag register (EFLAGS). During real mode operation, only the rightmost 16 bits of EIP contain the offset address of the next instruction executed in a program. In protected mode operation, all 32 bits of EIP are used to address segments that may contain a program or data that are up to 4G bytes in length. This is a significant improvement over the 64K-byte segments available in the 80286.

EXAMPLE 13–1

```
                                        .386

                        ;Example 80386 instructions using a variety of
                        ;addressing modes.

0000                    CODE      SEGMENT  USE16

0000  66¦ BB 00001234             MOV      EBX,1234H
0006  66¦ BF 00000034             MOV      EDI,34H
000C  65: 8A 0D                   MOV      CL,GS:[DI]
000F  66¦ 8B D8                   MOV      EBX,EAX
0012  66¦ 8B F3                   MOV      ESI,EBX
0015  66¦ F7 E6                   MUL      ESI
0018  65: 67¦ 88 040B             MOV      GS:[EBX+ECX],AL
001D  64: 67¦ 8B 07               MOV      AX,FS:[EDI]


0021                    CODE      ENDS

                                  END
```

Example 13–1 lists a variety of instructions that use the 32-bit registers. Any instruction operating in real or protected mode can use any 32-bit register. The example begins with a .386 that designates to the assembler that the program is an 80386 program. The USE 16 directive tells the assembler to use standard 16-bit offset addresses for real mode operation. In protected mode we often include a USE 32 directive, which tells the assembler to use 32-bit offset addresses. More discussion of the USE 16 or USE 32 directive appears in Appendix A.

The EFLAG register is pictured in Figure 13–12. Notice that the rightmost 16 bits are identical to the 80286 flag register. The RF and VM flag bits are new to the 80386. The RF (resume flag) is used with debugging to temporarily disable debugging for the next instruction. The VM (virtual mode) flag bit selects virtual 8086 mode while the 80386 is operated in the protected mode. This special mode is discussed in a later section of this chapter.

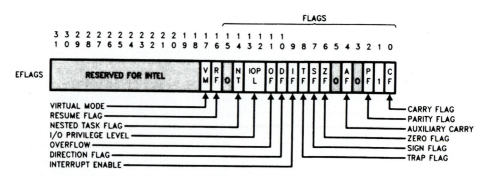

FIGURE 13–12   The EFLAG register. (Courtesy of Intel Corporation)

System Address Registers

The system address registers are GDTR (global descriptor table register), LDTR (local descriptor table register), IDTR (interrupt descriptor table register), and TR (task register). All system address registers are program invisible registers that are not directly accessed, except for loading or storing. The first three are used to address areas of memory that contain the global, local, and interrupt descriptor tables used during protected mode operation. The task register (TR) is used to address a selector that defines the current task in the form of the TSS (task state segment). These registers perform the same functions as they did in the 80286 microprocessor, except the base address is 32 bits wide instead of 24 bits and the limit is 20 bits instead of 16 bits.

Control Registers

In addition to the EFLAGS and EIP as described earlier, there are other control registers found in the 80386. Control register 0 (CR0) is identical to the MSW (machine status word) found in the 80286 microprocessor, except it is 32 bits wide instead of 16 bits. Additional control registers are CR1, CR2, and CR3.

Figure 13–13 illustrates the control register of the 80386. Control register CR1 is not used in the 80386, but is reserved for future products. Control register CR2 holds the linear page address of the last page accessed before a page fault interrupt. Finally, control register CR3 holds the base address of the page directory. The right-most 12 bits of the 32-bit page table address contain zeros and combines with the remainder of the register to locate the start of the 4K-long page table.

Register CR0 contains a number of special control bits that are defined as follows in the 80386:

1. PG—selects page table translation of linear addresses into physical addresses when PG = 1. Page table translation allows any linear address to be assigned any physical memory location.
2. ET—selects the 80287 coprocessor when ET = 0 or the 80387 coprocessor when ET = 1. This bit was installed because when the 80386 first appeared, there was

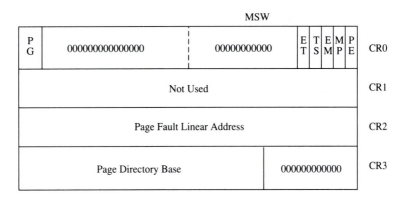

FIGURE 13–13 The control register structure of the 80386 microprocessor.

no 80387 available. In most systems, ET is set to indicate that an 80387 is present in the system.

3. TS—indicates that the 80386 has switched tasks. If TS = 1, a numeric coprocessor instruction causes a type-7 (coprocessor not available) interrupt.

4. EM—is set to cause a type-7 interrupt for each ESC instruction. (ESCape instructions are used to encode instructions for the 80387 coprocessor.) We often use this interrupt to emulate, with software, the function of the coprocessor. Emulation reduces the system cost, but execution of the emulated coprocessor instructions takes at least 100 times longer.

5. MP—set to indicate that the arithmetic coprocessor is present in the system.

6. PE—set to select the protected mode of operation for the 80386. It may also be cleared to reenter the real mode. Recall that this bit could only be set on the 80286.

Debug and Test Registers

A new series of registers not found in the 80286 appear in the 80386 as debug and test registers. Registers DR_0–DR_7 facilitate debugging and registers TR_6 and TR_7 are used to test paging and caching.

Figure 13–14 shows the sets of debug and test registers. The first four debug registers contain 32-bit linear breakpoint addresses. (A *linear address* is a 32-bit address that generates by a microprocessor instruction that may or may not be the same as the physical address.) The breakpoint addresses, which may locate an instruction or datum, are constantly compared with the addresses generated by the program. If a match occurs, the 80386 will, if directed by DR_6 and DR_7, cause a type-1 interrupt

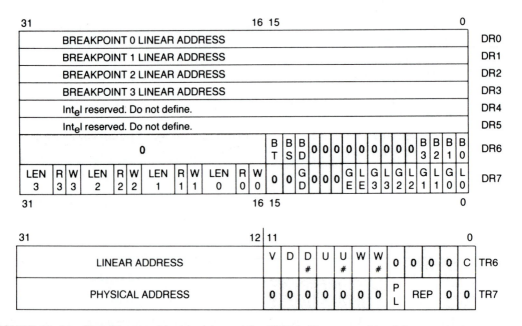

FIGURE 13–14 The debug and test registers of the 80386. (Courtesy of Intel Corporation)

(TRAP or debug interrupt) to occur. These breakpoint addresses are very useful in debugging faulty software. The control bits in DR_6 and DR_7 are defined as follows:

1. BT—if set, the debug interrupt was caused by a task switch.
2. BS—if set, the debug interrupt was caused by the TF bit in the flag register.
3. BD—if set, the debug interrupt was caused by an attempt to read the debug register with the GD bit set. The GD bit protects access to the debug registers.
4. B_3–B_0—indicate which of the four debug breakpoint addresses caused the debug interrupt.
5. LEN—each of the four length fields pertains to each of the four breakpoint addresses stored in DR_0–DR_3. These bits further define the size of access at the breakpoint address as 00 (byte), 01 (word), or 11 (double word).
6. RW—each of the four read/write fields pertains to each of the four breakpoint addresses stored in DR_0–DR_3. The RW field selects the cause of action that enabled a breakpoint address as 00 (instruction access), 01 (data write), and 11 (data read and write).
7. GD—if set, GD prevents any read or write of a debug register by generating the debug interrupt. This bit is automatically cleared during the debug interrupt so the debug registers can be read or changed if needed.
8. GE—if set, selects a global breakpoint address for any of the four breakpoint address registers.
9. LE—if set, selects a local breakpoint address for any of the four breakpoint address registers.

The test registers, TR_6 and TR_7, are used to test the translation lookaside buffer (TLB). The TLB is used with the paging unit within the 80386. The TLB holds the most commonly used page table address translations. The TLB reduces the number of memory reads required for looking up page translation table entries. The TLB holds the most common 32 entries from the page table, and it is tested with the TR_6 and TR_7 test registers.

Test register TR_6 holds the tag field (linear address) of the TLB, and TR_7 holds the physical address of the TLB. To write a TLB entry, perform the following steps:

1. Write TR_7 for the desired physical address, PL, and REP values.
2. Write TR_6 with the linear address, making sure that C = 0.

To read a TBL entry:

1. Write TR_6 with the linear address, making sure that C = 1.
2. Read both TR_6 and TR_7. If the PL bit indicates a hit, then the desired values of TR_6 and TR_7 indicate the contents of the TLB.

The bits found in TR_6 and TR_7 indicate the following conditions:

1. V—shows the entry in the TLB is valid.
2. D—indicates the entry in the TLB is invalid or dirty.
3. U—a user bit for the TLB.
4. W—indicates that the area addressed by the TLB entry is writable.
5. C—selects a write (0) or immediate lookup (1) for the TLB.
6. PL—indicates a hit if a logic 1.
7. REP—selects which block of the RLB is written.

Refer to the section on memory management and the paging unit for more details on the function of the TLB.

13–3   THE 80386 INSTRUCTION SET

The instruction set of the 80386 contains all of the instructions discussed for the 80286 plus a vast number of additional instructions and addressing modes that are new to the 80386. Many of the new variations are due to the 32-bit extended registers found in the 80386 microprocessor. In addition to the 8- and 16-bit registers found in the 80286, we also have the following 32-bit extended registers: EAX, EBX, ECX, EDX, ESP, EBP, EDI, and ESI along with two new segment (selector) registers: FS and GS. These additional registers increase the number of valid instructions for the 80386.

These new registers are used with instructions just as the 8- and 16-bit registers are used with the 80286 instruction set. The 32-bit registers may be accessed in either the real or protected mode of operation. Appendix B, which describes the entire instruction set of all variations of the Intel family, lists many examples of the 80386 instructions. In addition to the new 32-bit registers and new segment registers, there are also 14 new instructions (see Table 13–1) and many new addressing modes.

Bit Scan Instructions (BSF and BSR)

The bit scan forward and reverse instructions are similar in function so they are explained together. The bit scan forward (BSF) instruction scans a word or a double word from the rightmost bit toward the leftmost bit, and bit scan reverse (BSR) scans a word or double word from the leftmost bit toward the rightmost bit. If a bit is encountered that is set to a logic 1, the scanning ceases. If a logic 1 is found, the number of its bit position is stored in the destination register. If no bit is set, the contents of the destination register remain unknown.

TABLE 13–1 New 80386 instructions

Instruction	Comment	Example
BSF	Bit scan forward	BSF EAX,DATA
BSR	Bit scan reverse	BSR EAX,LIST
BT	Bit test	BT DATA,EAX
BTC	Bit test and complement	BTC AX,WATER
BTR	Bit test and reset	BTR EBX,4
BTS	Bit test and set	BTS BX,2
LFS	Load FS	LFS DI,DATA
LGS	Load GS	LGS SI,FIELD
LSS	Load SS	LSS SP,STACK
MOVZX	Move with zero extend	MOVZX EAX,CX
MOVSX	Move with sign extend	MOVSX ECX,DL
SETcd	Set byte on condition	SETNC AL
SHLD	Double-precision shift left	SHLD AX,BX,8
SHRD	Double-precision shift right	SHRD AX,BX,4

Suppose the contents of EAX are scanned for a logic 1. A BSF ECX,EAX instruction scans EAX from the right toward the left, searching for a logic 1. If bit positions 6, 9, and 12 contain logic 1s, the instruction returns with a 6 in register ECX. If none of the bits are a logic 1, the zero flag indicates a zero condition and ECX is undefined. These instructions are useful in converting numbers to floating-point form if a numeric coprocessor is unavailable.

Example 13–2 illustrates a short procedure that converts the 32-bit integer in EAX into a 32-bit single-precision floating-point number found in EAX upon return from the procedure. Notice how the BSR instruction is used to normalize EAX, along with a shift left, and how it generates the exponent. In this example, we should have shifted left 32 places, but the shift instructions only allow a maximum count of 31, so we shift by up to 31 and then shift an extra place to adjust the result.

EXAMPLE 13–2

```
                              .386
                              ;Procedure that converts the integer value of EAX
                              ;into a single-precision floating-point number.

0000                  CONV    PROC FAR

0000 66¦ 53                   PUSH  EBX              ;save registers
0002 66¦ 51                   PUSH  ECX
0004 66¦ 52                   PUSH  EDX

0006 66¦ 8B C8                MOV   ECX,EAX
0009 66¦ 81 E1 80000000 AND   ECX,80000000H         ;get sign-bit

0010 66¦ 0B C0                OR    EAX,EAX          ;test sign
0013 0F 89 001A R             JNS   CONV1            ;if positive
0017 66¦ F7 D8                NEG   EAX              ;make positive

001A                  CONV1:

001A 66¦ 0F BD D8             BSR   EBX,EAX          ;find 1
001E 0F 85 002E R             JNZ   CONV2            ;if not zero
0022 66¦ B8 00000000          MOV   EAX,0            ;get + 0.0
0028 66¦ 0B C1                OR    EAX,ECX          ;set sign-bit
002B EB 25 90                 JMP   ENDC             ;return

002E                  CONV2:

002E 66¦ 8B D3                MOV   EDX,EBX          ;form exponent
0031 66¦ 83 C2 7F             ADD   EDX,7FH          ;add bias
0035 66¦ C1 E2 17             SHL   EDX,23           ;position biased exponent
0039 66¦ 03 D1                ADD   EDX,ECX          ;form biased exponent and sign
003C 66¦ 83 C3 E1             ADD   EBX,-31
0040 66¦ F7 DB                NEG   EBX
0043 8A CB                    MOV   CL,BL            ;get shift count
0045 66¦ D3 E0                SHL   EAX,CL
0048 66¦ D1 E0                SHL   EAX,1
```

```
004B 66¦ C1 E8 09              SHR    EAX,9
004F 66¦ 03 C2                 ADD    EAX,EDX          ;combine

0052                   ENDC:

0052 66¦ 5A                    POP    EDX              ;restore registers
0054 66¦ 59                    POP    ECX
0056 66¦ 5B                    POP    EBX
0058 CB                        RET

0059                   CONV    ENDP
```

Bit Test Instructions (BT, BTC, BTR, and BTS)

The bit test instructions test a bit in any register or memory location. In addition to testing a bit, some of these instructions clear, set, or invert a bit. The bit test (BT) instruction tests a bit position for a logic 1 or 0. The bit test and complement (BTC) instruction tests the bit and then inverts it. The bit test and set (BTS) instruction tests the bit and then sets it (1). The bit test and clear (BTC) instruction tests the bit and then clears it (0). These instructions give the 80386 complete control over any bit position in any register or memory location. The bit control operations are often useful in control systems where bit positions represent various functions used to control machines.

With all four bit manipulation instructions, the bit tested changes the carry flag to the value of the bit under test. This test occurs before the bit changes, as with some bit manipulation instructions. The *destination operand* is the location of the bit under test, and the *source operand* is a register of immediate data that contains the bit position number under test.

For example, suppose that we must test bit position 4 of memory location DATA and then set it after the test. This is accomplished by the BTS DATA,4 instruction. The state of bit position 4 before being set is moved into the carry flag, then it is set to a logic 1. Example 13–3 shows a short procedure that sets bit 2, clears bit 7, and inverts bit 12 of the AX register.

EXAMPLE 13–3

```
                        .386
                        ;Procedure that sets bit 2, clears bit 7, and
                        ;inverts bit 12 of AX.

0000            CHNG    PROC    FAR

0000 0F BA E8 02        BTS     AX,2
0004 0F BA F0 07        BTR     AX,7
0008 0F BA F8 0C        BTC     AX,12
000C CB                 RET

000D            CHNG    ENDP
```

Load Segment Register and Pointer Instructions (LFS, LGS, and LSS)

The load segment register and pointer instructions are an extension of two other instructions of this type: LDS and LES. The LFS, LGS, and LSS instructions load a segment register and a pointer from a double word in the memory, just as LDS and LES do.

For example, the LSS SP,DATA instruction loads both SS (segment register) and SP (stack pointer) with the 32-bit contents of memory location DATA. The first two bytes of DATA are loaded into SP and the last two bytes are loaded into SS. The LFS and LGS instructions function in exactly the same fashion except that FS or GS is the segment register addressed instead of SS. These instructions are ideal for loading offset and segment-selector addresses into a pointer and segment register.

MOVZX and MOVSX Instructions

The MOVZX and MOVSX instructions are used to either zero extend or sign extend a number from 8 to 16 bits, 8 to 32 bits, or 16 to 32 bits. These instructions supplement the CBW and CWD instructions already found in the 80286 microprocessor. Recall that CBW sign extends AL into AX and that CWD sign extends AX into DX–AX. There are no zero extend instructions in the 80286 instruction set.

The MOVSX instruction sign extended data, just as CBW and CWD instructions did in the 80286. The main difference is that with CBW and CWD we were restricted to sign extending AL or AX. The MOVSX instruction allows any register or memory location to be sign extended and stored into any register. For example, the MOVSX ECX,BL instruction takes the 8-bit contents of BL and sign extends them into a 32-bit number stored at ECX. Likewise, the MOVSX DX,DATA instruction sign extends the byte contents of DATA into a 16-bit number stored at DX. (This assumes data is defined as a byte.)

The MOVZX instruction functions as the MOVSX instruction, but instead of sign extending the source operand, it zero extends it. We often use sign extension before a signed division and zero extension before an unsigned division. Example 13–4 lists two procedures that divide the 8-bit number at location TOP by the 8-bit number at location BOT and stores the 16-bit result at ANS. To accomplish this process one procedure (SIG) sign extends TOP into a 16-bit number before loading it into AX, and the other procedure (USIG) zero extends it.

EXAMPLE 13–4

```
                            .386
                            ;Procedures that use MOVSX and MOVZX.

0000                        SIG     PROC NEAR

0000  67¦ OF BE 05 00000008 R       MOVSX AX,TOP
0008  67¦ F6 35 00000009 R          DIV   BOT
000F  67¦ A3 0000000A R             MOV   ANS,AX
0015  C3                            RET

0016                        SIG     ENDP
```

```
0016                              USIG    PROC  NEAR

0016 67¦ 0F B6 05 00000008   R            MOVZX AX,TOP
001E 67¦ F6 35 00000009 R                 DIV   BOT
0025 67¦ A3 0000000A R                     MOV   ANS,AX
002B C3                                    RET

002C                              USIG    ENDP
```

Set Byte on Condition (SETcd)

The set byte on condition instruction is available in many forms. The SETcd instruction tests all of the conditions tested by the conditional jump instructions. Table 13–2 lists all forms of the SETcd instruction.

Each SETcd instruction tests a condition and sets a byte to 01H if the condition is true and clears it to 00H if the condition is false. For example, the SETE AL instruction places a 00H into AL on equal and a 01H into AL on not equal. These instructions are useful for setting a flag that indicates a condition for later use in a program. The SETcd instruction must use a byte-sized register or memory location.

Double-Precision Shifts (SHLD and SHRD)

The 80386 has added two double-precision shift instructions to the instruction set: SHLD and SHRD. These instructions shift left (SHLD) or right (SHRD) either a pair of words or a pair of double words. For example, the SHLD AX,BX,8 instruction shifts the 32-bit number located in AX and BX left eight binary places. If AX =

TABLE 13–2 The SETcd instructions

Instruction	Function	Example
SETO	Set on overflow	SETO AL
SETNO	Set on no overflow	SETNO CL
SETB	Set on below	SETB DATA
SETAE	Set on above or equal	SETAE BYTE PTR [DI]
SETE	Set on equal	SETE AL
SETNE	Set on not equal	SETNE BL
SETBE	Set on below or equal	SETBE CH
SETA	Set on above	SETA AH
SETS	Set on sign	SETS DL
SETNS	Set on no sign	SETNS DH
SETP	Set on parity	SETP AL
SETNP	Set on no parity	SETNP BYTE PTR FS:[BX]
SETL	Set on less than	SETL DL
SETGE	Set on greater or equal	SETGE CL
SETLE	Set on less or equal	SETLE CH
SETG	Set on greater than	SETG DL

1234H and BX = 5678H before the shift, they are AX = 3456H and BX 7800H after the instruction executes. Thirty-two bit operands may also be used, such as the SHRD EAX,ECX,19 instruction that shifts EAX and ECX right 19 places. All vacated bit positions are filled with zeros after the shift.

The double-precision shift instructions use a modulo-32 shift count, as do the shift and rotate instructions. This means that if the count is 34, the actual shift is 2 (34/32 = remainder of 2).

Notes on Older Instructions

In the 80286 microprocessor, the LMSW instruction loads the machine status word (MSW). On the 80386 the MSW is CR0. If you plan to modify the contents of CR0, don't use the LMSW instruction. Use the MOV EAX,CR0 instruction to move CR0 into EAX and then change it with the AND or OR instruction. After changing the image of CR0 in EAX, move it back into CR0 with the MOV CR0,EAX instruction. Likewise the SMSW instruction should never be used in 80386 programs.

In general most of the 80286 instructions can be adjusted for use with 32-bit registers on the 80386 microprocessor. For example, if you need to load EAX with a 12H, use the MOV EAX,12H instruction. Refer to Appendix B for a multitude of examples of instruction usage. Almost any instruction that uses an 8- or 16-bit register or pointer can use a 32-bit register or pointer.

New Addressing Modes

The number of addressing modes has been increased from the modes allowed by the 80286 microprocessor. The additional modes found in the 80386 microprocessor include using extended (32-bit) registers as 32-bit offset addresses and pointers. Also some additional forms of indexing, called *scaling,* have been added.

The most obvious of the new addressing modes use the new segment registers with the segment override prefix (FS: or GS:). The MOV AL,FS:[DI] instruction loads AL with the data stored in segment FS at offset address DI. Any instruction that can be prefixed, can use either FS or GS to address these two additional memory segments.

In addition to the indirect memory-addressing modes used with the 80286 microprocessor, the 80386 contains additional modes, as illustrated in Table 13–3. Notice that quite a few additional indirect addressing modes are added to the 80386 instruction set. The 80286 allowed memory to be indirectly addressed through only DI, SI, BX, or BP. These are still allowed in the 80386, but we may also use any of the new modes listed in Table 13–3. If these new addressing modes are used in the real mode, they can only access the first 1M byte of memory.

Notice that memory can be indirectly addressed using a 32-bit register or directly addressed using a 32-bit displacement. This increases the possible number of instructions available to the 80386 by a tremendous factor.

In the 80286 microprocessor, we can combine only certain pointers to indirectly address memory: [BX + DI], [BX + SI], [BP + DI], and [BP + SI]. In the 80386 any two 32-bit registers (except ESP) can be combined to address memory

TABLE 13–3 Additional indirect addressing modes for the 80386 microprocessor

Mode	Default Segment	Example
[EAX]	DS	ADD ECX,[EAX]
[EBX]	DS	SUB [EBX],AL
[ECX]	DS	MOV AX,[ECX]
[EDX]	DS	MOV AL,[EDX]
[EBP]	SS	MOV CL,[EBP]
[EDI]	DS	MOV [EDI],ECX
[ESI]	DS	MOV [ESI],EDI
d32	DS	MOV AL,DATA
[EAX + d8]	DS	ADD ECX,[EAX + 9]
[EBX + d8]	DS	SUB [EBX + 10H],AL
[ECX + d8]	DS	MOV AX,[ECX − 2]
[EDX + d8]	DS	MOV AL,[EDX − 12H]
[EBP + d8]	SS	MOV CL,[EBP + 1]
[EDI + d8]	DS	MOV [EDI − 33],ECX
[ESI + d8]	DS	MOV [ESI + 9],EDI
[EAX + d32]	DS	ADD ECX,TABLE[EAX]
[EBX + d32]	DS	SUB [EBX + 10000H],AL
[ECX + d32]	DS	MOV AX,ARRAY[ECX]
[EDX + d32]	DS	MOV AL,[EDX − 200000H]
[EBP + d32]	SS	MOV CL,[EBP + 1]
[EDI + d32]	DS	MOV TABLE[EDI],ECX
[ESI + d32]	DS	MOV TABLE[ESI + 92],EDI

Notes: d8 = 8-bit signed displacement and d32 = 32-bit signed displacement.

data. These additional addressing modes (see Table 13–4) use the following form [E?? + scaled index], where E?? is any 32-bit register except ESP and scaled index is any scaled 32-bit register except ESP. The MOV EAX,[EBX + ECX] instruction is an example of this new addressing mode. This instruction loads EAX with memory data stored in the data segment at the location address by the sum of EBX and ECX.

The term *scaled index* means that the second 32-bit register can be scaled (multiplied) by a factor of 1X, 2X, 4X, or 8X. A scaling factor of 1X is never used and is implied as in the MOV EAX,[EBX + ECX] instruction. The scaling factor multiplies the second register by 1, 2, 4, or 8, but it does not change the value in the register.

The scaling factor is used to address elements within arrays of data. Suppose that ECX addresses an array called ARRAY and that the element number is located in EDX. If the ARRAY is a byte-sized array, then EDX addresses the array element. If the ARRAY is word-sized, EDX must be multiplied by a factor (scale) of 2 to address the correct memory location for the array element. In a word-sized array, element 0 is at offset addresses 0 and 1; element 2 is at offset addresses 2 and 3; and so forth. Scaling factors of 4X and 8X are used to index array elements in double-word and quad-word arrays.

Example 13–5 lists a short procedure that adds floating-point single-precision numbers in LIST1 and LIST2 and stores the result in LIST3. Each array contains 100H double words of data in this example procedure that uses scaled indexed

TABLE 13–4 Scaled index addressing mode for the 80386 microprocessor

Mode	Default Segment	Example
[EAX + scaled index]	DS	MOV BH,[EAX + 2*ECX]
[EBX + scaled index]	DS	ADD AL,[EBX + EAX]
[ECX + scaled index]	DS	INC BYTE PTR [ECX + 4*EAX]
[EDX + scaled index]	DS	MOV [EDX + 8*EAX],SP
[EBP + scaled index]	SS	MOV AL,[EBP + ECX]
[EDI + scaled index]	DS	MOV BL,[EDI + ESI]
[ESI + scaled index]	DS	SUB BYTE PTR [ESI + EBX],22H
[EAX + scaled index + d8]	DS	MOV BH,[EAX + 2*ECX + 3]
[EBX + scaled index + d8]	DS	ADD AL,[EBX + EAX − 2]
[ECX + scaled index + d8]	DS	INC BYTE PTR [ECX + 4*EAX − 9]
[EDX + scaled index + d8]	DS	MOV [EDX + 8*EAX − 10H],SP
[EBP + scaled index + d8]	SS	MOV AL,[EBP + ECX + 1AH]
[EDI + scaled index + d8]	DS	MOV BL,[EDI + ESI − 2]
[ESI + scaled index + d8]	DS	SUB BYTE PTR[ESI + EBX − 4],22H
[EAX + scaled index + d32]	DS	MOV BH,[EAX + 2*ECX + 200000H]
[EBX + scaled index + d32]	DS	ADD AL,TABLE[EBX + EAX]
[ECX + scaled index + d32]	DS	INC BYTE PTR ARRAY[ECX + 4*EAX]
[EDX + scaled index + d32]	DS	MOV ARRAY[EDX + 8*EAX + 100H],SP
[EBP + scaled index + d32]	SS	MOV AL,LIST[EBP + ECX]
[EDI + scaled index + d32]	DS	MOV BL,LIST[EDI + ESI + 10000H]
[ESI + scaled index + d32]	DS	SUB BYTE PTR ARRAY[ESI + EBX],22H

Notes: d8 = 8-bit signed displacement, d32 = 32-bit signed displacement, and scaled index = EAX, EBX, ECX, EDX, EBP, EDI, or ESI with a scaling factor of 1X, 2X, 4X, or 8X.

addressing to access the array elements. If the scaling factor is changed from 4X to 8X, double-precision floating-point data are added. Also notice that a 4 is subtracted inside of each indirect addressing mode because the last count in CX is a 1, not a zero. Note that this software is written assuming real-mode operation in a DOS-based system, and that no attempt is made to place numbers inside of the two source arrays LIST1 and LIST2.

EXAMPLE 13–5

```
                    .386
                    .387
                    ;Procedure that adds lists of floating-point data

0000                CODE    SEGMENT USE16

                    ASSUME  CS:CODE,DS:CODE

0000 0100 [         LIST1   DD      100H DUP (?)
       00000000
              ]
```

```
0400  0100 [              LIST2     DD        100H DUP (?)
          00000000
                  ]
0800  0100 [              LIST3     DD        100H DUP (?)
          00000000
                  ]

0C00                ADDS     PROC      FAR

0C00  1E                     PUSH      DS
0C01  8C C8                  MOV       AX,CS
0C03  8E D8                  MOV       DS,AX

0C05  66¦ 33 C0              XOR       EAX,EAX          ;clear registers
0C08  66¦ 33 DB              XOR       EBX,EBX
0C0B  66¦ 33 C9              XOR       ECX,ECX
0C0E  66¦ 33 D2              XOR       EDX,EDX

0C11  B8 0000 R              MOV       AX,OFFSET LIST1  ;address data
0C14  BB 0400 R              MOV       BX,OFFSET LIST2
0C17  BA 0800 R              MOV       DX,OFFSET LIST3

0C1A  B9 0100               MOV       CX,100H          ;load count

0C1D                REPS:

0C1D  67& D9 44 88 FC        FLD       DWORD PTR [EAX + 4*ECX -4]
0C22  67& D8 44 8B FC        FADD      DWORD PTR [EBX + 4*ECX -4]
0C27  67& D9 5C 8A FC        FSTP      DWORD PTR [EDX + 4*ECX -4]

0C2C  E2 EF                 LOOP      REPS
0C2E  1F                    POP       DS
0C2F  CB                    RET

0C30                ADDS     ENDP

0C30                CODE     ENDS

                          END       ADDS
```

Interrupts

Although this topic contains hardware interfacing information, it also contains instructions, so it is presented with the instruction set. Figure 13–15 shows the predefined interrupts for the 80386. These interrupts should be compared to the interrupts
found in the 80286 in Section 10–1. The 80386 contains interrupt-type numbers 14
and 16 that do not appear in the interrupt table for the 80286. Type 14 occurs for a
page mechanism fault and type 16 for a coprocessor error.

We often call interrupts generated by the INTR and NMI inputs *hardware
interrupts,* while any other type is called an *exception.* Exceptions are generated by

Function	Interrupt Number	Instruction Which Can Cause Exception	Return Address Points to Faulting Instruction	Type
Divide Error	0	DIV, IDIV	YES	FAULT
Debug Exception	1	any instruction	YES	TRAP*
NMI Interrupt	2	INT 2 or NMI	NO	NMI
One Byte Interrupt	3	INT	NO	TRAP
Interrupt on Overflow	4	INTO	NO	TRAP
Array Bounds Check	5	BOUND	YES	FAULT
Invalid OP-Code	6	Any Illegal Instruction	YES	FAULT
Device Not Available	7	ESC, WAIT	YES	FAULT
Double Fault	8	Any Instruction That Can Generate an Exception		ABORT
Coprocessor Segment Overrun	9	ESC	NO	ABORT
Invalid TSS	10	JMP, CALL, IRET, INT	YES	FAULT
Segment Not Present	11	Segment Register Instructions	YES	FAULT
Stack Fault	12	Stack References	YES	FAULT
General Protection Fault	13	Any Memory Reference	YES	FAULT
Page Fault	14	Any Memory Access or Code Fetch	YES	FAULT
Coprocessor Error	16	ESC, WAIT	YES	FAULT
Intel Reserved	17–32			
Two Byte Interrupt	0–255	INT n	NO	TRAP

* Some debug exceptions may report both traps on the previous instruction, and faults on the next instruction.

FIGURE 13–15 The predefined interrupt vectors for the 80386 microprocessor. (Courtesy of Intel Corporation)

internal events, while interrupts are generated by external events. An *exception* is an exception to the normal progress of a program. The predefined interrupts and exceptions above level 5 are defined in the following list:

1. Type 6—any illegal instruction causes a type-6 interrupt.
2. Type 7—if the EM bit in the CR_0 is set, the type-7 interrupt occurs for any arithmetic coprocessor instruction. If the MP bit of CR_0 is set and TS is set by a task switch, the WAIT instruction will also cause a type-7 interrupt.
3. Type 8—a double fault or abort exception occurs whenever the 80386 detects a type 10, 11, 12, or 13 interrupt at the same time an interrupt other than a type 14 occurs.
4. Type 9—this exception occurs if the operand address for an arithmetic coprocessor instruction wraps around from location FFFFH to 0000H or 0000H to FFFFH on the real mode. In the protected mode, this exception occurs if the address wraps around from FFFFFFFFH to 00000000H or from 00000000H to FFFFFFFFH.

5. Type 10—if an invalid TSS is accessed, the type-10 exception occurs. An invalid TSS occurs whenever the selector is outside the table limit, if a code in stack segment is outside the table limit, if a stack is not writable, or if the requested privilege level is not equal to the current privilege level of the accessed TSS.

6. Type 11—occurs if the P-bit of the descriptor indicates that the segment is not present (P = 0).

7. Type 12—occurs if the SS descriptor accesses a segment that is not present or if any stack operation causes a limit violation.

8. Type 13—occurs for any of the following reasons: exceeding segment limit, writing to a read-only data segment or code segment, loading a selector with a system descriptor, reading an execute-only code segment, switching to a busy task, violating privilege level for a data segment, or loading CR_0 with PG = 1 and PE = 0.

9. Type 14—a page fault exception occurs if PG = 1 and the privilege level is incorrect or the page table or directory contains a zero.

10. Type 16—the $\overline{ERROR}$ pin on the 80387 causes a type-16 exception.

Hardware interrupts for the 80386 are the same as for the 80286. To refresh your understanding of the INTR and NMI inputs refer to Chapter 10 for a complete discussion of these interrupt inputs.

13–4   80386 MEMORY MANAGEMENT

The memory-management unit (MMU) within the 80386 is similar to the MMU inside the 80286, except the 80386 has a paging unit not found in the 80286. The MMU performs the task of converting logical addresses as they appear as outputs from a program, into physical addresses that access a physical memory location located anywhere within the memory system. The 80386 can use a paging mechanism to allocate any physical address to any logical address. What this means is that even though the program is accessing memory location A0000H with an instruction, the actual physical address could be memory location 100000H, or any other location if paging is enabled. This allows virtually any software, written to operate at any memory location, to function in an 80386 because any physical location can become any logical location. The 80286 did not have this flexibility. Paging is used in DOS 5.0 to relocate 80386 and 80486 memory at addresses above FFFFFH into spaces between ROM at locations D0000–DFFFFH and other areas as they are available.

Descriptors and Selectors

Before the memory paging unit is discussed, descriptors and selectors for the 80386 microprocessor are discussed. The 80386 uses descriptors in much the same fashion as the 80286 does. In both microprocessors, a *descriptor* is a series of 8 bytes that describe and locate a memory segment. A *selector* (segment register) is used to index a descriptor from a table of descriptors. The main difference between the 80286 and 80386 is that the 80386 has two additional selectors (FS and GS). The

80386 descriptors also use a 32-bit base address and a 20-bit limit instead of a 24-bit base address and a 16-bit limit, as found on the 80286.

The 80286 addresses a 16M-byte memory space with its 24-bit base address and has a segment length limit of 64K bytes due to the 16-bit limit. The 80386 addresses a 4G-byte memory space with its 32-bit base address and has a segment length limit of 1M byte or 4G bytes due to a 20-bit limit that is used in two different ways. The 20-bit limit can access a segment with a length of 1M byte if the granularity bit (G) = 0. If G = 1, the 20-bit limit allows a segment length of 4G bytes.

The granularity bit is found in the 80386 descriptor. If G = 0, the number stored in the limit is interpreted directly as a limit, allowing it to contain any limit between 00000H and FFFFFH for a segment size up to 1M byte. If G = 1, the number stored in the limit is interpreted as 00000XXXH through FFFFFXXXH, where the XXX is 000H. This allows the limit of the segment to range between 0 bytes to 4G bytes in steps of 4K bytes. A limit of 00001H indicates that the limit is 4K bytes when G = 1, and 1 byte when G = 0.

Figure 13–16 shows the way that the 80386 addresses a memory segment in the protected mode using a selector and a descriptor. Notice that this is identical to the way that a segment is addressed by the 80286. The difference is the size of the segment accessed by the 80386. The selector uses its leftmost 13 bits to access a descriptor from a descriptor table. The TI bit indicates either the local (TI = 1) or global (TI = 0) descriptor table. The rightmost two bits of the selector define the requested privilege level of the access.

Because the selector uses a 13-bit code to access a descriptor, there are at most 8,192 descriptors in each table, local or global. Since each segment in an 80386 can be 4G bytes in length, we can access 16,384 segments at a time with the two descriptor tables. This allows the 80386 to access a virtual memory size of 64T bytes. Of course, only 4G bytes of memory actually exist in the memory system. (One T byte = 1,024G bytes.) If a program requires more than 4G bytes of memory at a time, it can be swapped between the memory system and a disk drive or other form of large-volume storage.

As with the 80286, the 80386 uses tables for both global (GDT) and local (LDT) descriptors. Both machines also use a third table for interrupts (IDT) descriptors or gates. The descriptors for the 80386 are different from the 80286, as illustrated in the comparison of these descriptors in Figure 13–17. Notice how both descriptors use the same data for the first six bytes. This allows the 80286 software to be upward

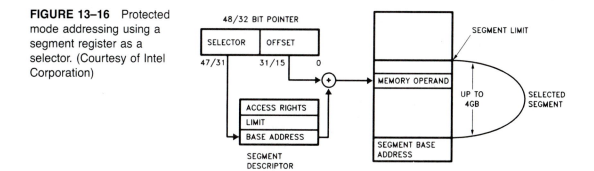

FIGURE 13–16 Protected mode addressing using a segment register as a selector. (Courtesy of Intel Corporation)

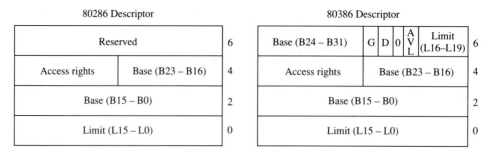

FIGURE 13–17 The descriptors for the 80286 and 80386 microprocessors.

compatible with the 80386 software. (Recall that an 80286 descriptor used 00H for its most significant two bytes.) The base address is 32 bit in the 80386, the limit is 20 bits, and a G bit selects the limit multiplier (1 time or 4K times). The fields in the descriptor for the 80386 are defined as follows:

1. Base (B_0–B_{31})—defines the starting 32-bit address of the segment within the 4G-byte physical address space of the 80386 microprocessor.
2. Limit (L_0–L_{19})—defines the limit of the segment in units of bytes if the G bit = 0, or in units of 4K bytes if G = 1. This allows a segment to be of any length from 1 byte to 1M byte if G = 0 and from 4K bytes to 4G bytes if G = 1. Recall that the limit indicates the last byte in a segment.
3. Access Rights—determines privilege level and other information about the segment. This byte varies with different types of descriptors and is elaborated with each descriptor type.
4. G—the granularity bit selects a multiplier of 1 or 4K times for the limit field. If G = 0, the multiplier is 1, and if G = 1, the multiplier is 4K.
5. D—selects the default register size. If D = 0, the registers are 16 bits wide as in the 80286, and if D = 1, they are 32 bits wide as in the 80386. This bit determines whether prefixes are required for 32-bit data and index registers. If D = 0, then a prefix is required to access 32-bit registers and to use 32-bit pointers. If D = 1, then a prefix is required to access 16-bit registers and 16-bit pointers. The USE16 and USE32 directives appended to the SEGMENT statement in assembly language control the setting of the D bit. In the real mode, it is always assumed that the registers are 16 bits wide so any instruction that references a 32-bit register or pointer must be prefixed. Note that current versions of DOS and OS/2* assume that D = 0.
6. AVL—this bit is available to the operating system to use in any way that it sees fit. It often indicates that the segment described by the descriptor is available.

Descriptors appear in two forms in the 80386 microprocessor: the segment descriptor and the system descriptor. The segment descriptor defines data, stack, and code segments, and the system descriptor defines information about the system's tables, tasks, and gates.

---

*OS/2 (Operating System 2) is a registered trademark of IBM.

FIGURE 13–18 The format
of the 80386 segment
descriptor.

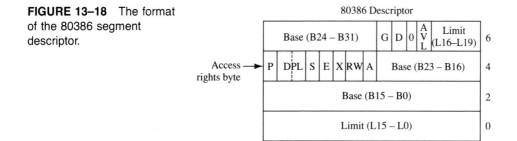

Segment Descriptors. Figure 13–18 shows the segment descriptor. This descriptor fits
the general form as dictated in Figure 13–17, but the access rights bits are defined to
indicate how the data, stack, or code segment described by the descriptor functions.
Bit position 4 of the access rights byte determines whether the descriptor is a data
or code segment descriptor (S = 1) or a system segment descriptor (S = 0).

Following is a description of the access rights bits and their function in the
segment descriptor:

1. P—Present: a logic 1 to indicate that the segment is present. If P = 0 and
   the segment is accessed through the descriptor, a type-11 interrupt occurs. This
   interrupt indicates that a segment was accessed that is not present in the system.
2. DPL—Descriptor Privilege Level: sets the privilege level of the descriptor where
   00 has the highest privilege and 11 has the lowest. This descriptor is used to
   protect access to segments. If a segment is accessed with a privilege level that
   is lower (higher in number) than the DPL, a privilege violation interrupt occurs.
   Privilege levels are used in multiuser systems to prevent access to an area of the
   system memory.
3. S—Segment: indicates a data or code segment descriptor (S = 1) or a system
   segment descriptor (S = 0).
4. E—Executable: selects a data (stack) segment (E = 0) or a code segment (E =
   1). E also defines the function of the next two bits (X and RW).
5. X—if E = 0, then X indicates the direction of expansion for the data segment.
   If X = 0, the segment expands upward as in a data segment, and if X = 1, the
   segment expands downward as in a stack segment. If E = 1, then X indicates
   whether the privilege level of the code segment is ignored (X = 0) or observed
   (X = 1).
6. RW—Read/Write: if E = 0, then RW indicates that the data segment may be
   written (RW = 1) or not written (RW = 0). If E = 1, then RW indicates that
   the code segment may be read (RW = 1) or not read (RW = 0).
7. A—Accessed: this bit is set each time that the microprocessor accesses the segment. It is sometimes used by the operating system to keep track of which segments have been accessed.

System Descriptor. The system descriptor is illustrated in Figure 13–19. There are
16 possible system descriptor types (see Table 13–5 for the different descriptor
types), but not all are used in the 80386 microprocessor. Some of these types are defined for the 80286 so that the 80286 software is compatible with the 80386. Some of

FIGURE 13–19 The general format of an 80386 system descriptor.

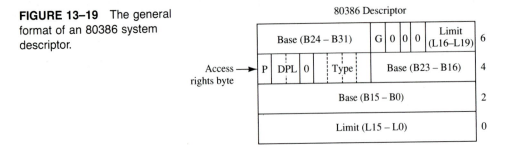

the types are new and unique to the 80386. Some have yet to be defined, and are reserved for future Intel products.

Descriptor Tables

The descriptor tables define all the segments used in the 80386 when operated in the protected mode. There are three types of descriptor tables: the global descriptor table (GDT), the local descriptor table (LDT), and the interrupt descriptor table (IDT). The registers used by the 80386 to address these three tables are called the global descriptor table register (GDTR), the local descriptor table register (LDTR), and the interrupt descriptor table register (IDTR). These registers are loaded, respectively, with the LGDT, LLDT, and LIDT instructions.

The *descriptor table* is a variable-length array of data with each entry holding an 8-byte-long descriptor. The local and global descriptor tables hold 8,192 entries each, and the interrupt descriptor table holds 256 entries. A descriptor is indexed from either the local or global descriptor table by the selector that appears in a

TABLE 13–5 80386 system descriptor types

Type	Description
0000	Invalid
0001	Available 80286 TSS
0010	LDT
0011	Busy 80286 TSS
0100	80286 call gate
0101	Task gate (80286 or 80386)
0110	80286 interrupt gate
0111	80286 trap gate
1000	Invalid
1001	Available 80386 TSS
1010	Reserved for future Intel products
1011	Busy 80386 TSS
1100	80386 call gate
1101	Reserved for future Intel products
1110	80386 interrupt gate
1111	80386 trap gate

FIGURE 13–20 Any
segment register showing the
selector, TI bit, and RPL bits.

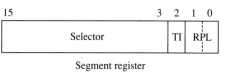

segment register. Figure 13–20 shows a segment register and the selector that it holds
in the protected mode. The leftmost 13 bits index a descriptor, the TI bit selects either
the local (TI = 1) or global (TI = 0) descriptor table, and the RPL bits indicate the
requested privilege level.

Whenever a new selector is placed into one of the segment registers, the 80386
accesses one of the descriptor tables and automatically loads the descriptor into the
invisible cache portion of the segment register. As long as the selector remains the
same in the segment register, no additional accesses are required to the descriptor
table. The operation of fetching a new descriptor from the descriptor table is program
invisible because the microprocessor automatically accomplishes this each time that
the segment register contents are changed in the protected mode.

Figure 13–21 shows how a sample global descriptor table (GDT), which is
stored at memory address 00010000H, is accessed through the segment register
and its selector. This table contains four entries. The first is a null (0) descriptor.
Descriptor 0 must always be a null descriptor. The other entries address various
segments in the 80386 protected mode memory system. In this illustration, the data

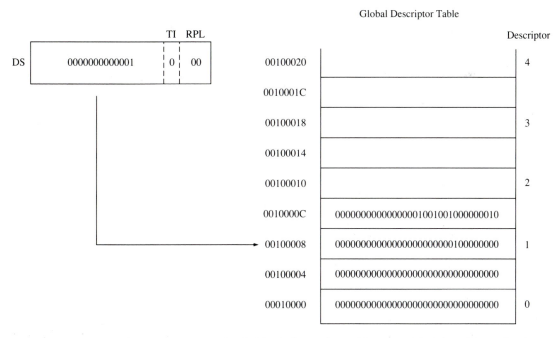

FIGURE 13–21   The data segment used to hold a selector that addresses global descriptor entry 1.

segment register contains a 0008H. This means that the selector is indexing descriptor location 1 in the global descriptor table (TI = 0), with a requested privilege level of 00. Descriptor 1 is located 8 bytes above the base descriptor table address at location 00010008H. The descriptor located in this memory location accesses a base address of 00200000H and a limit of 100H. This means that this descriptor addresses memory locations 00200000H–00200100H. Because this is the DS (data segment) register, this means that the data segment is located at these locations in the memory system. If data are accessed outside of these boundaries, an interrupt occurs.

The local descriptor table (LDT) is accessed in the same manner as the global descriptor table (GDT). The only difference in access is that the TI bit is cleared for a global access and set for a local access. Another difference exists if the local and global descriptor table registers are examined. The global descriptor table register (GDTR) contains the base address of the global descriptor table and the limit. The local descriptor table register (LDTR) contains only a selector and is 16 bits wide. The contents of the LDTR address a type 0010 system descriptor that contains the base address and limit of the LDT. This scheme allows one global table for all tasks, but also many local tables, one or more for each task, if necessary. Global descriptors describe memory for the system, while local descriptors describe memory for applications or tasks.

The interrupt descriptor table (IDT) is addressed, as is the GDT, by storing the base address and limit in the interrupt descriptor table register (IDTR). The main difference between the GDT and IDT is that the IDT contains only interrupt gates rather than segment and system descriptors, as do the GDT and LDT.

Figure 13–22 shows the gate descriptor, a special form of the system descriptor described earlier. (Refer back to Table 13–5 for the different gate descriptor types.) Notice that the gate descriptor contains a 32-bit offset address, a word count, and a selector. The 32-bit offset address points to the location of the interrupt service procedure or other procedure. The word count indicates how many words are transferred from the caller's stack to the stack of the procedure accessed by a call gate. The word count field is not used with an interrupt gate. The selector is used to indicate the location of the task state segment (TSS) in the GDT or LDT if it is a local procedure.

When a gate is accessed, the contents of the selector are loaded into the task register (TR). The acceptance of the gate depends on the privilege and priority levels. A return instruction (RET) ends a call gate procedure, and a return from interrupt

FIGURE 13–22 The gate descriptor for the 80386 microprocessor.

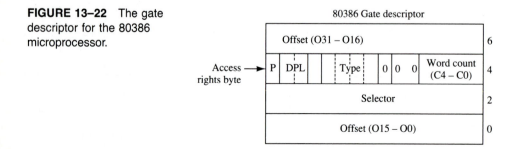

instruction (IRET) ends an interrupt gate procedure. Tasks are usually accessed with a CALL or an INT instruction.

The difference between real mode interrupts and protected mode interrupts is that the interrupt vector table is an IDT in the protected mode. The IDT still contains up to 256 interrupt levels, but each level is accessed through an interrupt gate instead of an interrupt vector. Thus interrupt type number 2 is located at IDT descriptor number 2 at 16 locations above the base address of the IDT. This also means that the first 1K byte of memory no longer must contain interrupt vectors as it does in the real mode. The IDT can be located at any location in the memory system.

The Task State Segment (TSS)

The task state segment (TSS) descriptor contains information about the location, size, and privilege level of the task state segment, just like any other descriptor. The difference is that the TSS described by the TSS descriptor does not contain data or code, but it does contain the state of the task and linkage so tasks can be nested, that is, one task that can call a second, which can call a third, and so forth. The TSS descriptor is addressed by the task register (TR), the contents of which are changed by the LTR instruction or whenever the protected mode program executes a far JMP or CALL instruction. The LTR instruction is used to initially access a task during system initialization. After initialization, the CALL or JUMP instructions normally switch tasks. In most cases we use the CALL instructions to initiate a new task.

The TSS is illustrated in Figure 13–23. As can be seen, the TSS is quite a formidable section of memory containing many different types of information. The first word of the TSS is labeled back-link. This is the selector that is used on a return (RET or IRET) to link back to the prior TSS by loading the back-link selector into the TR. The following word must contain a 0. The second through the seventh double words contain the ESP and ESS values for privilege levels 0–2. These values are required in case the current task is interrupted so these privilege level (PL) stacks can be addressed. The eighth word (offset 1CH) contains the contents of CR_3 that stores the base address of the prior state's page directory register. This address must be restored if paging is in effect. The contents of the next 17 double words are loaded into the registers indicated. Whenever a task is accessed, the entire state of the machine is stored in these memory locations and then reloaded from the same locations in the new TSS. The last word (offset 66H) contains the I/O permission bit map base address.

The I/O permission bit map allows the TSS to block I/O operations to inhibited I/O port addresses via an I/O permission denial interrupt. The permission denial interrupt is type number 13, the general protection fault interrupt. The I/O permission bit map base address is the offset address from the start of the TSS. This allows the same permission map to be used by many TSS's.

Each I/O permission bit map is 64K bits (8K bytes) in length beginning at the offset address indicated by the I/O permission bit map base address. The first byte of the I/O permission bit map contains I/O permission for I/O ports 0000H–0007H. The rightmost bit contains permission for port number 0000H and the leftmost for port number 0007H. This sequence continues for the very last port address (FFFFH)

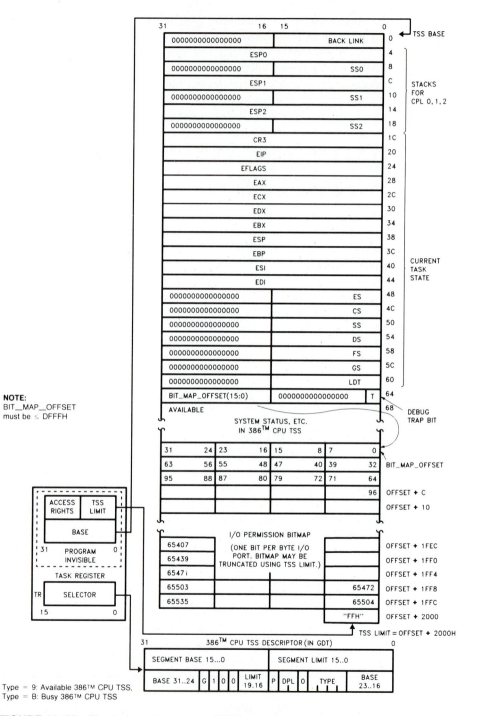

FIGURE 13–23 The task state segment (TSS) descriptor. (Courtesy of Intel Corporation)

stored in the leftmost bit of the last byte of the I/O permission bit map. A logic 0 placed in an I/O permission bit map bit enables the I/O port address, while a logic 1 inhibits or blocks the I/O port address.

In review of the operation of a task switch, which requires only 17 μs to execute, we list the following steps:

1. The gate contains the address of the procedure or location jumped to by the task switch. It also contains the selector number of the TSS descriptor and the number of words transferred from the caller to the user stack area for parameter passing.
2. The selector is loaded into TR from the gate. (This step is accomplished by a CALL or JMP that refers to a valid TSS descriptor.)
3. The TR selects the TSS.
4. The current state is saved in the current TSS and the new TSS is accessed with the state of the new task (all the registers) loaded into the microprocessor. The current state is saved at the TSS selector currently found in the TR. Once the current state is saved, a new value (by the JMP or CALL) for the TSS selector is loaded into TR and the new state is loaded from the new TSS.

The return from a task is accomplished by the following steps:

1. The current state of the microprocessor is saved in the current TSS.
2. The back-link selector is loaded to the TR to access the prior TSS so the prior state of the machine can be returned to and be restored to the microprocessor. The return for a called TSS is accomplished by the IRET instruction.

13–5 MOVING TO PROTECTED MODE

In order to change the operation of the 80386 from the real mode to the protected mode several steps must be followed. Real mode operation is accessed after a hardware reset or by changing the PE bit to a logic 0 in CR0. Protected mode is accessed by placing a logic 1 into the PE bit of CR_0, but before this is done some other things must be initialized. The following steps accomplish the switch from the real mode to the protected mode:

1. Initialize the interrupt descriptor table so it contains valid interrupt gates for at least the first 32 interrupt-type numbers. The IDT may contain up to 256, 8-byte interrupt gates defining all 256 interrupt types and often does.
2. Initialize the global descriptor table (GDT) so it contains a null descriptor at descriptor 0, and valid descriptors for at least a one code, one stack, and one data segment.
3. Switch to protected mode be setting the PE bit in CR_0.
4. Perform an intrasegment (near) JMP to flush the internal instruction queue and load the TR with the base TSS descriptor.
5. Load all the data selectors (segment registers) with their initial selector values.
6. The 80386 is now operating in the protected mode using the segment descriptors that are defined in GDT and IDT.

FIGURE 13–24 The memory map for Example 13–6.

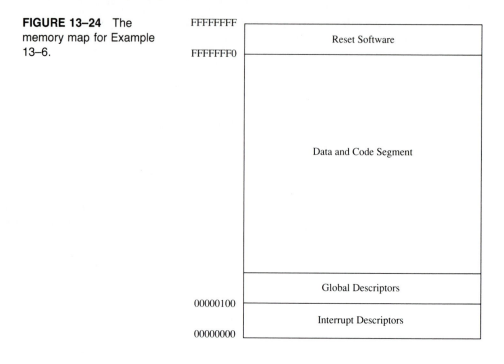

Figure 13–24 shows the protected system memory map set up using steps 1–5. The software for this task is listed in Example 13–6. This system contains one data segment descriptor and one code segment descriptor with each segment set to 4G bytes in length. This is the simplest protected mode system possible, loading all the segment registers, except code, with the same data segment descriptor from the GDT. The privilege level is initialized to 00, the highest level. This system is most often used where one user has access to the microprocessor and requires the entire memory space.

EXAMPLE 13–6

```
                         .386p
                         ;This software causes the 80386 to enter the protected mode.
                         ;It does not illustrate the interrupt descriptors or any
                         ;software that will be executed in the protected mode.

0000                     DATA    SEGMENT  AT 0000H    ;segment address = 0000H

0000                             ORG    0000H

                                 ;first 32 interrupt vectors placed here

0100                             ORG    0100H

                         ;Global Descriptor Table
```

```
0100  0000000000000000       DES0    DQ    0                  ;null descriptor

                             ;Code Segment Descriptor

0108  FFFF                   DES1    DW    0FFFFH             ;limit 4 G
010A  0000                           DW    0                  ;base address = 00000000H
010C  00                             DB    0
010D  9E                             DB    9EH                ;code segment
010E  8F                             DB    8FH                ;G = 1
010F  00                             DB    0

                             ;Data Segment Descriptor

0110  FFFF                   DES2    DW    0FFFFH             ;limit 4 G
0112  0000                           DW    0                  ;base address = 00000000H
0114  00                             DB    0
0115  92                             DB    92H                ;data segment
0116  8F                             DB    8FH                ;G = 1
0117  00                             DB    0

                             ;IDT table data

0118  00FF                   IDT     DW    0FFH               ;set limit to FFH
011A  00000000                       DD    0                  ;base address 0H

                             ;GDT table data

011E  0017                   GDT     DW    17H                ;set limit to 17H
0120  00000100                       DD    100H               ;base address 100H

0124                         DATA    ENDS

0000                         CODE    SEGMENT  USE16

                                     ASSUME   CS:CODE,DS:DATA

0000  B8 ---- R              START:  MOV   AX,DATA            ;load DS
0003  8E D8                          MOV   DS,AX

0005  67¦ 0F 01 1D 00000118 R        LIDT  FWORD PTR IDT  ;load IDTR
000D  67¦ 0F 01 15 0000011E R        LGDT  FWORD PTR GDT  ;load GDTR

0015  0F 20 C0                       MOV   EAX,CR0            ;set PE
0018  0C 01                          OR    AL,1
001A  0F 22 C0                       MOV   CR0,EAX

001D  EB 01 90                       JMP   START1             ;near jump

0020                         START1:

0020  B8 0010                        MOV   AX,10H             ;selector 2
```

```
0023 8E D8                          MOV    DS,AX
0025 8E C0                          MOV    ES,AX
0027 8E D0                          MOV    SS,AX
0029 8E E8                          MOV    GS,AX
002B 8E E0                          MOV    FS,AX
002D 66¦ BC FFFFFFFF                MOV    ESP,0FFFFFFFFH

                            ;at this point we are in the protected mode

0033                        CODE    ENDS

                            END     START
```

In more complex systems, the steps required to initialize the system in the protected mode are more involved. For complex systems that are often multiuser systems, the registers are loaded using the task state segment (TSS). The steps required to place the 80386 into protected mode operation for a more complex system using a task switch follow:

1. Initialize the interrupt descriptor table so it refers to valid interrupt descriptors with at least 32 descriptors in the IDT.
2. Initialize the global descriptor table so it contains at least two task state segment (TSS) descriptors and the initial code and data segments required for the initial task.
3. Initialize the task register (TR) so it points to a valid TSS, because when the initial task switch occurs and accesses the new TSS, the current registers are stored in the initial TSS.
4. Switch to protected mode using an intrasegment (near) jump to flush the internal instruction queue. Load TR with the current TSS selector.
5. Load the TR with a far jump instruction to access the new TSS and save the current state.
6. The 80386 is now operating in the protected mode under control of the first task.

Example 13–7 illustrates the software required to initialize the system and switch to the protected mode using a task switch. The initial system task operates at the highest level of protection (00) and controls the entire operating environment for the 80386. In many cases, it is used to boot (load) software that allows many users to access the system in a multiuser environment.

EXAMPLE 13–7

```
0008                        DESC    STRUC                   ;define descriptor structure

0000 0000                   LIMIT_L DW      0
0002 0000                   BASE_L  DW      0
0004 00                     BASE_M  DB      0
0005 00                     ACCESS  DB      0
0006 00                     LIMIT_H DB      0
0007 00                     BASE_H  DB      0
```

```
                    DESC    ENDS

0068                TSS     STRUC                                    ;define TSS structure

0000 0000           BACK_L  DW      0
0002 0000                   DW      0
0004 00000000       ESP0    DD      0
0008 0000           SS0     DW      0
000A 0000                   DW      0
000C 00000000       ESP1    DD      0
0010 0000           SS1     DW      0
0012 0000                   DW      0
0014 00000000       ESP2    DD      0
0018 0000           SS2     DW      0
001A 0000                   DW      0
001C 00000000       CCR3    DD      0
0020 00000000       EIP     DD      0
0024 00000000       TFLAGS  DD      0
0028 00000000       EEAX    DD      0
002C 00000000       EECX    DD      0
0030 00000000       EEDX    DD      0
0034 00000000       EEBX    DD      0
0038 00000000       EESP    DD      0
003C 00000000       EEBP    DD      0
0040 00000000       EESI    DD      0
0044 00000000       EEDI    DD      0
0048 0020           EES     DW      20H
004A 0000                   DW      0
004C 0018           ECS     DW      18H
004E 0000                   DW      0
0050 0020           ESS     DW      20H
0052 0000                   DW      0
0054 0020           EDS     DW      20H
0056 0000                   DW      0
0058 0020           EFS     DW      20H
005A 0000                   DW      0
005C 0020           EGS     DW      20H
005E 0000                   DW      0
0060 0000           ELDT    DW      0
0062 0000                   DW      0
0064 0000                   DW      0

0066 0000           BIT_MAP DW      0

                    TSS     ENDS

0000                STACK   SEGMENT STACK

0000 0400 [                 DW      400H DUP (?)
          0000
               ]
```

0800		STACK	ENDS		
		.386P			
0000		CODE	SEGMENT USE16		
			ASSUME CS:CODE,SS:STACK		

0000 0000 0000 00000000		TSS1	TSS	< >	;task state segment 1
	0000 0000 00000000				
	0000 0000 00000000				
	0000 0000 00000000				
	00000000 00000000				
	00000000 00000000				
	00000000 00000000				
	00000000 00000000				
	00000000 00000000				
	0020 0000 0018				
	0000 0020 0000				
	0020 0000 0020				
	0000 0020 0000				
	0000 0000 0000				
	0000				

0068 0000 0000 00000000		TSS2	TSS	< >	;task state segment 2
	0000 0000 00000000				
	0000 0000 00000000				
	0000 0000 00000000				
	00000000 00000000				
	00000000 00000000				
	00000000 00000000				
	00000000 00000000				
	00000000 00000000				
	0020 0000 0018				
	0000 0020 0000				
	0020 0000 0020				
	0000 0020 0000				
	0000 0000 0000				
	0000				

00D0 0800 [		IDT	DB	8*256 DUP (?)	;interrupt descriptor table
	00				
	]				
08D0 0000 0000 00 00		GDT	DESC	< >	;null descriptor
	00 00				
08D8 0000 0028 00 85		TG1	DESC	<0,28H,0,85H,0,0>	;task gate 1
	00 00				
08E0 0000 0030 00 85		TG2	DESC	<0,30H,0,85H,0,0>	;task gate 2
	00 00				
08E8 FFFF 0000 00 9A		CS	DESC	<-1,0,0,9AH,0CFH,0>	;code segment (4G)
	CF 00				
08F0 FFFF 0000 00 92		DS1	DESC	<-1,0,0,92H,0CFH,0>	;data segment (4G)
	CF 00				

```
08F8 FFFF 0000 00 89   TSS1      DESC      <-1,0,0,89H,0CFH,0>    ;TSS1 available
     CF 00
0900 FFFF 0000 00 89   TSS2      DESC      <-1,0,0,89H,0CFH,0>    ;TSS2 available
     CF 00
0908 2000 [            IOBP      DB        2000H DUP (0)          ;enable all I/O
          00
     ]
2908 FF                          DB        0FFH                   ;end of I/O bit map

0006                   GDT_A     STRUC

0000 0000              A         DW        0
0002 0000              B         DW        0
0004 0000              CC        DW        0

                       GDT_A     ENDS

2909 0000 0000 0000    GDT_AD    GDT_A     < >                    ;address of GDT

290F                   MAIN      PROC      FAR

290F 8C C8                       MOV       AX,CS
2911 8E D8                       MOV       DS,AX
2913 E8 0098                     CALL      DO_IDT                 ;set up IDT
2916 B8 0908 R                   MOV       AX,OFFSET IOBP         ;set up I/O bit maps
2919 2E: A3 0066 R               MOV       TSS1.BIT_MAP,AX
291D 2E: A3 00CE R               MOV       TSS2.BIT_MAP,AX

2921 66¦ 33 C0                   XOR       EAX,EAX                ;get linear start address
2924 8C C8                       MOV       AX,CS
2926 66¦ C1 E0 04                SHL       EAX,4
292A 66¦ 33 DB                   XOR       EBX,EBX
292D BB 29AE R                   MOV       BX,OFFSET TASK1
2930 66¦ 50                      PUSH      EAX
2932 66¦ 03 C3                   ADD       EAX,EBX
2935 66¦ 2E: A3 0088 R           MOV       TSS2.EIP,EAX           ;setup TASK1 as start address
293A 66¦ 58                      POP       EAX
293C 66¦ 50                      PUSH      EAX
293E BB 0000 R                   MOV       BX,OFFSET TSS1         ;load TSS1 address
2941 66¦ 03 C3                   ADD       EAX,EBX
2944 2E: A3 0002 R               MOV       TSS1.BASE_L,AX
2948 66¦ C1 E8 10                SHR       EAX,16
294C 2E: A2 0004 R               MOV       TSS1.BASE_M,AL
2950 2E: 88 26 0007 R            MOV       TSS1.BASE_H,AH
2955 66¦ 58                      POP       EAX
2957 66¦ 50                      PUSH      EAX
2959 BB 0068 R                   MOV       BX,OFFSET TSS2         ;load TSS2 address
295C 66¦ 03 C3                   ADD       EAX,EBX
295F 2E: A3 006A R               MOV       TSS2.BASE_L,AX
2963 66¦ C1 E8 10                SHR       EAX,16
```

```
2967  2E: A2 006C R              MOV      TSS2.BASE_M,AL
296B  2E: 88 26 006F R           MOV      TSS2.BASE_H,AH

2970  66¦ 58                     POP      EAX
2972  B8 FFFF                    MOV      AX,-1
2975  2E: A3 290B R              MOV      GDT_AD.B,AX
2979  66¦ 58                     POP      EAX
297B  66¦ C1 E0 04               SHL      EAX,4
297F  BB 08D0 R                  MOV      BX,OFFSET GDT
2982  66¦ 03 C3                  ADD      EAX,EBX
2985  2E: A3 2909 R              MOV      GDT_AD.A,AX
2989  66¦ C1 E8 10               SHR      EAX,16
298D  2E: A3 290D R              MOV      GDT_AD.CC,AX     ;set up GDT address
2991  2E: 0F 01 16 2909 R        LGDT     GDT_AD           ;load GDT register
2997  0F 20 C0                   MOV      EAX,CR0          ;set PM
299A  66¦ 83 C8 01               OR       EAX,1
299E  0F 22 C0                   MOV      CR0,EAX          ;protected mode
29A1  EB 00                      JMP      NEXT

29A3                NEXT:

29A3  B8 0008                    MOV      AX,8
29A6  0F 00 D8                   LTR      AX               ;address TSS1
29A9  B8 0010                    MOV      AX,10H
29AC  FF E0                      JMP      AX               ;jump to TSS2

29AE           MAIN     ENDP

29AE           DO_IDT   PROC     NEAR

               ;set up interrupts (not shown here)

29AE           DO_IDT   ENDP

29AE           TASK1:                                      ;main program starts here

29AE           CODE     ENDS
               END      MAIN
```

13–6   VIRTUAL 8086 MODE

One special mode of operation not discussed thus far is the virtual 8086 mode. This special mode is designed so multiple 8086 real mode software applications can execute at one time. Figure 13–25 illustrates two 8086 applications mapped into the 80386 using the virtual mode. If the operating system allows multiple applications to execute, it is usually done through a technique called *time-slicing,* wherein the operating system allocates a set amount of time to each task. For example, if three tasks are executing, the operating system can allocate 1 ms to each task. This means

FIGURE 13–25 Two tasks resident to an 80386 operated in the virtual 8086 mode.

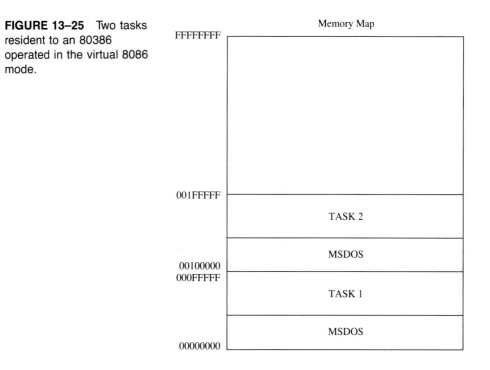

that after each millisecond, a task switch occurs to the next task. In this manner all tasks receive a portion of the 80386 execution time, resulting in a system that appears to execute more than one task at a time. The task times can be adjusted to give any task any percentage of the microprocessor execution time.

A system that can use this technique is a print spooler, which can function in one DOS partition and be accessed 10 percent of the time. This duality allows the system to print using the print spooler, but it doesn't detract from the system because it only uses 10 percent of the system's time.

The main difference between 80386 protected mode operation and the virtual 8086 mode is the way the segment registers are interpreted by the microprocessor. In the virtual 8086 mode, the segment registers are used as they are in the real mode, that is, as a segment address and offset address capable of accessing a 1M-byte memory space from location 00000H–FFFFFH. Access to many virtual 8086 mode systems is made possible by the paging unit that is explained in the next section. Through paging, the program still accesses memory below the 1M-byte boundary, yet the microprocessor can access a physical memory space at any location in the 4G-byte range of the memory system.

Virtual 8086 mode is entered by changing the VM bit in the EFLAG register to a logic 1. This mode is entered via an IRET instruction if the privilege level is 00. This flag bit cannot be set in any other manner. An attempt to access a memory address above the 1M-byte boundary will cause a type-13 interrupt to occur.

The virtual 8086 mode could be used to share one microprocessor with many users by partitioning the memory so each user has its own DOS partition. User 1 could be allocated memory locations 00100000H–001FFFFFH, user 2 locations

0020000H–002FFFFFH, and so forth. The system software located at memory locations 00000000H–000FFFFFH could then share the microprocessor between users by switching from one to another to execute software. In this manner, one microprocessor is shared by many users.

13–7   THE MEMORY PAGING MECHANISM

The paging mechanism allows any linear (logical) address, as it is generated by a program, to be placed into any physical memory page, as generated by the paging mechanism. A *linear memory page* is a page that is addressed with a selector and an offset in either the real or protected mode. A *physical memory page* is a page that exists at some actual physical memory location. For example, linear memory location 20000H could be mapped into physical memory location 30000H, or any other location, with the paging unit. This means that an instruction that accesses location 20000H actually accesses location 30000H.

Each 80386 memory page is 4K bytes in length. Paging allows the system software to be placed at any physical address with the paging mechanism. Three components are used in page address translation: the page directory, the page table, and the actual physical memory page.

The Page Directory

The page directory contains the location of up to 1,024 page translation tables. Each page translation table translates a logic address into a physical address. The page directory is stored in the memory and accessed by the page descriptor address register (CR_3). Control register CR_3 holds the base address of the page directory, which starts at any 4K-byte boundary in the memory system. The MOV CR3, reg instruction is used to initialize CR_3 for paging. In a virtual 8086 mode system, each 8086 DOS partition would have its own page directory.

The page directory contains up to 1,024 entries that are each 4 bytes in length. The page directory itself occupies one 4K-byte memory page. Each entry in the page directory (refer to Figure 13–26) translates the leftmost 10 bits of the memory address. This 10-bit portion of the linear address is used to locate different page tables for different page table entries. The page table address (A_{32}–A_{12}), stored in a page directory entry, accesses a 4K-byte-long page translation table. To completely translate any linear address into any physical address requires 1,024 page tables that are each 4K bytes in length plus the page table directory, which is 4K bytes in length. This translation scheme requires up to 4M plus 4K bytes of memory for a full address translation. Only the largest operating systems support this size address translation. Many well-known operating systems translate only the first 16M bytes of the memory system if paging is enabled. This includes programs such as Windows 3.0.*

---

*Windows is a program produced by Microsoft Corporation.

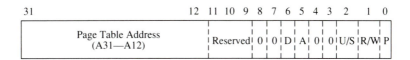

FIGURE 13-26 The page table directory entry.

The page table directory entry control bits, as illustrated in Figure 13–26, perform the following functions:

1. D—Dirty: undefined for page table directory entries by the 80386 microprocessor and is provided for use by the operating system.
2. A—Accessed: set to a logic 1 whenever .the microprocessor accesses the page directory entry.
3. R/W and U/S—Read/Write and User/Supervisor: both are used in the protection scheme as listed in Table 13–6. Both bits combine to develop paging priority level protection for level 3, the lowest user level.
4. P—Present: if a logic 1, indicates that the entry can be used in address translation. If P = 0, the entry cannot be used for translation. A not present entry can be used for other purposes, such as indicating that the page is currently stored on the disk. If P = 0, the remaining bits of the entry can be used to indicate the location of the page on the disk memory system.

Page Table

The page table contains 1,024 physical page addresses accessed to translate a linear address into a physical address. The format for the page table entry is exactly the same as for the page directory entry (refer to Figure 13–26). The main difference between them is that the page directory entry contains the physical address of a page table, while the page table entry contains the physical address of a 4K-byte physical page of memory. The other difference is the D (dirty bit), which has no function in the page directory entry, but indicates that a page has been written to in a page table entry.

Figure 13–27 illustrates the paging mechanism in the 80386 microprocessor. Here, the linear address 00C03FFCH, as generated by a program, is converted to physical address XXXXX3FCH, as translated by the paging mechanism. (*Note:* XXXXX is any 4K-byte physical page address.) The paging mechanism functions in the following manner:

1. The 4K-byte-long page directory is stored as the physical address located by CR_3. This address is often called the *root address*. One page directory at a time exists in

TABLE 13-6 Protection for level 3 using U/S and R/W	U/S	R/W	Access Level 3
	0	0	None
	0	1	None
	1	0	Read only
	1	1	Read/write

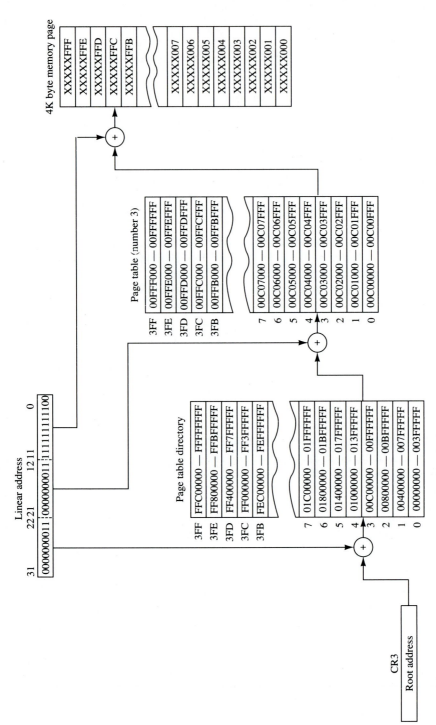

FIGURE 13–27 The translation of linear address 00C03FFC to physical memory address XXXXXFFC. The value of XXXXX is determined by the page table entry (not shown here). *Note:* 1. The address ranges illustrated in the page directory and page table represent the linear address ranges selected and not the contents of these tables. 2. The addresses (XXXXX) listed in the memory page are selected by the page table entry.

a system. In the 8086 virtual mode, each task has its own page directory allowing different areas of physical memory to be assigned to different 8086 virtual tasks.

2. The upper 10 bits of the linear address (bits 31–22), as determined by the descriptors described earlier in this chapter or by a real address, are applied to the paging mechanism to select an entry in the page directory. This maps the page directory entry to the leftmost 10 bits of the linear address.

3. The page table is addressed by the entry stored in the page directory. This allows up to 4K page tables in a fully populated and translated system.

4. An entry in the page table is addressed by the next 10 bits of the linear address (bits 21–12).

5. The page table entry contains the actual physical address of the 4K-byte memory page.

6. The rightmost 12 bits of the linear address (bits 11–0) select a location in the memory page.

The paging mechanism allows the physical memory to be assigned to any linear address through the paging mechanism. For example, suppose that linear address 20000000H is selected by a program, but this memory location does not exist in the physical memory system. The 4K-byte linear page is referenced as locations 20000000H–20000FFFH by the program. Because this section of physical memory does not exist, the operating system might assign an existing physical memory page such as 12000000H–12000FFFH to this linear address range.

In the address translation process, the leftmost 10 bits of the linear address select page directory entry 200H located at offset address 800H in the page directory. This page directory entry contains the address of the page table for linear addresses 20000000H–203FFFFFH. Linear address bits (21–12) select an entry in this page table that corresponds to a 4K-byte memory page. For linear addresses 2000000H–20000FFFH, the first entry (entry 0) in the page table is selected. This first entry contains the physical address of the actual memory page, or 12000000H–12000FFFH in this example.

Take, for example, a typical DOS-based computer system. The memory map for the system appears in Figure 13–28. Notice from the map that there are unused areas of memory that could be paged to a different location, giving a DOS real mode application program more memory. The normal DOS memory system begins at location 00000H and extends to location 9FFFFH, which is 640K bytes of memory. Above location 9FFFFH we find sections devoted to video cards, disk cards, and the system BIOS ROM. In this example, however, an area of memory just above 9FFFFH is unused (A0000H–AFFFFH). This section of the memory could be used by DOS, which means that the total applications memory area is 704K instead of 640K.

This section of memory can be used by mapping it into extended memory at locations 102000H–11FFFFH. Software to accomplish this translation and to initialize the page table directory and page tables required to set up memory are illustrated in Example 13–8. Note that this procedure initializes the page table directory, a page table, and loads CR_3. It does not switch to protected mode, though it does enable paging. Note that paging functions in real mode memory operation.

FIGURE 13–28 Memory
map for an AT-style clone.

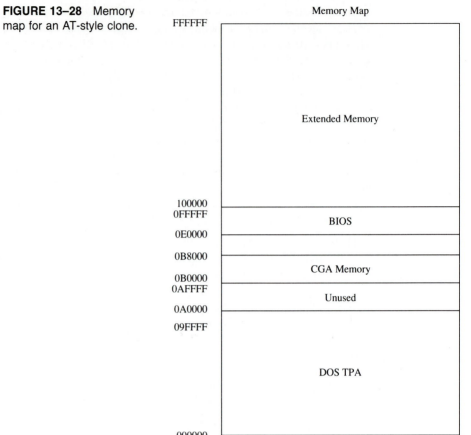

```
                      .386P
                      ;Software that sets up a paged memory system
                      ;that accesses memory above location FFFFFH.
                      ;
                      ;Page Directory

0000                  DATA    SEGMENT

0000 = 0000           PG_DIR  EQU     $

0000 00001000 R       TAB0PT  DD      TAB0
0004 03FF [                   DD      1023 DUP (?)
           00000000
                    ]

                      ;Page Table

1000 0400 [           TAB0    DD      1024 DUP (?)
```

EXAMPLE 13–8

```
                    00000000
                          ]

2000                DATA    ENDS

0000                CODE    SEGMENT USE16

                            ASSUME  CS:CODE,DS:DATA

0000                PAGES   PROC    FAR

0000 1E                     PUSH    DS
0001 06                     PUSH    ES
0002 FC                     CLD
0003 B8 ---- R              MOV     AX,DATA             ;load segment registers
0006 8E D8                  MOV     DS,AX
0008 8E C0                  MOV     ES,AX
000A BF 0000 R              MOV     DI,OFFSET PG_DIR    ;address page table
000D 66¦ 83 05 07           ADD     DWORD PTR [DI],7
0011 B9 0100                MOV     CX,256
0014 BF 1000 R              MOV     DI,OFFSET TAB0
0017 66¦ B8 00000007        MOV     EAX,7

001D                PAGES1:

001D 66¦ AB                 STOSD                       ;fill page table
001F 66¦ 05 00001000        ADD     EAX,4096
0025 E2 F6                  LOOP    PAGES1
0027 BF 1280 R              MOV     DI,OFFSET TAB0+4*0A0H
002A 66¦ B8 00102007        MOV     EAX,00102007H
0030 B9 0010                MOV     CX,16

0033                PAGES2:

0033 66¦ AB                 STOSD                       ;remap A0000H-AFFFFH
0035 66¦ 05 00001000        ADD     EAX,4096            ;to 102000H-11FFFFH
003B E2 F6                  LOOP    PAGES2

003D 66¦ 33 C0              XOR     EAX,EAX
0040 8C D8                  MOV     AX,DS
0042 66¦ C1 E0 04           SHL     EAX,4
0046 0F 22 D8               MOV     C3,EAX ;address page directory

0049 07                     POP     ES
004A 1F                     POP     DS
004B CB                     RET

004C                PAGES   ENDP

004C                CODE    ENDS

                            END
```

13–8   INTRODUCTION TO THE 80486 MICROPROCESSOR

The 80486 microprocessor is a highly integrated device containing well over 1,200,000 transistors. Located within this powerful integrated circuit are a memory-management unit (MMU); a complete numeric coprocessor that is compatible with the 80387; a high-speed cache memory that contains 8K bytes of space; and a full 32-bit microprocessor that is upward compatible within the 80386 microprocessor. The 80486 is currently available as a 25-, 33-, 50-, or 66-MHz device. Intel has demonstrated a 100-MHz version of the 80486, but it has yet to be released. The 80486 comes as an 80486DX or an 80486SX. The only difference between these devices is that the 80486SX does not contain the numeric coprocessor, which reduces its price. The 80487SX numeric coprocessor is available as a separate component for the 80486SX microprocessor.

This section details the differences between the 80486 and 80386 microprocessors. These differences are few, as shall be seen. The most notable differences apply to the cache memory system and parity generator.

Pinout of the 80486DX and 80486SX Microprocessors

Figure 13–29 illustrates the pinout of the 80486DX microprocessor, a 168-pin PGA. The 80486SX, also packaged in a 168-pin PGA, is not illustrated because only a few differences exist. Note that pin B_{15} is NMI on the 80486DX and pin A_{15} is NMI on the 80486SX. The only other differences are that pin A_{15} is $\overline{\text{IGNNE}}$ on the 80486DX (not present on the 80486SX), pin C_{14} is $\overline{\text{FERR}}$ on the 80486DX, and pins B_{15} and C_{14} on the 80486SX are not connected.

When connecting the 80486 microprocessor, all V_{cc} and V_{ss} pins must be connected to the power supply for proper operation. The power supply must be capable of supplying 5.0 V $\pm$ 10 percent, with up to 1.2 A of surge current for the 33-MHz version. The average supply current is 650 mA for the 33-MHz version. Logic 0 outputs allow up to 4.0 mA of current, and logic 1 outputs allow up to 1.0 mA. If larger currents are required, as they often are, then the 80486 must be buffered. Figure 13–30 shows a buffered 80486DX system. In the circuit shown, only the address, data, and parity signals are buffered.

Pin Definitions

1. A_{31}–A_2 (Address Outputs): provide the memory and I/O with the address during normal operation and during a cache line invalidation. A_{31}–A_4 are used to drive the microprocessor.
2. $\overline{A_{20}}$M (Address Bit 20 Mask): used to cause the 80486 to wrap its address around from location 000FFFFFH to 00000000H, as does the 8086 microprocessor. This provides a memory system that functions like the 1M-byte memory in the 8086 microprocessor.
3. ADS (Address Data Strobe): becomes a logic 0 to indicate that the address bus contains a valid memory address.
4. AHOLD (Address Hold Input): causes the microprocessor to place its address bus connections at their high-impedance state, with the remainder of the buses

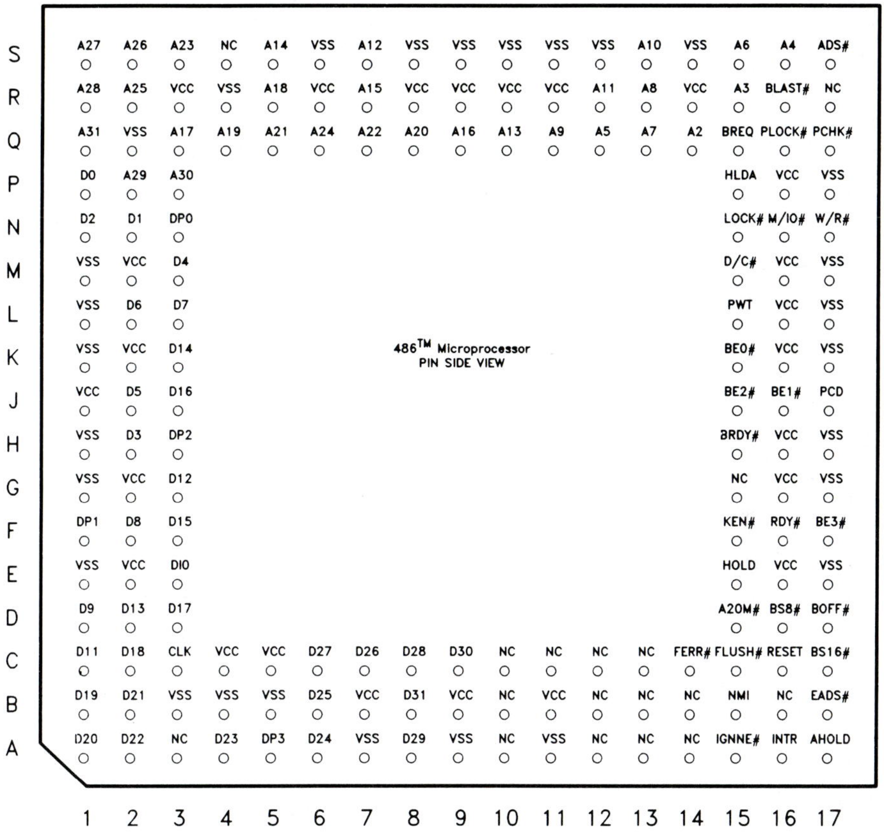

	1	2	3	4	5	6	7	8	9	10	11	12	13	14	15	16	17
S	A27	A26	A23	NC	A14	VSS	A12	VSS	VSS	VSS	VSS	VSS	A10	VSS	A6	A4	ADS#
R	A28	A25	VCC	VSS	A18	VCC	A15	VCC	VCC	VCC	VCC	A11	A8	VCC	A3	BLAST#	NC
Q	A31	VSS	A17	A19	A21	A24	A22	A20	A16	A13	A9	A5	A7	A2	BREQ	PLOCK#	PCHK#
P	D0	A29	A30												HLDA	VCC	VSS
N	D2	D1	DP0												LOCK#	M/IO#	W/R#
M	VSS	VCC	D4												D/C#	VCC	VSS
L	VSS	D6	D7												PWT	VCC	VSS
K	VSS	VCC	D14					486™ Microprocessor							BE0#	VCC	VSS
J	VCC	D5	D16					PIN SIDE VIEW							BE2#	BE1#	PCD
H	VSS	D3	DP2												BRDY#	VCC	VSS
G	VSS	VCC	D12												NC	VCC	VSS
F	DP1	D8	D15												KEN#	RDY#	BE3#
E	VSS	VCC	DIO												HOLD	VCC	VSS
D	D9	D13	D17												A20M#	BS8#	BOFF#
C	D11	D18	CLK	VCC	VCC	D27	D26	D28	D30	NC	NC	NC	NC	FERR#	FLUSH#	RESET	BS16#
B	D19	D21	VSS	VSS	VSS	D25	VCC	D31	VCC	NC	VCC	NC	NC	NC	NMI	NC	EADS#
A	D20	D22	NC	D23	DP3	D24	VSS	D29	VSS	NC	VSS	NC	NC	NC	IGNNE#	INTR	AHOLD

FIGURE 13–29 The pinout of the 80486. (Courtesy of Intel Corporation)

staying active. Often used by another bus master to gain access for a cache invalidation cycle.

5. $\overline{BE3}$–$\overline{BE0}$ (Byte Enable Outputs): select a bank of the memory system when information is transferred between the microprocessors and its memory and I/O space. The $\overline{BE3}$ signal enables D_{31}–D_{24}, $\overline{BE2}$ enables D_{23}–D_{16}, $\overline{BE1}$ enables D_{15}–D_8, and $\overline{BE0}$ enables D_7–D_0.

6. $\overline{BLAST}$ (Burst Last Output): shows that the burst bus cycle is complete on the next activation of the $\overline{BRDY}$ signal.

7. $\overline{BOFF}$ (Backoff Input): causes the microprocessor to place its buses at their high-impedance state during the next clock cycle. The microprocessor remains in the bus hold state until the $\overline{BOFF}$ pin is placed at a logic 1 level.

8. $\overline{BRDY}$ (Burst Ready Input): used to signal the microprocessor that a burst cycle is complete.

9. BREQ (Bus Request Output): indicates that the 80486 has generated an internal bus request.

10. $\overline{BS8}$ (Bus Size 8 Input): causes the 80486 to structure itself with an 8-bit data bus to access byte-wide memory and I/O components.

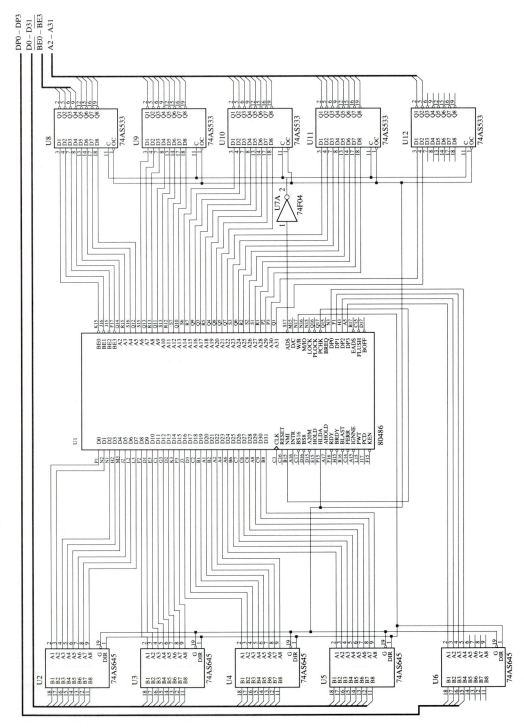

FIGURE 13–30 An 80486 microprocessor showing the buffered address, data, and parity buses.

11. $\overline{BS16}$ (Bus Size 16 Input): causes the 80486 to structure itself with a 16-bit data bus to access wordwide memory and I/O components.

12. CLK (Clock Input): provides the 80486 with its basic timing signal. The clock input is a TTL-compatible input that is 25 MHz to operate the 80486 at 25 MHz.

13. D_{31}–D_0 (Data Bus): transfers data between the microprocessor and its memory and I/O system. Data bus connections D_7–D_0 are also used to accept the interrupt vector type number during an interrupt acknowledge cycle.

14. $D/\overline{C}$ (Data/Control): indicates whether the current operation is a data transfer or control cycle. Refer to Table 13–7 for the functions of $D/\overline{C}$, $M/\overline{IO}$, and $W/\overline{R}$.

15. DP_3–DP_0 (Data Parity I/O): provide even parity for a write operation and check parity for a read operation. If a parity error is detected during a read, the $\overline{PCHK}$ output becomes a logic 0 to indicate a parity error. If parity is not used in a system, these lines must be pulled high to +5.0 V.

16. $\overline{EADS}$ (External Address Strobe Input): used with AHOLD to signal that an external address is used to perform a cache invalidation cycle.

17. $\overline{FERR}$ (Floating-Point Error Output): indicates the floating-point coprocessor has detected an error condition. Used to maintain compatibility with DOS software.

18. $\overline{FLUSH}$ (Cache Flush Input): forces the microprocessor to erase the contents of its 8K-byte internal cache.

19. HLDA (Hold Acknowledge Output): indicates that the HOLD input is active and that the microprocessor has placed its buses at their high-impedance state.

20. HOLD (Hold Input): used to request a DMA action. It causes the address, data, and control buses to be placed at their high-impedance state and also, once recognized, causes HLDA to become a logic 0.

21. $\overline{IGNNE}$ (Ignore Numeric Error Input): causes the coprocessor to ignore floating-point errors and to continue processing data. This signal does not affect the state of the $\overline{FERR}$ pin.

22. INTR (Interrupt Request Input): requests a maskable interrupt, as it does on all other family members.

23. $\overline{KEN}$ (Cache Enable Input): causes the current bus to be stored in the internal cache.

24. $\overline{LOCK}$ (Lock Output): becomes a logic 0 for any instruction that is prefixed with the lock prefix.

TABLE 13–7 Bus cycle identification

$M/\overline{IO}$	$D/\overline{C}$	$W/\overline{R}$	Bus Cycle Type
0	0	0	Interrupt acknowledge
0	0	1	Halt/special
0	1	0	I/O read
0	1	1	I/O write
1	0	0	Code cycle (opcode fetch)
1	0	1	Reserved
1	1	0	Memory read
1	1	1	Memory write

25. M/$\overline{\text{IO}}$ (Memory/$\overline{\text{IO}}$): defines whether the address bus contains a memory address or an I/O port number. It is also combined with the W/$\overline{\text{R}}$ signal to generate memory and I/O read and write control signals.
26. NMI (Nonmaskable Interrupt Input): requests a type-2 interrupt.
27. PCD (Page Cache Disable Output): reflects the state of the PCD attribute bit in the page table entry or the page directory entry.
28. $\overline{\text{PCHK}}$ (Parity Check Output): indicates that a parity error was detected during a read operation on the DP_3–DP_0 pins.
29. $\overline{\text{PLOCK}}$ (Pseudolock Output): indicates that the current operation requires more than one bus cycle to perform. This signal becomes a logic 0 for arithmetic coprocessor operations that access 64- or 80-bit memory data.
30. PWT (Page Write Through Output): indicates the state of the PWT attribute bit in the page table entry or the page directory entry.
31. $\overline{\text{RDY}}$ (Ready Input): indicates that a nonburst bus cycle is complete. The $\overline{\text{RDY}}$ signal must be returned or the microprocessor places wait states into its timing until $\overline{\text{RDY}}$ is asserted.
32. RESET (Reset Input): initializes the 80486 as it does in other family members. Table 13–8 shows the effect of the RESET input on the 80486 microprocessor.
33. W/$\overline{\text{R}}$ (Write/Read): signals that the current bus cycle is either a read or a write.

Basic 80486 Architecture

The architecture of the 80486DX is almost identical to the 80386 plus the 80387 math coprocessor and an 8K-byte cache, and the 80486SX is almost identical to an 80386 with an 8K-byte cache. Figure 13–31 illustrates the basic internal structure of the 80486 microprocessor. If this structure is compared to the architecture of the 80386, no differences are observed. The most prominent difference between the 80386 and the 80486 is that almost half of the 80486 instructions execute in one

TABLE 13–8 The effect of the RESET signal

Register	Initial Value (With Self-test)	Initial Value (Without Self-test)
EAX	00000000H	?
EDX	00000400H + ID*	00000400H + ID
EFLAGS	00000002H	00000002H
EIP	0000FFF0H	0000FFF0H
ES	0000H	0000H
CS	F000H	F000H
DS	0000H	0000H
SS	0000H	0000H
FS	0000H	0000H
GS	0000H	0000H
IDTR	Base = 0, limit 3FFH	Base = 0, limit = 3FFH
CR_0	60000010H	60000010H
DR_7	00000000H	00000000H

* Revision ID number supplied by Intel for revisions to the microprocessor.

FIGURE 13–31 The internal programming model of the 80486. (Courtesy of Intel Corporation)

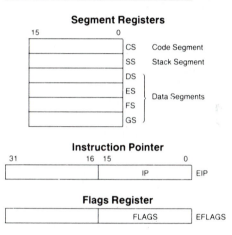

clocking period instead of the two clocking periods needed by the 80386 to execute like instructions.

As with the 80386, the 80486 contains eight general-purpose 32-bit registers: EAX, EBX, ECX, EDX, EBP, EDI, ESI, and ESP. These registers may be used as 8-, 16-, or 32-bit data registers or to address a location in the memory system. The 16-bit registers are the same set as found in the 80286 and are assigned AX, BX, CX, DX, BP, DI, SI, and SP. The 8-bit registers are AH, AL, BH, BL, CH, CL, DH, and DL.

In addition to the general-purpose registers, the 80486 also contains the same segment registers as the 80386, which are CS, DS, ES, SS, FS, and GS. Each are 16 bits wide, as in all earlier versions of the family.

The IP (instruction pointer) addresses the program located within the 1M byte of memory in combination with CS, or as EIP (extended instruction pointer) to address a program at any location within the 4G-byte memory system. In protected-mode operation, the segment registers function to hold selectors as they did in the 80286 and 80386 microprocessors.

The 80486 also contains the global, local, and interrupt descriptor table register and memory management unit as the 80386. These registers are not illustrated in Figure 13–31, but are present as in the 80386. The function of the MMU and its paging unit are described in Sections 13–4 and 13–7.

The extended flag register (EFLAGS) is illustrated in Figure 13–32. As with other family members, the rightmost flag bits perform the same functions for compatibility. Following is a list of each flag bit with a description of its function:

1. AC (Alignment Check): new to the 80486 microprocessor, used to indicate that the microprocessor has accessed a word at an odd address or a double word stored at a non-double-word boundary. Efficient software and execution require that data are stored at word or double-word boundaries.

2. VM (Virtual Mode): entered by setting this bit while the 80486 is operated in the protected mode. This bit is always cleared by a PUSHF instruction, even if the 80486 is operating in the virtual mode.

3. RF (Resume): used in conjunction with the debug registers as defined in Section 13–2 for the 80386 microprocessor.

4. NT (Nested Task): set to indicate that the 80486 is performing a task that is nested within another task.

5. IOPL (I/O Privilege Level): indicates the current maximum privilege level assigned to the I/O system.

6. OF (Overflow): indicates that the result of a signed arithmetic operation has overflowed the capacity of the destination. It is also used with the multiply instruction.

7. DF (Direction): selects auto-increment (DF = 0) or auto-decrement (DF = 1) operation for the string instructions.

8. IF (Interrupt Enable): enables the INTR pin if this bit is set.

9. TF (Trap): set to enable debugging as described by the debug registers.

10. SF (Sign): indicates that the sign of the result is set or cleared.

11. ZF (Zero): indicates that the result of an arithmetic or logic operation is zero (ZF = 1) or nonzero (ZF = 0).

12. AF (Auxiliary): used with the DAA and DAS instructions to adjust the result of a BCD addition or subtraction.

13. PF (Parity): indicates the parity of the result of an arithmetic or logic operation. If the parity is odd, PF = 0, and if the parity is even, PF = 1.

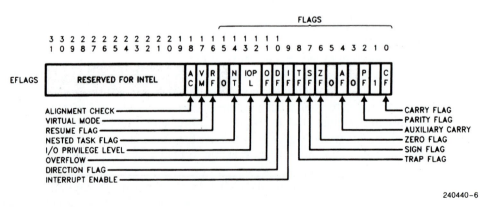

240440–6

NOTE:
0 indicates Intel Reserved: do not define; see Section 2.1.6.

FIGURE 13–32 The EFLAG register of the 80486. (Courtesy of Intel Corporation)

14. CF (Carry): shows whether a carry has occurred after an addition or a borrow after a subtraction.

80486 Memory System

The memory system for the 80486 is identical to the 80386 microprocessor. The 80486 contains 4G bytes of memory beginning at location 00000000H and ending at location FFFFFFFFH. The major change to the memory system is internal to the 80486 in the form of an 8K-byte cache memory that speeds the execution of instructions and the acquisition of data. Another addition is the parity checker/generator built into the 80486 microprocessor.

Parity Checker/Generator.   *Parity* is often used to determine whether data are correctly read from a memory location. To facilitate this determination, Intel has incorporated an internal *parity generator/detector.* Parity is generated by the 80486 during each write cycle. Parity is generated as *even parity* and a parity bit is provided for each byte of memory. The parity check bits appear on pins $DP_0–DP_3$, which are also parity inputs as well as outputs. These are typically stored in memory during each write cycle and read from memory during each read cycle.

On a read, the microprocessor checks parity and generates a parity check error, *if it occurs,* on the $\overline{PCHK}$ pin. A parity error causes no change in processing unless the user applies the $\overline{PCHK}$ signal to an interrupt input. Interrupts are often used to signal a parity error in DOS-based computer systems. Figure 13–33 shows the organization of the 80486 memory system that includes parity storage. Note that this organization is the same as for the 80386, except for the parity bit storage. If parity is not used, Intel recommends that the $DP_0–DP_3$ pins be pulled up to +5.0 V.

Cache Memory.   The cache memory system caches (stores) both data used by a program and also the instructions of the program. The *cache* is organized as a four-way set associative cache with each location (line) containing 16 bytes or four double words of data. The cache operates as a *write-through* cache. Note that the cache only changes if a miss occurs. This means that data written to memory location not already cached, is not written to the cache. In many cases, much of the active portion of a program is found completely inside the cache memory. This causes execution to

FIGURE 13–33 The organization of the 80486 memory showing parity.

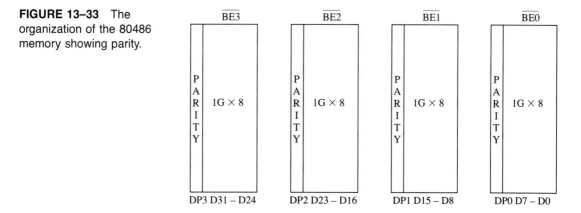

occur at the rate of one clock cycle for many of the instructions that are commonly used in a program. About the only way that these efficient instructions are slowed is when the microprocessor must fill a line in the cache. Data are also stored in the cache, but they have less of an impact on the execution speed of a program because data are not referenced repeatedly as many portions of a program are.

Control register 0 (CR_0) is used to control the cache with two new control bits not present in the 80386 microprocessor. (Refer to Figure 13–34 for CR_0 in the 80486 microprocessor.) The CD (*cache disable*) and NW (*noncache write-through*) bits are new to the 80486 and are used to control the 8K-byte cache. If the CD bit is a logic 1, all cache operations are inhibited. This setting is only ever used for debugging software and normally remains cleared. The NW bit is used to inhibit cache write-through operation. As with CD, cache write-through is only inhibited for testing. For normal program operation, CD = 0 and NW = 0.

Because the cache is new to the 80486 microprocessor and is filled using burst cycles not present on the 80386, some information is required to understand bus filling cycles. When a bus line is filled, the 80486 must acquire four 32-bit numbers from the memory system to fill a line in the cache. Filling is accomplished with a *burst cycle*. The burst is a special memory cycle where four 32-bit numbers are fetched from the memory system in five clocking periods. This assumes that the speed of the memory is sufficient and that no wait states are required. If the clock frequency of the 80486 is 33 MHz, we can fill a cache line in 167 ns, which is very efficient considering a normal, nonburst 32-bit memory read operation requires two clocking periods.

Memory Read Timing.   Figure 13–35 illustrates the read timing for the 80486 for a nonburst memory operation. Note that two clocking periods are used to transfer data. Clocking period T_1 provides the memory address and control signals, and clocking period T_2 is where the data are transferred between the memory and the microprocessor. Note that the $\overline{RDY}$ must become a logic 0 to cause data to be transferred and to terminate the bus cycle. Access time for a nonburst access is determined by taking two clocking periods minus the time required for the address to appear on the address bus connection minus a setup time for the data bus connections. For the 20-MHz version of the 80486, two clocking periods require 100 ns minus 28 ns for address setup time and 3 ns for data setup time. This yields a nonburst access time of 100 ns − 31 ns or 69 ns. Of course if decoder time and delay times

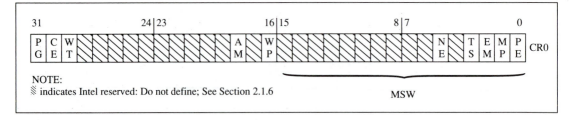

FIGURE 13–34   Control register zero (CR0) for the 80486 microprocessor. (Courtesy of Intel Corporation)

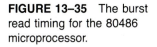

FIGURE 13–35 The burst read timing for the 80486 microprocessor.

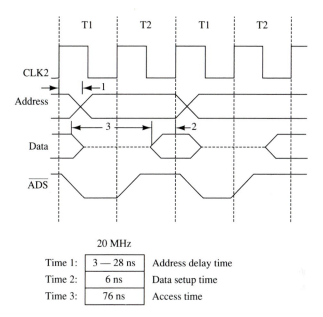

	20 MHz	
Time 1:	3 — 28 ns	Address delay time
Time 2:	6 ns	Data setup time
Time 3:	76 ns	Access time

are included, the access time allowed the memory is even less for no wait state operation. Also, if a higher frequency version of the 80486 is used in a system, memory access time is still less.

Figure 13–36 illustrates the timing diagram for filling a cache line with four 32-bit numbers using a burst. Notice that the addresses (A_{31}–A_4) appear during T_1 and remain constant throughout the burst cycle. Also notice that A_2 and A_3 change during each T_2 after the first two address four consecutive 32-bit numbers in the memory system. As mentioned, cache fills using bursts require only five clocking periods (one T_1 and four T_2) to fill a cache line with four double words of data. Access time using a 20-MHz version of the 80486 for the second and subsequent

FIGURE 13–36 A burst cycle that reads four double words in five clocking periods in the 80486 system.

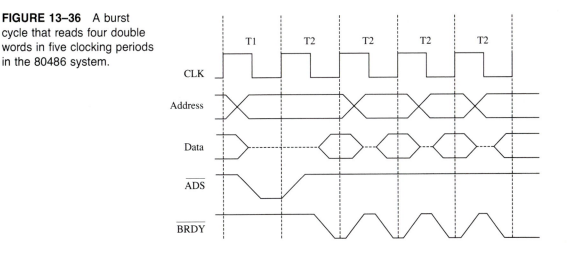

31		12	11 10 9	8	7	6	5	4	3	2	1	0
Page table or Page frame			OS Bits	0	0	D	A	P C D	P W T	U S	R W	P

FIGURE 13–37   The page directory or page table entry for the 80486 microprocessor.

double words is 50 ns − 28 ns − 3 ns or 19 ns, assuming no delays in the system. To use burst mode transfers, we need high-speed memory. Because DRAM memory access times at best are 40 ns, we are forced to use SRAM for burst cycle transfers. Even with SRAM we are pushing the limit of the technology for even a 20-MHz 80486 microprocessor. Note that the $\overline{\text{BRDY}}$ pin acknowledges a burst transfer rather than the $\overline{\text{RDY}}$ pin that acknowledges a normal memory transfer.

80486 Memory Management

The 80486 contains the same memory-management system as the 80386. This includes a paging unit to allow any 4K-byte block of physical memory to be assigned to any 4K-byte block of linear memory. The descriptor types are exactly the same as for the 80386 microprocessor. In fact, the only difference between the 80386 memory-management system and the 80486 memory-management system is paging.

The 80486 paging system can disable caching for sections of translated memory pages, while the 80386 could not. Figure 13–37 illustrates the page table directory entry and the page table entry. If these are compared with the 80386 entries in Figure 13–26, the addition of two new control bits is observed (PWT and PCD). The page write-through (PWT) and page cache disable (PCD) control caching.

The PWT controls how the cache functions for a write operation of the external cache memory. It does not control writing to the internal cache. The logic level of this bit is found on the PWT pin of the 80486 microprocessor. Externally, it can be used to dictate the write-through policy of the external cache.

The PCD bit controls the on-chip cache. If the PCD = 0, the on-chip cache is enabled for the current page of memory. Note that 80386 page table entries place a logic 0 in the PCD bit position, enabling caching. If PCD = 1, it disables the on-chip cache. Caching is disabled regardless of the condition of $\overline{\text{KEN}}$, CD, and NW.

13–9   80486 INSTRUCTION SET

The instruction set of the 80486 is almost identical to the instruction set of the 80386 except for a few additional instructions. The main difference is that the 80486 executes many instructions in one clocking period, whereas the 80386 requires two clocking periods. This increase accounts for an overall speed improvement of about 50 percent for the 80486 when compared to the 80386 microprocessor. Table 13–9 lists the instructions that are new to the 80486 microprocessor. Note that since

TABLE 13–9 New instructions for the 80486 microprocessor.

Instruction	Function
BSWAP	Swaps the bytes in a register
CMPXCHG	Compare and exchange
INVD	Flushes the internal cache memory
INVLPG	Invalidates a TLB entry
WBINVD	Flushes the internal cache memory after writing dirty lines to the memory
XADD	Exchange and add

the 80486 also includes an integrated 80387 numeric coprocessor, the coprocessor instructions listed in Chapter 12 also apply to the 80486 instruction set.

The BSWAP instruction allows bytes to be swapped in any 32-bit extended register. When the BSWAP instruction executes, it exchanges the rightmost byte with the leftmost byte and also exchanges the two middle bytes. For example, if EAX = 01234567H and the BSWAP EAX instruction executes, the result is 67452301H.

The CMPXCHG compares the destination operand to the contents of the accumulator (EAX, AX, or AL). If the destination operand is equal to the accumulator, the source operand is copied to the destination operand. If the destination operand is not equal to the accumulator, the destination operand is copied to the accumulator. An example is a CMPXCHG CX,DX, which copies DX into CX if DX = AX; otherwise, it copies CX into AX. In all cases the CMPXCHG instruction changes the flag bits to indicate the outcome of the comparison. Another example is CMPXCHG CL,DATA, which copies the contents of memory location DATA into CL if CL = AL; otherwise, it copies CL into AL.

The INVD (invalidate data cache) instruction empties the contents of the current data cache without writing changes to the memory system. Care must be exercised when using this instruction because data can be lost if INVD is executed before data are written to the memory system from the cache. This instruction is primarily used at the system software level.

The INVLPG (invalidate TLB entry) instruction invalidates an entry in the translation lookaside buffer (TLB) used by the demand-paging system in a virtual memory system. The instruction calculates the address of the operand and removes it from the TBL if the entry has been mapped into the TLB. As with the INVD instruction, this instruction is used at the operating system level instead of the application level.

The WBINVD (write before invalidating data cache) instruction functions as the INVD instruction, except the contents of any dirty location in the data cache is first written to memory before the cache is flushed. This instruction is normally found at the system level.

The XADD instruction exchanges and adds data in two registers or between memory and a register. For example, the XADD EAX,EBX instruction adds EBX to EAX and stores the sum in EAX, just as an add instruction. The difference is that the original value in EAX is moved into EBX. Just as addition affects the flags, so does the XADD instruction.

Cache Test Registers

Although not instructions, the cache test registers are placed in this section to illustrate the use of the cache test registers and some software for the 80486 microprocessor. The 80486 cache test registers are TR_3 (cache data register), TR_4 (cache status test register), and TR_5 (cache control test register), which are undefined for the 80386 microprocessor. These three registers are illustrated in Figure 13–38.

The cache data register (TR_3) is used to access either the cache fill buffer for a write test operation, or the cache read buffer for a cache read test operation. This register is a window into the 8K-byte cache memory located within the 80486 and is used for testing the cache. In order to fill or read a cache line (128 bits wide) TR_3 must be written or read four times.

The contents of the set select field in TR_5 determine which internal cache line is written or read through TR_3. The 7-bit test field selects one of the 128 different 16-byte-wide cache lines. The entry select bits of TR_5 select an entry in the set or the 32-bit location in the fill/read buffer. The control bits in TR_5 enable the fill buffer or read buffer operation (00), perform a cache write (01), a cache read (10), or flush the cache (11).

The cache status register (TR_4) holds the cache tag, LRU bits, and a valid bit. This register is loaded with the tag and valid bit before a cache write operation and contains the tag, valid bit, LRU bits, and four valid bits on a cache test read.

The cache is tested each time that the microprocessor is reset if the AHOLD pin is high for two clocks prior to the RESET pin going low. This causes the 80486 to completely test itself with a built-in self-test or BIST. The BIST uses TR_3, TR_4, and TR_5 to completely test the internal cache. Its outcome is reported in register

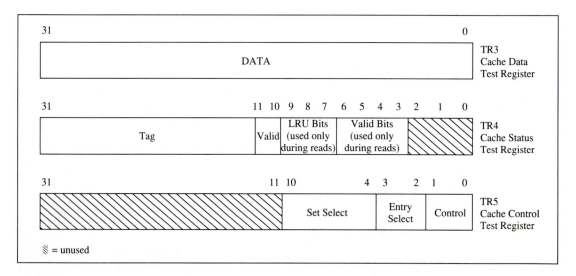

FIGURE 13–38   Cache test registers for the 80486 microprocessor. (Courtesy of Intel Corporation)

EAX. If EAX is a zero, the microprocessor, coprocessor, and cache have passed the self-test. The value of EAX can be tested after a reset to determine if an error is detected. In most cases we do not directly access the test registers unless we wish to perform our own tests on the cache or TLB.

13–10   SUMMARY

1. The 80386 microprocessor is an enhanced version of the 80286 microprocessor that includes a memory-management unit that is enhanced to provide memory paging. The 80386 also includes 32-bit extended registers and a 32-bit address and data bus. A scaled-down version of the 80386DX with a 16-bit data bus and 24-bit address bus is available as the 80386SX microprocessor.

2. The 80386 has a physical memory size of 4G bytes that can be addressed as a virtual memory with up to 64T bytes. The 80386 memory is 32 bits in width and is addressed as bytes, words, or double words.

3. When the 80386 is operated in the pipelined mode, it sends the address of the next instruction or memory data to the memory system prior to completing the execution of the current instruction. This allows the memory system to begin fetching the next instruction or data before the current is completed. This system increases access time, thus reducing the speed of the memory.

4. A cache memory system allows data that are frequently read to be accessed in less time because they are stored in high-speed semiconductor memory. If data are written to memory, they are also written to the cache so the most current data are always present in the cache.

5. The I/O structure of the 80386 is almost identical to the 80286, except that I/O can be inhibited when the 80386 is operated in the protected mode through the I/O bit protection map stored with the TSS.

6. The register set of the 80386 contains extended versions of the registers introduced on the 80286 microprocessor. These extended registers include EAX, EBX, ECX, EDX, EBP, ESP, EDI, ESI, EIP, and EFLAGS. In addition to the extended registers, two supplemental segment registers (FS and GS) are added. Debug registers and control registers handle system debugging tasks and memory management in the protected mode.

7. The instruction set of the 80386 is enhanced to include instructions that address the 32-bit extended register set. The enhancements also include additional addressing modes that allow any extended register to address memory data. Scaling has been added so an index register can be multiplied by 1, 2, 4, or 8. New instruction types include bit scan, string moves with sign or zero extension, set byte upon condition, and double-precision shifts.

8. Interrupts in the 80386 microprocessor have been expanded to include additional predefined interrupts in the interrupt vector table. These additional interrupts are used with the memory-management system.

9. The 80386 memory manager is similar to the 80286, except the physical addresses generated by the MMU are 32-bits wide instead of 24 bits. The 80386 MMU is also capable of paging.

10. The 80386 is operated in the real mode (8086 mode) when it is reset. The real mode allows the microprocessor to address data in the first 1M byte of memory. In the protected mode, the 80386 addresses any location in its 4G-byte physical address range.

11. A descriptor is a series of eight bytes that specify how a code or data segment is used by the 80386. The descriptor is selected by a selector that is stored in one of the segment registers. Descriptors are only used in the protected mode.

12. Memory management is accomplished through a series of descriptors stored in descriptor tables. To facilitate memory management, the 80386 uses three descriptor tables: the global descriptor table (GDT), the local descriptor table (LDT), and the interrupt descriptor table (IDT). The GDT and LDT each hold up to 8,192 descriptors each, while the IDT holds up to 256 descriptors. The GDT and LDT describe code and data segments and also tasks. The IDT describes the 256 different interrupt levels through interrupt gate descriptors.

13. The TSS (task state segment) contains information about the current task and also the previous task. Appended to the end of the TSS is an I/O bit protection map that inhibits selected I/O port addresses.

14. The memory paging mechanism allows any 4K-byte physical memory page to be mapped to any 4K-byte linear memory page. For example, memory location 00A00000H can be assigned memory location A0000000H through the paging mechanism. A page directory and page tables are used to assign any physical address to any linear address. The paging mechanism can be used in the protected mode or the virtual mode.

15. The 80486 microprocessor is an improved version of the 80386 microprocessor that contains an 8K byte cache, an 80387 arithmetic coprocessor, and executes many instructions in one clocking period.

16. The 80486 microprocessor executes a few new instructions that control the internal cache memory and allow addition (XADD) and comparison (CMPXCHG) with an exchange and a byte swap (BSWAP) operation. Other than these few additional instructions, the 80486 is 100 percent upward compatible with the 80386 and 80387.

17. A new feature found in the 80486 is the BIST (built-in self-test) that tests the microprocessor, coprocessor, and cache at reset time. If the 80486 passes the test, EAX contains a zero.

18. Additional test registers are added to the 80486 to allow the cache memory to be tested. These new test registers are TR_3 (cache data), TR_4 (cache status), and TR_5 (cache control). Although we seldom use these registers, they are used by BIST each time that a BIST is performed after a reset operation.

13–11   QUESTIONS AND PROBLEMS

1. The 80386 microprocessor addresses _____ bytes of physical memory when operated in the protected mode.

2. The 80386 microprocessor addresses _____ bytes of virtual memory through its memory-management unit.

3. Describe the differences between the 80386DX and 80386SX.
4. Draw the memory map of the 80386 when operated in the
   a. protected mode
   b. real mode
5. How much current is available on various 80386 output pin connections? Compare these currents with the currents available at the output pin connection of an 80286 microprocessor.
6. Describe the 80386 memory system and explain the purpose and operation of the bank selection signals.
7. Explain the action of a hardware reset on the address bus connections of the 80386.
8. Explain how pipelining lengthens the access time for many memory references in the 80386 microprocessor-based system.
9. Briefly describe how the cache memory system functions.
10. I/O ports in the 80386 start at I/O address _____ and extend to I/O address _____.
11. What I/O ports communicate data between the 80386 and its companion 80387 coprocessor?
12. Compare and contrast the memory and I/O connections found on the 80386 with those found on the 80286.
13. If the 80386 operates at 20 MHz, what clocking frequency is applied to the CLK2 pin?
14. What is the purpose of the $\overline{\text{BS16}}$ pin on the 80386 microprocessor?
15. What two additional segment registers are found in the 80386 programming model that are not present in the 80286?
16. List the extended registers found in the 80386 microprocessor.
17. List each 80386 flag register bit and describe its purpose.
18. Define the purpose of each of the control registers (CR_0, CR_1, CR_2, and CR_3) found within the 80386.
19. Define the purpose of each 80386 debug register.
20. The debug registers cause which level of interrupt?
21. Describe the operation of the bit scan forward instruction.
22. Describe the operation of the bit scan reverse instruction.
23. Describe the operation of the SHRD instruction.
24. Form an instruction that accesses data in the FS segment at the location indirectly addressed by the DI register. The instruction should store the contents of EAX into this memory location.
25. What is scaled index addressing?
26. Is the following instruction legal? MOV AX,[EBX+ECX]
27. Explain how the following instructions calculate the memory address:
   a. ADD [EBX+8*ECX],AL
   b. MOV DATA[EAX+EBX],CX
   c. SUB EAX,DATA
   d. MOV ECX,[EBX]
28. What is the purpose of interrupt type number 7?
29. Which interrupt vector type number is activated for a protection privilege violation?

30. What is a double interrupt fault?
31. If an interrupt occurs in the protected mode, what defines the interrupt vectors?
32. What is a descriptor?
33. What is a selector?
34. How does the selector choose the local descriptor table?
35. What register is used to address the global descriptor table?
36. How many global descriptors can be stored in the GDT?
37. Explain how the 80386 can address a virtual memory space of 64T bytes when the physical memory contains only 4G bytes of memory.
38. What is the difference between a segment descriptor and a system descriptor?
39. What is the task state segment (TSS)?
40. How is the TSS addressed?
41. Describe how the 80386 switches from the real mode to the protected mode.
42. Describe how the 80386 switches from the protected mode to the real mode.
43. What is virtual 8086 mode operation of the 80386 microprocessor?
44. How is the paging directory located by the 80386?
45. How many bytes are found in a page of memory?
46. Explain how linear memory address D0000000H can be assigned to physical memory address C0000000H with the paging unit of the 80386.
47. What are the differences between an 80386 and 80486 microprocessor?
48. What is the purpose of the $\overline{\text{FLUSH}}$ input pin on the 80486 microprocessor?
49. Compare the register set of the 80386 with the 80486 microprocessor.
50. What differences exist in the flags of the 80486 when compared to the 80386 microprocessor?
51. What pins are used for parity checking on the 80486 microprocessor?
52. The 80486 microprocessor uses _____ parity.
53. The cache inside the 80486 microprocessor is _____ K bytes.
54. A cache line is filled by reading _____ bytes from the memory system.
55. What is an 80486 burst?
56. Define the term cache write-through?
57. What is a BIST?
58. Can 80486 caching be disabled by software? (Explain your answer.)
59. Explain how the XADD EBX,EDX instruction operates.
60. The CMPXCHG CL,AL instruction compares CL with AL. What else occurs when this instruction executes?
61. Compare the INVD instruction with the WBINVD instruction.
62. What is the purpose of the PCD bit in the page table directory or page table entry?
63. Does the PWT bit in the page table directory or page table entry affect the on-chip cache?

APPENDIX A

The Assembler and Disk Operating System

This appendix is provided so the use of the assembler can be understood and also to show the DOS (disk operating system) and BIOS (basic I/O system) function calls that are used by assembly language to control the IBM-PC or its clone. The function calls control everything from reading and writing disk data to managing the keyboard and displays. The assembler represented in this text is the Microsoft ML (Version 6.0) and MASM (version 5.10) macro assembler programs.

ASSEMBLER USAGE

The assembler program requires that a symbolic program be first written, using a word processor, text editor, or the workbench program provided with the assembler package. The editor provided with version 5.10 is M.EXE, and it is strictly a full-screen editor. The editor provided with version 6.0 is PWB.EXE and is a fully integrated development system that contains extensive help. Refer to the documentation that accompanies your assembler package for details on the operation of the editor program. If at all possible use version 6.0 of the assembler because it contains a detailed help file that guides the user through assembly language statements, directives, and even the DOS and BIOS interrupt function calls.

If you are using a word processor to develop your software, make sure that it is initialized to generate a pure ASCII file. The source file that you generate must use the extension .ASM that is required for the assembler to properly identify your source program.

Once your source file is prepared, it must now be assembled. If you are using the workbench provided with version 6.0, assembly is accomplished by selecting the compile feature with your mouse. If you are using a word processor and DOS command lines with version 5.10, see Example A–1 for the dialog for version 5.10 to assemble a file called FROG.ASM. Note that this example shows the portions typed by the user in italics.

EXAMPLE A–1

A>*MASM*

Microsoft (R) Macro Assembler Version 5.10
Copyright (C) Microsoft Corp 1981, 1989. All rights reserved.

Source filename [.ASM]: *FILE*
Object filename [FILE.OBJ]: *FILE*
Source listing [NUL.LST]: *FILE*
Cross reference [NUL.CRF]: *FILE*

Once a program is assembled, it must be linked before it can be executed. The linker converts the object file into an executable file (.EXE). Example A–2 shows the dialog required for the linker using a MASM version 5.10 object file. If the ML version 6.0 assembler is in use, it automatically assembles and links a program using the COMPILE or BUILD command from workbench. After compiling with ML, workbench allows the program to be debugged with a debugging tool called code view. Code view is also available with MASM, but CV must be typed at the DOS command line to access it.

EXAMPLE A–2

A>*LINK*

Microsoft (R) Overlay Linker Version 3.64
Copyright (C) Microsoft Corp 1983-1988. All rights reserved.

Object Modules [.OBJ]: *TEST*
Run File [TEST.EXE]: *TEST*
List File [NUL.MAP]: *TEST*
Libraries [.LIB]: *SUBR*

ASSEMBLER MEMORY MODELS

Memory models and the .MODEL statement are introduced in Chapter 6. Here we completely define the memory models available for software development. Each

TABLE A–1 Memory models for the assembler

Type	Description
Tiny	All data and code fit into one segment, the code segment. Tiny model programs are written in the .COM file format, which means that the program must be originated at memory location 0100H. This model is most often used with small programs.
Small	All data fit into a single 64K-byte data segment, and all code fits into another single 64K-byte code segment. This allows all code to be accessed with near jumps and calls.
Medium	All data fits into a single 64K-byte data segment, and code fits into more than one code segment. This allows code to exist in multiple segments.
Compact	All code fits into a single 64K-byte code segment, and data fits into more than one data segment.
Large	Both code and data fit into multiple code and data segments.
Huge	Same as large, but allows data segments that are larger than 64K bytes.
Flat	Not available in MASM version 5.10. The flat memory model uses one segment with a maximum length of 512M bytes to store data and code.

model defines the way that a program is stored in the memory system. Table A–1 describes the different models available with MASM and also ML.

Note that the tiny model is used to create a .COM file instead of an execute file. The .COM file is different because all data and code fit into one code segment. A .COM file must have the program originated to start at offset address 0100H. A .COM file loads from the disk and executes faster than the normal execute (.EXE) file. For most applications we normally use the execute file (.EXE) and the small memory model.

When models are used to create a program, certain defaults apply, as illustrated in Table A–2. The directive in this table is used to start a particular type of segment for the models listed in the table. If the .CODE directive is placed in a program, it indicates the beginning of the code segment. Likewise, .DATA indicates the start of a data segment. The name column indicates the name of the segment. Align indicates whether the segment is aligned on a word, double word, or a 16-byte paragraph. Combine indicates the type of segment created. The class indicates the class of the segment, such as 'CODE' or 'DATA'. The group indicates the group type of the segment.

Example A–3 shows a program that uses the small model. The small model is used for programs that contain one DATA and one CODE segment. This usage applies to many programs that are developed. Notice that not only is the program listed but so is all the information generated by the assembler. Here the .DATA and .CODE directives indicate the start of segments. Also notice how the DS register is loaded in this program.

TABLE A–2 Defaults for the .MODEL directive

Model	Directive	Name	Align	Combine	Class	Group
Tiny	.CODE	_TEXT	Word	PUBLIC	'CODE'	DGROUP
	.FARDATA	FAR_DATA	Para	Private	'FAR_DATA'	
	.FARDATA?	FAR_BSS	Para	Private	'FAR_BSS'	
	.DATA	_DATA	Word	PUBLIC	'DATA'	DGROUP
	.CONST	CONST	Word	PUBLIC	'CONST'	DGROUP
	.DATA?	_BSS	Word	PUBLIC	'BSS'	DGROUP
Small	.CODE	_TEXT	Word	PUBLIC	'CODE'	
	.FARDATA	FAR_DATA	Para	Private	'FAR_DATA'	
	.FARDATA?	FAR_BSS	Para	Private	'FAR_BSS'	
	.DATA	_DATA	Word	PUBLIC	'DATA'	DGROUP
	.CONST	CONST	Word	PUBLIC	'CONST'	DGROUP
	.DATA?	_BSS	Word	PUBLIC	'BSS'	DGROUP
	.STACK	STACK	Para	STACK	'STACK'	DGROUP
Medium	.CODE	name_TEXT	Word	PUBLIC	'CODE'	
	.FARDATA	FAR_DATA	Para	Private	'FAR_DATA'	
	.FARDATA?	FAR_BSS	Para	Private	'FAR_BSS'	
	.DATA	_DATA	Word	PUBLIC	'DATA'	DGROUP
	.CONST	CONST	Word	PUBLIC	'CONST'	DGROUP
	.DATA?	_BSS	Word	PUBLIC	'BSS'	DGROUP
	.STACK	STACK	Para	STACK	'STACK'	DGROUP
Compact	.CODE	_TEXT	Word	PUBLIC	'CODE'	
	.FARDATA	FAR_DATA	Para	Private	'FAR_DATA'	
	.FARDATA?	FAR_BSS	Para	Private	'FAR_BSS'	
	.DATA	_DATA	Word	PUBLIC	'DATA'	DGROUP
	.CONST	CONST	Word	PUBLIC	'CONST'	DGROUP
	.DATA?	_BSS	Word	PUBLIC	'BSS'	DGROUP
	.STACK	STACK	Para	STACK	'STACK'	DGROUP
Large or Huge	.Code	name_TEXT	Word	PUBLIC	'CODE'	
	.FARDATA	FAR_DATA	Para	Private	'FAR_DATA'	
	.FARDATA?	FAR_BSS	Para	Private	'FAR_BSS'	
	.DATA	_DATA	Word	PUBLIC	'DATA'	DGROUP
	.CONST	CONST	Word	PUBLIC	'CONST'	DGROUP
	.DATA?	_BSS	Word	PUBLIC	'BSS'	DGROUP
	.STACK	STACK	Para	STACK	'STACK'	DGROUP
Flat	.CODE	_TEXT	Dword	PUBLIC	'CODE'	
	.FARDATA	_DATA	Dword	PUBLIC	'DATA'	
	.FARDATA?	_BSS	Dword	PUBLIC	'BSS'	
	.DATA	_DATA	Dword	PUBLIC	'DATA'	
	.CONST	CONST	Dword	PUBLIC	'CONST'	
	.DATA?	_BSS	Dword	PUBLIC	'BSS'	
	.STACK	STACK	Dword	PUBLIC	'STACK	

EXAMPLE A–3

Microsoft (R) Macro Assembler Version 6.00   07/30/91 22:21:45


```
                        .MODEL SMALL
                        .STACK 100H
0000                    .DATA

0000 0A                 FROG    DB      10
0001 0064 [             DATA1   DB      100 DUP (2)
          02
        ]

0000                    .CODE

0000 B8 ---- R          BEGIN:  MOV     AX,DGROUP           ;set up DS
0003 8E D8                      MOV     DS,AX
                                .
                                .
                                .
                                END     BEGIN
```

Segments and Groups:

N a m e	Size	Length	Align	Combine Class
DGROUP	GROUP			
_DATA	16 Bit	0065	Word	Public 'DATA'
STACK	16 Bit	0100	Para	Stack 'STACK'
_TEXT	16 Bit	0005	Word	Public 'CODE'

Symbols:

N a m e	Type	Value	Attr
@CodeSize	Number	0000h	
@DataSize	Number	0000h	
@Interface	Number	0000h	
@Model	Number	0002h	
@code	Text		_TEXT
@data	Text		DGROUP
@fardata?	Text		FAR_BSS
@fardata	Text		FAR_DATA
@stack	Text		DGROUP
BEGIN	L Near	0000	_TEXT
DATA1	Byte	0001	_DATA
FROG	Byte	0000	_DATA

```
                0 Warnings
                0 Errors
```

Example A–4 lists a program that uses the large model. Notice how it differs from the small-model program of Example A–3. Models can be very useful in developing software, but often we use full-segment descriptions as depicted in Chapter 6.

EXAMPLE A–4

Microsoft (R) Macro Assembler Version 6.00   07/30/91 22:38:58

```
                          .MODEL LARGE
                          .STACK 1000H
0000                      .FARDATA?

0000 00                   FROG     DB      ?
0001 0064 [               DATA1    DW      100 DUP (?)
         0000
               ]

0000                      .CONST

0000 54 68 69 73 20 69 MES1     DB      'This is a character string'
     73 20 61 20 63 68
     61 72 61 63 74 65
     72 20 73 74 72 69
     6E 67
001A 53 6F 20 69 73 20 MES2     DB      'So is this!'
     74 68 69 73 21

0000                      .DATA

0000 000C                 DATA2    DW      12
0002 00C8 [               DATA3    DB      200 DUP (1)
         01
               ]

0000                      .CODE

0000                      FUNC     PROC    FAR
                                   .
                                   .
                                   .
                                   .
0000  CB                           RET

0001                      FUNC     ENDP

                                   END     FUNC
```

Segments and Groups:

N a m e	Size	Length	Align	Combine Class	
DGROUP	GROUP				
_DATA	16 Bit	00CA	Word	Public 'DATA'	
STACK	16 Bit	1000	Para	Stack 'STACK'	
CONST	16 Bit	0025	Word	Public 'CONST'	ReadOnly
EXA_TEXT	16 Bit	0001	Word	Public 'CODE'	
FAR_BSS	16 Bit	00C9	Para	Private 'FAR_BSS'	
_TEXT	16 Bit	0000	Word	Public 'CODE'	

Procedures, parameters and locals:

N a m e	Type	Value	Attr	
FUNC	P Far	0000	EXA_TEXT	Length= 0001 Public

Symbols:

N a m e	Type	Value	Attr
@CodeSize	Number	0001h	
@DataSize	Number	0001h	
@Interface	Number	0000h	
@Model	Number	0005h	
@code	Text		EXA_TEXT
@data	Text		DGROUP
@fardata?	Text		FAR_BSS
@fardata	Text		FAR_DATA
@stack	Text		DGROUP
DATA1	Word	0001	FAR_BSS
DATA2	Word	0000	_DATA
DATA3	Byte	0002	_DATA
FROG	Byte	0000	FAR_BSS
MES1	Byte	0000	CONST
MES2	Byte	001A	CONST

0 Warnings
0 Errors

DOS FUNCTION CALLS

EXAMPLE A–5

```
0000 B4 06              MOV    AH,6
0002 B2 41              MOV    DL,'A'
0004 CD 21              INT    21H
```

In order to use DOS function calls, place the function number into register AH and load all other pertinent information into registers as described in the table. Once this is accomplished, follow with an INT 21H to execute the DOS function. Example A–5 shows how to display an ASCII A on the CRT screen at the current cursor position with a DOS function call. Following is a complete listing of the DOS function calls. Note that some function calls require a segment and offset address indicated as DS:DI, for example. This means the data segment is the segment address and DI is the offset address. All of the function calls use INT 21H, and AH contains the function call number. Note that functions marked with an @ should not be used unless DOS version 2.XX is in use. As a rule, DOS functions calls save all registers not used as exit data, but in certain cases some registers may change. In order to prevent problems, it is advisable to save registers where problems occur.

00H	TERMINATE A PROGRAM
Entry	AH = 00H CS = program segment prefix address
Exit	DOS is entered
01H	READ THE KEYBOARD
Entry	AH = 01H
Exit	AL = ASCII character
Notes	If AL = 00H the function call must be invoked again to read an extended ASCII character. Refer to Chapter 6, Table 6-1, for a listing of the extended ASCII keyboard codes. This function call automatically echoes whatever is typed to the video screen.
02H	WRITE TO STANDARD OUTPUT DEVICE
Entry	AH = 02H AL = ASCII character to be displayed
Notes	This function call normally displays data on the video display.
03H	READ CHARACTER FROM COM1
Entry	AH = 03H
Exit	AL = ASCII character read from the communications port
Notes	This function call reads data from the serial communications port.
04H	WRITE TO COM1
Entry	AH = 04H

	DL = character to be sent out of COM1
Notes	This function transmits data through the serial communications port.

05H	WRITE TO LPT1
Entry	AH = 05H DL = ASCII character to be printed
Notes	Prints DL on the line printer attached to LPT1

06H	DIRECT CONSOLE READ/WRITE
Entry	AH = 06H DL = 0FFH or DL = ASCII character
Exit	AL = ASCII character
Notes	If DL = 0FFH on entry, then this function reads the console. If DL = ASCII character, then this function displays the ASCII character on the console video screen. If a character is read from the console keyboard, the zero flag (ZF) indicates whether a character was typed. A zero condition indicates no key is typed and a not-zero condition indicates that AL contains the ASCII code of the key or a 00H. If AL = 00H, the function must again be invoked to read an extended ASCII character from the keyboard. Note that the key does not echo to the video screen.

07H	DIRECT CONSOLE INPUT WITHOUT ECHO
Entry	AH = 07H
Exit	AL = ASCII character
Notes	This functions exactly as function number 06H with DL = 0FFH, but it will not return from the function until the key is typed.

08H	READ STANDARD INPUT WITHOUT ECHO
Entry	AH = 08H
Exit	AL = ASCII character
Notes	Performs as function 07H, except it reads the standard input device. The standard input device can be assigned as either the keyboard or the COM port. This function also responds to a control-break, where function 06H and 07H do not. A control-break causes INT 23H to execute.

09H	DISPLAY A CHARACTER STRING
Entry	AH = 09H DS:DX = address of the character string
Notes	The character string must end with an ASCII $ (24H). The character string can be of any length and may contains control characters such as carriage return (0DH) and line feed (0AH).

0AH	BUFFERED KEYBOARD INPUT
Entry	AH = 0AH DS:DX = address of keyboard input buffer
Notes	The first byte of the buffer contains the size of the buffer (up to 255). The second byte is filled with the number of characters typed upon return. The third byte through the end of the buffer contains the character string typed followed by a carriage return (0DH). This function continues to read the keyboard (displaying data as typed) until either the specified number of characters are typed or until a carriage return (enter) key is typed.

0BH	TEST STATUS OF THE STANDARD INPUT DEVICE
Entry	AH = 0BH
Exit	AL = status of the input device
Notes	This function tests the standard input device to determine if data are available. If AL = 00, no data are available. If AL = 0FFH, then data are available that must be input using function number 08H.

0CH	CLEAR KEYBOARD BUFFER AND INVOKE KEYBOARD FUNCTION
Entry	AH = 0CH AL = 01H, 06H, 07H, or 0AH
Exit	see exit for functions 01H, 06H, 07H, or 0AH
Notes	The keyboard buffer holds keystrokes while programs execute other tasks. This function empties or clears the buffer and then invokes the keyboard function located in register AL.

0DH	FLUSH DISK BUFFERS
Entry	AH = 0DH
Notes	Erases all file names stored in disk buffers. This function does not close the files specified by the disk buffers, so care must be exercised in its usage.

0EH	SELECT DEFAULT DISK DRIVE
Entry	AH = 0DH DL = desired default disk drive number
Exit	AL = the total number of drives present in the system
Notes	Drive A = 00H, drive B = 01H, drive C = 02H, and so forth.

0FH	@OPEN FILE WITH FCB
Entry	AH = 0FH

	DS:DX = address of the unopened file control block (FCB)
Exit	AL = 00H if file found AL = 0FFH if file not found
Notes	The file control block (FCB) is only used with early DOS software and should never be used with new programs. File control blocks do not allow path names as do the newer file access function codes presented later. Figure A-1 illustrates the structure of the FCB. To open a file, the file must either be present on the disk or be created with function call 16H.

FIGURE A–1 Contents of the file-control block (FCB).

Offset	Contents
00H	Drive
01H	8-character filename
09H	3-character file extension
0CH	Current block number
0EH	Record size
10H	File size
14H	Creation date
16H	Reserved space
20H	Current record number
21H	Relative record number

10H	**@CLOSE FILE WITH FCB**
Entry	AH = 10H DS:DX = address of the opened file control block (FCB)
Exit	AL = 00H if file closed AL = 0FFH if error found
Notes	Errors that occurs usually indicate that either the disk is full or the media is bad.
11H	**@SEARCH FOR FIRST MATCH (FCB)**
Entry	AH = 11H DS:DX = address of the file control block to be searched
Exit	AL = 00H if file found AL = 0FFH if file not found
Notes	Wild card characters (? or *) may be used to search for a file name. The ? wild card character matches any character and the * matches any name or extension.
12H	**@SEARCH FOR NEXT MATCH (FCB)**

Entry	AH = 12H DS:DX = address of the file control block to be searched
Exit	AL = 00H if file found AL = 0FFH if file not found
Notes	This function is used after function 11H finds the first matching file name.

13H	**@DELETE FILE USING FCB**
Entry	AH = 13H DS:DX = address of the file control block to be deleted
Exit	AL = 00H if file deleted AL = 0FFH if error occurred
Notes	Errors that most often occur are defective media errors.

14H	**@SEQUENTIAL READ (FCB)**
Entry	AH = 14H DS:DX = address of the file control block to be read
Exit	AL = 00H if read successful AL = 01H if end of file reached AL = 02H if DTA had a segment wrap AL = 03H if less than 128 bytes were read

15H	**@SEQUENTIAL WRITE (FCB)**
Entry	AH = 15H DS:DX = address of the file control block to be written
Exit	AL = 00H if write successful AL = 01H if disk is full AL = 02H if DTA had a segment wrap

16H	**@CREATE A FILE (FCB)**
Entry	AH = 16H DS:DX = address of an unopened file control block
Exit	AL = 00H if file created AL = 01H if disk is full

17H	**@RENAME A FILE (FCB)**
Entry	AH = 17H DS:DX = address of a modified file control block
Exit	AL = 00H if file renamed AL = 01H if error occurred

Notes	Refer to Figure A-2 for the modified FCB used to rename a file.

FIGURE A–2 Contents of the modified file-control block (FCB).

Offset	Content
00H	Drive
01H	8-character filename
09H	3-character extension
0CH	Current block number
0EH	Record Size
10H	File size
14H	Creation date
16H	Second file name

18H	NOT ASSIGNED

19H	RETURN CURRENT DRIVE
Entry	AH = 19H
Exit	AL = current drive
Notes	AL = 00H for drive A, 01H for drive B, and so forth.

1AH	SET DISK TRANSFER AREA
Entry	AH = 1AH DS:DX = address of new DTA
Notes	The disk transfer area is normally located within the program segment prefix at offset address 80H. The DTA is used by DOS for all disk data transfers using file control blocks.

1BH	GET DEFAULT DRIVE FILE ALLOCATION TABLE (FAT)
Entry	AH = 1BH
Exit	AL = number of sectors per cluster DS:BX = address of the media-descriptor CX = size of a sector in bytes DX = number of clusters on drive
Notes	Refer to Figure A-3 for the format of the media-descriptor byte. The DS register is changed by this function so make sure to save it before using this function.

FIGURE A–3 Contents of
the media-descriptor byte.

7	6	5	4	3	2	1	0
?	?	?	?	?	?	?	?

Bit 0 = 0 if not two-sided
        = 1 if two-sided

Bit 1 = 0 if not eight sectors per track
        = 1 if eight sectors per track

Bit 2 = 0 if nonremovable
        = 1 if removable

1CH	GET ANY DRIVE FILE ALLOCATION TABLE (FAT)
Entry	AH = 1CH DL = disk drive number
Exit	AL = number of sectors per cluster DS:BX = address of the media-descriptor CX = size of a sector in bytes DX = number of clusters on drive
1DH	NOT ASSIGNED
1EH	NOT ASSIGNED
1FH	NOT ASSIGNED
20H	NOT ASSIGNED
21H	@RANDOM READ USING FCB
Entry	AH = 21H DS:DX = address of opened FCB
Exit	AL = 00H if read successful AL = 01H if end of file reached

	AL = 02H if the segment wrapped AL = 03H if less than 128 bytes read
22H	@RANDOM WRITE USING FCB
Entry	AH = 22H DS:DX = address of opened FCB
Exit	AL = 00H if write successful AL = 01H if disk full AL = 02H if the segment wrapped
23H	@RETURN NUMBER OF RECORDS (FCB)
Entry	AH = 23H DS:DX = address of FCB
Exit	AL = 00H number of records AL = 0FFH if file not found
24H	@SET RELATIVE RECORD SIZE (FCB)
Entry	AH = 24H DS:DX = address of FCB
Notes	Sets the record field to the value contained in the FCB.
25H	SET INTERRUPT VECTOR
Entry	AH = 25H AL = interrupt vector number DS:DX = address of new interrupt procedure
Notes	Before changing the interrupt vector, it is suggested that the current interrupt vector is first saved using DOS function 35H. This allows a back-link so the original vector can later be restored.
26H	CREATE NEW PROGRAM SEGMENT PREFIX
Entry	AH = 26H DX = segment address of new PSP
Notes	Figure A-4 illustrates the structure of the program segment prefix.

FIGURE A–4 Contents of the program-segment prefix (PSP).

Offset	Content
00H	INT 20H
02H	Top of memory
04H	Reserved
05H	Opcode
06H	Number of bytes in segment
0AH	Terminate address (offset)
0CH	Terminate address (segment)
0EH	Control break address (offset)
10H	Control break address (segment)
12H	Critical error address (offset)
14H	Critical error address (segment)
16H	Reserved
2CH	Environment address (segment)
2EH	Reserved
50H	DOS call
52H	Reserved
5CH	File control block 1
6CH	File control block 2
80H	Command line length
81H	Command line

27H	**@RANDOM FILE BLOCK READ (FCB)**
Entry	AH = 27H CX = the number of records DS:DX = address of opened FCB
Exit	AL = 00H if read successful AL = 01H if end of file reached AL = 02H if the segment wrapped

	AL = 03H if less than 128 bytes read CX = the number of records read
28H	@RANDOM FILE BLOCK WRITE (FCB)
Entry	AH = 28H CX = the number of records DS:DX = address of opened FCB
Exit	AL = 00H if write successful AL = 01H if disk full AL = 02H if the segment wrapped CX = the number of records written
29H	@PARSE COMMAND LINE (FCB)
Entry	AH = 29H AL = parse mask DS:SI = address of FCB DS:DI = address of command line
Exit	AL = 00H if no file name characters found AL = 01H if file name characters found AL = 0FFH if drive specifier incorrect DS:SI = address of character after name DS:DI = address first byte of FCB
2AH	READ SYSTEM DATE
Entry	AH = 2AH
Exit	AL = day of the week CX = the year (1980—2099) DH = the month DL = day of the month
Notes	The day of the week is encoded as Sunday = 00H through Saturday = 06H. The year is a binary number equal to 1980 through 2099.
2BH	SET SYSTEM DATE
Entry	AH = 2BH CX = the year (1980—2099) DH = the month DL = day of the month
2CH	READ SYSTEM TIME
Entry	AH = 2CH
Exit	CH = hours (0—23) CL = minutes DH = seconds DL = hundredths of seconds

2DH	SET SYSTEM TIME
Entry	AH = 2DH CH = hours CL = minutes DH = seconds DL = hundredths of seconds

2EH	DISK VERIFY WRITE
Entry	AH = 2EH AL = 00H to disable verify on write AL = 01H to enable verify on write

2FH	READ DISK TRANSFER AREA
Entry	AH = 2FH
Exit	ES:BX = contains DTA address

30H	READ DOS VERSION NUMBER
Entry	AH = 30H
Exit	AH = fractional version number AL = whole number version number
Notes	For example, DOS version number 3.2 is returned as a 3 in AL and a 14H in AH.

31H	TERMINATE AND STAY RESIDENT (TSR)
Entry	AH = 31H AL = the DOS return code DX = number of paragraphs to reserve
Notes	A paragraph is 16 bytes and the DOS return code is read at the batch file level with ERRORCODE.

32H	NOT ASSIGNED

33H	TEST CONTROL-BREAK
Entry	AH = 33H AL = 00H to request current control-break AL = 01H to change control-break DL = 00H to disable control-break DL = 01H to enable control-break
Exit	DL = current control-break state

34H	GET ADDRESS OF InDOS FLAG

Entry	AH = 34H
Exit	ES:BX = address of InDOS flag
Notes	The InDOS flag is available in DOS versions 3.2 or newer and indicates DOS activity. If InDOS = 00H, DOS is inactive or 0FFH if DOS is active.

35H READ INTERRUPT VECTOR

Entry	AH = 35H AL = interrupt vector number
Exit	ES:BX = address stored at vector
Notes	This DOS function is used with function 25H to install/remove interrupt handlers.

36H DETERMINE FREE DISK SPACE

Entry	AH = 36H DL = drive number
Exit	AX = FFFFH if drive invalid AX = number of sectors per cluster BX = number of free clusters CX = bytes per sector DX = number of clusters on drive
Notes	The default disk drive is DL = 00H, drive A = 01H, drive B = 02H, and so forth.

37H NOT ASSIGNED

38H RETURN COUNTRY CODE

Entry	AH = 38H AL = 00H for current country code BX = 16-bit country code DS:DX = data buffer address
Exit	AX = error code if carry set BX = counter code DS:DX = data buffer address

39H CREATE SUBDIRECTORY

Entry	AH = 39H DS:DX = address of ASCII-Z string subdirectory name
Exit	AX = error code if carry set
Notes	The ASCII-Z string is the name of the subdirectory in ASCII code ended with a 00H instead of a carriage return/line feed.

3AH ERASE SUBDIRECTORY

Entry	AH = 3AH DS:DX = address of ASCII-Z string subdirectory name
Exit	AX = error code if carry set

3BH	CHANGE SUBDIRECTORY

Entry	AH = 3BH DS:DX = address of new ASCII-Z string subdirectory name
Exit	AX = error code if carry set

3CH	CREATE A NEW FILE

Entry	AH = 3CH CX = attribute word DS:DX = address of ASCII-Z string file name
Exit	AX = error code if carry set AX = file handle if carry cleared
Notes	The attribute word can contain any of the following (added together): 01H read-only access, 02H = hidden file or directory, 04H = system file, 08H = volume label, 10H = subdirectory, and 20H = archive bit. In most cases a file is created with 0000H.

3DH	OPEN A FILE

Entry	AH = 3DH AL = access code DS:DX = address of ASCII-Z string file name
Exit	AX = error code if carry set AX = file handle if carry cleared
Notes	The access code in AL = 00H for a read-only access, AL = 01H for a write-only access, and AL = 02H for a read/write access. For shared files in a network environment, bit 4 of AL = 1 will deny read/write access, bit 5 of AL = 1 will deny a write access, bits 4 and 5 of AL = 1 will deny read access, bit 6 of AL = 1 denies none, bit 7 of AL = 0 causes the file to be inherited by child, and if bit 7 of AL = 1 file is restricted to current process.

3EH	CLOSE A FILE

Entry	AH = 3EH BX = file handle
Exit	AX = error code if carry set

3FH	READ A FILE

Entry	AH = 3FH BX = file handle CX = number of bytes to be read DS:DX = address of file buffer to hold data read
Exit	AX = error code if carry set

		AX = number of bytes read if carry cleared
40H	WRITE A FILE	
Entry	AH = 40H BX = file handle CX = number of bytes to write DS:DX = address of file buffer that holds write data	
Exit	AX = error code if carry set AX = number of bytes written if carry cleared	
41H	DELETE A FILE	
Entry	AH = 41H DS:DX = address of ASCII-Z string file name	
Exit	AX = error code if carry set	
42H	MOVE FILE POINTER	
Entry	AH = 42H AL = move technique BX = file handle CX:DX = number of bytes pointer moved	
Exit	AX = error code if carry set AX:DX = bytes pointer moved	
Notes	The move technique causes the pointer to move from the start of the file if AL = 00H, from the current location if AL = 01H and from the end of the file if AL = 02H. The count is stored so DX contains the least significant 16-bits and either CX or AX contains the most significant 16 bits.	
43H	READ/WRITE FILE ATTRIBUTES	
Entry	AH = 43H AL = 00H to read attributes AL = 01H to write attributes CX = attribute word (see function 3CH) DS:DX = address of ASCII-Z string file name	
Exit	AX = error code if carry set CX = attribute word of carry cleared	
44H	I/O DEVICE CONTROL (IOTCL)	
Entry	AH = 44H AL = code (see notes) AL = 01H to write attributes BX = file handle or device number CX = number of bytes DS:DX = data or address	
Exit	AX = error code if carry set AX and DX = parameters	
Notes	The codes found in AL are as follows:	

	00H = read device status (DX = status) 01H = write device status (DX = status written) 02H = read data from device (DS:DX = buffer address) 03H = write data to device (DS:DX = buffer address) 04H = read data from disk drive 05H = write data to disk drive 06H = read input status (AL = 00H ready or 0FH not ready) 07H = read output status (AL = 00H ready or 0FH not ready) 08H = removable media? (AL = 00H removable, 01H fixed) 09H = local or remote device? (bit 12 of DX set for remote) 0AH = local or remote handle? (bit 15 of DX set for remote) 0BH = change entry count 0CH = generic I/O control for character devices 0DH = generic I/O control for block devices 0EH = return number of logical devices (AL = number) 0FH = change number of logical devices
45H	DUPLICATE FILE HANDLE
Entry	AH = 45H BX = current file handle
Exit	AX = error code if carry set AX = duplicate file handle
46H	FORCE DUPLICATE FILE HANDLE
Entry	AH = 46H BX = current file handle CX = new file handle
Exit	AX = error code if carry set
Notes	This function works like function 45H except function 45H allows DOS to select the new handle while this function allows the user to select the new handle.
47H	READ CURRENT DIRECTORY
Entry	AH = 47H DL = drive number DS:SI = address of a 64 byte buffer for directory name
Exit	DS:SI addresses current directory name if carry cleared
48H	ALLOCATE MEMORY BLOCK
Entry	AH = 48H BX = number of paragraphs to allocate CX = new file handle
Exit	BX = largest block available if carry cleared

49H	RELEASE ALLOCATED MEMORY BLOCK
Entry	AH = 49H ES = segment address of block to be released CX = new file handle
Exit	Carry indicates an error if set

4AH	MODIFY ALLOCATED MEMORY BLOCK
Entry	AH = 4AH BX = new block size in paragraphs ES = segment address of block to be modified
Exit	BX = largest block available if carry cleared

4BH	LOAD OR EXECUTE A PROGRAM
Entry	AH = 4BH AL = function code ES:BX = address of parameter block DS:DX = address ASCII-Z string command
Exit	Carry indicates an error if set
Notes	The function codes are: AL = 00H to load and execute a program and AL = 03H to load a program but not execute it. Figure A-5 shows the parameter block used with this function.

FIGURE A–5 The parameter blocks used with function 4BH (EXEC). (a) For function code 00H. (b) For function code 03H.

(a)

Offset	Contents
00H	Environment address (segment)
02H	Command line address (offset)
04H	Command line address (segment)
06H	File control block 1 address (offset)
08H	File control block 1 address (segment)
0AH	File control block 2 address (segment)
0CH	File control block 2 address (offset)

(b)

Offset	Contents
00H	Overlay destination segment address
02H	Relocation factor

4CH	TERMINATE A PROCESS
Entry	AH = 4CH AL = error code
Exit	Returns control to DOS
Notes	This function returns control to DOS with the error code saved so it can be obtained using DOS ERROR LEVEL batch processing system. We normally use this function with an error code of 00H to return to DOS.

4DH	READ RETURN CODE
Entry	AH = 4DH
Exit	AX = return error code
Notes	This function is used to obtain the return status code created by executing a program with DOS function 4BH. The return codes are: AX = 0000H for a normal—no error—termination, AX = 0001H for a control-break termination, AX = 0002H for a critical device error, and AX = 0003H for a termination by an INT 31H.

4EH	FIND FIRST MATCHING FILE
Entry	AH = 4EH CX = file attributes DS:DX = address ASCII-Z string file name
Exit	Carry is set for file not found
Notes	This function searches the current or named directory for the first matching file. Upon exit, the DTA contains the file information. See Figure A-6 for the disk transfer area (DTA).

FIGURE A–6 Data transfer area (DTA) used to find a file.

Offset	Contents
15H	Attributes
16H	Creation time
18H	Creation date
1AH	Low word file size
1CH	High word file size
1EH	Search file name

4FH	FIND NEXT MATCHING FILE

Entry	AH = 4FH
Exit	Carry is set for file not found
Notes	This function is used after the first file is found with function 4EH

50H	SET PROGRAM SEGMENT PREFIX (PSP) ADDRESS

Entry	AH = 50H BX = offset address of the new PSP
Notes	Extreme care must be used with this function because no error recovery is possible.

51H	GET PSP ADDRESS

Entry	AH = 51H
Exit	BX = current PSP segment address

52H	NOT ASSIGNED

53H	NOT ASSIGNED

54H	READ DISK VERIFY STATUS

Entry	AH = 54H
Exit	AL = 00H if verify off AL = 01H if verify on

55H	NOT ASSIGNED

56H	RENAME FILE

Entry	AH = 56H ES:DI = address of ASCII-Z string containing new file name DS:DX = address of ASCII-Z string containing file to be renamed
Exit	Carry is set for error condition

57H	READ FILE'S DATE AND TIME STAMP

Entry	AH = 57H AL = function code BX = file handle CX = new time DX = new date

Exit	Carry is set for error condition CX = time if carry cleared DX = date if carry cleared
Notes	AL = 00H to read date and time or 01H to write date and time.

58H	NOT ASSIGNED

59H	GET EXTENDED ERROR INFORMATION

Entry	AH = 59H BX = 0000H for DOS version 3.X
Exit	AX = extended error code BH = error class BL = recommended action CH = locus
Notes	Following are the error codes found in AX: 0001H = invalid function number 0002H = file not found 0003H = path not found 0004H = no file handles available 0005H = access denied 0006H = file handle invalid 0007H = memory control block failure 0008H = insufficient memory 0009H = memory block address invalid 000AH = environment failure 000BH = format invalid 000CH = access code invalid 000DH = data invalid 000EH = unknown unit 000FH = disk drive invalid 0010H = attempted to remove current directory 0011H = not same device 0012H = no more files 0013H = disk write-protected 0014H = unknown unit 0015H = drive not ready 0016H = unknown command 0017H = data error (CRC check error) 0018H = bad request structure length 0019H = seek error 001AH = unknown media type 001BH = sector not found 001CH = printer out of paper 001DH = write fault 001EH = read fault 001FH = general failure 0020H = sharing violation 0021H = lock violation 0022H = disk change invalid 0023H = FCB unavailable 0024H = sharing buffer exceeded 0025H = code page mismatch 0026H = handle end of file operation not completed 0027H = disk full 0028H — 0031H reserved 0032H = unsupported network request 0033H = remote machine not listed 0034H = duplicate name on network 0035H = network name not found 0036H = network busy

0037H = device no longer exists on network
0038H = netBIOS command limit exceeded
0039H = error in network adapter hardware
003AH = incorrect response from network
003BH = unexpected network error
003CH = remote adapter is incompatible
003DH = print queue is full
003EH = not enough room for print file
003FH = print file was deleted
0040H = network name deleted
0041H = network access denied
0042H = incorrect network device type
0043H = network name not found
0044H = network name exceeded limit
0045H = netBIOS session limit exceeded
0046H = temporary pause
0047H = network request not accepted
0048H = print or disk redirection pause
0049H — 004FH reserved
0050H = file already exists
0051H = duplicate FCB
0052H = cannot make directory
0053H = failure in INT 24H (critical error)
0054H = too many redirections
0055H = duplicate redirection
0056H = invalid password
0057H = invalid parameter
0058H = network write failure
0059H = function not supported by network
005AH = required system component not installed
0065H = device not selected

Following are the error class codes as found in BH:

01H = no resources available
02H = temporary error
03H = authorization error
04H = internal software error
05H = hardware error
06H = system failure
07H = application software error
08H = item not found
09H = invalid format
0AH = item blocked
0BH = media error
0CH = item already exists
0DH = unknown error

Following is the recommended action as found in BL:

01H = retry operation
02H = delay and retry operation
03H = user retry
04H = abort processing
05H = immediate exit
06H = ignore error
07H = retry with user intervention

Following is a list of locus in CH:

01H = unknown source
02H = block device error
03H = network area
04H = serial device error
05H = memory error

| 5AH | CREATE UNIQUE FILE NAME |

Entry	AH = 5AH CX = attribute code DS:DX = address of the ASCII-Z string directory path
Exit	Carry is set for error condition AX = file handle if carry cleared DS:DX = address of the appended directory name
Notes	The ASCII-Z file directory path must end with a backslash (\). On exit the directory name is appended with a unique file name.

5BH   CREATE A DOS FILE

Entry	AH = 5BH CX = attribute code DS:DX = address of the ASCII-Z string contain the file name
Exit	Carry is set for error condition AX = file handle if carry cleared
Notes	The function only works in DOS version 3.X or higher.

5CH   LOCK/UNLOCK FILE CONTENTS

Entry	AH = 5CH BX = file handle CX:DX = offset address of locked/unlocked area SI:DI = number of bytes to lock or unlock beginning at offset
Exit	Carry is set for error condition

5DH   SET EXTENDED ERROR INFORMATION

Entry	AH = 5DH AL = 0AH DS:DX = address of the extended error data structure
Notes	This function is used by DOS version 3.1 or higher to store extended error information.

5EH   NETWORK/PRINTER

Entry	AH = 5EH AL = 00H (get network name) DS:DX = address of the ASCII-Z string containing network name
Exit	Carry is set for error condition CL = netBIOS number if carry cleared
Entry	AH = 5EH AL = 02H (define network printer) BX = redirection list CX = length of setup string DS:DX = address of printer setup buffer
Exit	Carry is set for error condition
Entry	AH = 5EH AL = 03H (read network printer setup string) BX = redirection list

	DS:DX = address of printer setup buffer
Exit	Carry is set for error condition CX = length of setup string if carry cleared ES:DI = address of printer setup buffer

62H	GET PSP ADDRESS
Entry	AH = 62H
Exit	BX = segment address of the current program
Notes	The function only works in DOS version 3.0 or higher.

65H	GET EXTENDED COUNTRY INFORMATION
Entry	AH = 65H AL = function code ES:DI = address of buffer to receive information
Exit	Carry is set for error condition CX = length of country information
Notes	The function only works in DOS version 3.3 or higher.

66H	GET/SET CODE PAGE
Entry	AH = 66H AL = function code BX = code page number
Exit	Carry is set for error condition BX = active code page number DX = default code page number
Notes	A function code in AL of 01H gets the code page number and a code of 02H sets the code page number

67H	SET HANDLE COUNT
Entry	AH = 67H BX = number of handles desired
Exit	Carry is set for error condition
Notes	This function is available for DOS version 3.3 or higher

68H	COMMIT FILE
Entry	AH = 68H BX = handle number
Exit	Carry is set for error condition Else, the date and time stamp is written to directory
Notes	This function is available for DOS version 3.3 or higher

6CH	EXTENDED OPEN FILE

Entry	AH = 6CH AL = 00H BX = open mode CX = attributes DX = open flag DS:SI = address of ASCII-Z string file name
Exit	AX = error code if carry is set AX = handle if carry is cleared CX = 0001H file existed and was opened CX = 0002H file did not exist and was created
Notes	This function is available for DOS version 4.0 or higher

BIOS FUNCTION CALLS

In addition to DOS function call INT 21H, some other BIOS function calls prove useful in controlling the I/O environment of the computer. Unlike INT 21H, which exists in the DOS program, the BIOS function calls are found stored in the BIOS ROM. These BIOS functions directly control the I/O devices with or without DOS loaded into a system.

INT 10H

The INT 10H BIOS interrupt is often called the video services interrupt because it directly controls the video display in a system. The INT 10H instruction uses register AH to select the video service provided by this interrupt.

Video Mode Selection.   The mode of operation for the video display is selected by placing a 00H into AH followed by one of many mode numbers in AL. Table A–3 lists the modes of operation found in video display systems using standard video modes. The VGA can use any mode listed, while the other displays are more restrictive in use. Additional higher resolution modes are explained later in this section.

Example A–6 lists a short sequence of instructions that place the video display in mode 03H. This mode is available on CGA, EGA, and VGA displays. This mode allows the display to draw a test with 16 colors at various resolutions dependent upon the display adapter.

EXAMPLE A–6

```
0000 B4 00          MOV     AH,0        ;select mode
0002 B0 03          MOV     AL,3        ;mode is 03H
0004 CD 10          INT     10H
```

TABLE A–3 Video display modes

Mode	Type	Columns	Rows	Resolution	Standard	Colors
00H	Text	40	25	320 × 200	CGA	2
00H	Text	40	25	320 × 350	EGA	2
00H	Text	40	25	360 × 400	VGA	2
01H	Text	40	25	320 × 200	CGA	16
01H	Text	40	25	320 × 350	EGA	16
01H	Text	40	25	360 × 400	VGA	16
02H	Text	80	25	640 × 200	CGA	2
02H	Text	80	25	640 × 350	EGA	2
02H	Text	80	25	720 × 400	VGA	2
03H	Text	80	25	640 × 200	CGA	16
03H	Text	80	25	640 × 350	EGA	16
03H	Text	80	25	720 × 400	VGA	16
04H	Graphics	40	25	320 × 200	CGA	4
05H	Graphics	40	25	320 × 200	CGA	2
06H	Graphics	80	25	640 × 200	CGA	2
07H	Text	80	25	720 × 350	EGA	4
07H	Text	80	25	720 × 400	VGA	4
0DH	Graphics	80	25	320 × 200	CGA	16
0EH	Graphics	80	25	640 × 200	CGA	16
0FH	Graphics	80	25	640 × 350	EGA	4
10H	Graphics	80	25	640 × 350	EGA	16
11H	Graphics	80	30	640 × 480	VGA	2
12H	Graphics	80	30	640 × 480	VGA	16
13H	Graphics	40	25	320 × 200	VGA	256

Cursor Control. Table A–4 shows the function codes used to control the cursor on the video display. These cursor control functions will work on any video display from the CGA display to the latest super VGA display.

If an SVGA (super VGA), EVGA (extended VGA), or XVGA (also extended VGA) adaptor is available, the super VGA mode is set by using INT 10H function call AX = 4F02H, with BX = to the VGA mode for these advanced display adaptors. This setup conforms to the VESA standard for VGA adaptors. Table A–5 shows the modes selected by register BX for this INT 10H function call.

INT 11H

This function is used to determine the type of equipment installed in the system. To use this call, the AX register is loaded with an FFFFH, and then the INT 11H instruction is executed. In return, an INT 11H provides information as listed in Figure A–7.

TABLE A–4   Cursor control functions

AH	Description	Parameters
01H	Sets the cursor type	CH = start line and CL = end line
02H	Sets cursor position	DH = row, DL = column, and BH = page number
03H	Read cursor position	BH = page number, DH = row, DL = column, CH = cursor start line, and CL = cursor end line
04H	Read light pen	DH = row, DL = column, CX = pixel row, and BX = pixel column
05H	Select display page	AL = page number (0–7)
06H	Scroll page up	AL = number of lines to scroll (0 clears window), BH = attribute, CH = top scroll window row, CL = left scroll window column, DH = bottom scroll window row, and DL = bottom scroll window column
07H	Scroll page down	same as function 06H
08H	Read current cursor position	BH = page number, AL = ASCII character, and AH = attribute
09H	Write cursor position	BH = page number, AL = ASCII character, BL = attribute, CX = number of characters
0AH	Same as 09H except no attribute is written	
0BH	Set color palette	BH = palette color and BL = background in graphics mode or border color in text mode
0CH	Write dot	AL = color, BH = page number, CX = pixel column, and DX = pixel row
0DH	Read dot	BH = page number, CX = pixel column, and DX = pixel row, AL = color

TABLE A–5   Extended VGA functions

BX	Function
100H	640 × 400 with 256 colors
101H	640 × 480 with 256 colors
102H	800 × 600 with 16 colors
103H	800 × 600 with 256 colors
104H	1,024 × 768 with 16 colors
105H	1,024 × 768 with 256 colors
106H	1,280 × 1,024 with 16 colors
107H	1,280 × 1,024 with 256 colors
108H	80 × 60 in text mode
109H	132 × 25 in text mode
10AH	132 × 43 in text mode
10BH	132 × 50 in text mode
10CH	132 × 60 in text mode

FIGURE A–7 The contents of AX as it indicates the equipment attached to the computer.

15	14	13	12	11	10	9	8	7	6	5	4	3	2	1	0
P1	P0		G	S2	S1	S0	D2	D1							

P1, P0 = number of parallel ports
G = 1 if game I/O attached
S2, S1, S0 = number of serial ports
D2, D1 = number of disk drives

INT 12H

The memory size is returned by the INT 12H instruction. After executing the INT 12H instruction, the AX register contains the number of 1 K-byte blocks of memory (conventional memory in the first 1M byte of address space) installed in the computer.

INT 13H

This call controls the diskettes ($5\frac{1}{4}''$ or $3\frac{1}{2}''$) and also fixed or hard disk drives attached to the system. Table A–6 lists the functions available to this interrupt via

TABLE A–6 Disk I/O function via INT 13H

AH	Function
00H	Reset disk system
01H	Get disk system status into AL
02H	Read sector
03H	Write sector
04H	Verify sector
05H	Format track
06H	Format bad track
07H	Format drive
08H	Get drive parameters
09H	Initialize fixed disk characteristics
0AH	Read long sector
0BH	Write long sector
0CH	Seek
0DH	Reset fixed disk system
0EH	Read sector buffer
0FH	Write sector buffer
10H	Get drive status
11H	Recalibrate drive
12H	Controller RAM diagnostics
13H	Controller drive diagnostics
14H	Controller internal diagnostics
15H	Get disk type
16H	Get disk change status
17H	Set disk type
18H	Set media type
19H	Park heads
1AH	Format ESDI drive

TABLE A–7 COM port
interrupt INT 14H

AH	Function
00H	Initialize communications port
01H	Send character
02H	Receive character
03H	Get COM port status
04H	Extended initialize communications port
05H	Extended communications port control

register AH. The direct control of a floppy disk or hard disk can lead to problems. Therefore we provide only a listing of the functions without details on their usage. Before using these functions refer to the BIOS literature available from the company that produced your version of the BIOS ROM.

INT 14H

Interrupt 14H controls the serial COM (communications) ports attached to the computer. The computer system contains two COM ports, COM1 and COM2, unless you have a newer AT-style machine where the number of communications ports is extended to COM3 and COM4. Communications ports are normally controlled with software packages that allow data transfer through a modem and the telephone lines. The INT 14H instruction controls these ports, as illustrated in Table A–7.

INT 15H

The INT 15H instruction controls many of the various I/O devices interfaced to the computer. It also allows access to protected mode operation and the extended memory system on an 80286, 80386, or 80486 system. Table A–8 lists the functions supported by INT 15H.

INT 16H

The INT 16H instruction is used as a keyboard interrupt. This interrupt is accessed by DOS interrupt INT 21H, but can be accessed directly. Table A–9 shows the functions performed by INT 16H.

INT 17H

The INT 17H instruction accesses the parallel printer port usually labeled LPT1 in most systems. Table A–10 lists the three functions available for the INT 17H instruction.

DOS System Memory Map

Figure A–8 illustrates the memory map used by a DOS computer system. The first 1M byte of memory is listed with all the areas containing different devices and programs used with DOS. The transient program area (TPA) is where DOS applications

TABLE A–8 The I/O subsystem interrupt INT 15H

AH	Function
00H	Cassette motor on
01H	Cassette motor off
02H	Read cassette
03H	Write cassette
0FH	Format ESDI drive periodic interrupt
21H	Keyboard intercept
80H	Device open
81H	Device closed
82H	Process termination
83H	Event wait
84H	Read joystick
85H	System request key
86H	Delay
87H	Move extended block of memory
88H	Get extended memory size
89H	Enter protected mode
90H	Device wait
91H	Device power on self-test (POST)
C0H	Get system environment
C1H	Get address of extended BIOS data area
C2H	Mouse pointer
C3H	Set watch-dog timer
C4H	Programmable option select

TABLE A–9 Keyboard interrupt INT 16H

AH	Function
00H	Read keyboard character
01H	Get keyboard status
02H	Get keyboard flags
03H	Set repeat rate
04H	Set keyclick
05H	Push character and scan code

TABLE A–10 Parallel printer interrupt INT 17H

AH	Function
00H	Print character
01H	Initialize printer
02H	Get printer status

FIGURE A–8   Memory map of DOS illustrating the first 1M byte of memory.

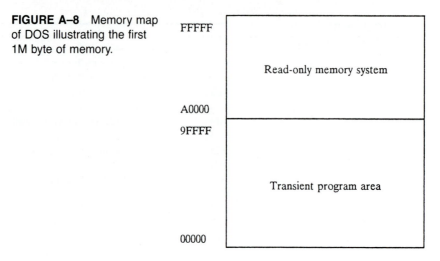

programs are loaded and executed. The size of the TPA is usually slightly over 500K bytes, unless many TSR programs and drivers fill memory before the TPA.

DOS Low Memory Assignments

Table A–11 shows the low memory assignments (00000H–005FFH) for the DOS-based microprocessor system. This area of memory contains the interrupt vectors, BIOS data area, and the DOS/BIOS data area illustrated in Figure A–8.

TABLE A–11   DOS low memory assignments

Location	Purpose
00000H–002FFH	System interrupt vectors
00300H–003FFH	System interrupt vectors, power on, and bootstrap area
00400H–00407H	COM1–COM4 I/O port base addresses
00408H–0040FH	LPT1–LPT4 I/O port base addresses
00410H–00411H	Equipment flag word, returned in AX by an INT 11H

	Bit	Purpose
	15–14	Number of parallel printers (LPT1–LPT4)
	13	Internal MODEM installed
	12	Joystick installed
	11–9	Number of serial ports (COM1–COM4)
	8	Unused
	7–6	Number of disk drives
	5–4	Video mode
	3–2	Unused
	1	Math coprocessor installed
	0	Disk installed

TABLE A–11   (*continued*)

Location	Purpose
00412H	Reserved
00413H–00414H	Memory size in kilobytes (0–640K)
00415H–00416H	Reserved
00417H	Keyboard control byte

Bit	Purpose
7	Insert locked
6	Caps locked
5	Numbers locked
4	Scroll locked
3	Alternate key pressed
2	Control key pressed
1	Left shift key pressed
0	Right shift key pressed

Location	Purpose
00418H	Keyboard control byte

Bit	Purpose
7	Insert key pressed
6	Caps lock key pressed
5	Numbers lock key pressed
4	Scroll lock key pressed
3	Pause locked
2	System request key pressed
1	Left alternate key pressed
0	Right control key pressed

Location	Purpose
00419H	Alternate keyboard entry
0041AH–0041BH	Keyboard buffer header pointer
0041CH–0041DH	Keyboard buffer tail pointer
0041EH–0043DH	32-byte keyboard buffer area
0043EH–00448H	Disk drive control area
00449H–00466H	Video control data area
00467H–0046BH	Reserved
0046CH–0046FH	Timer counter
00470H	Timer overflow
00471H	Break key state
00472H–00473H	Reset flag
00474H–00477H	Hard disk drive data area
00478H–0047BH	LPT1–LPT4 timeout area
0047CH–0047FH	COM1–COM4 timeout area
00480H–00481H	Keyboard buffer start offset pointer
00482H–00483H	Keyboard buffer end offset pointer
00484H–0048AH	Video control data area
0048BH–00495H	Hard drive control area

TABLE A–11   *(continued)*

Location	*Purpose*
00496H	Keyboard mode, state, and type flag
00497H	Keyboard LED flags
00498H–00499H	Offset address of user wait complete flag
0049AH–0049BH	Segment address of user wait complete flag
0049CH–0049DH	User wait count (low word)
0049EH–0049FH	User wait count (high word)
004A0H	Wait active flag
004A1H–004A7H	Reserved
004A8H–004ABH	Pointer to video parameters
004ACH–004EFH	Reserved
004F0H–004FFH	Applications program communications area
00500H	Print screen status
00501H–00503H	Reserved
00504H	Single drive mode status
00505H–0050FH	Reserved
00510H–00521H	Used by ROM BASIC
00522H–0052FH	Used by DOS for disk initialization
00530H–00533H	Used by MODE command
00534H–005FFH	Reserved

DOS VERSION 5.0 MEMORY MAP

Microsoft DOS version 5.0 has a slightly different memory map than earlier versions of DOS because of its ability to load drivers and programs in the system area. If the microprocessor is an 80386 or 80486, memory between the ROM memory located between addresses A0000H and FFFFFH can be backfilled with extended memory for drivers and programs. In many systems memory area D0000H–DFFFFH is unused, as is E0000H–EFFFFH. These areas can be filled with extended memory through memory paging found in the 80386 and 80486 microprocessors. This new memory area can then be filled with and addressed by normal real mode memory programs extending the memory available to DOS applications.

The drivers HIMEM.SYS and EMM386.SYS are used to accomplish the backfilling. If we want to use memory area E0000H–EFFFFH, we must load EMM386.SYS as EMM386.SYS I = E000-EFFF. Using these drivers increases the DOS TPA to more than 600K bytes. Typical CONFIG.SYS files and AUTOEXEC.BAT for DOS 5.0 appear in Example A–7. Notice that drivers after EMM386.SYS are loaded in high memory with the DEVICEHIGH directive instead of the DEVICE directive. Programs are loaded using the LOADHIGH or LH directive in front of the program name.

EXAMPLE A–7

(CONFIG.SYS file)

```
FILES=30
BUFFERS=30
STACKS=64,128
FCBS=48
SHELL=C:\DOS\COMMAND.COM C:\DOS\ /E:256 /P
DEVICE=C:\DOS\HIMEM.SYS
DOS=HIGH,UMB
DEVICE=C:\DOS\EMM386.EXE I=C800-EFFF NOEMS
DEVICEHIGH SIZE=1EB0 C:\LASERLIB\SONY_CDU.SYS /D:SONY_001 /B:340 /Q:* /T:* /M:H
DEVICEHIGH SIZE=0190 C:\DOS\SETVER.EXE
DEVICEHIGH SIZE=3150 C:\MOUSE1\MOUSE.SYS
LASTDRIVE = F
```

(AUTOEXEC.BAT file)

```
PATH C:\DOS;C:\;C:\MASM\BIN;C:\MASM\BINB\;C:\UTILITY;C:\WS;C:\LASERLIB
SET BLASTER=A220 I7 D1 T3
SET INCLUDE=C:\MASM\INCLUDE\
SET HELPFILES=C:\MASM\HELP\*.HLP
SET INIT=C:\MASM\INIT\
SET ASMEX=C:\MASM\SAMPLES\
SET TMP=C:\MASM\TMP
SET SOUND=C:\SB
LOADHIGH C:\LASERLIB\MSCDEX.EXE /D:SONY_001 /L:F /M:8
LOADHIGH C:\LASERLIB\LLTSR.EXE ALT-Q
LOADHIGH C:\DOS\FASTOPEN C:=256
LOADHIGH C:\DOS\DOSKEY /BUFSIZE=1024
LOADHIGH C:\LASERLIB\PRINTF.COM
DOSKEY GO=DOSSHELL
DOSSHELL
```

APPENDIX B

Instruction Set Summary

The instruction set summary, which follows this introduction, contains a complete listing of all instructions for the 80286, 80386, and 80486 microprocessors. Note that numeric coprocessor instructions for the 80486 appear in Chapter 12.

Each instruction entry lists the mnemonic opcode plus a brief description of the purpose of the instruction. Also listed is the binary machine language coding for each instruction plus any other data required to form the instruction, such as displacement or immediate data. Next to the binary machine language version of the instruction appears the flag register bits and any change that might occur for a given instruction. In this listing a blank indicates no change, a ? indicates a change with an unpredictable outcome, an * indicates a predictable change, a 1 indicates the flag is set, and a 0 indicates the flag is cleared.

Before the instruction listing begins, some information about the bit settings in the binary machine language versions of the instructions is required. Table B–1 shows the modifier bits, coded as oo in the instruction listings, so instructions can be formed with a register, displacement, or no displacement.

Table B–2 lists the memory-addressing modes available with the register/memory field, coded as mmm. This table applies to all versions of the microprocessor.

Table B–3 lists the register options (rrr) when encoded for either an 8-bit or a 16-bit register. This table also lists the 32-bit registers used with the 80386 and 80486 microprocessors.

TABLE B–1 The modifier bits, coded as oo in the instruction listing

oo	Function
00	If mmm = 110, then a displacement follows the opcode; otherwise, no displacement is used
01	An 8-bit signed displacement follows the opcode
10	A 16-bit signed displacement follows the opcode
11	mmm specifies a register instead of an addressing mode

Table B-4 lists the segment register bit assignements (rrr) for the MOV, PUSH, and POP instructions, which use these segment registers.

When the 80386 and 80486 microprocessors are used, some of the definitions provided in the prior tables will change. Refer to Tables B–5 and Table B–6 for these changes as they apply to the 80386 and 80486 microprocessors.

TABLE B–2 Register/memory field (mmm) description

mmm	Function
000	DS:[BX+SI]
001	DS:[BX+DI]
010	SS:[BP+SI]
011	SS:[BP+DI]
100	DS:[SI]
101	DS:[DI]
110	SS:[BP]
111	DS:[BX]

TABLE B–3 Register field (rrr) options

rrr	W = 0	W = 1	reg32
000	AL	AX	EAX
001	CL	CX	ECX
010	DL	DX	EDX
011	BL	BX	EBX
100	AH	SP	ESP
101	CH	BP	EBP
110	DH	SI	ESI
111	BH	DI	EDI

TABLE B–4 Register field assignments (rrr) that are used to represent the segment registers

rrr	Register
000	ES
001	CS
010	SS
011	DS

TABLE B–5 Index registers are specified with rrr in the 80386 and 80486 microprocessor

rrr	Index Register
000	EAX
001	ECX
010	EDX
011	EBX
100	No index
101	EBP
110	ESI
111	EDI

TABLE B–6 Possible combinations of oo, mmm, and rrr for the 80386 and 80486 instruction set using the 32-bit addressing mode

oo	mmm	rrr	Function
00	000	—	DS:[EAX]
00	001	—	DS:[ECX]
00	010	—	DS:[EDX]
00	011	—	DS:[EBX]
00	100	000	DS:[EAX+scaled−index]
00	100	001	DS:[ECX+scaled−index]
00	100	010	DS:[EDX+scaled−index]
00	100	011	DS:[EBX+scaled−index]
00	100	100	SS:[ESP+scaled−index]
00	100	101	DS:[disp32+scaled−index]
00	100	110	DS:[ESI+scaled−index]
00	100	111	DS:[EDI+scaled−index]
00	101	—	DS:disp32
00	110	—	DS:[ESI]
00	111	—	DS:[EDI]
01	000	—	DS:[EAX+disp8]
01	001	—	DS:[ECX+disp8]
01	010	—	DS:[EDX+disp8]
01	011	—	DS:[EBX+disp8]
01	100	000	DS:[EAX+scaled−index + disp8]
01	100	001	DS:[ECX+scaled−index + disp8]
01	100	010	DS:[EDX+scaled−index + disp8]
01	100	011	DS:[EBX+scaled−index + disp8]
01	100	100	SS:[ESP+scaled−index + disp8]
01	100	101	SS:[EBP+scaled−index + disp8]
01	100	110	DS:[ESI+scaled −index + disp8]
01	100	111	DS:[EDI+scaled−index + disp8]
01	101	—	SS:[EBP+disp8]
01	110	—	DS:[ESI+disp8]
01	111	—	DS:[EDI+disp8]
10	000	—	DS:[EAX+disp32]
10	001	—	DS:[ECX+disp32]
10	010	—	DS:[EDX+disp32]
10	011	—	DS:[EBX+disp32]
10	100	000	DS:[EAX+scaled−index + disp32]
10	100	001	DS:[ECX+scaled−index + disp32]
10	100	010	DS:[EDX+scaled−index + disp32]
10	100	011	DS:[EBX+scaled−index + disp32]
10	100	100	SS:[ESP+scaled−index + disp32]
10	100	101	SS:[EBP+scaled−index + disp32]
10	100	110	DS:[ESI+scaled−index + disp32]
10	100	111	DS:[EDI+scaled−index + disp32]
01	101	—	SS:[EBP+disp32]
01	110	—	DS:[ESI+disp32]
01	111	—	DS:[EDI+disp32]

Notes: disp8 = 8-bit displacement, disp32 = 32-bit displacement.

The instruction set summary that follows lists all of the instructions, with examples, for the 80286, 80386, and 80486 microprocessors. Missing are the segment override prefixes: CS (2EH), SS (36H), DS (3EH), ES (26H), FS (64H), and GS (65H). These prefixes are one byte in length and are placed in memory before the instruction that is prefixed.

The D-bit, in the code segment descriptor, indicates the default size of the operand and the addresses for the 80386 and 80486 microprocessors. If D = 1, then all addresses and operands are 32 bits and if D = 0, all addresses and operands are 16 bits. In the real mode, the D-bit is set to zero by the 80386 and 80486 microprocessors, so operands and addresses are 16 bits.

The address-size prefix (67H) must be placed before instructions in the 80386 and 80486 to change the default size as selected by the D-bit. For example, the MOV AX,[ECX] instruction must have the address-size prefix placed before it in machine code if the default size is 16 bits. If the default size is 32 bits, the address prefix is not needed with this instruction. The operand-override prefix (66H) functions in much the same manner as the address-size prefix. In the previous example, the operand size is 16 bits. If the D-bit selects 32-bit operands and addresses, this instruction requires the operand-size prefix.

INSTRUCTION SET SUMMARY

AAA	ASCII adjust after addition		
00110111		O D I T S Z A P C ? ? ? * ? *	
Example			Clocks
AAA		80286	3
		80386	4
		80486	3

AAD	ASCII adjust before division		
11010101 00001010		O D I T S Z A P C ? * * ? * ?	
Example			Clocks
AAD		80286	14
		80386	19
		80486	14

AAM	ASCII adjust after multiplication		

11010100 00001010			O D I T S Z A P C ? * * ? * ?
Example			Clocks
AAM		80286	16
		80386	17
		80486	15

AAS   ASCII adjust after subtraction

00111111			O D I T S Z A P C ? ? ? * ? *
Example			Clocks
AAS		80286	3
		80386	4
		80486	3

ADC   Addition with carry

000100dw oorrrmmm disp			O D I T S Z A P C * * * * * *
Format	Examples		Clocks
ADC reg,reg	ADC AX,BX ADC AL,BL ADC EAX,EBX ADC CX,SI ADC ESI,EDI	80286	2
		80386	2
		80486	1
ADC mem,reg	ADC DATA,AL ADC LIST,SI ADC DATA[DI],CL ADC [EAX],AL ADC [EBX+2*ECX],EDX	80286	7
		80386	7
		80486	3
ADC reg,mem	ADC BL,DATA ADC SI,LIST ADC CL,DATA[DI] ADC CL,[EAX] ADC EDX,[EBX+100H]	80286	7
		80386	6
		80486	2

100000sw oo010mmm disp data			
Format	Examples		Clocks
ADC reg,imm	ADC CX,3 ADC DI,1AH ADC DL,34H ADC EAX,12345 ADC CX,1234H	80286	3
		80386	2
		80486	1
ADC mem,imm	ADC DATA,33 ADC LIST,'A' ADC DATA[DI],2 ADC BYTE PTR [EAX],3 ADC WORD PTR[DI],669H	80286	7
		80386	7
		80486	3

0001010w data

Format	Examples		
ADC acc,imm	ADC AX,3 ADC AL,1AH ADC AH,34 ADC EAX,3 ADC AL,'Z'	80286	3
		80386	2
		80486	1

ADD Addition

000000dw oorrrmmm disp

	O	D	I	T	S	Z	A	P	C
	*				*	*	*	*	*

Format	Examples		

ADD reg,reg	ADD AX,BX
	ADD AL,BL
	ADD EAX,EBX
	ADD CX,SI
	ADD ESI,EDI
		80286	2

		80386	2
		80486	1

ADD mem,reg	ADD DATA,AL
	ADD LIST,SI
	ADD DATA[DI],CL
	ADD [EAX],AL
	ADD [EBX+2*ECX],EDX
		80286	7

		80386	7
		80486	3

ADD reg,mem	ADD BL,DATA
	ADD SI,LIST
	ADD CL,DATA[DI]
	ADD CL,[EAX]
	ADD EDX,[EBX+100H]
		80286	7

		80386	6
		80486	2

100000sw oo000mmm disp data

Format	Examples		

ADD reg,imm	ADD CX,3
	ADD DI,1AH
	ADD DL,34H
	ADD EAX,12345
	ADD CX,1234H
		80286	3

		80386	2
		80486	1

ADD mem,imm	ADD DATA,33
	ADD LIST,'A'
	ADD DATA[DI],2
	ADD BYTE PTR [EAX],3
	ADD WORD PTR[DI],669H
		80286	7

		80386	7
		80486	3

0000010w data

Format	Examples		

ADD acc,imm	ADD AX,3
	ADD AL,1AH
	ADD AH,34
	ADD EAX,3
	ADD AL,'Z'
		80286	3

		80386	2
		80486	1

AND Logical AND

001000dw oorrrmmm disp

	O	D	I	T	S	Z	A	P	C
	0				*	*	?	*	0

Format	Examples		Clocks
AND reg,reg	AND CX,BX AND DL,BL AND ECX,EBX AND BP,SI AND EDX,EDI	80286	2
		80386	2
		80486	1
AND mem,reg	AND BIT,CH AND LIST,DI AND DATA[BX],CL AND [ECX],AL AND [EDX+4*ECX],EDI	80286	7
		80386	7
		80486	3
AND reg,mem	AND BL,DATA AND SI,LIST AND CL,DATA[DI] AND CL,[EAX] AND EDX,[EBX+100H]	80286	7
		80386	6
		80486	2

100000sw oo100mmm disp data

Format	Examples		Clocks
AND reg,imm	AND BP,1 AND DI,10H AND DL,34H AND EBP,12345 AND SP,1234H	80286	3
		80386	2
		80486	1
AND mem,imm	AND DATA,33 AND LIST,4 AND DATA[SI],2 AND BYTE PTR[EAX],3 AND WORD PTR[DI],669H	80286	7
		80386	7
		80486	3

0010010w data

Format	Examples		Clocks
AND acc,imm	AND AX,15 AND AL,1FH AND AH,34 AND EAX,3 AND AL,'R'	80286	3
		80386	2
		80486	1

ARPL   Adjust requested privilege level

01100011 oorrrmmm disp		O D I T S Z A P C *	

Format	Examples		Clocks
ARPL reg,reg	ARPL AX,BX ARPL BX,SI ARPL CX,DX ARPL BX,AX ARPL DI,SI	80286	10
		80386	20
		80486	9
ARPL mem,reg	ARPL NUMB,AX ARPL LIST,DI ARPL DATA[BX],CX ARPL [ECX],AX ARPL EDX+4*ECX],DI	80286	11
		80386	21
		80486	9

BOUND   Check array bounds

01100010 oorrmmm disp		O D I T S Z A P C	
Format	**Examples**		**Clocks**
BOUND reg,mem	BOUND AX,BETS BOUND BX,SAID BOUND CX,DATA BOUND BX,[DI] BOUND DI,[BX+2]	80286	13
		80386	10
		80486	7

BSF   Bit scan forward

00001111 10111100 oorrmmm disp		O D I T S Z A P C 　　　　　*	
Format	**Examples**		**Clocks**
BSF reg,reg	BSF AX,BX BSF BX,SI BSF ECX,EBX BSF EBX,EAX BSF DI,SI	80286	—
		80386	10+3n
		80486	6—42
BSF reg,mem	BSF AX,DATA BSF BP,LISTG BSF ECX,MEMORY BSF EAX,DATA6 BSF DI,[ECX]	80286	—
		80386	10+3n
		80486	7—43

BSR   Bit scan reverse

00001111 10111101 oorrmmm disp		O D I T S Z A P C 　　　　　*	
Format	**Examples**		**Clocks**
BSR reg,reg	BSR AX,BX BSR BX,SI BSR ECX,EBX BSR EBX,EAX BSR DI,SI	80286	—
		80386	10+3n
		80486	6—103
BSR reg,mem	BSR AX,DATA BSR BP,LISTG BSR ECX,MEMORY BSR EAX,DATA6 BSR DI,[ECX]	80286	—
		80386	10+3n
		80486	7—104

BSWAP   Byte swap

00001111 11001rrr		O D I T S Z A P C	
Format	**Examples**		**Clocks**
BSWAP reg	BSWAP EAX BSWAP EBX BSWAP ECX BSWAP EDX	80286	—
		80386	—

	BSWAP EDI	80486	1

BT   Bit test

00001111 10111010 oo100mmm disp data			O D I T S Z A P C*

Format	Examples		Clocks
BT reg,imm8	BT AX,2 BT CX,4 BT BP,10H BT CX,8 BT BX,2	80286	—
		80386	3
		80486	3
BT mem,imm8	BT DATA1,2 BT LIST,2 BT DATA[DI],2 BT [BX],1 BT FROG,3	80286	—
		80386	6
		80486	3

00001111 10100011 disp			

Format	Examples		Clocks
BT reg,reg	BT AX,CX BT CX,DX BT BP,AX BT SI,CX BT CX,BP	80286	—
		80386	3
		80486	3
BT mem,reg	BT DATA1,AX BT LIST,DX BT DATA3,CX BT DATA9,BX BT DATA[DI],AX	80286	—
		80386	12
		80486	8

BTC   Bit test and complement

00001111 10111010 oo111mmm disp data			O D I T S Z A P C*

Format	Examples		Clocks
BTC reg,imm8	BTC AX,2 BTC CX,4 BTC BP,10H BTC CX,8 BTC BX,2	80286	—
		80386	6
		80486	6
BTC mem,imm8	DATA1,2 BTC LIST,2 BTC DATA[DI],2 BTC [BX],1 BTC FROG,3	80286	—
		80386	8
		80486	8

00001111 10111011 disp			

Format	Examples		Clocks
BTC reg,reg	BTC AX,CX BTC CX,DX BTC BP,AX BTC SI,CX BTC CX,BP	80286	—
		80386	6
		80486	6

BTC mem,reg	BTC DATA1,AX	80286	—
	BTC LIST,DX		
	BTC DATA3,CX	80386	13
	BTC DATA9,BX		
	BTC DATA[DI],AX	80486	13

BTR   Bit test and reset

00001111 10111010 oo110mmm disp data		O D I T S Z A P C *	
Format	**Examples**		**Clocks**
BTR reg,imm8	BTR AX,2	80286	—
	BTR CX,4		
	BTR BP,10H	80386	6
	BTR CX,8		
	BTR BX,2	80486	6
BTR mem,imm8	BTR DATA1,2	80286	—
	BTR LIST,2		
	BTR DATA[DI],2	80386	8
	BTR [BX],1		
	BTR FROG,3	80486	8

00001111 10110011 disp			
Format	**Examples**		**Clocks**
BTR reg,reg	BTR AX,CX	80286	—
	BTR CX,DX		
	BTR BP,AX	80386	6
	BTR SI,CX		
	BTR CX,BP	80486	6
BTR mem,reg	BTR DATA1,AX	80286	—
	BTR LIST,DX		
	BTR DATA3,CX	80386	13
	BTR DATA9,BX		
	BTR DATA[DI],AX	80486	13

BTS   Bit test and set

00001111 10111010 oo101mmm disp data		O D I T S Z A P C *	
Format	**Examples**		**Clocks**
BTS reg,imm8	BTS AX,2	80286	—
	BTS CX,4		
	BTS BP,10H	80386	6
	BTS CX,8		
	BTS BX,2	80486	6
BTS mem,imm8	BTS DATA1,2	80286	—
	BTS LIST,2		
	BTS DATA[DI],2	80386	8
	BTS [BX],1		
	BTS FROG,3	80486	8

00001111 10101011 disp			
Format	**Examples**		**Clocks**

BTS reg,reg	BTS AX,CX	80286	—
	BTS CX,DX		
	BTS BP,AX	80386	6
	BTS SI,CX		
	BTS CX,BP	80486	6
BTS mem,reg	BTS DATA1,AX	80286	—
	BTS LIST,DX		
	BTS DATA3,CX	80386	13
	BTS DATA9,BX		
	BTS DATA[DI],AX	80486	13

CALL   Call procedure (subroutine)

11101000 disp   O D I T S Z A P C

Format	Examples		Clocks
CALL label (near)	CALL FOR_FUN	80286	7
	CALL HOME		
	CALL ET	80386	7
	CALL WAITING		
	CALL SAME	80486	3

10011010 disp

Format	Examples		Clocks
CALL label (far)	CALL FAR PTR DATES	80286	13
	CALL WHAT		
	CALL WHERE	80386	17
	CALL FARCE		
	CALL WHOM	80486	18

11111111 oo010mmm

Format	Examples		Clocks
CALL reg (near)	CALL AX	80286	7
	CALL BX		
	CALL CX	80386	7
	CALL DI		
	CALL SI	80486	5
CALL mem (near)	CALL ADDRESS	80286	11
	CALL [DI]		
	CALL DATA	80386	10
	CALL FROG		
	CALL HERO	80486	5

11111111 oo011mmm

Format	Examples		Clocks
CALL mem (far)	CALL FAR_LIST[SI]	80286	16
	CALL FROM_HERE		
	CALL TO_THERE	80386	22
	CALL SIXX		
	CALL OCT	80486	17

CBW   Convert byte to word

10011000   O D I T S Z A P C

Example	Clocks	
CBW	80286	2
	80386	3
	80486	3

CDQ Convert double word to quad word

10011001	O D I T S Z A P C

Example	Clocks	
CDQ	80286	—
	80386	2
	80486	2

CLC Clear carry flag

11111000	O D I T S Z A P C 0

Example	Clocks	
CLC	80286	2
	80386	2
	80486	2

CLD Clear direction flag

11111100	O D I T S Z A P C 0

Example	Clocks	
CLD	80286	2
	80386	2
	80486	2

CLI Clear interrupt flag

11111010	O D I T S Z A P C 0

Example	Clocks	
CLI	80286	3
	80386	3
	80486	5

CLTS   Clear task switched flag

00001111 00000110		O D I T S Z A P C
Example		**Clocks**
CLTS	80286	2
	80386	5
	80486	7

CMC   Complement carry flag

10011000		O D I T S Z A P C *
Example		**Clocks**
CMC	80286	2
	80386	2
	80486	2

CMP   Compare operands

001110dw oorrrmmm disp		O D I T S Z A P C * * * * * *
Format	**Examples**	**Clocks**

CMP reg,reg	CMP AX,BX
	CMP AL,BL
	CMP EAX,EBX
	CMP CX,SI
	CMP ESI,EDI
		80286	2

		80386	2
		80486	1

CMP mem,reg	CMP DATA,AL
	CMP LIST,SI
	CMP DATA[DI],CL
	CMP [EAX],AL
	CMP [EBX+2*ECX],EDX
		80286	7

		80386	5
		80486	2

CMP reg,mem	CMP BL,DATA
	CMP SI,LIST
	CMP CL,DATA[DI]
	CMP CL,[EAX]
	CMP EDX,[EBX+100H]
		80286	6

		80386	6
		80486	2

100000sw oo111mmm disp data		
Format	**Examples**	**Clocks**

CMP reg,imm	CMP CX,3
	CMP DI,1AH
	CMP DL,34H
	CMP EBX,12345
	CMP CX,1234H
		80286	3

		80386	2
		80486	1
CMP mem,imm	CMP DATA,33 CMP LIST,'A'	80286	6

	CMP DATA[DI],2 CMP BYTE PTR [EAX],3 CMP WORD PTR[DI],669H	80386	5
		80486	2

0011110w data

Format	Examples		Clocks

CMP acc,imm	CMP AX,3
	CMP AL,1AH
	CMP AH,34
	CMP EAX,3
	CMP AL,'Z'
		80286	3

		80386	2
		80486	1

CMPS   Compare strings

1010011w   O D I T S Z A P C
                                           *   * * * * *

Format	Examples		Clocks
CMPSB CMPSW CMPSD	CMPSB CMPSW CMPSD CMPS DATA1 REPE CMPSB	80286	8
		80386	10
		80486	8

CMPXCHG Compare and exchange

00001111 1011000w 11rrrrrr   O D I T S Z A P C
                                           *   * * * * *

Format	Examples		Clocks
CMPXCHG reg,reg	CMPXCHG EAX,EBX CMPXCHG ECX,EDX	80286	—
		80386	—
		80486	6

00001111 1011000w oorrrmmm

Format	Examples		Clocks
CMPXCHG mem,reg	CMPXCHG DATA,EAX CMPXCHG DATA2,EBX	80286	—
		80386	—
		80486	7

CWD   Convert word to double word

10011001   O D I T S Z A P C

Example		Clocks
CWD	80286	2
	80386	2
	80486	3

CWDE   Convert word to extended double word

10011000		O D I T S Z A P C
Example		Clocks
CWDE	80286	—
	80386	3
	80486	3

DAA   Decimal adjust after addition

00100111		O D I T S Z A P C ? * * * * *
Example		Clocks
DAA	80286	3
	80386	4
	80486	2

DAS   Decimal adjust after subtraction

00101111		O D I T S Z A P C ? * * * * *
Example		Clocks
DAS	80286	3
	80386	4
	80486	2

DEC   Decrement

1111111w oo001mmm disp		O D I T S Z A P C * * * * *
Format	Examples	Clocks
DEC reg8	DEC BL DEC BH DEC CL DEC DH DEC AH	80286	2
		80386	2
		80486	1
DEC mem	DEC DATA DEC LIST DEC DATA[DI] DEC BYTE PTR [EAX] DEC WORD PTR [DI]	80286	7
		80386	6
		80486	3

01001rrr		
Format	Examples	Clocks

DEC reg16 DEC reg32	DEC AX DEC EAX	80286	2
	DEC CX DEC EBX	80386	2
	DEC DI	80486	1

DIV Unsigned division

1111011w oo110mmm disp

O D I T S Z A P C
?   ? ? ? ? ?

Format	Examples		Clocks
DIV reg	DIV BL DIV BH	80286	22
	DIV ECX DIV BH	80386	38
	DIV CH	80486	40
DIV mem	DIV DATA DIV LIST	80286	25
	DIV DATA[DI] DIV BYTE PTR [EAX]	80386	41
	DIV WORD PTR [DI]	80486	40

ENTER Create a stack frame

11001000 data

O D I T S Z A P C

Format	Examples		Clocks
ENTER imm,0	ENTER 4,0 ENTER 8,0	80286	11
	ENTER 100,0 ENTER 200,0	80386	10
	ENTER 1024,0	80486	14
ENTER imm,1	ENTER 4,1 ENTER 10,1	80286	15
		80386	12
		80486	17
ENTER imm,imm	ENTER 3,6 ENTER 100,3	80286	12
		80386	15
		80486	17

ESC Escape

11011nnn oonnnmmm

O D I T S Z A P C

nnnnnn = opcode for coprocessor

Format	Examples		Clocks
ESC imm,reg	ESC 5,AL ESC 5,BH	80286	20
	ESC 6,CH	80386	var

		80486	var
ESC imm,mem	ESC 2,DATA ESC 3,FROG FADD DATA FMUL FROG	80286	20
		80386	var
		80486	var

HLT   Halt

11110100	O D I T S Z A P C

Example		Clocks
HLT	80286	2
	80386	5
	80486	4

IDIV   Signed division

1111011w oo111mmm disp	O D I T S Z A P C ? ? ? ? ?

Format	Examples		Clocks
IDIV reg	IDIV BL IDIV BH IDIV ECX IDIV BH IDIV CH	80286	25
		80386	43
		80486	43
IDIV mem	IDIV DATA IDIV LIST IDIV DATA[DI] IDIV BYTE PTR [EAX] IDIV WORD PTR [DI]	80286	28
		80386	46
		80486	44

IMUL   Signed multiplication

1111011w oo101mmm disp	O D I T S Z A P C * ? ? ? ? *

Format	Examples		Clocks
IMUL reg	IMUL BL IMUL CL IMUL CX IMUL ECX IMUL EBX	80286	21
		80386	38
		80486	42
IMUL mem	IMUL DATA IMUL LIST IMUL DATA[DI] IMUL BYTE PTR [EAX] IMUL WORD PTR [DI]	80286	24
		80386	41
		80486	42

011010sl oorrrmmm disp data

Format	Examples	Clocks

IMUL reg,imm	IMUL CX,16 IMUL DX,100 IMUL EAX,20	80286	21
		80386	38
		80486	42
IMUL reg,reg,imm	IMUL DX,AX,2 IMUL CX,DX,3 IMUL BX,AX,33	80286	21
		80386	38
		80486	42
IMUL reg,mem,imm	IMUL CX,DATA,4	80286	24
		80386	38
		80486	42

00001111 10101111 oorrrmmm disp			
Format	Examples		Clocks
IMUL reg,reg	IMUL CX,DX IMUL DX,BX IMUL EAX,ECX	80286	—
		80386	38
		80486	42
IMUL reg,mem	IMUL DX,DATA IMUL CX,FROG IMUL BX,LISTS	80286	—
		80386	41
		80486	42

IN   Input data from port

1110010w port number		O D I T S Z A P C	
Format	Examples		Clocks
IN acc,pt	IN AL,12H IN AX,12H IN AL,0FFH IN AX,0FFH IN EAX,10H	80286	5
		80386	12
		80486	14

1110110w			
Format	Examples		Clocks
IN acc,DX	IN AL,DX IN AX,DX IN EAX,DX	80286	5
		80386	13
		80486	14

INC   Increment

1111111w oo000mmm disp		O D I T S Z A P C * * * * *	
Format	Examples		Clocks
INC reg8	INC BL	80286	2

	INC BH INC CL INC DH		
	INC CL	80386	2
	INC DH		
	INC AH	80486	1
INC mem	INC DATA INC LIST	80286	7
	INC DATA[DI]	80386	6
	INC BYTE PTR [EAX] INC WORD PTR [DI]	80486	3

01000rrr			
Format	Examples		Clocks
INC reg16 INC reg32	INC AX INC EAX	80286	2
	INC CX INC EBX	80386	2
	INC DI	80486	1

INS   Input string from port

0110110w		O D I T S Z A P C	
Format	Examples		Clocks
INSB INSW INSD	INSB INSW	80286	5
	INSD INS DATA	80386	15
	REP INSB	80486	17

INT   Interrupt

11001101 type		O D I T S Z A P C	
Format	Examples		Clocks
INT type	INT 10H INT 255	80286	23
	INT 21H INT 20H	80386	37
	INT 15H	80486	30

11001100		
Example		Clocks
INT 3	80286	23
	80386	33
	80486	26

INTO   Interrupt on overflow

11001110	O D I T S Z A P C
Example	Clocks

INTO		80286	24
		80386	35
		80486	28

INVD   Invalidate data cache

00001111 00001000		O D I T S Z A P C	
Example		Clocks	
INVD		80286	—
		80386	—
		80486	4

INVLPG   Invalidate TLB entry

00001111 00000001 oo111mmm		O D I T S Z A P C	
Format	Examples	Clocks	
INVLPG mem	INVLPG DATA INVLPG LIST	80286	—
		80386	—
		80486	12

IRET   Interrupt return

11001101 data		O D I T S Z A P C * * * * * * * * *	
Format	Examples	Clocks	
IRET IRETD	IRET IRETD IRET 10H	80286	17
		80386	22
		80486	15

Jconditional   Conditional jump

0111cccc disp		O D I T S Z A P C	
Format	Examples	Clocks	
Jcc label	JA BELOW JB ABOVE JG GREATER JE EQUAL JZ ZERO	80286	7/3
		80386	7/3
		80486	3/1
00001111 1000cccc disp			

Format	Examples	Clocks	
Jcc label	JNE NOT_MORE JLE LESS_THAN	80286	—
		80386	7/3
		80486	3/1

Condition Codes	Mnemonic	Flag	Description
0000	JO	O = 1	Jump if overflow
0001	JNO	O = 0	Jump if no overflow
0010	JB/JNAE	C = 1	Jump if below
0011	JAE/JNB	C = 0	Jump if above or equal
0100	JE/JZ	Z = 1	Jump if equal/zero
0101	JNE/JNZ	Z = 0	Jump if not equal/not zero
0110	JBE/JNA	C = 1 + Z = 1	Jump if below or equal
0111	JA/JNBE	C = 0 • Z = 0	Jump if above
1000	JS	S = 1	Jump if sign
1001	JNS	S = 0	Jump if no sign
1010	JP/JPE	P = 1	Jump if parity even
1011	JNP/JPO	P = 0	Jump if parity odd
1100	JL/JNGE	S • O	Jump if less than
1101	JGE/JNL	S = O	Jump greater or equal
1110	JLE/JNG	Z = 1 + S • O	Jump if less than or equal
1111	JG/JNLE	Z = 0 + S = O	Jump if greater

JCXZ/JECXZ   Jump if CX (ECX) equals zero

11100011	O D I T S Z A P C

Format	Examples	Clocks	
JCXZ label JECXZ label	JCXZ LOTSA JCXZ OVER JECXZ UPPER JECXZ UNDER JCXZ NEXT	80286	8/4
		80386	9/5
		80486	8/5

JMP   Unconditional jump

11101011 disp	O D I T S Z A P C

Format	Examples	Clocks	
JMP label (short)	JMP SHORT UP JMP SHORT DOWN JMP SHORT OVER JMP SHORT CIRCUIT JMP SHORT ARM	80286	7
		80386	7
		80486	3

11101001 disp

Format	Examples	Clocks	
JMP label (near)	JMP VER JMP FROG JMP UNDER	80286	7
		80386	7
		80486	3

11101010 disp

Format	Examples		Clocks
JMP label (far)	JMP VER JMP FROG JMP UNDER JMP FAR PTR THERE	80286	11
		80386	12
		80486	17

11111111 oo100mmm

Format	Examples		Clocks
JMP reg (near)	JMP AX JMP EAX JMP CX JMP DX	80286	7
		80386	7
		80486	3
JMP mem (near)	JMP DATA JMP LIST JMP DATA[DI]	80286	11
		80386	10
		80486	5

11111111 oo101mmm

Format	Examples		Clocks
JMP mem (far)	JMP WAYOFF JMP TABLE JMP UP	80286	15
		80386	12
		80486	13

LAHF   Load AH from flags

10011111		O D I T S Z A P C

Example		Clocks
LAHF	80286	2
	80386	2
	80486	3

LAR   Load access rights

00001111 00000010 oorrrmmm disp		O D I T S Z A P C *

Format	Examples		Clocks
LAR reg,reg	LAR AX,BX LAR CX,DX LAR EAX,ECX	80286	14
		80386	15
		80486	11
LAR reg,mem	LAR CX,DATA LAR AX,LIST LAR ECX,FROG	80286	16
		80386	16

		80486	11

LDS   Load far pointer

11000101 oorrrmmm		O D I T S Z A P C

Format	Examples		Clocks

LDS reg,mem	LDS DI,DATA
	LDS SI,LIST
	LDS BX,ARRAY
	LDS CX,PNTR
		80286	7

		80386	7
		80486	6

LES   Load far pointer

11000100 oorrrmmm		O D I T S Z A P C

Format	Examples		Clocks
LES reg,mem	LES DI,DATA LES SI,LIST LES BX,ARRAY LES CX,PNTR	80286	7
		80386	7
		80486	6

LFS   Load far pointer

00001111 10110100 oorrrmmm disp		O D I T S Z A P C

Format	Examples		Clocks
LFS reg,mem	LFS DI,DATA LFS SI,LIST LFS BX,ARRAY LFS CX,PNTR	80286	—
		80386	7
		80486	6

LGS   Load far pointer

00001111 10110101 oorrrmmm disp		O D I T S Z A P C

Format	Examples		Clocks
LGS reg,mem	LGS DI,DATA LGS SI,LIST LGS BX,ARRAY LGS CX,PNTR	80286	—
		80386	7
		80486	6

LSS   Load far pointer

00001111 10110010 oorrrmmm disp		O D I T S Z A P C

Format	Examples	Clocks	
LSS reg,mem	LSS DI,DATA LSS SI,LIST LSS BX,ARRAY LSS CX,PNTR	80286	—
		80386	7
		80486	6

LEA   Load effective address

10001101 oorrrmmm disp		O D I T S Z A P C	
Format	Examples	Clocks	
LEA reg,mem	LEA DI,DATA LEA SI,LIST LEA BX,ARRAY LEA CX,PNTR LEA BP,ADDR	80286	3
		80386	2
		80486	2

LEAVE   Leave high-level procedure

11001001	O D I T S Z A P C	
Example	Clocks	
LEAVE	80286	5
	80386	4
	80486	5

LGDT   Load global descriptor table

00001111 00000001 oo010mmm disp		O D I T S Z A P C	
Format	Examples	Clocks	
LGDT mem64	LGDT DESCRIP LGDT TABLE	80286	11
		80386	11
		80486	11

LIDT   Load interrupt descriptor table

00001111 00000001 oo011mmm disp		O D I T S Z A P C	
Format	Examples	Clocks	
LIGT mem64	LIDT DATA LIDT DESCRIP	80286	12
		80386	11
		80486	11

LLDT   Load local descriptor table

00001111 00000000 oo010mmm disp		O D I T S Z A P C	
Format	Examples		Clocks
LLDT reg	LLDT AX LLDT CX	80286	17
		80386	20
		80486	11
LLDT mem	LLDT DATA LLDT LIST	80286	19
		80386	24
		80486	11

LMSW   Load machine status word

00001111 00000001 oo110mmm disp		O D I T S Z A P C	
should only be used with the 80286			
Format	Examples		Clocks
LMSW reg	LMSW AX LMSW CX	80286	3
		80386	10
		80486	2
LMSW mem	LMSW DATA LMSW LIST	80286	6
		80386	13
		80486	3

LOCK   Lock the bus

11110000		O D I T S Z A P C	
Format	Examples		Clocks
LOCK inst	LOCK:XCHG AX,BX LOCK:MOV AL,AH	80286	0
		80386	0
		80486	1

LODS   Load string operand

1010110w		O D I T S Z A P C	
Format	Examples		Clocks
LODSB LODSW LODSD	LODSB LODSW LODSD	80286	5
		80386	5

	LODS DATA LODS ES:DATA	80486	5

LOOP   Loop until CX = 0

11100010 disp		O D I T S Z A P C

Format	Examples		Clocks
LOOP label	LOOP DATA LOOP BACK	80286	8/4
		80386	11
		80486	7/6

LOOPE   Loop while equal

11100001 disp		O D I T S Z A P C

Format	Examples		Clocks
LOOPE label LOOPZ label	LOOPE NEXT LOOPE AGAIN LOOPZ REPEAT	80286	8/4
		80386	11
		80486	9/6

LOOPNE   Loop while not equal

11100000 disp		O D I T S Z A P C

Format	Examples		Clocks
LOOPNE label LOOPNZ label	LOOPNE AGAIN LOOPNE BACK LOOPNZ REPL	80286	8/4
		80386	11
		80486	9/6

LSL   Load segment limit

00001111 00000011 oorrrmmm disp		O D I T S Z A P C *

Format	Examples		Clocks
LSL reg,reg	LSL AX,BX LSL CX,BX LSL DX,AX	80286	14
		80386	25
		80486	10
LSL reg,mem	LSL AX,LIMIT LSL EAX,NUMB	80286	16
		80386	26
		80486	10

LTR   Load task register

00001111 00000000 oo001mmm disp		O D I T S Z A P C

Format	Examples		Clocks
LTR reg	LTR AX LTR CX LTR DX	80286	17
		80386	23
		80486	20
LTR mem	LTR TASK LTR EDGE	80286	19
		80386	27
		80486	20

MOV   Move data

100010dw oorrrmmm disp		O D I T S Z A P C

Format	Examples		Clocks

MOV reg,reg	MOV CL,CH
	MOV BH,CL
	MOV CX,DX
	MOV EAX,ECX
	MOV EBP,ESI
		80286	2

		80386	2
		80486	1

MOV mem,reg	MOV DATA,DL
	MOV NUMB,CX
	MOV TEMP,EBX
	MOV TEMP1,CH
	MOV DATA2,CL
		80286	3

		80386	2
		80486	1

MOV reg,mem	MOV DL,DATA
	MOV DX,NUMB
	MOV EBX,TEMP
	MOV CH,TEMP1
	MOV CL,DATA2
		80286	5

		80386	4
		80486	1

1100011w oo000mmm disp data		

Format	Examples		Clocks

MOV mem,imm	MOV DATA,23H
	MOV LIST,12H
	MOV BYTE PTR [DI],2
	MOV NUMB,234H
	MOV DWORD PTR [SI],100
		80286	3

		80386	2
		80486	1

1011wrrr data		

Format	Examples		Clocks

MOV reg,imm	MOV BX,23H
	MOV CX,12H
	MOV CL,2
	MOV ECX,123423H
	MOV DI,100
		80286	3

		80386	2
		80486	1

101000dw disp		

Format	Examples		Clocks

MOV mem,acc	MOV DATA,AL
	MOV NUMB,AX
	MOV NUMB1,EAX
		80286	3

		80386	2
		80486	1

MOV acc,mem	MOV AL,DATA
	MOV AX,NUMB
	MOV EAX,TEMP
		80286	5

		80386	4
		80486	1

100011d0 oosssmmm disp

Format	Examples		Clocks

MOV seg,reg	MOV SS,AX
	MOV DS,DX
	MOV ES,CX
		80286	2

		80386	2
		80486	1

MOV seg,mem	MOV SS,DATA
	MOV DS,NUMB
	MOV ES,TEMP1
		80286	2

		80386	2
		80486	1

MOV reg,seg	MOV AX,DS
	MOV DX,ES
	MOV CX,CS
		80286	2

		80386	2
		80486	1

MOV mem,seg	MOV DATA,SS
	MOV NUMB,ES
	MOV TEMP1,DS
		80286	3

		80386	2
		80486	1

00001111 001000d0 11rrrmmm

Format	Examples		Clocks

MOV reg,cr	MOV EAX,CR0
	MOV EBX,CR2
	MOV ECX,CR3
		80286	—

		80386	6
		80486	4

MOV cr,reg	MOV CR0,EAX
	MOV CR2,EBX
	MOV CR3,ECX
		80286	—

		80386	10
		80486	4

00001111 001000d1 11rrrmmm

Format	Examples		Clocks

MOV reg,dr	MOV EBX,DR6
	MOV EAX,DR6
	MOV EDX,DR1
		80286	—

		80386	22
		80486	10

MOV dr,reg	MOV DR1,ECX
	MOV DR2,ESI
	MOV DR6,EBP
		80286	—

		80386	22
		80486	11

00001111 001001d0 11rrrmmm

Format	Examples		Clocks
MOV reg,tr	MOV EAX,TR6 MOV EDX,TR7	80286	—
		80386	12
		80486	4
MOV tr,seg	MOV TR6,EDX MOV TR7,ESI	80286	—
		80386	12
		80486	6

MOVS   Move string data

1010010w   O D I T S Z A P C

Format	Examples		Clocks
MOVSB MOVSW MOVSD	MOVSB MOVSW MOVSD MOVS DAT1,DAT2 REP MOVSB	80286	5
		80386	7
		80486	7

MOVSX   Move with sign extend

00001111 1011111w oorrrmmm disp   O D I T S Z A P C

Format	Examples		Clocks
MOVSX reg,reg	MOVSX BX,AL MOVSX EAX,DX	80286	—
		80386	3
		80486	3
MOVSX reg,mem	MOVSX AX,DATA MOVSX EAX,NUMB	80286	—
		80386	6
		80486	3

MOVZX   Move with zero extend

00001111 1011011w oorrrmmm disp   O D I T S Z A P C

Format	Examples		Clocks
MOVZX reg,reg	MOVZX BX,AL MOVZX EAX,DX	80286	—

		80386	3
		80486	3
MOVZX reg,mem	MOVZX AX,DATA MOVZX EAX,NUMB	80286	—
		80386	6
		80486	3

MUL Unsigned multiplication

1111011w oo100mmm disp

O	D	I	T	S	Z	A	P	C
*				?	?	?	?	*

Format	Examples		Clocks
MUL reg	MUL BL MUL CX MUL ECX	80286	21
		80386	38
		80486	42
MUL mem	MUL DATA MUL BYTE PTR [SI] MUL WORD PTR [SI] MUL DWORD PTR [ECX]	80286	24
		80386	41
		80486	42

NEG Negate

1111011w oo011mmm disp

O	D	I	T	S	Z	A	P	C
*				*	*	*	*	*

Format	Examples		Clocks
NEG reg	NEG AX NEG CX NEG EDX	80286	2
		80386	2
		80486	1
NEG mem	NEG DATA NEG NUMB NEG WORD PTR [DI]	80286	7
		80386	6
		80486	3

NOP No operation

10010000

O	D	I	T	S	Z	A	P	C

Example		Clocks
NOP	80286	3
	80386	3
	80486	3

NOT One's complement

1111011w oo010mmm disp		O D I T S Z A P C	
Format	Examples		Clocks
NOT reg	NOT AX NOT CX NOT EDX	80286	2
		80386	2
		80486	1
NOT mem	NOT DATA NOT NUMB NOT WORD PTR [DI]	80286	7
		80386	6
		80486	3

OR   Inclusive-OR

000010dw oorrrmmm disp		O D I T S Z A P C 0 * * ? * 0	
Format	Examples		Clocks
OR reg,reg	OR CL,BL OR CX,DX OR ECX,EBX	80286	2
		80386	2
		80486	1
OR mem,reg	OR DATA,CL OR NUMB,CX OR [DI],CX	80286	7
		80386	7
		80486	3
OR reg,mem	OR CL,DATA OR CX,NUMB OR CX,[SI]	80286	7
		80386	6
		80486	2

100000sw oo001mmm disp data			
Format	Examples		Clocks
OR reg,imm	OR CL,3 OR DX,1000H OR EBX,100000H	80286	3
		80386	2
		80486	1
OR mem,imm	OR DATA,33 OR NUMB,4AH OR NUMS,123498H OR BYTE PTR [ECX],2	80286	7
		80386	7
		80486	3

0000110w data			
Format	Examples		Clocks
OR acc,imm	OR AL,3 OR AX,1000H OR EAX,100000H	80286	3
		80386	2

		80486	1

OUT — Output data to port

1110011w port number		O D I T S Z A P C	

Format	Examples		Clocks
OUT pt,acc	OUT 12H,AL OUT 12H,AX	80286	3
	OUT 0FFH,AL OUT 0FEH,AX	80386	10
	OUT 10H,EAX	80486	10

1110111w			

Format	Examples		Clocks
OUT DX,acc	OUT DX,AL OUT DX,AX	80286	3
	OUT DX,EAX	80386	11
		80486	10

OUTS — Output string data to port

1110011w port number		O D I T S Z A P C	

Format	Examples		Clocks
OUTSB OUTSW OUTSD	OUTSB OUTSW	80286	5
	OUTSD OUTS DATA	80386	14
	REP OUTSB	80486	10

POP — Pop data from stack

01011rrr		O D I T S Z A P C	

Format	Examples		Clocks
POP reg	POP CX POP AX	80286	5
	POP EBX	80386	4
		80486	1

10001111 oo000mmm disp			

Format	Examples		Clocks
POP mem	POP DATA POP LISTS	80286	5
	POP NUMBS	80386	5
		80486	4

00sss111			

Format	Examples		Clocks
POP seg	POP DS POP ES POP SS	80286	5
		80386	7
		80486	3

00001111 10sss001

Format	Examples		Clocks
POP seg	POP FS POP GS	80286	—
		80386	7
		80486	3

POPA/POPAD   Pop all registers from stack

01100001	O D I T S Z A P C

Example		Clocks
POPA POPAD	80286	19
	80386	24
	80486	9

POPF/POPFD   Pop flags from stack

10011101	O D I T S Z A P C * * * * * * * * *

Example		Clocks
POPF POPFD	80286	5
	80386	5
	80486	6

PUSH   Push data onto stack

01010rrr	O D I T S Z A P C

Format	Examples		Clocks
PUSH reg	PUSH CX PUSH AX PUSH ECX	80286	3
		80386	2
		80486	1

11111111 oo110mmm disp

Format	Examples		Clocks
PUSH mem	PUSH DATA	80286	5

| | PUSH LISTS
PUSH NUMB
PUSH DWORD PTR [ECX] | 80386 | 5 |
| | | 80486 | 4 |

00sss110

Format	Examples		Clocks
PUSH seg	PUSH DS PUSH CS PUSH ES	80286	3
		80386	2
		80486	3

00001111 10sss000

Format	Examples		Clocks
PUSH seg	PUSH FS PUSH GS	80286	—
		80386	2
		80486	3

011010s0 data

Format	Examples		Clocks
PUSH imm	PUSH 2000H PUSH 5322H PUSHW 10H PUSHD 100000H	80286	3
		80386	2
		80486	1

PUSHA/PUSHAD   Push all registers

01100000		O D I T S Z A P C

Example		Clocks
PUSHA PUSHAD	80286	17
	80386	18
	80486	11

PUSHF/PUSHFD   Push flags onto stack

10011100		O D I T S Z A P C

Example		Clocks
PUSHF PUSHFD	80286	3
	80386	4
	80486	3

RCL/RCR/ROL/ROR   Rotate

1101000w ooTTTmmm disp			O D I T S Z A P C
			* *

TTT = 000 = ROL
TTT = 001 = ROR
TTT = 010 = RCL
TTT = 011 = RCR

Format	Examples		Clocks
ROL reg,1 ROR reg,1	ROL CL,1 ROL DX,1 ROR CH,1 ROL SI,1	80286	2
		80386	3
		80486	3
RCL reg,1 RCR reg,1	RCL CL,1 RCL SI,1 RCR AH,1 RCR EBX,1	80286	2
		80386	9
		80486	3
ROL mem,1 ROR mem,1	ROL DATA,1 ROL BYTE PTR [DI],1 ROR NUMB,1 ROR DWORD PTR [ECX],1	80286	7
		80386	7
		80486	4
RCL mem,1 RCR mem,1	RCL DATA,1 RCL BYTE PTR [DI],1 RCR NUMB,1 RCR WORD PTR [ECX],1	80286	7
		80386	10
		80486	4

1101001w ooTTTmmm disp			
Format	Examples		Clocks
ROL reg,CL ROR reg,CL	ROL CH,CL ROL DX,CL ROR CH,CL ROL SI,CL	80286	5+n
		80386	3
		80486	3
RCL reg,CL RCR reg,CL	RCL DL,CL RCL SI,CL RCR AH,CL RCR BX,CL	80286	5+n
		80386	9
		80486	8
ROL mem,CL ROR mem,CL	ROL DATA,CL ROL BYTE PTR [DI],CL ROR NUMB,CL ROR WORD PTR [ECX],CL	80286	8+n
		80386	7
		80486	4
RCL mem,CL RCR mem,CL	RCL DATA,CL RCL BYTE PTR [DI],CL RCR NUMB,CL RCR WORD PTR [ECX],CL	80286	8+n
		80386	10
		80486	9

1100000w ooTTTmmm disp data			
Format	Examples		Clocks
ROL reg,imm ROR reg,imm	ROL CL,4 ROL DX,5 ROR CH,12 ROL SI,9	80286	5+n
		80386	3

		80486	2
RCL reg,imm RCR reg,imm	RCL CL,2 RCL SI,3 RCR AH,5 RCR BX,13	80286	5+n
		80386	9
		80486	8
ROL mem,imm ROR mem,imm	ROL DATA,4 ROL BYTE PTR [DI],2 ROR NUMB,2 ROR WORD PTR [ECX],3	80286	8+n
		80386	7
		80486	4
RCL mem,imm RCR mem,imm	RCL DATA,6 RCL BYTE PTR [DI],7 RCR NUMB,6 RCR WORD PTR [ECX],5	80286	8+n
		80386	10
		80486	9

REP   Repeat prefix

11110010 1010010w		O D I T S Z A P C	
Format	**Examples**		**Clocks**
REP MOVS	REP MOVSB REP MOVSW REP MOVSD REP MOVS DATA1,DATA2	80286	5+4n
		80386	8+4n
		80486	12+3n

11110010 1010101w			
Format	**Examples**		**Clocks**
REP STOS	REP STOSB REP STOSW REP STOSD REP STOS DATA3	80286	4+3n
		80386	5+5n
		80486	7+4n

11110010 0110110w			
Format	**Examples**		**Clocks**
REP INS	REP INSB REP INSW REP INSD REP INS DATA4	80286	5+4n
		80386	13+6n
		80486	16+8n

11110010 0110111w			
Format	**Examples**		**Clocks**
REP OUTS	REP OUTSB REP OUTSW REP OUTSD REP OUTS DATA5	80286	5+4n
		80386	12+5n
		80486	17+5n

REPE/REPNE   Repeat conditional

| 11110011 1010011w | | | | O D I T S Z A P C |
| | | | | * |
Format	Examples			Clocks
REPE CMPS	REPE CMPSB REPE CMPSW REPE CMPSD REPE CMPS DATA6,DATA7		80286	5+9n
			80386	5+9n
			80486	7+7n

| 11110011 1010111w | | | | |
Format	Examples			Clocks
REPE SCAS	REPE SCASB REPE SCASW REPE SCASD REPE SCAS DATA8		80286	5+8n
			80386	5+8n
			80486	7+5n

| 11110010 1010011w | | | | |
Format	Examples			Clocks
REPNE CMPS	REPNE CMPSB REPNE CMPSW REPNE CMPSD REPNE CMPS DATA9,DATA10		80286	5+9n
			80386	5+9n
			80486	7+7n

| 11110010 1010111w | | | | |
Format	Examples			Clocks
REPNE SCAS	REPNE SCASB REPNE SCASW REPNE SCASD REPNE SCAS DATA11		80286	5+8n
			80386	5+8n
			80486	7+5n

RET   Return from procedure

| 11000011 | | O D I T S Z A P C |
Example		Clocks
RET (near)	80286	11
	80386	10
	80486	5

| 11000010 data | | |
Format	Examples		Clocks
RET imm (near)	RET 4 RET 100H	80286	11
		80386	10
		80486	5

| 11001011 | |
| Example | Clocks |

RET (far)		80286	15
		80386	18
		80486	13

11001010 data

Format	Examples		Clocks
RET imm (far)	RET 4 RET 100H	80286	11
		80386	10
		80486	5

SAHF   Store AH into flags

10011110	O D I T S Z A P C * * * * *

Example		Clocks
SAHF	80286	2
	80386	3
	80486	2

SAL/SAR/SHL/SHR   Shift

1101000w ooTTTmmm disp TTT = 100 = SHL/SAL TTT = 101 = SHR TTT = 111 = SAR	O D I T S Z A P C * * * ? * *

Format	Examples		Clocks
SAL reg,1 SHL reg,1 SHR reg,1 SAR reg 1	SAL CL,1 SHL DX,1 SHR CH,1 SAR SI,1	80286	2
		80386	3
		80486	3
SAL mem,1 SHL mem,1 SHR mem,1 SAR mem,1	SAL DATA,1 SHL BYTE PTR [DI],1 SHR NUMB,1 SAR WORD PTR [ECX],1	80286	7
		80386	7
		80486	4

1101001w ooTTTmmm disp

Format	Examples		Clocks
SAL reg,CL SHL reg,CL SHR reg,CL SAR reg,CL	SAL CH,CL SHL DX,CL SHR CH,CL SAR SI,CL	80286	5+n
		80386	3
		80486	3
SAL mem,CL SHL mem,CL SHR mem,CL	SAL DATA,CL SHL BYTE PTR [DI],CL SHR NUMB,CL	80286	8+n
		80386	7

SAR mem,CL	SAR WORD PTR [ECX],CL		
		80486	4

1100000w ooTTTmmm disp data

Format	Examples		Clocks
SAL reg,imm SHL reg,imm SHR reg,imm SAR reg,imm	SAL CL,4 SHL DX,5 SHR CH,12 SAR SI,9	80286	5+n
		80386	3
		80486	2
SAL mem,imm SHL mem,imm SHR mem,imm SAR mem,imm	SAL DATA,6 SHL BYTE PTR [DI],7 SHR NUMB,6 SAR WORD PTR [ECX],5	80286	8+n
		80386	7
		80486	4

SBB   Subtract with borrow

000110dw oorrrmmm disp			O D I T S Z A P C * * * * *
Format	Examples		Clocks
SBB reg,reg	SBB CL,DL SBB AX,DX SBB CH,CL SBB EAX,EBX	80286	2
		80386	2
		80486	1
SBB mem,reg	SBB DATA,CL SBB BYTES,CX SBB NUMBS,ECX SBB [EAX],CX	80286	7
		80386	6
		80486	3
SBB reg,mem	SBB CL,DATA SBB CX,BYTES SBB ECX,NUMBS SBB CX,[EDX]	80286	7
		80386	7
		80486	2

100000sw oo011mmm disp data

Format	Examples		Clocks
SBB reg,imm	SBB CL,4 SBB DX,5 SBB CH,12 SBB SI,9	80286	3
		80386	2
		80486	1
SBB mem,imm	SBB DATA,6 SBB BYTE PTR [DI],7 SBB NUMB,6 SBB WORD PTR [ECX],5	80286	7
		80386	7
		80486	3

0001110w data

Format	Examples		Clocks
SBB acc,imm	SBB AL,4 SBB AX,5 SBB AH,12	80286	3
		80386	2

	SBB AX,9		
		80486	1

SCAS Scan string

1010111w		O D I T S Z A P C * * * * * *

Format	Examples	Clocks	
SCASB SCASW SCASD	SCASB SCASW	80286	7
	SCASD SCAS DATA	80386	7
	REP SCASB	80486	6

SET Set on condition

00001111 1001cccc oo000mmm		O D I T S Z A P C

Format	Examples	Clocks	
SETcd reg8	SETA BL	80286	—
	SETB CH SETG DL	80386	4
	SETE BH SETZ AL	80486	3
SETcd mem8	SETE DATA SETLE BYTES	80286	—
		80386	5
		80486	3

Condition Codes	Mnemonic	Flag	Description
0000	SETO	O = 1	Set if overflow
0001	SETNO	O = 0	Set if no overflow
0010	SETB/SETNAE	C = 1	Set if below
0011	SETAE/SETNB	C = 0	Set if above or equal
0100	SETE/SETZ	Z = 1	Set if equal/zero
0101	SETNE/SETNZ	Z = 0	Set if not equal/not zero
0110	SETBE/SETNA	C = 1 + Z = 1	Set if below or equal
0111	SETA/SETNBE	C = 0 • Z = 0	Set if above
1000	SETS	S = 1	Set if sign
1001	SETNS	S = 0	Set if no sign
1010	SETP/SETPE	P = 1	Set if parity even
1011	SETNP/SETPO	P = 0	Set if parity odd
1100	SETL/SETNGE	S • O	Set if less than
1101	SETGE/SETNL	S = O	Set greater or equal
1110	SETLE/SETNG	Z = 1 + S • O	Set if less than or equal
1111	SETG/SETNLE	Z = 0 + S = O	Set if greater

SGDT/SIDT/SLDT Store descriptor table

00001111 00000001 oo000mmm disp		O D I T S Z A P C

Format	Examples	Clocks	
SGDT mem	SGDT MEMORY	80286	11

	SGDT GLOBAL	80386	9
		80486	10

00001111 00000001 oo001mmm disp

Format	Examples		Clocks
SIDT mem	SIDT DATAS SIDT INTERRUPT	80286	12
		80386	9
		80486	10

00001111 00000000 oo000mmm disp

Format	Examples		Clocks
SLDT reg	SLDT CX SLDT DX	80286	2
		80386	2
		80486	2
SLDT mem	SLDT NUMBS SLDT LOCALS	80286	3
		80386	2
		80486	3

SHLD/SHRD   Double precision shift

00001111 10100100 oorrrmmm disp data		O ?	D	I	T	S *	Z *	A ?	P *	C *

Format	Examples		Clocks
SHLD reg,reg,imm	SHLD AX,CX,10 SHLD DX,BX,8 SHLD CX,DX,2	80286	—
		80386	3
		80486	2
SHLD mem,reg,imm	SHLD DATA,CX,8	80286	—
		80386	7
		80486	3

00001111 10101100 oorrrmmm disp data

Format	Examples		Clocks
SHRD reg,reg,imm	SHRD CX,DX,2	80286	—
		80386	3
		80486	2
SHRD mem,reg,imm	SHRD DATA,CX,3	80286	—
		80386	7
		80486	3

00001111 10100101 oorrrmmm disp

Format	Examples		Clocks
SHLD reg,reg,CL	SHLD DX,BX,CL	80286	—
		80386	3
		80486	3
SHLD mem,reg,CL	SHLD DATA,AX,CL	80286	—
		80386	7
		80486	3

00001111 10100101 oorrrmmm disp

Format	Examples		Clocks
SHRD reg,reg,CL	SHRD DX,BX,CL	80286	—
		80386	3
		80486	3
SHRD mem,reg,CL	SHRD DATA,AX,CL	80286	—
		80386	7
		80486	3

SMSW   Store machine status word

00001111 00000001 oo100mmm disp   O D I T S Z A P C

(should only be used by the 80286)

Format	Examples		Clocks
SMSW reg	SMSW AX SMSW DX SMSW CX	80286	2
		80386	10
		80486	2
SMSW mem	SMSW DATA	80286	3
		80386	3
		80486	3

STC   Set carry flag

11111001   O D I T S Z A P C
                                                                           1

Example		Clocks
STC	80286	2
	80386	2
	80486	2

STD   Set direction flag

11111101		O D I T S Z A P C 1
Example		**Clocks**
STD	80286	2
	80386	2
	80486	2

STI   Set interrupt flag

11111011		O D I T S Z A P C 1
Example		**Clocks**
STI	80286	2
	80386	3
	80486	5

STOS   Store string data

1010101w			O D I T S Z A P C
Format	**Examples**		**Clocks**
STOSB STOSW STOSD	STOSB STOSW STOSD STOS DATA REP STOSB	80286	3
		80386	4
		80486	5

STR   Store task register

00001111 00000000 oo001mmm disp			O D I T S Z A P C
Format	**Examples**		**Clocks**
STR reg	STR DX STR CX STR AX	80286	2
		80386	2
		80486	2
STR mem	STR DATA	80286	3
		80386	2
		80486	3

SUB   Subtract

001010dw oorrrmmm disp			O D I T S Z A P C * * * * * *	
Format	**Examples**			**Clocks**

SUB reg,reg	SUB CL,DL
	SUB AX,DX
	SUB CH,CL
	SUB EAX,EBX
		80286	2	

		80386	2	
		80486	1	

SUB mem,reg	SUB DATA,CL
	SUB BYTES,CX
	SUB NUMBS,ECX
	SUB [EAX],CX
		80286	7	

		80386	6	
		80486	3	

SUB reg,mem	SUB CL,DATA
	SUB CX,BYTES
	SUB ECX,NUMBS
	SUB CX,[EDX]
		80286	7	

		80386	7	
		80486	2	

100000sw oo101mmm disp data				
Format	**Examples**			**Clocks**

SUB reg,imm	SUB CL,4
	SUB DX,5
	SUB CH,12
	SUB SI,9
		80286	3	

		80386	2	
		80486	1	

SUB mem,imm	SUB DATA,6
	SUB BYTE PTR [DI],7
	SUB NUMB,6
	SUB WORD PTR [ECX],5
		80286	7	

		80386	7	
		80486	3	

0010110w data				
Format	**Examples**			**Clocks**

SUB acc,imm	SUB AL,4
	SUB AX,5
	SUB AH,12
	SUB AX,9
		80286	3	

		80386	2	
		80486	1	

TEST Test operands (logical compare)

1000011w oorrrmmm disp			O D I T S Z A P C 0 * * ? * 0	
Format	**Examples**			**Clocks**
TEST reg,reg	TEST CL,DL TEST CX,DX TEST CL,CH TEST ECX,EBX	80286	2	
		80386	2	
		80486	1	
TEST reg,mem mem,reg	TEST DATA,CL TEST CL,DATA	80286	6	
		80386	5	
		80486	2	

1111011w oo000mmm disp data

Format	Examples		Clocks
TEST reg,imm	TEST CL,4 TEST DX,5 TEST CH,12H TEST SI,256	80286	3
		80386	2
		80486	1
TEST mem,imm	TEST DATA,6	80286	6
		80386	5
		80486	2

1010100w data

Format	Examples		Clocks
TEST acc,imm	TEST AL,4 TEST AX,5 TEST AH,12 TEST AX,9 TEST EAX,2	80286	3
		80386	2
		80486	1

VERR/VERW   Verify read or write

00001111 00000000 oo100mmm disp			O D I T S Z A P C *

Format	Examples		Clocks
VERR reg	VERR BX VERR CX VERR DX	80286	14
		80386	10
		80486	11
VERR mem	VERR DATA	80286	16
		80386	11
		80486	11

00001111 00000000 oo101mmm disp

Format	Examples		Clocks
VERW reg	VERW AX VERW CX VERW DX	80286	14
		80386	15
		80486	11
VERW mem	VERW DATA	80286	16
		80386	16
		80486	11

WAIT   Wait for coprocessor

10011011	O D I T S Z A P C

Examples		Clocks	
WAIT FWAIT		80286	3
		80386	6
		80486	6

WBINVD   Write back and invalidate data cache

00001111 00001001		O D I T S Z A P C	

Example		Clocks	
WBINVD		80286	—
		80386	—
		80486	5

XADD   Exchange and add

00001111 1100000w 11rrrrrr		O D I T S Z A P C * * * * *	

Format	Examples	Clocks	
XADD reg,reg	XADD EBX,ECX XADD EDX,EAX XADD EDI,EBP	80286	—
		80386	—
		80486	3

00001111 1100000w oorrrmmm disp			
Format	Examples	Clocks	
XADD mem,reg	XADD DATA,EAX XADD [DI],EAX XADD [ECX],EDX	80286	—
		80386	—
		80486	4

XCHG   Exchange

1000011w 1oorrrmmm		O D I T S Z A P C	

Format	Examples	Clocks	
XCHG reg,reg	XCHG BL,CL XCHG DX,CX XCHG EDI,EBP	80286	3
		80386	3
		80486	3
XCHG reg,mem mem,reg	XCHG CL,DATA XCHG DATA,CL XCHG DX,[DI] XCHG ECX,[EBP]	80286	5
		80386	5

		80486	5

10010reg

Format	Examples		Clocks
XCHG acc,reg XCHG reg,acc	XCHG DATA,AL XCHG AX,FRIED XCHG EAX,MONEY	80286	3
		80386	3
		80486	3

XLAT   Translate

11010111   O D I T S Z A P C

Example	Clocks
XLAT	80286	5
	80386	5
	80486	4

XOR   Exclusive-OR

001100dw oorrrmmm disp

O D I T S Z A P C
0   * * ? * 0

Format	Examples		Clocks
XOR reg,reg	XOR BL,CL XOR CX,DX XOR CH,CL XOR EAX,EBX	80286	2
		80386	2
		80486	1
XOR mem,reg	XOR DATA,CL XOR BYTES,CX XOR NUMBS,ECX XOR [EAX],CX	80286	7
		80386	6
		80486	3
XOR reg,mem	XOR CL,DATA XOR CX,BYTES XOR ECX,NUMBS XOR CX,[EDX]	80286	7
		80386	7
		80486	2

100000sw oo110mmm disp data

Format	Examples		Clocks
XOR reg,imm	XOR CL,4 XOR DX,5 XOR CH,12 XOR SI,9	80286	3
		80386	2
		80486	1
XOR mem,imm	XOR DATA,6 XOR BYTE PTR [DI],7 XOR NUMB,6 XOR WORD PTR [ECX],5	80286	7
		80386	7
		80486	3

0011010w data			
Format	Examples		Clocks
XOR acc,imm	XOR AL,4 XOR AX,5 XOR AH,12 XOR AX,9	80286	3
		80386	2
		80486	1

APPENDIX C

Flag Bit Changes

This appendix shows only the instructions that actually change the flag bits. Any instruction not listed does not affect any of the flag bits.

Instruction	Flags								
	O	D	I	T	S	Z	A	P	C
AAA	?				?	?	*	?	*
AAD	?				*	*	?	*	?
AAM	?				*	*	?	*	?
AAS	?				?	?	*	?	*
ADC	*				*	*	*	*	*
ADD	*				*	*	*	*	*
AND	0				*	*	?	*	0
ARPL						*			
BSF						*			
BSR						*			
BT									*
BTC									*
BTR									*
BTS									*
CLC									0
CLD		0							
CLI			0						
CMC									*
CMP	*				*	*	*	*	*
CMPS	*				*	*	*	*	*
CMPXCHG	*				*	*	*	*	*
DAA	?				*	*	*	*	*
DAS	?				*	*	*	*	*

Instruction									
DEC	*				*	*	*	*	
DIV	?				?	?	?	?	?
IDIV	?				?	?	?	?	?
IMUL	*				?	?	?	?	*
INC	*				*	*	*	*	
IRET	*	*	*	*	*	*	*	*	*
LAR						*			
LSL						*			
MUL	*				?	?	?	?	*
NEG	*				*	*	*	*	*
OR	0				*	*	?	*	0
POPF/POPFD	*	*	*	*	*	*	*	*	*
RCL/RCR	*								*
REPE/REPNE						*			
ROL/ROR	*								*
SAHF					*	*	*	*	*
SAL/SAR	*				*	*	?	*	*
SHL/SHR	*				*	*	?	*	*
SBB	*				*	*	*	*	*
SCAS	*				*	*	*	*	*
SHLD/SHRD	?				*	*	?	*	*
STC									1
STD		1							
STI			1						
SUB	*				*	*	*	*	*
TEST					*	*	?	*	0
VERR/VERW						*			
XADD	*				*	*	*	*	*
XOR	0				*	*	?	*	0

APPENDIX D

Bus Standards

This appendix illustrates the bus standards found in most clone and IBM PC systems. These buses are usually called ISA (IBM standard architecture). Although other bus standards exist, these represent the two that are most often found in computer systems.

Figure D–1 illustrates the 8-bit ISA standard found in the XT computer. Figure D–2 illustrates the 16-bit ISA standard found in the AT computer. Notice that the top connector in the AT standard is identical to the XT standard. This allows older 8-bit boards to be plugged into any 16-bit AT slot in an AT-style computer system.

FIGURE D–1   The 8-bit
XT-style edge connector.

Rear of computer

GND	B1	A1	$\overline{\text{IO CHCK}}$
RESET DRV	B2	A2	SD7
+5VDC	B3	A3	SD6
IRQ9	B4	A4	SD5
-5VDC	B5	A5	SD4
DRQ2	B6	A6	SD3
-12VDC	B7	A7	SD2
$\overline{\text{OWS}}$	B8	A8	SD1
+12VDC	B9	A9	SD0
GND	B10	A10	$\overline{\text{IO CHRDY}}$
$\overline{\text{SMEMW}}$	B11	A11	AEN
$\overline{\text{SMEMR}}$	B12	A12	SA19
$\overline{\text{IOW}}$	B13	A13	SA18
$\overline{\text{IOR}}$	B14	A14	SA17
$\overline{\text{DACK3}}$	B15	A15	SA16
DRQ3	B16	A16	SA15
$\overline{\text{DACK1}}$	B17	A17	SA14
DRQ1	B18	A18	SA13
$\overline{\text{REFRESH}}$	B19	A19	SA12
CLK	B20	A20	SA11
IRQ7	B21	A21	SA10
IRQ6	B22	A22	SA9
IRQ5	B23	A23	SA8
IRQ4	B24	A24	SA7
IRQ3	B25	A25	SA6
$\overline{\text{DACK2}}$	B26	A26	SA5
T/C	B27	A27	SA4
BALE	B28	A28	SA3
+5VDC	B29	A29	SA2
OSC	B30	A30	SA1
GND	B31	A31	SA0

Component side edge connector

FIGURE D–2 The 16-bit
AT-style bus connector.

Rear of computer

GND	B1	A1	IO CHCK
RESET DRV	B2	A2	SD7
+5VDC	B3	A3	SD6
IRQ9	B4	A4	SD5
-5VDC	B5	A5	SD4
DRQ2	B6	A6	SD3
-12VDC	B7	A7	SD2
OWS	B8	A8	SD1
+12VDC	B9	A9	SD0
GND	B10	A10	IO CHRDY
SMEMW	B11	A11	AEN
SMEMR	B12	A12	SA19
IOW	B13	A13	SA18
IOR	B14	A14	SA17
DACK3	B15	A15	SA16
DRQ3	B16	A16	SA15
DACK1	B17	A17	SA14
DRQ1	B18	A18	SA13
REFRESH	B19	A19	SA12
CLK	B20	A20	SA11
IRQ7	B21	A21	SA10
IRQ6	B22	A22	SA9
IRQ5	B23	A23	SA8
IRQ4	B24	A24	SA7
IRQ3	B25	A25	SA6
DACK2	B26	A26	SA5
T/C	B27	A27	SA4
BALE	B28	A28	SA3
+5VDC	B29	A29	SA2
OSC	B30	A30	SA1
GND	B31	A31	SA0

MEMCS16	D1	C1	SBHE
IOCS16	D2	C2	LA23
IRQ10	D3	C3	LA22
IRQ11	D4	C4	LA21
IRQ12	D5	C5	LA20
IRQ15	D6	C6	LA19
IRQ14	D7	C7	LA18
DACK0	D8	C8	LA17
DRQ0	D9	C9	MEMR
DACK5	D10	C10	MEMW
DRQ5	D11	C11	SD08
DACK6	D12	C12	SD09
DRQ6	D13	C13	SD10
DACK7	D14	C14	SD11
DRQ7	D15	C15	SD12
+5VDC	D16	C16	SD13
MASTER	D17	C17	SD14
GND	D18	C18	SD15

Component side edge connector

APPENDIX E

Answers to Even-Numbered Questions and Problems

Chapter 1

2. Primitive video games, microwave ovens, dishwashers, and washing machines.
4. Execution speeds have increased from 50,000 instructions per second on the 4-bit microprocessor to over 33 million instructions per second on the 80486.
6. 4G bytes.
8. The instruction unit is used to execute the instructions as they are fetched from the bus unit.
10. The pipeline aids in execution because it breaks the task of fetching and executing the program into multiple phases.
12. 000000H to FFFFFFH.
14. 2.
16. The logical memory system is the memory as viewed by a programmer that is always an 8-bit-wide memory. The physical memory can be any width and it is the memory system as viewed by the hardware.
18. 1G byte.
20. Four. AX, BX, CX, and DX.
22. The DX register holds data before a division and after a multiplication.
24. Offset.
26. Real memory is 1M byte addressed between locations 000000H and 0FFFFFH, while protected memory is 16M bytes addressed between locations 000000H and FFFFFFH.
28. 16 bytes or a paragraph.
30. 14340H.
32. Data and Extra.
34. CF (carry) holds a carry after an addition, subtraction, and shift and rotate instructions. SF (sign) holds the sign after an addition or subtraction. ZF (zero) indicates that the result is zero (ZF = 1). PF (parity) holds the parity of the result expressed as even (PF = 1) or odd (PF = 0). AC (auxiliary carry) holds the carry or borrow between the least-significant 4 bits and most-significant 4 bits of AL after an addition or subtraction. OF (overflow) indicates that an arithmetic overflow has occurred. DF (direction) used with a string instruction

to select the auto-increment or auto-decrement operation. IF (interrupt) enables (IF = 1) the INTR pin on the 80286 microprocessor. IOPL (I/O privilege level) used in protected mode to indicate the maximum privilege level allowed for I/O instructions. NT (nested task) shows that a task is nested within another task.

36. 100000H.
38. The transient program area (TPA) holds the operating system, drivers, and applications software.
40. A selector that indicates which table and which descriptor. The selector also indicates the requested privilege level.
42. The limit indicates the end of the segment or last location in the segment.
44. (a) -128. (b) $+81$. (c) -89. (d) $+34$. (e) -1.
46. (a) 57 65 6C 6C. (b) 77 61 74 65 72 20 69 73 20 63 6F 6C 64 21. (c) 53 6F 20 77 68 61 74 2E. (d) 53 68 61 6C 6C 20 77 65 3F. (e) 57 68 6F 20 73 61 69 64 20 73 6F 3F.
48. 04000H = 34H, 04001H = 12H, 04002H = 00H, and 04003H = 10H.
50. (a) $+12.0$. (b) -0.5. (c) $+116$. (d) -0.203125. (e) -15.75
52. Processor control instructions.

Chapter 2

2. AH, AL, BH, BL, CH, CL, DH, and DL.
4. CS, DS, ES, and SS.
6. You cannot move data from one segment register to another segment register.
8. (a) MOV AL,12H. (b) MOV AX,123AH. (c) MOV CL,0CDH. (d) MOV SI,1000H. (e) MOV BX,1200H.
10. A displacement is a distance. The memory address is determined by adding the 2000H to the contents of code segment register, appended with 0000_2.
12. (a) 3234H. (b) 2300H. (c) 2400H.
14. The MOV BX,DATA instruction transfers the word contents of memory location DATA into BX, while the MOV BX,OFFSET DATA instruction loads BX with the address of DATA.
16. (a) 12100H. (b) 12350H. (c) 12200H.
18. (a) 14200H. (b) 15400H. (c) 13000H.
20. Direct, relative, and indirect.
22. An intersegment jump allows a jump to any location in the memory, and an intrasegment jump allows a jump to any location within the segment.
24. (a) Short. (b) Near. (c) Short. (d) Far.
26. JMP [BX] if BX contains address TABLE.
28. The PUSH [DI] instruction addresses word data at the location addressed by DI in the data segment and pushed it onto the stack.

Chapter 3

2. The D-bit indicates the direction of flow for some instructions. If D = 0, data flow from the REG field to the R/M field, and if D = 1, the data flow from the R/M field to the REG field. The W-bit indicates the size of the transfer. If W = 1, the transfer is a word, and if W = 0, the transfer is a byte.
4. The DL register.

6. (a) Stack segment. (b) Data segment. (c) Data segment. (d) Stack segment. (e) Data segment.
8. MOV BX,[004CH]
10. Nothing is wrong with this instruction.
12. 16
14. AX, BX, CX, DX, SP, BP, SI, and DI.
16. Location 20FFH = BH and 20FE = BL. After these data are stored, the stack pointer changes to 00FEH.
18. SP = 200H and SS = 0200H is one possible combination.
20. There is no difference except MOV SI,OFFSET NUMB executes faster than LEA SI,NUMB.
22. This instruction removes the first two bytes of location NUMB and places them into BX. It then loads the next two bytes into DS.

24. **MOV   BX,NUMB**
    MOV   DX,BX
    MOV   SI,BX

26. The CLD instruction clears DF and STD sets it.
28. The LODSB instruction copies the 8-bit contents of the memory location addressed by SI in the data segment into AL. It then either increments or decrements SI by 1.
30. The OUTSB instruction copies the contents of the data segment memory location addressed by SI to the I/O device addressed by DX.

32. **MOV   SI,OFFSET SOURCE**
    MOV   DI,OFFSET DEST
    MOV   CX,12
    REP MOVSB

34. XCHG BX,SI
36. The XLAT instruction adds the AL register to BX to form the translation memory address within the data segment. It then copies the contents of this address into AL to complete the translation.
38. The OUT DX,AX instruction copies AX into the I/O device addressed by DX.
40. MOV AH,ES:[BX]
42. The DB directive defines bytes, the DW directive defines words, and the DD directive defines double words.
44. The EQU directive equates values, addresses, or labels to labels.
46. The .MODEL directive selects one of the assembly language memory models.
48. Full-segment definitions.
50. The PROC directive indicates the start, and the ENDP indicates the end.

Chapter 4

2. You may not add a 16-bit number to an 8-bit number.
4. Sum = 3100H, SF = 0, ZF = 0, CF = 0, AF = 1, OF = 0, and PF = 0.

6. ADD AX,BX
   ADD AX,CX
   ADD AX,DX
   ADD AX,SP
   MOV DI,AX

8. INC SP

10. (a) SUB CX,BX. (b) SUB DH,0EEH. (c) SUB SI,DI. (d) SUB SP,3322H. (e) SUB CH,[SI]. (f) SUB DX,[SI+10]. (g) SUB FROG,AL.

12. SUB AX,DI
    SUB AX,SI
    SUB AX,BP
    MOV BX,AX

14. This instruction subtracts DX with carry (CF) from the data segment memory location addressed by DI − 4. The difference is stored in memory at the data segment location addressed by DI − 4.

16. AX.

18. The overflow and carry flags indicate whether the most-significant half of the product is zero or not.

20. MOV AL,DL
    XOR AH,AH
    MUL DL
    MUL DL

22. AX

24. Either a divide by zero or a divide overflow.

26. AH

28. DAA and DAS

30. It accomplishes this conversion by dividing by 10.

32. (a) AND BX,DX. (b) AND DH,0EAH. (c) AND DI,BP. (d) AND AX,1122H. (e) AND [BP],CX. (f) AND DX,[SI − 8]. (g) AND WHAT,AL.

34. OR AH,BL. (b) OR CX,88H. (c) OR SI,DX. (d) OR BP,1122H. (e) OR [BX],CX. (f) OR AL,[BP + 40]. (g) OR WHEN,AH.

36. (a) XOR AH,BH. (b) XOR CL,99H. (c) XOR DX,DI. (d) XOR SP,1A23H. (e) XOR [BX],DX. (f) XOR DI,[BP + 60]. (g) XOR DI,WELL.

38. Both instruction AND data, except the TEST instruction does not return a result in the destination register.

40. (a) SHR DI,3. (b) SHL AL,1. (c) ROL AL,3. (d) RCR DX,1. (e) SAR DH,1.

42. Extra.

44. It repeats the SCAS or CMPS instruction until either CX reaches zero or until a not equal condition exists.

46. The CMPSB instruction compares the bytes stored in memory addressed by DI and SI.

Chapter 5

2. The near jump instruction.
4. The far jump instruction.
6. The IP register.
8. The jump AX instruction moves the contents of AX into IP when it executes, causing the microprocessor to continue execution at this new offset address. The JUMP AX instruction is a near jump.
10. The JUMP [DI] instruction removes a word from the memory location addressed by DI in the data segment and places it into IP to accomplish a near jump. The JMP FAR PTR [DI] instruction removes a 32-bit number from the data segment memory location addressed by DI and places it into both IP and CS to accomplish a far jump.
12. The jump above (JA) instruction jumps if the unsigned number in the destination register is above the number specified by the source.
14. JG, JL, JGE, JLE, JE, and JNE.
16. JA.
18. CX.

20.
```
              MOV   CX,150H
              MOV   DI,OFFSET DATA
     HERE:
              STOSB
              LOOP  HERE
```

22. A procedure is a group of instructions that perform one task. This group is stored once in the memory, but used as many times as needed.
24. The RET instruction removes the return address from the stack and places it into either IP or IP and CS.
26. PROC.
28. The RET 6 instruction adds a 6 to the stack pointer before returning.

30.
```
MULTS         PROC  FAR

              PUSHF
              PUSH  DX
              PUSH  CX
              MOV   AX,SI
              MUL   DI
              MOV   CX,100H
              DIV   CX
              POP   CX
              POP   DX
              POPF
              RET

MULTS         ENDP
```

32. INT, INTO, and INT 3.
34. A divide error interrupt.

36. The difference is that the IRET instruction pops the IP and CS register plus (unlike RET) the contents of the flag register.
38. At locations 100H–103H.
40. The WAIT instruction.
42. 16 bytes.
44. The ESC or escape instruction passes opcodes to the 80287 coprocessor.
46. The LGDT instruction loads the global descriptor table register.

48.
```
CGATE       STRUC

LIM         DW     ?
BASL        DW     ?
BASH        DB     ?
RI          DB     ?
            DW     0

CGATE       ENDS
```

50. You must define the null descriptor and at least one descriptor for the code and stack segments.
52. The TSS contains the entire state of the machine plus backlinkage.

Chapter 6

2. TEST.LST, TEST.OBJ, and TEST.CRF.
4. The PUBLIC directive indicates that a label or segment is public so it can be used by other modules.
6. BYTE, WORD, DWORD, NEAR, or FAR.
8. The MACRO directive indicates the start of a macro sequence and the ENDM directive indicates the end.
10. Parameters are passed to a macro through the MACRO directive.
12. The LOCAL directive must be placed immediately after the MACRO statement without any intervening spaces. The LOCAL directive declares labels within the macro as local labels.
14. The INCLUDE statement allows a file containing macro sequences to be included in any other file.

16.
```
DISP        PROC   FAR

            MOV    SI,DX
DISP1:
            LODSB
            OR     AL,AL
            JE     DISP2
            MOV    AH,06H
            MOV    DL,AL
            INT    21H
            JMP    DISP1
DISP2:
            RET
```

```
        DISP            ENDP

18.  MOVCU           PROC  NEAR

                     MOV   DH,3
                     MOV   DL,6
                     MOV   BH,0
                     MOV   AH,2
                     INT   10H
                     RET

        MOVCU           ENDP
```

20. By repeatedly dividing the number by 10 and saving each remainder as a significant digit of the BCD result.

22. 30H.

```
24.  CONVS           PROC  NEAR

                     CMP   AL,'a'
                     JB    CONVS1
                     CMP   AL,'z'
                     JA    CONVS1
                     SUB   AL,20H
        CONVS1:
                     RET

        CONVS           ENDP
```

```
26.                  MOV   SI,OFFSET TABLEJ
                     XOR   AH,AH
                     SUB   AL,6
                     ADD   AX,AX
                     ADD   SI,AX
                     JMP   CS:[SI]

        TABLEJ:         DW    ONE,TWO,THREE
```

28. The boot sector contains a program called a bootstrap loader that takes the DOS from the disk and loads it into the memory system. The FAT (file allocation table) contains the assignment and location of all the disk files. The root directory contains the main system files and also subdirectory file names for other disk directories.

30. The bootstrap loader is found in the boot sector on the disk and is responsible for loading the operating system into the memory.

32. The attribute byte indicates that the directory entry is a file name (read, write, or read/write), a subdirectory name, or the name of the disk (disk volume).

34. $2^{32} - 1$.

```
36.  REN             PROC  NEAR

                     PUSH  DS
```

```
                    PUSH   ES
                    MOV    AX,CS
                    MOV    DS,AX
                    MOV    ES,AX
                    MOV    DI,OFFSET NEW
                    MOV    DX,OFFSET OLD
                    MOV    AH,56H
                    INT    21H
                    POP    ES
                    POP    DS
                    RET

        NEW         DB     'TEST.LIS',0
        OLD         DB     'TEST.LST',0

        REN         ENDP

38. PROG        SEGMENT
                ASSUME        CS:PROG

        MAIN        PROC  FAR

                    MOV    CX,7
                    CALL   DIPS
                    LOOP   MAIN
                    MOV    AH,4CH
                    INT    21H

        MAIN        ENDP

        DIPS        PROC  NEAR

                    CALL   NEW
                    MOV    AL,7
                    SUB    AL,CL
                    ADD    AL,30H
                    CALL   DIP
                    MOV    AL,'^'
                    CALL   DIP
                    MOV    AL,'2'
                    CALL   DIP
                    MOV    AL,'='
                    CALL   DIP
                    MOV    AL,7
                    SUB    CL
                    PUSH   CX
                    MOV    CL,AL
                    MOV    AL,1
                    SHL    AL,CL
                    POP    CX
                    CALL   DISP
                    RET
```

```
DIPS        ENDP

DIP         PROC  NEAR

            MOV   AH,6
            MOV   DL,AL
            INT   21H
            RET

DIP         ENDP

NEW         PROC  NEAR

            MOV   AL,13
            CALL  DIP
            MOV   AL,10
            CALL  DIP
            RET

NEW         ENDP

DISP        PROC  NEAR

            MOV   BL,10
            PUSH  CX
            XOR   AH,AH
            XOR   CX,CX
            MOV   DX,CX
DISP1:
            DIV   BL
            PUSH  AX
            INC   CX
            OR    AL,AL
            JNZ   DISP1
DISP2:
            POP   AX
            MOV   AL,AH
            ADD   AL,30H
            CALL  DIP
            LOOP  DISP2
            POP   CX
            RET

DISP        ENDP

PROG        ENDS
            END   MAIN

40. PROG        SEGMENT
            ASSUME      CS:PROG

MAIN        PROC  FAR
```

```
                    CALL    GET_ADR
                    CALL    NEW
                    CALL    DISP
                    MOV     AH,4CH
                    INT     21H

MAIN                ENDP

MES1                DB      13,10,'Enter the starting address: $'

GET_ADR             PROC    NEAR

                    PUSH    DS
                    MOV     AX,CS
                    MOV     DS,AX
                    MOV     DX,OFFSET MES1
                    MOV     AH,9
                    INT     21H
                    POP     DS
                    CALL    READ
                    RET

GET_ADR             ENDP

READ                PROC    NEAR

                    XOR     CX,CX
READ1:
                    CALL    GET
                    CMP     AL,13           ;enter key
                    JE      READ3
                    CMP     AL,'0'
                    JB      READ1
                    CMP     AL,'9'
                    JBE     READ2
                    SUB     AL,7
                    CMP     AL,'A-7'
                    JB      READ1
                    CMP     AL,'F-7'
                    JA      READ1
READ2:
                    SUB     AL,'0'
                    PUSH    AX
                    INC     CX
                    JMP     READ1
READ3:
                    XOR     DX,DX
                    XOR     BX,BX
                    OR      CX,CX
                    JE      READ5
READ4:
```

```
                    POP     AX
                    SHL     BX,1
                    RCL     DX,1
                    SHL     BX,1
                    RCL     DX,1
                    SHL     BX,1
                    RCL     DX,1
                    SHL     BX,1
                    RCL     DX,1
                    ADD     BL,AL
                    LOOP    READ4
                    SHR     DX,1
                    RCR     BX,1
                    SHR     DX,1
                    RCR     BX,1
                    SHR     DX,1
                    RCR     BX,1
                    SHR     DX,1
                    RCR     BX,1
READ5:
                    MOV     DS,BX
                    XOR     SI,0
                    RET

READ                ENDP

NEW                 PROC    NEAR

                    MOV     AL,13
                    CALL    DIP
                    MOV     AL,10
                    CALL    DIP
                    RET

NEW                 ENDP

DIP                 PROC    NEAR

                    MOV     AH,6
                    MOV     DL,AL
                    INT     21H
                    RET

DIP                 ENDP

GET                 PROC    NEAR

                    MOV     AH,6
                    MOV     DL,0FFH
                    INT     21H
                    JE      GET
                    RET
```

```
GET         ENDP

DISP        PROC  NEAR

            MOV   CX,256
DISP1:
            MOV   AX,SI
            AND   AX,0FH
            JNZ   DISP2
            CALL  ADDR
DISP2:
            LODSB
            CALL  DIPS
            MOV   AL,20H
            INT   21H
            LOOP  DISP1
            RET

DISP        ENDP

DIPS        PROC  NEAR

            PUSH  AX
            SHR   AX,4
            ADD   AL,30H
            CMP   AL,'9'
            JBE   DIPS1
            ADD   AL,7

DIPS1:
            CALL  DIP
            POP   AX
            ADD   AL,30H
            CMP   AL,'9'
            JBE   DIPS2
            ADD   AL,7
DIPS2:
            CALL  DIP
            RET

DIPS        ENDP

ADDR        PROC  NEAR

            CALL  NEW
            MOV   AX,DS
            PUSH  AX
            MOV   AL,AH
            CALL  DIPS
            POP   AX
            CALL  DIPS
            MOV   AL,':'
```

```
                        CALL    DIPS
                        MOV     AX,SI
                        MOV     AL,AH
                        CALL    DIPS
                        MOV     AX,SI
                        CALL    DIPS
                        MOV     AL,20H
                        CALL    DIPS
                        RET

ADDR                    ENDP

PROG                    ENDS
                        END     MAIN
```

42. ;software assumes DS:DI addresses the memory block.

```
    ;
    DISP                PROC    NEAR

                        MOV     CX,256

    DISP1:
                        CALL    DISP_AD
                        MOV     AL,[DI]
                        INC     DI
                        CALL    DISP_N
                        MOV     AL,' '
                        CALL    DISP_A
                        LOOP    DISP1

                        RET

    DISP                ENDP

    DISP_AD             PROC    NEAR

                        TEST    DI,0FH
                        JNZ     DISP_AD1
                        MOV     AX,DS
                        MOV     AL,AH
                        CALL    DISP_N
                        MOV     AX,DS
                        CALL    DISP_N
                        MOV     AL,'0'
                        CALL    DISP_A
                        MOV     AL,' '
                        CALL    DISP_A

    DISP_AD1:

                        RET
```

```
DISP_AD      ENDP

DISP_A       PROC  NEAR

             MOV   AH,6
             MOV   DL,AL
             INT   21H
             RET

DISP_A       ENDP

DISP_N       PROC  NEAR

             PUSH  AX
             SHR   AL,4
             AND   AL,0FH
             ADD   AL,'0'
             CALL  DISP_A
             POP   AX
             AND   AL,0FH
             ADD   AL,'0'
             CALL  DISP_A
             RET

DISP_N       ENDP
```

Chapter 7

2. 24.
4. +5.0 V.
6. 350 mV.
8. 10.
10. A_0.
12. The M/$\overline{\text{IO}}$ signal selects memory when it is a logic 1 and I/O when a logic 0.
14. The status bits define the function of the current bus cycle.
16. The CLK signal is 12 MHz and the PCLK signal is 6.0 MHz.
18. The EFI (external frequency input) is a timing source that is used in lieu of the crystal timing source.
20. Whenever power is applied, the capacitor is discharged to zero volts. This applies a logic 0 to the $\overline{\text{RES}}$ input of the 82284 clock generator, causing the RESET output to reset the microprocessor. After a short time, the capacitor charges toward 5.0 V, where it places a logic 1 on the $\overline{\text{RES}}$ input. This causes RESET out to become a logic 0, allowing the microprocessor to operate.
22. $\overline{\text{MRDC}}$ and $\overline{\text{MWTC}}$.
24. 32 mA.
26. The buffer goes to its high-impedance state.
28. Either the 74LS373 or 74AS533 octal latch.
30. 1.
32. The control bus information and address are presented.

34. Memory.
36. 110 ns.
38. READY.
40. At the end of T_c.
42. The address signals are generated by an external logic circuitry for two complete banks of memory.

Chapter 8

 2. (a) 10. (b) 12. (c) 16. (d) 18. (e) 20.
 4. $CE_1 = 1$, $\overline{CED_2} = 0$, and $CE_3 = 1$.
 6. A ROM is programmed at the factory as it is manufactured, and the EPROM is programmed in the field on an EPROM programmer.
 8. Static RAM stores data for as long as power is applied.
10. Every 2 ms for most DRAM devices.
12. The row address is entered through the address pins on the DRAM at the time the DRAM receives the $\overline{RAS}$ signal.
14. 1K.
16. The address must be decoded so the microprocessor can address more than one memory device.
18. The low bank.
20. A_0.
22. 8M words.
24. See Figure E–1.
26. See Figure E–2.
28. See Figure E–3 on page 721.
30. See Figure E–4 on page 722.
32. See Figure E–5 on page 724.
34. See Figure E–6 on page 726.
36. Parity is a count of the number of 1s expressed as even or odd.
38. 5.
40. Yes. In fact, software is used for refreshing memory in most systems.
40. Yes. In fact, software is used for refreshing memory in most systems today. This is accomplished through a periodic interrupt that calls a procedure to read each row of the DRAM memory in the system.
42. See Figure E–7 on page 728.
44. $\overline{WAIT} = 1$.
46. The access times for an interleaved memory system are about the same as the access time allowed by a standard memory system with one wait state.

Chapter 9

 2. On address bits A_7–A_0, with A_{23}–A_8 equal to logic 0s.
 4. On address bits A_{15}–A_0, with A_{23}–A_{16} equal to logic 0s.
 6. The OUTSB instruction copies the byte contents of the data segment memory location addressed by SI to the I/O port addressed by DX. After the transfer, SI is incremented or decremented by 1.

FIGURE E–1

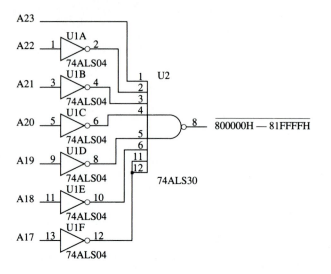

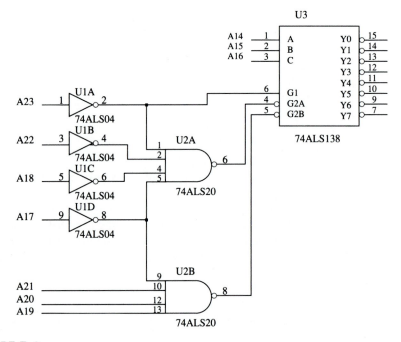

FIGURE E–2

FIGURE E–3

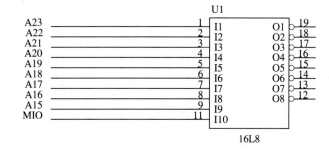

16L8

TITLE   Question 28

PATTERN   Test 28

REVISION   A
AUTHOR   Barry B. Brey
COMPANY   Symbiotic Systems
DATE   1/27/92
CHIP   QUEST28 PAL16L8

;pins 1   2   3   4   5   6   7   8   9   10
      A23 A22 A21 A20 A19 A18 A17 A16 A15 GND
;pins 11   12   13   14   15   16   17   18   19   20
      MIO O1   O2   O3   O4   O5   O6   O7   O8 VCC

EQUATIONS

/O8 = A23 * /A22 * A21 * A20 * A19 * A18 * /A17 * /A16 * /A15 * MIO
/O7 = A23 * /A22 * A21 * A20 * A19 * A18 * /A17 * /A16 * A15 * MIO
/O6 = A23 * /A22 * A21 * A20 * A19 * A18 * /A17 * A16 * /A15 * MIO
/O5 = A23 * /A22 * A21 * A20 * A19 * A18 * /A17 * A16 *A15 * MIO
/O4 = A23 * /A22 * A21 * A20 * A19 * A18 * A17 * /A16 * /A15 * MIO
/O3 = A23 * /A22 * A21 * A20 * A19 * A18 * A17 * /A16 * A15 * MIO
/O2 = A23 * /A22 * A21 * A20 * A19 * A18 * A17 * A16 * /A15 * MIO
/O1 = A23 * /A22 * A21 * A20 * A19 * A18 * A17 * A16 * A15 * MIO

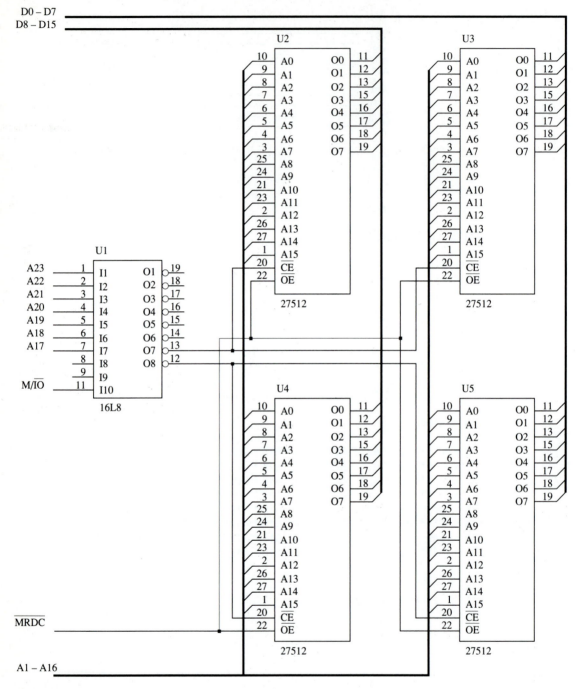

FIGURE E–4

```
TITLE           Question 30
PATTERN         Test 30
REVISION        A
AUTHOR          Barry B. Brey
COMPANY         Symbiotic Systems
DATE            1/27/92
CHIP            QUEST30 PAL16L8

;pins 1    2    3    4    5    6    7    8   9   10
      A23 A22 A21 A20 A19 A18 A17 NC  NC  GND
;pins 11   12   13   14   15   16   17   18   19   20
      MIO  O1  O2  NC  NC  NC  NC  NC  NC  VCC
```

EQUATIONS

/O1 = /A23 * /A22 * A21 * A20 * /A19 * A18 * /A17 * MIO
/O2 = /A23 * /A22 * A21 * A20 * /A19 * A18 * A17 * MIO

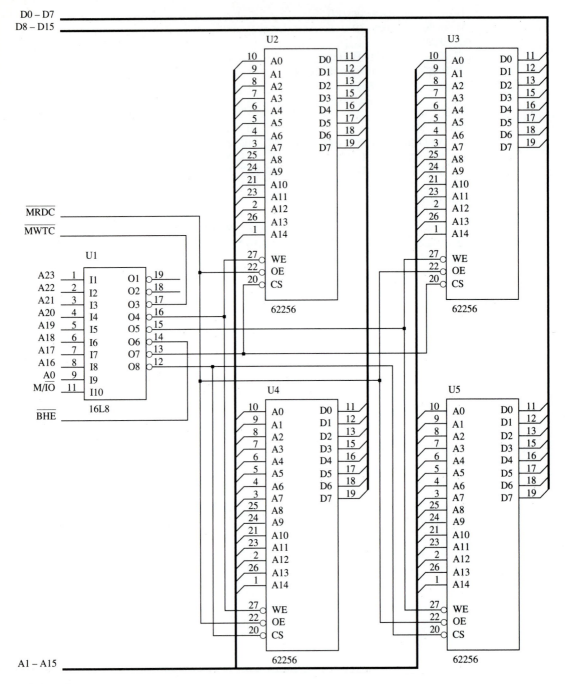

TITLE   Question 32
PATTERN   Test 32
REVISION   A
AUTHOR   Barry B. Brey
COMPANY   Symbiotic Systems
DATE   1/27/92
CHIP   QUEST32 PAL16L8

;pins 1   2   3   4   5   6   7   8   9   10
      A23 A22 A21 A20 A19 A18 A17 A16 A0 GND
;pins 11 12 13 14 15 16   17   18 19 20
      MIO O1 O2 BHE LWR HWR MWTC NC NC VCC

EQUATIONS

/O1 = A23 * /A22 * /A21 * /A20 * /A19 * A18 * /A17 * /A16 * MIO
/O2 = A23 * /A22 * /A21 * /A20 * /A19 * A18 * /A17 * A16 * MIO
/LWR = /A0 * /MWTC
/HWR = /BHE * /MWTC

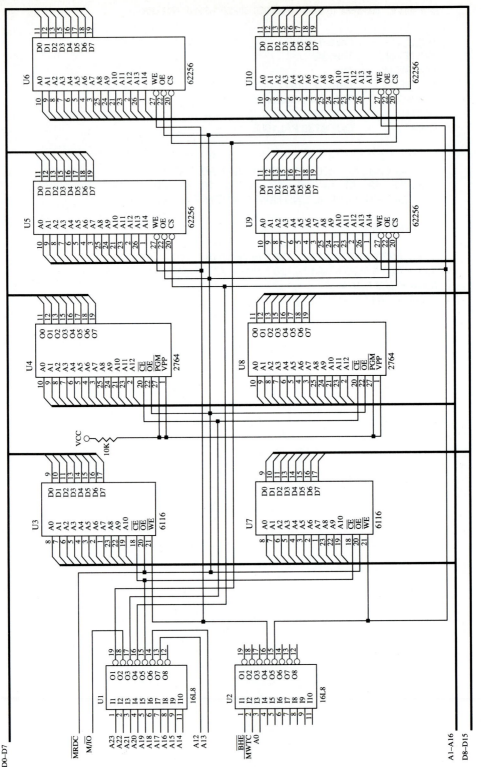

FIGURE E-6

```
TITLE          Question 34 (PAL U1)
PATTERN        Test 34
REVISION       A
AUTHOR         Barry B. Brey
COMPANY        Symbiotic Systems
DATE           1/27/92
CHIP           QUEST34 PAL16L8
```

```
;pins 1    2    3    4    5    6    7    8    9    10
      A23 A22 A21 A20 A19 A18 A17 A16 A15 GND
;pins 11   12   13   14   15   16   17   18   19   20
      A14 NC  A13 A12 O1  O2  O3  MIO O4  VCC
```

EQUATIONS

/O1 = /A23*/A22*/A21*/A20*/A19*/A18*/A17*/A16*/A15*/A14*/A13*/A12*MIO
/O2 = /A23 * /A22 * A21 * /A20 * /A19 * /A18 * /A17/A16 * MIO
/O3 = A23 * A22 * A21 * A20 * A19 * A18 * A17 * A16 * A15 * A14 * MIO
/O4 = /A23 * /A22 * A21 * /A20 * /A19 * /A18 * /A17 A16 * MIO


```
TITLE          Question 34 (PAL U2)
PATTERN        Test 34
REVISION       A
AUTHOR         Barry B. Brey
COMPANY        Symbiotic Systems
DATE           1/27/92
CHIP           QUEST34 PAL16L8
```

```
;pins 1    2      3    4    5    6    7    8    9    10
      BHE MWTC A0  NC  NC  NC  NC  NC  NC  GND
;pins 11   12   13   14    15    16   17   18   19   20
      NC  NC  NC  HWR LWR NC  NC  NC  NC  VCC
```

EQUATIONS

/HWR = /BHE * /MWTC
/LWR = /A0 * /MWTC

FIGURE E–7

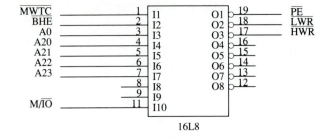

16L8

TITLE   Question 42
PATTERN   Test 42
REVISION   A
AUTHOR   Barry B. Brey
COMPANY   Symbiotic Systems
DATE   1/27/92
CHIP   Decode42 PAL16L8

;pins 1   2   3   4   5   6   7   8   9   10
         WE BHE A0 A20 A21 A22 A23 NC NC GND
;pins 11   12 13 14 15 16 17   18 19 20
         MIO NC NC NC NC NC HWR LWR PE VCC

EQUATIONS

/HWR = /BHE * WE
/LWR = /A0 * WE
/PE = A20 * /A21 * /A22 * /A23 * MIO

FIGURE E–8

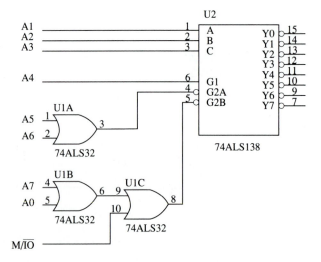

FIGURE E–9

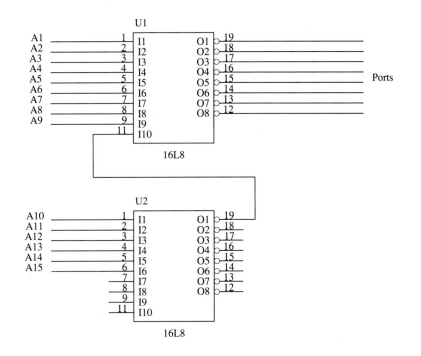

TITLE   Question 16 -- U1
PATTERN   Test 16
REVISION   A
AUTHOR   Barry B. Brey
COMPANY   Symbiotic Systems
DATE   1/27/92
CHIP   Decode16 PAL16L8

;pins 1   2   3   4   5   6   7   8   9   10
       A1   A2   A3   A4   A5   A6   A7   A8   A9   GND
;pins 11   12   13   14   15   16   17   18   19   20
       U2   O8   O7   O6   O5   O4   O3   O2   O1   VCC

EQUATIONS

/O1 = /U2 * /A1 * /A2 * /A3 * /A4 * /A5 * /A6 * /A7 * /A8 * /A9
/O2 = /U2 * A1 * /A2 * /A3 * /A4 * /A5 * /A6 * /A7 * /A8 * /A9
/O3 = /U2 * /A1 * A2 * /A3 * /A4 * /A5 * /A6 * /A7 * /A8 * /A9
/O4 = /U2 * A1 * A2 * /A3 * /A4 * /A5 * /A6 * /A7 * /A8 * /A9
/O5 = /U2 * /A1 * /A2 * A3 * /A4 * /A5 * /A6 * /A7 * /A8 * /A9
/O6 = /U2 * A1 * /A2 * A3 * /A4 * /A5 * /A6 * /A7 * /A8 * /A9
/O7 = /U2 * /A1 * A2 * A3 * /A4 * /A5 * /A6 * /A7 * /A8 * /A9
/O8 = /U2 * A1 * A2 * A3 * /A4 * /A5 * /A6 * /A7 * /A8 * /A9

TITLE   Question 16 -- U2
PATTERN   Test 16
REVISION   A
AUTHOR   Barry B. Brey
COMPANY   Symbiotic Systems
DATE   1/27/92
CHIP   Decode16 PAL16L8

;pins 1   2   3   4   5   6   7   8   9   10
      A10 A11 A12 A13 A14 A15 NC NC NC GND
;pins 11 12 13 14 15 16 17 18 19 20
      NC NC NC NC NC NC NC NC U2 VCC

EQUATIONS

/U2 = /A15 * /A14 * /A13 * A12 * /A11 * /A10

FIGURE E–10

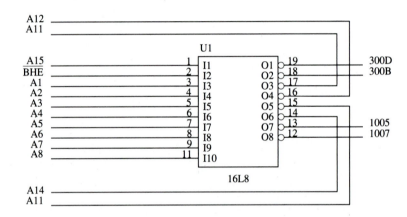

TITLE   Question 18
PATTERN   Test 18
REVISION   A
AUTHOR   Barry B. Brey
COMPANY   Symbiotic Systems
DATE   1/27/92
CHIP   Decode18 PAL16L8

;pins 1   2   3   4   5   6   7   8   9   10
      AX BHE A1 A2 A3 A4 A5 A6 A7 GND

;pins 11 12 13 14 15 16 17   18 19 20
      A8 O7 O5 AY A11 A12 A13 OB. OD VCC

EQUATIONS

/O7 = /AX*/A13*A12*/A11*/AY*/A8*/A7*/A6*/A5*/A4*/A3*A2*A1
/O5 = /AX*/A13*A12*/A11*/AY*/A8*/A7*/A6*/A5*/A4*/A3*A2*/A1
/OB = /AX*A13*A12*/A11*/AY*/A8*/A7*/A6*/A5*/A4*A3*/A2*A1
/OD = /AX*A13*A12*/A11*/AY*/A8*/A7*/A6*/A5*/A4*A3*A2*/A1

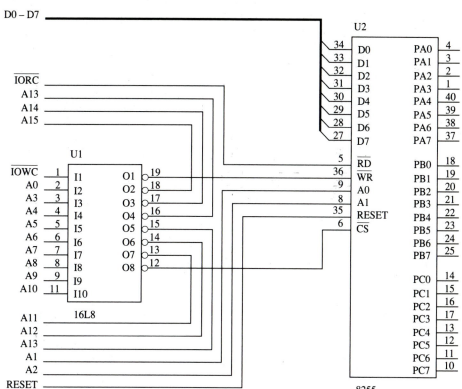

FIGURE E–11

TITLE   Question 26
PATTERN   Test 26
REVISION   A
AUTHOR   Barry B. Brey
COMPANY   Symbiotic Systems
DATE   1/27/92
CHIP   Decode26 PAL16L8

;pins 1   2   3   4   5   6   7   8   9   10
      IOWC A0 A3 A4 A5 A6 A7 A8 A9 GND
;pins 11 12 13 14   15   16   17   18   19   20
      A10 CS A11 A12 A13 A14 A15 NC WR VCC

EQUATIONS

/WR = /IOWC * /A0
/CS = /A15*/A14*/A13*/A12*/A11*/A10*A9*A8*A7*/A6*/A5*/A4*/A3

8. The memory-mapped I/O system uses a portion of the memory map for I/O device addresses, while the isolated I/O system has its own separate I/O space. Memory-mapped I/O uses any instruction that addresses memory to transfer data between the microprocessor and the I/O device, while isolated I/O uses IN and OUT for the transfer.

10. The basic output interface is a latch that captures data during the execution of the OUT instruction.

12. Low.

14. See Figure E–8 on page 728.

16. See Figure E–9 on page 729.

18. See Figure E–10 on page 730.

20. Because the I/O port address is even it is connected to the low bus (D_7–D_0).

22. 24.

24. A_1 and A_0.

26. See Figure E–11 on page 731.

28. Mode 0 (buffered input/latched output), Mode 1 (strobed I/O), and mode 2 (bidirectional I/O).

30. The IBF line is set when the strobe input changes from a 1 to a 0.

32. By setting bit PC_4 (INTEA) for port A and by setting bit PC_2 (INTEB) for port B.

34. The $\overline{OBF}$ (output buffer full) signal is cleared (to indicate a full condition) when data are written to the port with the $\overline{WR}$ signal.

36. Port A.

38. A signal that is 3.125 MHz or less in frequency.

40. If CLK is connected to a 3.0-MHz external clock, a divide by number 30 is used.

42. The encoded mode places a binary number in the select lines for an external decoder. The decoded mode performs the function of the external decoder.

44. See Figure E–12.

46. 6.

48. 301.

50. The read back control word is programmed to latch the count and/or status from any combination of the three counters at a time. This allows the counters to be read and latched simultaneously.

52. It attempts to make the motor spin in one direction for half the time, and then the other direction half the time, causing a net rotational speed of zero.

54. Synchronous serial data are data that are sent with a synchronizing clock signal.

56. **MOV   AL,01110101B**
    OUT   22H,AL

58. Simplex operation occurs when data are always transmitted in one direction only. Half-duplex operation occurs when data are transmitted in both directions, but in one direction at a time. Full-duplex operation occurs when data are transmitted in both directions simultaneously.

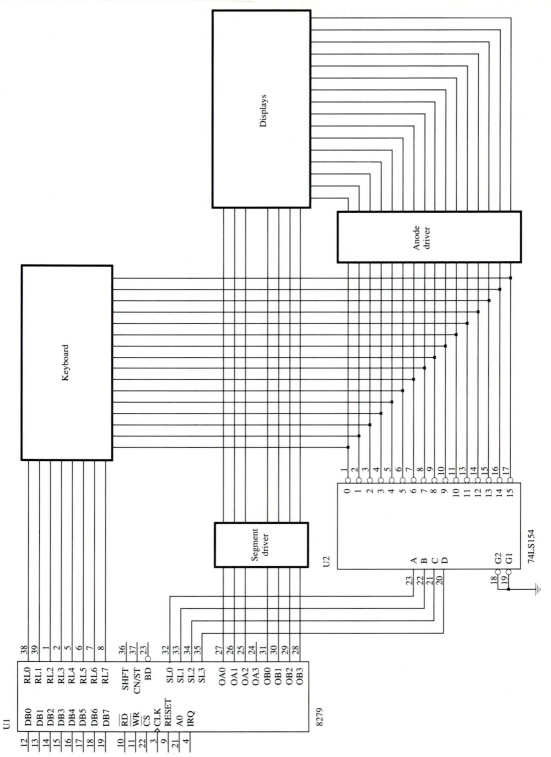

FIGURE E-12

Chapter 10

2. An interrupt is either a hardware- or software-initiated call to an interrupt service procedure.

4. An interrupt provides additional software execution time to the microprocessor because the I/O device no longer must be polled. Polling consumes much of the microprocessor's execution time.

6. INT, INT 3, BOUND, IRET, and INTO.

8. At memory locations 000000H–0003FFH.

10. Vectors 0–31.

12. The BOUND instruction compares a register with the boundaries stored in memory. If the contents of the register are greater than or equal to the first word in memory and less than or equal to the second word, no type-5 interrupt occurs.

14. 110H–113H.

16. Interrupt 7 is often used to emulate a numeric coprocessor.

18. The interrupting flag (IF) enables the INTR pin when set, or disables INTR when cleared.

20. The interrupt flag is cleared with the CLI instruction and set with the STI instruction.

22. Interrupt vector number 2.

24. Active high-level sensitive.

26. Type or vector.

28. See Figure E–13.

30. These resistors cause the machine to see an FFH in response to an INTA pulse, because the bus becomes receptive to the logic 1s placed on it by the pullup resistors.

32. The daisy chain is a serial connection that indicates an interrupt has occurred. It does not indicate which serial device caused the interrupt.

34. 9.

36. These pins are used to cascade 8259A interrupt controllers.

38. The initialization command word for the 8259A PIC.

FIGURE E–13

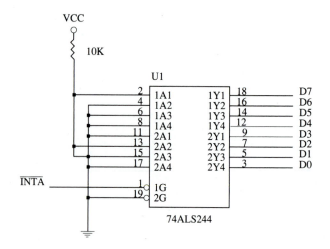

40. 2.
42. ICW0.
44. A nonspecific end of interrupt signals an end of interrupt, but not the interrupting device that caused it.
46. This allows the interrupt inputs to be interrogated before they are enabled.

Chapter 11

2. The 80286 microprocessor stops executing the program within a few clocking periods; floats the data, address, and control buses; and signals that a DMA is accepted by placing a logic 1 on the HLDA pin.
4. I/O to memory.
6. The $\overline{\text{DACK}}$ (DMA acknowledge) pin.

8. The 80286 holds and the DMA controller has access to the system buses.
10. 4 channel.
12. The local bus is the bus connected directly to the microprocessor before any system buffers or latches.
14. The ADMA general burst and delay registers are programmed to allow DMA accesses less than 100 percent of the time.
16. 2.
18. CPR and then GCR, assuming the channel control block exists at the location addressed by the CPR.
20. A type-1 command controls the type of DMA actions that occur.
22. The length of the channel control block is determined by the type-1 command.
24. Up to 16M bytes.

```
26. GCR    EQU    1000H           ;GCR port
    CPR3   EQU    10E0H           ;CPR1 port


    MEMT   PROC   FAR

    MOV    AX,CS                  ;get linear address
    MOV    BX,AX
    SHL    AX,4
    SHR    BX,12
    ADD    AX,OFFSET CB1          ;address control block
    ADC    BX,0

    MOV    DX,CPR3                ;address CPR3
    OUT    DX,AX
    ADD    DX,2
    MOV    AX,BX
    OUT    DX,AX

    MOV    DX,GCR                 ;address GCR
    MOV    AL,22H                 ;start channel 3
    OUT    DX,AL
```

```
        RET

        MEMT  ENDP

;Type 1 command

        CB1:
        DW    0C0DDH              ;type 1 command
        DW    2000H               ;source address
        DW    0
        DW    3000H               ;destination address
        DW    0
        DW    1000H               ;byte count
        DW    0
        DW    0                   ;channel status

;Type 2 STOP command

        CB2:
            DW    0000H           ;STOP command
            DW    0
            DW    0
```

28. Microfloppy disk.
30. Sectors
32. Because it automatically erases old data as new data are recorded.
34. See Figure E–14.
36. Because when heads crash on the surface of a hard disk they can eventually cause damage to the surface.
38. A write-once/read-mostly memory.
40. A TTL monitor has a restriction of 16 colors, while the analog monitor can display an infinite number of colors.
42. Cyan, yellow, and magenta.
44. 600 and 800.
46. The voltage level of each color video input can be any value between 0.0 V and 0.7 V.
48. It can display 256 colors at a time because its palette memory contains 256 locations.

Chapter 12

2. Word is 16 bits with a value of $\pm 32K$, short is 32 bits with a value of -2×10^9 to $+2 \times 10^9$, and a long is 64 bits with a value of -9×10^{18} to $+9 \times 10^{18}$.

FIGURE E–14

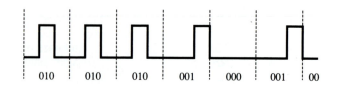

010   010   010   001   000   001   00

4. Single-precision (32 bits), double-precision (64 bits), and temporary (80 bits).

6. (a) −7.0. (b) +0.5625. (c) +306. (d) +2.0. (e) +10. (f) +0.0.

8. BUSY.

10. The coprocessor either continues executing a prior coprocessor instruction or remains idle.

12. They indicate the outcome of a comparison with the stack top and zero.

14. FSTSWAX.

16. Zero.

18. Affine allows a signed infinity, and projective is an unsigned infinity.

20. (a) FROG DD 23.44. (b) DATA3 DD −123. (c) DATA1 DD −23.8. (d) DATA2 DQ ?.

22. Loads an integer from memory location DATA to the top of the stack.

24. The FADD instruction adds the ST and ST(1) together and removes both original numbers from the stack. The sum is found at the top of the stack after the FADD instruction.

26. Stores a BCD number and memory location DATA and pops the top of the stack.

28. FTST compares against zero, while FXAM tests the stack top.

30. FLDPI.

32. FSTENV.

34.
```
FLD     W
FMUL    L
FSTP    A
```

36.
```
              MOV       DI,OFFSET TABLE      ;address table
              FLD1
              FADD      ST,ST(0)
              FSTP      TEMP
              MOV       CX,9
LOOPS:
              FLD       TEMP
              FSQRT
              FSTP      DWORD PTR [DI]
              ADD       DI,4
              FLD       TEMP
              FLD1
              FADD
              FSTP      TEMP
              LOOP      LOOPS
```

38.
```
FLD     R2
FLD1
FDIV
FLD     R3
FLD1
FDIV
FLD     R4
FLD1
FDIV
```

```
FADD
FADD
FLD1
FDIV
FADD        R1
FSTP        RT
```

Chapter 13

2. 64T bytes.
4. See Figure E–15.
6. The 80386 memory system is 32 bits (four 8-bit banks) wide. The bank selection signals allow any 8-bit data to be addressed, any 16 bit, or any 32 bit.
8. The pipeline allows more access time because as one intruction is executing, the microprocessor outputs the address for the next, allowing additional access time to the memory.
10. 0000H-FFFFH.
12. The main difference is the 32-bit address and data buses in the 80386, whereas athe 80286 has only a 24-bit address and a 16-bit data bus.
14. This causes rthe bus size to become 16 bits wide.
16. EAX, EBX, ECX, EDX, ESP, ESI, EDI, EBP, EIP, and EFLAGS.
18. CR_0 is used to switch to protected mode and replaces the machine status register in the 80286. CR_1 is not used. CR_2 holds the linear page address accessed before a page fault interrupt. CR_3 holds the base address of the page directory.
20. Type-2 interrupt.
22. BSR shifts a number to the left until a 1 is moved into the leftmost bit position.
24. MOV EAX,FS:[DI].

FIGURE E–15

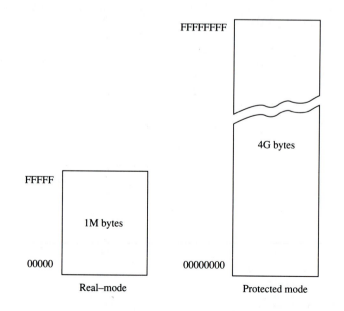

26. This instruction is legal on the 80386 or 80486 microprocessor.
28. This interrupt is a trap that is used to emulate numeric coprocessor instructions in a system that doesn't contain a coprocessor.
30. An interrupt (vector type 8) that occurs whenever the 80386 detects a type 10, 11, 12, or 13 interrupt at the same time that an interrupt other than a type 14 occurs.
32. A descriptor describes a segment of protected mode memory.
34. The TI bit is set in the selector to access the local descriptor table.
36. 8,192
38. A segment descriptor describes a segment of memory, while the system descriptor is used to access a procedure, task, or interrupt.
40. The TSS is addressed through the TSS descriptor that is accessed by the task register (TR).
42. The 80386 switches from protected to real mode by clearing the rightmost bit of CR_0.
44. The contents of CR_3 select the paging directory.
46. The linear address accesses the page directory that accesses a page table containing the new physical memory address of C0000000H.
48. The FLUSH input erases the internal cache memory.
50. The alignment check flag is new to the 80486 and it indicates that a word or double word is stored at a nonword or non-double-word boundary.
52. Even.
54. 16.
56. This term applies to a cache where data are written to both the cache and memory each time that a write occurs.
58. Yes, the paging unit allows the cache to be disabled for any 4K byte page of memory.
60. The CMPXCHG compares the destination operand to the accumulator. If the destination operand is equal to the accumulator, the source operand is copied to the destination. Otherwise, the destination operand is copied to the accumulator.
62. It controls whether data are stored in the internal cache memory.

INDEX